Devenishki Book; Memorial Book
(Dieveniškės, Lithuania)

Translation of
Sefer Divenishok; yad vashem le-ayara yehudit

Memorial Book to a Jewish Shtetl

Original Yizkor Book Edited by: David Shtokfish

Published by the Divenishok Societies in Israel and the US
1977

Published by JewishGen

An Affiliate of the Museum of Jewish Heritage—A Living Memorial to the Holocaust
New York

Devenishki Book; Memorial Book
(Dieveniškės, Lithuania)
Translation of: *Sefer Divenishok; yad vashem le-ayara Yehudit*
Memorial Book to a Jewish Shtetl

Copyright © 2020 by JewishGen, Inc.
All rights reserved.
First Printing: October 2020, Tishrei 5781

Editor of the Original Yizkor Book: David Shtokfish
Project Coordinator and Translation Editor: Adam Cherson
Translation Layout, Cover Design, and Indexing: Adam Cherson

This book may not be reproduced, in whole or in part, including illustrations in any form (beyond that copying permitted by Sections 107 and 108 of the U.S. Copyright Law and except by reviewers for public press), without written permission from the publisher.

Published by JewishGen, Inc.
An Affiliate of the Museum of Jewish Heritage
A Living Memorial to the Holocaust
36 Battery Place, New York, NY 10280

JewishGen, Inc. is not responsible for inaccuracies or omissions in the original work and makes no representations regarding the accuracy of this translation. Digital images of the original book's contents can be seen online at the New York Public Library website.

The mission of the JewishGen organization is to produce a translation of the original work, and we cannot verify the accuracy of statements or alter facts cited.

Printed in the United States of America by Lightning Source, Inc.

Library of Congress Control Number (LCCN): 2020947185
ISBN: 978-1-939561-94-7 (hard cover: 660 pages, alk. paper)

Cover Credits:

Cover Art Used by Permission and Courtesy of Natan Karczmar

Front Cover: *Market [Detail] by Shimon Karczmar*

Back Cover: *Prayer to the Moon [Detail] by Shimon Karczmar*

Both paintings depict the artist's childhood memories of Divenishok c. 1900.

For More Information Please Visit: www.karczmart.org

JewishGen and the Yizkor Books in Print Project

This book has been published by the **Yizkor Books in Print Project**, as part of the **Yizkor Book Project** of JewishGen, Inc.

JewishGen, Inc. is a non-profit organization founded in 1987 as a resource for Jewish genealogy. Its website [www.jewishgen.org] serves as an international clearinghouse and resource center to assist individuals who are researching the history of their Jewish families and the places where they lived. JewishGen provides databases, facilitates discussion groups, and coordinates projects relating to Jewish genealogy and the history of the Jewish people. In 2003, JewishGen became an affiliate of the **Museum of Jewish Heritage—A Living Memorial to the Holocaust** in New York.

The **JewishGen Yizkor Book Project** was organized to make more widely known the existence of Yizkor (Memorial) Books written by survivors and former residents of various Jewish communities throughout the world. Later, volunteers connected to the different destroyed communities began cooperating to have these books translated from the original language—usually Hebrew or Yiddish—into English, thus enabling a wider audience to have access to the valuable information contained within them. As each chapter of these books was translated, it was posted on the JewishGen website and made available to the general public.

The **Yizkor Books in Print Project** began in 2011 as an initiative to print and publish Yizkor Books that had been fully translated, so that hard copies would be available for purchase by the descendants of these communities and also by scholars, universities, synagogues, libraries, and museums.

These Yizkor books have been produced almost entirely through the volunteer effort of researchers from around the world, assisted by donations from private individuals. The books are printed and sold at near cost, so as to make them as affordable as possible. Our goal is to make this important genre of Jewish literature and history available in English in book form, so that people can have the personal histories of their ancestral towns on their bookshelves for themselves and for their children and grandchildren.

A list of all published translated Yizkor Books in the project with prices and ordering information can be found at:
http://www.jewishgen.org/Yizkor/ybip.html

Lance Ackerfeld, Yizkor Book Project Manager
Joel Alpert, Yizkor-Book-in-Print Project Coordinator

This book is presented by the
Yizkor-Books-In-Print Project
Project Coordinator: Joel Alpert

Part of the Yizkor Books Project of JewishGen. Inc.
Project Manager: Lance Ackerfeld

These books have been produced solely through efforts of volunteers from around the world. The books are printed using the Print-on-Demand technology and sold at near cost, to make them as affordable as possible.

Our goal is to make this intimate history of the destroyed Jewish shtetls of Eastern Europe available in book form in English, so that people can experience the near-personal histories of their ancestral town on their bookshelves and those of their children and grandchildren.

All donations to the Yizkor Books Project, which translated the books, are sincerely appreciated.

Please send donations to:

Yizkor Book Project
JewishGen, Inc.
36 Battery Place
New York, NY, 10280

JewishGen, Inc. is an affiliate of the
Museum of Jewish Heritage
A Living Memorial to the Holocaust

Notes to the Reader:

We apologize ahead of time for the poor quality of images in the book. Often these images had been scanned from the original Yizkor books, which were of poor quality to begin with, being copies of old photographs. Each transfer results in loss of quality. We have done the best we could, given the original material and the resources and technology at hand. Even though images often appear of higher quality on computer screens, that does not transfer to high quality images in print. A reader can view the original scans on the web sites listed below.

Within the text the reader will note "{34}" standing ahead of a paragraph. This indicates that the material translated below was on page 34 of the original book. However, when a paragraph was split between two pages in the original book, the marker is placed in this book after the end of the paragraph for ease of reading.

Also please note that all references within the text of the book to page numbers, refer to the page numbers of the original Yizkor Book.

The original book can be seen online at the New York Public Library site:

https://digitalcollections.nypl.org/search/index?utf8=%E2%9C%93&keywords=divenishok

or at the Yiddish Book Center web site:

https://www.yiddishbookcenter.org/search/collection/%22NYPL-Yid-dish%2520Book%2520Center%2520Yizkor%2520Book%2520Collection%22?search_api_views_fulltext=divenishok&Submit+search=&restrict=

In order to obtain a list of all Shoah victims from Divenishok, the reader should access the Yad Vashem web site listed below; one can also search for specific family names using family name option. These lists are continually updated by Yad Vashem, so it is worthwhile to periodically search these lists.

There is much valuable information available on this web site, including the Pages of Testimony, etc.
http://yvng.yadvashem.org

A list of this book and all books available in the Yizkor-Book-In-Print Project along with prices is available at:
http://www.jewishgen.org/Yizkor/ybip.html

Geopolitical Information:

Dieveniškės, Lithuania

The town is located at 54°12' N 25°37' E 36 miles SSE of Vilnius

Period	Town	District	Province	Country
Before WWI (c. 1900):	Devenishki	Oshmyany	Vilna	Russian Empire
Between the wars (c. 1930):	Dziewieniszki	Oszmiana	Wilno	Poland
After WWII (c. 1950):	Dieveniškės			Soviet Union
Today (c. 2000):	Dieveniškės			Lithuania

Alternate names: Dieveniškės [Lith], Devenishki [Rus], Dziewieniszki [Pol], Divenishok [Yid], Dzievianiški [Bel], Dzevenishki, Dewenishki

Belarusian: Дзевянішкі. Yiddish: דיווענישאק. Russian: Девянишки / Дзевенишки. Hebrew: דז'יוויינישקי

Nearby Jewish Communities:
- Byenyakoni, Belarus 11 miles WNW
- Šalčininkai 12 miles NW
- Voranava, Belarus 12 miles WSW
- Traby, Belarus 13 miles ESE
- Lipnishki, Belarus 14 miles S
- Halshany, Belarus 17 miles ENE
- Iwye, Belarus 19 miles SSE
- Ashmyany, Belarus 20 miles NE
- Laibiškės 20 miles N
- Jašiunai 21 miles NW
- Gav'ya, Belarus 24 miles S
- Eišiškes 25 miles W
- Vishneva, Belarus 25 miles E
- Lida, Belarus 25 miles SSW
- Zhuprany, Belarus 26 miles NE
- Radun, Belarus 27 miles WSW
- Krevo, Belarus 28 miles ENE
- Rudamina 29 miles NNW
- Bakshty, Belarus 29 miles SE

Jewish Population in 1897: 1,225

Map of Lithuania with Divenishok Indicated

Title Page of Original Hebrew/Yiddish Book

ספר דיבנישוק
יד ושם לעיירה יהודית

DEVENISHKI BOOK
MEMORIAL BOOK

ספר דיוועניש‌אָק
געשיכטע פון א שטעטל

Translation of the Title Page of the Original Hebrew/Yiddish Book

Sefer Divenishok

Memorial to Jewish Shtetl

העורך : • רעדאקטאָר :
דוד שטוקפיש

ועד הספר : • בוך-קאָמיטעט :
מאיר-יוסף איצקוביץ,
יעקב בלוך, שרגא בלאכר,
בנימין דובינסקי, שמואל שרון

ציור המפות והשער :
די מאפעס און שערבלאט :
מאיר-יוסף איצקוביץ

המו״ל : • ארויסגעבער :
ארגוני יוצאי דיבנישוק בישראל
ובארצות-הברית
די לאנדסמאנשאפטן אין ישראל
און אין די פאר. שטאטן

PRINTED IN ISRAEL

נדפס בישראל, 1977 — תשל״ז

דפוס רייתן בע״מ טל. 480-827

Divenishok Memorial Book

Translation of previous page

Editor:
David Shtokfish

Book Committee:
Meir Yosef Itskovitsh
Yaakov Bloch, Shraga Blyakher
Benjamin Dubinski, Shmuel Sharon

Maps and Title Page:
Meir Yosef Itskovitsh

Publisher:
Organizations of former residents of Divenishok in Israel and the US

Printed in Israel – 1977 - 5737
Reitan Printing Inc.

Contents

Article	Author	Page
Introduction to the Translation	Adam Benyakonski Cherson	1
Map of Devenishki		3
The Jewish Town (Introduction to the Devenishki Book)	Shmuel Sharon	6
A. The Development of the Town		9
Devenishki - From The Founding	Binyamin Dubinski	10
Thoes Days Are Well Remembered (Photos Only)	Yakov Bloch	21
Under Confinement With Russians, Poles, and Germans	Eliohu Wiener	24
My Town and My Family	Orit Kaplan	28
The Civil Guard ("Varte")	Meir Yosef Itskovitsh	32
Divenishok: A Charming Town	Dr. Menachem Weisenfeld	33
I Treated Divenishok and its People With Fondness	Shlomo Levine	37
I Bonded With Divenishok	Frume Kaplan	40
Social and Political Life (Photos Only)	Shraga Blyakher	42
Institutions and Organizations in Divenishok	Avraham Abir (Rudnik)	46
Maccabi HaTzair	Natan Kaplan	54
My Path to Betar	Meir Yosef Itskovitsh	56
Zionist and Cultural Activity (Reference Only)	Avraham Aloni	65
The Hebrew School in Divenishok	Shmuel Dubkin	65
Memories of the "HeKhaluts" Society	Shalom Rosenblum	67
The Revival Period in Divenishok	Dov Ben Shalom (Popisko)	70
HeKhaluts Organization in Our Town	Eliahu Netaneli (Itskovitsh)	72
Trivia From Our Town	Moshe Mintz	77
The Torah Reading Was Stopped	Eliahu Itskovtish (Itzkovitz)	80
In the Service of the Jewish Homeland	Natan Kaplan, son of Mordechai and Khasye	81
Memories from Two World Wars	Aryeh Olkenitski	85
The Youth Was Imbued With A Zionist Consciousness	Esther Gordon	87
The Theater in the Town	Binyamin Dubinski	88
Revolutionary Activity Against the Czar	D. Binyamin	91
With Love and Nostalgia	Khayeh Garvey (Khayeh Broine's)	93
The Mitzvah of Linat Zedek	Miriam Herman	96

From Divenishok to *Eretz-Israel*	Khenye Harari	98
How I Reached Israel	Dvora Rakhl	100
My Contribution to the Building of the Country	Elimelech Rudnik	102
The Monument in Divenishok Honoring the Unknown Soldier	Boris Rabinovitsh	104

B. The Holocaust and Fighting — 106

We Will Not Forget You!	Yakov Bloch	106
Gloom Fell on the Town	Taiba Griner	108
In the Ghettos and the Woods with Partisans	Tsvi Novopolanski	114
In the Claws of the Nazi Beast	Kalmen Kartshmer	138
I Fought the Germans with the Partisans	Lucia Rubin	142
In Battle Against the Nazi Enemy	Zelig Rogol	146
A Partisan's Story	Eliahu Blyakher	152
Under the German Occupation	Sara Hinda Movshovitsh	163
The Forest Was Our Home....	Sholem Bronshtayn	168
I Was Left Alone and Isolated	Shulamit Fuchs	171
From Partisan Unit to the Palmach Brigade	Michael Dubinski	177
I'm The Only One Left From My Family	Yeshayahu Vulfovitsh	193
Where Are All of Them? Where?....	Tzvi (Hirshel) Krizovski	195
Days of Hardship and Suffering	Tsvi Ahuvi	196
The Amputee of Divenishok	Meir Yosef Itzkovitsh	203
Our Loved Ones Did Not Go As Lambs to Slaughter	Meir Yosef son of Natan Itskovitsh	206
The Story of an 11 Year Old Boy	Pinchas Lipkunski	219
I Got to See a Picture of the People I Love	Nili Itskovitsh	225

C. Images — 228

My Father, the Great Rabbi Yosef Rudnik	Avraham Abir (Rudnik)	228
In Memory of Rabbi Rudnik	Shraga Blyakher	240
Rabbi Yisrael Movshovitsh	Yosef Movshovitsh	241
My Father's House	Shmuel Sharon	245
Ben–Zion Schneider	Avraham Aloni	251
The Zionist Activist Yudel Satkolshtsik	Avraham Aloni	253
Eulogy for My Father of Blessed Memory	Yosef Meir Itskovitsh	254
About My Father and My Family	Shulamit Fuchs [Rogol]	259
Dov Zandman	("Memorial" Book)	261
Dov of Blessed Memory	Rivke Zandman	263
Reb Moshe Ben Zion Khasman		265
The Daughters Tell About Their Father	Sarah Itskovitsh and Grunye Bronshtayn	269

HaRav Ben-Zion Khasman	Eliahu Netaneli (Itskovitsh)	271
Sarah Disha Horvits: A Righteous Woman	Henye Harari	272
Hirshl Krizovski	Shlomo Gordon	273
Tzvi (Hirshl) Krizovski	Khaye Rivke and Menukha Krizovski	275
Working for the Community	Eliohu Blyakher	278
My Father and Grandfather Loved Working the Land	Yosef Kaplan	280
In Memory of My Father Leyb Dubin, May He Rest in Peace	Rachel Zuvitshki (Dubin)	282
Mordechai Blyakher, Of Blessed Memory	Moshe Mintz	284
My Family	Kheyne Sutskever	286
On Those Who Escaped to Soviet Russia	Rivke Krizovski	287
In Memory of Our Mother Shoshana (Reyzl) Ben-Dov	Amnon and Yaffa	288
About A Jewish Family	Dina Lebizuvski	289
R' Leyb Aharon Engle, Of Blessed Righteous Memory	Eliahu Netaneli (Itskovitsh)	291
Eliahu Chaim Shkolnik	Eliahu Netaneli (Itskovitz)	291
One of the Ancient Families	Esther Ala (Blyakher)	293
My Husband Yosef Levine: A Multifaceted Man	Yehudit Levin	294
Tsvi Rogol	Shulamit Fuchs (Rogol)	296
About My Parents and Grandfather	Shlomo Gordon	297
Yehuda Satkoltshtsik, Of Blessed Memory	Shlomo Aviel	302
My Father Provided Much Aid to Jews	Yehuda Katz	303
Our Mother Zipporah (Rashke) of the Levine Family	Shoshana Yudenfreund	305
In Memory of Itteh Blyakher	Eliahu Netaneli (Itskovitsh) & Bella Ashman (Itskovitsh)	307
About My Husband and Our Family	Ida Kaplan	309
In Memory of My Parents, Brothers, Sister, and Family	Bella Ashman	310
A Daughter and Granddaughter Speaks	Sarah Hinde Movshovitsh [Blyakher]	318
My Mother Immigrated to Israel in 1922	Sara Kaplan	349
A Family of Blacksmiths	Zalmen Bronshtayn	320
A Typical Jewish Home	Zipporah Yudenfreund (Levine)	322
A Brief Biography of My Friend Avraham Kartshmer	Avraham Aloni	324
Khaneh	Khonen Eyshishki	325
About the Family of Tsvi Schmidt (Hershl the Stableman)	Zalmen Dan Kushtilski	328
Our Mother Khayne, Daughter of Avraham Eliezer and Miriam Levine	Eliahu Netaneli [Itskoztish]	328

They Were So [Series of Brief Biographies]	Binyamin Dubinski	330
My grandfather R' Yitzchak (Itshe) Binyamin Rudnik	Yakov Bloch	393
The 'Tel-Hainik': M[eir] Y[osef] Itskovitsh	Chaim Lazar	395

Yiddish Section
1. The Town and its Development

		410
Dieveniskes [Divenishok] - The History of a Town (Photos Only)	Binyamin Dubinski	410
The Shtetele Divenishok	Meir Yoshke Nathan's (Itskovitsh)	414
A Jewish Life that is No More...	Motke (Moshe Leyzer's) Kartshmer	428
Social and Political Life	Shraga Blyakher	435
Zionist and Cultural Activity	Avraham Aloni	443
How I Remember You, Divenishok...	Khanan Lefkovitsh	451
Those Days Are Well Remembered	Yakov Bloch	453
On Communal Life	Lolik Sutskever	463
The "Bees" and "Vilbig" Organizations	Khaye-Rivke Krizovski	469
The Torah Reading was Stopped ...	Eliahu Itskovitsh (Netaneli)	471
Jewish "Parnoses" [Livelihoods] in Divenishok		473

2. Destruction and Bravery

		476
All That Remains is a Name	Solomon Levine	478
How I Remember You, Divenishok...	Shoel ben Natl Kaplan	479
The Amputee of Divenishok (Reference Only)	Meir Yosef Itskovitsh	482
A Dream ...	Meir Yosef Itskovitsh	482

3. Figures

		486
The Rabbi and Great Scholar Yosef Rudnik, May His Memory Be For a Blessing		486
Aaron-Leyb Baron		487
Reb Moshe Ben-Zion Hasman, May His Memory Be For a Blessing		488
Krizovski, Aaron Yakov-- Of Blessed Memory		492
Two poems by Aaron Yakov Krizovski		493
The Poet Aaron Krizovski	Menukha Peykhova (Krizovski)	494
Our Poet A. Y. Krizovski	Binyamin Dubinski	495
Shtetelech (Poem)	Shloyme Kazjimirovski	498
One Cannot Forget Them	Sore-Teybke & Nakhum Levine	499
My Shtetl, Home, and Family	Moshe & Perke Levine-Kartshmer	500

In Memory of My Father, My Mother, and My Family	Sore-Toyve Hershovitsh-Levi	503
In Memory of My Father	Sore Shklar	505
Horav Khaim Yehudah Horvits, Of Blessed Memory	Nisan Gordon	505

4. Landsmanshaftn — 516

Our *Landsmanshaft* in Israel	Khaya Garvey	516
American Relief Creates the *Gmiles Khesed* Fund	Tsvi Ahuvi (Lieb)	518
An Appeal From Former Divenishok Residents in the Land of Israel to their Townspeople in America	(A Document)	520
Landsman in Israel Tells About the *Landsmanshaft* in America	Yakov Bloch	522
10th Anniversary of the Divenishok *Landslayt* in New York	(Various)	528
30th Anniversary of the Divenishok Society of Greater New York	(Various)	531
35th Anniversary of the Divenishok Society	(Various)	533
Greetings to the 45th Anniversary of the Divenishok Society of Greater New York	Yosef Levey	535
The 70th Anniversary of the Divenishok Relief in America	Binyamin Dubinski	538
Report from the Divenishok Ladies Auxiliary	Nellie Brown	543
Organization of Former Divenishok Residents in Israel	Tsvi Ahuvi (Lieb)	545

List of Martyrs — 548

In Memoriam (Photos) — 558

Index For **Original** Hebrew/Yiddish Yizkor Book
Annotated Name Index — 567

Index For this English **Translation**
Names and Places Index — 624

Introduction to the Translation

I have known about the Divenishok Yizkor Book since I was a young boy. My grandparents gave me a copy of the book when I was about twelve and it has moved with me, going from shelf to shelf, largely unread for decades. However, as I began to have the time to delve into my own ancestry I soon realized how much invaluable and otherwise unobtainable information was hiding within these pages. Since nearly forty years had passed without an English translation, my only option was to produce a translation of my own. And so I volunteered for the task via the JewishGen Yizkor Book Project and have been rewarded a thousand times over for the effort.

I cannot claim to be an expert on the subject of Yizkor Books, but I suspect that among Yizkor Books, this one is especially compelling. There are two main reasons why I feel confident about making such a statement. The first is that the writers and editors of the original volume took great care to include not only the tales of heroism and suffering that are staples in the Yizkor book literature, but also numerous articles about everyday life and everyday people. The result is one of the most authentic eyewitness accounts ever written of what genocide looks like and feels like from inside the hunted community.

The other major achievement contained in this work is its photographic richness. One of the town's residents, Tsvi Krizovski, became fascinated with photography in the early 20th Century, assuming the role of unofficial town photographer. Over 100 photos accompany the articles, in many instances depicting the persons mentioned in the text.

For genealogists. the amount of family tree information contained in this volume is extraordinary, and I have assimilated these data into a Divenishok Ancestral Tree containing over 14,000 entries that researchers may use to find their roots in this and surrounding towns. Researchers interested in delving further into Divenishok kinships are welcomed to visit the "Dieveniskes Kehilalinks" page, via online search, to access these and other materials.

While I have made every effort to remain faithful to the intentions and dialects of the book's original authors, there are three areas which depart from this principle:

- ❖ for the sake of indexing, the spellings of town names have been standardized throughout the book to conform with the Yiddish language versions of these names,

- ❖ similarly, the spellings of recurring names and surnames have been standardized to conform with the most commonly used versions of these names, and

- ❖ for the five articles which appear in both Hebrew and Yiddish language versions in the original book, only one translation is published here: in these instances, the article is placed where the original language version was placed (i.e., if the Hebrew version was used for the translation then the article appears in the Hebrew section, and vice versa); the duplicative articles have been omitted from the book; the titles of each of the omitted articles continue to appear in the text at their original locations, along with a note giving the page number where the article may be found; the photographs associated with the ommited articles continue to appear under their titles in their original locations (they have not been moved).

I am forever grateful to the extraordinary translators who have moonlighted for pittances on this project. Their names may be found below the title of each of their articles and they should be honored. I am also eternally indebted to the many generous, individual contributors whose funding made this translation possible.

Adam Benyakonski Cherson, 21 November 2020
Project Coordinator and Translation Editor

Map of Devenishki

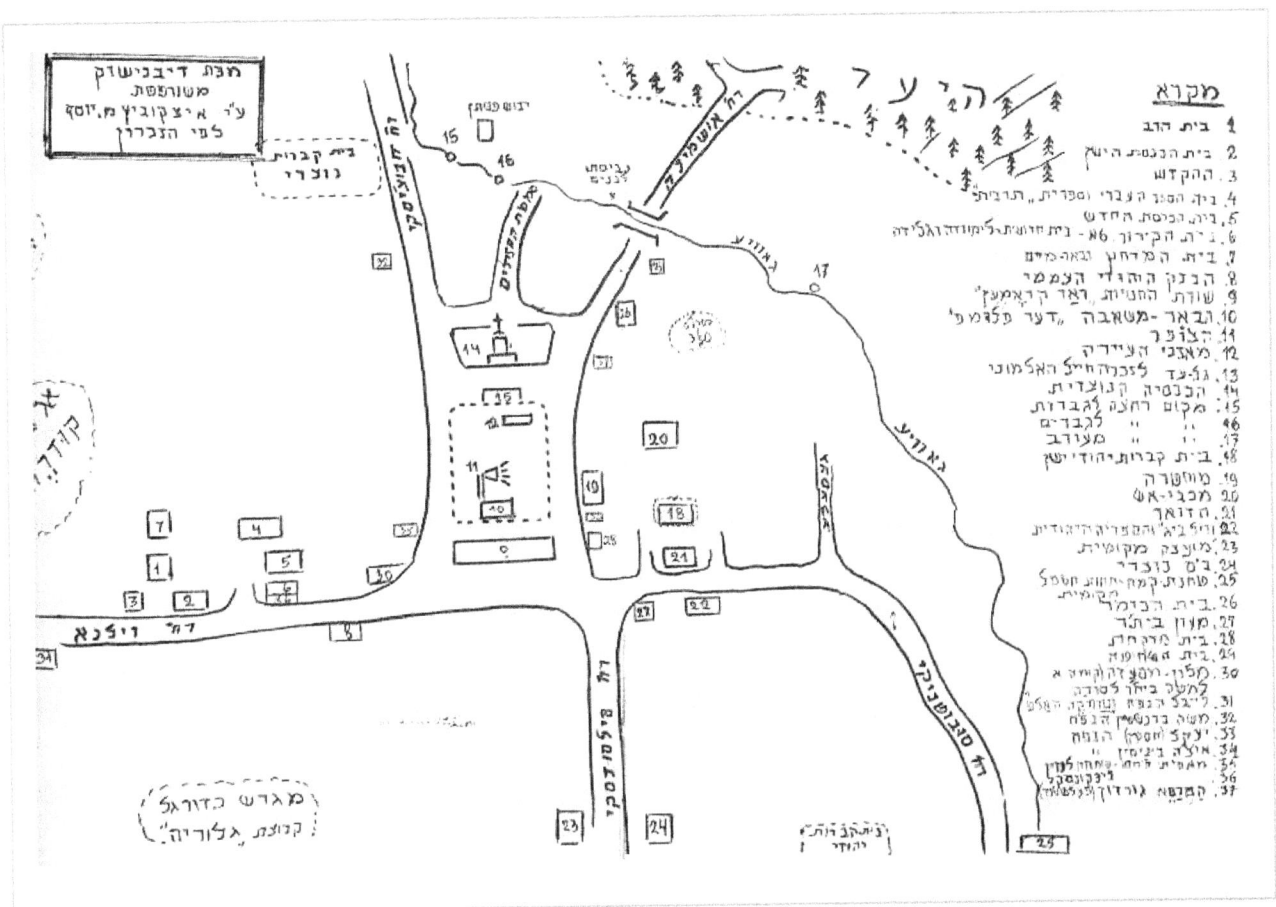

Other Notations on Map: a) lower left corner in dotted oval to left of 23: Soccer Field "Gloria", b) dotted oval between 24 and 25: Jewish Cemetery

Key to Map of Devenishki

1. Rabbi's House
2. Old Synagogue
3. Hey-Hey-Kuf-Daled-Shin (meaning unknown)
4. 'Tarbut' Hebrew School and Library
5. New Synagogue
6. Ice House (6a: Lemonade and Ice Cream Factory)
7. Public Bath House and Well
8. Jewish Bank
9. Row of Stores "Rad Kramets" (meaning unknown)
10. Well and Pump "Der Plump"
11. Hey-Tzadek-Vov-Pey-Reysh (meaning unknown)
12. City scales
13. Memorial for Unknown Soldier
14. Christian Church
15. Wash House for Women
16. Wash House for Men
17. Co-Ed Bath House
18. Old Jewish Cemetery
19. Police
20. Fire Department
21. Post Office
22. Jewish Library
23. City Hall
24. Christian School
25. Wheat Station (Silo?)/ Electricity Generating Plant
26. Priest's House
27. Betar House
28. Pharmacy
29. Slaughterhouse
30. Hotel and Restaurant
31. Leybl the Blacksmith and Nekhehmka the Tile Maker
32. Moshe Bernshteyn the Blacksmith
33. Yakov Khasman the Blacksmith
34. Yitzach Binyamin the Blacksmith
35. Bakery- Simkha Leyzer
36. Bakery- Lipkunski
37. Hey-Mem-Reysh-Pey-Aleph (meaning unknown) Gordon the Medic

Tombstone for a Divenishok martyr, murdered during the Shoah

The Jewish Town

(Introduction to the Devenishki Book)

Translation by Alma Cahn

How did the Jewish town appear and in what way did it differ from a Jewish settled area in the big city in the Diaspora? The small town was different from the life of the Jews who congregated in the big city. They were shut off from the wide world. The town lay in a high, natural setting surrounded by woods, fields, and gardens in a pastoral atmosphere, open except for the blessings and curses from the world around them. There were no ghetto walls for these Jews to protect them from neighboring enemies, nor were there any doors to lock against pogroms and robbers. Their fort was their security and their faith in their religion. Their wealth lay in their courage and fortitude in times of pogroms and never ending trouble. In the center of the town, on a high place, was a market where trading and business transactions took place. Everyone recalls the get-together on the market days where the Jewish merchants gathered with the peasants of neighboring areas and sold their products. Jewish houses attached to each other surrounded the market. In the side streets and a bit further from the center lived the non-Jews. The town was divided between Jewish and non-Jewish quarters because, in that way, it was easier to protect their religion, to be careful with their customs and rituals, and give respect to the celebrations of the Sabbath and the holidays. Within this closed community the Jews felt as if they were in a fort, just believing that their world is strong, impenetrable, as if they were in their own country.

Among the Jewish townspeople were craftsmen who worked with great energy to earn their daily bread. They loved their work and worked from morning 'til night. Only Jews performed certain occupations: tailors, shoemakers, capmakers, and blacksmiths. It should be emphasized that in the town there were also lumber merchants and wheat dealers who were very diligent workers. Their work, however, did not exclude them from upholding their spiritual values and religion, maintaining their family ties, raising their children to do good deeds, and studying Torah.

The writer Sholem Asch gives a very vivid description of wealthy Jewish craftsmen in the various Jewish town who acted like the nobility. This caused a great deal of resentment amongst their Gentile neighbors who envied them because they lived in luxurious homes. The Gentiles wanted to destroy the Jews and their possessions. Unfortunately, they were successful.

Most of the Jews were poor craftsmen, peddlers and general storekeepers, selling dishes and other general goods. They were not always able to eke out a living or make ends meet. They had to contend with going by foot in all kinds of weather, on unpaved roads, and peddling with old clothes in order to make a living to support their families.

The majority of the downtrodden Jews, however, did not lose their hope for a better future and [were] known in Jewish literature for their piousness and devotion to their religion. One sees the picture of a Jewish merchant sitting on the threshold of his store, anxiously awaiting a customer, and holding a prayer book in his hand. In spite of the fact that the town underwent many economic crises such as poverty, unpaid debts, lack of money, and bankruptcy, they never lost their hopes and expectations for a better future. The inhabitants of the town were very devout Jews. They believed in doing good deeds [mitzvot]. Before the town was devastated, most of the people attended the synagogue daily to study Torah and relax after a hard days' work. To the very end they followed the Jewish traditions and all of it ramifications. Saturdays and Jewish holidays were very eventful days for the Jews in the town. They forgot all their worries and problems. The holidays were observed in the usual Jewish tradition, especially during the Jewish New Year (Rosh Hashonah), Yom Kippur, Succot, and Simchat Torah. Passover was celebrated with the arrival of spring. The children celebrated the holiday of Lag B'Omer in the woods. Shevuot was the holiday where the homes were decorated by greenery.

It was a hard life in the town and a very sad existence. The town had its own lifestyle. The aspirations and ideals that prevailed in the Jewish homes gave them incentive and encouragement to go on with their lives. They looked forward to the Jewish holidays and the Sabbath. Special preparations were made months in advance for the Passover holiday so that the Jews should not be left without matzot and wine during the holiday. Weekdays, the people of the town were very depressed, with very little hope for the future or expectation for their liberation.

The Jewish children in the village looked forward eagerly with great expectation and anticipation to the various Jewish holidays such as Chanukah and the lighting of the Chanukah candles on the menorah. They looked forward to the holiday of Purim where noisemakers were distributed, Purim gifts were exchanged, and the traditional Purim pastry (Hamentashen) eaten. They also looked forward to the two Passover Seder evenings, Lag B'Omer, Shevuot, the holiday of Tisha B'ov, and the Jewish New Year. The shofar was blown in the synagogue during Rosh Hashonah. They also looked forward to the holiday of Yom Kippur, the Day of Atonement, and Simchat Torah, when they danced in the street around the Torah. There were many customs in the village that gave much meaning to the people, even though their life was filled with despair and struggle for existence. The wonderful family life and devotion to their religion gave them the courage to carry on. On the other hand, they contended with poverty, denigration, unemployment and helplessness, the difference between reality and fantasy to improve conditions and escape from reality. Benjamin Hashlishe, the Yiddish writer, represented a special character of Mendele Mocher Sefarim's [?] stories of Jews in the small towns. Benjamin wants to go to Israel but cannot differentiate between dream and reality. He imagines he is Alexander the Great and is convinced of his own strength. He yearns for the Holy Land. There is no obstacle in his path that keeps him from getting there. He keeps on dreaming and fantasizing without having the practical means to travel. There were many such dreamers in the village who were preoccupied with the legends and miracles in the stories they read. These stories gave the townspeople courage and hope. Was the hero Benjamin Hashlishe in reality a dreamer? Many of the so-called dreamers had illusions and expectations to escape from the misery of their conditions in their town. These dreamers felt that they were in exile and that there was no future for them in the shtetl. They were trapped and looked for a way out. They had the strength and fortitude to work for a higher standard of living. They were devoted to their families and to their religion and Jewish heritage.

Such heroes as Benjamin Hashlishe represented the tower of strength of Jewish independence in their homeland. Amongst the group of heroes were prominent leaders, liberation fighters, revolutionaries, poets and writers, scientists, spiritual leaders and creative people on all fronts. They also represent the Jewish town.

The Holocaust annihilated our people and wiped out the Jewish shtetl in Europe. 'Our town is burning' was not merely a folksong, but a reminder of the traditional Jewish lifestyle. Also, the Jewish town of "Divenishok" was affected by the Holocaust. We the "saving remnant" or survivors of that town who found refuge in their new homes in Israel and the U.S.A. did not want to forget our town where we were born, raised and received our education and knowledge. Due to their pride in their Jewish heritage and concern and responsibility for future generations, they establish the memorial book for the town of Divenishok. The yizkor now is distributed to the former inhabitants of Divenishok and to those interested [in] reading about the history of the sociology and psychology of the Jewish town of Divenishok. "Sefer Divenishok" is the product of many years of research, [...?...] regarding a small Jewish community. The book consists of five parts depicting chronologically the existence, development, and annihilation of the Jewish town of Divenishok. We express our thanks and recognition to our (landsleit) former residents or inhabitants of Divenishok to the following: Milton Kartshmer, Frank Barnett, and the former inhabitants of Divenishok who are now living in Israel and to editorial co-workers, Meir Jacob Itskovitsh, Shraga Blyakher, Jacob Bloch, Benjamin Dubinski, the editor of the book, David Shtokfish, and all others who assisted in providing the material for this book. When we planned our memorial book, we did not have the slightest idea that we would reach over five hundred pages in Yiddish, Hebrew and English. However, the desire to establish a memorial in honor of those Jews whose grave sites remain unknown, spurred us to our work of writing this book, "Sefer Divenishok".

Signed Samuel Sharon
in the name of the Book Committee
Tel Aviv, June 1977

A. The Development of the Town

[Page 16]

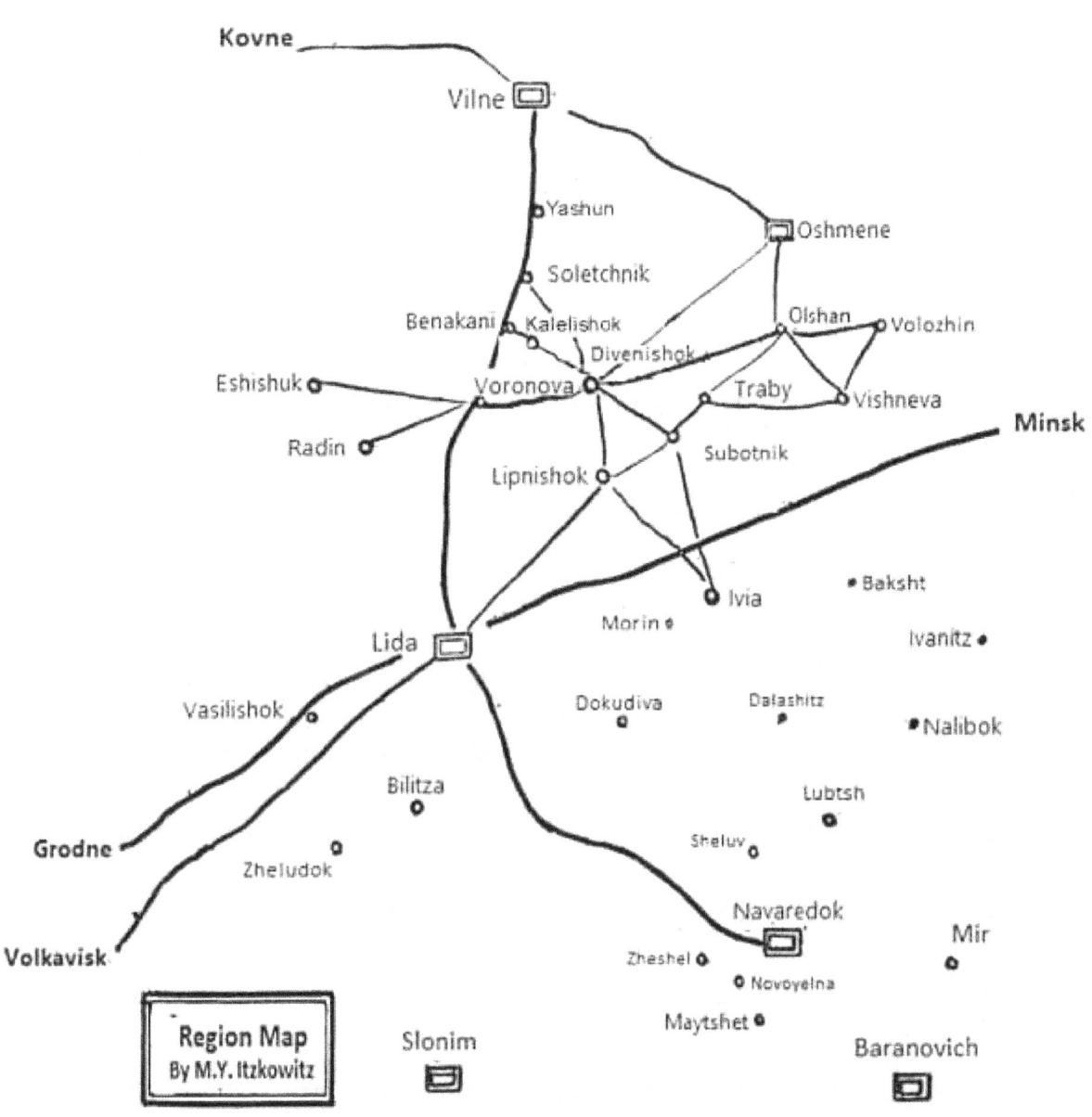

Region Map By M.Y. Itzkowitz

Divenishok-From The Founding

Binyamin Dubinski
Translation by Martin Jacobs

Geographic, Demographic, and Statistical Data

The town has had many names, although phonetically they all have one source. In Hebrew it was called Divenishok; in Yiddish, Dzivenishok; in Russian, Dyevenishki = Девенишки; in English, Devenishki; in Polish, Dziewieniszki; and in Lithuanian, Deveniskas.

The town is situated on the bank of the Gavya River, which has its sources about 15 km from the town. The entire region is rich in springs of water. The Gavya River flows into the Neman River.

Divenishok is situated on a plateau about 150 meters above sea level, at 54° 12' latitude, 43° 16' E longitude. It is about 30 km southwest of Oszmiana, 63 km from Vilne, 12 km from Subotniki, 21 km from the Benakani railroad station, and about 50 km from Lida.

The origin of the town's name is not sufficiently clear but it is related to the Polish word "dzwon" (bell). On all official documents the bell appears as the official symbol of the town.

The Founding of Divenishok; Its Owners

According to the *Slownik Geograficzny*, [Ed. Note: geographical dictionary of the former kingdom of Poland and other Slavic lands] in 1433 Divenishok, as well as other properties in Lithuania, passed into the possession of the well known Gasztold[Tr. Note: Goštautas] family, by order of the Lithuanian Grand Duke Sigmund Kiejstutowicz. In 1500 a Catholic church was established in the town by one of this family. After the last of the Gasztolds, Stanislaw, died, the town passed to the guardianship of King Sigmund; that was in 1542. And so it was transformed into a state possession, administered by a *starost*.[Tr. Note: governor of a province in Poland]

In 1782 Marshal Jadka ruled Divenishok. ("Marshal" was a designation for Polish nobility; he was a descendant of a convert to Christianity, who was given a noble title.) Rental on his estate brought him a yearly income of 1,184 zlotys.

In the 19th century there was a distribution of town lands, as a result of which agricultural parcels were divided among the Christian residents (called *mieszczanin*),[Tr. Note: burghers, townspeople] except for the hundred *desyatin*[Tr. Note:

obsolete Russian land unit, one desyatin is equal to 2.7 acres] of land granted to Nazaretski, a state official.

3In 1880, 843 Christians lived in the town; their principal occupation was agriculture. Jews formed the majority of the town's population, and they were in trade and handicrafts. They made a good living, especially at the weekly market days and at the two great yearly fairs.

The community included nine rural areas with 90 villages and 5,796 residents. It is surprising that the *Geographic Dictionary* gives no information on the number of Jews in Divenishok, since it does have information about the number of Jews in other towns.

The Founding of Jewish Towns in Lite

[Tr. Note: Here 'Lite' designates not just Lithuania but also surrounding areas, such as Belarus and Northeast Poland]

The beginnings of the Jewish settlement in Divenishok are shrouded in darkness, as is the blossoming of all the small towns on the broad plain between the Neman, Gavya, and Vilija Rivers. For the most part this area is covered with virgin forest, green meadows, and flowing streams, extending over a terrain of thousands of kilometers.

There are creditable documents attesting to the presence of Jews in Lithuania as early as the ninth century. Bishop Adalbert of Prague, sent in 997 to preach the Gospel to the pagans in Lithuania, relates that "many Christian prisoners are sold to Jews for money and he was not able to ransom them". It is also known that there was a large Jewish emigration from western Europe to Lithuania in the 14th century, during the rule of Gediminas (1316-1341), who expanded the borders of the Lithuanian state to the Neman and the Bug. Gediminas was a pagan, free of anti-Jewish complexes, and he opened the gates of his land to the persecuted Jews of western Europe. His grandson, Witold Vytautas (1392-1430), Grand Duke of Lithuania, also had a sympathetic relationship with the Jews. He even published a "Jewish Law" of 37 paragraphs which granted special rights to the Jews. Witold's laws for the Jews of Lithuania essentially resembled the charters of Duke Boleslaw of Kalisz for the Jews of Poland and recognized their civil, religious, and commercial rights, and granted permission to move freely across the entire land. The Lithuanian population, pagan until the second half of the 14th century, knew nothing of anti-Semitism and had honorable and tolerant relations with Jews.

Market day in the town: farmers brought their produce to the market every Thursday

The Beginning of the Jewish Settlement in Vilne and Environs

Vilne was founded in 1323 by Gediminas, Grand Duke of Lithuania. From that time on Jews little by little began to settle in the city and basically engaged in trade and brokerage. The Jewish population of Vilne grew very slowly. In 1520, when the Council of Four Lands was formed, only three communities of Lithuanian Jews were represented in it: Brisk, Horodne, and Pinsk. The size of the Jewish population of Vilne at the time did not justify representation in the Council. Only after 1623 were the communities of Vilne and Slutsk included in the Council of Lithuanian Jews. This means that only more than 300 years after the founding of Vilne had its population increased significantly enough to justify its joining the Council of Lithuanian Jews.

The development of the Jewish settlement in the Vilne area paralleled that of the city itself. Individual Jews settled in each administrative center and wherever a Catholic church had been built. There they had the prospects of a decent living. Jews settled in the villages near the center and so began the spread of Jewish settlement in the region and in Vilne.

A decisive factor in the growth of the Jewish population in the Vilne region were the massacres of 1648 and 1649. At that time Bogdan Khmelnytsky lead the Cossacks in a holy war against the Polish land owners. In their bloody path the Cossacks destroyed entire Jewish communities in the Ukraine and Podolia. A stream of Jewish refugees began to flow west, many of them coming to our region. Survivors of these pogroms also settled in Divenishok.

The Polish grocery store set up by anti-semites with the slogan "Buy only from Poles"

The Russian-Swedish War

The Jews in the area lived through hard times during the war between Russia and Sweden at the end of the 17th century. The Russian army swept across Poland and Lithuania and in 1655 it occupied Vilne and its environs. There were pogroms against Jews in Vilne and Grodne, but there are no historical reports of pogroms also taking place in the surrounding small towns such as Divenishok.

Carl Gustav X, King of Sweden, who was then at the height of his military power, exploited the anarchy in Poland to launch a surprise attack on Russia. His armies took all of Lithuania by storm and reached Vilne and even areas to the south. To the present day there are testimonies to the Swedish presence in our town. About five kilometers from Divenishok, on the highway from Vilne that goes through the Dubink forest, lies swampy terrain which makes passage difficult, especially on rainy days. The Swedes solved the problem as they did in Sweden in those days. They sawed pine from the forest into planks and covered the roadway with layer upon layer, and in this way created a bridge over the swamp and solved the problem of crossing the mud. The remains of that bridge are still visible and the locals call it "shvedska greblia". [Ed. Note: the Swedish embankment]

The Period of the Russian Occupation

Three times, in 1772, 1789, and 1795, Russia, Prussia, and Austria partitioned the Polish state among themselves. After the third partition the largest part of Poland came under Russian rule and the Jews of Lithuania found themselves subject to Catherine the Great, the "enlightened" empress, who immediately defined a Pale of Settlement for Jews and issued harsh decrees against them, such as an absolute prohibition of living in villages. The Jews who in the course of generations had put down roots in the villages, and had their own land, were forced to leave everything and move into the towns empty handed.

In 1804 the expulsion began. It was interrupted by Napoleon's invasion of Russia. The expulsions were renewed after Napoleon's defeat and continued intermittently throughout the 19th century. These expulsions led to a flow of population into the cities and towns; this is one of the reasons for the increase in the Jewish population of Divenishok.

The Russian occupation also had positive aspects: Large markets in Russia opened up for the Jews of Lithuania. This led to economic prosperity in the Lithuanian towns. The religious and cultural connections between the Jews of Lithuania and Russia were also broadened, as is shown by the distribution of newspapers and the publication of religious books and research books.

The Age of Upheaval and Change

The years from 1914 to 1945 were full of difficulties and afflictions, because power passed from hand to hand. In 1915 the Germans occupied the town and were in control for two years. After that the Bolsheviks were in control; they stayed briefly, until the Poles expelled them. In 1919 the Poles set up their administration in the town, which lasted until 1939, when Divenishok was taken by the Soviets. In 1941 the Germans again took the town. In 1943 the Germans transferred it to the Lithuanians. When the region was taken by the Soviets in 1945, the town was finally transferred to the Lithuanian Soviet Republic, to which it still belongs.[Ed. Note: Divenishok is currently in the Republic of Lithuania]

Development of the Jewish Community in Divenishok

As a result of the break in communications with Poland we have no documents which can shed light on the beginning of the Jewish settlement in Divenishok. The only authoritative source we possess is the *Yevreiskaya*

Entsiklopedia[Tr. Note: Jewish Encyclopedia] by Katzenelson and Ginzburg, according to which there were 94 Jews[Ed. Note: could mean 94 families] in Divenishok in 1766. In 1847 the town had 240 Jews[Ed. Note: could mean 94 families] and in 1897[Ed. Note: 1897 is probably an error since the Jewish encyclopedia reports this date as 1898] there were 1,897 residents in the town, 1,225 of them Jews.

It should not be inferred from this that there was no Jewish settlement in Divenishok many years earlier. The fact that in 1500 a Catholic church was established there and the place was designated a regional center raises the possibility that individual Jews were already living there in the sixteenth century, since they could live and develop peacefully there. It also seems reasonable that individual Jews, engaging in brokerage and agriculture, lived in the surrounding villages.

There is reason to believe that in 1652, with the inclusion of Vilne as an independent area in the Committee of Lithuanian Jewry, the population in Vilne increased at the same rate as the population in the area as a whole, including our town, although this cannot be proven from the historical data, since the head-tax which the Jews of the small towns paid was included in the total accounts of Vilne and the region.

Some data can, to a certain extent, throw light on the beginning of a Jewish settlement in our town. As is the general custom, cemeteries are at somewhat of a distance from settlements. In Divenishok the cemetery was located in Magazin, more than a kilometer from the town. However, at the same time, an old cemetery was located in the town center, about ten meters from the market. It had not been used for more than a hundred years. The grave stones were half sunk into the ground and overgrown with vegetation, showing beyond all doubt that the town was first built far from its present location and for unknown reasons was moved to where the town cemetery was located. Even the most elderly townspeople did not know where the town had first been. They could only say that the cemetery had graves from the year 5450,[Tr. Note: 1690] that is, about 300 years ago.

I remember that there was a special synagogue for praying in summer in Divenishok. In its women's section there was an inscription carved into the wood: "This synagogue was built in the year 5500",[Tr. Note: 1740] 235 years earlier. That it was able to build a special summer synagogue for itself shows the economic strength and spiritual vigor of the Jewish settlement in the town.

The synagogue collapsed in the twenties and was replaced by a Hebrew school. In order not to destroy the holiness of the spot the rabbi decreed that an ark with a Torah scroll be placed in one of the classrooms, and there people prayed from time to time.

I remember that in the study house there were several bookcases with ancient volumes of the Talmud, which had been printed in Livorno, Italy. There were yellow drops of candle wax on them, proving that hundreds of years before, many scholars had lived in the town and spent their days in the study of the Talmud and Mishna.

From everything mentioned above it follows that a Jewish settlement in Divenishok was forming in the 16th century. At first it was very small in scope, only a few dozen families in the town and the surroundings. Because of the persecutions of Jews both in the east and the west the settlement continually grew and developed into a typical town. It is difficult to determine if the dominant majority in the town consisted of Jews who came from the east, from Russia, or German Jews who came from the west. In the opinion of Rabbi Joseph Movshovitsh the great stream of Jews came from Germany. He cited as proof the great number of family names which sound German, like Levine, Kuhn, Becker, Pludermacher[Tr. Note: could also be Fludermacher, indeterminate from original text], and others. The Rabbi had also heard that the grandfather of Justice Frankfurter of the United States Supreme Court had once lived in Divenishok and had owned the Pushpeshk farm. But many Jews changed their names, so as not to serve in the Czar's army, thus hiding their true identity. In addition Jews in Germany had close commercial ties with Jews in the Baltic lands; in time of trouble they of course found a refuge in tranquil Lithuanian towns.

In the seventeenth century the town was in its beginnings and only towards the eighteenth century did it begin to crystallize into an ordinary Jewish settlement. In that century the development of the town was dynamic and economically strong. In the nineteenth century the town grew in size and in quality because of the expulsion of the Jews from the villages. After that, however, the town lost population as a result of the mass migration to America, which continued into the twentieth century.

For over 400 years the quiet charming town existed in the thick forests of Lithuania, until the German enemy came and wiped it from the face of the earth. May the curse of generations cling to him forever.

Municipal Affiliation

During the Polish-Lithuanian Union Divenishok belonged administratively to the region of Lida and was under the jurisdiction of the regional court in Lipnishok. It received its mail by way of Subotniki, a town 12 km away. After the last partitioning of Poland (1795) the Russian authorities did everything they could to Russify the region. An Orthodox church was set up at the market place in Oszmiana and a Russian school was opened in the city. Oszmiana was designated a regional seat, taking in five towns, including Divenishok. According to the 1880 census a total of 11,131 Jews lived in the entire Oszmiana region.

Starting with the Russian occupation Divenishok belonged to the Vilne gubernia (region) and the Oszmiana oyezd (district). When the Vilne-Baranovich railway line was opened mail began to come to Divenishok from the Benakani railway station, 21 km away.

In the period of Polish rule (1919-1939) Divenishok belonged administratively to the Vilne voyevod (region) and Oszmiana powiat (district). During Soviet rule it belonged to the Oszmiana Rayispolkom (Regional Executive Committee) and the Grodne Oblast (region), within the framework of the Belorussian Soviet Socialist Republic, with its capital in Minsk. Since the Soviet occupation Divenishok has belonged to Lithuania and administratively to its capital Vilne.

Employment and Economy

The economy of the town was principally based on commerce and crafts. Agriculture supplemented the income of land owners. The *Slovnik Geograficzny*[Ed. Note: geographical dictionary of the former kingdom of Poland and other Slavic lands] indicates that the town included nine rural regions, which included 90 villages. Trade was in the hands of the Jews, who made up a dominant majority of the town's population. Commerce brought the Jews a good living during the regular market days and the two great semi-annual fairs. The situation did not change in the 20th century. Trade with the surrounding villages served as an essential basis for Jewish existence in the town. Such a situation characterized all towns in Lithuania from their founding.

The market days were days of strenuous administrative and physical activity which determined the extent of Jewish earnings for the week. Bearded burghers would stand at the thresholds of their shops looking for customers. Merchants, coachmen, and traders urgently hurried to buy produce from the farmers before the competition could get there. Peddlers and salesmen invited customers by calling and gesturing. People bought and sold everything they had. The other days of the week the town was quiet and life was lazy. Everyone was getting ready for the next market day.

Before the 20th century we have no data on the occupational make up of the population. The *Jewish Encyclopedia* has information on this matter basically for the end of the 19th century and the beginning of the twentieth. The 1898 census reports a population of 1,877, of whom 1,283 were Jews. There were 277 craftsmen in the town; about 66 women made their living from knitting socks which were sold in Vilne. Approximately ninety three people were day laborers and the rest of the population was in commerce. Charitable organizations in the town included the shelter for poor travelers, a free loan fund, and the society for visiting the sick. In addition there was a library with

Yiddish books, a school with 84 students, a Jewish religious school with 20 pupils, and five Jewish elementary schools with 56 children.

It should be noted that knitting socks was an exceptional occurrence in the town and only a temporary one. Only three towns were engaged in this occupation: Molodetchno, Kobilnik, and Divenishok, and only until the large knitting mills were set up in Vilne and other cities.

Life in the town followed the same fixed patterns as in all the Lithuanian towns. For hundreds of years life flowed by "beside the still waters", unchanged and undisturbed.

Employment and one's economic situation determined the status of everyone in society. Wealthy people and established shopkeepers were considered the most respectable. Most of the town's residents hunted for work and lived by the toil of their hands. Despite difficulties in making a living the Jews were proud, with a strong Jewish and national consciousness. Many of them emigrated, looking for a better life.

The Fires

Our town experienced two large fires and several smaller ones. In 1912 a big fire broke out in the marketplace and almost destroyed the whole town. There was a second fire in 1932, in which many houses in the market burned. The fires impoverished the townspeople, but thanks to mutual help those who suffered from the fires were able to rebuild. We should emphasize that helping each other in the event of a fire was taken for granted in Lithuanian towns. So we find in the newspaper "HaMelits" in the year 5652 (1891) that Divenishok is listed among the towns which gave valuable assistance to the Jews in Lida after the great fire in that city.

In the First World War

With the outbreak of the First World War the situation in the town worsened, especially after the Germans came in 1915. They seized the young people in the town for forced labor (in the so-called "Fonye battalion") and stole food from the villages. The situation worsened daily. On top of this typhus was spreading through the surrounding area and many fell victim.

In the registry book for Y.K.P.[Tr. Note: Yevreski Komitet Pomoshchy (Jewish Aid Committee)] for that period we find a report from Divenishok: M. and S., 10 and 13 years of age. Father died of typhus. Mother blind. S., her 13 year old daughter, runs the household. The house is not fit to be lived in and might collapse. By pleading, the girl can get a little firewood from good hearted neighbors to warm the family. There is suffering, distress, and poverty in the town.

The Y.K.P., a well known philanthropic organization, undertook the task of helping the town. Urgent meetings in Vilne were arranged; delegates from Divenishok, Arye Leyb Rogol and Rabbi Movshovitsh, participated. Urgent assistance was sent to the towns of the area, including Divenshok. A public kitchen was opened for the poor; the needy received help with food and clothing. This situation continued with the arrival of the Bolsheviks in the town and improved when the Poles came.

Firefighters unit made up entirely of Jewish youths (1932)

Polish Rule

Polish rule can be divided into two periods. The first was the time of Marshal Pilsudski. He treated the Jews with tolerance; their economic situation achieved a certain stability. In the second period, which succeeded Pilsudski, the position of the Jews worsened more and more as a result of an increasing wave of anti-Semitism. The Poles began to remove business from Jewish hands; they opened shops and cooperatives in every town and village; they organized a boycott of the Jews with the slogan "swój do swego" (everyone for his own people).

We read in the report of the Y.K.P. about the position of the Jews in Divenishok at that time: There are 250 families in Divenishok, 140 of them Jewish. Principal occupations: shop keeping, trade with the villages, crafts, sewing workshops, and clothing manufacture. There were 60 shops in the town owned by Jews and two Polish cooperatives which received financial aid from the local government.

Merchandise in the cooperatives was brought from the central warehouse in Benakani. The Jewish merchants brought their merchandise by wagon from Vilne. Because of the expense of the transportation, the excessive number of shops, and the fierce competition from the Polish cooperatives, the Jewish shops were in a very difficult position. The weekly market day was held every Thursday. About 20 to 30 families made their living dealing in produce from the villages *korobelnikes*.[Tr. Note: peddlers] There were five sewing workshops for clothing manufacture in the town, employing 40 men and women, who earned 20 - 30 zlotys a week. Their products were marketed in the neighboring towns of Vishneva, Trok, Olszanica, Oszmiana, etc.

Two expert Polish shoemakers and one carpenter also worked in the town, but no builders. Five Jewish families had five *desyatin* each of agricultural land. They tilled the land themselves or with the help of day laborers. There were also Jews "who lived from the air" ("luftmentshn"): brokers, match makers, peddlers, etc.

From 1939 to 1941 the town was under Soviet rule. It took just a few days for the Red Army to make off with everything in the shops. Business stopped completely and most of the Jews lived from hand to mouth. They engaged in illegal trade and in selling what was left from Polish times. Life became gloomy and oppressive.

In July of 1941 the Germans entered Divenishok and our community was cruelly destroyed.

Bibliography:
1. Dr. Raphael Mahler, Toledoth haYehudim bePolin, "Siphrith haPoalim", 1946.
2. Prof. Sh. Dubnov, Pinkas haMedina shel Vaad haKehiloth haRishioth beMedina Lita, Berlin, 5688 [1928].
3. Prof. Sh. Dubnov, Dibhré yemé olam, Debhir publishers, Tel-Aviv 5710 [1950].
4. Moshe Shalit, Af di khurves fun milkhomes un mehumes, Pinkas fun gegnt komitet Y.K.P., Vilne 5691 [1931].
5. Sepher Yahaduth Lita, Tel-Aviv 5727 [1967].
6. Sepher Oszmiana, Tel-Aviv.
7. Sepher Lida, Tel-Aviv.
8. [Ed. Note: skipped]
9. "HaMelits", 5662 [1902].
10. Tsaytshrift far geshikhte, demografye un ekonomik, Minsk 1928.
11. Slownik geograficzny, Bronislaw and Filip Chlebowski, Warsaw 1882.
12. Yevreiskaya entsiklopedya [Jewish encyclopedia], Dr. Katzenelson and Baron Ginzburg, Peterburg 1912.

13. Yevreiskaya entsiklopedya [Jewish encyclopedia], Brockhaus and Efron, Peterburg 1912[Tr. Note: may refer to "Entsiklopeditcheskiy slovar" [Encyclopedic Dictionary] published by Brockhaus and Efron in St. Petersburg (1890-1907)]
14. Jewish encyclopedia, New York and London, 1903-1916.

[Page 28]

Those Days Are Well Remembered

Yakov Bloch

Ed. Note: This article appears in both Hebrew and Yiddish in the original Yizkor Book; only the Yiddish version has been translated and published in this book and may be found at page 453 of this book. Photos appearing within the Hebrew version of the original book are included here without their accompanying text.

[Page 31]

The HaShomer HaTsair "nest" (group) in Divenishok (1930)

[Page 32]

The HaShomer HaTsair[Tr. Note: Young Guard] "nest" with the teacher Betsalel Petukhovski z"l[Tr. Note: of blessed memory] (1930)

[Page 33]

Members of HaShomer HaTsair at an agricultural camp in a village near Smorgon, 1932

[Page 34]

Agricultural summer camp in a village near Smorgon where members of HaShomer HaTsair participated (1931)

[Page 35]

'Gloria' football team [Tr. note: soccer] founded by students in 1923

[Page 36]

Under Confinement
With Russians, Poles, and Germans

Eliohu Wiener

Translation by Meir Bulman

When the Bolsheviks occupied Poland in 1920, a harsh famine took hold of Divenishok. The situation had not improved much even after the Bolsheviks retreated and the Polish regained control. Skyve's home we knew had burned down, and so we had to move to Chaim Gershovitsh's house, which was previously used as a school.

Wandering, Starving, Dying

I remember an episode from those days. Nathan Kaplan's grandfather had a large plot of land behind his house, where he grew potatoes. Since the famine was so severe, the cobbler's son, Hershl Pinchas Katz, and I snuck into the garden, took out the planted potatoes, cooked and ate them, skin and all.

After a while, the hunger at home became unbearable. My mother Sarah, my brother Leybkeh, Yitzchak Schneider (whose brother was Leyzer "Der Voyevada",[Ed. Note: A *voyevode* is a Provincial Governor, which in this case could be a tongue-in-cheek epithet] and I decided to head to Grodne. We had heard by way of a rumor that the situation there was better. My sick father stayed at home and my sister Tzirah Leah stayed to care for him.

We wandered from town to town and asked for food. We were not ashamed at all, since it was a time of mass-wandering. When we got to Grodne, we contracted Typhus and were hospitalized in town. I was the weakest among us and spent a year in the hospital.

On our way back, we traveled through Shtutchin, a city near Lida. My brother, who was 16, landed a job as a tanner. Thanks to him we had the chance to lodge in the corner of the room where skins were dried. The stench of the skins was overwhelming, but we saw a positive aspect in having a place to rest our heads. Shortly we were informed that our father Yoel had passed away, and my sister Tzirah Leah moved to Vilne, so we decided to not return to Divenishok and to stay put in Shtutchin. In 1934 death came for my mother too. My brother married and worked as a cobbler, but his hobby was writing poems. He was an intelligent young man and locals came to him to write addresses in America for them.

In 1931 I traveled to Vilne to attend a trade school, "Hilf Dorkh Arbet" (Assistance Through Labor), where subjects like carpentry, tailoring, drawing, and more were taught. I chose drawing. I was accepted to the school as an orphan and received three zloty a month as spending money, as well as vouchers for the soup kitchen on Vilner Street. Because the availability of sustenance worsened at school, I decided to work as a tailor's apprentice and learned that trade.

Escape to Russia

In the early 30's the situation in Poland was at a low point. Mass unemployment and heavy taxation burdened the Jewish population. As a result, a movement began of Jewish youth emigration to Russia, and I too decided to cross the border.

My friend Zelda, another friend, and I, connected with a farmer who lived on the border. Upon his recommendation, we arrived at a hotel in Ivanitz and transferred from there to the farmer's house. We hid three days with him until the weather became rainy and dusty, and on a dark and misty night, the farmer took us beyond the river and instructed us to walk towards a field whose trees looked pale through the mist.

We crossed the border and Russian guards led us to Koydenovah Camp, where there were about 200 people, mostly Jews, as well as some Poles and Lithuanians.

After a staying a few days in the camp, we realized that we had been foolish and had gotten ourselves into a venture for which we might pay with our lives. The sanitary conditions were atrocious, and all the prisoners were hungry, exhausted, and crawling with lice. The Russian prisoners were wearing rags, and we learned from them about the terrible situation in the Soviet Union. Many young men were on the brink of despair. It seemed that what the Poles had been unable to carry out in the way of torture and detention camps, the Russians had accomplished in a mere few days. The dreams of a Russian utopia vanished, and everyone had but one dream: the return to capitalist Poland.

I was lucky, as I began to work in the kitchen and at least could have access to larger food portions. A meager 200-gram slice of bread, and soup containing horse's head and carcass were our nourishment, and even that was scarce.

Along with that, the Russian were experts at interrogation. For six weeks various officials interrogated us daily. Once I was even interrogated by a Jewish man from Radin, who had probably already arrived in Russia by WWI. Interrogations were meticulous and thorough, and every detail was written. In all interrogation sessions we were offered a return to Poland for a spying mission.

During my interrogations I claimed repeatedly that I had escaped from Poland due to a lack of employment and the rumor was that in Russia all youths are given the opportunity to learn and progress. I feared a trap and maintained my position stubbornly, and the interrogators failed to break me.

The early interrogation sessions were conducted gently, but as time went by they acquired an increasingly confrontational tone and were accompanied by swears, threats, and insults. Our spirit was suppressed because we had not expected this "warm welcome" for youth such as ourselves, full of ideals of justice and brotherhood. The cat was out of the bag and we were now acquainted with this "progressive" regime.

The Release

After six weeks my friend and I were summoned from the holding cell to one of the interrogators, our clothes were returned and we were told we were being sent back to Poland. Later we were joined by our friend Zelda who came to Russia with us. At night we were led to a location near the border by a Russian woman wearing a military uniform. The woman gestured where we should head to cross the Polish border.

We were fearful since we had heard of young men who had snuck into Russia, and then when crossing back were thought by Polish officials to be spies and were brutally tortured. One man from Mir was tortured to death in Baranovich, and as a cover–up the prison guards hung him, claiming he committed suicide by hanging.

While being aware of all this we changed course with the clear intention of being captured by Polish border control. We knew that we would remain imprisoned for a while and then would be released. And indeed, border patrol captured and imprisoned us. My interrogation sessions were uneventful, but other prisoners notified me that my friend was being harshly tortured because of the few dollars that were found on his person. I understood what the issue was and decided to rescue him (he was suspected of surveillance), and asked for an interview with the chief interrogator.

At the meeting with the chief I said that we had come to the town of Ivanitz even before crossing the border to Russia, and there we had stayed for a day at a Jewish hotel. We exchanged our Polish money for ten dollars we could use in Russia, and my friend had sewn the bill into his shirt collar. The Russians were unable to find the bill, but the Poles had succeeded, and so this is why he is being accused of spying. "The truth is," I told the interrogator, "that the guy did so with no ill intent". To prove my claim, I provided him with the hotel owner's name. The Poles confirmed it and my friend was saved from tragedy.

A few days later we were tried for illegally crossing the border and were sentenced to two months in prison. Compared to the Russian camp it was a luxury hotel.

After our release from Stolpce prison, we wandered without wages or a means to return home. A certain detective who saw us aimlessly wandering a border town like Stolpce suspected we were trying to cross the border to Russia. He arrested us at the train station and promptly sat us on the train to the Vilne police. We had not told him a thing, because we were interested in reaching Vilne, but once there we told the truth and confirmed our claims with documentation. We were released to the detective's shame: he had inadvertently assisted us in reaching our destination.

For many years, the reason for our release by the Russians was a mystery to me, since many of our acquaintances were sent to Siberia where their souls departed them. But only thirty years later in Israel the mystery was solved. I happened to meet a childhood friend from Zheludok, which is not far from Shtutchin. I knew that he too had been in Russia and we got to discussing the old days. He told me he had escaped death by "activating" a spy. The interrogator in Russia had given him half a kerchief of some girl named Zelda and had told him to show it her and inform her of her mission. That is how it became apparent why we had been released. Zelda could not withstand the pressure and had accepted a surveillance mission. To not raise any suspicion, my friends and I were let go too since we had crossed the border with her. Of course, Zelda later suffered for her recklessness. After my return home, I presented myself for military duty, but was declined for political reasons. Due to the lesson I had learned in Russia, I abandoned my political work and began training as a tailor.

As WWII erupted in 1939, I visited my relatives by Leybeh Eydel's daughter Bilha in Divenishok. After the collapse of the Polish regime, it was difficult to return to Vilne, since it was unknown who would control it. With many difficulties, I made it to a restless Vilne. The Poles had vanished and the town was without a government. The Jews feared that the gentiles would launch massacres against them. To maintain order until some sort of government could form, the Culture Department of Professional Unions organized the Workers' Civilian Guard, "Rabochaya Gvardia," to operate governmental functions until commands were clarified. I was among the active members of this organization. The leaders were two Jewish men, Kroshkin and Shuchman, and they took hold of police warehouses, distributing weapons among members who went to patrol the town's sensitive regions. That arrangement continued until the Lithuanians entered, when the civilian guard disbanded, with some members joining the Russians and others remaining in Vilne.

I left Vilne on my way to Lida, where I married my wife Sarah. Together we returned to Vilne where I worked as a tailor until the war commenced. In the days of German control I was in various detention camps. After being liberated, I arrived with my wife in Israel, and here my two daughters were born.

The teachers, and sisters, Breyne[Ed. Note: top row, center] and Sheynele Rudnik z"l, [Ed. Note: top row, right] with a group of students from the Hebrew school

[Page 41]

My Town and My Family

Orit Kaplan

Translation by Meir Bulman

In 1923, in a town named Divenishok, which was located 63 kilometers south of Vilne, on Rosh Hashanah, the youngest child was born to an established Jewish family. That child would later become my father. He had four sisters and one brother– and of course his older sisters pampered him. His father– my grandfather– was the town's bank manager, a landowner who employed Christians from the nearby villages as land workers. He also owned a food supply store and was the synagogue administrator.

Polish state school ("Powszechna") on Geranion Street built in 1927

There were 5000 Jewish residents in the town, aside from a number of Poles who worked in local government and the police force. There were a few Christian families that made their living providing janitorial services to Jews.

Once a week a market day took place in the town. The nearby farmers brought their produce to sell and would buy their necessary products. The entire town profited from the business generated by market day. The noise level was high' auctioneers and jugglers performed too. All of that made market day a great economic and social event.

The town had a large synagogue and nearby was a Hebrew School with 7 classrooms. On Fridays, the Sabbath, and on holidays, town Jews gathered there for prayers. My grandfather had a designated honorary spot by the ark, which had been inherited for generations, and my father was obliged to join him there. As a young boy the reciting of the prayers was a burden to him, and he would sneak out with the other children to play in the synagogue yard. Before prayers concluded he would sneak back into the synagogue. His father would usually scold him for his mischief. The synagogue was a meeting spot for many Jews, who came to pray three times daily. Jews who did not have time to attend services prayed at home.

After my father completed sixth grade at the Hebrew school he transferred to the local Polish public school named for Adam Mickiewicz, a well-known Polish poet. The school was attended by Jewish children who had completed Hebrew school, as well as the Christian farmers' children. The percentage of Jewish students in that school was small. There were usually 5 to 8 Jewish students and between 30 and 40 Christians. The Jewish children excelled at their studies, especially in mathematics. There was a tense atmosphere at school and there were few social interactions between the Jewish and Christian students. There were occasional squabbles between Jews and Christians. Once a quarrel erupted between my father and one of the Poles, whose parent was employed by the town. Although neither child had complained, the matter was brought to the principal's attention. As punishment they were forced to carry rocks on a stretcher from the school yard to the field. After they worked cooperatively for two hours they were released by the principal, and since then, despite incitements by other Christians, they remained good friends until my father emigrated to Israel.

Market Street in the center of the town

Even as a child my father excelled at athletic activities and thus the principal appointed him director of team sports. In one of the volleyball competitions he added five Jews to the school team, as well as his Christian friend. The school principal objected to that, adding two more Poles. Only after he realized that his line-up is causing the team to lose did he agree to my father's line-up, who then led the team to victory.

On Polish Independence Day, annual prize-granting sports competitions took place, in which Jews did not participate. At the age of twelve, a year before my father emigrated to Israel, he decided to participate in the boys' 60-meter sprint. He had to run numerous times before the finals and the organizers realized that his competitors did not stand a chance;, they added two young men, but their plan failed, and my father was the first past the finish post. Additionally, he won first place in the long jump. An important noteworthy fact is that the Christian mayor, who was an anti-Semite, had to announce the victory of a Jewish boy, and his face flushed with rage, he shook my father's hand in the presence of the Polish aristocracy. My father still recalls that they murmured in wonderment: "How is it that no Pole succeeded in catching up to the Jew?"

The mill in Divenishok

As news of the event spread through town, my grandfather, who was a fundamentalist, Orthodox Jew, came to the field looking for my father, who was afraid his father would be angry. But my grandfather approached him, and though his eyes were radiant, he did not say anything, took his hand affectionately, and with a heart filled with satisfaction said: "Nu? Come home".

A year later my father emigrated to Israel with his parents.

In Israel he attended "Ahad Ha'am" high school in Petah Tikva, and lived with his parents at Kfar Ma'as. This period was a bloody chapter in the history of Israel. His parents' house was right on the border. Beyond the fence there was an Arab orchard from which shots were fired at night. Residents guarded positions to prevent Arabs from breaching into the village. Since my grandfather was an elderly man and could not participate in guard duty, my father replaced him on many nights, and as a result had to cope with drowsiness during school hours. He once earned a teacher's scolding who had sensed his lack of alertness in class and his desire to doze.

My father's home was a traditional one where religious commands and customs were strictly adhered to. My grandfather was also an enthusiastic Zionist basking in the glory of the Kingdom of Israel. During his childhood my father inherited from his father a pride in the bravery of the Kings of Israel in the spirit of the Bible, where prophets and kings are described as visionary heroes, glorifying the Kingdom of Israel.

Considering this education, it was natural for my father and grandfather to make Aliyah, and afterwards for my father to fight for Israel's independence, following which he founded a family in Israel.

[Page 45]

The Civil Guard ("*Varte*")

Meir Yosef Itskovitsh

Translation by Meir Bulman

I put the term in the title as we all knew it, both Jews and gentiles. It essentially means what we know today as a civil guard.

Every night, four people, each one from a different household, would patrol the streets of town until dawn. The role of the *varte* was to guard the lives and possessions of the residents of Divenishok. In case of a burglary, the police had to be woken, and in case of fire, the siren had to be sounded and the fire department summoned. The next night, four people from the homes next in line patrolled and so on until the final person at the edge of town was reached and the cycle began again. Usually, a member of the households would patrol, but when it could be afforded, a gentile would be hired for the task.

I remember one night when I returned home for summer vacation from gymnasium. The duty of *varte* reached our house. I approached father and asked him to hire me instead of a gentile, since I would patrol town into the late hours of the night anyway. To my delight father agreed.

At midnight I was on *varte* duty joined by my great–uncle, and the daughter of Alexander (Oless) Pezkovski the tailor. As a typical young man, I could not walk calmly and withstand the temptation of blonde–haired Helenka, and on the balcony (ganek) of Nachum Lipkunski the bakery owner, we made a connection. I do not remember what we discussed or did not discuss, but I remember that we were so absorbed in conversation that we did not notice that on the horizon, from Dubtshinski Street, the sky turned red and an entire village burned, without us noticing.

The next day, a ruckus was raised: How could it be? How did the *varte* not notice the fire? Why was the siren not sounded? Who was on watch?

The Polish police in town (1932)

Imagine what I went through. I shook in fear, but as they say, 'oysgekrenkt dem gantsen fargenign.[1] Who knows how the whole ordeal would have ended if not for my father, who was a member of the town council and accepted and respected by the authorities. Thanks to his intervention the sad events of the *varte* night were put to rest.

Editor's footnote:

1. Yiddish expression used when a turn of events ruins a pleasant mood or experience.

[Page 47]

Divenishok: A Charming Town

Dr. Menachem Weisenfeld

Translation by Martin Jacobs

I was born in Galicia, in the town of Zuravna, located between Lemberik and Stanisle. There I completed elementary and middle school and then went on to study medicine at the University of Vilna. I was one of the students who supported themselves by giving lessons. Among my pupils were the children of Slonimski, the well known attorney, one of the leading Zionists in Vilna.

Beginning of Geranion Street

When I finished my studies at the university I learned that Divenishok needed a "sejmikowy" (regional) government physician. A permit for this was given only by the *starosta*[Ed. Note: district administrator] responsible for the district, who lived in the city of Oshmene. The Poles never have distinguished themselves by their love of Jews and the *starosta* had never certified a Jewish physician for this position. But I tried my luck and sought an appointment with him. The man gave me a penetrating look and spoke with me briefly. He apparently liked my "non-Jewish" face and my fluent Polish; he directed me to his secretary to have the certification forms filled out. When the secretary read my diploma, in which my given name, Menachem Mendel, was recorded, her eyes went dark, but without a word she filled out the documents and the *starosta* signed the contract.

At the end of December 1928 I arrived in Divenishok, where I stayed with the pharmacist Aryeh Leyb Rogol. He was already seriously ill and the pharmacist N_ [Ed. Note: accurate name translation not possible as written in text: nun-mem-yud-vov-tes] was working with him at that time. In addition to my work as a physician, I was responsible for the sanitary and hygienic conditions in the town, and it was my job to go out with the chief of police to inspect businesses and courtyards for cleanliness.

Before I came this had been done by the public health doctor of the district seat, Oszmiana, and the Jews had to put up with a lot from him, especially the restaurant owners, bakers, and business owners. Depending on how good his mood was, he wrote summonses right and left – "let the Jews put a bit of money into the state treasury" – he used to say. The appearance of this *sejmikowy* physician in the town was like a visit from a ghost, because the Jews were terrified of him, since most of them were very poor and it wasn't just once that they had to run around wherever they could to borrow a fortune to pay the fines.

With my appearance in the town a great feeling of trust came upon the Jews there. My wife was very friendly with the family of Noah Kartshmer, and if the townspeople found it difficult to get close to him, my wife, Rosa Ostrinski, found him approachable. She was known in the town as the daughter of Ostrinski, the well known Vilne merchant, and it was due to Noah Kartshmer that she could let the townspeople know when the sanitation commission was about to make an appearance.

The police chief used to say to me: "The townspeople must be afraid of you. Since you've been the physician here hygiene has been exemplary and it hasn't been necessary to write summonses."

Once a week I visited schools in the villages in the vicinity to investigate sanitary conditions. In this capacity I checked on the health of the Polish teachers to see if they were fit to be teaching. A carriage with two horses and a coachman was at my disposal. The townspeople were overjoyed when I went through the streets of the town in the carriage. I was in close contact with the police officer and the Christian priest, a man of Lithuanian origin named G_. [Ed. Note: possibly Gedgaudas; accurate name translation not possible as written in text: gimel-daled-gimel-vov-beyz-daled] We visited with each other, and took walks together through the streets of the town. The Jews were very pleased that the priest was friendly with the Jewish physician.

At government ceremonies, which were celebrated with great pomp, I appeared on the reviewing platform in the uniform of a Polish officer, in sight of thousands of Poles who crowded around the platform. This raised the esteem of the Jews in the eyes of the Poles and raised the sense of pride of the Jews.

S_,[Ed. Note: accurate name translation not possible as written in text: samekh-tes-reysh-vov-gimel-tsadek-apostrophe] a well known man of wealth from Oshmene, brought me into the center of the Party of Independents, set up by Pilsudski to bring the Jews closer to himself. This was a party without any obligation either to the right or to the left. Its sole aim was to work together with the government. I represented Divenishok and I was consulted on town matters more than the "Wojt" (head of the council) Motskovitz.

Most of townspeople were poor. They roamed around the surrounding villages buying produce from the farmers to sell in Vilne. It was said about

Divenishok: "Divenishok of the forty beaters", meaning that the town had forty horse owners, known as "beaters" because they whipped their horses.

*

Divenishok was charming. I loved it because of the enchanting landscape and its delightful people. Every one was attached to tradition, even the irreligious. I remember an incident concerning Sholem Yakov Olkenitski, whose 19 year old son Aharon came down with pneumonia and whose condition was very serious. Despite the fact that this Sholem Yakov was a devout communist he wrapped himself in *talis* and *tefilin* and in the middle of the night ran to the synagogue, opened the holy ark, kissed the holy Torah scrolls, prostrated himself before the ark, wept bitter tears, and implored mercy for his son.

To my great sorrow I was unable to fulfill my duties for long in Divenishok. The Poles, who were saturated with venomous hatred toward the Jews, and could not tolerate a Jewish physician serving in such a high position, began to undermine me; they sent petitions to the government opposing a Jew serving as "sejmikowy physician". A Polish physician named Raszko was especially out to get me. He was a landowner in the vicinity of Benakani who was eager to take my place. He organized a venomous propaganda campaign against me and, since he had connections with the land-owners, he had great influence with the authorities. This Raszko was not a certified physician. At most he had completed some sort of school for "feltshers", [Tr. Note: old-time barber-surgeon (cf. Weinreich), or assistant surgeon (cf. Harkavy)] but, as people said, he was an unadulterated *goy* and a great anti-Semite, and that was what was most important. I became convinced that it was not worthwhile for me to remain in Divenishok. It was with great regret that I left the town. I decided to go to Vienna to qualify as an ear, nose, and throat specialist.

In 1939 I enlisted in the Polish army and fought the Nazis. When the Nazis occupied Poland I was in labor camps in Slonim and Bialystok. Some time before the end of the war I went out to the village of B_ [Ed. Note: possibly Benakani] disguised as a Christian, and worked in the sawmill. Everything that happened to me in that period is recorded in Isaac Nimsevic's book "For Their Sake – Likenesses from the Journal" under the heading "Secretary to the Gestapo – A Jewish Partisan" (published by the Ministry of Defense, January 1968).

When I reached Israel I joined the war of independence and was decorated by the state. I also joined "Mission Kadesh" as a doctor in the army hospital. I was decorated both for fighting for the state and for fighting against the Nazis.

The market place – in the center is the pump which the Germans constructed during the First World War

[Page 50]

I Treated Divenishok and its People With Fondness

Shlomo Levine

Translation by Meir Bulman

Our family came to Divenishok from the nearby village of Geranion, where we had lived for many years. After WWI, most of our family members emigrated to the United States, and my father remained in Geranion.

In 1920 Anti–Semitism in the region escalated, as evident by the murders of Jews. Among others, the Poles murdered my uncle, and he was buried as a martyr in Divenishok. Tsvi Novoplanski's maternal grandfather was also brutally murdered in Geranion. My uncle, who was visiting from the United States, demanded that we move to Divenishok, and thus we arrived at the town in 1921. My father purchased a large home in the center of the market place and we made our living from a café and from rent for lodging paid by people who came for market day.

My father got involved in all aspects of the village's public life. He was a member of the charity foundation board, was active in the synagogue board, a member of the school parents' committee, and generously supported the town's institutions.

My family consisted of my two sisters Paye and Khaya, and my older brother Gad. Paye married before we moved to Divenishok and resided in the Ivia area, where she perished along with her family. My brother Gad, along with his wife and two children, died in Geranion one day before liberation, savagely murdered by Poles. My parents and my sister Khaya were murdered in the Voronova ghetto.

When we arrived at Divenishok, I was seven years old, and was accepted to the Hebrew school at Abba the Shoemaker's house. The teachers I can recall are Engle, and the Hebrew studies instructor Leyb Aryeh. In 1928 under the influence of Rabbi Rudnik I traveled to the Radin Yeshiva. Khaykl Itskovitsh and Yeshayahu Moshe Katz traveled with me. I studied there for one year. I remember that all of us yeshiva pupils visited the Chofetz Chaim on Saturday nights to hear Torah lessons. We were all impressed by his humility and simple nature. He would tell us to write "year of redemption and salvation" as the header for each letter. Every year he awaited the Geulah[1] with complete confidence that salvation was right around the corner.

After that I transferred to the Rabbi Elchonen Wasserman Yeshiva in Baranovich, where I studied for a year before returning home.

I experienced an interesting event in Baranovich: Once, as I sat pondering a difficult Talmudic passage, two yeshiva guys held me down and shaved the front of my head in accordance with the Halachic commandment of a smooth surface providing no interference to the Tefilin.

After returning from yeshiva at age 15, I joined the *HaShomer HaTsair* youth group, and along with Yakov Bloch, Aharon Kaganovitsh, and Moshe Levine, we departed to a village near Vilnea where we learned agricultural skills.

After that I left *HaShomer HaTsair* with some friends and we established *HeKhaluts HaTsair* (The Young Pioneers). In 1932 I joined training with *HeKhaluts* in Lida and later in Grodne. A year later I received an immigration certificate and emigrated to Israel in July of 1933.

Right off the boat I joined the Tel Yosef Kibbutz in Jezreel Valley, and later the Ramat Rachel Kibbutz near Jerusalem. After that I married my wife Tova Leshchinski and established a home. Two children were born, the eldest daughter Khaya, and a son, Yehezkel, and I was privileged enough to see grandchildren too, praise God.

The Gmina House[Tr. Note: Town Hall] on Geranion Street, built in 1926

I always regarded the Divenishok alumnus in Israel with great fondness and did my best to befriend and assist them as much as possible. Many of our town people spent their first days in Israel with me until they managed to get on their feet.

The first gathering of the Divenishok reunion took place in my home on Bar Kochba Street in Tel Aviv in 1936, to mark the visit of my uncle Betzalel Levine from America. It was a good start, and as a greater stream of Divenishok folk began moving to Israel after the war, we began conducting the gatherings at Beit Ha'haluzot.

Footnote

1. In Jewish theology, Geulah refers to the period of final redemption that will occur when the Messiah comes.

[Page 52]

I Bonded With Divenishok

Frume Kaplan

Translation by Meir Bulman

My parents lived and breathed the town's atmosphere as children. That is where they were born, where they received their traditional education, and where they got married.

My father's name was Yitzchak ben Note (Note the Miller's Son), and my mother's name was Esther. She was Yitzchak Leyb's daughter. They wed in 1909 and moved to Vilne, where my father began work building houses.

Even though I was born and raised in Vilne, I was bound to Divenishok with special cords of love. Every summer our family would travel to Divenishok to spend time off and get some rest. There, our kind grandfather Yitzchak Leyb's spacious house awaited us.

Spending summers in Divenishok was an unforgettable experience for me. In Vilne I had friends, but only a select few. Here, I had a chance to meet the entire village's youth population, since everyone knew one another. All were friendly, and despite any differences in political opinions, they were a cohesive, sociable unit, happy and cheerful. Spending summer vacations with them was very enjoyable. All the youth sought my company, because I was from the big city. Let it be known that the youth in town longed for the big city, and all they wanted was to bask in the glory of the great city. I harbored no feelings of superiority towards them, but I still found their approach to me charming.

I spent my vacations trekking in the area, which contained golden grain fields, and I particularly enjoyed the pine forest, where we inhaled its wonderful scent. My mother would bring food and we would all spend the day together, resting and napping on hammocks. The serenity and pastoral silence would project a good mood and relaxation.

We spent the evenings together in song and dance. The world was so good, so pleasant, that when vacations ended I did not want to leave the town.

I was especially proud of my grandfather Yitzchak Leyb. He was a tall Jewish man, adorned with a flowing white beard. He was well presented, handsome and cordial. He was respected by the youth and his pockets were always filled with candy that he gave out to the children, and he would pinch their cheeks with affection and happiness.

A children's party, with organ grinder and his parrot that "casts lots"

Parting ways with him when summer ended was difficult for me. Grandfather loved us and did all he could to make our stay pleasant and provide us with a home–like feeling. Grandfather was a man who loved conversation and companionship and I detected a sense of loneliness in him when we bid him farewell. "You're departing and I'm staying here all by my lonesome." "Please stay a bit longer," he would plead to my mother and me.

Indeed, summer vacations at my parents' birthplace was packed with adventure and pleasant feelings, and my heart was full of love for the town, even when I was in Vilne.

Those were the happy days of my youth and the experience remains in my heart to this day. My father worked as a trader in Vilne and in addition owned a "Lombard" (pawn shop). Our financial status was quite stable until the war.

I was the youngest daughter of the family. I arrived in Israel at the behest of Natan Kaplan, whom I married.

Aside from my parents, my older sister Gita who completed her agronomy studies, and my younger brother Herzel stayed at home. Lithuanian collaborators who received money from the Germans for every Jew they kidnapped, captured my brother in our yard and killed him on the spot. His innocent blood was scattered on the ground in front of our window, as my parents witnessed helplessly the horror of their only son, a 17-year-old handsome and distinguished boy, being brutally murdered. My mother perished in Stutthof concentration camp, and my father passed away in the same camp, two weeks before it was liberated. My sister Gita perished in Klooga, Estonia.

"The Kidre" (lake) from Vilne Street

[Page 55]

Social and Political Life

by Shraga Blyakher

Ed. Note: This article appears in both Hebrew and Yiddish in the original Yizkor Book; only the Yiddish version has been translated and published in this book and may be found at page 435 of this book. Photos appearing within the Hebrew version of the original book are included here without their accompanying text.

[Page 56]

The Tarbus School and its teachers (1930)

[Page 57]

A group of young people, teachers and students, on the Oszmian Street bridge, a meeting place for the young

[Page 58]

*Friends saying goodbye to Sarah Kartshmer, z"l,
on the occasion of her emigration to America*

[Page 59]

The Drama Circle after a performance of the play "The Kidnapper"

[Page 60]

Winter in the town – young people enjoying the snow

[Page 61]

The "Vilbig"[Tr. Note: Vilna Jewish Educational Association] Library for Yiddish Books on Subotnik Street (1931) – standing in the doorway: Yosele Levine, z"l, behind him Hirshel Krizovski, z"l

[Page 62]

Institutions and Organizations in Divenishok

Avraham Abir (Rudnik)

Translation by Meir Bulman

In my memoirs of a number of institutions and organizations in our town I would like to stress the positive and active involvement of my father, the great Rabbi Yosef Rudnik, may he rest in peace. He was not satisfied with activity in the religious field alone, but also acted to develop and expand most institutions in Divenishok.

Students, teachers, and the parents committee of the Tarbus School in Divenishok (1932) – in the center: Rabbi Rudnik, z.ts"l, Dr. Weisenfeld, Ben-Zion Schneider, Zisha Yakov Shkolnik, Nathan Itskovitsh, Moshe Yakov Rogol, and Krivitski

The School

Most of Rabbi Rudnik's concern was for rearing future generations and educating the children. That is why he devoted energy and effort to establish a school for Jewish children. At the school there was a parental committee that was elected by a general assembly in the synagogue, usually on the Sabbath before the recitation of the Torah. The school administration was comprised of observant Orthodox Jews. The Rabbi brought an instructor from Vishneva to teach the upperclassmen *Talmud* and *Mishnah*. The instructor received a small salary and ate on a rotation with the students' parents.

At first the school took place in rented homes. Then my father decided to build a beautiful modern school building, so it could compete with the public school.

It was decided the school would be built in place of the old synagogue that had collapsed due to age, but a Halachic[Ed. Note: the *halacha* is the Jewish law] issue arose surrounding the demotion of a building from a synagogue to a school. My father solved that by selling the building to a different Jew to abrogate its holy status.

A group of young people in the town: Standing, from the left: Leah and Isaiah Wiener z"l, Itka Mintz, Tuvya Blyakher, Reyzl Yutan, Duba Bernshteyn Seated: Itka Blyakher, Itka Wiener z"l, Sarah Hinda Blyakher Movshovitsh, Khaya Blyakher-Lifsha

To raise the large sum necessary my father worked on Friday, the day following market day, along with the synagogue administrator Shmuel Kherson and Yeshayahu Kaplan. In a few hours a large sum in cash and commitments was raised. Especially active were Ben Tsion Schneider and Yeshayahu Kaplan, the Judaism teacher at the local Polish public school.

My father often conducted site visits at the new school to be assured the children were not cold or hungry, and to ensure their studies were progressing. Children spent more time at school than at home so a proper environment needed to be solidified, allowing them to study and thrive with ease.

Almost every Sabbath before the recitation of the Torah, the Rabbi lectured on the weekly portion and paralleled the concepts discussed with contemporary issues then in the public mind. In his talks he always highlighted his address specifically for his audience of Lithuanian Jews, the elite among Jewry. Our forefathers, he said, went as far as to pawn their candle sticks to pay tuition, and so we too must bear the burden of education so as to convey the values of Judaism to the younger generation.

His efforts bore fruit. The school was of top-shelf quality and excellent teachers taught there. Among them was Avraham Aloni, who had completed Dr. Cherno's Yeshiva in Vilne. He managed the school quite successfully. Afterwards he immigrated to Israel and married my sister Breyne. Today he is the principal of *Tel Nordoy* School in Tel Aviv.

It must be noted that in terms of financial and practical feasibility it was easier to send children to the Polish public school, where they would not have to pay tuition, in addition to acquiring skills in the then-important Polish language. The Rabbi stood on guard and ensured that no child quit the community. Poor children studied for free when they studied at the Hebrew school. Notably, my father succeeded in that mission.

Youth Groups

The town had some Zionist and non-Zionist youth organizations. The Rabbi maintained good relationships with them all and tried to influence them to not steer too far off the path of Jewish tradition. Due to a lack of facilities most of these youth's activities took place at the school. Once, the school committee decided to remove these young folks from the school campus. The youth greeted the committee members by standing at attention and singing the "*HaShomer HaTsair*"[Ed. Note: Zionist self-defense movement] anthem. The singing did not conclude until the committee had left the premises. Ben Tsion Schneider told the members, "let us not disturb them, they are reciting their '*Kaddish*'".[Ed. Note: a well known prayer] The youth's scheme had succeeded and the old folks' anger subsided; they quit disturbing the youth ever since.

Bikur Holim[1]

There was no health maintenance organization in town, instead there was a *Bikur Holim* whose committee provided medical assistance to the poor when they could not afford a doctor. *Bikur Holim* also provided medical instruments for home health assistance. Of special note, they provided ice on summer days. For that purpose an ice storeroom was constructed in the synagogue yard. Small ice chunks were placed in the basement and water would be poured on to them, turning them into a single large block of ice which endured even during the hot summers. An ill person who needed ice received it from the basement. Some people also stored food items there so the heat would not spoil them.

Yosef Zhizhemski was the *Bikur Holim* administrator for many years. My father always encouraged him to stay on the job despite difficulties like a limited budget and instrument disappearance. After that, Yaakov Eliashkovitsh served as administrator. A group of young men volunteered their services to the *Bikur Holim* organization. They raised funds in the town every Friday. The income was not miniscule, but the main component in their activities was educational.

Linat Hatzedek[2] and *Gemilut Hasadim*[3]

A special organization, where young men volunteered, operated in the town. These men visited the severely ill to assist family members, especially in overnight stays with the sick. It was of great assistance to family members who were exhausted by caring for the sick.

The Rabbi established a charity bank in town that loaned money to local Jews. With the money received from the zero-interest charity bank, individuals bought merchandise from local farmers and sold it in Vilne. The Rabbi oversaw that the money was distributed fairly. Every person was eligible for a loan, with no formal limitations. His presence at the charity bank prevented squabbles, fights, and hostility, since people knew he would stand guard and verify that distribution had been just, equal, and free of discrimination.

Religious Activity

Diverse religious activities took place in town. Two synagogue buildings were built in one yard, called the "*Shulhoyf*".[Ed. Note: synagogue courtyard] The synagogues were always busy. Many daily services took place for morning, noon, and evening prayers. On the Sabbath, nearly all the town residents visited the synagogue. The synagogue was used not only for prayers, but also functioned as the town's spiritual center. Many Torah teaching groups continuously convened there, dealing with such Torah subjects as *Mishnah*, *Talmud*, Psalms, and *Chayei Adam*.

I remember once as I prayed the morning-prayer in one of the synagogue's corners, I heard my father's voice, weeping. I approached to see what happened and saw some town Jews gathered around a long table, and my father teaching *Mishnah* to his flock. He had reached the passage describing how our forefathers brought with glorious splendor the *Bikkurim*, the First

Fruit, to the temple in Jerusalem. The described passage concludes "when they reached the Temple Mount even King Agrippa would take the basket..." [Ed. Note: King Agrippa refers to Herod Agrippa, King of Judea from 41 to 44 A.D., by many accounts a friendlier monarch to the Jews of Judea] Overwhelmed with yearning and exhilaration Father began to cry, and tears rolled down the elders' beards too. That image remains with me to this very day.

Between the noon and evening prayers my father taught Jewish law from the book *Chayei Adam* to a few groups. Following the evening prayers my father gave a Talmud lecture, joined by important local Torah scholars.

Due to his clear explanations and his magnetism, participants thoroughly enjoyed his teaching, and even talented youths enjoyed the classes. Among his school-aged pupils there were those who continued to post-secondary and higher education Torah studies. One of those pupils, Yeshayahu Moshe Katz, was one of the best students at the Radin Yeshiva. I fondly remember Yaakov Cohen, orphaned of both parents, who was among the most distinguished students in the Mir Yeshiva. On vacation days, he taught Ethics of Our Fathers at the old synagogue.

It should be noted, that despite the heavy financial burden the town folks diligently devoted time for Torah studies. The Synagogue had a large Torah library which was open to the public. After completing any study of a book, a festive *Seudat Mitzva*[Ed. Note: an obligatory and festive meal following the fulfillment of a *mitzvah*, or commandment] took place.

The Libraries and the... Leftists

The Synagogue had a large Torah library, but a new generation emerged in town that was interested in secular literature as well, mainly Yiddish literature. That is how a large library containing important Yiddish books was established. The library's dimensions were larger than would be expected for a town this size, due to generous contributions by "Relief" donations in America, where activists originally from Divenshok now resided; they maintained a special relationship and provided for its existence and expansion.

Local youths also devoted some of their time to maintain and organize the library. The life force behind these youths was Reuven Kartshmer, a pharmacy owner who read many books. He transferred his knowledge to the youth and awakened in them the desire to read and learn. But as time went by Kartshmer veered off the path of Jewish tradition, became a leftist and corrupted the youth with his opinions. Dozens among the youth became avid communists and were smitten with Soviet Russia. Several left town and sneaked across the border to Russia. Rumor told that they met a bitter fate there.

But all that did not curb the growth of the Leftist tidal wave. Heading this wave was Hirshl Krizovski, a son to a devout Jew. Hirshl was a zealot and so as expected he opposed the Rabbi and the community organizers around him.

The Rabbi and the other residents, who feared for the fate of their children, frowned upon these activities. The two rival camps waged a fierce war of ideas, which came to fruition especially in the education field. The Leftists wanted to appoint their own teachers at the school and desired to establish a pre-school where the teacher would conform to their views. But the Rabbi and his staff would not allow them to infiltrate those institutions. Ben Tsion Schneider, a kind-hearted Jew who cared for the children, found time for public interaction with and combat against the leftists.

Father was deeply wounded that talented, quality youth withdrew from their religious roots. He actively countered them and attracted the youth to Torah study.

The leftists took over the acclaimed library and filled it with anti-religious and anti-Zionist books; all efforts to transfer the library to the Zionist camp were unsuccessful. That's when the Zionist youth decided to establish a Hebrew library. Very active in this task were Gad Levine (Shlomo's brother), David Leybke Berkovitsh, among others. They approached the Rabbi to assist them with American donations. The leftist activists were well established in the United States, and father knew that every dollar allocated toward the new library would stir a controversy in both New York and Divenishok. They had funded a library, and what right does the Rabbi have in giving Relief funds to a new library?

After debates and deliberation it was decided that $15 would be devoted to the new library. It was established and was a resource in combating the leftists in town. And indeed, many among the Divenishok youth emigrated to Israel as pioneers.

Governmental Relations

My father maintained good relationship with the Christian leadership in town. Once, the postmaster, a Christian, told him: "Rabbi, you see? I must work on Sunday, which is my Sabbath!" so the rabbi replied, "The bulk of my work also takes place on the Sabbath. On the Sabbath I participate in public prayers, I give lectures, and I teach Torah to the community." The Christian thought it was peculiar that adults attended Torah lessons as well.

In the days of Polish rule, an important guest visited town, and both the Christians and Jews festively greeted him: the archbishop from Vilne visited Divenishok. The welcoming ceremony took place on Vilne Street, near the synagogues. As the guest approached he was greeted with bread and salt. The

Rabbi greeted him with the Priestly Blessing in Hebrew, "May the LORD bless you and guard you..." to which the archbishop responded in Hebrew as well, "Amen and Thank You."

I remember that my father and the Jewish village notables once went to greet the county governor. After a long wait it began drizzling. My father told the notables, "Apparently this gentile hasn't studied Torah and is not aware of the duty to not cause the public trouble, to which a public official must adhere to more than the common man"...

After my father passed, and while my brother Aharon Tayts served as chief town rabbi, a decorative, honorary entrance gate was erected near the synagogue. In those days anti–Semitism was increasing in Poland and the Polish teacher Kutilah commanded the "Steshlach" (a Polish military organization) to take down the Star of David atop the gate. The Jews objected and a large quarrel erupted. Kutilah, wearing a Polish military uniform, began waving his sword above the heads of Jews. Yekl the Blacksmith approached him, forcibly removed the sword from Kutilah's hand, and broke it in front of the astonished Jews and Poles. The gentiles recoiled and decided to erect their own honor gate at the town entrance, 200 meters ahead of the Jewish gate.

In the days of Polish control, Jews depended on the mercy of police officials, since every policeman could greatly harm Jewish income.

To damage the Jews, a law was introduced that Sunday is a day of rest and businesses open that day would be fined. The law was mainly aimed at the Jews, who did not open their shops on the Sabbath. The church was at the center of town. Every Sunday many of the local farmers arrived to pray in church and after services would go to Jewish businesses to shop. Naturally, any police officer could incriminate that Jew and issue a ticket, which would cost more than his daily earnings.

To avoid such events Father maintained a relationship with the police chief. Father would explain the situation to every new chief that arrived in town: If a Jew is issued a report he is denied his living and can't feed his family. A smack to the face would not be as harsh a punishment as a Sunday report. The Rabbi requested that the chief ignore the Sunday rules and allow Jews to conduct their business on Sundays. Usually things worked out just fine. Certainly no smacks were issued, and no tickets were issued either.

I remember when we sat around the table on Sabbath day once, Father was informed that the new chief of police had inspected the market place, and had slapped Lubetski for the lack of cleanliness in the establishment. Father smiled and said, "I told other chiefs in town that a ticket would be tougher on Jews than a smack to the face, and it worked. But already from my first conversation with this one, I realized he is not the brightest light in the harbor, and if I tell him he can slap— he'll actually do it. What our Sages told us is true, 'Sages, be careful with your words'. The situation could have been much worse..."

Hebrew public school in Divenishok (1931)

Support from America

All the town's institutions were supported by former Divenishok residents – the "Relief" from America. My father conducted a correspondence with the Relief, especially with Rabbi Chaim Yudl Horvits. Father would distribute the funds to the institutions and sent back a detailed report. Without assistance from the Relief the institutions would have faced a crisis.

Most of our town's members received assistance from relatives in America. Many times the Rabbi was the one coordinating these familial bonds. If the relationship between the family in town and the one overseas dwindled, the Rabbi wrote to them and explained how important it is to support one's relatives. My father's letter would usually make a strong impression and help would be received.

I recall an anecdote where an anti-religious Jewish man who opposed Father was in a crisis and could not make a living. The Rabbi was told that the man had relatives in America that could assist him, but the Divenishok family dared not ask the Rabbi to write overseas. When he heard this the Rabbi right away sent a letter to the man's relatives in New York and assistance was provided.

Footnotes

1. Bikur Holim is literally the commandment which says to visit and aid the sick; societies going by that name have arisen to carry out this commandment

2. Visitation of the Sick

3. Interest–free charity loans

4. A famous Halachic work by Rabbi Avraham Danzig (1748–1821). *Chayei Adam* deals with the laws of daily conduct, prayer, Shabbat, and holidays, the laws discussed in the Orach Chaim section of the *Shulchan Aruch.*

[Page 70]

Maccabi HaTzair

Natan Kaplan

Translation by Meir Bulman

Starting in the 20's, Avraham Kartshmer, Nakhum Movshovitsh, Moshe Stul, Moshe Lubetski, Avraham Kotler, myself, and many others were in Vilne. Among other activities we did sports and we were regular members at "Maccabi HaTzair" in Vilne [Ed Note: Maccabi HaTzair is Zionist youth organization emphasizing Jewish values together with athleticism and camping]. We learned Judo, swimming, wrestling, and soccer. When we returned home for vacation we set up a soccer field behind the Gmina County Building where we practiced. Naturally, establishing the field attracted the best of the youth in town and so we established a team.

To improve our skills we played local Polish teams, with whom we enjoyed great relationships. After we made some progress and reached a satisfactory skill level in soccer we connected with all the area towns, like Voronova, Vishneva, Lida, Ivia, Oshmene, Traby, Olshan, Lipnishok, and their soccer players responded to invitations to compete.

The games that took place in town were at the center of attention for local youth and attracted a large audience. After the game, young people stormed the field in song and dance, singing with the players in Yiddish. After that we would invite the rival team's players to one of the houses and spend time together singing and eating well— as I accompanied the audience with a mandolin.

We were enthusiastically greeted in towns nearby. In Lida and Oshmene a fire department band accompanied the game, playing marches. It should be noted that the toughest games were with Lida, Ivia, and Oshmene, who had talented teams.

Purim performance in the Hebrew School in 1931, directed by the teachers A. Aloni (Zolondz), Bruria Rudnik-Aloni z"l, Dubkin, and others

At Maccabi HaTzair in Vilne we learned swimming and during our vacation we practiced in the Gavya River that ran through the outskirts of town. During summer breaks some vacationers visited town, among them college students who joined us for swimming training.

In Israel I met a doctor who had studied medicine in Vilne, and as we spoke he became aware that I come from Divenishok. He hugged and kissed me with happiness, and when he noted my wonderment, he told me that the good days he spent in our company swimming and picnicking in the Divenishok woods were an experience he will never forget.

That was our town, then, one that excelled in its unique charm and was supportive and friendly to all who entered its gates, and the experience of visiting there is forever cherished in the hearts of many who enjoyed that experience.

[Page 72]

My Path to *Betar*
(Youth Society Named after Yosef Trumpeldor)

Meir Yosef Itskovitsh

Translation by Meir Bulman

Youth Movements of All Shades

The *Betar*[Ed. Note: A right-wing leaning Zionist youth movement] branch of Divenishok was organized and established after there were already various youth groups operating in town, starting with VILBIG ("*Vilner Yidishe Bildung Gezelshaft*"),[Tr. Note: Vilne Jewish Educational Society] that was comprised of Yiddishists, Folkists;[Ed. Note: a political party that sought Jewish national autonomy within the Diaspora] many members of the communist party also found refuge from the Polish government in that organization. The VILBIG was anti-Zionist. Heading it was Hirshl Tzvi Krizovski, the town photographer. The driving ideological force was Yosef Levine ("Yosele Dem Mulers"[Ed. Note: Joseph the Bricklayer's Son]) who was fortunate enough to end his exile in Russia and come to the Land of Israel to witness the fruition of Zionism – the establishment of the Jewish state in the fatherland.

Near the Vilbig was "*Di Bin*" (The Bee), comprised of communist youth. It was named "Bee" for the collective living style of bee colonies. The organizer and educator was Yisroelke Munem (Yisrael Kherson), the sworn heretic, who now lives in Philadelphia, US, and has turned enthusiastic Zionist.

Aside from these anti-Zionist organizations, there was *HeKhaluts*,[Ed. Note: literally 'the pioneer'; a Zionist youth movement] whose members were also devoted Socialists, but unlike the anti-Zionists, their goal was a return to Zion and enact socialism in Israel. Along with *HeKhaluts*, there was *HeKhaluts HaTsair*, which was aimed at younger youths...[Ed. Note: the boy-scout and girl-scout branch of *HeKhaluts*]

Above all was the *HaShomer HaTzair* branch,[Ed. Note: a Zionist self-defense movement] which was the most active, and whose members included a majority of the town's youth. The active members were Yankele (Yaakov) Bloch, Fayvke (Shraga) Blyakher, Shloymke (Shlomo) Levine (who lives with us in Israel) and Aharke (Aharon) Kaganovitsh (who was not fortunate enough to arrive in Israel; his place of rest is unknown).

I was among the youngest members of *HaShomer HaTzair*. I was party to all the social mixers and meetups with the branches of nearby towns. I remember an interesting event at a meeting in Zhizhimi Villlage, near Lipnishok. In the village forest, we met up with the Voronova chapter of *HaShomer HaTzair*. They lit a bonfire on Friday night. My friend Tevye Blyakher, ז״הי[Tr. Note: hashém yikóm damó; used after the name of someone killed because he was Jewish, as a prayer to God that He avenge the death], an observant, god-fearing young man, approached me and remarked, "Look! They are violating the Sabbath by lighting a fire!" and so we decided not to drink the coffee around the fire.

At the Hebrew Gymnasium in Vilne

In 1931, my father decided to send me to continue my education in Vilne. I was accepted to the Dr. Epshteyn Hebrew Gymnasium.[Tr. Note: a gymnasium is a college preparatory school]

There was a rich boy from Vilne in my class by the name of Leybke Bloch. He targeted me for some unknown reason, and taunted me with the nickname "Provintser Khazer" (provincial pig). At recess he would chase me down the long hallway as he mocked me. He thoroughly angered me, yet I hesitated to respond. One day, during the lunch break, when he bothered me to the extreme, and in the presence of other students repeated his Provintser Khazer insult, I could not hold back. My patience had expired and I raised my right hand and punched him square in the face. His nose bled and his face was covered in blood. That raised a commotion and the school doctor, Dr. Bizheski, was summoned, and I was honorably led to the class instructor Steinberg. I poured my heart out to him and told him of all the hardships and persecution. The instructor said, "That's how a person defending his honor reacts" – and to everyone's surprise dismissed me without punishment.

The biggest surprise was that my assailant, injured by me, started greeting me when we crossed paths. The rest of my classmates followed suit and began treating me respectfully. Overnight my state had changed from being harassed, battered, and humiliated: I proceeded to walk with my head held high and the foreign surroundings slowly but surely treated me differently. I began seeing many things I had not been previously aware of, and began to understand things I hadn't thought of before. The thought of the revolution that had happened because of the punch stayed with me and did not leave me. I began to ponder the phenomena in individual life and its impact on the broader group.

The time was not encouraging to Jews. Anti-Semetism had spread and at the Vilne University Christian students rioted and denied entrance to their Jewish schoolmates. Young Jewish men who worked at the slaughterhouse, "Shtarke Yingalakh" (Strong Youngsters) organized, wore student hats, and mixed in with the Jewish students. To sum up, thanks to their intervention many injured anti–Semites were sent to the hospital, and one of them died. We, the students at the Hebrew Gymnasium, collected a whole heap of coal stones on the rooftop, ready to greet the Polish protestors. This bold response from the Jewish youngsters left a strong impression on me and I began to wonder if my path at *HaShomer HaTzair* was the right one to take.

Meanwhile in British Mandated Palestine, Jewish leaders announced a "restraint" policy.[Ed. Note: the *Havlagah* policy, supported by David Ben–Gurion among others, was premised on the principle of self-defense and abstention from seeking revenge against innocent Palestinian civilians] I had a hard time understanding the policy. I asked myself, "How will we look and what will we achieve if we are not wise enough to respond? Will restraint lead us to establish the Jewish State?" and my answer was, "No!"

Another thing influenced my future political path. In one of the Hebrew classes we learned about the poet David Frishman, and the instructor read us one of Frishman's poems.[Ed. Note: David Frishman 1865–1922 was an important poet, author, journalist, and translator in the European diaspora] If I am not mistaken, it goes something like this:

> The Silver Said: all is mine!
> The Iron Responded: all is mine!
> The Silver Said: I will buy all!
> The Iron Responded: I will take all!

I thought a lot about those lines, and realized how right they were. I reached the conclusion that my place was among the ranks of *Betar*, and with some other classmates I joined the *Betar* chapter in Vilne.

How the Divenishok Chapter of *Betar* Was Established

On the floor above the *Betar* chapter resided the Revisionist student union, *HaShmonai*.[Ed. Note: literally the Hasmoneans, named after the Dynasty that ruled Judea between c.140 and 116 BCE; Revisionist Zionism, usually accredited to Ze'ev Zhabotinsky and Joseph Trumpeldor, called for a 'revision' of Ben–Gurion's and Weizman's practical Zionism] One evening, I met a fellow town member, the law student Moshe Lubetski, Dovid Khaim Lubetski's son. We decided to devote our summer break to establishing the Divenishok chapter of *Betar*.

We decide to invite town residents to a community gathering on a Sabbath day in the grand synagogue during the hours between noon and evening prayers. Once we received permission from the Rabbi and the synagogue administrator we prepared posters and hung them in the entrance to the old and new synagogues and the school building. The keynote speaker was Moshe Lubetski, and I followed. A few friends joined us, among them Myshke Solts, Arke (Aharon) Solodukhe, Gotlib–Shkolnik and some others:, the Levine brothers from the Danoyke village, and Feygele Kaplan (now in Canada), who had transferred from the ranks of *HaShomer HaTzair*. The next day we met in one of the rooms at the Hebrew school for the establishment meeting. We established the chapter's command structure with me serving as the first commander. Moshe Lubetski prepared a request to the district executive in Oshmene for a youth group operating license – for the Joseph Trumpeldor Youth Organization –*Betar*. The purposes of the organization were stated in the organization's objectives: National education, military preparation for *Aliyah*,[Ed. Note: literally flying up; term used to describe emigration to and settlement in Israel] and the founding of a Hebrew state on both banks of the Jordan river. The request was signed by three of the town's distinguished gentleman, Avraham Noakh the ritual-slaughterer who was an avid National Zioinist, Natan Itskovitsh, and Ben Tsion Schneider. Letters were sent to *Betar* command in Warsaw requesting informational literature. When we received the first delivery we were quite happy. It included the *HaMedinah* (The State) Hebrew newspaper, (that was published by *Betar* in Riga, Latvia, birthplace of *Betar*), and the weekly Yiddish publication De Velt (The World), edited by Uri Zvi Greenberg. His weekly columns "*Fun Vokh Tsu Vokh*" (From Week to Week) were electrifying. The shipment also included booklets, newsletters, and communication forms. We consumed the material as if quenching our thirst.

Updated and encouraged, we approached the town's youth in order to befriend them. In face to face debates and conversations we convinced many youths, and we attained more than 20 members. That did not satisfy us and so we requested help from the Voronova chapter of *Betar*, and their talented commander Aharon Kalmenovitsh, whose speeches in the simple and understandable mother lounge attracted a large crowd. Aharon appeared several times at large gatherings, and after every appearance chapter memberships increased.

In the summer of 1932 the first meetup with the Vornova and Divenshok chapters of *Betar* took place in the Dovinski Forest, everyone wearing the *Betar* uniform. The joint formation was festive and remarkable. After that we gathered around the campfire and sang *Betar* and Israeli songs, and afterwards a joint conversation took place in which all attending participated. Questions were asked and opinions exchanged. After the conversation, the official ceremony concluded and each member attempted to get acquainted with someone from the other chapter. Pairs sat by their tents into the late hours of the night.

Without a Roof Over our Heads

Most of the Zionist youth organizations convened in the Hebrew school building. When *Betar* was established and organized we too demanded to convene there. This led to arguments and quarrels which sometimes even led to physical altercations. To maintain the peace in town the parents committee decided to ban future club meetings at the school, thus we remained without a roof over our heads.

During the summer, that problem was easily solved because gatherings and formations took place outdoors in the great forest surrounding town. We routinely met on a wonderful, large, grassy square that nature had created deep within the woods. But as the Fall arrived and Winter approached, we had to rent space in a private apartment, but did not have money. The cash shortage always trailed us. Most of us were poor, and even the "rich" folks in town had limited cash on hand. Occasionally, the ritual-slaughterer Avraham Noakh Shlomovitsh (an avid Zionist of the Abba Ahimeir school of thought[Ed. Note: Ahimeir founded the Maximalist faction within the Zionist Revisionist Movement]) provided financial support. We purchased a space in Aryeh Olkenitski's house, a vacant apartment on Subotniki Street. The small room hosted the command center and in the remaining two rooms were the chapter's classrooms. The walls were decorated with pictures of Benjamin Ze'ev Herzl, *Betar* head Ze'ev Jabotinski, Joseph Trumpeldor in the battalion uniform, and an additional illustration of Trumpeldor's fall in *Tel Hai*. The illustration was a gift from a *Betar* member in Ivia. Above the pictures were slogans such as "Two Banks has the Jordan – This is ours and, that is as well", "In blood and fire Judea fell – And in blood and fire Judea will rise again", and "It does not matter, it is good to die for our country."

Various and Expanded Activities

Each evening meetings took place devoted to educational activity. Each meeting began with standing in formation in full uniform. Following that, information from headquarters or regional command was read, current events were discussed, Israel studies and conversation, and debate on the settlement of the Land of Israel. A special emphasis was placed on organizational maneuvers, exercise, and bodybuilding.

On Saturdays chapter drills took place involving all units within the chapter. We were supplied with various periodicals including newspapers, pamphlets, and above all – Jabotinski's weekly column in the Warsaw publication *Haynt*,[Ed. Note: a Yiddish daily newspaper published in Warsaw from 1906 until 1939] and later in the *Der Moment* newspaper,[Ed. Note: a daily Yiddish newspaper published in Warsaw from 1910 until 1939] which we would read out loud, explain and comment on, followed by a lively discussion of the issues raised in the article.

On Fridays, a pair of *Betar* members patrolled the town from end to end, fundraising for the *Tel Hai* Fund, holding blue copper boxes with the charity's logo on the side. The boxes were triangular, distinguished from the squares of *Keren Kayemet*[Ed. Note: Jewish National Fund] box. Occasionally we distributed Zionist Revisionist literature to homes in the town.

Flag Dedication

With the purchase of our fixed dwelling we began to prepare for the flag-dedication festivities. To complete this task we recruited some non-*Betar* reinforcements. The flag was 120x100 centimeters, in two colors: one side in silk white, and the other blue. On the white side there was a figure of a lion and on the other the *Betar* logo, a Menorah with the words "*Betar* in Poland" above it and "Divenishok Chapter" underneath. My sister Bilkhe was asked to embroider the lion. Feygele Kaplan and her sisters (also *Beitar* membrs) embroidered the Menorah. My father prepared the lion, which was composed of brown fabric, and sewed according to my sketch on the fabric. A properly sized wooden pole was ordered from Yankele the carpenter. We prepared a list of homeowners willing to host *Betar* members from nearby towns. Once the flag was ready we sent invitations to all *Betar* chapters in the region for the Saturday night ceremony.

Despite the bitter cold of the 1933 winter many envoys from all the nearby towns joined. Divenishok was festive and crowded. The first to show up were *Betar* members from the small nearby town of Baksht, who arrived Friday so they would not violate the Sabbath. The delegation included a wind-instrument band. Imagine in a small town back in those days, an entire marching band all wearing *Betar* uniforms, with a blue and white flag ahead of the parade, followed by the *Betar* flag. Our happiness knew no limits. The Jewish town residents were beside themselves, and even the gentiles were astonished and watched respectfully. The parade passed through town and members formed into neat straight lines. It was a spectacular and unforgotten sight. Following the parade, a bazaar took place, with all proceeds directed to the Tel Hai Fund and the establishment of *Metzudat Ze'ev* building in Tel Aviv.[Ed. Note: this building, also known as Beit Jabotinski, houses the Jabotinski Museum and the headquarters of the modern Likud Party] I remember we had a special promotional placard bearing the future building's model.

We held special seminar events with out-of-town guest speakers on *Lag BaOmer*, 29 *Tamuz*, and 11 *Adar*. The town residents, even those opposed to *Betar*, attended the events. When *Betar* leader Ze'ev Jabotinski visited Vilne, many went to witness his speeches, much like the Hasids listen to their Rebbe. Along with *Betar* member Aryeh (Leybke) Botvinik from Eshishuk ה"יד,[Tr. Note: hashém yikóm damó; used after the name of someone killed because he was Jewish, as a prayer to God that He avenge the death] I had the good fortune to meet Jabotnisky at the Bristol Hotel. I presented him with a flower bouquet on behalf of the Dr. Cherno Teaching Seminary in Vilne.

On holidays the *Betar* facilities were decorated in holiday themes and appropriate slogans. The conversations during the Passover days were devoted to the Exodus – from slaves to liberation, and on *Hannukah* we discussed the

Hasmonean uprising – war of the few against the many. We drew encouragement and faith from the distant past, looking towards the future.

One of our primary obstacles was purchasing the *Betar* uniforms. The uniform was made up of a brown khaki shirt, with golden metallic buttons bearing the *Betar Menorah* logo. The fabric necessary was not available in town and had to be specially ordered. What vendor would invest his own money into this unpopular fabric?

But THE vendor was found, none other than Hinde Sareh, Ben Tsion's wife and Shmuel Sharon's mother (who now lives with us in Israel). This woman with valor was the "foreign minister" in Ben Tsion's large business, and she brought the first fabric roll. The vendor Shalom Garvey followed and took the risk of purchasing *Betar*'s shiny golden buttons.

Once the shirts were sewn we approached Aharon Bloch the hat maker to sew the *Betar* caps. It was not a simple task and only Aharon's hands of gold succeeded.

The Split Came to Divenishok Too

Adorned in uniforms, with pride and honor we walked the town streets with our heads held high and our hearts full of glee and hope— but then a crisis struck. A split occurred between *Betar* leader Jabotinski and his right hand man Meir Grossman. Grossman withdrew from the Revisionist movement and established the *Brit HaKa'naim*, (The Zealots' Covenant) youth group, as a competitor to *Betar*. And then Michael Solodukhe, who was Aharon's (the town's *Betar* commander) brother, established the Zealots' Covenant chapter— but less than a dozen became members. Michael emigrated with his brother to the United States then fought and was wounded in the Korea War, receiving many valor awards. He passed away unexpectedly in 1975.

In the Area Villages

When the number of members topped 40 we set out to "conquer" the Jewish youth in the nearby villages. The "stranded" Jews, aside from observing Torah commandments, were not connected to the events unfolding in the Jewish world and had not even heard at all of the Jewish settlement in Palestine.

The Levine family lived in the Danoyke village, and their son Chaim (the town's windmill administrator) and his brothers Yosef and Chanan joined *Betar*. Near our town, on the way to Benakani, was Konvalishki with 14 Jewish families who lived amongst the gentiles. One Saturday I walked there with two other *Betar* members. When we got there we gathered about ten participants in the small synagogue's women's section and I lectured about *Betar* and its role. They absorbed our talk and that was not surprising. They were so distant from all that was happening in the outside Jewish world. Our appearance there brought a ray of light to the small, Gentile–dominated town. We were asked to teach the *Betar* anthem and songs of the Promised Land. We established a local *Betar* chapter which had 8 members. After refreshments including *Challah* and the famous Yudelevitsh lemonade, we kindly departed.

An additional attempt to establish a *Betar* chapter in Lipnishok was unsuccessful. In the grass field between house and barn a large crown gathered on a Saturday and we were happy, but it turned out those were *HaShomer HaTzair* loyalists. When our speaker Aharon Kalmenovitsh attempted to talk he was interrupted by heckling and whistling. I approached the ruckus raisers, mostly former friends I had met at *HaShomer HaTzair*, in an attempt to calm them, but I failed. My friend Naftali Kartshmer (a close friend to this day, living in Israel), and simply told me, "Meir Yoshke, a *Betar* will never ever be established here!", and unfortunately, he was right.

The WWII days

While *Betar* members were busy dreaming up their plans to migrate to the land of Israel, dark clouds gathered and the earth was darkened. The war erupted and Poland was occupied. The Soviet–Nazi alliance split the spoil. Our town was transferred to Soviet hands. A government crackdown began on Zionist youth groups, especially *Betar*. Many were summoned before the NKVD[Ed. Note: leading Soviet secret police organization from 1934 to 1946] and were interrogated entire nights. The interrogator would take a photo of Jabotinski out of his drawer and inquire, "Do you know who this is? Who was he?" and would repeat the question louder, accompanied by juicy Russian swear. "This is the biggest fascist Jew, correct?"

Yaakov Schneider, the last *Betar* commander, gathered the *Betar* flag, the photos and informational literature, and hid them at home for brighter days to come. His mother discovered the "treasure" and informed her husband, who commanded Yaakov to destroy the materials. But Yaakov could not bring himself to obey the command, and to his assistance came his Brother, 15 year old Shmuel, who packed his bike with the materials and distributed it to passers–by along and across town.

Someone passed along the information of his counter–revolutionary acts to the NKVD, and Shmuel was summoned for interrogation. In the stairway he encountered a former *Betar* member who had becpme an informant. Shmuel shot him a look of disdain as he passed by. The interrogation lasted two hours and he was then released. They were likely convinced that the young boy had acted in good faith and was not accountable for his actions.

Hanuka party in the home of the Satkolshtsik family in Subotnik Street– Samuel Sharon is a descendant of the family

The evidence against *Betar* members piled up and they faced a known destination: Siberia. They were saved by a rumor that I had died in combat while fighting against the Germans with the Polish military. Their way out was to put the blame on me. I was the one that had misled them, who had tricked them— I, being an expert in persuasion and rhetoric, had blinded them and had led them astray, etc. etc.

What the Soviet "liberators" could not destroy was destroyed by the German invaders.

I often tell myself, "If those Zionist youths were alive today, if they were here with us in Israel, we would not feel so alone, we would not be so constantly heavy hearted. We miss them."

May these words be a monument in memory of all Zionist youth movements – the loyal, honest, gentle, innocent town residents, serene lovers of God and mankind, who dreamed day and night of Zion, who prayed: "may our eyes witness the Lord's return to Zion".

May these words be an everlasting shrine to those who were not fortunate enough to make their dreams come true and who fell on foreign soil.

May their souls be bound up in the bond of everlasting life.

[Page 81]

Zionist and Cultural Activity

Avraham Aloni

Ed. Note: This article appears in both Hebrew and Yiddish in the original Yizkor Book; only the Yiddish version has been translated and published in this book and may be found at page 443 of this book.

[Page 85]

The Hebrew School in Divenishok

Shmuel Dubkin

Translation by Meir Bulman

"'Touch not my anointed' referring to school children"
--Babylonian Talmud, Tractate Shabbath

I had the good fortune to convey Torah and knowledge in various towns in the Vilne area, and to educate children in the National Hebrew spirit for love of the Torah, for the People of Israel, and for the Land of Israel.

As I attempt to shake off the dust from that time, an era steeped in the dust of the past, my mind's eye witness all those towns, their Hebrew schools and their students which I instructed and educated. Allegedly, all towns in Eastern Europe were similar in their external build and their spiritual and financial build, but, every town had its own unique character.

Among those towns where I served as teacher, Divenishok, in the Vilne region, especially stands out. Many impressions and experiences from my work at the Hebrew school remain in my memory to this day.

I arrived in Divenishok in 1930. Ahead of my arrival there was an interesting meeting in Vilne with the town rabbi, Rabbi Yosef Rudnik, may he rest in peace. His firm character and noble personality left a strong impression on me. As I discussed the school and local conditions, he asked if I could guide young people. "What kind of young people?" I asked. "Zionist pioneering youth: *HaShomer HaTzair* and *HaKhalutz*, especially *HaShomer Hatzair*," he responded.

I was embarrassed by his answer. What business does an Orthodox rabbi have with *HaShomer HaTzair*? The Rabbi, who sensed my discomfort, said with his unique humor and in a fatherly tone, "You must be wondering why a

Rabbi is concerned about *HaShomer*? Well, you should know that our *Shomer* is unlike any other *Shomer*. In our town, *HaShomer HaTzair* members come to the synagogue for the three daily prayers".

In town I stayed in the home of the Kosher slaughterer Avraham Noakh (may God avenge his blood). His family members greeted me kindly and warm feeling of residing among my own people surrounded me.

My impression of the school was also very positive. A spacious, beautiful building, filled with light, large classrooms, with windows wide open, overlooking the green fields. The building was at the center of the *Shulhoyf*–[Ed. Note: the Synagogue's courtyard] the town's spiritual center. The school was blessed with a devoted teaching staff and heading them was Mr. Avraham Aloni, the school principal (now principal of *Tel Nordoy* in Tel Aviv), his wife Bruria (rest in peace), and Yeshayahu Kramer (now living in Haifa), and I joined that staff. We all did our best to promote this educational institution to top–tier educational quality.

An important part of our work was the school plays that brought a festive and happy feeling to the students and their parents.

The school was not just a place of learning for the children, but also a cherished spot, filled with light and joy of life, where many could forget the day–to–day troubles of their parents at home.

I must positively mention the school committee, headed by town chief rabbi Yosef Rudnik: Ben Tzion Schneider, Mintz Kaplan, Natan Itskovitsh, Avraham Krivitski, Avrahm Noakh and more, who were involved in much activity for the school and Hebrew education in town.

For my entire time at work I was active in the Pioneering Zionist organization *HaShomer HaTzair*, a majority of which was composed of school alumni, which was an active, lively place, where I found vast ground for cultural activity and spiritual guidance. During the school day the building was full of children's cheer, and in the evening, the building was reignited and taken over by *HaShomer* members who came to conduct various educational tasks, and waves of Hebrew song and Hora dance were heard into the late hours of the night. Here within the school walls great intellectual experiences and a longing for Israel were developed.

An important part of the educational work at *HaShomer* were the field trips to the surrounding natural grounds. The town was surrounded by enchanting pine forests, frequently visited. Meetups with Pioneering Zionist groups from the nearby towns were conducted, leading to an awakening in those towns. Standing out in my memories are two such gatherings that left a strong impression on us, one in nearby Traby, and the other in Oshmene for the *Keren Kayemet* conference.

I shake as I remember that Nazi forces of destruction defiled and destroyed such a dear and holy community as Divenishok. The heart aches – a pure community is no more, and its song of life was interrupted.

In the words of R. Weintraub:

"The wind of the abyss will silently weep

For annihilation, destruction, and desolation

Will roil and rage, for the blood holocaust

Will never be forgiven, forever and eternity"

May this collection of memories serve as living letters on the written tombstone in memory of the Divenishok community.

[Page 87]

Memories of the "Khaluts" Society

Shalom Rosenblum

Translation by Rabbi Israel Rubin

Our house was in the neighborhood of "Patzlof" near the flour depot. We lived in one part of the house, and rented the other part to the parents of Yakov Khasman (Yankel the blacksmith). They lived in our home for 28 years. My mother's name was Menucha, and my father was Tzvi, her second husband. My father died in WWI and the burden was placed on my mother to raise the orphans.

My first teacher was Kalman Shepsel (the father of Tzvi Krizovski). We, the students, would sit around the table, and he would wear the tallis–katan, holding the pointer–stick in his hand while conducting the children. After I grew up a little, I studied tailoring. At first I worked for Nasan the tailor, and afterward I went to work for Groinam the tailor.

When the "Khaluts" ("Pioneer") started, I enlisted as a member and was sent (in 1925) to "preparation" (preparatory farming study done in anticipation of farming the land of Israel) in the area of Sventzion. We worked there on all kinds of back–breaking labor and were often subjected to starvation. After half a year I sent in a request to make *aliyah* to Israel and was sent to Warsaw for a fitness examination. There they had a pressure machine to measure my tendons and overall strength...to my good fortune, the instrument was flawed, and after all this I was authorized to make *aliyah*.

HeKhaluts (Ed. Note: boy/girl scouting group) organization in Divenishok, 1932

From Warsaw to Constanta we traveled by train, and from there by the Roman boat [named] "Datsia" to Israel. In Kolonie Lvovo something unpleasant occurred to me. I hired a porter to bring my bag through a tunnel. He hid the number and wanted to run away, so I grabbed the bag from him by force and continued on my way.

When I arrived in Israel, I was sent to the Kibbutz HaCovesh in Petach-Tikva. There I worked in the orchard, I dug holes for new plants, and pruned and fertilized the orchard. There I learned what menial handiwork was. One time we needed to carry the fertilizer on our shoulders, and my shirt tore. I, understandably, continued to carry my sack of fertilizer until evening. When I got home, I felt terrible burns on my back from the heat and fertilizer. I was unable to eat or sleep for three days as a result of my wounds.

After 1929, when the German *aliyah* began, the situation improved and I began regular (permanent) work as a tailor.

HeKhaluts membership card, Divenishok, 1925

I visited Divenishok in 1938, after being away for 12 years. The youth were very reclusive. I searched hard for good, lively youth with an awareness of Zionism that were ready to make *aliyah* to Israel. While they were ready for *aliyah*, the gates of Israel were closed.

I became especially friendly with Yekusiel Zhizhemski, who wanted to experience the atmosphere of the Jewish Land, and to learn the proper Sephardic pronunciation. I loved Zhizhemski. He was a wondrous young man, pleasant, brilliant, and an excellent teacher. I really miss him. After several months I left Divenishok and returned to Israel full of impressions.

Post Office on Subotnik Street, in the house of the Kivelevitsh-Krivitski family

[Page 90]

The Revival Period in Divenishok

Dov Ben Shalom (Popisko)

Translation by Meir Bulman

I was born in Eshishuk, and arrived in Divenishok before Purim of 1923. The story goes like this: as the Poles entered the town, I joined the army. I bought a fake passport in Lida, which stated I was older, and so I had to serve on reserve duty only half the time.

When I returned home on vacation, a Polish police officer ratted me out and I had to escape to Divenishok, where my sister, who was married to Eliahu Melamed the tailor, lived. They had seven children. My sister Chava was in Divenishok as well, as she had married Eliahu's brother Grunem. They all perished in Voronova.

I resided in Divenishok for two years. I worked as a tailor with my brother–in–law Eliahu Melamed. On my first month living there, I met my wife Reyzl (Shoshana). I was registered with *HaKhalutz* at the end of the seventh month by Eliahu Itskovitsh (Netaneli), who was the branch chairman.

I should note that a revival period began in our town with the establishment of *HaKhalutz*. The youth sprang into activity and were influenced by the pioneering Zionism.

We met weekly, mostly in the women's section in the synagogue, and occasionally in private homes. At the start of the meeting we would read the correspondence from the regional *HeKhaluts* headquarters. Then we would discuss current events or conduct a public debate on a book that members had read prior to the discussion.

A group of Jewish youths in the woods near Divenishok (1930)

I remember a debate on *Di Goldene Keyt*, the Golden Chain, by I. L. Peretz. Eliahu Itskovitsh was taken by Hassidic enthusiasm and lectured on the topic for three hours. To this day the concluding remarks of the speech ring in my ears: "the golden chain continues and will continue until we reach the renewed Land of Israel."

Occasionally, guest speakers would appear. I remember Yhoshua Manoakh from Dganya, who was a gifted speaker, Bardichevski from Yagur, who was very active in the *HaKhalutz* organization in the Vilne district. They were both sent from Palestine to organize the Vilne district branch.

The gatherings were attended by large crowds and conducted in the spirit of pioneering. Especially uplifting were the new songs of the Land of Israel that the delegates would bring. I visited *HaKhalutz* in Eshishuk and other towns, but the Divenishok branch excelled with its organizational and cultural activities.

I must make note of the teachers in Divenishok, especially Mr. Engle, who was director of Zionist and cultural activity at *HaKhalutz*. He also traveled with me to Mr. Tiktniski at the "Zion Youngsters" (*Tz'eerey Zion*) in Vilne and helped me get an immigration certificate to Palestine. It was quite an accomplishment for me, since only 400 such certificates were issued in the whole of Poland that year, and only 15 in the Vilne region.

I arrived in this land in 1925 with my wife Shoshana. I did not want to continue working as a tailor, but to be an actual pioneer and literally participate in developing the land— but due to the harsh conditions I had to quickly return to tailoring.

Since my Aliyah 50 years ago I have lived in Haifa. In this city I established a family. I have three children who established their own homes. My wife was a great companion in life, but died two years ago, unfortunately for me. That is how I lost my most loyal and closest life friend.

[Page 92]

HeKhaluts Organization in Our Town

Eliahu Netaneli (Itskovitsh)

Translation by Meir Bulman

I was born in 1906 in Divenishok to my parents Natan, son of Dov, and Khiene. My father was a Voronova native, and my mother was from the family of Avraham Eliezer Levine, an ancient Divenishok family. I know of four generations because on the prayer book in my father's house it said, "This prayer book is the property of Avraham Eliezer son of Meir son of Yitzchak."

About My Family

I do not remember my grandfather, but the memory of my grandmother Miriam is etched deep in my consciousness, perhaps due to her unique personality. I remember that every Thursday at dawn my grandmother would gather many vegetables into a basket with her quick hands and disappear into the morning mist. I followed her once out of curiosity and saw her rushing with the basket towards one of the homes, climbing rapidly, almost floating, onto a balcony of a neighbor in need - and then disappear. Her actions were a well-kept secret even among members of her family so as to fulfill the mitzvah of *matan b'seter*[1] without a single flaw.

My mother, despite being the daughter of a poor tailor, strived for Torah and knowledge. She was the only girl in town to complete art, embroidery, and design studies, with honors, in Vilne in 1903, and receive a diploma.

My father was good-natured man and liked helping his fellows. He had a majestic appearance, with a permanent smile. He was a kind man and involved himself with those around him. He was among the leaders of the community in town and devoted much of his time to public activism.

I remember that once while we sat down for Friday lunch, Meir Rogol entered the home and told father that Leyzer the coachman's horse had fallen. Father moved aside the beef stew with challah bread and left the house. An hour or two passed, and father returned with a smile on his face and said, "Moshe Leyzer already has a horse," and returned to eating calmly.

Father was faithfully devoted to community matters for many a day, from when he married my mother to the day he died. I remember a number of episodes which were typical of my father from my childhood, the era of the Tsar.

In the time of the Tsar, a special judge was appointed to handle Divenishok and the surrounding area. The residence of the judge was by Malinovke, on Giranyoon Street. I would fill with pride when I saw the judge pull up to our home on a coach harnessed to two horses. The judge would enter, shut himself in the room with my father, and consult with him regarding complex legal matters. As my father told it, the judge would accept his advice and make rulings accordingly.

I remember another event, in the 1920s, when the Poles occupied the town. As was their custom, they appointed a city commander, who in this case was an anti-Semitic commander from Galicia. He entered our home on a Saturday and announced that the Jews must immediately go out and clean the marketplace. "But today is the Sabbath," my father replied. "This is an order," the commander said. I do not know from where my father drew the courage, but he angrily approached the commander and told him, "When you speak to me, nobody can hear. But when I begin talking to you the whole town will hear. Sabbath is holy to us and we will not work today." The commander left.

Father was very talented and influential. Had he studied, he certainly would have been a successful lawyer, but in his youth he did not have the opportunity to study at school and had to help his parents with tailoring. He took advantage of his talents for community work in town, which brought him satisfaction and was of much help to the residents. Our town was without change for decades; its life proceeded peacefully without fateful events. The source for the news we received about events occurring out in the big world was Aryeh Leyb Rogol, the pharmacist who was subscribed to two Warsaw newspapers: *Haynt* and *Moment*. Later on the newspapers were also in my parents' home. My rabbi and teacher Rabbi Leib Aharon Engle, the well-known lecturer, was subscribed to *HaZfira*.

Out in the world events were taking place that drastically altered human history. During WWI our territory exchanged hands many times. The February Revolution erupted, and then the Bolshevik Revolution, which was rooted in ideals of freedom for humanity, and independence and freedom for small weakened states.

And in the Jewish world – The Balfour Declaration, in which many Jews saw 'Athalta D'Geula'[2], prayed for British victory over the Turkish, but many were not satisfied with hopes and prayers alone, and these got involved in helping the British in their war. The message of redemption intoxicated the Jewish community. Vilne, a leading Jewish city, celebrated the start of a new era in the life of the Jewish people magnificently. Parades by all Zionist organizations took place. In Vilne I saw the joy and abundant faith which overtook the whole of Jewry. I, the *cheder* student, saw in that declaration the fruition of the prayer, "May our eyes witness Your return to Zion in compassion." I wept with tears of happiness and joy. I conceived an idea of establishing a Zionist organization in our town, to take action for *aliyah* and put an end to life in exile.

I poured my heart and ideas out to my father. We stood on our balcony and saw Lithuanian cavalry approaching the market place from Dowichitzki Street, passing by on their horses with expressions of glee and happiness on their faces. I was very envious and told my father, "Look, that small faltering nation is fortunate to have its own military, why should we not make Aliyah to fight for our freedom?" My father was not influenced by my enthusiasm.

After some time, I returned to my studies in Vilne. My young spirit was attached to the Zionist movement, to *HeKhaluts*. And with my youthful passion I made up my mind: *HeKhaluts* will be established in Divenishok! I decided to discuss the issue and consult with Zionist leaders. The goal I set for myself gave me wings. I dared and approached the important leader Dr. Yakov Vigudski. He greeted me warmly, listened to me and directed me to Mr. Bankover, the driving force behind *HeKhaluts* in Vilne, who was the representative from Israel to organize the *HeKhaluts* movement in Poland.

The 4 Clauses

When I returned home, I was equipped with guidance and materials I received from Mr. Bankover. The *HeKhaluts* plan focused on four main objectives:

1. *HeKhaluts* must be subject to the World Zionist Organization and fulfill the roles to which its members are appointed.

2. The study of the Hebrew language, its literature, and Zionist doctrine.

3. Publicizing the Zionist idea, and professional and agricultural training.

4. Aliyah

I brought with me various documents and newspapers in Hebrew, among them the *HeKhaluts* paper *HaAtid*[Tr. Note: the future] which was published in Warsaw. In Divenishok I discussed matters with my good and close friend Dov Zandman (who fell at Mount Scopus with his envoy), along with Avraham Kartshmer, Nakhum Movshovitsh, son of the town rabbi. We decided to establish a *HeKhaluts* organizational chapter. Our town residents were feeling energized and in our vision we saw the dream of an independent Israel taking shape. In our mind's eye we were already in *Eretz* Israel.

Then 1921 arrived. From Israel came stunning news: about the *Tel Hai* incidents-- of the death of a man with a hero's stature, Yosef Trumpeldor. It was also the time of awful news concerning a massacre of Jews in the Ukraine, and the flurry of emotion in the Jewish street had not yet quieted. We, the youth, compared the helplessness of the Jews in exile with the heroic standing of Jews in Israel.

The initial group gathered around us more youth. Few days went by before we were a group of dozens, imbued with the spirit of Zionism. We did not have a permanent place to convene. We would gather in one of the yards, or at times in the large garden of the elderly Kaplan family, or on Saturdays while hiking through the woods. I read them correspondence and newspapers in Hebrew, still with Ashkenazic pronunciation. Our parents and town elders treated us dismissively: "What? Where? Eretz Israel? Parched Palestine? The *Geula* has not yet come... you... you who have not left your fathers' home to enter the vast world, you, the children, will establish a state? (You, the people of my town who will read these words – I swear I am not writing out of boastfulness but for the sake of historic accuracy alone.)

I was the first founder of *HeKhaluts* and its main activist in town. I would lecture in front of my friends for hours on end. I passed to them my great love for Hebrew literature which fed into the love of country. The *Keren Kayemet* collection box was holy to us. The movement began to take shape. My family's stable financial situation helped me carry on with my Zionist activism. With the allowance I got I could afford writing utensils, rubber stamps, and more. After a while an administration was elected and I was appointed its chairman. The secretary was Y. Satkolshtsik and the treasurer Mordechai Abramovitsh. *HeKhaluts* became an organization recognized by the authorities. We corresponded with Israel and envoys from Israel began visiting us. I still remember some of them: Yehoshua Manoakh from Dganya, Aharon Bardichevski and others.

After a while, Rabbi Movshovitsh – the sympathetic and friendly rabbi – allowed us to conduct our meetings at the women's section in the New Synagogue. It was very good to gather on a summer or winter night for information and culture sessions, games and sing-a-longs, etc.

I served as chairman for four years, until I made *Aliyah* in 1925. We busied ourselves with various activities, especially devoting ourselves to establishing a quite large library. From the income of 10-20 grush[3], we purchased books in Hebrew and Yiddish. Later we also purchased books from funds provided by the town's first Zionist Aryeh Leyb Rogol.

From funds sent for constructive purposes by former residents of our town living in America, a portion was budgeted for the library.

Within three years approximately fifty youths joined us and to this day I do not understand from where I took the strength and mental capacity to break down conservative walls to establish *HeKhaluts* in our town and turn it into an influential factor in the town's life. Later, when Kibbutz *HaKovesh*,[4] consisting of pioneers from Vilne and the surrounding area, made Aliyah, a few people from our town joined them.

At the time of the Mandate, in the days of the *Aliyah* suspension, and the unemployment in Israel, the first of our townfolks, made *Aliyah* and served as the bedrock for the future Divenishok alumni in Israel.

In 1903 and 1905, various revolutionary organizations were established in our town, like the *Bund* and others. But they did not last long and were destroyed by the Tsarist regime. Most of their members emigrated to the United States, where they established an organization of former Divenishok residents. But *HaHaluz* presented to them with the question, "And now when shall I provide for my own house also?" [Gen. 30: 30] and the answer was clear, "The time has come to act for our country, the land of Zion and Jerusalem!"

My Aliyah

After I established *HeKhaluts* and became one of its chief spokespersons, I was smitten by the fire of Zionist activism and decided to not only say but also to do as I was saying. In 1925 I left a well-established, wealthy home to make Aliyah. Here I suffered want and hunger, struggled hard for each work day; with my frail body I had to do back-breaking labor, so I would not trail behind friends, and I struggled daily for survival.

Father rained letters on me, "Dear son! My eldest son, return home, you will lack nothing, you are physically weak, you cannot withstand the immense effort." But I, a fire blazing in my heart, was tired of exile and humiliation, and the striving to reconstruct the homeland was the center of my life. I suffered and was burning out, yet I withstood temptation and did not return to Poland.

After years of difficult physical labor, I had to transfer to teaching and was fortunate to educate the younger generation with a love of nation and land, until I retired for health reasons.

In Israel I met my wife Khaya, who became a loyal friend through the twists and turns of my life. Despite the harsh conditions, she kept my sister Bilkhe with us and encouraged her to not return to the diaspora, and thanks to her, she remained in Israel and was fortunate to establish a new generation.

Despite all I endured, my heart is full with praises of God, who has blessed me to live in our free country, who blessed me in seeing its renewal, and blessed me with starting home in it.

Translator's Footnotes

1. Anonymous charity

2. Aramaic for: beginning of redemption

3. An obsolete Israeli currency

4. :iterally, 'the conqueror'

[Page 97]

Trivia From Our Town

Moshe Mintz

Translation by Martin Jacobs

My parents lived in the "*magazin*" (warehouse) on Geranion Street. It got its name of *magazin* from the large granaries a kilometer away. In the days of the Czar there was also a courthouse there. In the First World War the Germans burnt down the storehouses and the courthouse.

*

The cemetery was behind our house. Our lands were separated from the cemetery by the lands of the farmers of Subotnik Street. There were two cemeteries in the town, the old one, on which a beautiful pine grove grew, and the new one, purchased in 1928. It took much effort to acquire this land, since the farmers knew that the Jews would pay any price they asked so as to have the plot for this use. They refused to sell for less than triple its value.

When the Jews finally succeeded in acquiring the land there was much joy in the town and the burial society hosted a dinner in honor of the event. To this day I remember how large wooden posts were brought, smeared with pitch, and passed through a fire, so that they would not decompose in the ground, and a high wire fence was put up all around.

It was always the practice in the town to carry the deceased to the cemetery on a stretcher. With the purchase of the new cemetery a new practice was put into effect: the burial society purchased a cart on which a black wooden coffin was set out, and the deceased was placed into it. A horse was harnessed to the cart and the coffin and horse were covered with a velvet covering embroidered with a white Star of David and verses from the Psalms.

I remember an interesting episode in connection with the cart. Members of the burial society had difficulty deciding what length to make the coffin. On the one hand, it had to fit every body, on the other, it had to have an aesthetic form. Itza Binyamin the Blacksmith, a member of the burial society himself, lay down so that they could measure him for the coffin – as he said, there is no man taller in the town – and his measurements were accepted.

I learned reading and writing from Shaul the Dyer. He was a strict man in whose hand an oak ruler was always at the ready – and when he hit "no grass would grow in that place". The pupils were dreadfully afraid of him, but he devoted himself more to the dying business, which his wife managed, than to teaching.

After that I went on to the school which opened in the town. I recall that for a while the school was in Chaim Hershovitsh's house and then in the house of Abba the Shoemaker.

*

I joined HeKhaluts when I was 16 years old. In 1923 I went to a pioneer training camp near Wiszniewo. There my task was to chop down trees and prepare them for shipment to Germany. Although my brother sent me papers for travel to America I chose to go to Palestine, since I wanted to participate in building the land.

I arrived in Palestine at the beginning of 1926, before Rosh Hashana. The economic conditions there were not good. I barely got work with Kantrowitz, the orange grower, in Petach-Tikva. For digging a pit I got a piaster and a mil per meter. I dug twenty pits a day.

Once when I had been there a year I met David Lipka Berkovitsh on the street. He had arrived in Palestine a year before me. To my great surprise he said to me: "Do you know what? I have decided to return home." I went with him to buy a present for my mother and sister. Suddenly I was overcome with longing to see my family and the city of my birth. I said to David Lipka, "Have a good trip. Give my regards to my family and tell them that I too will soon be going home." And so it was: I went to Jerusalem, got a six-week visa, and in spring of 1928 I returned to Divenishok.

*

In the town they were then building the Hebrew school and Zionist activity was quite strong. I myself joined the Zionist labor circle and we were beginning to set up a Hebrew library after the Yiddishists had gained control of the municipal library. We collected money and went to Vilna, where we bought as many as 500 books with cash and on credit. We organized appeals at all festive occasions and arranged question and answer evenings, with a guest lecturer. We organized raffles and we emptied Jewish National Fund collection boxes. The teachers of the school did their utmost for all cultural and Zionist activities.

Daughters of Moshe Aaron Katz and their friends

Because of my family situation I put off my return to Palestine from day to day, until the visa expired. To this day I cannot forgive myself for the two serious mistakes I made in my life, that I left Palestine, and, more seriously, that I did not return in the time specified. Several years later I tried to return, but unsuccessfully. I even went to the commune in Glubok, where I stayed for three and a half years, but all my efforts to return to Palestine came to naught.

I paid very dearly for my mistakes. For seventeen years I endured countless troubles and hardships. Not just once did I face death. Only in 1956, broken and crushed, did I succeed in reaching Palestine. Here I needed to start all over again, and with God's help I was able to get on with my life.

[Page 100 – Hebrew] [Page 439 – Yiddish] (original book pagination)

The Torah Reading Was Stopped

Eliahu Itskovitsh

Translation by Leybl Botwinik

Stopping the Torah reading was one of the best and quickest ways to achieve what one wished for according to law, when an injustice had been done to someone. A person who saw himself discriminated against would come to *shul*[Tr. Note: Synagogue] on *shabes*[Tr. Note: Sabbath, the Jewish day of rest] morning during the *shakharis*[Tr. Note: Morning prayer] service, and place himself directly in front of the *orn koydesh*[Tr. Note: Holy ark where the Torah scrolls are kept, usually on a raised platform or stage] and not let anyone take the Torah out for the reading – until the Rabbi, the community leader and the rest of the congregation heard out his complaints and claims, and promised to carry out his requests. Then he would descend from the stage.

This system was also often used by swindlers and informers that wanted to force the community to give them money.

During the Czarist reign, every able-bodied male who reached the age of 21 had to join the army, and if someone did not report for duty or ran away, then his family would be fined 300 Rubles.

One *shabes*, as the *shakharis* prayer ended and the words "*veyehi binsoya ho-oroyn*"[Tr. Note: Prayer said while the Torah ark is being opened] were said by the *khazn*,[Tr. Note: Cantor who leads the prayer] there was heard a sudden outcry. The worshipers were alarmed. Within moments, two young scholars appeared and argued the following: "In two months' time, we are to be enlisted into the army. We have decided to travel to America. Our desire is that you will give us funds for our fare and 600 Rubles, the fine that will be put on our parents."

The brazen pair shouted that they wanted to reach an agreement immediately, even before the reading of the Torah – and if not, they would inform on the Rabbi and on other community leaders to the authorities, that they are plotting against the regime – and other such false charges.

The delay in the reading of the Torah depressed and embittered my father greatly, but did not shake him. He went up onto the stage, and in a beautiful speech explained to them that they had no right to demand the monies. If they would speak honorably, it would be seen what could be done about their voyage to America. Tactfully and with words that spoke to the heart, he pointed out that the two young scholars were yet innocents. The worshippers in the *shul* were satisfied with his words and the young men left the house of worship with downcast eyes.

[Page 101]

In the Service of the Jewish Homeland

Natan Kaplan, Son of Mordechai and Khasye

Translation by Meir Bulman

The Jewish football[Tr. note: soccer] *team Gloria after a match with the local police team (1924)*

I was born in Divenishok, a small town in the Vilne area. My father Mordechai and my mother Khasye excelled in their pleasant traits and good deeds, like all residents in our town. My mother and father, may they rest in peace, were near and dear to my heart and I loved them very much.

My father was a *gabbai* at the synagogue, and with the rest of the members of the community worked to improve his financial state. The main basis for livelihood in town was market day and Sunday. On those days, the residents of nearby villages would bring their merchandise to town, and with the money they earned, bought various goods at the Jewish-owned stores.

At a young age, my father sent me to study in Vilne. I studied there, along with my friends from town, at the "knowledge disseminating" schools, and then later at the *Gymnasia* Realit.

In Vilne we devoted ourselves also to boxing, soccer and other sports. We also apprenticed in firefighting so that later we could be accepted as volunteers at the firehouse. Each year during summer vacation, we returned to our town and there too we busied ourselves with sports. We played teams from nearby towns: Oshmene, Olshan, Voronova, Lida, and Ivia. We also trained in swimming in the river. I dedicated a few hours a week to singing. I sang in Vilne with the *Slepp* choir, and with a religious chorus at the Old Synagogue, in the days of Cantor Hershman. On evenings we gathered sometimes in my room and spent a number of hours singing – and I accompanied the singing by strumming the mandolin.

I was very pleased with my studies in Vilne, but there was one think I could not accept– that my teachers and counselors were members of the Yiddishist movement, and strived to establish a Jewish Yiddish center within the Polish borders. Most of them rejected Zionism while my heart was drawn only towards Zionist youth movements.

*

By 1942, Vilne had become a large Zionist and Hebrew center. The *HeKhaluts* movement was established while at the same time many of my friends continued studying there and also left for the university towns in Europe. I joined *HeKhaluts* and burned behind me my contacts with teachers and counselors who opposed Zionism.

In 1925, *HaKovesh* was established. Hundreds of members, including me, organized the *Aliyah* kibbutz with *HeKhaluts,* whose role it was to arrange for emigration to Israel and to oversee labor in the colonies.

In September of 1925 I reached the land with the first platoon of *HaKovesh*, now the *Ramat Hakovesh* kibbutz, which had only twenty members, and began work in Petah Tikvah. By the end of the year in which I reached Israel, *HaKovesh* established a foothold also in Kfar Saba, which began rebuilding from the ruins of the war as well as the 1921 Jaffa riots. *HaKovesh*, and I among them, dealt with public matters regarding labor in Kfar Saba, establishing a blueprint for organized Hebrew labor in Kfar Saba and the area.

At the beginning of 1927 I enlisted in the police, pursuant to an order from the highest institutions, headed by Mr. Ben Zvi. I knew neither tiring nor fear. I was always optimistic. If I fell down I did not despair: I got up again and prevailed. I did not disdain any role assigned to me-- if it was for the good of the Jewish people and their state.

The collection of memoirs which I wrote encompasses 22 years of working as a commander in the British Mandate police, at a time when the regime was clearly pro-Arab and hostile towards us. I handled a whirlwind of events in the land, until our State was established with blood and flames.

*

I was a member of *HaGana,* commanding units, participating in its actions, and being always willing to risk my life for *HaGana* and for the entire nation. I gave the full extent of my support to organizations which worked to penetrate every industry in the economy. I also assisted *Keren Kayemet* in redeeming the land. When I search my conscience I can assess with confidence that I gave exemplary service to my nation and my land. In the places where I served as an officer no one was ever court-martialed, even if caught with an illegal weapon. I was alert night and day ensuring that no illegal weapons be seized.

Young people boating on the Gavye River (1930) [Ed. Note: Gauja River]

On thirteen occasions I assisted *HaGana* in the unloading of illegal *olim* from illegal ships at Shfayim beach, helping them reach internal territory. When an illegal ship approached I pulled the British policemen far from shore with various excuses, so the beach would be free for action. (Those matters were published in *The Hebrew Policeman in the Time of the Mandate,* where details appear of my bold actions during the war against gangs of Arab belligerents).

On this occasion I would like to also mention several valuable actions I took during that fateful period. Before the "Black Sabbath" in 1946, I was commander of the police station on Yehuda HaLevi Street in Tel Aviv. I became aware that the Brits were about to arrest the leaders of the *Yishuv* and to search for illegal weapons. I immediately notified those in charge and efforts were made to thwart the plan. Another time, a group of Jews who had been brought illegally by men of The Jewish Brigade feared they would be deported, since they had no documents. I immediately approached the district commander Mr. Gobernik, who had once assisted me in a similar instance. A group of Jewish soldiers who reached Israel with the Polish military from Russia, among them a resident of my town, Zvi, left the Polish army and wanted to settle in Israel. I then approached Mr. Gobernik, and after I signed that I have known them for over five ears, I received identification documents for them.

*

When the War of Independence began and the suburbs of Tel Aviv were attacked, I went out with the policemen and *HaGana* for a counter-attack. We managed to counter the Arab attacks from mostly Jordanian legionnaires and Syrian soldiers. After that we established 23 defense posts in the suburbs of Tel Aviv in the Mnashye area. It was a war of the few against the many until we occupied Jaffa, and I had the good fortune of entering Jaffa among those who liberated the city from a foreign invader and blood thirsty gangs.

*

To my delight I achieved my wish when in 1937 I brought my parents and brother Yosef from Divenishok to Israel and prepared a home for them in the Ma'as Village near Petah Tikva. But, unfortunately, I was unable to bring my three married sisters with their husbands and children from Divenishok, and they were executed by Hitler's men, damn them. I should note that I had prepared a passport, had arranged for time off, and had intended to travel to Divenishok to bring them to Israel illegally. As bad luck would have it, the war erupted, the British cancelled my vacation, and did not permit me to leave the country.

*

In the State of Israel, I was a high-ranking police official. I am happy because I was able to see the fruition of the vision of the State of Israel. I always adhered to the principle of "the job comes first," while maintaining good and fair relationships with the public at large without exception. It seems to me that public security roles were the spice of my life, every day and every hour. I think I never felt any weakness nor was I fatigued by the burden of care that rests on a policeman dealing with national security. I should note that we succeeded not only in bringing security to the Israeli public, but also in maintaining the moral integrity of the police force.

On July 1, 1969 I retired and parted with my commanding officers who remained by the wheel, and I am certain they will ensure the national stability and the fairness of public relations.

[Page 105]

Memories from Two World Wars

Aryeh Olkenitski

Translation by Meir Bulman

In my youth, my grandfather Leyb was the owner of a glassmaking workshop in Soletchnik. After Jews were forbidden to live in the villages, he relocated to Divenishok and purchased a large home on the corner of Geranion and Subotnik, which was used as a motel for passers-by. It was there that grandfather and grandmother passed away.

My mother Zippa, of the Sharashevski family from Kovne, died in the prime of her life in 1912, and we small children were left behind. In order to stop my eldest brother from being enlisted in the Tsarist military, my father sold a horse and a cow, and sent him to England.

Next in line was my sister Khayeh whom married Yitzhak Levine. After her, Shifra, married Avraham Kotler. After her, my brother Yosef who married Radke Moshe Aharon's, and I, the youngest in the home, married Zemakh Masukutnik's daughter.

I learned the alphabet by Kalman Shepsel, Zvi Krizovski's father. Later I studied with Shaul "the Varnish," and later I transferred to more modern teachers who acquired a reputation in town: Yitzach, Sarah Disya's; Shmuel "Kesele's" (Shmuel Kramer), Slava "Kesele's" brother. Shmuel Kramer's father arrived in Divenishok after the big fire and built a two-story brick home. It was the only two-story home in Divenishok. He later returned to America.

During WWI, Yitzach and Shmuel established a school in that home, where they taught Hebrew and History.

Some members of Vilbig [Tr. Note: Vilna Jewish Educational Association; Ed. Note: Yankel and Jaimorke Benyakonski, far right]

In WWI we suffered much at the hands of the Germans. There were times when there was literally not even a piece of bread in the house. To gain something for the orphans, my father traveled to Lida, purchased matches, and then brought them to Divenishok. The Germans captured him on the road, and led him to Zakrevtsizne, near Geranion. Berl, who was a warm-hearted Jew, took pity on my father and bought the matches from the Germans, and payed them heftily, so that they would release my father. By the way, a monument should be built in memory of Berl, who was murdered by the Count of Zakrevtsizne, from whom Berl leased the flour-mill. Berl had many promissory notes from the Count and his three brothers. He was buried as a martyr in the Divenishok cemetery. He was succeeded by two daughters who traveled to America.

Many changes occurred with the entrance of the Russians to town during WWII. Trade, which was the town's main source of income, was completely frozen, and the state of affairs for Jews worsened considerably. Merchants still attempted to trade with gentiles, but did so in secret because it was an offense that carried with it a lengthy prison sentence. My brother Yosef was caught on his way from Lida with some merchandise, and was jailed for a month. We barely managed to release him. Had the matter reached court he would have certainly been tried as a profiteer and sentenced to five years in prison.

When the Germans entered I encountered many troubles. I escaped home, hid in the woods, and worked in various labor camps until liberation.

From my entire family remain only myself and my brother Shaul, who now resides in England. All of them perished in the Voronova ghetto, aside from my brother Yosef, who perished in the Lida ghetto.

[Page 107]

The Youth Was Imbued With A Zionist Consciousness

Esther Gordon

Translation by Meir Bulman

I visited Divenishok in 1937, after I married my husband Syoma Gordon, when he came from *Eretz* Israel to visit his family. I was very impressed by the alert and excited youth, who were imbued with a deep Zionist consciousness. I was surprised by the friendship and harmony that existed within the youth, and was especially impressed by the social and Zionist activities.

The Divenishok "nest" of HaShomer HaTsair [Tr. Note: Young Guard] at a summer camp in the village of Juraciski in 1937

Syoma's appearance in his white suit was an attraction in the town and everyone accepted us with admiration and excitement. All the youth crowded around us to breathe and enjoy the atmosphere of the Land of Israel.

The Zionist youth organized parties in our honor. I remember one party in Sara-Disya's home. Sara-Disya's two granddaughters, Shime-Etke and Yehudit, threw us a party, and Syoma sang new Hebrew songs from *Eretz* Israel. The atmosphere in town was electrifying and everyone envied us for being able to travel to *Eretz* Israel. That was unsurprising since the state of Jewry was terrible then, anti-Semitism increased with each passing day, and the youth was depressed, hopeless for the future. The gates of the Land were shut, but the youth desired, if not to make *Aliyah*, than at least to hear a word about the Land and enjoy its spirit.

[Page 108]

The Theater in the Town

Binyamin Dubinski

Translation by Martin Jacobs

The Drama Circle in a performance of "Der Batlen" (1931)

[Tr. Note: "The Idler"; Ed. Note: Bilke Kherson top row, 4th from left]

Our town was a small one, but the Jewish youth there eagerly took an interest in culture and in various ways tried to satisfy their hunger for art and culture. There was no cinema in the town and no other place of entertainment, and so they had to find entertainment in original ways through the town's theatrical life. For this purpose they organized a group of theater lovers, which included all the talented youth, no matter what their viewpoint or political party. It was a necessity of life that the few dramatic resources not be fragmented and that attention be given, from an economic point of view, for what performances were desirable.

Neither the "Zionists" nor the "leftists" were capable, by themselves, of staging any performances whatsoever, and the main principle was to insure that performances would be successful economically. The profits were divided among the parties in accordance with the power of the performance.

Despite the fact that none of the youths in the town was qualified in stagecraft or make-up, resourceful and talented young people could always be found to stage plays, to apply make-up, and to create suitable scenery. Performances were very successful because these youths put all their enthusiasm into them. So it is no surprise that the townspeople were very excited about the actors and each event became the talk of the day in every home.

The general Drama Circle group under the direction of Hershel Krizovski (1930) [Ed. Note: Yankel Benyakonski with mandolin; Bilke Kherson top row, 5th from right]

Among those who stood out in the area of staging we must mention with distinction Avraham Kartshmer, Moshe Stul, Avraham Aloni, Shmuel Dubkin, and Sholem Sonnenson. But excelling all others in this field was Tsvi Krizovski, who was the major force behind most of the performances: as director, stage-manager, and producer.

Ten productions, all in Yiddish, were successfully staged during these years, including "Der Batlen",[Tr. Note: The Idler] "Di Makhsheyfe",[Tr. Note: The Witch]

"Khoshe di Yesoyme",[Tr. Note: Khoshe The Orphan Girl] "Der Vilder Mentsh",[Tr. Note: The Wild Man], "Di Puste Kretshme",[Tr. Note: The Empty Inn] "Got Mentsh un Tayvl",[Tr. Note: God, Man, and Devil] "Foter un Zun",[Tr. Note: Father and Son] "Der Foter",[Tr. Note: The Father] "Ye Khasene Hobn, nit Khasene Hobn",[Tr. Note: To Marry or Not to Marry] and more.

One of the classic performances which was staged in Divenishok was "The Selling of Joseph," with Peyshe the cobbler in the role of Jacob, Yosele the builder's son as Joseph, and Yankel the blacksmith as Reuben. Outstanding in other performances were Fayvke (Shraga Blyakher), Bilke Itskovitsh, Ester-Rokhke Shkolnik, Kheynke Blyakher, Nekhemke Katsev, Shtirke Leybe the boilermaker's son, Shloymke Levine ("The Prodigy"), Gotlib Shkolnik, and others. Fayvke, who played the lead in the performances and was the principal actor, was renowned in the town for his impressive acting. And so when a Jewish troupe called "Yidishe Trupe" arrived in town and one of its actors, who played the role of the father in "Di Rumenishe Khasene",[Tr. Note: The Romanian Wedding] suddenly became ill, Fayvke was recommended to them as a substitute. This was just one day before the performance and Fayvke had doubts about accepting the role without any preparation. The director calmed him down, encouraged him, and as for the text – he was told to follow the prompter. Fayvke scored a great success and was rewarded by the director.

There was no hall suitable for theatrical performances in the town, so they used to rent the barn next to Felix in Subotnik Street. Afterwards they performed in Shmuel Olkenitski's tavern, at the corner of Subotnik and Geranion Streets. After the firehouse was built they put on their performances there permanently.

The many long rehearsals forced rivals from different parties to meet with each other and forge bonds of friendship and camaraderie. This was an especially positive influence on social relations in the town. The animosity and the sharp debates between Zionists and Yiddishists ceased almost completely, and certainly did not lead to sharp exchanges as in other towns. Travelers visiting our town expressed surprise at the friendly and amicable relations found among our youth. We see this in the story of the traveler from Erets-Yisrael. He saw young men walking together in friendship, one wearing the tie of HaShomer HaTsair,[Ed. Note: one of several Zionist youth organizations], a second with the cap of Betar,[Ed. Note: one of several Zionist youth organizations], a third in the red shirt of Vilbig.[Ed. Note: 'Vilner Yidisher Bildungs Gezelshaft', a Yiddishist youth organization]. He couldn't believe his eyes, and didn't move from the spot until he had taken photographs of the sight.

Reports of the performances also reached the Poles. Most days they too flocked to the performances. Some of them understood Yiddish, the rest came out of sheer curiosity. This of course encouraged the producers in their activity, filled them with pride, and spurred them on to continue their wonderful work.

The purpose of this article is to commemorate the talented and courageous young people who devoted countless hours of their time to theater in the town and worked hard and with a sincere will to raise the level of Jewish culture in our town. This they did voluntarily, without receiving any compensation, just from love of culture and of art for its own sake and from the joy of creation.

[Page 111]

Revolutionary Activity Against the Czar

D. Binyamin

Translation by Meir Bulman

Clean up of the market place after market day (1929)

Our town was naturally tranquil, conservative, and adhered to Jewish values. There were no large factories or workshops in it and so a special class of laborers formed and organized.

Nonetheless, there is testimony that the revolutionary tide which flooded Russia since the events in 1905 did not skip our town. Indeed, no protests or violent outbreaks against the Czarist regime took place in our town, but the youth was organized in the revolutionary *Bund* organization, which conducted cultural and organizational activities among the youth. Those activities were quiet, civilized, and polite. There are many testimonials of the organization's activity.

Rachel Zuvitshki testified that seventy years ago, in 1905, she was a member of the *Bund* and the leader of *Bund* was Bezalel the Hasid's son.

Another witness, Zalmen Bernshteyn, said that his beautiful sister, Tsira-Leah (Lyke), was active in the *Bund* in those days. At one of the meetings held in the woods, while Lyke was lecturing, Russian *Okhrana* men appeared and began hitting indiscriminately. Lyke panicked and became ill with epilepsy, spent a few months on her deathbed, and then passed.

From the above testimonies, and others, we can learn that there indeed was a revolutionary uprising against the Czar in our town at the start of the Twentieth Century.

Oszmiana Street Bridge over the Gavya River, constructed in 1928 [Ed. Note: Gauja River]

One of the *Bund* leaders in town, near the time of WWII, was the teacher Moshe Stutski, from the nearby town of Ivia. In the Yizkor Book about his town of Ivia the following words can be found: "Moshe Stutski, who was then a teacher in Divenishok, got up on a table at Wednesday market day and gave a passionate speech against Russian Czar Nikolai. He instructed the peasants to go chop wood in the rich men's forests. The peasants asked him for a license, and he, as if the owner of the woods said, 'No need for license, I'm responsible.' "

Stutski the teacher was a passionate revolutionary, conducted intensive propaganda against the Czarist regimes among the town's youth, and preached for the toppling of the regime.

My mother told me with nostalgia of those days, when Stutski the teacher gathered the youth in the woods on Saturdays, would lecture, and then they all sang revolutionary songs, among them the French 'La Marseillaise'.

Menukha, Zvi Krizovski's daughter, said that her father's sister Shayne was also a revolutionary and conducted propaganda against Czar Nikolai and his regime. In 1905 she was imprisoned and charged with revolutionary activity. At that time it was custom to beat prisoners and she also was quite so unfortunate. She was a member in the R.S.D. revolutionary movement, where she met her husband Avraham Moisevitsh, and in 1917 when the Russians retreated from Vilne, she joined them with her husband, and her whereabouts since are unknown.

Though there were few impressive or influential revolutionary movements in the area, there was organizational activity by the youth, which desired freedom and release from the oppressive Czarist regime. The eyes of the youth were raised to the big towns where a persistent bloody struggle took place against the Czarist regime, which especially excelled in its hatred of Jews.

[Page 115]

With Love and Nostalgia

Khayeh Garvey (Khayeh Broine's)

Translation by Meir Bulman

My family resided in a small wooden home on Subotnik Street. My father, Broine Levine, my mother Feigeh, my grandfather Eliahu Levine, my brother Yosef Yehuda, and my beautiful sister Liba made staying in that house pleasant. I remember the long winter nights when we sat by the warm fireplace and asked grandfather to tell us his life stories, to which he responded positively by sailing away into tales of the past. My great-grandfather, Meir Levine, was a humble school teacher, whose livelihood was difficult, like the splitting of the sea was difficult for the Israelites, because he was "rich" in offspring: eight sons and three daughters.

The branches of our family tree spread throughout town, and of the descendants of my great-grandfather I should mention Peysakh Levine (Peyse the shoemaker); Shmuel Yakov Levine and his son Alter; Eliahu Chaim Shkolnik; Shoshe-Yente, Eliahu and Michel Mazeh's mother, Moshe Leyser Kartshmer, Motl Kartshmer's father, and others.

In his youth, my grandfather attended the *Rammyles Yeshiva* in Vilne. When the Enlightenment period began and my great-grandfather became aware of the "tragedy" of his son Eliahu learning Russian, he traveled hastily to Vilne, returned his "lost" son home and married him to my grandmother. Because two sons of my great-grandfather married two sisters, and there was another girl left in the home, there was no issue: my grandfather was married to her. My grandfather, the youngest of the family, was 18 when he married.

At the wedding my great-grandfather Meir did not feel well. He called over his children and in-laws and commanded them to keep dancing, and instructed the musicians to continue playing, because it is not permitted to disrupt Jewish festivities. He went home, where he then died, and in the morning he was eulogized.

My grandfather also told us that his brother Velvel (Ze'ev) was kidnapped for the Russian military when he was 12. As is common knowledge, that was the time of the Cantonists, and a kidnapped child had to serve in the Czarist military for 25 years. After a ransom was payed to the kidnapers, he was released, and in order to avoid the recurrence of that event he had to be married immediately. On the Sabbath when he celebrated his Bar Mitzvah, his wedding also took place.

My grandfather said jokingly that when his brother, the young married man, would walk with his *tallit* and *tefillin* to the synagogue and saw children his age playing *falankas* and *fikers*[1], he quickly abandoned the prayer, *tallit* and *tefillin*, and joined the games. His young wife had to search for him and return him from the world of childhood to the company of family men.

Life in town until the outbreak of WWI progressed with tranquility. As the war erupted, my father was enlisted in the Russian army, and we relocated to live with my mother's family in Vishneva. Unfortunately, fierce battles between the Russians and Germans took place in the Vishneva area. Because it was on the front, we suffered starvation, and had to escape town into the woods more than once.

After the Germans retreated my father was released from German captivity and returned us to Divenishok. In the town we got a new lease on life after the Polish regime stabilized. Life went back to its normal course and the population began breathing a sigh of relief. My father, as a merchant, earned a nice living for his family, and we, the children, grew up, developed, and attended school.

In our town a wonderful younger generation was raised, who were cultural, and aspired for a better world, and love of our fellow man and humanity, but we were especially imbued with a Zionist–pioneering spirit and longing for the homeland.

I joined the *Herut U'Tnua*[2] organization, which was organized by Pethovski[A] the teacher, and recived an immigration certificate through *HeKhaluts*; in 1925 I made Aliyah along wth David Leybke Berkovitsh, Michael Mazeh, a young woman from Traby, Dov Zandman, and Shifra Blyakher.

When I arrived in Israel I went to work in Acre. We were a group of girls who worked at the *Noor* match factory, and at *Gan Ha'Memshala*[3]. I then relocated to Tel Aviv where I worked paving roads and mining gravel on Ben Yehuda Street. From Tel Aviv I moved to Jerusalem, and there I married Yehuda Garvey, a pioneer from Russia, who arrived in Israel after the Bolshevik revolution, and worked with me in guiding Hebrew labor. In Jerusalem I trained as a pharmacist and worked at the Sha'are Zedek hospital, where I also had my eldest son Uri. We returned from Jerusalem to Tel Aviv, and our daughter Sophia was born there. My son currently works as an aeronautics engineer in the United States, and my daughter Sophia also lives there, married to an engineer and raising her two children.

Gate of the old cemetery on Geranion Street

I missed my children very much, and in 1962 I joined them in the United States, where I befriended Rohkl Leah Movshovitsh, the rabbi's wife, a righteous, wise, and kind woman. I liked spending my spare time with her, because she brought back memories of life in our town. I discovered at her home a notebook detailing life in town, where it was written that my father contributed 100 Zlotys for community needs.

From time to time she would raise figures from town and describe them with much creativity, love, and admiration. "Consider Moshe Leizer, Mordechai Kartshmer's father, for example. Do you know who he was?" That is how she would begin her descriptive stories. "He was a righteous man, showed great respect for his father. For the eight years his father was paralyzed, he took him to the bathhouse every Friday to wash him, and even Moshe's wife cared for her father-in-law with love and devotion." She also described and praised Barukh Leyb "the Beard" (Berkovitsh), an ordinary man, but secretly righteous. He founded the bathhouse with his own money, and gathered firewood all year for the bathhouse and the rabbi's home.

And: Shoshe Yente (Eliahu and Michael Mazeh's mother), a widow who raised her two sons in the ways of the Torah and good deeds. She was a seamstress and made a living with difficulty, but was a kind woman. A poor girl who married in town would receive a wedding dress which Shoshe Yente purchased and would pay for on installment. It was anonymous charity which no one knew about.

I liked visiting Rokhl Leah often and listening to her wise stories, her humor, and the love of life in her descriptions. After every visit my longing for my town, which exists no longer, would reemerge, and I would cling to the past with love and nostalgia: I remembered the image of my father, who once returned home barefoot, because he gave away his boots to a poor Jewish man whose legs were swollen from the cold; the image of my dear mother, whom every Friday would send me to the poor neighbors to check on the situation and send me to give them *challah* and milk for the Sabbath; the images of my brother Yudel and my sister Liba, sitting around the festive sabbath table and giggling about the guest eating the soup and even the compote with *challah*. The heart aches for the beautiful and good thing which was lost and is no more.

Translator's Footnotes

1. Literally, politicians and fishermen; a children's game of some type

2. Literally, 'Freedom and Movement'

3. The 'Government Garden'

Editor's Footnote

A. Also spelled Pethukovski elsewhere in this book

[Page 118]

The Mitzvah of *Linat Zedek*

Miriam Herman

Translation by Meir Bulman

The *Linat HaZedek*[1] institution was established in our town with the purpose of assisting families in need with caring for a patient who was bedridden for a prolonged period-- by providing care at night.

Before I made *aliyah* I wanted to fulfill the mitzvah of *Linat HaZedek*, so that God would bless my journey. I was sent along with Leyzer the Miller to Berl the Cobbler, whose wife Feigeh Reyzl was bedridden for a long time, and he, the tired elderly man, cared for her to the best of his abilities.

My eyes turned dark at the sight of Feigeh Reyzl who lay paralyzed in bed, sighing bitterly. Berl stood helpless, crying about his misfortune and bitter fate. The sanitary conditions were intolerable.

I was deeply saddened by what was occurring and decided to do my best to help them. Leyzer and I worked non-stop through the night; we changed the bedding, I bathed Feigeh Reyzl and changed her robe. After that we thoroughly cleaned the house. I went out to the yard and cleaned around the house and the yard. After that, I went to the well at the marketplace and filled a water barrel for them. I didn't complete my work until 6 in the morning. Berl was beside himself with joy; he just stood there and cried. His wife, who did not know me, mumbled the whole time, "Who are you? You are so kind! Who are you?"

When I arrived by Natan Itskovitsh's house for work at 7, all were surprised by my quickness, and praised me for the good deed I had done.

*

My sister Zilpeh's *aliyah* intensified the desire in our home to make *aliyah*, but it was impossible, because the gates to the Land were shut.

One day, in the well-known daily Yiddish newspaper *Moment*, published in Warsaw, we read about the organizing of a group of tourists for a tour in Israel. I feared missing such a rare opportunity, and my mother sold a lot she owned and with the money funded my registration for the trip. I was 22.

The trip, dubbed *Excursion Moment*, aroused great interest throughout Poland. Jewish youth, always searching for ways to make *aliyah*, found in the trip a onetime opportunity to fulfill their desires. It was thought by everyone that those entered the Land were sure not to be expelled by the British.

My brother Shraga accompanied me to Warsaw where we parted ways. I traveled by train to the port of Trieste where I boarded a ship that sailed to Israel. 600 tourists from all over Poland boarded the ship, most of whom intended to stay in Israel.

My sister Zilpeh waited for me in Haifa and took me to her home in Tel Aviv. At that time, my future husband, Dov, arrived at my sister's, and a friendship formed between us the result of which was our marriage, after two months.

After the wedding our home was open to any former Divenishok resident who arrived in Israel, who we would supply food and shelter until on their feet.

Translator's Footnote

1. Literally, Slumber of Justice

[Page 119]

From Divenishok to Eretz-Israel

Khenye Harari

Translation by Meir Bulman

My Family

My father, Yitzach Binyamin, or as he was known in town, Itshe Binyamin, was a blacksmith and worked hard to provide a living for his large family. My mother, Rivkeh, was his second wife, with whom he had four girls. The eldest, Beileh, perished with her husband and children at the Voronova Ghetto. Pesye also perished in Voronova, and her husband Gedalye was murdered by Polish rioters. The third daughter, Malkeh, married in Lida, and perished there with her husband and children. And I, Khenye, am the fourth.

My Father's Brave Deed

My kind-hearted father loved doing acts of kindness unto his fellow man, with money or action. I remember a very unique instance when my father saved the town from a literal pogrom. In 1918, with the retreat of the Bolsheviks and the Poles' entrance into town, a peasant from the Duvitsishuk[1] sat at Naftali Delatishki's tavern and drank to intoxication. Suddenly he fell and died as a result of a heart attack.

A fear arose of a pogrom. The infamous Poles of general Heller's army were in town cutting beards and mercilessly assaulting, and would of course pounce on the incident to exploit a riot. The Jews hastily approached my father to devise a plan.

My father did not hesitate long. He got a horse from Leyzer Kartshmer the coachman, loaded the deceased on horseback, sat behind the body and held on to it. He galloped quickly to the Christian cemetery, threw the body in the ditch, and returned to town by 1 am. It was a hard winter: snow covered the footsteps. The Jewish residents breathed a sigh of relief.

Graduates of HaShomer HaTsair [Tr. Note: Young Guard]
at pioneer training in the commune BaDerekh [Tr. Note: "On the Way"]
in Grodno before emigrating to Israel (1933)

Aliyah

In my youth I was a member of the *HeKhaluts* organization, and as a devoted Zionist, participated in all its activities. After the passing of my father in 1932, I traveled to a *kibbutz* in Bialystok, and after staying there for a year got a certificate and made *aliyah*. We traveled as a group of hundreds of Polish pioneers and were very happy. Every time we danced the *Hora* on deck, the passengers from first class came down to watch us and draw inspiration.

We arrived in *Eretz* Israel shortly before Passover. The World Zionist Organization held a Passover Seder at the Mograbi Theater, and after that I transferred to *Bet HeKhalutzot*, where I stayed for two weeks before going to work.

After a while, I married my Husband Eliezer, and we had three children: Rina, Khanita, and the son, Binyamin, and I had the good fortune of having and enjoying my grandchildren.

Editor's Footnote

1. The location of this place has yet to be determined; in the original text the name is spelled: daled-vov-veyz (or beyz)-yud-tsadek-yud-shin-vov-kuf

[Page 121]

How I Reached Israel

by Dvora Rakhl

Translation by Meir Bulman

All my life, I aspired to reach Israel. My brother Yehuda, who was already in Israel, sent me a Yemeni man to fictitiously marry and then bring me to Israel as his "wife." The British council was not stupid and did not grant me an entrance permit.

With the arrival of the Russians in September of 1939, I submitted a request to the authorities to make *aliyah*. I was naïve and did not understand that that action carried with it a risk of imprisonment. The Soviets rejected my request and began surveilling me. I felt like the ground was burning under my feet and looked for a way to sneak across the border to Vilne, which was under Lithuanian control. From there the roads to the free world were still open.

Meir Dubinski encouraged me to cross the border towards Stashiles, where his uncle Yonah Tener resided, and he would ensure that I reach Vilne.

On a dark night, I crossed the border to Lithuania with a smuggler and reached Yonah Tener's house exhausted. Yonah Tener and his wife Alta treated me very well and provided me guidance on how to board the train and get to Vilne.

I boarded the train and an undercover policeman sat next to me trying to get me to talk. I was scared to death that the Lithuanians would discover me and hand me to the Russians, whereupon I would arrive in Siberia instead of Israel. I wrapped myself in a scarf as if I had a toothache and did not respond to him. From time to time I gestured towards my teeth, meaning "they hurt very much and I cannot speak, I'm rushing to the dentist." That is how I arrived in Vilne, shaking.

In Vilne, a certificate from my brother awaited me. I then approached the Jewish Council and requested funding for my journey to Israel. A man from the Israel Affairs Office named Less helped me. He also brought me to the train and sat me in the correct train car, the one designated for travelers to

Israel. I left Lithuania at the last minute, immediately before it was declared a Soviet Republic.

And so after wandering and fear, I arrived in Israel satiated by troubles. Here I married and was fortunate to get some rest and happiness, and was blessed with two children; the eldest, Shoshana, and a son, Avraham.

*

My father was known in Divenishok by his name, "David the Cobbler." His parents were not from Divenishok, they relocated to that town from a different town. My paternal grandfather was known as Leyb Katz. My maternal grandfather was Yakov Kagan.

During the days of Bolshevik control, in 1918, my father was chair of the *Revcom* (Revolutionary Committee.) I was nevertheless a devoted member of *HaShomer HaTzair*. Despite his nickname David the Shoemaker, my father worked processing wooden roofing tiles. The forest guard from Zhizimi Village, with whom he had connections, helped him gather materials for that purpose.

My father was an ordinary man, but with great talents. He excelled in spinning stories and anecdotes about everything that happened – or did not happen - or had ever been recounted in our town or the world over. When David the Cobbler would begin one of his famous stories, Jews gathered around, mouths agape, listening carefully so they did to miss a single word that left his mouth.

One of my father's interesting stories remains in my memory:

There was a couple who were without a child. Gypsies came and promised them children by witchcraft. One gypsy, who presented himself as group leader, told the woman, "Put your head through the chimney and you will start having children." What won't parents do to have children? The innocent woman stuck her head in the chimney and waited! And waited! And did not get permission from the gypsy to take out her head. After she waited in vain for a while, she took out her head. It is unknown if the woman was ever blessed with offspring! But one thing was clear: the gypsies disappeared from her house – and with them all the gold and silver utensils from the home.

Washing clothes in the river at Oszmiana Street

[Page 123]

My Contribution to the Building of the Country

Elimelech Rudnik

Translation by Meir Bulman

I was born in 1895 in Divenishok. I remember my grandfather, Shmuel Aaron, as if in a dream. He lived in Kosholova, near Navaredok, and was a property owner and merchant.

My father married a Divenishok woman by the name of Sarah Malkeh Bernshteyn and moved to Divenishok. He bought lands on Oshmene Street, established a home, and built a smithy where he worked for the rest of his life.

Five children were born from the marriage of my parents: Yehoshua, the oldest who married in Olshan and perished there with his family, Sheineh Yokhl Bernshteyn who married, and perished with her family, the third daughter, Khasyeh, lives in New York, the fourth daughter, Freidel - Yakov Bloch's mother who perished in Voronova, and I, Elimelech Rudnik, live in Giv'atayim.

A year after the outbreak of the WWI, following a bloody battle, the frontline was situated between Russia and Germany on the Berezina River, near Vishneva. To strengthen the front, the Germans enlisted thousands of Jews into forced labor along the frontline. For the first time these Jews heard the term "Fonye Battalion" as in "Fonye, come work at the battalion."[1]

Committee for Keren Kayemes [Ed. Note: Jewish National Fund] and the Tarbus School, 1930

Those enlisted were held in poor conditions. The work was exhausting, accompanied by curses and assaults, a hostile attitude, and food rations which consisted of roasted barley and 200 grams of bread for breakfast and dinner, and a watered-down bean soup for lunch. Lodging was in temporary, terribly crowded huts.

I worked for two years in the Fonye Battalion, and would have died of starvation and the backbreaking labor, as thousands of others did, if not for my father who brought me food packages. With me worked Yekusiel Lubetski, and Dovke- Meir Zalman's. The camp was fenced and every morning an attendance formation was conducted. In my camp there were 250 people and escape was difficult. I still managed to escape five times and each time I was returned. Matters continued like that until the Polish entered our town in 1918.

A battle between the Poles and the Bolsheviks took place on our street, where the Bolsheviks were on the right bank of the Gavia river which passed near our house, and the Poles attacked from the direction of the town. My father was at home at the time and busied himself by cutting tobacco for cigarettes. A bullet shot from the Russian side penetrated the wall and exited through the window, right by my father's nose. The Poles, who stormed our home, saw me wearing a Russian shirt and wanted to shoot me, thinking I was a Bolshevik, but a Polish neighbor prevented them from doing so.

After the war, I married my wife Khaye and moved to live in her parents' home in Oshmene. I worked hard at her father's smithy and earned my living with dignity. With Hitler's rise to power in 1933, things changed for the worse: in Poland anti-Semitism rose significantly and Poles began rioting against Jews. On market day in the nearby town of Ostrovits, a riot took place and Poles flipped all the stands owned by Jews, and began hitting them indiscriminately. I barley managed to escape. After I witnessed that, I made up my mind that I must make *aliyah* no matter what. I approached my Zionist friends and they obtained a certificate for me, and in 1934 I made *aliyah*. Times were tough: riots, unemployment, competition with cheap Arab labor, but we overcame despite all that.

During all my years in Israel I labored productively and installed machines in water wells at kibbutzim and villages. I did my work with love and devotion, feeling that I was contributing to building the Land.

In Israel I had three children, and was also blessed with grandchildren.

Editor's Footnote

1. The word 'fonye' is believed to be a derogatory term in Yiddish for 'Russians', derived from the nickname Vanye, for Ivan (see, Ribak, Gil. Gentile New York: The Images of Non-Jews among Jewish Immigrants, p. 24, Rutgers University Press, 2012); the use of 'fonye' in this context may have been a recruitment tactic employed by the Germans.

[Page 125]

The Monument in Divenishok Honoring the Unknown Soldier

Boris Rabinovitsh (Painter and Sculptor from Smorgon)

Translation by Meir Bulman

In 1928, the district-city of Oshmene held a conference for all district mayors. On that occasion, Divenishok mayor Shaul Mashkevitsh asked the mayor of Smorgon if he knew a sculptor who would be willing to sculpt a statue to be stationed at City Hall, in memory of the unknown soldiers who fell in the years 1918-1920 while liberating Poland from the burden of the foreigners. The mayor of Smorgon recommended me and so I was invited to Divenishok.

Monument to the Unknown Soldier, erected in 1929 next to the Polish State Elementary School in Geranion Street – the round stones are from a nearby archaeological dig

After signing a contract wherein City Hall committed to paying me 700 Zlotys for completing the task, I stayed in Divenishok until I finished sculpting the monument.

There was much historical value to the stones that decorated the edges of the monument. They were round stones, in bright-red colors, etched with great skill, and left a great impression on the viewer. They were found by a peasant as he plowed his field, located a kilometer from town. Their purpose and origin were shrouded in mystery, but they were [likely] used as ballistic objects canons by the Swedish, who arrived in Divenishok in the second half of the 17th century. Those claims were based on the fact that the stones were composed from a granite made up of hard quartz, feldspar, and mica, such as is abundant in the Swedish mountains.

The stones were of two different sizes: some were 20 centimeters in diameter, some 30. The corners of the monument were decorated with the smaller stones, and the eagle, symbol of Poland which adorned the top, stood on a stone 30 centimeters in diameter. A special compartment was built at the base of the monument in which the founding document was placed, signed by Polish officials and Jewish town luminaries, among them Rabbi Rudnik and Rabbi Tayts.

The square surrounding the monument was used as a gathering place for every national and public event. It was also the spot where the finish line for festive parades was placed. To this day I keep in my heart the good days when Poles and the Jews coexisted in harmony, harmony which was expressed by the unveiling of the monument.

I clearly remember the few months I spent in pleasant and kind Divenishok, which left an unforgettable mark on me.

[Page 127]

B. The Holocaust and Fighting

[Page 129]

We Will Not Forget You!

Yakov Bloch

Translation by Meir Bulman

Divenishok, our native town, the hundreds-of-years-long intermediate station for Jews on their long journey from Eretz Israel to the State of Israel – we will not forget you. We, whose years of youth were passed in you, we who were blessed to reach a Jewish state - we will not forget you.

We remember your narrow roads paved with rocks, and the dirt alleyways in which our bare feet were injured during our childhood. We remember your houses built of either wood, brick, or mortar, pressed together, hugging one another, as if expressing the love of Israel within them.

We remember you Jews, whose faces were adorned by sidelocks and beards, who carried Judaism as a crown, the crown of "your people Israel" [2 Samuel 7:23]. We remember you, wonderful Jews, who placed no barriers between yourselves and those who had observed a tradition passed from generation to generation.

A group of girl scouts (1932) from HaShomer HaTsair[Tr. Note: Young Guard] who were killed by the German murderers: Standing, from the right: Khayke Levine, Rebecca Solts, Minka Rogol, Yehudis Levine, Mashka Shapiro. Seated: their leader Yakov Bloch; he is now in Tel-Aviv

You, who upon your exile from your land, took with you its Torah and culture, and observed them as if still in the Homeland, each and every one of you was willing to become a soldier to guard and protect them, and always willing to die for them – because of you we made it this far.

Jews of Divenishok, those adhering to their faith, and even those who objected, we will not forget your synagogues, the Old and the New, where you read three times a day, "May our eyes witness your return to Zion in mercy."

We will not forget the glory of the Sabbath days, when you demonstrated your independence among the gentiles, we will not forget your holidays and festivals, when you sanctified and observed the freedom of the Nation in days of bondage.

Jews of Divenishok! We will not forget your sons, encouragers of the messianic era, for the faith which you planted in our hearts was faith in the redemption of man, the world, and Israel. At their clubs, libraries, and gathering spots they worked altruistically for the sake of the town's Jews.

We will not forget your suffering, torment, horrible torture, and your cruel deaths. We will bind your souls in the bond of our souls in the Homeland, and in each of our endeavors you are one with us. You are a party to the redemption, partners in the effort, partners in the building, and partners in plowing, planting and harvesting, partners in night-watches and partners in the wars.

[Page 130]

We will remember our parents, brothers and sisters, our friends, and relatives who perished by cruelty. We will remember that our lives, loves, and hopes came from them. We will remember that we are their ambassadors to the Homeland, and they fell during the journey. We will mix their living souls in our living souls.

[Page 131]

Gloom Fell on the Town

Taiba Griner

Translation by Meir Bulman

I left my parents' home in 1938, after I married a relative in the town of Koblynik, by the famous Narach Lake. It was a quiet and peaceful town, crowded in the summer with vacationers and tourists who came to sail on the lake.

When the Germans entered gloom fell on the town. A curfew was announced and exiting a home after four in the afternoon was forbidden. Anyone who violated the curfew was shot on the spot. The town's Jews were forced into unpaid labor. In the spring of 1942 the Germans began exterminating the town's Jews. Every day a number of families were executed following "witness testimony" by the gentiles that the condemned were "communists." Jews, including women and children, were led to the cemetery, and after they were tormented, were shot inside the greaves they had dug for themselves. Once, the Germans shot our neighbor during work, then came to his house and took his wife, Iyta Reider, and her two children, a six year old girl and a two year old girl, and led them to the cemetery. I tremble as I recall Iyta walking with her baby in her arms and the older girl attached to her body, the Germans following behind and clubbing them. The six-year-old girl probably understood their fate, and as she walked she wept bitterly and pulled out her hair. The defenseless girl's crying only intensified the Germans' cruelty and they continued beating them. The blood of the mother and her daughters trickled from them the whole way to the cemetery, marking the trail of torture of a Jewish mother in the hands of predatory beasts who craved the blood of the innocent.

After a few days of staying with the children by my mother-in-law, I saw through the window the Germans leading my husband towards the cemetery, striking him with their guns. I understood the end has come. I left the children with the mother-in-law and decided to hide until the storm would pass.

At the time, I employed a domestic worker named Khenye Sipka, from a village 16 kilometers from Kobilnik. Her parents visited her every Sunday and we became close friends. "If something happens," they told me, "come to us." In the morning I left for the village, anxious and fearful. I often turned back my head, fearing that I was being chased; with every rustle I hid in the forest. I felt dizzy, my knees were weak, my legs failed me, and I dragged them heavily.

The road was endless. I reached the farmer's home only at nightfall. He greeted me kindly and hid me in the cellar. The Germans threatened the townspeople that if they did not turn me in all the residents would be executed. Three Jewish women came by and searched for me. I wanted to go with them because I did not want the blood of the town's Jews on my hands, but the farmer would not let me. "They'll kill the Jews no matter what," he said, "it's better if you don't leave."

After some time I became aware that the Germans had captured my children, a four year-old boy and a one year old girl, and had viciously murdered them.

The farmer led me to an abandoned hut in the marshlands where I stayed for three weeks. One day the farmer told me he would continue to shelter me only if I gave myself to him. He was an old farmer, ugly and disgusting. I shivered as I heard those words. I decided I would rather die than give myself to such a disgusting gentile.

I ran from the farmer's house to a mansion located approximately 15 km from the village. Jews from Svir were working there so I joined them and worked with them until we were returned to Svir.

The men of the Jewish Police did not allow me to stay there, as they claimed that would harm the Jewish residents. For lack of any other option I joined a labor camp in the village of Loshe[1] where the Germans were paving a new road. Since I am a professional seamstress, I asked the German overseeing the camp if I could work for the local peasants, and in return I would give him butter and eggs as a gift.

He agreed, and every week I would send him eggs and butter– very valuable items at the time. I managed to befriend the peasants and word spread of what a good seamstress I am. That is how I arrived at the Lotovits home. I sewed him a shirt and he admired my work very much. "Such golden hands, the Germans could die. I must save you, no matter what." And indeed, he and his wife Carolina saved my life.

The camp held on until the fall. Some Jews managed to escape, but most were executed. The Lotovits family continued to hide me. They taught me Christian prayers, especially the blessing when the priest enters the church. The first time I got confused and recited the prayer backwards, as the priest looked at me with curious eyes.

My benefactor Lotovits recommended me as an employee to other peasants. I lived for a few weeks with one peasant and sewed for the family, and then relocated to another peasant's home and worked for a while and managed to save up some money. Lotovits arranged a forged Polish identity card for me, with the aid of another Pole, for which I gave 20 pods of grain and 12 litters *smogon*[2]— quite a hefty sum.

Since then my name became "Lonya", as was written on the ID card. I felt safer and even dared to go out and look for work.

Once when I visited the Lotovits residence, I saw from the window two Polish policemen approaching the home. Suddenly they changed course and approached the neighbors' house, but the house was closed. They briefly consulted one another and then turned towards the village. After a while, I learned that the policemen would not have been satisfied by capturing me, but were also searching for a way to execute the Lotovitses, but needed two witnesses to sign the required document.

Carolina knew the risks, gave me a fur coat – it was a cold, stormy day – and encouraged me to quickly escape to the woods. Before long the policemen, accompanied by collaborators, followed my trail and meticulously searched the house, the yard, and the barn, and left the place, cursing.

I hid in the woods all day. The cold gnawed my bone marrow, the hunger and thirst bothered me to death, and I breathlessly waited for nightfall.

At nightfall, I arrived at the nearby Kano Village[3] and knocked at the first house on the edge of the village. An elderly woman opened the door and asked what I wanted. I told her I wanted to reach Vilne but missed the train. After I showed her my Polish passport she relaxed and showed me in. At night, her daughter came with her lover and brought *smogon*, drank to intoxication and poured some for me, but I spilled mine under the table. In his intoxicated state, the man began telling how he worked for the Germans, and his role is to deliver Jews to the Germans. As he spoke, he cursed the Jews. He boasted that he had sent more than one Jew to the next world. "What did I fall into?" I thought, "What should I do? Where to run?"

I could not sleep all night, my mind was racing, and suddenly I recalled Kasatshenkova the teacher, maybe I could find shelter with her? I knew Kasatshenkova for a long time, while in my parents' home. In Divenishok I was a well-known seamstress and all the Polish nobles hired me. Among those customers was Mrs. Kasatshenkova. She taught Polish at the Hebrew school in our town and was acquainted and friendly with all. She and I developed a special bond because she was very satisfied with my work. I learned that Mrs. Kasatshenkova was living in a remote home in Renkatsinski[4] near Vileyka, not far from Vilne.

The next morning I began walking towards Renkatsishok Village, 150 kilometers away. My journey spanned a few days because I traveled on foot and on various side roads until I reached her.

She greeted me warmly, not out of much love for me as a Jew, but out of a desire to exploit me, and what more, a seamstress in those days was a "very valuable commodity." I stayed with her for five months and sewed clothes for the whole family. I worked day and night to meet her demands, all for no pay, in exchange for food only.

Once, we needed a fashion journal for women's dresses. She proposed we travel together to Vilne and pick out the right designs for her. It was a rare opportunity to visit Vilne, the Jerusalem of Lithuania. I passed through the streets and occasionally saw a Jew walking in the middle of the road (Jews were forbidden from walking on the sidewalk) with a yellow patch on the arm. I will never forget the sight; their appearance was oppressed, hunched over, worn and torn, starving, wretched and miserable. Their appearance awoke fear and horror in me.

The teacher would tell me nonstop that the Germans were murdering the Jews, and with what joy and light she would say that, I felt the hatred boiling in her, and I – my heart would weep in secret. Once, I wept bitterly when I learned the fate of the Vilne Jews, and the teacher found me like that with my eyes shedding tears and she said, "Why are you crying, for your life or maybe mine?"

After I completed the sewing for all family members, Kasatshenkova told me, "I can no longer hold you, got to the forest, the forest!"

I decided to return to the Lotovitses, who greeted me nicely, but they proposed I look for work with the peasants and not stay in their house, to not arouse suspicion by the authorities. I constantly worked with the peasants, but occasionally visited my benefactors the Lotovitses. The situation continued like that until the "White Poles" appeared, and my situation took a turn for the worse. The Poles gained the admiration of the population who collaborated with them and would assist them in finding Jews. They would take out Jews from hiding spots and savagely execute them. The Lotovitses hid me for seven weeks in the cowshed attic. Twice a day Carolina brought me food with the food she brought the chickens, so I would not be detected. Interestingly, the White Poles chose the Lotovits home as their headquarters, which instilled in me a feeling of safety, because they would not think a Jewess was there. Through the cracks in my hiding spot I saw them coming and going on their missions. Those Poles were terrible! Once they captured a Jew name Levine who was taken out of a bunker, laid him on the table, tormented him, hit him, and tortured him until his soul passed.

They told the farmers, "Give us the Jews, hand over the Communists, and we will settle the score with them. Now we will be masters of the land! We will divide the lands among you." They would rebuke the peasants and say, "What kind of loyal Poles are you that don't want to give us the Jews." Once, probably influenced by the Poles, Carolina told me, "Maybe you should go to the Narats[5] River, there are many Jews there."

"No!" I told her, "I will not leave you again, I am staying here, it is better if they kill me here in your yard, and you will bury me here and pray at my grave."

My cry probably influenced her and she began crying. As a thankful gesture I requested wool to knit sweaters for her and her husband.

In the final weeks before Liberation she would tell me, "We might stay alive, the Russians are nearly here."

After Liberation I traveled to Vilne and arrived once more at Kasatshenkova's, where I met Bezalel from Vileyka, I married him and we traveled to Poland and from there to Israel.

In 1957 I visited Divenishok with my husband and two daughters. The town was abandoned and burnt, only a row of houses remaining at the marketplace. We also visited the cemetery, where the tombstones were ruined and broken, shards of tombstones spread throughout the territory, surrounded by wilderness and abandonment. I searched for my mother's grave. Where there was once a tombstone surrounded by a concrete belt, now I could find nothing. The fence was in disrepair, the trees uprooted, and the peasants working the fields as of yore, sitting to rest on the tombstones, their cows grazing between the graves. I could find no marks on the graves, everything uprooted, broken and ruined. All the trees in the cemetery were chopped by the peasants and used as building material for their homes.

I shed many tears for the loss of my family and the destruction of our town. My tears were absorbed in the ground of the Jewish cemetery of Divenishok.

Footnotes

1. This place could be the village of Losha but seems quite far from the previous location of Kobilnik; in the original text the name is spelled: lamed–aleph–shin–ayin.

2. Tr. Note: Moonshine

3. Ed. Note: The location of this place has not yet been identified.

4. Ed. Note: The location of this place has not yet been identified.

5. Ed. Note: The location of this river has not yet been identified; in the original text the name is spelled: hey–nun–reish–langer tsadek.

[Page 136]

In the Ghettos and the Woods with Partisans

Tsvi Novoplanski
Translation by Meir Bulman

I was not at home on the day the Germans stormed Divenishok. At the time I was working at *Ziamya Slava*, a large estate located about 10km from Divenishok where we built a large airport with underground hangers for the Soviet defense infrastructure.

The people in our town who were mostly merchants and traded with local peasants were left unemployed after the Russians invaded. They did contractual work to collect stones and bring them to be made into gravel for the fortification, so they could make a living.

Most of the workers were prisoners who had committed minor crimes like *frugul* (arriving late to work) and the like. About 10,000 people worked there. I worked as a technical clerk in the warehouse. There were several large military bases in the area.

It was a Sunday morning and all the *nachal'nik* (commanders) lay stinking drunk in their beds. I was glued to the radio and heard of the German declaration of war on Russia and about the lethal bombings on Russian military pockets. I took a horse and rode quickly to the main officer and told him: "War! The Germans are bombing!" and he, drunk as a skunk, turned on his side and mumbled: "Forget that nonsense", and kept on napping. The next day all workers were declared recruits and the work resumed as usual. I sent a letter home with Yitzach Levine: "We have all been enlisted and I am staying here." The next day we packed everything and began traveling east.

The road was busy with vehicles and people. Conditions became unbearable around Radoshkovichi, which was a border passage between Poland and Russia until 1939. The road was packed and the Germans picked us off from the air. I met many Divenishok townspeople, among them Tsvi Krizovski and Yosef Levine. We continued to Minsk where there was a roadblock; military personnel unloaded civilians from cars and loaded them with soldiers.

Minsk was in flames. German bombers came and dropped bombs periodically on the city. It is hard to describe the turmoil and shock, the sighs and screams of the wounded. The road was flooded with blood, maimed men and women sighed in pain, blood gushing from their wounds, yelling for help but to no avail. It was a truly horrific scene. I jumped from the truck, crouched in a ditch, and covered my head with the two loaves of bread I bought on the road.

After I calmed a bit I raised my head and saw a Jewish woman from Minsk that I worked with at *Ziamya Slava*. "Go back to your small town it will be calmer there," she told me, "As you see, Minsk is burning."

I listened to her and started to make my way back home. The swarm of people moved eastward and I was walking westward. I traveled a distance and encountered a group of young men and women from Oshmene, about 17 people. "You have no reason to return to Divenishok," they said, "The Germans are already there." I decided to join them. The Germans bombed us nonstop. We reached the town of Lahoisk on the Minsk–Bobroisk road. Older Jews from the National Guard greeted us as their sons (among them were some army recruits) and gave us food and drink. People joined together in defending the spot, dug trenches, and prepared to meet the enemy with weapons. We helped them to the best of our abilities. The Germans would not occupy the town until they brought in tanks and conducted an aerial bombing. After they occupied the town they retaliated with cruel revenge on the population: they killed all the men and burned the houses. We decided to return home since the Germans were everywhere anyway. With the help of two young Polish women who accompanied us we received a permit from a German officer saying we were Polish workers at the Polish *Electrit* electronics factory, returning home.

"We Are Not Jews"

The German army rapidly moved East as we traveled West. When we reached the town of Lvidov[1] a German yelled, "There are Yudeh!" We were surrounded and hit with gun muzzles, and were led straight to the synagogue where we found Jews wearing *talits* and *tefillin*, praying, crying, reciting loudly "'Hear O Israel, the Lord our God is One Lord." German soldiers surrounded the yard. Officers were giving orders, Torah scrolls spread across the road and trampled on by wheels. The Germans gathered Jews from the area, rushing them with curses and blows.

The Polish sisters approached the German officers and said, "We are not all Jews; here is a certificate saying we are returning from Minsk to Vilne. Why are we kept here?"

Five German officers came to examine us. One of them looked at my head, turned it right and left, and yelled, "Yudeh! Yudeh!" as in, Jew! Jew! I erupted with wild laughter (I played the part), and another officer told him, "Stupid man this is not a Jew." They still suspected the rest of the people. Eventually they decided we were not Jews. We were given cigarettes and coffee. Our belongings were returned and they sent us on our way.

Rumors reached us later that a big massacre had taken place in the synagogue and that the remaining people had been sent to an unknown destination. From there we continued to Horodok and on the way, we saw stacks of burnt cars. Here we met the second line of Germans who moved slowly as they transported supplies. They had enough time to murder and plunder and they did so with great joy. When we reached Horodok we decided not to enter the town for safety reasons. We entered a farmer's house at the edge of the road and sent the girls to survey the situation. I was very tired and fell asleep. I awoke to the screams of the Gentile, "The Germans are searching door to door, looking for Jews and foreigners."

I left everything including my backpack and hat, and ran out into the street. With no backpack I looked like a local and could move freely. Germans surrounded the town and no one could enter or leave. I blended in with the Gentiles who had come to rejoice and watch Jews being exterminated.

I saw all the Jewish men being led to the marketplace, ordered to lay face down in the dirt, and then ordered to rise. The Rabbi and other bearded men had their beards plucked and shaved. The Germans were obviously not careful and they cut flesh with the beards. The blood dripped slowly, soaked into the *kapoteh*,[2] and swallowed up the golden sand as the crowd cheered in joy.

I was very disturbed at that sight and left the place. I recognized one of the girls who was with our group and asked about the fate of the others from Oshmene. "Escape quickly," she said, "all the guys are already captured."

Standing there not knowing what to do, I met a young Polish man wearing a student's hat. "Tell me, young man," I approached him, "where can a Polish guy like me stay for the night?" "Come, let us ask the German officer," he answered. I was out of options so we approached the "*feld comandant*" who directed me to the priest. I told the priest my name was Yampolski, a day laborer from Vilne, and happened to come across the town and wish to return home.

The priest gave me food and a place to sleep. The next day at sunrise I managed to sneak through the barrier around the priest's home, and with a staff in hand continued towards Oshmene. The state of affairs in Oshmene was poor; Jews were broken and afraid. I did not stay there long and hurried home. I finally arrived at the river that crosses Oshmene Street after three eventful weeks. I went to Yakov Bloch's mother, ate, rested, and shaved, and at night I arrived at home.

Divenishok Under German Rule

The Nazi criminals and thieves now controlled the governance of our town. The police were composed of criminals. All the criminal types were now in positions of power, like Kasiuk Skyviss, Gvidon, Treshkavits and others. They entered a different Jewish home every night, assaulted, tormented, and left. Cries were often heard from Jewish houses, "Help! Robbers!" but nobody dared go outside.

When Gvidon learned I had returned he came up with the idea to reunite the school orchestra that had entertained them before holidays (I played violin). He gathered all the musicians; Getsl Kherson, Binyamin Lipkunski, Eliahu Rogol, and others, and brought us the Polish school hall and where we played all night.

Afterward, Gvidon approached me and accused me, "You ran to the Russians, you are a communist," and arrested me. When my father learned of that he brought him a few bottles of vodka and I was released.

We lived on Dovizishok Street not far from the *mogilnok* (the Christian cemetery.) I once passed by the cemetery and saw a long row of graves. I asked my mother for an explanation and she replied, "On the third day of their invasion, the Germans brought hundreds of Russian soldiers and their officers on freight trucks to the cemetery, forced them to dig long ditches, shot them into the ditches, and covered them." The Geneva Convention did not exist for the Germans.

A German radio unit was parked on Dovizishok Street, whose role it was to disturb Russian radio communications. They would appear periodically and impose ransom (*contrevuzia*) on the Jews, demanding furs, silver, and gold. The *Yudenrat*[3] would gather what they wanted from the Jews and give it to them.

Once, members of the radio unit demanded 14 young Jews for labor. I was sent along with Avraham Meyshke Kotler, Meir Yosef Itskovitsh, Zeytske Shvintolski and others. They had a radio tower and wanted shacks built for them [near it]. They brought poles and hammers, and told us to place the poles in the ground. I began to hammer and the handle broke off, was given a second hammer which also broke, as did the third. The German was angered and told me to climb the 35–meter high tower. "This is the end," I thought. "Bring down the antenna!" the Germans yelled at me. I did so. "Now come down!" I was relieved. After two weeks we were released.

One day a German unit appeared in town accompanied by Polish collaborators. The Jewish men were gathered in the market place and were ordered to lie on the ground facing the church and bow to the cross. After that we were instructed to perform different tasks and then instructed to run towards City Hall. There, a German officer instructed us to stand in formation and announced, "From this day forward you start work."

Then started the *zvengas arbet* (forced labor) in town. Every morning we were organized, given various tasks such as cleaning gutters, fixing the road, and the like, all of course without pay. An order was given to wear a Star of David patch. The situation continued like that until winter.

Several farmers from Divenishok headed by the *kakerakes* who were Lithuanian, petitioned the Germans for Divenishok to be transferred to Lithuania, and indeed, in January 1942 our town was handed over to Lithuania. The Jews were frightened, as the fate of the Lithuanian Jews was well known to us.

Zalmen Leyb Lieb (Tsvi Ahuvi's brother) chairman of the *Yudenrat*, who had lived in Danzig for many years and mingled with the Germans, knew their mentality, and spoke fluent German. He was connected to the *Gvits Commisar* in Lida and bribed him into issuing a decree transferring all the Divenishok Jews to the nearby Voronova, which was in Belarus where the Jews were not yet being exterminated.

It should be noted that the *Yudenrat* officials in Divenishok were good, and did their best to help not only town residents but also the refugees who had escaped Vilne and other places, and found refuge in Divenishok. With the help of the *Gvits Commisar* documents were forged for all the refugees present in Divenishok. They transferred to Voronova along with the town's Jews. Residents of our town treated the refugees faithfully and respectfully, helped them as best they could, and shared their last piece of bread with them.

My dear mother Sheineh will be fondly remembered for hosting many Jewish refugees from Vilne in her home, and thanks to her many survived. One of them was a dear friend of ours, Dr. Tsvi Yoffe, who served as an army doctor with the Red Army in Vilne and married Khayeh of Yitzach's family. During the 'actions' in Vilne he escaped to Divenishok and stayed at our house. He managed to escape, with his wife, from Voronova to the partisans and survived (Dr. Yoffe later served for a time as the chief doctor for the IDF.)

In the Voronova Ghetto

In January 1942 the Jews of Divenishok packed their belongings, loaded them on wagons and traveled to Voronova. All the houses in Voronova were full because the Germans had transferred all local Jews there and placed them in a designated quarter. In addition, they added the Jews from Divenishok, Benakani, Soletchnik, and surroundings, to the crowding. We huddled with people from Geranion who were our relatives.

In Voronova I was tasked with tree–clearing around the village of Yanushevits. It was backbreaking labor but had one advantage to it: we were housed in farmers' homes of the many [farmers] were detained or had escaped.

The farms were abandoned and had nobody to work on them. We befriended the farmers and helped them in our free time, and they helped us too. I would take the risk, dressed in peasant's fur, of loading wood on a sled and bringing it home. This was a significant help since firewood was very scarce in the ghetto.

In the village we met Russian soldiers who were hiding from the Germans. They were strong men who worked nicely so the farmers did not turn them in. Among them were officers who had hidden their weapons in the woods, and when the Germans came searching for them they escaped to the woods. They created the first partisan groups. The Russians were experts in making wool overshoes (*woolenki*), a very important product to the farmers who had no shoes.

Dismantlement of the Voronova Ghetto

A month before the dismantlement of the Voronova ghetto, an order was issued to return all workers to the Ghetto. On the evening of May 7 a curfew was announced. Documents were strictly examined. On the morning of May 8 we saw from our home a row of police officers as reinforcements to the SS, and behind them stood another row of police and volunteers.

Many people attempted to escape. Some encountered guards and were killed; many managed to escape. On May 1[4] *Yudenrat* officials patrolled the streets and announced on a loud speaker that Jews must leave their houses and gather in the market place with their families. If anyone were to be missing from a family, the rest would be punished. Frightened Jews gathered in the marketplace, while gangs of rioters passed door to door, robbing, hitting, and killing. Farmers armed with pitchforks, sickles, axes, and knives gathered near the houses and plundered joyously.

During the three days we were enclosed inside the Ghetto, farmers dug deep pits in the Belaruski Woods at the end of Lida Street and prepared chlorine and lime for disinfecting the bodies. According to the original plan, the Germans intended for Jews to dig the pits themselves. But they had learned their lesson in Radin, where the Germans had tasked 300 Jews headed by Meirke der Shmid (Meir the Blacksmith) to dig the graves; he organized an uprising and a large battle ensued which lasted a few hours. The Jews managed to kill police with their shovels and waged a persistent battle on the arriving reinforcements. Meirke did exceptionally well, hid behind a pile of stones, and fought persistently. And thus hundreds of young men from Radin managed to escape to the woods and formed the first core of the Jewish partisans. In Voronova the Germans organized matters so that there would be no surprise.

For three days I built myself a *melina* (hiding spot) in the attic. Father did not want to go in there and said, "We are a strong and healthy people. We will surely survive. We should give it to weak and disabled people who would be otherwise executed." We placed 10 people in the hiding spot and they indeed survived.

The marketplace was surrounded by Germans armed with machine guns and grenades. Germans stood at the intersection of the main roads, lead by headquarters' commander Windisch, and directed those destined to live to go to the right and to the left, and those for destined for death to go straight. My father wanted to go straight but the officer pointed him right. "Stupid guy, I told you to go right."

After a while we heard faint gunshots and shouting. We understood what was happening.

After a few days, when I left the ghetto for work, the farmers told me that all along that [death] path had stood Gentiles with axes, pitchforks, and sickles, and were hitting Jews until they bled, in order to stun them. When they reached the graves, they were laid on their faces, and waited in line for their deaths. Group by group they were unclothed, entered the graves, and were shot in the neck. The dead were covered with lime and chlorine, and the horrific acts were continued with the next group. The murders continued until all the Jews were exterminated.

Despite all the safety measures the Germans had taken there were a few men who tried to resist. Gentiles told me of an unusual heroic act by Zalmenke Shrira. He was led to the grave with his mother Mineh and his sisters Mashke and Esther. He jumped and stunned the Germans, broke the chain, and began running towards the woods. A few Germans chased him riding motorbikes and caught up to him. He jumped on and flipped a bike, shoved its rider to the ground, and took his gun. A second German rider came up and he flipped him too. He took a position and pointed the weapon to the Germans who surrounded him and fought them until a bullet pierced his heart. A few days later farmers found his body a kilometer from the graves, riddled with bullets. People confirmed it was indeed Zalmen Shrira's body.

After the extermination the Germans spread a sheet and commanded the Jews who had survived to toss their silver and gold onto the sheet. "Later we will conduct a search," the murderers said, "and anyone found with silver or gold will be killed." The sheet was filled with silver, gold, and jewelry.

Of all the Voronova Jews, only seven hundred people remained, transferred after a few days to the Lida Ghetto.

At the Lida Ghetto

A calculated dismantling of the ghettos in the Navaredok and Lida districts took place in May. *Zunder commando* units passed from town to town and exterminated Jews. Those who remained were transferred to the Lida Ghetto. Before that operation began, 6000 Jews were killed in Lida, to make room for the survivors from the area towns. Before that, about 8000 Jews were killed near the army base. The rest of the Jews were placed in a small and limited ghetto. The rest of the area Jews were placed in that dense and narrow parcel.

The Lida Ghetto made a very depressing impression on me. I felt like we had arrived in the valley of death, everything ruined and broken. Every step and corner highlighted the murder, the robbery, and the plunder. Jews were crammed into houses with much overcrowding under a strict ghetto regime: the yellow patch, the walking in the middle of the road, licenses to leave the ghetto, and difficult compulsory labor.

In the first days of our stay at the Lida Ghetto we were very pessimistic because German success at the Russian front was at its height, and we could see no way out. We put all our hopes into joining the partisans and avenging the Jewish bloodshed.

We heard from Gentiles that there were partisans in the Nalibok and Lipnishok areas, but how would we reach them? It was also clear to us that the partisans accepted only people with weapons. But where would one get a weapon? As luck would have it, a group of Divenishok people was sent to work at the train station where a train loaded with many weapons arrived on its way to Germany. Despite the station teeming with Germans, a group of Divenishok men including Dovid Schneider (Dovid Zekkel's[5] son), Leyzer Shklar, Tuvye Blyakher, Meir Levine and his brother Sender from Soletchnik, and I, decided to put on a performance. We approached the train cars while pretending our job was to transfer weapons between cars. We chose gun parts and hid them under our long rain coats. We made an effort to ensure barrels were functional. We hid the weapons and after work we smuggled them into the Ghetto. Getting the guns into the Ghetto was not easy, but each person improvised to his ability. One tied the weaponry to his leg and pretended to limp, one tied the weapon to his shoulder under the coat, another in his sleeve, and we managed to smuggle various parts into the Ghetto. We set up a workshop in our basement to fix and upgrade the guns.

We began developing ties with the Partisans at that point, including several Divenishok people like Eltsik Blyakher. Eltsik came to the ghetto a little later to rescue Jews, but I was prevented from joining him because although I wanted to leave with my cousin Schneider using the same gun, he [Schneider] unexpectedly contracted typhus.

Meir Levine from Soletchnik arrived later at the Ghetto to extract his family (he took the weapons from the train station with him) and took with him a group of youths from the Ghetto including several Divenishokers: Dovid Schneider, Avraham Kotler and his wife Leah, his brother Shlomo Kotler, Tuvye Blyakher, and I. My father knew I had a weapon, but my mother was surprised by it. I will never forget the moment we parted ways. My mother prepared my package for the road and when she saw the weapon she handed it to me and said, "My son, take the weapon and go take revenge on the Germans!" and began crying. It was a very shocking separation from my family.

40 people left the ghetto that night. There was harmony among us and everything went well. In one night we reached the village of Sagli,[6] about 20km from Lida. That village was under Partisan control and served as a front position and passage spot for the combat troops. We felt like we had been born again as free people and not human dust.

On our way to Bielski the next day we encountered a horse dragging a wagon and a dairy cow. A man slept in the wagon with his rifle next to him. We woke him and to my surprise it was Shmuel Schneider my cousin from Ivia (he was also called Kalmen Vigosh[7]). He told us he was an assistant to the *Isscara* commander and his task was to supply milk for a Jewish baby living with his parents and hosted by a Gentile in the small village *hutur*.[8] We accompanied him and gave the cow to the farmer. From there we traveled to *Sstara Huta*, commander Bielski's base. We did not find Bielski's units and instead saw some of his men patrolling on horseback; they told us the Germans were about to attack. They took us to the Zhorabalnik woods, 30 km from there.

And indeed the next morning a German assault began aided by Polish units. We had to escape. Hershl from Oshmene's (Zalmen Kushes' father-in-law) daughter Rachel was injured there. We then traveled to Baksht but the Germans attacked us there too. Bielski led from there to the Naliboki Woods (*Naliboker Puscza*.)

The three Bielski brothers were blessed with rare gifts that were manifested in their operations as partisans. They had great leadership abilities when conducting military operations, but they particularly excelled in their love for the people of Israel. They could have joined any Russian partisan battalion, but their primary mission was not only to fight the Germans but to save as many Jews as possible, and indeed, Bielski gave shelter to children and the elderly, who were not deserted.

We were given two tasks: one, to go on revenge missions against German collaborators, and the second to go on estate missions, meaning supplying food to the combatants and to the family camp which expanded daily.

I knew no satisfaction during my stay in the Naliboki Woods. The German drive to destroy the partisans was at its height and we were in a constant fearful retreat from the enemy. I was tasked with transferring the families deep into the woods and we had to pass through swamps to cover our tracks. Walking was done only at night and with much tension. We were freezing, barefoot, and starving. After two weeks we arrived deep into the woods and felt relieved.

Bielski summoned me one day and said, "I know your father, he will be a brave fighter, take a friend and bring your parents and any Jew who wants to join the partisans."

I chose Leybke Kaplan (Alter Yashe Nashe's son) and traveled 150 km until we reached Sagli village which was the buffer zone between German and partisan controlled territory. There we learned the Germans had reinforced the Lida Ghetto perimeter.

We decided to enter the Ghetto. We hid in the bushes whenever we observed dark figures. We held our breaths and realized those were German troops wearing rain ponchos preparing for an ambush. We waited until morning and with the help of a farmer managed to enter the Ghetto.

Once inside the Ghetto, we began gathering people. We gathered 100 people, but extraction was postponed. The Germans began an all-out assault on the Partisans. We saw villages burning in the distance. Chaos erupted among the Partisans, gangs of thieves formed and began attacking Jews. People were killed for a pair of shoes or a weapon. People who were sick, injured, or infected returned to the Ghetto after encountering trouble, dirt, and hunger. There was no hope of returning to the woods— the situation was dire with no way out.

After ten days of staying in the Ghetto, German troops surrounded it, and people were ordered to stay indoors. The next day an order was issued to pack clothes and food and go to the gathering point. My mother proposed we hide but my father strongly opposed, saying it was well known that in Byalistok the ghetto was burned after dismantlement and there was no point in hiding.

We offered the hiding spot to people from Ivia: Shmuel Geller, Dr. Gordon, Rachel and Chava Stotski entered and survived.

Escape from the Train Station

From the gathering point we were directed to the train station where we were to wait for the death train. My sister requested permission to bring water from the nearby yard, took advantage and escaped. I stayed with my parents. I saw Gentiles in the distance digging pits. I jumped in a pit, took a hoe, and began digging. After a while I put the hoe on my shoulder and began walking on the sidewalk. As I walked slowly in a cloud of sadness and heartbreak a Gentile stopped to look at me. My blood ran cold. I thought he recognized me. "Do not be afraid," he said, "your sister is with us and she sent me to search for you." He brought me to his house and we stayed there until the evening. He was an unfamiliar Gentile. He simply saw my sister wandering aimlessly, took pity on her, and brought her to his home. The reunion with my sister was very emotional; she cried and cried. "I have no time for this," I told her. "Let us go to the partisans."

On the Way to the Partisans

Near Lida there was a *hutur*[9] named Plashevitsi. A single man lived there with his mother. His name was Vladek Melkhovski. One day, he appeared at our house in the Ghetto and helped my sister bring some flour from the city. How did that happen? He saw a group of Jewish women clearing bricks from the ruins, among them my sister. He approached her and said, "I want to help you." At nightfall, after work was done, he joined the group and brought us flour. "I would like to meet the girl's family," he said. He offered to hide us at his farm for the duration of the war. We ignored him and did not take him seriously. He gave us his address and left.

At nightfall I left Lida with my sister and we headed to Melkhovski. I knew Plashevitsi was behind the train tracks. I asked people for directions. To this day I do knot know if I was mistaken or misled, but I was told to walk towards the forest where I would find the tracks. It was dark. We moved through the woods and saw trenches with empty food cans near them, and some pieces of paper. "This is a training spot," my sister said. I scolded her, "You just left the ghetto and already you know better than me." We kept walking, the trees thinned, and we suddenly heard an order, "Shty!" (Stop!), and gunfire rained down on us. My sister was probably hit on the spot because I heard her horrifying screams. I jumped in a trench. The Germans gathered around to search for me and when they were somewhat distant I jumped into a potato field. I lost contact with my sister then, but I am certain they executed her because I heard her screams from a distance and then she fell silent. I later found out that we were at the back side of a German military base, the infamous army camp where the Jews of Lida were executed.

I lay there shocked, did not know what to do, what to decide, or where to turn. I do not know how long I lay there but suddenly the moon rose. Lumps of fog rose and behind them the moon emerged. I saw a group of soldiers leaving the base, jumped out, and crossed the road towards the base; I thought they would not search for me there. I crawled into a natural grazing plot with rocks scattered across it, clung to one, and wanted to die. The suffering had depleted my strength and hope. It was too much to lose my parents and sister on the same day. I noticed a horse tied at a farm and thought it was the God-send that would save me. I got on the horse and let it walk. It reached a solitary, crumbling house and stopped. I got off the horse and knocked on the door. A pale, scared face appeared before me, and said, "Listen! A search was conducted here five minutes ago. They said I was hiding Jews. Hide nearby until morning and tomorrow I will tell you where to go."

I fell asleep in his garden due to exhaustion. Rain started falling in the morning and I awoke. I entered his house and the farmer cooked potatoes with lemon for me, and explained how to reach Plashevitsi. He gave me a hoe and a basket as a disguise— like I was going to gather potatoes.

I reached Vladek Melkhovski that same day. When he saw me he hugged me and wept as he asked about my family's fate. I told him about my sister and parents. He put me in the barn. He took a bike and patrolled all day, reached the base and gathered information. He learned the Germans had searched the area, captured Jews who escaped the Ghetto, and put them on the train which had been at the station for the past three days. A few days later in the afternoon hours he came to me beaming and said, "I found your family." It turned out those were the Jews from Ivia to whom we had given our hiding spot. They hid there until nightfall then exited the Ghetto to look for another hiding spot. The Pole had found them in the field and brought them to the barn.

There were already eight people in the barn and he cared for them all with friendship and devotion. We stayed with him for a few days until that wonderful man obtained weapons for us. As it turned, out the famous Sagla[10] Village was 15 km from our location, and our only hope to survive was in reaching the village. One foggy morning we packed our guns in a package of birch wood. We shouldered the package and made our way to Sagla. The group parted ways there, our group made its way to Bielski, and today are alive and well in Israel. I began walking towards my birth town, Divenishok.

The Search For Members of Our Town

While speaking to Partisans, I learned that the Divenishokers had decided to leave the Naliboki Woods where conditions had become unbearable due to the constant searching by Germans, and had moved to the woods near Divenishok because: first, things were calmer there, second so they could be masters if their own fate and not suffer anti-Semitism on the part of Russian Partisans, and third so they could take revenge against Gentiles in the Divenishok area for their robberies and killings of Jews.

I began traveling, dressed like a farmer, with a pistol and two grenades in my pockets. I approached Yanushevits village, the same village I worked at when I stayed at the Voronova Ghetto. On the road, I portrayed myself as a farmer wanting to buy a horse or carriage, and traveled among the peasants, inquiring as to the situation. The Gentiles told me there were many gangs of White Poles being particularly cruel to the Jews. "Here, in this yard, the Poles killed a Jew, and here they killed another," they pointed. Of course that news saddened me.

After a long investigation I found out that our group was in the Kalelishok area, but I was warned that the place was overrun by White Poles who were eager to hunt for Jews. After extensive searching in the Kalelishok Woods, I reached the Divenishokers' spot. They lived in a well-hidden dugout. The reunion was very emotional. We hugged and cried, bitterly mourning that so few of us remained. There I found Leyzerke Shklar, Tuvya Blyakher, the Kotler brothers Avraham and Shlomo, Avraham Kotler's wife Leah (from Lida), Kalmen Kartshmer, Dovid Schneider, Meir dem Zekl's[11] son, Chaim Levine (Chaim der Milners), his brother Yosef Levine from Danoyke village, and two brothers from Kalelishok. The experts on the area were the Levines from Soletchnik.

My friends told me a fascinating story about their first reunion with Kalmen Kartshmer. One night, when they came to Yurglan Village to search for food, a bearded dirty creature approached them and began begging from them, "Brothers! Do not take anything from this village. They are good people, I am Jewish and they look out for me; please, take pity on me and leave them alone."

"Kalmen? Is that you? What are you doing here?" The Divenishokers began yelling, "Come join us, come with us, brother."

Kalmen began crying and joined his friends. The Gentiles were shocked.

"What? You want Kalmen!? Take whatever you wish but leave Kalmen to us. Take pigs, take cows, but do not take Kalmen."

The valued Kalmen a lot, because he chased away the Partisans with his begging and then they would not take their *smogon* (moonshine).

Attacks by Germans and Poles

After we stayed with them for a few days (it was July at harvest time) we relocated to a forest near Sleski Village.[12] Since we had heard that local Gentiles had collaborated with the Germans, robbing Jewish homes in Divenishok and plundering their belongings, we decided to come even.

One night we attacked the village and conducted a search in the houses. We recognized mirrors, pantries, cabinets, and other items, and smashed them to smithereens. We beat them for what they had done to Jews. They were fearfully shaken, begged us to forgive them since they regretted their actions. We took bread and meat from them and returned to the woods.

At dawn, as we skinned the sheep, Germans and Polish police officers arrived and began to surround us. We left behind all the supplies and managed to retreat with our weapons, while dragging Shmuel Levine whose hand was injured. At night we brought him to the doctor in Kalelishok who extracted the bullet from his hand.

Preparations for the Winter of 44/45 in Stoki Forest

After that assault we decided to relocate to the Stoki Woods, hoping to find a stable, well-hidden *zhmlanke* (den) to gather food for winter and stay there until it was safe. We chose a spot in a *molodniak* (young forest), assuming the peasants avoided visiting there. We brought birch trees, built the *zhmlanke* with planks, uprooted trees, and replanted them atop the hiding spot so the spot was well hidden. Happy at the success of the mission we went to bed and the two women who were with us prepared a festive meal.

"Food is ready!" the girls called and we jumped from our spot. Only Tuvya Blyakher stayed asleep. We went to wake him. He lay covered in sweat and spoke Hebrew in his sleep. "Gentlemen!" he mumbled, "gentlemen, how do I get to Petah Tikva? My brother went to war, so what? He will fight for our freedom and we will win. We'll win, of course, we will. But why are you crying? Everyone is here with us! Everyone, everyone (and he began saying the names of everyone in the den). They are here with us. Together we were in the Partisans; we fought the Germans together. And here they all are in Israel, everyone! Everyone! We avenged the blood of our brothers and sisters! We took revenge on our enemies! And here we are in Israel," he wept in his sleep.

We stood around amazed and crying. It was the first time in years that we had heard Hebrew. All the pent up emotions in us erupted; we remembered the lively Jewish youths in our town walking about with the Hebrew language rising to the heavens. We remembered the cultural life, the lively youth movements, remembered our parents, our siblings, our relatives. Where are they? Why have they fallen silent? We felt orphaned, alone, without a past or a future, surrounded by bloodthirsty enemies who wanted to take our lives. And far away freedom awaits! Our friends await! But how can we reach them? How can we untangle the noose of the tragedy threatening our lives? How could we reach freedom? A stream of tears grew stronger and turned into bitter weeping, taking over our beings. When Tuvya awoke we asked him of what he had dreamed about? "I do not remember a thing. I do not remember," and he wiped the sweat from his face.

Chaim Levine, his wife, and his brother Yosef from the close-by Danoyke village joined us in the Stoki Forest. They hid in a *zhmlanke* located a few kilometers from us, and a friendly farmer supplied food. Two men from Kalelishok and two from Vilne joined us as well. A young Russian man named Mishka Lytnent who roamed the area joined us as well.

We hoped to form a large and powerful partisan force that would instill fear in Divenishok, and the region, becoming a strong supporter of Jews still hiding in various places.

We began to reorganize for that purpose. Mishka Lytnent was appointed as commander. The group was composed of 11 armed people and 7 unarmed. Our first mission was to obtain weapons for the remainder of the members. We were in contact with several farmers who lived around the woods whose farms served as bases where we could meet-up and exchange information. They also notified us where we could obtain weapons.

We had unique methods of obtaining weapons. When we learned a farmer had weapons we would appear and ask for them. When he refused, we threatened that we would search the house and if we found weapons we would burn the house down. To frighten him, we would order him to bring straw from the barn to burn the house, until he relented and brought the weapon. Then he would receive some blows for not complying.

We took unique measures to cover up our tracks. We constructed a small wooden bridge from the sleigh, raised it above some brush, and continued to our residence from there.

When the cold intensified we decided to go on a special mission to prepare food in case of emergency and to bring winter clothes for the people who had joined us and had nothing. Six armed men went on that mission. We prepared 3 horse-bound sleighs and traveled to a more distant and rich area, though we knew it was swarming with White Pole militias.

We reached the village and loaded the sleighs with bread, meat, and potatoes, and intended to turn back. Dovid Schneider and Leybke Kaplan from Voronova went into one of the homes to bring winter clothes. We suddenly noticed a woman's figure sneaking into the woods. The commander gave an order to immediately retreat since we knew of strong units of White Poles stationed in the area. As we turned the sleighs around, armed people came out of the woods on foot and on horseback and opened heavy fire. Commander Mishka gave an order to stop at the turn, return fire, and then get on the sleighs and escape.

Dovid Schneider and Leybke Kaplan who had stayed in that house, stormed out, and began a close combat with the Poles. The Poles left us and concentrated their fire on the two young men, probably assuming a large force of ours was stationed in the village. Leybke managed to break through and reach us. My cousin, Dovid Schneider, held a position by a pile of wood and fought bravely until a bullet pierced his heart.

The next evening we attempted to approach the village but learned that the Poles had placed guards by the body, hoping we would return to retrieve it. The man was not buried. It was our first casualty in the Stoki area.

The White Pole headquarters located our spot. To tighten their grip they took positions in nearby villages until only the woods remained for us. They waited for their first chance when we would emerge from hiding so they could attack us.

Headquarters then decided to locate the Partisans and clear Stoki from Partisans once and for all. To ensure results, they decided to wait until January, when the cold would be intense and partisans avoided missions. We sat in the bunker with nothing to do until January 11, 1944, when we ran out of supplies, and decided to go get food. Commander Mishka, Leyzer Shklar, Shlomo Kotler, Yosef Levine (from Danoyke), and I went out.

This time we went to the Kalelishok area since we knew a rich farmer lived there, a Jew-hater, who had handed two brothers from Kalelishok to the White Poles, after setting a trap. "I will introduce you to Partisans," he told them, and when they arrived, the Poles were waiting for them in his yard and executed them on the spot. That took place in the summer of 1943.

At this opportunity we decided to settle the score with him. We arrived there, recognized the people, and introduced ourselves as Polish partisans. We asked him to hitch two horses to sleighs, loaded them with meat and bread, and then we asked, "Do you know the two brothers from Kalelishok?" he turned pale. We put a bullet in his head, executed his family, and burned the farm. We left a white sheet on which we wrote in their blood, "Blood for blood, Jewish blood will not be disregarded! Dog death for dogs!"

At dawn a large snow storm started. A white coat covered the area and we feared the sleigh tracks would be visible to the Poles on the fresh-fallen snow. We decided to unload the supplies at a small abandoned bunker located 2 km from our bunker. The brothers Chaim and Yosef from Danoyke used to live in that bunker. Just as planned, Kalmen Kartshmer, Chaim Levine, and Avraham Kotler waited for us by the bunker. We gave them the sleighs with the supplies and they transported them to a distant location to prepare the meat for consumption. Chaim's wife and Avraham Kotler's wife who had arrived with their husbands were in the bunker then.

We five, exhausted by the mission, entered the bunker to rest a bit, but since the spot was narrow we decided to sleep in shifts. As fate would have it, Yosef Levine and I remained awake for the first shift, and the three brothers went to sleep. Suddenly we heard gunfire. Turns out, the Poles had planned the attack long ago; that morning they followed our tracks and came close. Luckily, the clothes we had out to dry confused them and they thought we were outside and began shooting. I took my gun, jumped out barefoot, and crashed into a Pole. I hit him with the gun handle and he fell. I had thus breached the chain of Poles. Yosef Levine and Leah, Avraham Kotler's wife, escaped through that gap. Fourth was Chaim Levine's wife, who was hit by a bullet and died immediately. They chased us. We managed to widen the gap between us. The three of us ran as a unit. My bare feet were suddenly wounded by some branches and I feared the blood tracks would be the end of it. Luckily, I had on cotton underwear. I stopped for a moment, took off the underwear and tied my feet with them. We looked for a clever way to trick the Poles. We probably ran in the same direction where a search had already taken place since we saw many footsteps on the way. That, of course, made things easier, but we were still in danger. I suddenly discovered a pine tree lying on the ground in the direction we were running, with its top inside a thicket facing us. We climbed on the pine, crossed it, and then jumped in the thicket. We remained there until nightfall. We feared to make a sound and held in our breath since there were many White Poles in the woods. We heard shots, orders, and even conversations. The only action we took was rubbing our hands and feet so we would not freeze.

After nightfall we heard a trumpet, probably a signal for the Poles to return to base. We had a Russian semi-automatic and a Russian rifle with bullets, and we pondered our next action. Yosef Levine proposed going to his hometown Danoyke, located not far from us, where a friendly farmer lived who had cared for him and his brother while they were in their bunker. "I have a feeling he escaped to him," he said.

We were out of options and accepted his proposal. We made our way towards Danoyke. We stopped about 500 meters from the village. That spot was great for observing, the village could be seen as if on the palm of the hand. From a distance the village seemed lively: lighted houses, we heard singing, yelling, and cheering. I left Yosef and Leah in the field and crawled towards the farmer's house to peak through the window. I crawled 100 meters and encountered a body in the snow, no boots on, frozen, stiff. At first I did not recognize him, but when I took a closer looked I saw it was Chaim. Turned out that Kalman Kartshmer, Avraham Kotler, and Chaim Levine, who had taken the supplies to prepare for storage, also encountered White Poles. Kalmen and Avraham had run deeper into the woods, while Chaim had run towards his hometown Danoyke, intending to reach the farmer. There was a sniper's mound on the pine hill and Chaim walked right into their crosshairs. They executed him on the spot.

I turned around, told my friends everything, and we decided to leave quickly. We changed course and headed to Kalelishok where the Levine family from Soletchnik was hiding. I should note the Levines greeted us kindly and said, "We will share our last piece of bread with you, whatever happens, happens, one fate for us all."

It was clear that there was no other way to survive than by joining an established partisan group. But first we wanted to know our friends' fate. We decided not to re-emerge and to conduct searches for the next two weeks.

Two weeks later, Yosef Levine and I took our weapons and went towards the forest to search for survivors. We had emphatically decided to gather all survivors and go to the Partisans. First we went to check on Yitzach from Voronova. It was a small, well camouflaged bunker where he lived with his wife, their daughter and her husband Tsvi Shatsitnitski from Turgel (cousin of the Shatsitniskis from Divenishok.) We had sponsored that bunker. They had no weapons and we supplied them food. On the last mission, during which my cousin Dovidke Schneider was killed, we managed to bring them food to last through the winter. They had not left the bunker since then and the Poles had not found them. Much to our surprise we also found Kalmen Kartshmer and Avraham Kotler there. We were very excited; they thought we had been killed and we thought they had been killed.

The Bitter Fate of Our Brothers in Stoki Forest

We then learned of the fate of our brothers in the main bunker. The bunker was discovered by the Poles when Leyzer Shklar, who was among the three who were attacked in their sleep in the *zhmalnke*, managed to break the chain of Poles, and in his shock began running towards the big bunker where the rest of our group were. He was shot near the bunker, which led to the discovery of the bunker, and a hopeless battle took place between our friends and the Poles. The men could not withstand the large enemy force, and all fell in battle, including Tuvya Blyakher, Dovid Schneider's girlfriend (he fell in an earlier mission,) and some people from Kalelishok and Soletchnik. The Poles blew up the bunker and took the bodies with them to show the Germans their heroic act.

The next day we went to see what had happened in the first bunker after I had escaped. Near the bunker we found the bodies of Mishka Lytnent, Shlomo Kotler, and Chaim from Danoyke's wife Esther, all frozen. Mishka's pants were down; they probably wanted to see if Mishka was Christian.

We dug three graves since Kalmen ruled it was not permitted to bury a man, a woman, and a Gentile in one grave. We carved their names on the trees above their graves. We sat atop their new graves and mourned. A low weeping sound echoed through the woods. We decided then to leave this damned place soaked with the blood of our brothers and to join the well-organized Partisans to avenge their deaths.

In the Rudniki Woods

All who were left in that area gathered and we made our way to Rudniki Woods. We were led by Shmuel Levine from Soletchnik and Yitzach from Voronova who were very familiar with the area. We walked all night and reached Salki[13] Village across the Vilne–Grodne train tracks the next morning. This was the point of entry and exit for the Partisans.

We knew that Borukh Levine from Soletchnik served as a major in Captain Protzhenov's combat company. He was related to Shmuel Levine and served as a contact to the Partisans. We reached the company on the front lines that guarded the entrance to the woods named *Perkunas* (thunder in Lithuanian). The unit commander was a Lithuanian redhead named Burakas. He was a quick and witty man who excelled in war tactics. After he fell in one of the battles against the Polish, we learned he was a Jewish man from a small Lithuanian town who had been parachuted in by the Red Army as a Lithuanian commander and founder of Lithuanian partisan companies. I would like to note that in the entire Lithuanian company I encountered almost no genuine Gentile Lithuanians: there were Russians and Jews. We found some Jews from Voronova in that company (Borukh Grevetski, now in Beer Sheba, and the two Arkin brothers.) The young among us, Yitzach Levine and Kalmen Kartshmer, joined combat operations, and the rest were in services. Kalmen Kartshmer was tasked with preparing sausage for winter.

Fighting with the Lithuanian Brigade

The youngest in the group joined combat operations and were included in all sabotage missions against German army bases and roads, including ambushing motor convoys, attacking roads, and ambushing German supply sources. We went to blow up bridges and railways every evening. We conducted thorough operations. Operations were hastened by the destruction of telegraph poles spanning 5 km and the destruction of train tracks for many kilometers.

We were considered an elite unit and our base was at the very front position, about 6–7 km from Salki Village. Due to that, we were familiar with all the units of the Vilne Brigade that passed through us. By that chance, we were familiarized with the two Jewish companies in the Vilne Brigade.

In the spring of 1944, when actions by the White Poles increased, we hoped to reach a compromise with them, that we fight the Germans individually and not point our weapons at each other. All fighting should be directed at the common enemy.

Since we were in the front position it was natural for meetings of the leadership to take place where our unit was located. Expert snipers guarded meetings. There I met the famous sniper Grisha Gorvits, who came with me to Israel where we were fortunate to fight alongside one another in the War of Independence.

I Was Appointed as an Expert Sniper

In April 1944, a unit comprised of five Jewish members headed by Russian commander Kostya was to blow up a train between Soletchnik and Vilne. We planted the dynamite sack under the tracks. An operational mechanism was inside the sack. We tied explosives to the sack and the mechanism was triggered by pulling a rope. Similar missions succeeded many times and sometimes we would derail up to 14 cars. This time, Lithuanian patrollers replaced the Germans and they took their task seriously, sending a crew of 18 people to scan the track. Some scanned the surface of the tracks while others went on foot and scanned the ditches with a mine detector.

The device was found by the Lithuanians and disposed of by the technicians. Hellfire rained down on us and we barely managed to return to base. Luckily, our commander was Kostya. Otherwise, the Jews would have been court-martialed.

Headquarters decided to retaliate against the Lithuanians and to destroy that unit at any cost. At night, we set out to ambush them with the full force of the 120-man company. Some took positions on one side of the tracks and others on the other side at some distance, myself included. The Lithuanian patrol arrived on time and much to our misfortune passed the first ambush heading towards us. We opened fire. The Lithuanians abandoned the tracks and took positions behind the mound and returned fire. An order was issued to move forward. The Lithuanians began throwing grenades and facing me lay a Lithuanian sharpshooter who fired heavily in my direction. I then heard him slamming the gun's handle and cursing that it had malfunctioned. I jumped over the track and killed him with a sub-machine gun. Once their marksman was gone, the Lithuanians started running towards Soletchnik. The ambush on the other side finally sprung into action and joined the chase. And so we killed all 18 Lithuanians as they attempted to escape.

We returned to base with a large haul and great satisfaction. I got a modern 1943 Bren light machine gun made in Czechoslovakia. The next day a festive formation took place and unit commander Sergei himself handed me the gun, praised me for my bravery and said, "Grisha! Hit the enemy so the tragedy of the ghetto will not be repeated." The stock of the ten Jewish men in the unit increased monumentally.

The machine gun was the weapon with the strongest firepower among the Partisans and its operator was the strongest, most experienced soldier in the company. The sharpshooter had special standing in the unit and it was no wonder the Russians' regard for us was changed for the better. I had many occasions to operate that machine gun and it was close to my chest for the duration of my stay with the Partisans. More than that, with the same Bren gun I participated in the War of Independence.

The Killing of Yosef Kaplan– A Disgrace to the Russian Partisans

The anti-Semitism hidden in the hearts of the Russians was uncovered in the next event: We departed for an assault on a large procession passing from Soletchnik to Vilne. A Jewish unit of 8 people took a position on the side of the road. Its role was to open fire on the approaching Germans so they would concentrate their fire on us while the assaulting force located at the edge of the woods would storm the procession and destroy it. I was positioned with my machine gun on a well camouflaged tree and awaited orders.

Three partisans, among them Yosef Kaplan, his brother, and another man from Voronova were on the look-out, and their role was to announce the arrival of the Germans. It was agreed that if tanks secured the procession we would not open fire since our weapons were not fit to fight armored troops. The Jewish men mistakenly announced the convoy was headed by tanks and an order was given to hold fire.

When the convoy approached I was surprised that it was headed by two wagons loaded with hay. German supply vehicles followed them and a German musical band [was] behind them. The entire convoy passed without a single shot being fired. A supply vehicle then approached from Vilne and we killed them. We left the overturned car on the road and returned to base.

The Kaplan brothers and the third man arrived at the base only the next morning. A formation of all companies was conducted, they were placed in front of the formation and were accused of three counts: A) not fulfilling their combat mission, B) false notice which led to the failure of the mission, and C) cowardice and late arrival at the base.

The verdict for all three was a death sentence. Yosef Kaplan, group commander was sentenced to death by firing squad, and the other two to a suspended death sentence.

Yosef Kaplan's claims were that the German tanks being grey like the color of hay had fooled him from a distance, and that the sun was in his eyes and obstructed his vision. In reply to the accusation of being late, Kaplan argued they were surrounded by Germans who had come to search the area after the mission, and they could not leave their hiding spot. All this to no avail: the young man was taken behind the formation and executed on the spot.

That sight haunts me to this day. The young Jewish man weeping and saying, "Brothers, I am innocent, do not shed innocent blood! I am your brother–in–arms, I risked my life for the sacred goal. I am young and want to live and see the triumph of good over evil. Please, brothers, avoid bloodshed!"

His pleading was ignored. As the Jewish man was led, his fiery gaze met our eyes as if pleading to the heavens, asking for mercy. And we felt as if our hearts were being cut by a sharp knife. Is there a God above? Why is fate so cruel to us? And Yosef's brother wept bitterly, tears streaming down his face. The sound of weeping merges with the sound of the forest and the ringing gunshots. We were stunned, angry, and sad, gritting our teeth in pain. Our hearts were ripped to shreds and we were inconsolable.

We felt the hatred of Jews expressed in all its might since we knew of worse incidents in which partisans had lost their lives due to negligence, but because those were Russian partisans they went unpunished. The Jews suffered the full consequences. I am certain that if that same event had taken place with a Russian partisan he would not have been shot.

When the Red Army approached Vilne we were ordered to join them in capturing the city. Battles in Vilne lasted 7 days. Many SS men were positioned in Vilne, as well as many Vlasovians[14] who fought bitterly. Combat in the city was difficult and very deadly. We fought door–to–door and many Russians were killed by German snipers positioned on the rooftops. I remember that when I passed through the *Ostra Brama* (a famous holy site in Vilne, where, according to Christian tradition, the Blessed Mother revealed herself, and where everyone passing through the gate, even Jews, had to take of their hats if they did not want to risk getting beaten), I saw a Russian soldier lying there soaking in his blood with a bottle of vodka in his pocket. Many fell prey to the vodka.

A tough battle was waged over the Blokshiki prison, where we captured 63 SS men. The company commander, a Jewish man from Minsk, told me, "Take them and finish them." It was at the height of battle. I did so; I put them up against the wall and finished them off with a large burst from the machine gun. That was a happy feeling I had not yet encountered. I waited my whole life to spill the blood of these prey animals and avenge the blood of my parents, my sister, and of all the shed Jewish blood. I was happy to fulfill the oath I swore to my mother as I held the gun when parting ways at the Lida ghetto.

After the conquest of Vilne, a formation was conducted at the Napoleon Yard and we were placed in various units. I was drafted as an accountant for the NKVD at Blokshiki Prison. I worked there for a year before making *aliyah*.

Visiting my Hometown Divenishok

I very much wanted to visit Divenishok, but I knew it was swarming with White Poles and thieves, so I approached my commander and told him. He took two NKVD squads and we drove to Divenishok in two trucks after spending the night with some Gentiles in Vilne. I was angered at the sight of the town in its abandonment. A fire burned in me when I witnessed the thieves and murderers walking around enjoying Jewish property. "Hast thou killed and also taken possession?" My heart screamed in pain. I walked around dazed. Where are my friends and family who filled the street with sound on holidays? Where is the lively and happy youth? All fell silent! Is this reality or a nightmare? Indeed, that was a reality as bitter as wormwood.

I met the infamous Gvidon on the street, he who had served as a policeman for the Germans. We took him with us and settled the score with him in the woods on the way to Vilne.

Activity in HaBricha

I then traveled to Poland from Vilne. I joined *Haganah* in Lodzh and was part of a special unit tasked with organizing Jewish exits to Italy. That organization was named PPS (initials for partisan, pioneer, soldier). We were sworn on the bible in a dark cellar near the Lodzh ghetto.

Our organization transferred Jews to Italy and from there they were transferred to Israel. We opened various paths of escape to Italy. We used various tactics for that purpose. In Krakow we gathered Greek passports and crossed the border to Hungary, claiming we were Greek POWs returning home from captivity. From Hungary we crossed the border to Austria through difficult paths in the mountains. The Jewish Brigade operated in Austria and they transported refugees to Israel. Meanwhile, the British detected the Brigade's activities and exiled them to the Benelux states.

HaBricha's efforts to bring Jews to Israel did not cease and we looked for new ways to transport Jews to Italy. I was sent in a group of 4 men to Yugoslavia to examine the option of transporting Jews to Italy through Trieste, but the border there was hermetically sealed.

Extermination of the Dachau Camp Commander's Son

One day, I was given an order to relocate to Villach, a large city near the Italian border at the foothills of the Alps. There was a large camp where refugees from multiple nations were living. One evening, I went out to the movies with three friends from *HaBricha*, including the brothers Pinto, and Shefern.[15] We stood in line to buy tickets and rain started pouring down. In front of me stood a young blonde man, who started to curse in Polish. He seemed suspicious to me and I decided to figure him out. We started talking and he told me his father was the commander of the Dachau concentration camp and that he himself was "uber murder fun kinder" meaning he was head–murderer of children. "Maybe you are joking," I told him. "No!" he swore and showed us photos of his horrifying acts. It boiled my blood and I decided to exterminate him at any cost.

After the film ended we invited him to a party with friends. "We have quality whisky and pretty women. We will spend a nice evening together. We are Polish too, we collaborated with the Germans." We convinced him until he agreed to come with us. At camp, we gave him vodka and then killed him. We wrapped him in an army blanket and threw the package in the middle of the street. We phoned the English police and notified them that an army vehicle had dumped a package in the road and left. The Police came, took the package, and left.

Aliyah

After that act we quickly left and relocated to Italy. There we boarded the *Aliyah Bet* ship *Enzo Serni* with 915 immigrants on board including 350 partisans. The British army discovered us by plane near the shore of Beirut and an hour later a British destroyer appeared and wanted to tow us to an unknown location. A message was delivered from the boat announcing we would not agree to be towed until we were promised to be brought to the port of Haifa. When we reached the shores of Israel, leaders from the *Yishuv*, including Moshe Sharet, David HaCohen, and Golda Meir arrived on a motorboat. They requested we not resist the Brits since negotiations were taking place to release us using previously unused certificates from wartime. We were the first illegal *olim*, which was an advantage. We were taken to Atlit and I was released two weeks later. That was in January 1946.

Then a new period in my life began, a period of renewed fighting, first with *Haganah* and later IDF— this time on our soil and for our People. That time was full of suspense and heroic acts that did not cloud the partisan period. But that is a separate ordeal and when the time comes will be written as a historic testimony for the generations to come.

Editor's footnotes:

1. The precise location of this town remains unconfirmed.

2. Long, dark overcoat worn by Jewish men at the time.

3. Jewish Councils mandated by German orders in the occupied communities of Eastern Europe during WWII

4. The number '1' is likely a typographical error since it does not follow from the prior dates given.

5. The nickname 'dem Zekl' is not yet understood.

6. The precise location of this town remains unconfirmed. In the original text the name is spelled: samekh–aleph–gimel–lamed–yud.

7. In the original text the name is spelled: vov–yud–gimel–shin.

8. The meaning of this word is not yet known. In the original text this word is spelled: khes–vov–tes–vov–reysh.

9. The meaning of this word is not yet known. In the original text this word is spelled: khes–vov–tes–vov–reysh.

10. The precise location of this town remains unconfirmed. In the original text the name is spelled: samekh–aleph–gimel–lamed–hey.

11. The nickname 'dem Zekl' is not yet understood.

12. The precise location of this village remains unconfirmed.

13. The precise location of this village remains unconfirmed.

14. Followers of the quisling general Andrey Vlasov's Russian Liberation Army.

15. In the original text this name is spelled: shin–fey (or pey)–reysh–lange nun.

[Page 162]

In the Claws of the Nazi Beast

Kalmen Kartshmer

Translation by Meir Bulman

The Jews of Divenishok were expelled to Voronova on Shvat of 5702 (December 1942). The apartments in Voronova were terribly crowded; four or five families lived in one house. After the life we had lived in Divenishok, where everyone lived in their own home, we felt as if we were in hell.

Ten days after we arrived in Voronova (it was Shvat 10th), we learned our first lesson about the cruelty of the Nazis. They put 28 elderly persons in a cellar, tormented them, and killed them on site. Among those was my father, Rest in Peace. Three days they lay in the cellar because we could not dig a grave for them, because it was very cold out and the ground was frozen. The horrific act was done to mark Hitler's birthday.[1] I sat by my dear father's corpse for three days, weeping and mourning for our bitter fate.

Those physically capable were sent to compulsory labor, without pay of course. I worked in the Bastuni area. Then a week before dismantling I was sent to work in the forest near Baltic Village, near Bastuni. There we worked on tree-cleaning and preparing wood for delivery to Germany.

Eleven people from Divenishok worked there. Among them were the brothers Meir and Tsvi Dubinski, the Shatsitnitski brothers, and Khaye Sarah Levine's husband. When the rumor reached us that Voronova was surrounded, we did not return to town, as we regularly did on Sunday, but waited for news of what was happening in Voronova.

The gentiles told us that the Germans had cruelly executed most of the Jews and left a small number for work. Two days after the slaughter we returned to Voronova and witnessed the tragedy that had befallen the people of our town. All those who worked with me could no longer find their families alive. I too could not find my wife and children. We were shocked and broken and did not know what to do and where to turn. I fondly remember Shimke, Avke David Leyb's sister, and Atke Meir Zalman's, who gave me a loaf of bread and said, "Escape quickly from here and save your life! We are lost no matter what."

I escaped to the Bastuni woods where I found a large group of Divenishok residents, among them those who worked with me at Baltic Village. I found again the brothers Meir and Tsvi Dubinski, the Shatsitnitski brothers, Chaim Hershovitsh, Leybl Varshever, and Maishke Gordsvatser.[2] After staying for a few days in the Bastuni area, we decided to return to the Divenishok area, assuming the peasants who knew us would be of assistance in getting through the difficult days.

We walked all night until we reached Andrei from Starrobieres[3] who was a well-known Russian and did not like the Polish. But we soon discovered that we must leave the place hastily if we wished to live. In the dead of night, we circumvented the town and arrived at Soltsin Village and hid in an oat field. We stayed there until evening and continued walking to Yurglan[4] Village. There we parted ways. Meir and Tsvi Dubinski went to Baltobitze to the forest ranger's house, their good friend, and innocently thought they would find shelter there. But they were sorely mistaken: after all their money was extorted they were executed. Two months later word reached us that they were no longer alive.

The remaining Divenishok folks dispersed in various directions to find shelter. I went to Lodvik, our old friend who lived in Spravstsishuk Village. He kindly greeted me and I stayed with him for six weeks. His neighbor Duvl became aware of that and informed the Germans that a Jew was hiding in Lodvik's home. One day, Kasiuk Skyviss, appeared in the village. During Polish times, he had been a famed thief, and now served as the Divenishok police chief. He arrested me. When we both walked through the woods he took pity on me and told me, "Run into the forest and I will shoot a few rounds in the air, so I can justify myself to the Germans." At first I hesitated since I feared he would stick a bullet in my neck, but I knew I had nothing to lose so I agreed. I wandered in the forest for a few days; the hunger gnawed at me and I wanted to die.

In the end I decided to walk to Hamutsi Village, to my father's friend. At night I knocked on Yozef Sobotsh's window. He opened the door and to my surprise, I found the Shatsitnitski brothers there. After staying with Sobotsh we wandered the area villages like gypsies and searched for shelter.

One day, the Shatsitnitski brothers disappeared. After Liberation I found out that they been hiding with a gentile in Sorktzi Village. The peasant lived in an isolated house and dug a bunker for them. They brought their sister Leah there too and stayed until two days before Liberation, when they were killed by the Poles.

I wandered amongst the gentiles all winter, and to each gentile I was forced to give one of the clothing items I had hidden with Lodvik. Occasionally I would send a messenger to Lodvik and he would give an item to the Gentiles. The young Poles tormented me often. Once, after a dance party, intoxicated by moonshine, they dragged me from the barn, brought me to the center of the village and began tormenting me, "Look at this bearded Jew!" said one.

"Good thing the Germans destroyed all the Jews!" said another.

"The Jews sucked our blood and their day has come!" a young woman spat.

"So why do we need this bearded Jew here?" Screaming erupted from all over and the drunken shouting mixed with the singing around me. The circle tightened more and grew more threatening, and blows rained on my head like a hail storm. My head began spinning, blood flowed from the wounds in a great tide. With my remaining strength I broke the chain and escaped to the woods.

That night I wished I was dead. Will God stay silent in the face of such a horrible act? I would rather be dead than live such a life. The debauchery and wild song reached me from a distance. I lay here and mourned my bitter fate. When a man is on the brink of destruction sometimes a spark of an idea guiding him towards his future shines in his mind. That was my case. Suddenly I got the idea to approach a paramedic who lived in a close–by village and request his help. With the rest of my strength I knocked on his door.

The paramedic was shocked and moved by my terrible appearance, and he immediately began caring for me. He pitied me and hid me with him for a few weeks until I healed a bit.

After that, the wandering from village to village and from peasant to peasant began again, and to each one I gave some of the belongings I had left with Lodvik. Once, a peasant demanded goose feathers. I sent a woman to the town priest and he informed the peasant that I had deposited with him 20 kilograms of feathers and that he would give the woman the feathers. Thanks to that I stayed with the peasant for a long while.

Whenever I felt the situation was worsening and I was in danger, I would escape to Lodvik and he would shelter me for a few weeks until the storm passed. I want to emphasize that I remained alive only thanks to Lodvik.

In the Spring I met partisans who were active in the area. I joined them and began operating. One of our important actions was burning the sawmill in Giluzh. As payback for that act, the Germans bombed the local forests for three days. I was wounded by shrapnel in one of those bombings, but healed.

Because of the bombings and the ambushes, the partisans dispersed in different directions, and once more I found shelter with my benefactor Lodvik. Afterwards, I met some people from my town and stayed with them in the Stoki Woods. There, I survived a most intense hunt by the White Poles. They destroyed most of the people from Divenishok, but with a few friends I managed to escape to the Rodnitski Woods, where we stayed until Liberation.

Editor's Footnotes

1. Hitler's birthday is actually in April, not December.

2. This surname is spelled in the original text as follows: gimmel–reysh–daled–zayin–tsvey vovn–tsadek–ayin–reysh.

3. This as of yet unidentified place is spelled in the original text as follows: mem–hey–samech–tes–aleph–reysh–vov–beyz–yud–ayin–reysh–ayin–samech.

4. In the original text the place name is spelled as follows: yud–vov reysh–gimmel–lamed–aleph–nun.

[Page 165]

I Fought the Germans with the Partisans

Lucia Rubin (of the Mendel Preski family)

Translation by Meir Bulman

When the Germans occupied, I was living with my parents at the Stashiles Station. It was a train station on the Baranovich–Lida–Vilne route, and all the Divenishok folks would travel to Vilne on that train, usually passing through Stashiles. A few Jewish families resided at the station: my parents' family who moved there from Vilne, and the family of Yonah and Alteh Tener, Binyamin Dubinski's uncle and our cousins.

We felt the horrors of war on our skin already by the second day when the Germans bombed the station. The atmosphere became very tense and the Gentiles began displaying signs of anti–Semitism. We felt bad days lay ahead and awaited the coming days in fear.

A week after the invasion, the Germans brought four Jews from Vilne to repair the bombed station. The Germans tormented them and paid them nothing nor gave them food.

My parents were, naturally, merciful; our home was open to anyone in need. They immediately went to task and provided soup to these suffering Jews. My husband the doctor and I peeled potatoes to feed the Jews.

After a few months, friends notified us that the Germans intended to jail us. We escaped to Soletchnik and from there to our cousin Shmuel Dubinski in Benakani. After a while we found ourselves in the Voronova Ghetto. We were miraculously saved from the fate of the rest of the Jews of Vilne who were concentrated at the city movie theater in Voronova and executed.

Those days are etched deep in my mind since an interesting event which must be mentioned took place. One of the prisoners in the theater sent my father a small bag containing valuable objects, money and diamonds, along with a message my father saying he [the sender] was lost anyway, and maybe my father could save our family with the money. That is evidence of the loving feelings that everyone had towards my father due to the many good deeds he had done for people during his life.

At the Voronova Ghetto

We lived in Voronova until the ghetto was disbanded. On that fateful, bitter day, we were led to the marketplace. I held my parents' hands, my husband walked beside me, while my sister Khayeh and her husband Avrashe Ashpon followed behind. The Germans asked my husband his profession. When they heard he was a doctor they sent us to the right. My sister Khayeh and her husband were sent to the left. I attempted to join my sister on the left side, but a German caught me, picked me up and tossed me to the right and shouted, "Jude, rechts zu lebendig!" (Jew, to the right means to stay alive!) Shots and the screams of the murdered echoed out from the distance, but I witnessed a horror which I will never forget: one of the rich men of Benakani, Avrashe the Miller, hid with his family and the Germans found him and brought them towards us. All the way they assaulted them, the blood trickled and Avrashe walked hunched. He did not scream, just placed his head in his hands and sighed bitterly. When they reached us, the Germans shot them before our eyes; they squirmed in pain and breathed their last.

After a few weeks, the remaining Jews from the Voronova Ghetto were led to the Bastuni train station, to be transferred to Lida. I was in the seventh month of my pregnancy and do not know from where I drew the energy and drive to help the Jews who had tripped on the road. I helped one carry his bag; another leaned on me so as not to fall. The whole way I encouraged the weak and depressed who wanted to die.

At the Lida Ghetto

At the Lida Ghetto, we were housed in homes from which the town Jews had been recently expelled and then executed. Overcrowding was awful. Eight people were stuffed into one room and the fear of death was instilled in the Jews. We had ample food. My father's farmer friends anonymously sent us various food items. Periodically, my sister [and I] would dress like a Gentile[s], leave the ghetto, and bring back necessary items. The Germans stopped other young women, recognizing them by the fear in their eyes. I attempted to remain calm. They never recognized fear in my eyes and I was never stopped.

In Lida we met our uncle Shmuel Dubinski and my cousins Yonah and Alteh Tener. They helped us to the best of their abilities, and we tried staying as close to one another as possible. After a few months rumors spread that the ghetto was to be dismantled. My husband and I decided to escape the ghetto and not go through that nightmare once more.

My parents decided to stay, but my husband and I joined a group, and on a dark night escaped the ghetto through the swamps. I was so afraid that I lost a shoe in the swamps. The next day the shoe as brought to my mother who was sure the Germans killed me. After a few days of troubles we reached the partisans in the "Nazi Forests" area. The commander accepted us willingly since he needed a doctor.

In the Woods with Partisans

Life in the woods was difficult: the Germans periodically tried to surround us. One night I felt the Germans were approaching. I remained calm, and before I left the spot I dumped sand on the fire so the Germans could not track us. That action saved the partisan *otriad*[1] from being surrounded. Had a Russian done that in my place, he would have received high praise, but thanking me at the general meeting was adequate in their eyes.

After a while, we were sent to Lipnishok Pustshe, accompanied by several Russians. On the road we observed that one of them was drunk and did not stop cursing Jews and spouting profane anti-Semitic expressions. We extricated ourselves from him with difficulty and reached our destination. I write this to demonstrate how much our lives were in danger— even by the Russian partisans.

Once, by chance, I learned of the location of our cousins – the Dubinski family. I arrived and found their mother Feigeh, Michael who was a patrolman at headquarters, and their little brother Yisroel. After a while, I learned that their mother was killed in a German attack and little Yisroel remained alone after his brother was sent on a distant mission. I got a coach from a peasant, loaded it with food items and brought them to Yisroel. The commander found out about that, and when I returned I was bound to a pine tree, and was to be shot. I was released only thanks to my husband's efforts.

After the situation at the front began to deteriorate for the Germans, a few hundred *Wolasovitz* troops joined our side. The commander sent them on daring missions such as blowing up bridges and the like. I joined them as a combat paramedic and participated in all missions. I fulfilled my duties very successfully and did not trail the soldiers in physical strength and bravery. They regarded me very positively and shielded me from harm.

In our camp there was a Jewish cobbler, a remarkably quick young man. In contrast, his wife was a big *schlemiel*. To my surprise, during the siege her husband fell and she remained alive. She had not left me since. She would claim, "If I will be near Lucy I might stay alive."

Once during a chase, we had to cross a deep stream. We began to swim and she held on to me and would not let go. Both of us were about to drown. A few soldiers came to our aid, but she did not let go of me. "Save the woman," I yelled at them, "I will rescue myself somehow." And thus we both survived. People always saw in me a saving light and would stick to me in times of trouble.

My fierce hatred for the Germans demanded revenge, and on one occasion my desire for vengeance was fulfilled. During a chase, we traveled through the woods, worn–out and tired. Suddenly we observed a bunker in the distance. We approached it silently and heard German speech. A quick partisan, Yitzhak Menski from Lida, snuck up to the bunker and threw grenades as we shot into the bunker. After we stormed the bunker we found seven bodies of S.S. men and found the clothes we so desperately needed.

On one of the missions a Russians general and paratrooper from Moscow was wounded. His life was in danger. My husband and I dragged him out of the line of fire and dressed his wounds, but since the Germans were attacking we had to retreat and we left him in place. After a while we learned the Germans had located him and he had blown himself up to not be taken alive by the Germans. A monument was erected in Slonim in his honor.

After Liberation

After liberation we returned to Stashiles to mourn our tragedy. There I learned that my brother Mulke (Shmuel) had snuck out of the Vilne ghetto to the Aryan side and was in contact with family members. A peasant named Rodzivits who lived in Stashiles and was a good friend of my father, accepted our belongings from my father for safekeeping until things were calmed. So as to steal our belongings, he informed the Gestapo of my brother, who was then captured and executed, and the peasant took all our belongings.

When I visited him [Rodzivits], I recognized our furniture and drapes. I was enraged and wanted to beat him and finish him off, but people stopped me. I sued the peasant, but did not want to wait for the verdict and decided to leave the defiled land which was soaked with ample Jewish blood. After a while I learned that the peasant was cleared of any wrongdoing and continued to enjoy the Jewish theft in broad daylight.

After many efforts we managed to leave Russia and reach Poland and then Germany. We did not want to stay in Germany for too long, and with the help of smugglers we reached Italy after many difficulties. In Rome my husband served as chair of the Vilne Jewish Organization and was busy with philanthropy for the refugees who were flooding in.

After a long stay in Rome we traveled to the United States. My husband worked as a doctor and I assisted him; our financial status was quite stable. There we had two sons: the eldest Alexander and the second Robert (Yerakhmiel).

Throughout our stay in the United States our hearts were lovingly bound to Israel and we would periodically visit the country to enjoy its beauty.

*

On the eve of Israel Independence Day in 1973 we arrived in Israel to celebrate, bask in the spirit of the holiday, and enjoy the impressive IDF parade. Unfortunately my husband Oscar suffered a heart attack and his heart stopped forever. He passed at the Sheraton Hotel in Tel Aviv.

My husband, Oscar, was a son of a respected Warsaw family. He completed medical school in Warsaw and at the time of Nazi occupation wound up in Vilne, where we met and our fates intertwined. He was a loyal husband and was devoted to his wife and children. In New York he helped many Jews and Gentiles who needed medical attention at his clinic.

He was not fortunate to witness the impressive IDF parade, but he was very fortunate to be buried in the soil of our land. He was honorably buried in Kirayt Shaul. May he rest eternally and the clouds of our land please him forever.

Editor's Footnote

1. A partisan detachment

[Page 169]

In Battle Against the Nazi Enemy

Zelig Rogol

Translation by Meir Bulman

After the Russians entered in 1939 the situation in town completely changed. The main sources of income were destroyed and disappeared. The shops were closed because the sources of supply disappeared. The Jews hid their remaining merchandise with the Gentiles and for a while sustained themselves from that. Cultural life in town completely ceased. The youth movements such as *Beitar*, *HeKhaluts*, and *HaShomer HaTzair* ceased operating.

The Hebrew school became a Yiddish school. Yekusiel Zhizhemsky was appointed principal and Yosef Levine became a teacher at the school. All Jewish institutions were destroyed and disappeared. Not a trace remained of the bank and the *Gemilut Hessed*.[1]

Before 1939 I had completed a bookkeeping course in Vilne, and during the time of Russian control I worked as an accountant in the hospital that opened in the priest's mansion. The church was active, but the priest was given more modest housing. The synagogues also still existed, but Rabbi Aharon Tayts had to escape to Vilne.

Eli Sutskever was appointed post office administrator, Zusman (Munye the tailor's son-in-law) was appointed a household manager at the hospital. Hirsh Krizovski was appointed mayor (Sel Soviet). When Vilne was transferred to Lithuania, some town residents escaped there. Some of them, among them Zalman Leyb Shchneider (Kalmen the Crippled's son), were captured at the border and exiled to Siberia. Zalman Leyb was saved and now resides in America. Our pharmacy was nationalized and my brother-in-law Herman Fuchs became an employee.

The Russians Leave and the Germans Enter

With the entrance of the Germans, Zusman pleaded with me that we escape eastward. I refused because my conscience would not let me abandon my ill father, who was bedridden for a few years then. The district government was in Oshmene, as it had been under the Poles. An anti-Semitic teacher was appointed the head of the local council. A directive was issued to choose *Yudenrat*[2] officers. It should be noted that the men of the *Yudenrat* tried to the best of their abilities to ease the peoples' suffering.

An order was issued that every Jew must wear a yellow patch with the Star of David. The council demanded the *Yudenrat* supply them with Jews for labor, unpaid of course. The *Yudenrat* would select people after considering age, family status, and profession. A Jewish police force was also established, whose role it was to maintain order.

I remember an incident which left a horrifying mark on the town. One day, a German officer appeared and gathered about 30 young Jews (I among them) in front of the church and commanded us to perform different tasks: get up, run, kiss the dirt, lay on our backs, and more. We thought he wanted to shoot us. It was the priest who probably came out and begged him for mercy and then the German left us.

After that, we were recruited to work at the sawmill in Giluzh. We worked there for a few months. Sometimes we would enter Tsvi Usishkin's house (Khanah from Giluzh's father) and we would receive some food. A large group of Divenishok folks worked in Giluzh: Yekusiel Zhizhmski, Khaykl Katzev, Meir and Tsvi Dubinski, and others. We tried to stay in one group.

In the fall of 1941 word reached us that several communities near Divenishok were destroyed: Radin, Eshishuk, Olkenik and other towns that were under Lithuanian jurisdiction. In January of 1942 we were commanded to leave behind our belongings and relocate to Voronova. We hired coaches, packed them with our bundles, and traveled to Voronova. There was much despair. The Germans were at the height of their success, close to Moscow and Leningrad, and no hope of rescue was on the horizon.

Conditions were very crowded. We were put in a house with Eliohu Blyakher's mother. The mother lived in that house with us, five people: my sister Mineh, my brother Eliohu, and I. Ra'aya, Eli Sutskever's sister, also joined us. She had escaped with the Russians and reached Smolensk. When the Germans reached there, she returned to Divenishok. Since she had no place to stay, and my sister Mineh was her close friend, she stayed with us.

The Germans operated in Voronova as they did in Divenishok. The physically able were sent to various compulsory labors. For the entire winter of 1942 I worked in Nibosha Village, approximately 9 kilometers from Divenishok. We uprooted trees, sawed and organized them in cubic meters – they were designated for heating. Four of us friends stayed in one peasant's house, with Meir Dubinski. When we finished work we would help the peasant and he would give us some food. Of course, we were always hungry.

Escape from Voronova

The situation continued like that until May. On May 9, heavy forces surrounded the Ghetto, no one could come or go. Rumors reached us about the elimination of all Jews in the Lida district. People were afraid and depressed because they felt something terrible was about to happen.

Eliohu Blyakher's brothers–in–law, who were merchants and were quite familiar with the area, organized a group to escape the ghetto. I gave a hand and joined the group. We bribed the guards and at night a group of 50 people left the ghetto. It was a dark night. We left at 11 and reached a forest approximately 10km from Voronova; we waited for news from the town.

After a few days we sent some people to find out what happened in Voronova. They returned and told us of the tragedy. My father was killed in bed, my sister Mineh, my brother Eliohu, and Sutszkever's sister Ra'aya were executed. My sister Shulamit and her husband Herman and their daughter Lilly, and my aunt Tsippeh Leah and her husband Yeshayahu Kaplan, and my friend Yitzhach Segal remained alive.

The few Jews who survived were concentrated on one street. After assessing, we reached the conclusion that given the situation there was no other option but to return to Voronova, and so we did. At night we snuck back in and joined the remaining Jews. One day, when we went out to work under police supervision, we passed by the house we lived in. I asked the policeman if I could enter the house, and I witnessed a horrifying scene: the floor was littered with ripped photographs and congealed marks of my father's blood on the walls and floor told of his persistent struggle for life in his final moments. I stood there and wept bitterly until the policeman's call woke me from my thoughts.

One day we were commanded to take our bundles and go to the Bastuni Station; from there we traveled to Lida.

In the Lida Ghetto

Life in the Lida ghetto followed the known pattern in ghettos; *Yudenrat*, Jewish police, compulsory labor. For a short while I worked at the sawmill and was then transferred to work at the German gendarmerie in Lida. I was put in charge of a few homes and my role was to heat the rooms. I would bring firewood and heat the rooms. SS men, who often went on missions, lived there. I saw them returning saddened from a mission: turned out one of their men had fallen in action.

My situation was relatively better than the rest of my family members in the Lida ghetto because I would eat the leftovers in the kitchen and did not have to work hard outdoors. I worked there for five months before a directive was given by the district commissioner forbidding Jews from working in such roles. All Jews were sent away from there, myself among them.

Under Partisan Control

I felt that the belt was tightening and a way must be found to escape the ghetto. Coincidentally, Yitzach Segal and I found $250 in an old mattress and, with the assistance of a man named Koppel from Ivia, we purchased a Belgian gun from a gentile, preparing our escape from the ghetto.

As luck would have it, Partisans from Bilitza came to the ghetto to pick up their relatives: I, Yitzchak Segal, and Shulamit joined them. We walked restlessly all night until we reached Neman, 35km from Lida. We crossed the Neman by boat and felt relieved because that territory was under Partisan control. A short distance away we found some families that had escaped Lida.

A young man from Warsaw named Max joined us, and together we put up a tent. Yitzach Segal, Max, and I would go out at night, knock on peasants' doors and ask for food. The peasants did not refuse. After staying there for three months, we decided for security reasons to join the Partisans. With the help of a young man from Zhtel we managed to exchange the Belgian handgun for a rifle. We assembled a second gun from parts we had purchased, and due to them, we were accepted into *Orlanski Otriad*.[3] We were accepted as fighters, and Shulamit as a pharmacist at the field hospital. The middleman presented us to the commander Pantzenko and he accepted us.

Our platoon was made up entirely of Jews. The platoon included experienced scouts who were well acquainted with the area so we were assigned household tasks, meaning we had to supply the Partisans with meat and other food items. We performed those tasks successfully and were greatly esteemed by the commander. When the situation at the front worsened for the Germans, the Ukrainians joined our battalion. A platoon was established composed entirely of Ukrainians. They were clear anti–Semites. Especially committed to anti–Semitism was the platoon commander Shekhne. He influenced headquarters to confiscate weapons from the Jews and hand them over to Gentiles. One day our weapons were confiscated and they wanted to expel us from the battalion. Coincidentally, a special Russian para–trooping unit was in the area, and their commander was a Jew named Davidov. We contacted him and told him about the anti–Semitic incident and he forced them to return our weapons.

A command was then issued to expand Partisan action in the Grodne forests and I was sent there and placed in one of the platoons. There, I participated in combat operations; blowing up bridges and rail tracks, disconnecting telephone lines, and doing food supply missions. One such food supply mission nearly cost me my life. It was when we were returning to base with a wagon filled with food items. We reached the bridge where an ambush of 80 police officers waited for us and began raining hellfire upon us. We abandoned the wagon and barely managed to escape to the woods through the marshlands.

Anti–Semitism Runs Wild

Anti–Semitism did not skip the Jews in the Grodne forests either. I remember a horrific incident when a Jew fell asleep while on guard duty. The next day he was brought in front of the formation where his death sentence was read to him. The man stood there pale as a ghost and tears streamed down his face. He pleaded to allow him a defense so he could explain the incident. His pleading was useless. The formation was ordered to not disperse until the verdict was carried out. Two Russians led the man about 50 meters from the spot and a shot rang through the air. I was deeply saddened as there were countless incidents of Russians sleeping on guard duty, yet they were not executed.

That horrific image stands before me as if happening now. The Jewish man led away, he looks at the Jews, his eyes pleading, "Save me! I am innocent! I fulfilled all my duties with devotion and sacrifice! Why do I deserve such punishment?"

Fate was very cruel to us Jews. We wanted to help him, but we could not. Our hearts secretly wept.

I left my dear and devoted friend Yitzach Segal with my sister Shulamit in the Lipiczanska woods and was not aware of their fate until after Liberation. My sister Shulamit survived and currently resides in Israel. I learned that Yitzchak Segal lost his weapon on a mission against the White Poles. He retreated through the Neman and lost his gun while doing so. As punishment he was expelled from the battalion and his whereabouts since are unknown.

Liberation

I remained in the Grodne Woods until Liberation. I actively participated in the attrition of German forces retreating from the frontlines and I did my best do unto them as they did to us.

After Liberation I was enlisted in the Red Army and was sent to the frontline where I was wounded and then taken to a hospital in Kovne. After I recovered I was placed in paramedic school. After the war ended I enlisted in the standing army for three years. I was discharged in 1959 and made *Aliya*.

In Israel, I was blessed to build a home with my wife Masha and we have two children. The eldest Aryeh and a daughter named Sarah, who are continuing their parents' heritage.

Visit in Divenishok

I visited my birth town of Divenishok twice. Once in 1948, with Pinyeh (Pinkhas) Lipkunski, and again in 1957 in a Red Army uniform. The town left a horrifying impression on me: most of the buildings were burned, only remnants of ruined walls remained, testifying to the great tragedy that had befallen our town. I sat among the remnants of our ruined pharmacy and sank into melancholy thoughts. "Where is my dear family? Where are the lively Jewish youths? Where are my friends from *HaShomer HaTzair* with whom I spent most of my beautiful years? Where are they?"

A deathly silence surrounded me. My hot tears covered the bricks, crying out from the wall. With deep pain and hateful rage I left my birthplace and homeland.

Editor's Footnotes

1. Institution providing interest–free loans

2. Yudenrats were Nazi–mandated town Councils composed of Jewish elders and responsible for carrying out Nazi orders upon the Jewish population.

3. The Orlanski brigade of Partisans

[Page 175]

A Partisan's Story

Eliahu Blyakher
Translation by Meir Bulman

The war between Germany and Russia began on June 22, 1941, and the next day the Germans were already in Divenishok. It was late afternoon, and my father was praying at the old synagogue whose windows faced the main road, Vilne St., where the German forces were making their way east.

The Germans, noticing the movement of bearded Jews in the synagogue, stormed the building, took out the Torah scrolls from the ark, and spread them along the street. Then the German tanks drove over them as riled up crowds cheered loudly.

My father, risking his life, begged the Germans to return the scrolls. A German pointed his pistol at him. Father was saved from certain death thanks to Vazek the lame peasant who happened to be at the synagogue. Father used his remaining strength to return home. Henceforth, fear increased in the town, and my father prayed at home. Secret group prayers took place in our home on holidays.

Mourning the Falling of My Eldest Brother Gershon

In addition to the sadness which befell the town, news reached us that my eldest brother Gershon, who had enlisted in the Polish military, fell while defending Warsaw along with Yeshayahu Moshe Katz and others. My father cried in private; at night a soft weeping emerged from his room. It was my father's sighing voice reciting *Tikkun Chatzot*[1] in memory of my brother who fell in battle fighting the Nazis. His voice echoed in the distance, merging with the loud wind blowing atop the oak trees across the church.

Fear and Depression

Because of its distance from the train station, the Germans postponed dealing with our town. Despite that, the Germans often appeared in town, demanding bribes. The *Yudenrat*[2] raised the funds necessary to compensate them. One day, a German group appeared in town seeking entertainment. They gathered the town's youth in the marketplace square, facing the church, and forced them to perform exercise tasks. They then forced them to run around the marketplace, followed by more tasks. After a few hours of torture, one German made a wild anti–Semitic speech, and the Germans got excited.

Thanks to the priest who came out and pleaded for us, sacrifices were then avoided.

To make life unbearable, Jews were forbidden from the first days to draw water from the pump at the center of the market. Once, my sister Leah snuck out to the pump and filled a bucket. A few hooligans attacked her and took the bucket. I went to the police station across the street to complain and was jailed. My father managed to rescue me after much effort, and some bribes to a few officers.

The First Victims

A few days after the Germans entered, the police publicly executed two Russian NKVD officers who had remained trapped in town. The next night the Germans killed Dovid Shklar (Dovid der Zekl[3]), while he attempted to reach his brother-in-law Delatishki's house via a shortcut. Fear in town doubled when we learned that the infamous robber Kasiuk Skyviss was appointed as chief of police. Our fears were confirmed when he assembled a gang of young Poles to torture us. Every evening they raided the homes of rich Jews and stole whatever they could lay their hands on. They mainly targeted the homes of merchants who had food stock. I remember once, Sarah Leah, Binyamin Mikelson's daughter, ran outside and cried, "Help! We are being robbed!" but all feared to come to her aid.

On one market day Thursday, Itshe Binyamin's[Ed. Note: Yitzach Binyamin Rudnik] house was raided, a young woman from Vilne who lived with them was killed, and her baby's head was hurled at the wall until his brains were splattered. Gedalye,[Ed. Note: Katz], Itshe Benyamin's son-in-law, tried to defend the woman but was killed in the same room. We were especially shocked at the sight of Russian prisoners who would pass near our house towards Dubizishok St. in route to the *moggilnik* (Christian cemetery) where they would be unloaded from the trucks and executed with a shot to the neck.

If the Germans do that to prisoners of war, to whom the Geneva Convention applies, what fate could we expect?

In January 1942 an order was given by the Gvits-Commissar to dismantle the Jewish settlement in Divenishok and to transfer Jews to nearby Voronova.

It was a rough snow-filled winter. We loaded families onto sleds. Each one packed a few belongings and we moved to Voronova. The Germans' intentions were clear: to concentrate the remaining Jews from the small towns into one place and then later finish them off at one fell swoop.

The ghetto horrified me. Overcrowding was unbearable. The Germans crammed 6–8 families in each house and there was barely enough space for each person to rest his head.

Life proceeded according to the well-known ghetto pattern: yellow patch, forced labor, intimidation, torment, and execution of Jews with great cruelty. All was done, of course, to inspire fear in Jews and humiliate them.

Dismantling of the Voronova Ghetto

On Saturday, May 8, 1942, we felt that something was about to happen, something irritating and suffocating. Concerned and afraid, people looked through cracks in the windows

We were jailed. Polish police officers and SS men surrounded the ghetto, no one was permitted to leave or enter. Fear gripped us. We felt like the end was near. Each person expressed his fear in a unique way: one bit his fingernails, another privately wiped tears from eyes expressing fear and horror. The hours dragged on endlessly.

After many hours of terror, the curfew was lifted, but the guarding around the ghetto continues. The general feeling was that 'the end is near'. Many attempted to escape at night, others attempt to bribe policemen to allow them to escape the ghetto. Many succeeded, yet others were captured and killed.

On 1/5/42[4] the sun's rays shone on the golden grain fields, and the fields are filled with light. It was a very lively sight, but for the Jews of Voronova it was a fateful and bitter day.

The ghetto saw an increased presence of SS officers and Polish police. Guarding around the ghetto tightened. Gentiles from local villages swarmed into town, armed with rakes, hoes, pitchforks, and metal rods. They boisterously marched through town.

The Germans, and their Lithuanian and Polish collaborators, went door to door, taking Jews of every age and dealing them blows before bringing them to the market square. Those who tried to evade were killed by axes and steel rods.

The marketplace is crowded with fearful Jews, kneeling, as the fear of death reflects in their eyes. The wild mob goes to each house, helping the Germans assault every Jew who falls into their hands, breaking into houses, plundering, destroying, and shattering everything they could put their hands on.

A German officer, Windisch, appears and gives a venomous speech: "The Jewish Nation is the biggest enemy of the German People and of all humanity, so a death sentence is given to them".

The Jews are chased from the marketplace to the intersections of Lida Street, Train Station Street, and Hermanishok Street. The German officers stand at the intersection, among them Windisch, Gvits–Comissar Warner and his deputy Hinds and begin dividing Jews into groups to life or death.

Those who will remain alive are directed to the right side to Train Station Street. A few important people were sent to the left as hostages. If something were to happen to the Germans, they would be immediately executed. Those who were directed straight to Lida Street were immediately abandoned; the mob of predators stood on both sides of the road and assaulted these Jews with whatever came to hand; axes, shovels, whips. The beards of the town's notables were plucked, and they were taunted before reaching the mass grave.

The Jews were brought in groups to the grave, ordered to disrobe, and to enter the graves. They were shot in the neck, placed in layers, and doused with chlorine and lime for disinfection. Among those buried were also people still alive who then suffocated. In that cruel manner, Jews of Voronova, Divenishok, Kalelishok, Soletchnik, Stashiles, Yashuny and Benakani were exterminated. At least 5000 Jews were executed that day.

My father's family hid in a bunker and was saved. My wife, mother in–law, and I were brought to the marketplace. My mother–in–law was sent forward to her death. Being a professional, I was sent to the right with my wife and two children.

The sounds of gunshots and the cries reaching the heavens still echoed when a German officer appeared before us and said: "Know that you remain alive as a privilege and not by right, so you must pay the price." As he spoke he spread a blanket and commanded that all valuables be placed on it. "Whoever hides silver or gold will be executed." The blanket was filled and taken by the Germans.

After the speech, all surviving Jews were registered. Horrific events took place during the registration. People wept like children, cried, and wailed. Many fainted. Some had been orphaned, others had lost children, some were now widowed.

The most horrific thing I witnessed was the sight of wagons filled with the clothes of the murder victims. People recognized their beloved's bloody clothes. Mental collapses were common; many people were terror stricken.

After the registration we were not allowed to return to our houses, which had been destroyed by the peasants. We were held on Lida Street, 8–10 families in one house. Mourning and bereaved we went back to forced labor until an order was received to transfer us to the Lida Ghetto. Those remaining took their few belongings with a heavy heart and deadly silent, and the caravan made its way to the Bastuni train station.

In the Lida Ghetto

After the dismantling of the Voronova ghetto we recived an order to walk to Bastuni and to take the train to Lida from there. We shouldered our belongings and accompanied by police walked to Bastuni. On the way we passed a mass grave. It was [approx.] 12 meters in length, 6 meters wide and 4 meters deep. The area was littered with papers, documents, and photos. Four pillars on which the Germans had smashed babies' skulls still stood next to the grave.

Schnapps and vodka bottles from which the executioners had drunk still rolled nearby. The grave seemed to be rising due to people still breathing. My heart wept at the enormity of the tragedy which had befallen our nation, but tears must not be shown to the Germans.

The Lida Ghetto has left a depressing impression. A constantly guarded 2-meter tall fence surrounded it. Every morning, the *Yudenrat* assembled a labor roster and I worked on various tasks. We suffered poverty and hunger, and my daughter died in the ghetto. I felt suffocated and decided to leave the ghetto come what may. Rumors of partisans reached us and I planned to join them. For that purpose I purchased a gun and waited for the first chance to leave the ghetto.

To the Bielski Otriad

After a few months of waiting, a partisan going by the name of Leybke Kadap arrived at the ghetto to take people to the Bielski Otriad. My brother-in-law Leybke and I joined him. We traveled on winding paths through the woods all night until we reached the partisans' area. We then continued to where Bielski was stationed. Bielski, who was a close acquaintance of ours, greeted me with open arms.

After remaining there for 7 days I received permission to return to the ghetto and bring my family. I received a gun, and with another friend, we made our way towards the Lida ghetto. 12km away from Lida I hired a trustworthy coachman, traveled to the ghetto, and told him to wait while I took out my wife and children. At 12 am I crawled under the wires and entered the ghetto. In the morning, with the help of the chief of Jewish police, Stolitski, I stood in line with my wife as if going to work and then left the ghetto. The coachman gave my wife peasants' clothes and handed her a sickle and they traveled to his house. At night I gathered 12 people and once more, aided by Stolitski, I left the Lida Ghetto at 1 AM and made my way to Bielski.

On a Mission to Rescue Jews

A week following my first mission, Bielski sent me again to rescue Jews from the Lida Ghetto, as well as restock on medication. I crawled under the barbed wire again and entered the ghetto. In the ghetto I had already become known as a partisan successfully transferring Jews to the Bielski Otriad. Within a short while I concentrated 46 people with weapons and some medication, and with the aid of commander Stolitski, I managed to sneak out of the ghetto and safely make it to the woods.

After a 10-day resting period, Bielski asked that I bring more Jews and medicine. I went alone this time and breached the ghetto at night. News of my arrival spread and over a few days I gathered a group of 76 people. On that visit I took with me commander Stolitski's only son as a reward for the great help in tricking the Germans into not noticing what was happening. I promised him that when the time came I would rescue him and his wife from the ghetto.

After the success of that mission I was again requested to return to the ghetto. Indeed, after a 2-week break, I returned and rescued 86 people, among them my sister Sarah Hinde, her husband David Movshovitsh, and their daughter Khenye, as well as my other brother-in-law Meir Olkenitski. That mission was a success too and two days later we were already in a safe place.

Due to my knowledge of the roads and considering my previous success, I was sent back to the ghetto. I must note that on all missions, especially the final ones, the aid of commander Stolitski was crucial. Without his help, I would not have been able to visit the ghetto that often and rescue that many people. In that particular mission, I transferred 33 people from the ghetto, among them Zeydke Lubetski.

My wife's sister was recovering from ear surgery and I left her in the ghetto, as well as my sister Leah, her husband, her three children, and my father who did not want to leave my sister. We agreed I would take them on the next visit. I had not managed to bring these people to Bielski when the big siege in *Naliboki Pushcha*[5] began, and we split up. Each person ran in a different direction. [I, along with] Zeydke Lubetski, Shmulik from Lida, someone from Soletchnik, and a Russian partisan made our way towards Divenishok. We did so for two reasons: first, we wanted to avoid the German chase which was larger than all the preceding manhunts. Second, we wanted to recover from the Gentiles property left with them by Jews.

The Divenishok Area

After we reached an area about 12km from Divenishok we entered a village and obtained a coach from a peasant, and traveled to Yokhenvitsh the Miller. We knew some town Jews had hidden clothes, silver, and gold with him. But most of all we searched for his son-in-law who had collaborated with the Germans and had much Jewish blood on his hands. His son-in-law probably sensed us coming and managed to sneak away from the house, but we found the miller. We intimidated him with our weapons and he placed some gold and silver in a small bag and gave us clothes and food for the road. From there we traveled to another village, where my brother-in-law Shayke [Wiener] had deposited clothes with a peasant, and Meir Rogol had left many fabrics with him. The peasant took the items out from a pit in the barn and returned them to us.

We patrolled the area until we reached a village about 8km from Divenishok, where we went to sleep. When I woke up in the morning I could find neither Zeydke nor the coach. He likely estimated that with the money he could live peacefully in the ghetto so why should he suffer in the woods? But he eventually perished with everyone at the Lida Ghetto. Fortunately, he left me the gun, otherwise my situation would have been very bad.

I returned to the woods to search for the Bielski Otriad. To my great disappointment I could no longer find them at the designated spot. Partisans there made me aware that they had left due to the siege.

Having no other choice I searched for a way to join a different otriad and was accepted to the Alexander Nevsky Otriad. I stayed there for ten days and was sent on a mission to place explosives under train tracks. My left eye area and fingers were injured on that mission. I remained at the camp for a short while I healed. There, I found out were my family was. I did not hesitate and began traveling. After much searching I found my family and the entire Bielski Otriad.

After the chase ended and things had calmed, I sent my brother-in-law to rescue my father, my sister Leah and family, and my sister-in-law and family. He entered the ghetto and decided to bring them all to Bielski the next day. Unfortunately, the ghetto was surrounded by a heavy guard at night no one entered nor left. His sister woke him at 4 am and said, "Yakov, the ghetto is surrounded. Get up and save yourself and your friends." They managed to cross the fence and hid in the foundry until the evening and slipped into the woods.

How I Saved a Jewish Partisan's Life

In recognition of my devotion to the Otriad and the successful completion of all my missions, I was appointed to by Bielski to serve as his adjutant. After that I accompanied Zusye on his journeys and meetings with Russian commanders.

Once, we arrived at the Alexander Nievski Otriad for an important meeting with the commander. I was told that a Jewish man named Tuvye was caught sleeping while on guard duty and might be put to death the next day.

I searched for a way to rescue him. At first I thought to ask the Otriad commander to pardon him but abandoned that thought since I knew he was a Jew–hater. I asked the company where Tuvye was being held and they showed me the bunker. A guard stood outside. I found out the bunker was divided into a few cells, one where the man was being held, and the other in which a cobbler worked. I entered the bunker as if to fix my shoes and approached the man and told him, "Listen, Tuvye, your fate is sealed! If you do not escape you are lost." He asked the guard permission to use the restroom, utilized the dark of night, and escaped to a designated spot where he hid until I came to take him.

I left the bunker and heard gunshots. When I asked, "What happened?" I was told, "Tuvye escaped." A while later, after Bielski and I had returned from the meeting, I came to the designated place and took the young man to our otriad. That is how I saved his life and he is with us today in Israel.

After I arrived in Israel, rumors reached me that there were ungrateful partisans who owed their lives to the Bielski brothers but were spreading fictional stories about Tuvye Bielski's behavior, and were trying to diminish his immense contribution to rescuing Jews.

In those days, when entire Jewish families roamed the woods without weapons or resources, subjected to starvation, robbery and looting, and Russian partisans would steal whatever little food they had and then send them away, Tuvye Bielski and his brothers risked their lives and allowed poor Jews and their wives and children to join them, gave them food and shelter, and were in constant conflict with headquarters which vehemently opposed these family camps. The Russian claims were justified in many aspects; the families were a burden to the Otriad and made it difficult to maneuver and strike the Germans. The family camps were weak spots in the partisan concealment.

Despite everything, the Bielski Otriad was the only one which accepted Jews without differentiation; men, women, children, with or without weapons.

I served for a while as Tuvia Bielski's adjutant and witnessed everything that took place at the Otriad and can definitively state that Bielski saved many Jews from certain death and risked his own life and his friends' lives for the one and only purpose of rescuing Jews from the ghettos.

I personally was sent by Bielski 5 times to the Lida Ghetto to bring Jews to the woods. That operation was very successful and in a short time, I was able to rescue 250 people from the Lida Ghetto.

In the Voronova book, M. Shamir (Shmerkovitsh) tells us that people from Navaredok refused to accept him when he arrived in the woods from Lida and he was accepted thanks only to Bielski.

In his words (page 89): "Fortunately, the Bielski brothers got people under control. The eldest Tuvye surpassed himself and did not cease bringing people in from the ghetto, thinking to rescue as many Jews as possible from imminent destruction. At that point the rescue issue was truly his life's purpose. He paid no mind to anyone, not even his family members. It made a tremendous impression on us."

After the partisan movement expanded and the Russians, with support from Moscow, took control of partisan headquarters, anti–Semitism began running wild in the woods; the Russians would steal weapons from weak Jews and expel them from battalions. Their situation was dire, and their only refuge was with Tuvye Bielski. I personally know of many cases in which Tuvye rescued partisans from the Russian claws.

Tuvye is accused of enacting a rigid discipline and conducting matters harshly. I would like to point out that at that time, when human life was [considered] worthless, Tuvye had to act and rule with an iron fist to take control of the rabble and to enact order and discipline, without which there could have been no sustainability even for the shortest time.

In some cases, Tuvye acted very harshly, but "a person is not held responsible when he is in distress".[6] In such circumstances any undermining of discipline would have caused the entire otriad to crumble and the consequences would have been unfathomable. He faced a choice "to be or not to be," and so he did not act otherwise.

On a Successful Mission

Towards the end of our stay in the woods we suffered greatly at the hands of the White Polish Army. They imposed a siege on us and we could not resupply the otriad. After the situation increased in severity I took on the mission of supplying food to the people.

I selected ten daring men, obtained 6 wagons, and traveled to the Navaredok area, which was distant from our base.

We surprised the peasants because the White Polish controlled the area; we encountered no resistance. We took meat from the peasants, entered a flour mill, and returned to base. Other equestrians and I rode ahead of the envoy.

We reached a village where we encountered a narrow bridge, difficult to cross. Those spots always posed obstacles to us. Our progress became slower and more cautious. I suddenly noticed cigarette smoke and heard them speaking Polish. We opened heavy fire on them and they were taken by surprise and left.

We changed course for security reasons, so we were late and did not return to base at the planned time. We were delayed for a whole day. The people thought we were killed on the road and so they were very happy [to see us]. They greeted us with kisses and dancing. We brought them wagons loaded with goods; bread, lamb, smoked beef, flour, and grains.

Towards the end, as the Germans began retreating, the Russians blocked their path and they had to retreat through the woods. We received an order to put to death any captured Nazi. I captured two Nazi officers and brought them to headquarters. One Nazi which we made stand by a tree understood what was about to take place and said, "I will not live but neither will the Jews." The Jewish partisans attacked him and ripped him to shreds. The second officer met a similar fate.

The Stay in Voronova

After Liberation, I traveled to Voronova and was accepted to be employed at the NKVD, where I tried to locate German collaborators. For whole days I sat with an NKVD commander and provided details on the actions of those people. I could not do much because the Russians feared the local population, which was hostile towards them.

In Voronova we took into our care two small orphaned children, one Yekutiel Boyarski and the other Berl Trivitski. I found them work and so they were exempted from service in the Red Army. Asael Bielski, brother of Zusye, the praised commander who went through all tribulations with us in the woods, found his death in the Red Army while in the Prussian wilderness. Pinkhas Lipkunski, then a young child on his own, stayed with me for a long time.

Chaim Hershovitsh and his young children hid for a long time with a Gentile near Yorzishok. The Gentile relentlessly extorted him and when his money ran out the Gentile handed him and his sons to the White Poles which cruelly tortured and murdered them.

A similar thing happened to Gotke Levine (Itshe from Geranion's son) and his family. He hid in a pit near the village Geranion. A peasant who knew extorted him and when there was no longer money to extort handed them to the White Poles. The Poles came to the field, removed Gotke Levine and his family from the pit and murdered him on the spot.

Moshe Kaganovitsh writes in his book that a senator in the Polish Senate who lived in Geranion led the White Poles and initiated the killing of Jews who hid in Geranion and surrounding area.

Visit in Divenishok

During my stay in Voronova, I traveled with 4 police officers to Divenishok. I found our house intact. Five families lived in it, among them Baoshke the drunk, who was appointed by the Russians chairman of the local council. He treated me courteously and helped gather some belongings we had deposited with the Gentiles. I patrolled my destroyed town, mortified. Every pile of rubble and destroyed building cried to me of the tragedy with a silent sense of loss. My heart was ripped to shreds at the sight of destruction and abandonment. "Master of the Universe!" my heart cried in pain, "please avenge of the blood of thy servants which is shed."[7]

The visit to my town depressed my spirit and I was determined to leave the bloody land, for my future and for my children. I was looking towards *Eretz Israel*.

I arrived in Israel in 1948 at the height of the battles. I soon enlisted in the IDF and participated in many battled across the country until I was injured in the back by shrapnel and was hospitalized at *Tel HaShomer* for about six months.

As I look back at the tumultuous events of my life, my heart is filled with thanks to God whose blessings have allowed me to reach this point and establish a family in Israel.

Translator's & Editor's Footnotes

1. "*Tikkun chatzos* is a midnight ritual which focuses on mourning over the destruction of the Beis Hamikdash and beseeching God to rebuild it speedily", Rabbi Avi Zakutinsky, "Tikkun Chatzos", https://www.ou.org/torah/halacha/practical-halacha/tikkun-chatzos-assorted-halachos/.

2. Jewish Councils mandated by German orders in the occupied communities of Eastern Europe during WWII.

3. The word 'zekl' means 'sack' in Yiddish. The meaning of this nickname is not yet fully understood.

4. The date written in the text does not follow logically from the prior date given of May 8, 1942.

5. Naliboki Forest

6. Tr. Note: Bava Batra 16b

7. Tr. Note: Psalm 79:10

[Page 186]

Under the German Occupation

Sara Hinda Movshovitsh

Translation by Sara Mages

The Germans entered Divenishok on Monday (May 24, 1941) after the outbreak of the war against the Soviet Union. It was quiet on Wednesday. As usual, in the morning of that day my father went to pray in the synagogue. The Germans, who passed convoy after convoy through Wilner Street, saw the Jews praying through the synagogue's windows. They broke into the synagogue, seized the Torah scrolls, spread them across the road, drove their tanks over them and tore them to pieces. My father opposed the removing of the Torah scrolls and the Germans wanted to kill him. Fortunately, Pyotr Shimanski, who lived across from the synagogue, entered the synagogue and asked the Germans to leave him alone. "He is a decent Jew – he said – please leave him alone". Shimanski brought my father home. We were already very anxious for the fate of our father because Meir Zalman came running to us earlier telling us in a tearful voice: "Your father is no longer"...

One of the Germans noticed that the Red Flag was hanging over the school building. Out of panic, Yekutiel Zhizhemski, who was the school principle, forgot to remove the flag from the flagpole. The Germans set fire to the school building and with it also two synagogues went up in flames.

The Germans advanced towards Subotnik where heavy fighting took place. Later, convoys of Russian prisoners began to flow toward Dowichitzki Street, and there, in the graveyard they eliminated them.

An Unusual Case

When the Germans entered, all the thugs raised their heads and started to harass the Jews.

From day to day conditions in the streets became more and more dense. At night, shouts were being heard from the homes that the thugs broke into. Truskevitsh, the well known robber, seized two hand grenades and ran to throw them on the Jews, but a Polish policeman prevented him from doing so. The robber harassed Gutka, the daughter of Yankel A. At night he was knocking on the door and making scandals. She was forced to flee from Divenishok.

A gang of robbers joined together under the leadership of Truskevitsh, Myopglen and Wazyock. Night after night they broke into the shops and robbed the merchandise. This gang also killed Gedalia the blacksmith (Itza Binyamin's son-in-law), and a woman and a boy from Vilna who were hiding in his house. At nightfall the whole town was immersed in the fear of death.

The praise of Zalman-Leyb Lieb, leader of Divenishok's Judenrat, should be noted. He has done a lot to ease the life of the town's Jews. He knew good German and used his personal charm to influence the Regional Commander. He used his influence and asked for help against the atrocities committed by the gang members. One day, a group of Germans arrived to town, brought the gang leaders to the market – and shot them. This was an exceptional case: Germans shooting gentiles because they robbed Jews.

Once, next to the police station, Zalman-Leib noticed that three refugees from Vilna were being loaded on a truck accompanied by beatings. They were two Yeshiva students and a teacher from Ivia who were hiding in town. Zalman-Leib knew well what was waiting for these Jews. He approached the German commander and promised him a pair of boots if he would release the Jews – they were released.

We suffered in particular from a German communication unit that was stationed in the village of Vasilishok on Dubizishok Street. Every Friday they were given a leave and came to Divenishok to have fun. To humiliate the Jews they collected the young people in the market, ran them through different exercises, threatened them with their firearms, and didn't spare punches. The Judenrat was forced to answer to their demands and give them ransom money.

Despite the difficult life, the town's people were united and mutual aid was their main concern. My husband David and my brother Eliahu carried rye on their backs to the flour mill, a distance of 2 kilometers, to grind flour for the poor. My sister Leah baked bread and distributed it to the poor

In Friendship and Brotherhood

In Voronova we lived with the town's cantor. There were 3 rooms in his apartment.

The cantor and his family lived in one room, we lived in the second and another family in the third – all together 19 people. The men were taken to force labor without pay, all of us lived from the sale of the clothes that we brought with us and waited for the future with anxiety.

Somehow the winter passed - we lived in friendship and brotherhood and shared everything that we had.

On May 9, the ghetto was surrounded by German and Polish heavy guards. The local farmers gathered with their axes and pitchforks and closed the city. The cantor prepared a shelter in his home, and on the day of the killing 58 people crammed inside. Among them were his mother and his sister. Shmuel Sharon, his father, was hiding in another bunker.

Doctor Gordon, who arrived to Voronova together with the people from Divenishok, also lived with us. He had a permit to walk freely even during the liquidation of the ghetto. He informed us of what was happening outside. After noon he knocked on the wall and said: "get out slowly, the Germans registered the names of those who remained and I registered yours". After we came out a policeman harassed my father, who was wrapped in his Tallith and Tefillin, and wanted to arrest him. My brother Eliahu bribed the policeman and saved my father.

My Brother Joins the Partisans

After a two week stay in Voronova we were transferred by train to Lida. Here they housed us in a barn on Klodna Street together with other families. I slept next to the family of Yona Tener, Binyamin Dubinski's uncle, from Stashiles. They ere rich and helped many. His wife Alta approached me and said: "Sara Hinda, maybe you need something? Maybe money? Take, don't be shy!" she helped me and also others in need. There was also a family from Traby with us, a husband, wife and daughter, she also helped them and kept them alive. She also helped Lizrka Avraham Meirs and his family. She was a dear soul, a real "angel from heaven".

We stayed in Lida's Ghetto for 13 months, and there history repeated itself: work quotas, threats and new decrees to humiliate and oppress the Jews. Meanwhile, my brother Eliahu left for Bielski's Otriad [partisan detachment] and returned every once in a while to take Jews out of the ghetto. I seriously debated what to do because I didn't want to leave my sister Leah and my old father in the ghetto.

In the Bielski Partisan Detachment

My brother visited Lida's Ghetto three times and for various reasons we were not able to leave with him. But, on the fourth time he took us out of there. My brother was already known in the ghetto as a trustworthy man who was familiar with all the winding paths that led to the partisans. And indeed, on the same operation my brother was able to take 86 people from the ghetto. Bielski received us well and also cared for the elderly and the children. Those who were capable of carrying weapons joined the fighters, and the rest stayed in the family camp. We lived in huts and everyone tried to help with the household chores.

It was early August 1943. The German Army and the Belarusian police started the most extensive hunt for the partisans. According to various estimates their number reached forty thousand. The Germans removed large forces from the front and directed them to the fight against the partisans. The Germans wanted to secure the Wehrmacht's withdrawal routes, and decided to eliminate the partisan at all costs. This roundup was the largest throughout the German occupation. Besides Naliboki forest they also surrounded Lipiczanska and Novogrudok forests.

The whole camp was placed on alert. Dziencielski was ordered to take the responsibly for the families, and retreat with them inside the forest. The gunfire got closer and indicated that the enemy was attacking from the rear. Seven hundred people were running in the woods – women, men, fighters and people without weapons. We sought refuge and retreat, but the enemy blocked all the roads.

An order arrived from the brigade's headquarters to retreat in the direction of the dense forests of Naliboki Pushcha [primeval forest]. The Pushcha was a continuous virgin forest hardly ever trampled by human feet and with large swamps. There were dry islands between the swamps, like "Krasnaya Gorka", but it was only possible to reach them during the winter. We set off and walked in a single file. First in line were those who carried the children because the swamps deepened as we progressed. The Germans rained machine-gun fire and mortar and their voices echoed in the woods. People moved forward through the swamps, in the meadows, and between tall grass that hid the movement – they were tired, hungry, barefoot, exhausted and thirsty. At rest time people tied themselves to a tree with a rope or a strap and dozed a little.

After ten days of wandering we finally arrived to a dry hill in the Krasnaya Gorka area.

Food ran out quickly but the Germans encircled us from all sides and the access to villages was blocked. Due to the hunger many started to show signs of bloating.

The shooting stopped several days later, and people started to return to the old camp. The road was very difficult. Most of the people were infected with ulcers and sores from eating grass, and barely dragged their feet. The women were on the verge of despair and collapse, but the will to live was so strong that we overcame all these hardships. The condition of Bella, my brother Eliahu's wife, was the most difficult. She was left alone without her husband who went to fulfill an important task: to bring Jews from Lida's Ghetto. She carried her baby in her arms in the boggy swamps and her suffering was unimaginable.

My brother Eliahu came back to us after the siege ended. We were together until we were liberated.

After the Liberation

After the liberation I lived in Ivia. On a Thursday, Divenishok's market day, I traveled to Divenishok with a farmer (the Tatars who lived in the area sold seeds). I arrived to the market, sat by the pump, and cried for my bitter fate. My heart shuddered when I saw a lot of people walking peacefully in the market. Farmers from the nearby villages were engaged in trade, and gentiles replaced the Jews in the stores. The world functioned as usual, as if the Jews had never existed there.

Most of the town was burnt. When I went to investigate how it happened, this was explained it to me: There was a large concentration of heavily armed White Poles in the vicinity of Divenishok. Their leader was Jacek, the cobbler from Subotniki Street. When the Germans retreated a battle developed between the retreating Germans and the Poles. There were many casualties in this battle. The Poles buried their dead in the market in front of the church, and indeed, a large cemetery is located the market square. In the heat of battle the Germans torched the town and it almost burned down.

When I passed the market the gentiles looked at me with astonishment, they didn't believe that Jews were still alive. Barsolka Staskes, the well known thief who lived in my father's house, approached me and said to me in Yiddish: "Surke, are you still alive?"

He took me in his hand and led me to our house. I didn't enter because I didn't want to increase the great pain that was infiltrating my whole being. I returned to Iwye and lay for two weeks with a high fever.

Our decision was made: to leave the field of slaughter and immigrate to Israel. And indeed, shortly after we traveled to Poland and from there to Israel.

I arrived to Israel together with my husband David and my two daughters, Henya and Hedva. I live in Motza Illit near Jerusalem.

[Page 190]

The Forest Was Our Home….

Sholem Bronshtayn

Translation by Sara Mages

I studied in the *Heder* with the teacher Leyb Arye. He slapped his students on the cheek and also beat them with his fists. I also studied at the Russian School which was in front our house. At the age of 17 I started to work in my grandfather's smithy. After I got married I lived in Aran which was half way between Vilne and Grodne. About fifty Jewish families lived there. It was right next to the border with Lida. Lithuanian Aran, where five thousand Jews lived, was located across the border. In Aran I was independent in my smithy. My wife's name was Miriam. We had four sons.

[Page 191]

When the Second World War began, and the Germans occupied Lida, they arrested my two sons, the eldest, 18 year old Tzvi, and the second, 16 year old Yehudah. They led them to Alita and shot them to death.

About a month later, they rounded up all the Jews from the area in the synagogue in Lithuanian Aran. The synagogue was filled to capacity. For lack of space they also filled the square in front of the synagogue with men, women and children and erected a barbed wire fence around it. In this way they held us for two days without food and drink. At times, the guards only brought a little water for the children. I shudder as I remember what took place in the synagogue: crying, shouting and wailing, women tore their hair and slammed their heads against the wall. It was a shocking tragedy. Two days later, they began to chase us in the direction of the forest where they prepared pits in advance. I, and several other young people, agreed that we wouldn't walk like sheep to the slaughter. Suddenly, we started to shout "Hurrah!" and escaped from the lines. Many fell and died and many got caught. I managed to escape to the forest and by indirect routing arrived to the village of Pakolishok. There, I entered the home of the widow Garishevich who kindly received me and put me in the barn. My wife and my two young sons perished on that day together with of all the Jews of Aran.

The next day, I sent the widow to my Lithuanian friend, Jonas Wilczyńskas, in the village of Kasheti. She took eggs with her and went as if she was going to exchange them for salt. In this way she reached my friend and told him that

I was staying with her. That evening he came to me, brought me food and clothes, and at my request took me to my relatives in Marzikanza Station. I stayed there for two days and was forced to flee together with my relatives, to Drosknik. A refugee aid committee was still active there.

*

I stayed in Drosknik for four months. Suddenly, the Germans surrounded the city. I felt that the end was near. I, along with seven other young men, crawled to the wooden buildings which were built on stilts and used for convalescence and recreation. We huddled under the stilts and spent the whole night there. The next day they took all the Jews, loaded them on freight cars, and led them to annihilation. After the Germans began to scour the city to search for fleeing Jews we divided into two groups. Four ran in one direction and got caught by the Germans who killed them on the spot. I, along with three other young men, escaped in the direction of the forest and managed to get away. Fortunately, two in our group, especially Heshil who was a merchant in this region, knew the area well. He brought us to a farmer who was his acquaintance and he gave us bread and onions. After an overnight stay at farmer's house we searched for a way to reach Dowicz Forest because, when we were in Drosknik a man told us that his son was there. The farmers from the area showed us the roads that the partisans crossed. We hid, waited, and indeed, they arrived and we joined them.

[Page 192]

We sat hungry and barefooted and winter was approaching. Luckily, I found out by chance that it was quiet in my hometown, Divenishok, there were no attacks on the Jews and life carried on as usual. I decided to return to my parents' house - and so I did. There, I found only women, my young brother, Zalman Yosef (who now lives in Hadera), fled with the Red Army for fear of the Germans. My brother-in-law Antek was hiding in the forests from the Pole, Durniak, who was from the village of Dowitshok who wanted to kill him because he was the manager of his flour mill during the communists' days. I found all of them confused and scared. They feared Durniak's young son who from time to time appeared in my parents' house and brutally beat my elderly mother and my sister Zirka, Antek's wife, with a thick stick, shouting: "Where is Antek hiding?" If you don't tell me - I will kill you here, on the spot. Since my arrival, Durniak's son stopped coming to us. I activated the smithy and in this way I supported the family.

*

It was quiet in the town throughout the week but we were especially anxious on market day, on Thursday, when all the farmers from the area gathered in town and used the opportunity to attack individual Jews. To this day I can't forget the case of Meir "*Der Warsawer*" who was attacked by several Poles and Germans. They beat him with great cruelty until he lost consciousness. His face was torn and he was bleeding.

At the same time we welcomed to our home a young couple from Vilne, Yitzchak and Liza Gogodzinski, who escaped from the ghetto and didn't have a place to turn. They spent seven months with us. They moved to Voronova with us and managed to survive. Now they are in Israel.

When we moved to Voronova I felt that the situation was very bad, but I didn't want to leave my family. And indeed, one day the Germans surrounded the ghetto. I knew what was going to happen and waited nervously for the evening. At nightfall, I crawled on my stomach, managed to get away through the guards, and made my way again to Dowicz Forest.

[Page 193]

After a lot of effort I joined the partisans in Dowicz Forest with one prayer in my heart: to avenge the spilled blood. My first task was - to get a rifle. I remember that a rich Jew from Aran entrusted his property with a gentile. We decided to take the property from him. We, ten partisans, went to him and demanded the property. The farmer resisted us with force so we killed him on the spot and took the clothes. We exchanged some of the clothes for rifles and returned to the forest.

At first, we were assembled in the forest in groups, Jews and Russians apart. Each group operated as it saw fit and cared for its needs. After a large number of Russians arrived to the forest and the partisans' forces increased, an order arrived from Moscow to consolidate the groups. A Russian *politruk* [political commissar] joined our group and tried to unite us together with a Russian group. He left us to make the arrangement - but didn't return. One of the partisans killed him on the spot.

Later, probably under Moscow's command, a Russian lieutenant came to us with seven other Russians to organize the groups into detachments. He was our commander. Thus began the organized work of the partisan detachments - and the forest became our home until the end of the war. In the forests we suffered greatly from the hunts, which were conducted by the Germans and the Lithuanians, and later from White Poles. These gangs murdered Stankvitsh and his staff sergeant, Leybkeh, a young Jewish man from the town of Olkenik.

A year and a half later, while Stankvitsh was still alive, an officer named Davidov came to us. He was a Russian Jew who was parachuted by Moscow to strengthen the partisan movement and report on events in the occupied territories. It was a very special intelligence mission. A radio station, with which he was in constant contact with Moscow, was also at his disposal.

Davidov sought excellent partisans at his disposal. I also joined when I found out that Lipa Sokolski left to join Davidov. In this manner a detachment of 12 men was organized under Davidov's command. We were happy with the change of command because Stankvitsh was an anti-Semite and sent the Jews on the most dangerous missions.

Davidov was in constant contact with Moscow. Soviet planes arrived to us and brought weapons, explosives and medicine. When a plane was about to arrive we lit three bonfires in an agreed order so the pilot would know our location. We left for action almost every evening. We blew up train tracks and toppled telegraph and electric poles. Twenty men left for this mission.

[Page 194]

I carried the explosives to the destination. After every successful mission we drank "*L'chaim*" in Davidov's company.

*

In this way the time passed until the end of the war. When the Germans started to flee, Davidov ordered us to scour the forest and search for Germans. We undressed those we caught and killed them. When the Red Army arrived, Davidov thanked us for the joint work and expressed his appreciation for our operations. Davidov was a wonderful commander, he was loved by all the partisans and we parted from him with great sorrow.

We arrived in Grodne after we parted from Davidov. There, I was appointed director of a brick factory. Sometime later I returned to Aran. There, I worked at the police station together with Lipa Sokolski. Our commander was Binyamin Rogovski (he passed away in Haifa). In our service we managed to find several Lithuanians who collaborated with the Germans. Among them were two policemen who participated in the liquidation of the Jews of Aran. These murderers were sentenced for long prison terms and returned to Aran after they served their sentences. Our loved ones - would never return…

I Was Left Alone and Isolated

Shulamit Fuchs

Translation by Meir Bulman

The First Days of German Occupation

The Lithuanians were very quick to destroy Jews and begin their despicable work on the first days of German occupation. Most of the towns in the Vilne area were part of the Lithuanian Republic. Our town was on the border but was part of Belarus, so Jews from Vilne and the surrounding area sought shelter in Divenishok. A large stream of refugees came to Divenishok and the residents did their best to assist with housing and documents. The *Judenrat*[1] was particularly successful at assisting in obtaining forged documents for the refugees.

Ra'aya Sutskever stayed in our home, as well as an intelligent woman from Vilne with her brother. The woman and her brother stayed for six weeks, relocated to Yashuny, where they perished. Dr. Gordon from Navaredok also stayed with us. We hid him for a long time in our cellar and after that I bribed the head of the town council to allow him to stay with us. Dr. Gordon joined the partisans in the woods and survived. He is now in Russia.

In the Voronova and Lida Ghettos

With the directive mandating expulsion to Voronova, my husband Herman, my daughter Lilly, and I relocated there. The Germans allowed my husband to open a pharmacy at the nearby town of Kalelishok to serve the local peasants. We stayed there for only six weeks, at which point we were returned to Voronova. There, we experienced the horrors of the Nazi massacre. From there we were transferred to Lida with the rest of the Jews.

Our situation in Lida was quite bad. My daughter became ill and was taken to the hospital. With the help of a nurse at the hospital I sent a letter to the Lithuanian teacher Pauleitiss in Voronova, with whom we had left many valuable objects— furs, and gold jewelry— to send us help to save our daughter in exchange for our valuables. But the teacher, instead of sending help, informed the Germans that my husband the chemist was preparing gas to poison the Germans. SS men arrived in our home and arrested him. I approached Zalmen Leyb Lieb who was a member of the Lida *Judenrat*, and he arranged a meeting with the *Gvits Commissar* himself. When I entered I presented him a golden ring with a half-carat sized diamond – an inheritance from my husband's parents – and requested the release of my husband. "Your husband is accused of a political crime and not a financial one," he told me, "so I cannot release him. I would be risking my own wellbeing." He took the ring but did not release my husband, who was torturously executed.

After liberation I returned to Voronova, and in a nearby village I located the teacher with whom we left our valuables and asked him to return my belongings. "Hast thou killed, and also taken possession?" [1 Kings 21:19]. He expelled me from the home. I approached the NKVD to complain, but the Soviet police did nothing on the matter.

Escape to the Woods

My daughter perished in the Lida ghetto. I remained alone and isolated, and so I decided to leave for the woods. On that occasion, Leyzer Meir from Bilitza arrived at the ghetto. He knew my brother Tsvi and when he saw me he said, "You're Tsvi's sister; I'm willing to take you to the woods."

And indeed, on a March day, 12 of us departed the Lida ghetto. On the way we encountered a German patrol and split up. The Germans captured some of the people and returned them to the ghetto. Only six of us evaded capture. We then met partisans on a mission who asked us for a password. Instead of telling them we were Jews from the Lida ghetto, we ran. They, of course, opened fire. We hid in a grain field.

I accompanied a tailor from Lida whose wife and two children waited in a nearby village. I joined him, and in the evening we reached the partisans' area. There, I met my brother Zelig and his friend Yitzhach Segal and another young man named Yeshayahu. My brother introduced me as a doctor and the peasants approached me for medical help. I gave one of the peasants a medication for worms and it helped immediately. In return we received bread and pork.

From there we continued to the village of Narodovitsh,[2] where we met Max Stavitski from Warsaw. He was a nice man, quick, and with a great sense of direction. He helped us a lot. We continued our wandering with him along the Neman River. The situation turned dangerous since the Germans began establishing police stations throughout the villages. We found some family camps but did not join them. We searched for partisans, so we might seek revenge against the Germans. Once a week we would go searching for food. We had no weapons so at night we would knock with a stick on a peasants' window, to scare him, and yell, "Partisans! Give food!" The peasants would throw us bread, potatoes, and sometimes meat. We obtained one gun, but to be accepted as partisans we needed at least one more. Max helped us buy parts, from which we assembled a *haloshykke* – which is what we called a rifle missing its butt. We then began to search for partisans.

The Orliani Otraid [3]

We met partisans at a village [where they were] leading wagons filled with food, and they said they were willing to accept us. We boarded the coaches and traveled for a while without reaching a destination. It seemed suspicious and we asked for a reason. They said it was a mobile *otriad* without a fixed location. I told them we did not have shoes and were not able to constantly walk. My brother Zelig, Max, and I left them at Dimiantsove Village.[4]

At the village, one of the farmers whispered to us that on the right side of the Neman were staying troops from the Orliani *Otriad*— to guard against White Poles crossing the river. We crossed the Neman and turned ourselves into the guards. We then waited for the commander who would determine our fate.

We stayed in the cold and rain for three days until the commander appeared. An unpleasant event occurred, which nearly cost me my life. One night, I felt I must go bathe in the Neman. It got dark and I could not find my clothes or the way back and had to wander naked in the woods all night. Adding to my misfortune, there had been a fire there not long before, and the area was full of soot: the trees were burnt and were frightening. In addition, swarms of mosquitoes attacked me and stung me mercilessly. I wept bitterly over my fate and wanted to die. Only the next morning was I able to find my way back. My brother did not recognize me because I was all blackened.

The commander accepted us to the *otriad*. My brother Zelig and Yitzchak Segal were placed in the combat squad and I was sent to work in the kitchen. We stayed there six months. Once, as I passed by headquarters, I heard an officer say, "Why do we need that girl with the green pants?" I understood something was about to take place.

Expulsion from the Otriad

Our fears came to fruition. One day, all the Jews in the *otriad* were gathered and were told the *otriad* had received special combat [orders] demanding much effort, so all the Jews are being expelled. Their weapons were confiscated and they were told to go wherever their eyes would take them. We were at a loss for ideas; where would we go? What could we do without weapons? How would we get food? How would we defend ourselves? A single German could destroy us in the blink of an eye.

Rumors reached us that a Jewish commander had parachuted into the forest for a special operation. He was of high rank and the partisan command centers respected his opinion. The officer's name was Davidov. We wandered the woods for a few days and found him sitting with three other officers around a birch wood table, eating canned food. We poured out our hearts to him and told him how our brothers in arms had abandoned us. I could not contain myself and began crying.

Our pleading touched his heart and there were tears in his eyes. "Wait a bit," he said, "I'll call Moscow to ask for guidance." A bit later he returned and sent a runner to the commander directing him to return the weapons to the Jews. "I have a special role for you," he told me, "we have a central hospital for the various partisans in the forest run by two doctors. That is where you will work."

The weapons were returned to the Jews, and commander Panchenko was relocated. Suddenly, a command arrived to send a unit to the Grodne woods, where the situation was dire and especially dangerous. Many Jews were sent on that mission, including my brother Zelig.

At the Hospital in the Lipnishok Woods

Every *otriad* was accompanied by a doctor who handled small scale issues. For larger-scale incidents which required dangerous operations and at times amputation, [patients] would be evacuated to the central hospital. The hospital was well hidden at the center of the Lipnishok woods. There was no direct path to the hospital. The injured were brought to an agreed upon spot and from there transferred to the hospital. Even the partisans were not aware of the hospital's location. Supplies and medicines were also placed at a distance from the hospital.

The hospital stood atop a hill surrounded by a swamp and there was no path to it. If needed, a small wooden bridge would be placed above the swamp, supplies loaded and the bridge then dismantled, so there was no direct contact with the outside world. The partisans knew there was a central hospital somewhere but did not know its location.

Two doctors ran the hospital: the head doctor was Dr. Miasnik from Lida (now in Brooklyn, United States) and the second was Dr. Rakover (who now serves as a head doctor in a hospital in Jerusalem).

The hospital was constructed as two bunkers with semi-separate rooms. One bunker served as a surgery ward and the other was for contagious diseases, ran by Dr. Rakover. Most of those hospitalized by Dr. Rakover had typhus or STDs. The Germans would send the partisans young women who had dangerous STDs to infect them. In our camp, three such women who admitted they were sent by the Germans, were executed.

Dr. Miasnik greeted me very kindly. Turned out we were old friends; he operated on me in Lida while it was still under Russian control. I lived in the same bunker as his wife and daughter until the last weeks before liberation.

I worked in the surgical ward under the guidance of Dr. Miasnik. Working conditions were very poor. Medicine and surgery tools were scarce. Once, when the situation was particularly dire, I went out with a partisan unit to search for medicine. We entered a pharmacy in a small town not far from Zhetl, tied up the pharmacist, and took all the medication. Each unit was obligated to supply us a certain amount of food and medication. The food would be left at an agreed upon spot three kilometers from the hospital and we would carry it on foot through the swamps to the base.

The Surgeries

Surgery was usually conducted at night since battles took place at nighttime and the wounded were brought to us immediately.

Surgery was done in the most primitive manner. Dr. Miasnik directed the bunker doors dismantled and placed them on thick wooden planks on which the wounded would be placed. Once, the doctor had to perform a surgery without anesthesia; surgery had to be performed immediately and we could not find anesthetics. The doctor proposed the patient bite my hand during the operation so he would not feel the pain. Surgery was successful even in those conditions since Dr. Miasnik was a very gifted surgeon.

Towards the end, our situation improved monumentally, thanks to the tight bond developed with Moscow. Russian planes would drop food and drugs for us. Every parachute contained 100 meters of silk which we used for clothing needs.

A radio station was established nearby, which was in constant contact with Moscow and informed it of the events on our end. In severe incidents, we would summon planes to transfer the injured to Moscow.

In addition to his difficult work at the hospital, Dr. Miasnik served the area villages, whose residents were allies, and provided us with much assistance. He would travel to the villages a few times a week and would cure, dress wounds, and operate. He was summoned for every urgent need and he never refused.

Sometimes we would work 20 hours a day. Surgery was performed at night and I would prepare the instruments and medication for operations. There was also a need to administer injections, change bandages, and carry food from afar.

Work was difficult and exhausting, but also very satisfying. While bitter battles were being waged between Germans and partisans, and gunfire echoed near us, we did our work as usual. We were afraid of being discovered, but believed our blessed work was saving lives.

Liberation

Two weeks before liberation, we dismantled the hospital, as we feared the Germans while retreating via the woods would surprise us. I was handed a few wounded people and was told too care for them. Those were such tough days for me; I was alone in the woods with the wounded and had to care for them and for myself. Fortunately, their conditions improved after a few days and I was able to search for Dr. Miasnik and join him. I found them after wandering through the woods for two days and stayed with them until liberation.

After liberation I arrived in Shutchin and got a job at a pharmacy. My salary was extremely low, winter was approaching, and I was wearing rags. Incidentally, a soldier offered me some morphine shots. I purchased them, then resold them on the black market, and bought shoes. The NKVD learned of the incident and came to arrest me, so I hid at a nearby village for a while. From there I traveled to Grodne and prepared for departure to Poland. I received an exit visa and crossed the border in 1945.

I was so fortunate to receive the visa quickly. Otherwise, I would have been arrested and would have spent many years in a Russian prison. Many partisans met such a fate, despite their heroics against the Germans.

I lived in Lodzh for some time and worked at a pharmacy. I then illegally crossed the border to East Germany. We were arrested there but released the next day. From there we continued to West Germany. I made *aliya* after staying at a refugee camp for a while.

Editor's Footnotes

1. Jewish Councils mandated by German orders in the occupied communities of Eastern Europe during WWII

2. The location of this town has not yet been determined.

3. An otriad is a detachment of partisans

4. The location of this village has not yet been determined.

[Page 200]

From Partisan Unit – to the *Palmach* Brigade

Michael Dubinski

Translation by Marion Stone and Meir Bulman

My father, born in Radin, married my mother Chaya Rivke (nee Rogov) while he was still teaching Hebrew in Kalelishok. Afterwards he moved to the Benakani train station, where he owned a leather shop.

We Decide to Escape to Russia

At the start of the War, the Red Army retreated by way of the railway station. The Germans, who had discovered this route of retreat, dropped many bombs over the railway station, but not even one Russian aircraft appeared in the sky. Pulitruk was positioned outside and fired toward the planes with his revolver, shouting *Grodi we Krastach a Glawa we Kostach*[1] (the chest is decorated with medals of heroism but the shoulders have no head).

A group of nine men and one woman was organized and we decided to escape to Russia riding bicycles. During the escape we passed by Kalelishok, and by early evening we reached Divenishok, where we slept overnight at my uncle's, Yosef Dubinski. The following morning we turned eastward and approached the Volozhin area. From dugouts near the cannon cells, Russian soldiers promised us excitedly that the Germans would not be able to pass here. Suddenly from behind us some German cyclists, and a few light tanks, burst through. The Russians began to flee over the wheat fields for their lives as the Germans cut across after them, slaughtering them with their machine guns.

I threw myself into a channel by the roadside and kept my head to the ground. The bullets flew above my head with threatening, shrieking sounds. After some time the shooting stopped and the girl who was with us, Dinah Rabinovitsh, informed us that what had happened to us wasn't a bad thing since the Germans didn't harm civilians. We went to the road and sat by the edge of the road. We watched how the Germans concentrated the Russian soldiers into a group, shouting at them and hitting them with their rifle butts. The City of Volozhin was already burning.

We decided to continue with the Germans toward Russia, believing that the Russians would stop the German attack. We went on our way when suddenly some Poles attacked us and began to curse and hit us. They took our bicycle. We managed to escape them and continued on our way by foot. After some 10 km the German tanks turned off the road and on to a side road. This was caught our interest, but we continued along the main road as far as the fortified Russian posts guarded by a large force.

I reported to the Soviet officer about the German force that had diverted to a side road in order to surround them. After he understood the new situation that had been created the officer ordered his soldiers to prepare for a planned attack from the estimated direction.

The Russians were still busy with their preparations to pre–empt the attack as a battle developed, and within minutes the Russian soldiers scattered hurriedly and frightened, in all directions. I stood in amazement at what I saw since the Russian force was ten times stronger than the German force.

We continued eastward. As we progressed toward Minsk the chaos grew. On the way we met thousands of refugees, and scared soldiers without weapons, escaping to Minsk, and among them thousands of criminal prisoners who had been involved with constructing fortifications at the front.

From time to time German planes appeared and sprayed a hellish inferno over the scared crowds of people. Every explosion left hundreds lying by the roadside.

After a week of wandering we saw Minsk burning in the distance. We moved closer towards the city even though it was already in German hands with a curfew was in place. The blinds of some houses that were not on fire were shuttered, and doors were locked. We found a house that was open and went inside, but German soldiers appeared and wanted to see our documents. We had no documents so we explained to the Germans that we were Poles and that the Russians had been transporting us by train to Siberia when the Germans had saved us by bombing the train. Our explanation satisfied them and they left us alone.

We found an uninhabited house; it seems that a Jew had lived there who had managed to escape, because we discovered religious books. Some of our group stayed to sleep there and with the other men, I went out to look for food. At the destroyed train station we found carriages loaded full of sugar lumps and we grabbed them, filling our backpacks with them.

One morning we discovered two Russian soldiers and an officer hiding in the attic. One of the soldiers was injured. We dressed his wounds and we brought the three of them downstairs. We gave them new clothes and sugar so that they could continue their journey eastward and avoid arrest.

We were in the town for a week when the Germans hung announcements instructing Jews over age 14 to present themselves to the commander in the town centre. Communists and NKVD were to go to a special camp by the river. Most of us obeyed the order, but my brother Nachum and I, and another pair of brothers refused to show up, and we continued eastward. Afterwards I heard that they were all killed, apart from Dinah Rabinovitsh, who managed to get to Voronova, but then she was killed with her parents.

We crossed the Berezina River and reached a *kolkhoz*,[2] but the members refused to take us in. They gave us some meager slices of bread and directed us toward the tractors parking area of the *kolkhoz*. There we met Russian soldiers who were hiding. We stayed with them for a week and a half until Germans suddenly appeared. In order to avoid being discovered we hid in piles of straw in the granary. The Germans were trying to find us and poked their bayonets into the hay. A terrible cry came from one of the soldiers who had been hit by a bayonet. As a result we showed ourselves. The Germans assembled us and took a census. They put us on to trucks and transported us to a wooded area near the command camp where we stayed until the following morning. A German officer along with two Ukrainian collaborators appeared and they began to interrogate us.

The soldiers were immediately put together on one side while the officers were put to a different side. We were taken to Minsk together with the soldiers; the officers stayed in place and apparently were shot to death. We feared that our Ukrainian interrogators would discover our Jewish origins and so we repeated the same "story" which we had fed to the Germans in Minsk.

In Minsk we were attached to a convoy of captives being taken in the direction of the river. Afraid that we were being led to our deaths I was able to convince my brother to leave the line at the first opportunity and run. We managed to evade the guard's watch and joined a group of civilians moving in the opposite direction. The two brothers who were with us in Minsk refused to leave the line and they disappeared; we never saw them again. In town we were told that Germans were murdering Jewish 'communists' and that the river was running red with blood.

Return to Divenishok

We decided to return home and left Minsk westward. During daylight hours we hid in the forests and survived on black grains and pieces of bread that we received from farmers. During nights we continued on our way until we reached Divenishok. My uncle Yosef had already left town on his way to rescue his son who had been arrested for being a Zionist and was being held in the Lokishki Prison. The Germans caught him while on the way and murdered him in Lipuvke, a suburb of Vilna.

The following day we continued to Kalelishok. My grandfather was out of his mind with joy because he had thought that we were no longer alive. I stayed at my grandfather's house until we left the house to go to Voronova.

On one of the *Shabbatot*[3] shooting was heard in the town. We were afraid for my grandfather's fate since he was at the synagogue. Polish police took Jews out of their homes to the church square. Afterwards they brought Jews who had been praying in the synagogue. The anti-Semitic Priest pronounced his verdict and the policemen hurried to fulfill his instructions. They took one Jew from the line, harnessed him to a cart, placed a non-Jewish woman, a Jew hater, on the cart, and she whipped the man's back to force him to pull the cart up the hill. He could not take the load and fell, and he couldn't get up again.

The other Jews were forced to run the length of the square back and forth by being hit with rifle butts. Whoever fell was subjected to further blows. These Jews were bleeding and helpless, but the police continued their cruel abuse.

While I was running alongside the twins, my Aunt Roykhl's sons, I sensed a policeman standing about to hit me. I glanced backwards while running and saw that the policeman was a former friend who had sat with me on the same bench at school; I had helped him with his lessons. I called his name. He recoiled, stopped, looked at me, and told me to step out of the row. I told him that I would not step out without my family. At my assertiveness, he took out my grandfather and my aunt and set us aside— as he constantly continued to hit Jews. This horrible performance lasted for two hours, which seemed to us an eternity. In the end, the beaten, bruised, broken and exhausted Jews were expelled to their homes, crawling on all fours.

When we returned home my grandfather told us about what had happened in the synagogue. As soon as the Polish police had appeared in the synagogue they had begun to shoot in all directions in order to frighten the Jews.

To worsen matters, they began to torment the parishioners. They forced them to open the ark and take out the Torah scrolls, spread them in the yard and dance on them, as they hit those who were not quick to fulfill their orders. A few hours later I went to the synagogue and saw Torah scrolls scattered in the yard, stained in the blood of Jews.

After our expulsion to Voronova, I met with my parents and moved in with them.

The Extermination of Vilne Jews

Jews from Vilne escaped to Voronova in hope of finding refuge, but the *Gestapo* gathered them one winter day in the movie theater and executed them after holding them for three days without food or water. I watched that event in horror from the roof of my house. In the morning, the Jews were ordered to dig trenches, and in the afternoon two cars arrived loaded with Lithuanian murderers joined by Polish police and assisted by the Germans. Jews were ordered out of the movie theater and organized in rows. My blood froze at the sound of horrific screams. The murderers dealt indiscriminate blows to women and children. The Polish police officers, well known for their cruelty, whipped in every direction in merciless bloodlust. I will never forget it.

Rows of Jews were led under heavy guard to a small patch of forest near the train station. The Jews were forced to unclothe and stand by the pits. They were shot and fell into the graves they had dug.

The Lithuanian murderers completed their work with their hands soaked in the blood of Jews, and with a song. They walked through town happy and joyful singing hateful venomous songs towards Jews and yelled anti-semetic slogans.

One day on my way back from work I encountered a horrifying scene. A wagon was being led loaded with a murdered woman and two children, their blood dripping along the street all the way to the cemetery. The horrific scene shocked me and I decided to investigate the matter. I found out that not far from where we lived there lived a Jewish man, a member of the underworld, whom the Germans decided to execute. The man probably managed to escape, but his wife and two small children were captured and murdered immediately, tossed like animal carcasses on a wagon which led them to the cemetery.

On the day the Jews of Voronova were exterminated I was working with a group of Jews on the water pump (wudu kachka) at the train station. Suddenly we heard shots from Voronova. The Gentiles told us the Jews were being killed and the ghetto being dismantled. Fortunately we were unguarded and immediately organized a group of eight friends who decided to escape to the woods in the Kalelishok area. The group was led by a young cobbler who traveled in the villages repairing shoes and was familiar with the area and its residents.

Bogoslav the Pole – A Righteous Gentile

We walked all night and reached a dense forest. The forest keeper was Bogoslav, who later helped us and rescued us from difficult situations. He was a righteous Gentile and helped us without expecting anything in return. He shared his last piece of bread with us and eventually paid with his life for helping us. The White Poles executed him on charges of collaborating with the Jews.

Bogoslav showed us hiding spots in the forest, and gave us a weapon and trained us in using it. We survived on left-overs we found, and potatoes brought to us by peasants.

One day police officers came to Bogoslav's home and conducted a thorough search, claiming that he was hiding Jews. After they found nothing to prove his guilt the police officers left. Bogoslav took his dog and after he verified he was not being followed, reached us, and warned us to leave immediately so the police would not soon discover us. After thanking him for his faithful help, we left the site for the Almpina Swamps, a large swampy area which was untouched by humans where we often hid.

As Fall approached we could no longer stay in the swamps. The cobbler led us to a poor farmer who lived in a lone *hutur* (small village) who agreed to host us over winter. The farmer had visited my parents in Lida Ghetto and they gave him gold in exchange for sheltering us. I remember the farmer had an eldest daughter who had many suitors. When they appeared the dog would bark, and we hid in fear of being discovered.

At nights we would go out to gather food for us and the farmer. I once came to Kallelishok and entered grandfather's house; the Gentile living in it cast me out.

One night we entered a farmer's home basement as we searched for food and to our surprise discovered a large barrel of pickled cabbage. We knew if we could get the barrel to the Gentile we were staying with we would solve the food problem for the entire winter. In a joint effort we took the barrel from the basement and rolled along the river bank, on the ice, a road of over 10 km. The operation was a success and we brought the barrel to our host. It was a very difficult operation which lasted the whole night.

In the Spring, we left the Gentile and returned to Bogoslav the forest keeper. A shepherd probably noticed us and reported to the police. In the evening we heard horsemen approaching us and left running towards the swamps to hide. A month later we returned to Bogoslav to take the kitchen utensils we had left behind as we ran. He told us the police had paid him a visit and assaulted him for hiding Jews.

The Sheep and the Wolf

All summer long we were in the swamps and hid in dense shrubbery behind a mighty, nearly uncrossable river. We discovered a spot where a tree had fallen across the river and we would climb on it. Passage was especially difficult at night and we had to illuminate our path to avoid drowning. That place served as a safe and comfortable hiding spot despite the difficulties.

Every time the guys went out to search for food I feared they would not return, and would be startled by rustling leaves. One time when I stayed alone I heard footsteps and saw two approaching spotlights. I hid behind a tree to examine the situation. I then heard intense running and dragging as the sound and light came closer. After a few minutes of terrible fear the light disappeared. When my friends returned I told them what happened and they calmed me, and promised it could not have been humans.

For safety reasons we searched the area the next morning. Less than 50 meters away we found a dead sheep, skinned and half-eaten. Apparently a wolf had hunted it and dragged it to safety. When he sensed my presence he was frightened and left the prey behind and vanished.

We were amazed that the wolf was able to skin the sheep so skillfully, beyond human capabilities. We cleaned the rest of the meat, rinsed it, and began cooking it. Much to our surprise, the meat softened only after two days of cooking.

How We Obtained Weapons

We knew we could not survive for long without weapons. One Gentile, as revenge against his neighbor, told us that his neighbor owned two quality Polish rifles. We went in a group of eight men to take the weapons. We reached the farmer's house at night and a few men remained outside to guard the men who entered the house carrying sticks resembling guns. We read an "order by partisan headquarters" which we wrote before we left. It said in Russian that he must give the rifles he owned to the Partisans. The Gentile shook in fear, denied he had weapons, crawled on the floor, and begged for his life. We attempted to influence him in any way to tell us where the weapons were, but to no avail. Even after sustaining an assault he continued saying that he had no weapons and was being framed. We took him out to the yard, bound his hands and legs with the rope from the well, and immersed him in water repeatedly, but he did not relent. I proposed scaring him with the lives of his wife and children. We placed his wife and children in the house and locked the door. We tied the farmer to a tree so he could watch his family burn. "After that," I threatened him, "I will kill you with this grenade I am holding." After he saw us approaching the house to burn it down he broke and fearfully announced he would hand over the guns. He led us to the swamps behind the village where the guns were hidden in a hollow tree; they were two new Polish rifles, still with grease. "Go to my brother who lives in a nearby *hutur* and he will give you 140 bullets." We thanked the Gentile and did so. We divided the guns among us and rushed to Bogoslav who then taught us to shoot.

Later, it turned out the Gentile was a leader in the White Poles movement and I have a reasonable suspicion he had a hand in the murders of my parents and family.

After we obtained weapons we felt safer and went on a counter–punitive operation against a farmer whose son had killed a Jewish man. In an area village there was an intelligent Jew from Vilne who posed as a Crimean thinking he would save himself that way. One day the Jew went out to graze sheep. The son knew the Jew had a pistol and asked him to show him the gun. The man did not suspect a thing and handed it to him. That naiveté cost him his life as the Gentile shot and killed him immediately. The story upset us and we went to punish the farmer, and to kill his son. We did not find the son at home and the farmer himself begged for his life. We gave up on our intention to burn the house so as not to alert the Gentiles. We broke and shattered all the furniture in the house and did much damage.

One day, a group of young men from Voronova appeared and were looking for weapons. We learned that at the intersection of Benakani, Kallelishok, and Oshmene there had been an intense battle between Russians and Germans, and many Russians had fallen and were buried with their weapons. At night we reached the spot with the men from Voronova, dug among the bodies, and extracted gun parts from which we were able to construct functional guns. We divided the weapons among us and parted ways with he Voronova group.

Partisans Took Our Weapons

In the fall, the men from Voronova reappeared asking for more guns, claiming that Russian partisans had taken their weapons. Of course, we could not oblige them so we refused. They tricked us: when we parted ways they asked that some armed men accompany them to the nearby forest. We agreed. Now the lowlifes attacked us and forcibly took our weapons. They fired warning shots in the air and left. Those men brought us double trouble: they not stole our defensive weapons, but they had also disclosed our location to the Gentiles with the shots they fired. Thus, we had to leave our devoted and loyal benefactor and search for another hiding spot in the middle of winter.

My grandfather had deposited his belongings with a Gentile. My cousin Shlomo Olkenitski and his brother the cobbler came to the Gentile to request that he replace the weapons taken from us. The Gentile greeted them nicely and invited them to return. A few days later they went to the agreed upon meeting place but were never seen again. Later we learned that the Gentile had set a trap for them and invited Lithuanian policemen. When the men appeared, the policemen presented themselves as Russian partisans and tried to discover the hiding spot of the entire group. The men recognized the trap and wanted to leave. The Lithuanians stopped them and murdered them in the Gentile's yard. Six months later we came at night and burned his barn. We could not storm his house because he opened heavy fire.

We learned from a Gentile that Russian partisans were searching for Jews to recruit. We asked the Gentile to introduce us. A short while later the Gentile announced, on behalf of the Partisans, a meeting time at his house. We arrived on time and found four Russian partisans. They chose four men among us who had good guns, placed them on a sled, and said they were going on an operation, promising they would return and take us all to Rodnitski Puscha.[Ed. Note: Forest]

After a short while the guys came back to us discouraged, and without weapons. They had been brought to the property of an anti-Semite and were commanded to each separately enter the home. When they entered they were each disarmed and commanded to leave. A year later, when I was at the Borba Otriad, I recognized them and tried to move against them, unsuccessfully.

The Death of My Brother Nachman

Before the disbandment of the Lida ghetto, I sent a Gentile there to transfer my parents, Aunt Sheinelle, Aunt Mosya, and her daughter. They hid with kind Gentiles, first the Gentile with whom we spent the first winter, and later, when the situation turned suspect, we transferred them to another Gentile who lived in a secluded *hutur*[4].

We visited them occasionally and brought them food. On our way to one of the visits, I, my brother Nachman, and some other men entered a bathhouse at the edge of the forest intending to wait until nightfall to visit my parents and aunts. The winter was heavy and the snow reached our waists. As we waited we cleaned our guns. Unfortunately, my brother Nachman could not dislodge the cleaning rod stuck in his barrel. He went outside to heat a wire so he could burn the rod. Suddenly, a single shot was heard from the direction of the forest. I immediately sprang up and ran towards the door; heavy fire rained on me from the forest. The shooters, White Poles, told us to hold our fire, and promised no harm would come to us.

We knew very well what would happen to us if we submitted. Horrifying rumors had reached us about the torture and inhumane torment inflicted on Partisans captured by the White Poles. We had heard of dismemberment while their captives were alive, of white hot metal into the eyes, of fingernail and toenail removal, of placing genitals in the mouth of a nursing calf, and other varied and strange tortures the White Poles' sick imaginations produced.

Four of us remained in the bathhouse: the cobbler, my friend Avraham Levine, a man from Kallelishok, and I. We decided to fight to our last bullet and not surrender under any conditions.

I called to my brother Nachman but did not hear a response. I understood that tragedy had befallen him; he was hit. I discovered his body outside and attempted to crawl to him, but hellfire rained on me from the forest.

We returned fire and tried to crawl towards the house where my parents and aunts were. Crawling was exhausting, since the snow was deep, and we had to attach the guns, our only protection, to our bodies since we feared they would get wet. We moved with significant difficulties, but the White Poles followed closely behind. I concluded that if we could not stop them we had no chance of escaping. I turned back, took out the only grenade I had, and threw it behind me with all my might towards the estimated source of the gunfire. I heard a tremendous explosion followed by terrible shouting, and then total silence. Apparently the grenade surprised the Poles who thought we had more grenades and stopped attacking us.

The Night of Horrors

We crawled to the Gentile's house where my parents were hiding. I saw my parents and aunts pacing nervously in the yard. They knew what was happening and feared for our fate. We suspected an ambush was set and decided to leave. It is fortunate we did so because we later learned that the sons of that Gentile were White Poles, and had not immediately murder my parents and aunts because they thought more Jews would be coming to them and they could finish them all off at once.

We took advantage of the darkness and began running into the forest. Our feet sank in the snow and we occasionally had to stop to extract those who were stuck in the heavy snow. My heart ached at the sight of my Aunt Mosya, pale as a ghost, as she dragged her little daughter with her remaining strength, my thin father, whose face was white and lips blue, his eyes blazing with the fire of life. My kind, dear mother crying and silently whispering, "God, why have you inflicted this upon us? How have we sinned? We have become a mockery to the nations and our lives and blood abandoned!" I led the group with a heavy heart, pressing the rifle against my chest with all my might and biting my lips in pain and anger.

At dawn, after an hours-long fearful run, we were exhausted as we reached a lone house at the edge of the woods. It was the home of the *wyat* (city council chairman) who was well acquainted with my family. He invited us into his home, gave us milk to calm us, and proposed we stay with him and build up our strength. He directed us towards the barn so that we would not be discovered.

The *wyat* seemed suspect to us and we did not trust his words. We constantly looked through the cracks of the barn to see what was happening in the yard.

It was not long before we heard voices approaching. Murderers began entering the yard on foot and on skis. Their numbers increased and reached about fifty. Our rescuer greeted them at the entrance and they saluted him as he invited them in. Not much time passed before we heard singing voices.

We sat still in the barn and expected the worst. We were prepared to die, but determined to fight, and charge the largest possible price for our lives.

After they drank to intoxication, the murderers left the house and began shooting into the air for entertainment. They then fastened their skis and prepared to travel. The homeowner showed them footsteps in the snow and sent them towards the footsteps to confuse them. After they left he came to us and instructed to escape quickly because his guests would most likely return to his house after they had given up on their decoy search. Much later we found out that man was the head of the Polish gangs and it [his conduct] remains a mystery.

At nightfall we left his house. We walked for some time before reaching a Gentile's house, who agreed to let us stay a few days. Throughout our stay there we were very concerned about being discovered. After much consideration we decided to go to Kallelishok and hide with Gentile friends.

To not attract extra attention, we divided into two groups. My parents, aunts, my friend Avraham Levine, and I, hid with a Gentile who was grandfather's neighbor in Kallelishok. The cobbler and two young men, and one woman, hid in a *hutur* one kilometer from the town.

A few weeks later we heard shots from the direction of the *hutur*. We had a bad feeling. Indeed, the gentile visited us that evening and told us our friends were compromised and attacked by Lithuanians. According to him, a lengthy battle took place. Our friends defended their position for some time and even struck a Lithuanian policeman. Their attackers had to bring reinforcements just to thwart their escape and managed to beat them only after their ammunition had run out. They then brought them out to the yard and killed them.

We knew then that we must leave this terrible place, and the farmer we were staying with encouraged us to leave his house. Avraham Levine and I went to search for a hiding spot. We ran towards the woods, but the winter was very cold and we hesitated for some time. On our way we met a Gentile acquaintance who agreed to host us until the end of the winter.

We learned that this Gentile was with the White Poles, and after staying for two days in a small, suffocating room we feared for our safety. My aunt Sheinele, Avraham Levine, and I went to search for another hiding spot. My father Shmuel, my mother Khayeh Rivkeh, my aunt Mosya and her daughter, Avraham's wife, and his eight-year-old son remained at the Gentile's house.

The Murder of My Parents and Family Members

The night was dark. We managed to reach fifty meters from the house before heavy fire was opened on us. We ran towards the woods and lost Sheinelle on the way. We later learned she hid with a Gentile who had previously worked with us, but the murderers tracked her footsteps and tortured her in an attempt to extract our hiding spot. She knew her torturers personally and pleaded for mercy, crying and begging, but to no avail. She was terminated after grim torture.

The murderers killed all the Jews in the house other than my father, who managed to escape under cover of darkness. He wandered among the Gentiles for days and was not harmed because they hoped he would bring them to me, and they could kill us both. After a few days, when they had given up hope, they killed him in a peasant's yard. Hid body was abandoned to forest predators, again in the hopes that I would come out to bury him and they would capture me as well.

Avraham Levine and I escaped through the woods towards Soletchnik. Freezing temperatures and heavy snow enclosed the woods. We dug under the snow with our fingers and lay in the holes like forest animals for a week with no food or drink. We were shocked by this tragedy and apathetic about death.

Sometimes when I think of the past I ask myself where I found the physical and mental strength to survive those days. To lie in the dark forest and survive on ice after all of my loved ones had been cruelly slaughtered. I answer myself that the drive to survive came from the desire for revenge and not let the flame of life be extinguished, in spite of our enemies threatening to destroy us; this was stronger than everything.

When exhausted by hunger we exited to search for food, and once we found some, returned to our dens. We lived like that until the spring arrived. Whilst wandering through the woods we met some young men and women from Voronova, including Elisha Hershovitsh. We returned with them to Almpinner Bloteess (the Swamps in Almpina), a spot where Jews never went and an ideal location for survival.

Our friend Elisha Hershovitsh began to suffer from intense scabies. We could not watch him suffer so we risked our lives one night and snuck into Dr. Melinovski in Kallelishok. We got an ointment from the doctor which saved the man's life.

To the Partisans in *Rudnizkia Pushcha*[5]

As the noose of the White Poles gradually tightened around us we decided to join the Partisans in *Rudnizkia Pushcha*. There were five of us, three men and two women. Only Avraham Levine and I had guns. One night we lost Leah Pupko from Voronova; four of us remained. We later learned she had exited the woods and Gentiles murdered her.

After weeks of wandering we reached the Partisans' location. Two partisans on observation duty led us to Commander Wasilniko, a Russian Jew and engineer by training who greeted us well. I was placed in a combat unit and participated in all battles involving the unit. There was a *polanka* (clearing with vegetation) in the forest where aircraft would drop weapons and explosives. I once went out to fetch food and received an order to bring a cow back to base. In one of the villages I stole a white cow from a peasant. When the Partisans saw the cow they mocked me, "a white cow can be seen at night from kilometers away; it will give away our location to the Germans." I covered the cow in mud and we arrived safely to the base. To this day, 30 years after the fact, when I meet the Nyunke[6] brothers and Yitzchak Telerent[7] from Vilne, my brothers in arms, they ask me, "Say, Michael, how is your white cow doing?"

The White Poles Occupy Vilne

Our first meeting with the Red Army was very emotional. We received an order to join them and move towards Vilne. We reached a forest near Vilne and stopped there. We heard a gun battle from the city and the Soviet officers told us that there was a battle between Germans and White Poles who had surfaced to occupy Vilne before Russia got control of the city. The Russians patiently waited at the edges of the woods so both sides would attrit one another and then they [the Russians] could enjoy the fruits of victory.

At the height of the battle some high ranking Russian officers appeared including the famed writer Ilya Ehrenburg. We told them what things the White Poles had committed against us and requested permission to enter the city and take revenge. We were denied. Ilya Ehrenburg told us that the actions of the White Poles were well-known, and that their day of retribution was approaching.

After the battling ceased we received an order to enter the city. At the entrance to the city the White Poles greeted us wearing white bands on their sleeves, holding a red-white flag, smiling and happy, as if to say, "Look! We have conquered the city." My blood boiled. I wanted to avenge the blood of my family and the blood of all Jews, but we received a strict order to not harm them.

After the Red Army gained control of Vilne we received an order to concentrate all the White Poles in a forest near Vilne, under the guise of enlisting them in the Wanda Wasilewska[8] army. We fulfilled the order enthusiastically; we knew what it meant. A few thousand Poles were gathered in the woods and a large NKVD force surrounded them. The Poles began to understand that they had been set up and attempted to escape, but to no avail. They were loaded onto cars, led to the train station, placed on train cars, and sent to an unknown destination.

In the Russian Militia

After the city was liberated I was appointed Secretary of the First Division of the militia and served as an interrogator of atrocities committed by White Poles. We captured many Poles who had hidden in the woods and pestered Soviet convoys. I did my best to retaliate, and although they begged for their life, I was fortunate to be able to take revenge.

While I was in Vilne I was appointed as translator for the Red Army Special Division, and accompanied the conquering army to Konigsberg, where we interrogated men of the SS and *Gestapo*. In one of the prisoner camps we located the commander of the Stutthof death camp and terminated him. In that role too I tried with all of my might to pay back the enemies of our People: many found their way to Siberian work camps.

Aliyah

After the war ended I traveled to Poland, and after much difficulty, reached Israel. The British captured our immigrant ship and expelled us to Cypress. I reached Israel with a forged passport at the height of the battle and was enlisted in the Third Palmach Battalion. For two consecutive years I served an active role in the War of Independence.

After I was released from the Palmach I established a home and family. I currently live in Tel Aviv with my wife Esther and my only daughter, Rivka'le. I am very thankful to God who has brought me here.

Editor's Footnotes

1. Original expression is in Polish.

2. A Russian collective farm

3. Plural of shabbat

4. Typical Lithuanian peasant cottage.

5. Rudnitki Forest

6. In the original text this name is spelled: nun–yud–vov–nun–kuf–hey.

7. In the original text this name is spelled: tes–lamed–resh–nun–tes.

8. What may be meant here is the 'Halszka Wasilewska' army since this is the Wasilewska sister who was and active combatant for the Polish side. Her sister Wanda was a novelist and activist.

The "valley of murder" of the Jews of Divenishok, not far from Voronova, in 1943 – in the background are Germans and Polish police – the picture was found, after the liberation, in the possession of a Pole who had collaborated with the Nazi murderers

[Page 215]

I'm The Only One Left From My Family

Yeshayahu Vulfovitsh

Translation by Sara Mages

I was born and raised in the town of Kollishok, a distance of about 12 kilometers from Divenishok. Around 20 Jewish families lived in that town. Naturally, this settlement couldn't function independently and therefore it had tight communal ties with Divenishok. I had a family connection with Divenishok: Hirshel the cobbler from Wilner Street was my uncle, and for that reason I visited the town frequently.

The conquest of the town by the Germans caused a sharp turn: we lived in fear not knowing what the day would bring. And indeed, immediately on *Shabbat Shuva*, a number of Polish policemen took all the Jews to the market and laid them in rows while others used the opportunity to steal valuables that they found in the Jewish homes.

Chaim Traub, who was the head of the village council, was harnessed to a wagon and the wife of Smulni's village leader was placed inside. She forced Traub to pull the wagon up the mountain, lashing him hard with a long whip. Chaim Traub pulled until he weakened and fell. They forced us to crawl back and forth, and when they realized that we were completely exhausted they ordered us to crawl back home.

On the next day, a number of Jewish women went to the Police Chief to complain about the act, but he, as if to complete the measure of bitterness, answered them rudely:

"You're lucky I wasn't there at that time. I would have poured kerosene on all of you and burned you alive".

Kollishok's Jews were ordered to move to Divenishok three weeks before Divenishok's Jews were transferred to Voronova. All that time I was staying with my uncle Hirshel the cobbler. However, before long, the Kollishok and Divenishok Jews were transferred to Voronova.

Before the liquidation I worked together with 30 other young men in the forests in the vicinity of Stashiles. Every night the forester in charge of us returned to sleep at his home. One evening, when he didn't return, we thought that something was going to happen. To investigate the situation we sent a young Polish woman to Voronova. She told us that the ghetto was surrounded by soldiers and the Jews were digging pits. We decided to escape immediately, and each one of us went on his way. I returned to Kollishok and started to associate with the gentiles until I met Avraham Goldensky.

Avraham and I left to seek help from a farmer who at one time sold us his crop. For many years this farmer supplied potatoes to the Jews who lived in Lipufka, a suburb of Vilne, and they sold them to the shops. When Vilne's Jews were transferred to the ghetto, a few of them were allowed to supply potatoes and flour to the ghetto.

In the Vilne Ghetto I was able to evade all the *Aktziot* – coincidence or good fortune helped me. When the ghetto was liquidated I found shelter in a pit under the bath-house in Stephen Street. After a few weeks stay in the pit, the gatekeeper discovered us and reported us to the Germans. I was captured and transferred to a work camp in Kalwariski Street, Vilne. It was one of the last labor camps to exist in Vilne. 150 Jews worked there overhauling and painting automobiles.

About two weeks before the end of the war, Gestapo men came and killed all the Jews on the spot. My friend Moshe Zukovski and I were lucky: we hid behind the oven's vent.

Moshe woke me in the early hours of the morning and ordered me to leave the place with him. His mother, may she rest in peace, appeared in his dream and told him that someone will find us in our hiding place. We left our location and moved to an adjacent room that was already searched by the Germans. This is how both of us survived and saved from the fate of the other Jews who were caught and shot in the yard.

As evening fell, we slipped from the place and hid in the forests in the vicinity of Yashny. After liberation I worked in Benakani. There, it became known to me that Pinkowski, the notorious Police Chief, was in a Grodne prison. I announced that I wanted to appear as a witness in his trial and my request was granted. I testified about all the atrocities that his officers committed, and his answer to the women who came to complain before him. After a brief discussion he was convicted and the death sentence was to be carried out in Voronova.

We traveled to Voronova in the district headquarters' car that escorted Pinkowski and another Polish policeman who murdered Resnic's son from Lida. We arrived to Voronova at ten in the morning and made our way directly to the market. Two gallows were already standing in the center of the market. After the sentence was carried out, the bodies were left hangings for a number of days, so the gentiles will see and know the fate waiting to the opponents of the regime.

I didn't want to stay any longer in a country awash in blood. I traveled to Poland and from there I immigrated to Israel. In Israel, I was inducted to the Israeli Army and fought in the War of Independence.

I was the only one left from my family. My father Reuven passed away before the German entered. My mother Rivka, my married sisters - Batya, Henya and Sheine, and my unmarried sister Chana, were murdered by the Germans. My brother Yisrael managed to escape from Lida Ghetto and hid among the farmers, but as far as I know, he was murdered by them.

[Page 217]

Where Are All of Them? Where?...

Tzvi (Hirshel) Krizovski

Translation by Sara Mages

On the second day of the war between Germany and Russia, that is to say, in the morning of 23 June, my father organized all the active people in our town - more than 50 people, to prepare wagons with horses to carry their baggage, and drive in the direction of Oshmene. On the third day we arrived to the town of Rakovi near the Russian border. We hid in the forest because German airplanes bombed us. We weren't able to continue on our way because the border was closed. We turned in the direction of Radoshkovits where the border police commander, my father's friend, was stationed. But, when we were informed on the road that the Germans were already in Radoshkovits – we returned to Rakovi.

The road was completely blocked with wagons, burnt cars and refugees who filled the whole area. We weren't able to advance, and we also didn't know where to go because everything was burning around us. My mother was in one wagon, the family of Ajzik Levine in the second, and we walked.

When my father realized that we reached a dead end, he told my mother: "try to return home, the children and I will walk to Russia because I prefer to die from a Russian bullet than a German bullet".

My mother returned to Divenishok and hid with Chaim Hershovitsh. From there, she traveled to her family in Ivia and perished there in the ghetto. My sister Keila returned to Vilna and perished there together with her husband's family. We moved in the direction of Rakovi and on the way we lost our father. According to what Meir Yosef Itskovitsh told us, our father got stuck between the Germans and became ill on the road. My brother Kalman took care of him and they managed to reach Krasnei Ghetto. There, he suffered from hunger and deprivation until he was killed together with all of Krasnei's people.

We advanced through the forest in an easterly direction. On the way we met two young Russian men and women who escaped from prison and returned home. We waked with them for ten days. We gave them money and they bought us food and milk in the villages. One day they stole a horse and a wagon from a farmer and escaped – and left us alone. We moved forward alone until we reached the city of Mogilev. There was a lot of confusion in the city. With difficulties we made our way to the train and traveled.

After a two week journey we arrived to the Tambov region. From there, they sent us to the city of Penza where we worked in a peat mine until we were inducted to the Lithuanian Brigade in 1943. There, we worked in the headquarters' restaurant until we were liberated. Immediately, on our first opportunity we traveled to Vilna.

My visit to Divenishok

After the war I visited Divenishok twice, the first time in 1950. I wanted to see my birthplace, the place where I spent my childhood. The town left a depressing impression on me. All the buildings were burnt, and here and there the protruding chimneys shouted the destruction. The silence reminded me of the stillness in a cemetery. I went to see our house, but to my sorrow I didn't find anything – only a few pitiful bushes stood here and there. The farmers recognized me and said: "Here is Krizovski's son ...look what the Germans have done to you"...and the expression of hypocrisy reflected from their faces.

On the occasion of my immigration to Israel I was forced to visit Divenishok again in order to obtain documents. It was in 1971 – meaning, twenty one years later. This time great changes took place. Beautiful brick houses with large windows, surrounded by lawns and gardens, stood where the Jewish houses used to be. There were streets and buildings in the area across from the church. The local municipality gave its residents the Jewish building plots for free, and also long-term loans so they could build houses in town. No wonder that the town was being built in a fast pace. My heart ached with pain when I saw Divenishok without Jews. I stood stunned in the market, looked around me, and my heart was crying, Where are all of them? Where?...

[Page 219]

Days of Hardship and Suffering

Tsvi Ahuvi (Lieb)

Translation by Meir Bulman

When I was four years old, I was sent to Kalmen Shepsel's *kheyder* on Subotniki Street.[1] He was a grey–bearded, tall, slender man who wore two pairs of glasses one on top of the other due to his poor eyesight. His unique appearance and the whip which he was always holding struck fear in us, his students. Occasionally we would sneak out of *kheyder* and run to Yozhke the peasant, who was an admirer of Jews, and pick 'beralakh' [berries] from a large tree which stood in his yard. After that I transferred to the *kheyder* run by Shaul der Forber [the dyer] (Shaul, Lipkunski's father–in–law). The *kheyder* was at the front of the house, and in the back room there were two barrels which were used to dye flax threads for the peasants' wives. Every time his wife would summon him to open paint boxes we would sneak up behind him and blow on the paint, which of course caused Shaul's beard to be painted in various colors, which thoroughly amused us.

From Shaul's *kheyder*, I transferred to Aryeh Leyb Engle's cheder. He was considered the best Torah instructor in town, and in his *kheyder* they already studied *Mishnah* and *Talmud*. He had a very talented daughter who sat behind the wall (it was forbidden for girls to study with boys) and listened in on the classes. When we the boys could not explain a chapter in the Bible, an answer echoed from behind the wall.

After that, *Bet Sefer Va'ad* was established in town. Classes took place in the synagogue. It was a novelty in town because the school, run by Zalmen Merlinski, also held classes on secular subjects such as Hebrew, mathematics, and history. The school existed until 1915.

After that school closed, I learned with Rabbi Yosef Movshovitsh's son at the Reines Yeshiva. My teachers were Rabbi Meir and Rabbi Yakov, who later became a rabbi in Traby. I studied there for only two years because the yeshiva closed due to a lack of funds. My parents wanted to provide me with a professional education so I was sent to *Ort* in Vilne.[2] I studied there for a year before returning home.

From all the events in my childhood the big town fire of 1912 left the deepest impression. I was a student at Aryeh Leyb's school. On Thursday, which was market day in town, we suddenly heard shouting on the streets. We exited the *kheyder* and saw frightened people quickly moving their belongings to the fields behind the synagogues. The fire spread everywhere and peasants took advantage, stealing what they could. Since I was young I was tasked with keeping an eye on our belongings behind the synagogue. I remember that I stood guard for a very long while. Night fell and Yehoshua Zandman appeared. He yelled, "Who has a match to light a cigarette?" I handed him the match and when he saw there were jelly jars near me he ripped the paper off one of them, stuck in three fingers, and began licking them. He was probably very hungry, but it was very funny to me, and I remember it to this day.

During the Polish period, I worked in forestry. After I married I ran a turpentine business, meaning we extracted turpentine from burned pine roots, [in a place] which we called the *smolarnye*³, and shipped it abroad. My factory was on Graf Omiastovsky's manor, 15 kilometers from Divenishok. The factory was quite profitable and I made a nice living.

After WWII Erupted

In 1939 the Polish military was defeated in a matter of days. Poland was divided between Russia and Germany, and the new border went through the Bialystok area. We were in Russian territory.

Immediately after the Russians entered, all Positronic (Polish Police) documents were burned publicly in the market. Afterwards, Russian airplanes appeared and dropped *olatkess* (leaflets) in broken Belarussian which said, "Because the Polish government escaped, citizens have requested that we liberate you." We began grasping the meaning of a communist regime; the lie was self-evident. The Polish government escaped **because of** the assault by the Red Army, nobody invited the Russians, the Polish cried a lot when they first saw the Russian tanks. The Russians simply invited themselves.

The Jews greeted the Russians with a mixed feeling of happiness and sadness. The words of Rabbi Tayts expressed their feelings, "It is better the Russians are here. We might have to give up some of the religion (*frumkeit*) but we will stay alive."

Immediately following the Russian invasion, the factory was confiscated and turned into a cooperative. Scarcity increased in town. The gentiles would gather on market day and curse the Communist regime but could not do more. Arrests increased and the regime instilled fear in the populace.

While I worked at the *Klevits* I developed a bond with the Graf Omiastovsky's forest manager, the *nadlishnitsi* Casimir Stotski.⁴ The fate of whether I would work at the *Klevits* factory was then in his hands since the Graf respected his opinion. One day after the Russian invasion, a peasant brought me a note from Stotski which said, "Local peasants broke into my house, robbed everything I owned, stripped my wife and I naked and expelled us from the house. Please, Tsvi, save us!" I immediately sent a coach and clothes and brought him and his wife to my house.

Casimir Stotski and his wife stayed in my house a month before the NKVD suddenly appeared and arrested him. A few days later his wife was arrested too. Years after, I learned a *leshnik* (forest guard) named Bogoshovitsh informed the Russians Stotski was hiding in my house, as revenge for once having fired him.

A month after the incident, as I walked with my son Khetzel to bring the horse to pasture, a few policemen appeared and asked me to accompany them to the *Gmine* (city council building). When I asked what the concern was, I was calmed and told it was a minor issue. I had a bad feeling, and I asked for permission to go tell my wife, but the policemen refused, saying I would return home soon anyway.

I was brought to the *gmine* where I was thrown into a truck and covered in canvas. I was brought to a ranch named Vonzdova, a 12km distance from Divenishok, and placed in a restroom where I spent the night. That was my first lesson in Communism.

When I did not return home my wife was shocked. For two whole days she ran around, for two days, before Krizovski, who was then the mayor, told her I was arrested and was at the Oshmene jail. My brother immediately traveled to Oshmene to rescue me, but his efforts were unsuccessful.

The next day I was interrogated. At first the interrogators were courteous. I was asked why I sheltered in my home the USSR hater, the *nadlishnitsi* Casimir Stotski. I told them the whole truth, I said he was my friend and that my income depended on him, I told of how the peasants tormented him and chased them to the forest naked. I tried to explain that my actions were not political in anyway, but purely humanitarian. My arguments were ignored, and the interrogators became increasingly hostile. One of the interrogators shouted at me, "Do not hide behind the veil of a humanist! You are a Polish fascist, just like your friend Stotski!" I realized that evil had befallen me and I was done for. After two days of interrogation and torture I was transported to the Oshmene jail.

In Oshmene Jail

In Oshmene I was placed in a dark and crowded cellar. People stepped on one another's feet and there was no air to breath due to the overcrowding. There was no room to sit, and of course, no space to lie down; at night we dozed off while standing. People fainted and fell, but the Russians did not notice those minor details and treated us like animals. The food we received was a slice of black bread and *balanda* (bland vegetable soup). After a few interrogation sessions I was transferred to the jail next door. There I found many acquaintances, including Shatsigloski who owned a flour mill in Mogovian,[5] the mayor under the Polish Zvedsky, the Dakh brothers, Rabbi Sorotzkin and his son Elkhanan who wanted to cross the border to Lithuania and were captured when they left Ben Zion Schneider's house, Vasilsky the teacher's father, and other notable Poles from Divenishok and the surrounding area.

Conditions in that prison were intolerable. Overcrowding was unbearable. The rooms were crowded beyond capacity in three story cells. The passageway was also full of mattresses. There was barely any air to breath and we almost suffocated. He who found a space by the window was happy. I stayed in that place for three months, and that whole time we did not change underwear. We suffered much from lice and inadequate food which included bland soup in which lone groats periodically floated.

On the Road to the Labor Camp

After a three month stay in Oshmene prison we were taken to the train station in Sol and transferred by train to Minsk. We stayed in the Minsk prison for a week. There I met many people from Vilne, including the notable lawyer Tchernikov who always appeared at trials as a defense attorney in favor of the communists, Count Diamont who was Countess Milvski's attorney, and others.

In that jail, we were finally permitted to bathe. We received old and patched clothes, and after we dressed we were taken out to the streets of Minsk, so its residents could see us. Here, a court notified me I was sentenced to ten years imprisonment and would be serving my term in the infamous Pitma Labor Camp.

The road to Pitma was accompanied by endless suffering and torture. We were transferred by train for two months. We waited at stations for long periods of time and lived on very harsh food and sanitary conditions. Dry toast and meager small fish were our food, and our suffering was unbearable, but there was no one to complain to. I prayed that God give me the strength to withstand the suffering so I can return home to my wife and children. After an exhausting journey, tired, hungry, and full of lice we reached Ural, a city that was used as the center for transferring prisoners from all over Russia. At Ural prisoners were divided into the various labor camps in Siberia.

Pitma Labor Camp

After a few days journey, we were brought to the infamous Pitma camp, which contained 300,000 prisoners. The conditions in the camp were very harsh, the regime strict and severe, and the work was backbreaking labor: tree-clearing in the bitter cold which at times reached forty degrees below zero. Thousands of prisoners died in the thick woods and the sound of their final shouting echoed into the distance.

To this day I cannot understand how I, the weak Jew who never did physical labor, broken and depressed, managed to clear centuries-old trees.

To my astonishment, I met at Pitma camp the *nadlishnitsi* Casimir Stotski, who I was jailed for. His situation was monumentally better than mine since he worked in his profession as a forest ranger and I had to work as a low-level laborer.

Conditions in the camp were especially worsened after the war between Russia and Germany began. The small food portions were reduced to miniscule, and if not for my wife's help, who sent food packages and clothes, I would have died. I remained at Pitma camp until 1943, thanks to the pardon which all Poles received after Russia recognized the exiled Polish government.

From the moment we received the pardon we refused to work, despite warnings by our superiors. We heaved a sigh of relief and once more began to feel like humans, since up to that moment we had been humiliated, tormented, and tortured like slaves, at times even worse than that.

From Pitma we were transferred to the halfway camp Yardova with our clothes and other belongings and then were sent to Dsalel–Abad in Uzbekistan. When we arrived there we were told we would be accepted to General Andreas' army and were guided to Kramina.

The officials at the Polish headquarters in Kramina immediately accepted the Poles who had been with me in Pitma, but I was refused admission due to my Jewish origin. I feared I would miss that opportunity to leave Russia, in addition to the famine which Uzbekistan suffered at the time; many Polish refugees died of starvation and lack of shelter. In the Polish army, on the other hand, the soldiers received ample food and sugar packets, cocoa, and American cigarettes which were then priceless.

Fortunately I encountered a Polish officer at headquarters, a longtime acquaintance who owned an estate near Divenishok, and I was accepted to the Andreas army on his recommendation.

We stayed a year in Uzbekistan and finally the happy moment we were waiting for [arrived]: we received an order to get in cars and cross the border to Iran. From there we were transferred to Iraq. In 1943[6] part of the Andreas army arrived in Gedara. I was very excited and happy I had finally managed to reach Israel and I asked for permission to meet my relative Natan Kaplan. The meeting was very exciting and I decided to desert the Andreas army.

After a while, we were transferred with the army to Gaza. A group of 12 men decided then to desert the Polish army. One evening we took our guns and traveled to Tel Aviv. We hid for a while with Khayeh Garvey and then relocated to Ra'anana where we handed our guns to *Hagana* man Wasserman.

At that time, I learned of the tragedy: my wife Devorah of the Deltishki family and my three children Khetzel, Moshe, and Tanyeh were murdered at the Voronova ghetto.

Now, after many years of suffering, I am married, and my wife Yafa and I have three children, Uri, Ruti, and Nekhma.

About My Family

My father David, Moshe Aryeh Leyb's, was from a family that resided in Divenishok for many generations. He was a man of the people, kind and traditional. He was always alert to the suffering of others and he was generous towards the needy and suffering.

My mother, Tanyeh, was a native of Ilia but acclimated to our town very well. My mother was very energetic and ran the household wisely. Our home was open to guests who wanted a rest or a warm meal.

My mother was a woman of valor, her hands full of work, and alert. She was full of energy and she always smiled. Many of the area nobles came to dine and rest with us. My mother also gave charity anonymously, and like all mothers was devoted to the family and religiously observant. My parents had five children: the eldest Zalmen Leyb, me Tsvi, and three sisters. The oldest sister married in Olshan to a son of the Voronovsky family. All but her daughter Feige perished in the Holocaust.

The second sister, Rivke, married Velvl Schwarts, a kind Jewish man, a Torah scholar, and an admirer of scholars.

The third sister Tzileh married Hershl Arkin in the town of Subotnik and perished with her husband and three children.

Editor's Footnotes

1. The text refers to Kalmen Shepsel Krizovski.

2. A system and network of vocational training schools.

3. A tar factory.

4. The word 'nadlishnitsi' is spelled as follows in the text: nun–aleph–daled–lamed–yud–shin–nun–yud–tsadek–yud. The meaning of this word is not yet known.

5. This place has not yet been found on a map.

6. The year given in the text cannot be correct.

[Page 225]

The Amputee of Divenishok

Meir Yosef Itskovitsh

Translation by Rabbi Israel Rubin

(Published in "*Persumei Muzeion HaLochamim VeHaPartiznim*"
Tel Aviv 1972, volume 19b, number 1 [16])

My hometown Divenishok (Oszmiana District, Province of Vilna) was one of the cities on the way to Vilna–Minsk. It was far from the railroad and highway, the approach was by dirt road and exclusively by wagon.

The Jewish residents had many great attributes: they kept the mitzvas, were hardworking and loved mankind, rose early to serve the Creator, and hurried to help those in need.

In this village and its surroundings Yakov Schneider grew up and was educated. He was the oldest son of the Schneider family, renowned and famous for their acts of kindness, charity, and concern for others.

Yakov received a "national-traditional" education. No wonder that as soon as he became aware of himself, he joined the ranks of "Beitar"[1] where he found what he was looking for – a place to express his inner feelings, dreams, and ideas. He dedicated [all] his spare time to "Beitar" and found satisfaction [spending] time in "Beitar" club with his friends. He teached "Beitar" ideology to his trainees and together with them hoped to fulfill the prophecy of reestablishing Malkhut Israel.[2]

In a short period of time Yakov stood out among his friend and he was appointed commander of "Beitar" – the last commander in our town before the rise of the butcher of the Jews of Eastern Europe.

I remember well the dream–laden youth who was the first commander of the "Beitar" group in our city, quiet but bursting [with energy], with a decisive character that would stand by him when the day would come.

The situation for the Jews of the city did not improve, and fell to the same circumstances as every Jewish city at the time of the Russian–German war: persecution, pogroms, torture, humiliation, and murder. Those who remained after the great slaughtering that took place in May 1942 in our city, and those surrounding it, moved to the Lida ghetto.

*Survivors from Divenishok, after the liberation,
at the memorial stone at the mass grave in Voronova*

In the ghetto barbershop run by Gordon (born in Vasilishok), the "Young Chalutz" group and the former JNF members would meet with the students of the Beitar movement, the Zionist Youth movement, the Shomer HaTza'ir movement, and others. At these meetings, they evaluated the situation, exchanged views, and collected experiences from the past, in order to draw inspiration, strength, and faith to continue on. They made one decision: To the forest!

One of the meetings left a deep impression on me and I remember it in great detail: There were stormy debates when we discussed the appropriate time to leave the ghetto. One of the participants did not voice his thoughts. He sat quietly engrossed in his thoughts. At the end of the session, I asked him "Yanke'le (as he was nicknamed in the city) why are you so quiet?" He answered me in Yiddish: "You have spoken a lot, but have not taken any action." Then he was quiet. The next morning I was told that Yakov left the ghetto the previous night and went toward the forest.

Yakov Schneider hi"d
[Tr. Note: May the Lord Avenge his Blood]

Two days later, the news arrived that Yakov's arm was wounded by a "dom–dom" bullet in the Dovinski forest on the way to the partisans. He was then returned to the ghetto by a point–man. I visited him and stood by his bed where his mother was crying. He turned to me and said quietly, "Commander, explain to my mother that Tromflador also lived with one arm and when needed he gathered up the strength to do wonders with just one arm." Those were the last words I heard from his mouth, while standing at his bedside in the Lida ghetto.

Under those conditions, it was impossible to obtain proper medical care in the ghetto. He was transferred to the city hospital, where they amputated his wounded arm. The news quickly spread to the German police that a wounded Jew was in the city hospital (!), and they did not hesitate to stop by. He was immediately taken to the local prison for interrogation. They wanted to know: how and where were you wounded? Who were the point–men, and where were they located? Who were the heads of the partisans?

Yakov was covered in blood, without bandages on his wounds or medication. He withstood [their interrogation] with super-human strength and refused to answer them. The questions were repeated again and again, the torture became more severe, the wounds became worse, and blood was flowing, but Yakov was silent. The police were prevented from executing their will, because Yakov was silent, silent forever.

We find a dedication to the Schneider family in the introduction to the book "Oznayim LaTorah" (Genesis) that was published by Rav Zalman ben Ben-Tzion Sorotzkin, the Rabbi of Lutsk, in Jerusalem 1969:

"I remember by G-d's grace, the holy Ben-Tzion Schneider HY"D, from the prominent members of Divenishok, a lover and friend of Torah and its learners, for the kindness he did for me during the Holocaust when he hid me, along with many rabbis in his house when we fled from the Communists when Poland was conquered by the Red Army. In his house, I found shelter and help to cross the border of Lite (Lithuania). Through him I merited, with the help of G-d to move to the holy land of Israel and be in the courtyard of G-d in Jerusalem."

Eventually, Rabbi Sorotzkin passed away, and the Schneider family were cruelly butchered by "friendly neighbors" during the Holocaust, with the exception of one son, Shmuel (the younger brother of Yakov), a student of Beitar, member of Atze"l, [who was] exiled (by the British) to Kenya.

The name of Yakov HY"D will shine forever among the names of the holy members of our nation and its heroes.

Footnotes:

1. Tr. Note: Jewish youth organization

2. Tr. Note: Kingdom of Israel

[Page 228]

Our Loved Ones Did Not Go As Lambs to Slaughter

Meir Yosef. Son of Natan Itskovitsh

Translation by Meir Bulman

I feel like I must return to the city of death to visit the absentees, memorialize the dead, stop by every Jewish home that is no more, stand by the souls of the martyrs, and recite a silent *kaddish*.

I want to stop by the *Shul–Hoyf* where two synagogues stood, the old and the new, and the Rabbi's house, the homeless shelter, and the Hebrew school. I see myself stationed in the abandoned yard, close my eyes, and imagine that the dear townspeople are gathering on holidays and festivals in the synagogues, cloaked in prayer shawls holding prayer books. We the children, wearing festive clothes, holding bags of fruit, running around as the *polish* (a room for resting and waiting between services) bustles, filled with congregants who desire a cigarette.

I hear the pleasant voice of R' Munye Kherson, "Munye the Tailor," the wonderful cantor, as the congregation accompanies him by humming.

The clear echoing voice of R' Avraham Noakh[1] the ritual slaughterer, standing at the podium and starting the recitation of "I called upon the LORD in distress,"[2] and the weeping sounds heard from the women's section.

I open my eyes and find myself as one of few remaining survivors, spared death, who only 34 years ago was a member of a large and extended family.

Therefore, we must attempt to explain and answer the question plaguing every Jew who was not in the valley of death; "How was an entire nation led as lambs to the slaughter?"

Well, it must be said once and for all in a loud voice to our brethren, the People of Zion, and the Sons of Ishmael should hear and listen: **our loved ones did not go as lambs to slaughter!**

The heroic acts by individuals, uprisings in the ghettos and death camps, the thousands of Jewish partisans who served the resistance movement across occupied Europe, 1.5 million volunteers, soldiers and officers on all fronts serving the Allied Forces are the answer to the big and terrible lie!

Our nation had a significant role in ending the Third Reich.

We have sinned an unforgivable sin against ourselves by overemphasizing the events of the Holocaust over the bravery in WWII.

The period of a written and signed agreement between the two allies from the left and the right ended in 1941. The Molotov–Ribbentrop Pact, a signed contract, was trampled on by the steel chains of the German army which encroached on Russian soil.

German army forces entered our town through Vilne Street, the street which housed the synagogues, the Hebrew school, and the Rabbi's house. Two tanks infiltrated directly in front of the Old Synagogue while afternoon prayers were taking place. German soldiers entered the synagogue, took Torah scrolls out of the ark, and tossed them in a pile in the yard. The tanks then trampled them. After the 'victory in battle,' they left the *Shul–Hoyf* and went onward.

That was their first step the first action, as if taunting, "Where is your God?" in front of the town's pious and faithful elders, the Spiritual leaders of the local Jewish community.

Humiliation and Breaking the Spirit

They moved to the next level after desecrating holy artifacts.

One bright day, all Jewish men were gathered in the market square at the center of town and ordered to weed between the gaps in the sidewalk. That task, whose sole purpose was a debasement of the Jews, was performed by the town's notables, as they kneeled, surrounded by Gentiles raucously mocking them as they kicked the behind of a random Jew.

After the stage of disrespect and humiliation came the stage of fright and terror.

And So, It Began

For some reason, it is common among Jews to believe that all troubles and edicts happen specifically on Fridays.

I do not remember the exact date, but I will remember that damned Friday as long as I live.

It was a pleasant sunny day with blue skies, without even the lightest of clouds. Distant shadows were seen moving in a long line approaching from the woods on Vilne Street. It slowly became apparent that those were German soldiers riding bicycles approaching the town. They reached the market square and parked by the church fence. The head of the city council (*wyat*) was summoned quickly, and after a brief conversation the Christian collaborators present went door to door and announced that all men from 14–60 must gather by the Church with hoes.

Confusion overtook the house. What to do? Present ourselves or not? I proposed that father not do so but hide in the attic, and my brother Eliezer and I went. When we arrived we found most local Jews there gripped with fear and pale as ghosts. Without saying a word the Germans stood us in two straight lines and the "concert" began.

An order given, "drop!" and immediately, "rise!" repeatedly. Gershon Shlovski, (nicknamed Gershon the Turk) was to my right. In one of the exercises, the German ordered us to kiss the ground. Gershon, the experienced soldier who remembered the Japanese–Turkish War asked me innocently, "What is with them? Are they normal or have they gone crazy?" Gershon did not imagine what those Germans would soon inflict on him. Exercises continued and intensified, to the amusement of local Gentiles, who observed like they were watching a circus act.

The breaking of our spirit and pride through our humiliation by the Gentiles began.

As we concluded the exercises, we were ordered to sprint towards the City Council (*gmina*) located a kilometer away. We were forbidden to look back and were told that anyone who disobeyed that order would get a bullet in his head.

We started running along the marketplace and Geranion Street, as joy and satisfaction–filled eyes observed us from the windows of the Gentiles' homes. While running, Yehezkel the butcher's (Chaikel Velvel Khaykl's) hat fell. Yehezkel, who was observant and would not run bare–headed, turned back and picked up his hat. Then he was dealt a blow from a German's gun handle. Remarkably, Yehezkel with his fragile weak body was not broken and continued running.

We reached the City Council building and were again placed in rows, faced by Council Chairman Kakraka, the German officer, and some German soldiers. The officer said," Yesterday, two German soldiers were killed as they passed through Dovinki Forest. They were killed by Soviet soldiers, remnants of the defeated army. We know the Jewish population is giving food, clothing, and hiding places to the retreating Soviets. We also know local Jews have weapons in their homes. You are required to hand over the weapons immediately, otherwise, we will execute every tenth Jew in each row."

He finished speaking and asked his men to pass by the rows and pick out every tenth man. Eliahu Blyakher suddenly left his spot and asked the councilman and the German officer to speak. Eliahu claimed the Jews have no weapons and that local Jewish residents were law and instruction abiding, and had been living here peacefully for decades while maintaining mutually respectful treatment of their Christian neighbors, which the local government officials could confirm.

I still do not know from where Eliahu had such courage to take that step and will not know if his honest words influenced the officer, or if it was part of the show the Germans had prepared for us.

After the desecration of national holy artifacts, breaking spirit, the accusations, threats, and frightening, began the period of planting delusions.

Those Lacking Identification Cards

Local Jews were issued ID cards (*Avsweis Karte*). There were refugees who came from near and far and with no possibility of proving their ties to the town and they were not issued cards.

One day an identification operation was declared for the local Jewish population with the explicit promise that its purpose was only to locate those without identification who were suspected as dangerous elements who might complicate matters and endanger local Jews.

13 people were captured and executed during that operation. Among them was an elderly Jewish man, Kalmen, son of Berl Kalman's, who had refused to obtain an ID card in the days of Tsar Nikolai and in the time of Pilsudski the Pole, and would say, "*Na, teshto, minia passport kali ya sam tot?*" (Why do I need a passport when I am here?"). When the Germans entered he did not obtain a passport either. He was found without one, and as "a dangerous element" he was sentenced to death. He was shot by the German occupiers who 'feared he might damage the Third Reich.'

The Chronically Ill and the Disabled

"As long as Germany is at war," it was repeatedly explained to us Jews, "it is impossible that the German soldier is deprived in favor of the ill and the disabled who contribute nothing to society." The true purpose was to convince us all that only healthy work-ready Jews who could contribute to the war effort had a right to life.

On one winter day, German soldiers from *Zunder Commando* units passed from house to house, and all Jews found bed-ridden were shot where they lay.

That is how the eldest among our Zionists, Aryeh Leyb Rogol, was murdered in cold blood. He was the owner of a local pharmacy. He was an enthusiastic Zionist from a young age and a talented speaker. Even though in his later days was afflicted with partial paralysis, he was careful to uphold the National Convention on Tamuz 20th. Once his illness worsened, he remained bed-ridden unable to move or speak.

That same day, Frumeh from the *Hekdesh* was murdered. Frumeh ("devout") knew much suffering and poverty. The *Hekdesh* was a small wooden structure whose walls were almost half sunken and sprouted mushrooms. It served as a shelter, a place where the impoverished who wandered from town to town could lodge free of charge. She was short statured, and due to her odd body structure was deemed by the representative of 'the superior race' as unable to contribute to society and sentenced to death.

In that operation they also murdered the town's water delivery man, Eliahu Portnoi (Elke the dumb) who was a deaf-mute from a young age and who made his living drawing water from the well and delivering buckets to homes. He was also an observant God-fearing Jew and would wear *tefillin* and pray enthusiastically.

A very elderly blind man staying with Yeshayhu Kaplan was also murdered.

Professionals and the Healthy

"All professionals will work in their field and will contribute to the war effort." "People with a healthy and strong body will do public work clearing rubble and do construction." Those were the slogans that gave hope to those imprisoned in the ghettos. After the desecration of national holy artifacts, the harming of human respect, and the suppression of spirit and thought, still a flicker of hope remained in their hearts.

But the Germans, who used volunteering collaborators, our neighbors and "friends" the Gentiles, to ease their own effort, had already planned the all-encompassing destruction. The first stage in the destruction approached. On 5/11/1942, when the Jews in Voronova awoke at dawn to pray, they found themselves surrounded in all directions by German soldiers and local Gentile police officers. Nobody knew what it meant, but there was a bad feeling. I noticed that across the street in the house of the Stul family from Benakani were two soldiers from the military phone station in town. We recognized them; they were Austrian natives, and though they wore the German uniform, they were unusual. They associated with the Jews and were uninterested in politics. Through the window I saw they said something to the residents who responded by putting their hands together and pulling out hair.

A rumor quickly spread (*tsum neyem plan*[Tr. Note: The new plan]) that we were to be killed and a deep pit was being dug for that purpose at the edge of town towards the woods on the road to Lida.

I managed to sneak out of my house and reach a nearby house where my friend Edelshteyn lived. He was a brave and proud Jew. He had taken 8 bullets in his left hand when the Poles attacked his family-owned flour mill in 1922. Movement in his hand was limited since then.

He had a young, pretty wife, and an only son, a beautiful 1-and-a-half-year-old who was born with an unstable spinal cord and a brain defect.

We deliberated our next action, and he proposed that at nightfall we and other friends escape through a gap in the siege. Edelshteyn said he had a weapon hidden near the flour mill (north of Benakani) and once we reached that spot we would decide our next steps.

Then arose the question of the baby. It was impossible to take him with us, but his mother did not want to leave him behind alive. The parents finally decided to poison the baby before they left.

At midnight I heard the bird whistle of Myshke the Grasshopper[3] who whistled our familiar password. I arose from my bed and accidentally touched my brother Yehezkel. In that house we lay clustered together, my father and my two brothers, Eliezer and Yehezkel (may God avenge their blood!) When Yehezkel awoke he woke Father, and when I reached the door he stood there, leaned on the doorway, and said, "You will not leave!" I replied, "Father, you should know that only death awaits us here! There is no way but to escape to the woods. In a dog–eat–dog world we need to become predatory animals!" My father answered, "Listen, son! I am your father and I raised you and educated you. I held food from myself just to teach you Torah and knowledge, and I will not allow you to disobey me!" and then added, "Know that there is a God above, there is still a vast free world, there is a humanity left. The world is not abandoned! You will not leave!"

I stayed. Did I do the right thing? I leave the answer to those who ask, "How did that happen? Is it possible?"

The next day, all Jews were ordered to leave their homes and gather in the yard facing the church. Among those who went was my cousin Eliahu (Yitzach der Sheindel Makher's) from Bastuni, a simple Jew, pure of heart and God-fearing. He was a villager, lived among the Gentiles far from any Jewish area, alone with his wife. He was not familiar with politics, did not read the paper nor did he listen to the radio. He lived with his prayer books and Psalms. He was a tailor. He would travel on foot through nearby villages, get homemade fabric from the villagers, record their measurements, and return later and get paid. He was an honest man among honest men. When the order to gather arrived, he cloaked himself in his prayer shawl, put on his *tefillin*, and silently prayed and recited the *Shehecheyanu* and thanked God for the opportunity to fulfill the *mitzva of Kiddush Hashem*,[4] "for thy sake are we killed all the day long."[5] He did not return.

As I walked to the concentration yard, I met my neighbor the miller and he approached me and offered me a hiding place. We quickly snuck between the houses and climbed to the attic in the house of the town's dental technician, Yitzach Katzenellenbogen. Inside he told me that when the time came had come for escape, he had approached his son, holding the poison, but his wife had caught his hand and stopped him. It spilled on the ground. They too had not escaped that night, but now we were determined to escape at any cost.

Through the cracks in the wooden wall we watched the death procession. Mothers held their babies, families held one another's hands, walking in a single line in one direction. Our Gentile neighbors stood on both sides of the road holding clubs and sticks and hit anyone who strayed aside. The procession continued, our acquaintances, relatives, neighbors, and friends passed. Suddenly, Edelshteyn the miller called out, "Listen! If my wife and son have not yet passed and I see them walking, I will leave and join them. I could not bear to see them abandoned and being led to their deaths as I escape to save my own life!"

Indeed, when he noticed his wife with the baby in her arms, he immediately jumped towards the exit and out of sight. He joined his loved ones knowing full well what they were walking towards.

Is that not a brave act? You answer the question if he acted correctly, gentlemen!

My Escape

On 11/5/1942, two thirds of the Jewish community in Voronova was exterminated. After being deemed as supposedly desirable professionals, those who were not shot and killed were given an arrogant speech by Gauleiter Mindits (his trial took place a few years ago and was attended by witnesses from Israel who said he remained a Hitlerist as before.) He said, "You hear the echoes of the gunshots carrying out the death sentences of your parents, brothers, and sisters, due to the guilt of World Jewry which has declared war on the Third Reich. You were left alive, for now, as collateral. If your brethren across the world continue their war against us, you will meet the same end. Mark my words!"

I must mention two figures among my town peers whose bravery was later described to me by a Pole who was present at the time. Menke the butcher, Velvel Khaykl's son, was a tall and strong man whose strike of the hand was feared by the Gentiles. When he saw what was about to take place he attacked his murderers and struck them. He broke the head of an SS officer with a rock and wounded two Lithuanian soldiers taking part in the extermination. But his strength and courage could not withstand the bullets fired upon him and he fell. The second is Zalmen Shrira, who jumped out naked (clothes were removed before the killing), skipped over the dead and dying, running in a curved path to evade the murderers' bullets, and managed to escape out of reach of the bullets until he reached a grazing field. A shepherd then approached him and while speaking supposedly kind words called his friends who captured Zalmen and returned him to the killing fields.

The few who survived [and heard what] the Gauleiter said were again concentrated in the Lida Ghetto, and survivors from nearby towns were brought there as well, and the Ghetto was once again packed with Jews as if nothing had happened.

After the bloody events of May 1942, in which Jewish communities were destroyed consecutively, inhabitants of the Ghetto began sobering from their delusions, their eyes were opened, and a shift began towards reexamining the situation and seeking an exit.

We began gathering in the evenings to discuss the situation. The attendees were young members of Zionist youth groups from various backgrounds and differing opinions. In one of the meetings devoted to *Hanukkah*, we discussed the miraculous bravery of the Maccabees who battled as few against the many and were victorious. After that meeting, I and another friend left the Ghetto without parting ways with our families and joined area partisans. After conducting several sabotage missions, such as sawing telephone poles and derailing or bombing trains, I met a friend, currently with us in Israel, Yakov Strudvorski, and we decided to return to the Ghetto and extract Jews from there. We were not alone in that sacred mission of rescuing Jews from the ghetto. Eliahu Blyakher and Hirshke Novoplanski also did so.

I will mention Leybke Kaplan, Feigeleh Kaplan's brother, who went to the Ghetto and could not leave.

Meeting in the Ghetto with My Father and Brother

We reached the ghetto area at dusk. We hid among the tombstones in the Jewish cemetery and waited for nightfall. We intended to cross the tile fence surrounding the ghetto under cover of darkness. Unfortunately, it was a bright moon-lit night which made infiltration difficult. We observed Polish patrol officers, the collaborators, patrolling the fence, and between rounds snuck in from our hiding spot. We searched for a more-or-less secure hiding place since the ghetto residents feared to host partisans and we did not wish to put them in danger.

The ideal spot was found in the apartment of Yosl 'the buttocks' (*der tukhest*). Yosl, a Jew originally from Vilne, was a member of the underworld. The nickname 'buttocks' was given to him due to the rumor that when he would climb to a top floor for a 'job' he would slide down the drainpipe and land safely on his buttocks.

Yosl greeted us with open arms, set a plentiful table for us, and promised that as long as we were his guests, not a single hair on our heads would be harmed. Yosl also served as a contact person and deliveryman. Nobody suspected he had other intentions besides stealing. Yosl was sent to call my father.

Father was not happy to greet a guest like him. It was "below his dignity" (he maintained his self-worth even in the ghetto) and was not willing to walk through the streets of the ghetto with Yosl. Yosl arrived first, followed by Father.

The meeting was shocking. The room was stuffy with smoke and the scent of homemade liquor. The image of his youngest son was unveiled through the smoke, his hair mussed, two grenades strapped to his belt, and a cigarette in his mouth.

Father approached me in small steps, hesitated a bit, and hugged me, silently weeping, and said, "Why did you return to hell? Why? Why did you not stay in the woods? I hoped God would save you there!"

After he had calmed, I told Father I had come to rescue them from the ghetto and he responded, "My son, you know your mother is ill and suffers pain in her feet and walks with difficulty. She is immobile and I will not leave her." My brother Eliezer (Leyzerke) asked many questions, "How do you live in the forest? Where do you sleep? And where does one get clothes?" Eliezer did his best to maintain an organized and pleasant appearance, and quality food; in short, he was the pampered member of the family. My proposition did not appeal to him and he claimed that relative to other ghettos life in the Lida Ghetto was decent so additional waiting was necessary.

My brother Yehezkel (Khaykl), the observant Yeshiva student, did not agree to abandon Mother and Father.

The question which haunts me and causes pangs of conscience is, "Did I act correctly?" Should I not have forced them, or at least one of them, with threats, as I had acted on others in the group we extracted? While holding a gun to Dr. Tenenbaum's head, a group of 29 people was extracted, including a young woman named Esther who later would become my wife. Only one from the group was killed, and the rest are alive, mostly living in Israel. They established families and their children served or are serving the homeland.

I do not know if my father should have left and abandoned mother to follow me. My brother Yehezkel was a Yeshiva student and ordained as a rabbi, God-fearing and observant, he was educated according to the Torah and the mitzvah "Honor your father and your mother." Should he have abandoned his parents? I will never know which is braver: escaping death or going to one's death fully knowing and conscious.

Meeting with the Yudenrat[6]

News of our presence in the ghetto reached the *Yudenrat*. Sure enough, one morning we suddenly heard a knock on the door. We did not open immediately. As the knocks intensified we heard Maness's voice (the administrator of the vegetable garden and fruit trees for the *gvits commissar*);

he had blocked the door from the outside with his hands and body and declared he would not allow their entrance under any circumstances.

The argument intensified and turned into yelling and we feared the commotion would raise the attention and suspicion of Polish and German police officers so we decided to open the door.

Eisenshtat, head of the *Yudenrat*, entered. He was a short-statured man from far-away Galicia; he approached us and said, "We, the Jews who remained after the big massacre, have two paths. The one you have chosen, and may God help you. The other is to stay put, to obey, gain time and trust in God. We were promised that what has happened will not be repeated and that our labor is needed: if we follow orders we will not be further harmed. We were also told that for every Jew who leaves the ghetto, a hundred others will be executed. So, I ask you, please, leave as you came, alone, and do not bring tragedy. I will not turn you in to the Germans in the hope that you will do as I requested." He then left.

We left the ghetto that night, 20 men and women.

We did not see Eisenshtat, head of the *Yudenrat*, again. He perished along with the other Jews of the ghetto.

Our loved ones were under siege conditions in a foreign land, surrounded by haters and German collaborators. They faced a powerful enemy which planned the extermination calmly with perfect German precision, utilizing science and modern technology. The extermination was planned by scientific geniuses, psychologists, experts in breaking the human spirit.

They operated against a peaceful and silent nation, scattered among the nations, honest and innocent, faithful believers in God and humanity, left leaderless and without hope of assistance. The "enlightened" world ignored them and did not even protest the horrors.

We will remember the sacrifices made by our loved ones, which are unprecedented in human history, but we will also learn a lesson from their errors and failures.

To end my memories from the valley of death I wish to tell the story of a heroic fighter who resisted the Germans.

Sholom Garvey

Sholom Garvey was not a local native, but a "foreigner" who married a Divenishok woman and established a family. In WWI, he volunteered in the Polish Liberation Army of Pilsudski (the Legionnaires) and enjoyed rights not usually afforded to Jews.

Sholom built his two-story house using *postakess* (bricks) at the center of the market place. He rented the top floor to the police, who used it to observe the town. The bottom story was his residence and a store selling sewing products and tobacco.

The Yiddish he spoke was very different from the one spoken in town. He regularly flipped punctuation marks and we often mocked him when we heard him speak.

Sholom also did not follow local customs, did not rise for the morning prayers, and attended synagogues only on High-Holy days. He did not fit in with the town Jews and was like a foreign implant. He befriended the Gentiles, whose language he knew well, and especially fraternized with his police-officer neighbors from the top floor. Due to that friendship, rumors spread that caution with him was advisable. Nobody bothered to verify the rumors. We will never know if there was a shadow of truth to that gossip.

[Page 240]

After the Germans invaded the town, the Christian population collaborated with them to humiliate local Jews. Sholom could not stomach his Polish acquaintances turning their backs on him, the same people for whom he had fought in the Polish Liberation Army, and it depressed his spirit. In a conversation I once had with him after [some] refugees from Soletchnik arrived in town ('great and tiny Soletchnik') and told of the massacre of the Jewish population, Sholom said, "The Germans will not lead me to my death. I will not give them that pleasure. If I reach that state, as an experienced fighter and a proud Jew, I will end my own life!"

After the massacre in Voronova (11/5/42) the lives of most of the Jews in our town and nearby towns were severed. *Zunder Commando units* and death squads from the Lithuanian army, accompanied by local Polish police officers, shot our loved ones next to a massive pit they had dug a few days prior. Local Gentiles dug the pit at the entrance to the forest on the road to Lida. Gauleiter Minditz gave his arrogant speech to the survivors who remained alive as we kneeled in the yard facing the church in Voronova and the gunfire echoed in the distance. That temporary remnant was then transported to the Lida Ghetto.

The Jews of the ghetto were given various tasks. Sholom worked at a gas station. One day a cigarette was thrown near the gas tank, the station burned, and Sholom disappeared. The German police arrived at the ghetto, searching for him and his family, which had gone into hiding after hearing of the fire. The policemen announced that if Sholom did not turn himself in by the next day they would execute one hundred Jews. The announcements reached Garvey and he asked the people to remain calm, promising to turn himself in.

M. Y. Itskovitsh (on the right) as a partisan in 1943, with a woman and a man from his unit

The next morning, Sholom Garvey "turned himself in" at the gas station; the Germans found his body hanging atop the charred remains of the gas station. Sholom hung himself using his striped gown. He kept his promise.

Blessed be his memory!

Footnotes:

1. Ed. Note: Refers to Avraham Noakh Shlomovitsh.

2. Tr. Note: Psalm 118:5 recited before *shofar* blowing on Rosh Hashana

3. Ed. Note: In the original text this word is spelled: gimel–reysh–yud–daled–zayen–ayen–veyz–tsadek–ayen–reysh.

4. Ed. Note: Literally 'sanctification of the name', the mitzvah involves the willingness to die in the name of the Jewish religion.

5. Tr. Note: From Psalm 44:22.

6. Ed. Note: Jewish Councils mandated by German orders in the occupied communities of Eastern Europe during WWII.

The Story of an 11 Year Old Boy

Pinkhas Lipkunski

Translation by Sara Mages

1

My father was called Nahum and he originated from the village of Dogalishok near Radin. My mother, Slova, from the Binyamin Schneider family, was devoted, and fearful of the fate of her children. She was tall, dark, beautiful - but a weak and sickly woman. Despite all that, she carried the burden of managing the home and the business.

[Page 241]

My father was a baker and our bakery was adjacent to our house.

As a villager, my father had no formal education, but as a self-educated man he acquired a basic knowledge of mathematics and geometry. In his youth, he studied for a short time at the Radin Yeshiva, but in his view he was a secular man - and that, as a result of his service in the Russian Army.

His participation in the First World War, and later in the Bolshevik Revolution, deepened his atheistic world view. He took an active part in battle and was wounded by shrapnel in his hand and legs.

In his youth he served in the Far East, near Vladivostok. He always told in his fascinating stories about the wonders of the Taiga and of a tiger hunt in which he participated. He was courteous and friendly and participated in conversations about politics and world affairs.

He loved to play chess; so much so, that he left his work to sit and play. My mother would get angry and shout: "Nahum! The bread is burning in the oven, why chess in the middle of work?" And he, calmly: "Soon Slova! Here- I'm almost done. Just one minute!"...

My sister, Hannah, was beautiful. She had long, blond hair and blue eyes. My brother, Binyamin, was a weak boy in his childhood and a poor student. However, at the age of Bar Mitzvah, it was discovered that he was a gifted child in all areas. He matured physically and played the violin and mandolin. He was a good boy and was accepted by his friends. His positive character was discovered in the Lida Ghetto: he left for work and managed to bring food, not only for our family, but also for all the tenants...

My brother was very enthusiastic about the partisans and smuggled an Obrez (short-barreled rifle) to the ghetto. My father encouraged him to leave for the partisans, but my mother opposed it: "It's forbidden to break up the family."

2

On the first day of the occupation, 22 June 1941, all the who's who of the town gathered to discuss the situation. There were fierce debates about the outcome of the war. All were optimistic and said that it's the end of Hitler.

On the second day of the war, in the evening, a unit of German Stormtroopers was already in the town. Five to six motorcyclists burst northwest of the town, from the direction of Divenishok, and then, for a week, troops of German soldiers moved eastward.

At the end of the summer of 1941, the Germans imposed a "contribution" on the town - to bring them gold. As collateral they arrested, Pina Kartshmer, the owner of the restaurant, my father and several other Jews. They returned them after they received the gold. My father's appearance was awful - weak, thin, stooped and completely broken from the torture at the prison in Oshmene.

[Page 242]

In Vilne, which was under Lithuanian rule, the persecution of the Jews had already begun in the first days. Many Jews from the city and refugees from Poland sought refuge in nearby towns. A young man named Shalom arrived to our house and asked to reside with us. We welcomed him as a family member.

The town's priest, who visited us, saw the young man and asked who he was. We told him the matter, and on the spot he expressed his willingness to save his life under the condition that he would convert. After the war he would be able to return to the fold of Judaism. The young man agreed - and then he disappeared without a trace.

When we arrived to Israel and settled in Ramot Remez in Haifa, we became friendly with our neighbors who were former residents of Vilne. Once, on Rosh Hashanah, we found a Jew at their home whose leg was amputated after being wounded at the front. He recounted the whole story before me: The priest got him a job as a laborer in a farm near Divenishok. When the Russians arrived, he returned to Judaism and volunteered to the Red Army. He was wounded in action and his leg was amputated. He was among the *ma'apilim* [illegal immigrants] in Cyprus and now he lives in Ashdod.

3

Our situation in the Lida Ghetto was very bad. We were hungry for bread and became ill from lack of food. In my external appearance I didn't look like a Jew. From time to time I snuck through the fence to the market, bought potatoes, carrots and onions and brought them home. Once, we were caught by Christian teenagers who took our vegetables. They gave us a severe beating and put us in the Judenrat's cellar where we were held for a week. My mother came every day to the prison and cried for her son. My beloved, what will be your fate? The hunger at home was unbearable. My father brought soup ("*Balanda*") when he returned from work to revive our souls.

My father worked in the road near the "*Gebietskommissar*" and became friendly with a Pole named, Mackevic, who supervised the Jewish slave laborers. My father became friendly with him. It turned out that Mackevic loved the Jews. I came to him from the Ghetto and he bought vegetables for me. This man saved me when I escaped from the Ghetto.

On September 1942, the Ghetto was surrounded by Gestapo sentinels. An order was issued for the Jews to gather in the streets. There, they were divided in groups of 100-150 people and led in differed directions. The gentiles stood in masses on both sides of the street and rejoiced. As fate would have it, our group was led between the tracks in the direction of a place called "The Green

Forest", where some of Lida's Jews had been slaughtered in 1942. When I realized this I told my parents: "see where they're leading us - to a certain death. I'll try to escape."

[Page 243]

My mother objected and said "you're too young, you will get lost" (I was only eleven then). My father, on the other hand, encouraged me and said: "try my son, try!" Since my mother held me tight, I bit her hand, and crept among the gentiles who stood crowded around us.

In the street I looked like one of the *shkotzim* and didn't draw attention to myself. I walked slowly, slowly until I arrived to our acquaintance, Mackevic, who lived on the other side of the city. They were frightened, but welcomed me, and were glad that I survived. They took me to the barn and hid me under piles of straw. I was there for three days.

The gentile's wife brought me food and drink on her way to milk the cows without saying a word for fear that the matter would be discovered. I lay in the straw and cried in secret: "what would be my fate? Where are my parents and my sister, are they still alive? Will the farmer keep me, or betray me?" These, and similar thoughts, pecked incessantly in my head. A lonely little boy is in a hostile environment - and the tears choked my throat. Suddenly, I remembered that I must not cry-- not allowed to say a word.

4

On the third day, at nightfall, the woman entered the barn and whispered that I would have to walk to a certain intersection in the forest where I'll meet two children. "Join them," she told me, "and they'll lead you to a safe place."

It turned out that they were a brother and sister, members of the Hochman family from Soletchnik. They had also been hidden by the same gentiles in a second barn. I joined them and we wandered in the forest until we reached a village where we saw figures walking around with rifles on their shoulders. I got closer to one of the figures and discovered, to my surprise, that it was Moshe Druck. He hugged me and took me to one of the buildings where I was given food and clothes. In this manner around one hundred people gathered in the village. A few days later they gathered us all and Yakov Druck, together with his friends, led us to "*Naliboki Puszcza.*"

After a journey of three days we reached the shore of the Berezina River, and there we met Russian partisans for the first time. They heard that Jews had arrived and searched for a doctor among them. By chance, there was a doctor from Baranovich in our group. On this occasion they took me and also two young men. In addition, they also took two young women from Lida, Tzila and Yehudit, apparently with the intention of exploiting them. However, the young women stood bravely and didn't give in to them. For this reason they were expelled and found refuge with Bielski's partisans.

[Page 244]

The core of our group was organized in Moscow and consisted of 20 men who underwent a long period of training for guerilla warfare. Among them there was a Jew, Yakov Smolovitski, from Homl. When he learned that they had brought a Jewish boy, he protected me and took care of me like a father. Two days after I arrived to the group he returned from a mission and brought me a pair of appropriate boots, underwear, and fur. He made sure to equip me with a short-barrel shotgun. The commander was Major Ruscinsky.

Our camp was situated behind Berezina River, at the entrance to the *Puszcza*. We were surrounded by swamps and the only passage to the *Puszcza* was through the lake (The Black Lake). We guarded the bridge and our people constantly patrolled the lake by boats.

We had been entrusted to guard the entrance to the *Puszcza*. It was one of the most critical and dangerous tasks. For that reason our people were very alert to what was happening outside and followed the Germans' movements.

5

After I integrated a little into the place they started to use me for acts of espionage and scouting. Rumors reached the Otriad that a hunt was about to happen. Then, they decided to send me to Lida, to sniff and see if there was any military movement. Sometimes, I sat for hours across from the German Gendarmerie and followed what was happening there. Sometimes, I watched a military camp and in the evening went to an agreed location from which a runner took me to the base.

Once, I met Jews who had escaped from the "Fort" in Kovne and were headed to Bielski's camp.

From Divenishok's people I only met Meir Yosef Itskovitsh. It was about two months after I arrived to the partisans, when I was on guard duty at the lake. Suddenly, a group of partisans arrived and their scout, who was riding on a white horse, moved back and forth in search of a place to cross. I got closer to him and to my great surprise - I couldn't believe what I saw: before me was Meir Yosef Itskovitsh. The meeting was emotional. We hugged, kissed, shared about two good hours and parted.

During my time with the partisans I also got to experience a hunt. It was in late autumn of 1943. The Germans surrounded us with great forces and started to advance into the *Puszcza*. We were forced to escape to the boggy marshes, deep in the forest. For a weak we lay in the marshes, hung the rifles on the bushes and survived by eating "*Brosnitzes*" (sour-flavored red berries that grow in the forests of Poland in the autumn). We drank the water from the swamp, like frogs.

The German intelligence made great efforts to plant spies among the partisans. The commanders tried not to accept local people, but, in spite of it, more than once, spies infiltrated our ranks. Some of them were exposed right before my eyes.

After the winter, they stopped my intelligence activities and attached me to the ranks of fighters. As a partisan I left for action together with all the members. I participated in several activities. I had great satisfaction in laying dynamite blocks under the train tracks and watch from afar how German soldiers and equipment rose in the air...

In one of the actions we destroyed a train that transported officers to a holiday. We caught five German officers, took them to the base so they could see everything with their own eyes. We told them to dig pits and undress, the Germans kept family pictures in a small pouch on their neck. When they got undressed the pictures fell and scattered in all directions. That reminded me of the pictures that were scattered near the death pits around Poland. The Germans begged and asked for mercy - but they were eliminated on the spot.

The yearly memorial service in Tel-Aviv for the martyrs of Divenishok – the executive committee together with guests from the United States, Meir and Fanny Bolinski z"l[Tr. Note: Of Blessed Memory] *(1960)*

[Page 246]

6

With liberation our company entered the city of Ivia. The vast majority were taken into the army, including my benefactor, Yakov Smolovitski, who fell in battle. Our commander was appointed mayor of the city of Lida. Moshe Druck and his family also lived in the city. I was sent to a vocational school where all the miserable people gathered. There was a feeling of discomfort in the institution. The Christian boys sensed that I was a Jew and started to harass me. Then, I made up my mind to escape. When everyone was taken to the bath house I dodged and escaped to Druck. I stayed with them for several days and in the meantime we learned that an orphanage for Jewish children was being organized in Vilne. Druck and his wife, Feigale, traveled with me to Vilne and handed me over to the director of the orphanage.

A Jewish school was organized near the orphanage. Children who grew up in Christian homes, or were educated in monasteries, or stayed, like me, with the partisans, studied there. The school had a team of Jewish educators whose only aspiration was to bring us back to the bosom of our nation and our homeland...

I Got to See a Picture of the People I Love

Nili Itskovitsh

Translation by Sara Mages

From the day I was born I was given everything I asked for. But, I lacked two things, a grandfather and a grandmother-- that my parents couldn't give me.

When I was little I didn't understand how precious they would be, but as I grew older I began to long for them. I longed for the little house that was built in the format of the time and was furnished in the old style, a grandmother who would sit on a rocking chair and knit me a pink sweater, and a grandfather with a beard, that I could sit on his lap when I would come to visit him and hear stories about my father, how he lived and behaved in his childhood, and then, come home and tell my parents: "you see, you always blame me, but grandfather told me that you, too, father, didn't sit idle," and the whole family will laugh with joy.

I missed the meal, in which the whole family would sit together and grandmother would serve antiquated but very tasty dishes. I wanted a grandfather who will come to our house with a bundle of gifts and repeat the question: "So, Nillinka, what to bring you next time?"

[Page 247]

That is all I wanted, and if it had been given to me I would've been one of the happiest girls in the world, but, God disappointed me and I would never get it.

Since I couldn't change the reality, I wanted, at lease, to see their picture, a small picture that would show me images that I'm so eager to see. One clear day I turned to my father with a question: father, can you show me a picture of grandfather and grandmother? But my father's answer was like a thunder on a clear day. "No, Nilli, to my great sorrow all of my parents' pictures were destroyed during the war, my brother also doesn't have a single picture." Imagine how great my disappointment, but suddenly I had a spark of hope: I would turn to my mother. And if you ask why I forgot to mention my mother's parents earlier, I will tell you, but I hope that you won't tell it to my mother. I liked my father's parents more from the stories he told me about them. But, it's possible, that if my mother sat and told me about her parents, their life, their house and their village, they would also attract my attention. Therefore, I turned to my mother, and as you may have imagined I received the same answer from her.

When I heard her answer I lay in bed and burst into tears.

And so, the days have passed. I was jealous at the children who had a grandfather and grandmother, and my desire to see their [my grandparents'] picture intensified.

One day, my father came home from work and announced: "a memorial service will be held today for my townspeople, and if Nilli will behave nicely, I'll take her with me." You can imagine how I behaved on that day. I imagined that I would get to hear interesting stories and tales about the Diaspora.

In the evening, my father and I got dressed in festive clothes and traveled to the hall where the memorial service would take place. The hall was filled to capacity. People talked to each other and reminisced. I sat in the corner and waited for the opening of the ceremony. The ceremony began exactly at six. The first part, which was a Yizkor prayer, didn't interest me, but I was very impressed from the second part. Pictures from the old days were shown on a screen. I looked at the pictures with great pleasure and suddenly, one of the pictures showed a middle-aged couple standing on the steps of a house and the name: "Nathan Itskovitsh the tailor and his wife" was announced. My eyes lit up; I looked at the picture with great interest. I looked at their facial features, the hairstyle, the clothes, and tears of joy burst from my eyes.

I engraved their image well within my heart, and then I didn't continue to look at the pictures. All that evening I saw before me a beautiful grandfather with fair hair and a bald spot in the middle of the head, long pants with suspenders, and a grandmother in a black dress. A black scarf was wrapped around her head and every crease and wrinkle in her face, which looked out of the scarf, was portrayed before me. I also managed to see the house, the pretty garden, the stairs leading to a wooden door, and the sign on which a pair of scissors was painted - a symbol for a tailor.

[Page 248]

There was no end to my happiness. The next day, I told all my girlfriends about my beloved grandfather and grandmother. Indeed, I got to see the picture of the people that I loved with my own eyes.

(From "*Davar le-Yeladim*" / 32/38, 22.5.1962

A section of the audience at the yearly memorial service in Tel-Aviv (1963)

[Page 249]

C. Images

[Page 251]

My Father, the Great Rabbi Yosef Rudnik

Avraham Abir (Rudnik)

Translation by Meir Bulman

The life of my father, and his story, were near and dear to my heart more than my own soul, and that fact is what deterred me from wanting to summarize in a writing what I remember and what I have heard from others.

From a young age my father excelled in talent and intelligence, good taste, and alertness and loyalty of heart. Everyone expected a great future for him. At an older age he was educated at the Volozhin Yeshiva (he studied alongside a young C.N. Bialik.) He then continued his studies at the Kovne Kollel and was ordained as a rabbi by the great Rabbi Shlomo HaCohen from Vilne, the President of the Rabbinic Court in Kovne– Rabbi Zvi Hirsch Rabinovitsh– and the President of the Slabodke Court– the great Rabbi Moshe Donshevski.

My father's father–in–law (my grandfather) was the great Rabbi Avraham Abali, Varzhan Rabbinic Court President, author of the *Ahavat Etan* commentary on the *Mishna* by Re'em Publishers. Grandfather is also mentioned in the book *Ohelei Shem* about the great rabbis of Russia.

*

My father's first steps in the rabbinate were in Horodok, near Byalistock, a wool manufacturing town, the home of the Chief Town Rabbi Nissan Broyde, a famous rabbi and activist in the <u>Hovevei Zion</u> movement,[1] by whom he was very much influenced in rabbinical administration.

My father–in–law Rabbi Shmuel Avinoam (Zuckerman) who lived then in Horodok, says of him in his memoirs, "In those days, the Great Rabbi Yosef became ill.[2] Before the doctors sent him abroad, he invited the ordained Rabbi Yosef Rudnik, a man of great traits and good deeds, to overlook the rabbinate in his absence. In a short time, Rabbi Yosef managed to become favored and acquired the admiration and hearts of the town residents, both from the devout and the more liberally minded, rich, and poor alike. We, the young Zionists, established a Talmud club in the Zionist Council house, and Rabbi Yosef volunteered to conduct classes. His classes were so interesting that in a short time the number of listeners increased significantly enough that the large hall was too small to contain everyone, and many listened through open windows. That was because his explanations were simple, full of content, palatable, and also spiced with allegory and contemporary matters in the right places."

"Those classes made a deep impression on me and many of my friends, who at that time were beginning to take a genuine interest in Talmud, leaving an unforgettable mark on their souls and consciousness. I will never forget the expression of joy on [the faces of] many of the listeners, who found a light in the Talmud which they had forgotten about for years, and if they had remembered seemed tasteless and dry. When they now saw proof of how much sense and logic there was to [the Talmud], it seemed like they had found a treasure, and they would often express those feelings afterwards."

"After Rabbi Nissan passed away many of the town residents demanded that Rabbi Yosef be appointed town rabbi, but Rabbi Yosef himself was among those who proposed finding a husband for the Rabbi's oldest daughter who would be worthy of the honor of chief town rabbi, and with that the question of the large orphaned family would be solved as well. And so they did."

Administration of the Tarbus School (1938 [according to the Yiddish]/ 1930 [according to the Hebrew]) at the time of the visit of Meir Bolinski and G. Levey from America. In the middle of the first row, Rabbi Rudnik z.ts"l[Tr. Note: May His Saintly Memory Be For a Blessing; Ed. Note: in the middle row, second from right, Munye Kherson]

The bond between Rabbi Nissan's family and my father's family continued for many years even after my father left Horodok, including contacts with his brother Rabbi Shlomo Meirson (who was chairman of the Torah Council for many years) who later brought Rabbi Nissan's daughter and her children to Israel and took an interest in their future until the children matured and settled in Israel.

After he completed his role in Horodok, my father was appointed rabbi at the town of Bilitza. There, his talent and understanding in community administration were uncovered. Under the harsh conditions of the Pale of Settlement, where concerns about economic wellbeing were elevated, where life was not protected from the danger of an attack by hostile Christians, and where malicious authorities sought to restrict and torment Jews, the role of town rabbi was very difficult. Aside from religious matters he also cared for other community matters, for the poor, for victims of fate, for the welfare and charitable institutions, *Bikur Holim*,[3] *Linat Zedek*,[4] *Gemilut Hesed*,[5] the burial society, the religious schools, as well as for the Torah scholars: the Talmud Society, the *Ein Yaakov*, the Mishnah, and so forth.[6] He was both the initiator and [operational] executive, because heads of household were busied by making a living and only few could be devoted to community matters.

*

Educating the Children of Israel in the ways of Torah and its labors was his main goal in life and he devoted much of his strength and funds to sending the talented to yeshiva. For those who did not fit that role he would ensure they could study a profession. Rabbi Sheftel the Shoe-Craftsman from Bilitza said at the funeral that when his son Yerakhmiel departed for yeshiva, he went to the rabbi to bid him farewell, and when he reached to shake his hand, a metallic object rolled into his hand. The boy was confused and, sensing this, the rabbi told him, "Don't worry, dear, take the money, it will be of help to you in a strange place."

My aunt, Ruth Shurin (U.S.) said that when he would donate to charity from his own funds he would give the money without counting it first. When he was asked, "Rabbi, why do you do that?" he replied, "Why should I count it? The pauper will count!

*

My father objected to the longwinded debate method of study customary in Lithuanian yeshivas, where even at a younger age the students were force-fed additional commentary and longwinded debate while ignoring the core, standard interpretation of the Talmud. According to his method, the pupil should begin with standard interpretation, then study added material pertaining to the standard interpretation, and once the student had already studied his fair share of Talmudic matters, then could be studied all the additional commentary.

He would say that students could find the answer to the commentator's question on the first page if his studies progressed to the tenth page.[7] He did not send me and friends my age to the yeshiva for younger ages, but brought us to the older-age-range Radin Yeshiva, where, following a consultation with the supervisor Rabbi Eliezer Kaplan, a teacher among the excellent students was designated for each younger student— who taught us separately the Talmud without complex commentary. The truth of his claims about the study method was proven because we made such progress that after a single year of study I was accepted to the upper-class at Rabbi Elchonen Wasserman's Yeshiva, whose study method was also based on standard interpretation excluding complex debate.

All throughout my stay at the yeshiva my father funded me generously. I did not have to rely on homeowners, as it was then the custom for a student to eat at a different home each day, and I did not need the yeshiva's funds, nor did I receive grants, even when I studied at the higher yeshiva.

*

My father was a loyal leader of his community, and I think that thanks to leaders and rabbis like him our nation were able to hold on through its long and bitter exile. Of course, he was also a good husband and a devoted father.

My mother told me that his whole life he would take out the trash at night and then bring back water buckets and chopped wood for heating and cooking— to save this trouble from my mother when there was no housekeeper. Indeed, the burden of maintaining the household, including the financial burden rested on her shoulders and she knew [how to] conduct the rabbi's home very well. In addition to her righteousness, her love for the Torah knew no bounds. She was a beautiful woman of valor, knew how to overcome all obstacles, and was of much help to Father including in rabbinate matters, to the point where it was said of her that she is a rebbetzin not just because she is the rabbi's wife but in her own right. From the experience of observing and listening she knew how to determine the *halachic*[8] verdict on many rules, but was very cautious to not rule or predict how my father would rule. If Father was absent, she would expertly deliver the contents of the question.

My father did not always have enough time to look after and care for his home and children, but he devoted special attention to orphans (perhaps because he himself grew up as an orphan.) When my sister Bruria was in the United States (with her husband Avraham Aloni), Yaakov Cohen, who was orphaned in childhood, told her that our father looked after his wellbeing and his education, and would often show him affection to fill the what he was missing the most, and he remembers it and feels it with every fiber of his being.

Once on Sukkot night, an orphan entered the synagogue wearing a ragged hat. When my father saw that he called the hatter and asked him to make a hat at his expense, which the hatter did.

My adopted brother Rabbi Aharon said while eulogizing our father, that through his entire life our father was careful to not show excessive affection to his biological sons and daughters, fearing his adopted son would be offended. Every time and in every situation he found the time to teach him Torah and the ways of life, though he did not always find the time for his biological children.

When our adopted brother arrived at our home, he was six years old and grew very attached to my father. He also inherited the role of town rabbi after father's death and fulfilled his role with great success because he followed in the footsteps of our father and followed his experience. After becoming well known among other rabbis he was destined for greatness if not for the bitter enemy who murdered him along with six dear souls from his family (in Ponary, Vilne). My efforts and the efforts of Rabbi Tzvik (his brother-in-law) to bring him to Israel were unsuccessful, but an orchard remains of him in Israel, which he managed to purchase in peacetime, thinking eventually he would succeed in making *aliyah* with his family since he was a great lover of Zion. Rabbi Kalmen Parvar, now the Ramla district officer, who was with him in Vilne and survived and got to Israel, told me of Aharon's final days. His friend from the Radin Yeshiva, now Netanya Chief Rabbi Moshe Levine, told me with much pain and suffering about Aharon's studiousness in Torah and his expansive education.

My father did not only look out for orphans but for all families in his community. One of his sacred duties was writing letters to America seeking assistance for relatives who had stayed behind in Russia, and there was barely a time when such requests were denied. He styled the letters in a brief and clear manner so as not to burden the receiving party, and would inject much warmth and emotion into his writing. Thanks to the support of relatives, Jews living in the Pale of Settlement were able to make a living and could educate their children, as well as sustain community institutions. My father had close relationships with activists in America who sent significant sums to the town.

Our family too was sustained mainly by the assistance we received from relatives in America, not from the low salary of a town rabbi. My aunt Chaya Henye was devoted to the role and contributed and urged others to contribute to their relative, the well-respected rabbi beloved by all. My uncle R' Yaakov sent immigration documents many times and implored him to emigrate to America, but out of concern for the children's education, and due to his personality, he was not interested in life in America and rejected the offer. In contrast, throughout his life, he desired to make *aliyah* and was delighted that thanks to his brother, Hedera mayor Shlomo Meirson, his daughters made *aliyah* during his lifetime and settled in Hedera (most of the *olim* from Bilitza followed them thus turning Hedera into a center for Bilitzians in Israel.)

My father was quite irritated by residents of our town who had shared relatives in the United States who saw each other as competitors risking one another's portion from their shared relative. There were incidents when one of them slandered the other with an accusation he did not need assistance since he had a substantial income, sufficient to maintain his household. At about the same time a relative from a neighboring town asked my father to write to a shared relative in America about a crisis and encourage assistance. My father immediately did as requested, writing a letter to the shared relative describing in heartfelt words the condition of the person who had requested help and asking for assistance. A short while later a response arrived thanking father for his efforts on behalf of his fellow man along with a check for both my father and the relative. Father then used that incident as evidence in rebuking those who had acted jealously, and explained to them how the opposite mindset was best: "One who solicits mercy for his fellow while he himself needs the same thing will be answered first."[9]

*

Father invested much effort and energy in caring for his community being tormented by the authorities whose sole purpose was to confiscate Jewish income sources, primarily based on market–day Wednesdays. Villagers would bring their produce for sale and would purchase goods from local workshops. The government demanded the relocation of the market to out of town. The excuse was hygiene, i.e., to clean–up the marketplace from trash and dirt, but the true intention was to sever the income of Jewish merchants since [it would be] Christians opening the stores out of town. Father made every effort, worked, and energized the town's activists, and appeared before the authorities to make his claims that [the policy] was an attempt to deprive Jews' of an income source. Eventually the authorities agreed that the market should stay in place and only the livestock market was moved out of town.

The authorities harassed the bakeries as well when they demanded bread be baked only in electric ovens, when there was no electricity in town. Father traveled to the district governor who expressed his wonder that an educated and wise man would object to such a helpful law which is for the benefit of the population's health maintenance. Father replied, "I have been here for decades and have never heard of someone in the area dying because of eating bread. And for this shadow of a concern certain death will be inflicted on dozens of souls." The governor was eventually convinced to postpone the edict until such time when there would be electricity in town and electric ovens could be installed.

On a similar topic, there was [the case of] a Jewish baker at the time of the Soviet invasion of Poland. At the end of WWI, this baker was accused by the Communist military of having baked bread for sale without receiving a permit to do so and was facing execution. Though father knew the Communists did not respect rabbis, he decided to attempt to convince them for the sake of saving a life. They asked him how long he had known the accused and father replied that he had known him to be an honest respectable man, and that this was the first offense, that he did not fully comprehend, and thus should be forgiven this time.

When the transcript was ready the interrogator told my father that everything would be done publicly, which is why they would go outside to announce the decision. A squadron of soldiers stood outside and the interrogator/officer, and Father, faced them. The transcript was read and when the officer finished he faced Father and said, "Your words indicated you are friends with the accused and we have the same verdict for the criminal and his friend." Father wanted to reply but a Jewish soldier from the squad put his hand over his mouth and hinted he should remain silent, thus probably saving his life. When father later told of the incident, which confirmed to him that the Communists considered a rabbi to be a criminal, he would add that peace is virtuous even for sinners and "I'm probably a rabbi to the Communists as well; they need a rabbi more than do all the town residents."

On a related note, a similar event was mentioned which took place in the era of the Czar. The Jews were hated then too, but religious representatives were respected. Once, the Patriarch vested Bilitza and the population went to greet him, among them Jews led by the rabbi who greeted him with bread and salt as was traditional, and with the *Birkat Cohanim*,[10] to which the patriarch responded in perfect Hebrew. That made a strong impression on the Christian population and raised esteem [for the Jews] in their eyes.

Father was popular among the Gentiles and had friends among their intellectuals. The Russian Pope was considered a friend. When the Poles occupied the region they banned the Pravoslav Church and inserted Catholic clergy in their place, and exiled the Pope, despite the population being overwhelmingly Pravoslav. The Pope came to my father to pour out his heart, complaining of the injustice done to his tribe, and wept bitterly. Father consoled him as was demanded by courtesy and when he left father said, "I am surprised he learned so well how to complain of his bitter fate and weep—just like a Jewish rabbi."

*

Advisees would come to the rabbi's home regarding questions on Kosher laws, as was customary. One Friday, while I passed with father through the market place, a woman approached us holding a chicken and apologized for bothering father on his way, but she wanted to ask a question. "You did well," Father replied, "why should you go through the trouble of walking all the way to my house on a Friday." As he spoke he entered a nearby home, was handed a knife, and he opened the chicken, checked, and gave his ruling.

*

Since childhood I loved helping father with building the *sukkah*, which he would construct on his own (I would go with him to get the covering). The *sukkah* was large because many [people] visited the rabbi's home during the festival, and on the Feast of Water-Drawing the whole community would come to the *sukkah* to eat and rejoice after reciting the Song of Ascents from the Psalms.

*

Every Friday, my father would go inspect the *eruv*[11] so that town residents would not, unknowingly commit the sin of carrying items from property to property on Shabbat, God forbid. There was a period when the eruv was getting torn every Friday and Father worked to repair it. A police complaint was filed since it was assumed that Gentles were doing it to torment the Jews, but eventually it became clear that policemen had done this themselves, for their own amusement, to irritate Jews.

*

I do not remember every detail about the relocation or the negotiations surrounding my father's agreement to accept the role in Divenishok, but the days of moving to the new town remain in my memory.

When news [emerged] that father had accepted the rabbinate in a different town, Bilitza was in turmoil. A strategy to prevent his exit was being planned. The salary was doubled and people came and asked him to stay, emphasizing that which was the will of the public, even among those who did not identify with the rabbi's administration of the town.

When the coaches for moving items and furniture arrived from Divenishok, the Bilitza community gathered together to prevent this, even if by force. However, my father explained to them that the parting of ways would be tough on him as well, but because he had accepted the rabbinate contract from the people of Divenishok and they had put much effort into setting up the rabbi's home, he could not renege.

Guarded by the coachmen, items were loaded, and when that was completed they went on their way while we traveled by train. Community members accompanied the rabbi, and on the way, the crowd detoured to the synagogue where the rabbi departed with a heartfelt speech quoting the Prophet Samuel [at his farewell address] after the ordination of King Saul, "Whose ox have I taken? Whose donkey have I taken?" etc. (1 Samuel 12:3), and added Rashi's commentary, "for their needs I used my own donkey" (and did not take theirs). As usual, the words fit the situation, since everyone knew that he had served his community with total devotion and for a minimal salary.

The community, men, women, and children, walked the rabbi and our family out of town, where the procession stopped and R' Eliahu Sokolvski made a speech and remarked, "The rabbi was the gold chain holding all of us and linked us to one another, and now as he leaves us we will all maintain that unity and walk the path given to us by God." Everyone parted ways in tears and wished [us] luck at the new place.

In all the tumult we forgot Itshe the synagogue custodian who was very close to the rabbi and our family, and now as we got closer [to the train station] we felt his absence from the crowd and Father was quite worried something had happened to him. We reached the Neiman train station and were about to board the train. As we stood there, very concerned, R' Itshe suddenly appeared, weeping and crying like an infant and unable to speak, not even a "shalom." He tried boarding the train car with us, but we convinced him to return home with the coachmen who brought us.

We traveled three hours before reaching Benakani, where town notables from Divenishok waited for us. We entered a well-lighted house arranged for us near the station; wine and refreshments were served. We sat around a table in an atmosphere of friendship and good conversation. I remember Shmuel Kherson the tailor and gabbai at the synagogue, who was also a cantor, pleased listeners with his beautiful voice. Zushe-Yankel the tar-workshop (the smalyarne) owner, Aryeh Leyb Rogol the pharmacist, and many more [were there]. Father had a conversation with Aryeh Leyb about his house that was being reconstructed after the fire and was happy to hear that it was built up to the roof and would be completed soon at that construction pace.

The next morning our journey continued and we made our way from Benakani to Divenishok (≈30 km) on a horse-pulled carriage. The road passed through pine forests and Gentile villages; a small town of only 20 Jewish families named Kalelishok was on the road. They told us they previously had a rabbi but after his death the town joined the Divenishok community.

We met Jews there who had walked from Divenishok to greet the rabbi. Among them I remember R' Pesach the synagogue custodian, a Jew with a quick sense of humor. He told us the entire community awaited us a few kilometers from Divenishok where an honor-gate was built for the arrival.

Father was deeply moved and said, "Jews who live in a sea of Gentile villagers ignore their everyday activities and cancel a work day to pay their respect to a representative of the Torah they live by, and appoint him rabbi according to their wishes. Is that not independence and freedom within subjection?"

We reached the meeting spot, where the whole town, old and young, women and children, all stood together. I remember my sister Bruria, then a student at the Epshteyn Gymnasium in Vilne, stood in the coach and made a speech in Hebrew. The procession continued from there straight to the synagogue which was illuminated by daylight which added festiveness. Father ascended the stage near the ark wrapped in a *tallit* and gave his speech to the townsfolk who packed the synagogue to capacity. I do not remember the content, but the joyful faces of the listeners nodding their heads in agreement appear before me. When my father descended the stage the crowd surrounded him to shake his hand. My father served that community for nearly a decade—to his last day.

Avraham Aloni, Avraham Abir (Israel), Rebitsin Rudnik, Sheyne Rudnik
[Ed. Note: top row, left] and Naomi z"l[Tr. Note: Of Blessed Memory]

I remember once as I stood and privately recited the morning prayer in a corner at the synagogue, I heard my father's voice choking back tears. I approached to check what had happened and found him sitting and speaking to his flock about the *Mishna in Bikkurim*,[12] describing how our forefathers had magnificently brought the sacrificial First Fruit "even King Aggripa mounted the basket on his shoulder and entered" [Bikkurim 3:4]. Father was overtaken by longing and excitement and cried, and his students, the working men, cried with him. To this day [I still can see] that image of grown men busy with their daily lives crying in longing for the glory days in *Eretz Israel*.

Father always emphasized his satisfaction with the honor that some of his descendants were in Israel, and would add, "People say that the wishes a man does not fulfil in his lifetime are fulfilled through his children. I was not fortunate to make *aliyah*, but was honored by my children doing so." While still in his prime he planned to visit his beloved brother Shlomo in Israel. He said, "After I return from my visit we will make *aliyah* as a family." He received a tourist visa and was fully prepared for his journey, but meanwhile, did not feel well and decided to visit Dr. Shabad in Vilne to examine his health. At that visit the doctor discovered terminal cancer.

My brother Aharon and my sister Bruria traveled with our father to Vienna, Austria where the greatest medical experts operated, followed by my sister Sarah and my uncle Shlomo who all did whatever possible to save his life. He was brought into the operating room and even administered anesthesia, but the doctors did not operate after closely examining the type of illness and the patient's state. He did not know he had not been operated on and said later that the operation had been very easy, but that he was not feeling relieved and healed.

Father returned from Vienna to his home in Divenishok shortly before Passover of 5693 [1933]. On Seder night he left his bed, barely ate a small portion of *matzah brei* and said he could not taste the flavor. Despite the worsening pain, he did not give up hope that he would be healed, and frequently repeated: "How nice and beautiful the world is."

He faded away with each passing day until on Sivan 23, 5693 [17/06/1933], a Friday afternoon, he returned his pure soul to his Creator.

M.H.S.B.B.E.L: From the booklet *Father's Home* by Avraham Abir (Rudnik.)

Editor's Footnotes

1. "The first *Hovevei Zion* (Lovers of Zion) organizations were established in 1881--1882 with the aim of furthering Jewish settlement, particularly agricultural settlement in Eretz–Israel. From its inception, the Hovevei Zion groups in Russia sought to erect a country¬wide legally recognized framework. After arduous negotiations, in which the authorities

demanded that the society be set up as a charitable body, its establishment was approved, early in 1890, as The Society for the Support of Jewish Farmers and Artisans in Syria and Eretz–Israel, which came to be known as The Odessa Committee. In 1892, the organization had approximately 14,000 sympathizers in Russia. Among its leaders were Rabbi Samuel Mohilever (1824¬1898), Moshe Leib Lilienblum (1843¬–1910) and Leon Pinsker (1821¬–1891). Following the publication of Herzl's *Der Judenstaat* in 1896, and the establishment of the World Zionist Organization, most of the branches of Hovevei Zion aligned themselves with the new movement." (From 'Zionism: Hovevei Zion' in Jewish Virtual Library, http://www.jewishvirtuallibrary.org/hovevei–zion, last accessed on 2 January 2018).

2. The quote addresses Rabbi Broyde as a Yosef, while in the prior paragraph he is named Nissan. This could be an error in the text or perhaps Rabbi Broyde was both a Nissan and a Yosef, i.e. Nissan Yosef Broyde, etc.

3. Literally, the commandment which says to visit and aid the sick; societies going by that name have arisen to carry out this commandment.

4. Literally, paupers' hostel— a society that provided overnight lodgings for poor travelers.

5. A charitable fund or service for the needy, also providing interest–free loans.

6. The list refers to various study groups focused on these particular texts.

7. It was therefore not necessary to read all the additional commentaries to the question on the first page before proceeding.

8. Halacha = Jewish Law

9. Tr. Note: The quotation is from the Babylonian Talmud, Baba Kama 92a

10. The Cohen's (priest's) benediction.

11. A fabricated perimeter around certain public areas that allows Jews to carry items within the perimeter during the Sabbath day.

12. The mishnah portion discussing the ritual of the first fruits.

[Page 259]

In Memory of Rabbi Rudnik

Shraga Blyakher
Translation by Meir Bulman

Like all Jewish communities in the Diaspora, spiritual leadership in our town was in the hands of the rabbi: halachic trials, representation before the authorities, administering the town's institutions, etc. He was responsible for all those matters since they demanded wisdom, flexibility, a strong personality, and the power to persuade and influence. With wisdom, he cared for the poor and always stood by the side of the weak, the working man, the poor.

The rabbi had a majestic appearance. He was tall, his face expressing kindness. Rabbi Yosef Rudnik was smart and worldly-wise.

He was attached to *Eretz Israel* with every fiber of his being, and in his fiery lectures he managed to bring many closer to Judaism, especially among the youth. Despite not being a self-declared Zionist, he was devoted to the Zionist ideal his whole life. He initiated the establishment of the Tarbut Hebrew School in our town, from which the youth learned the Hebrew language and a love of *Eretz Israel*.

It should be noted that hiring a teacher at the school was conditioned on their agreement to counsel members of *HaShomer HaTzair*, to which the teachers Aloni and Dubkin would testify. I, who was among those often present in the rabbi's home, regularly received counseling on how to conduct matters at *HaShomer HaTzair*.

I remember that when Moshe Lubetski, Yakov Schneider, and Meir Yosef Itskovitsh established the *Beitar* chapter in town and it was decided to kick us out of the school building. The rabbi rose against that decision, and indeed the decision was overturned.

The rabbi's death shocked us. My brother Tuvye and I sat all night with the deceased and read Psalms. The funeral took place the next day and he was eulogized by many rabbis from the region.

May his pure should be bound in the bond of everlasting life with all the sacred souls of Israel and their memory shall last forever.

Rabbi Yisrael Movshovitsh

Yosef Movshovitsh
Translation by Meir Bulman

Rabbi Yisrael Movshovitsh

Our family, Movshovitsh, is a family of distinguished lineage, which generated Torah Scholars and rabbis over many generations. Though it is difficult for me to reconstruct the family lineage due to lack of documentation in the family tree, I do know that my great-grandfather Rabbi Asher Shabbtai Rabinovitsh served as rabbi in Divenishok for approximately 30 years, from 1850–1880. After his death, his son Yosef Yehuda, (who had served previously as *Dayan* [Tr. Rabbinic judge] in Oshmene) was appointed town rabbi. He served in that role for 24 years, until 1904.

Rabbi Yosef Yehuda was a man of great wisdom and Torah knowledge, and was widely known. He was invited often to Beth Din[Ed. Note: rabbinical court] trials out of town. I have in my possession a few letters from Volozhin's Rabbi Rafael Shapiro, that began with the words "To the honored, brilliant, rabbi, "*Likhvod Harav HaGaon Khakima DeYehudae*".[Tr. Note: wise among the Jews]

After the death of my grandfather, his son-in-law *HaRav* Yisrael Movshovitsh was appointed as town rabbi. He was immersed in *Torah* and well versed in the *Poskim*.[Ed. Note: Jewish jurisprudence] In his youth he studied in the *Maltz Yeshiva* in Lithuania, but he was particularly praised at the *Slabodke (Lite) Yeshiva*, where my father excelled as an *Illui*,[Tr. Note: prodigy] and where many *Talmidei Hakhamim*[Ed. Note: wise Torah scholars] originated.

My father was ordained as rabbi by *HaRav HaGaon*[Ed. Note: title given to a Rabbi of exceptionally proud merit] Zalmen Sender, father of the well-known Rabbi Shapiro, AB"D[Tr. Note: Av Beth Din- Chief of Rabbinical Court; leading community rabbi of the community] of Kovne. My father administrated all spiritual and public life in town, and was particularly punctilious in lecturing on the daily *Talmud Daf*[Ed. Note: daily page from the Bablonian Talmud] to the community elders, who excelled in their deep knowledge of *Talmud* and the *Poskim*.

His public activity was not limited to the confines of the town, but encompassed much broader horizons. My father participated in public activities around the entire Vilne district, a district that was rightfully considered to be the spiritual and cultural center of the entire region dubbed *Cressy* (the north east district of Poland, bordering Lithuania and Russia). My father's tenure as a rabbi in Divenishok was accompanied by vicissitudes, turmoil, and change in the life of Russian Jewry. He began his tenure under a Czarist regime, a year before the Kishniev Pogrom. The progress and advancements of the enlightened world began penetrating Russia, and our town, though remote in the Lithuanian woods, began to awaken from its stillness. My father was the first to understand the importance of postal service. In 1907 he established a post office in town, and residents began to receive letters twice weekly. In 1908, my father established the Jewish bank, partly self-funded and partly funded by a loan from ICA[Ed. Note: Iddish Colonization Association] (a philanthropic company founded in 1891 by Baron Maurice de Hirsch, aimed at assisting Russian Jewry). The bank functioned as an important financial support system for Jewish town residents.

At that time, a big fire spread in Divenishok. The fire spread very rapidly through the market place, progressed south towards Subotnik and Geranion Streets, and to the north towards Vilne Street. The two synagogues were in grave danger. Chaim Alperovitsh (Aryeh Leyb Rogol's son-in-law), who was a great *Torah Scholar* and feared the fate of the synagogues, watched the flames as they sped towards Vilne Street, and said, "Do not despair, Jewish brothers! God will have mercy! It is not possible that the synagogues will burn. A miracle will happen and the fire will stop." And indeed, that miracle did occur; the fire stopped in front of the synagogues. The town residents saw this as the hand of God at work. After the fire, the bank served as a life-raft for town residents. The bank funded Jewish families in rebuilding their stores, as well as the brick homes in the market place.

My father initiated building a new bathhouse and *Mikveh*.[Ed. Note: Jewish ritual bath] Until then, the *Mikveh* had been a simple cistern.

Our town received substantial help from ICA, thanks to my father's close friendship with Efroykin, a senior ICA leader in Poland, who was his schoolmate in the *Slobodke Yeshiva*.

During the years of WWI, a famine struck the country, and my father labored without rest. He frequented aid institutions operating in Vilne, leading to substantial assistance in food and clothes to town residents. A soup kitchen was established for the town's poor.

After the war ended, aid from America intensified and increased. The *Yaakofu* organization was established then, and provided much assistance to Polish Jewry. *Yaakofu* had various and diverse functions, among them: aid to schools, clothing and food distribution for orphans and widows, and financial aid to children, the sick, and the disabled.

The regional center of *Yaakofu* was in Vilne, and my father was a member of the regional oversight committee. Thus, his requests for increased aid to our town were always answered with generosity.

My father was often invited to serve as mediator, or to complex *Beth Din* trials, and much of his time was spent out of town. Residents were occasionally angered by his absence, but at the bottom line they were proud that their rabbi was so respected and admired in the region and accepted his absence.

After serving for 20 years, he accepted an offer from the Jewish community in Trenton, capital of New Jersey, US, and in 1924 he left Divenishok and traveled to serve there as rabbi. In Trenton he was greeted with great admiration. Trenton has a large Jewish community, among them 60 families of former Divenishok residents. Shlomo Sholomovitsh, Avraham Noakh's brother, served as Kosher-slaughterer in Trenton after leaving Divenishok, and then transferred the job to his brother Avraham Noakh. Issac Horvits was Hebrew teacher there. My father remained active in public and cultural activities in Trenton too, and to this day the town residents praise his public services, the crown jewel of which is the *Gemilut Hesed*[Ed. Note: giver of interest-free loans] institution, still active to this day.

In 1929 he was appointed as rabbi in the *Zera Ya'akkov* Synagogue, and later served as rabbi in the *Ahavat Akhim* Synagogue. He eventually served as rabbi at *Beth Hamedrash Hagadol* on Forrest Avenue, Bronx, New York, where he lectured on Talmud to large audiences, and amazed all with his Talmudic knowledge and depth. There too, he did not cease his public service. He oversaw *Kashrut*,[Ed. Note: Jewish Dietatry Laws] and was active in *Relief for Divenishok*. He passed away in 1940.

After my father's passing, I was appointed as rabbi in the *Nezakh Yisrael* Synagogue in the Bronx, and served in that role until my retirement.

Rebitsin Movshovitsh with her sons and daughters

In the days of my youth, I studied in the Hebrew school, like all town children. After that, I attended grade school, where I studied Torah, arithmetic, Yiddish.and Hebrew. I remember that during the war years, the well-known Yiddish writer Glomb, and educator and writer Bastomski served as teachers in Divenishok. After that, I studied in *Kloyz Ramyless* in Vilne, and from there I transferred to a public gymnasium. After receiving my diploma, I traveled to Basel to study medicine. I studied medicine for two years, and then suddenly the Polish council demanded I return at once to Poland and present myself for military duty. I preferred to travel to the United States, and there I was accepted as a student to the Schechter Seminary. Concurrently, I studied chemistry at Columbia University. After four years of intensive study, I completed the seminary and was ordained as a rabbi, and also completed a master's degree. Until 1957 I worked in research, and since then I have been serving as a rabbi.

My eldest brother Nakhum completed his studies at the *Sofia Gorvits Gymnasium* in Vilne, where the language of instruction is Yiddish. After that, he traveled to Grenoble, France, where he completed an electrical engineering degree. He arrived in the United States in 1934, where he worked in his trade. He passed away in 1934.[Ed. Note: 1934 is given as both Nakhum's year of arrival and of death] My sister Reyzl passed away in 1967 in New York. My sister Blume lives in New York.

[Page 262]

My Father's House

Shmuel Sharon

Translation by Meir Bulman

My family members on my father's side – to my knowledge – lived in Divenishok over many generations.

My mother's family moved to town from neighboring Voronova after she married my father.

My paternal grandfather, Shepsel (Shabtai) was a dynamic man, industrious and active, with a firm body, bright, level headed, and was a sharp-minded merchant. He was a proud Jew, brave and self-confident. His gentile customers treated him with great honor and appreciation, and their confidence in him was absolute.

In his youth my grandfather labored intensively and worked at many trades. He particularly excelled in the building trade and built the home where we resided with his own two hands.

As was common in those days, my grandfather was married off right after his Bar Mitzvah. The first time he saw his bride was under the *Chuppah*. That had deeply wounded him, and when he reached independence he got divorced, without having had children by her.

From his second marriage he had an only daughter, who is Aunt Sarah Leah (Zeydke Lubetski's mother). My grandfather loved his grandson Zeydke very much, because of his athletic body type, his bravery and strength, perhaps he saw in him a mirror image of his younger self.

My father was his only son from his third marriage, and that's why his name was Ben Zion.

My grandmother Khaye Sorah was a righteous, merciful, and energetic woman. She oversaw the household until the day she died, leaving the store's operation to my mother. She accepted her destiny and took care of her blind sister Gitah Leah with love and devotion, until she passed away.

From the fruit of his labor my grandfather accumulated much wealth, and was a respected and admired member of the community. He passed before Passover of 1930 of old age and was brought to rest at the cemetery on Geranion Street. I remember that on his tombstone, prepared by Yaakov Olkenitski, were etched among others the words "by hard work he ate his bread"

My father, Ben Zion Schneider, continued to oversee the house and businesses he inherited from my grandfather, along with my mother Hinde Sarah, and they established a family worthy of pride. They had five children: the eldest Yaakov, myself, and my three sisters – Libke (Ahuva), Rozhke (Shoshana), and Leah ז"הי.

In addition to a big store (relatively big in terms of a small Eastern European town), my father owned lands in town and outside of town. Most of the fields were leased to gentiles, in exchange for part of the crops. On the rest of the land we labored ourselves and grew vegetables, potatoes, and fruits for our own consumption.

Though my father was busy with his family and businesses, he passionately devoted himself to involvement in public matters. That led to disagreements with my mother, who argued he was neglecting his livelihood for public involvement. My father was a Nationalistic Jew, an enthusiastic Zionist, and an observer of Jewish tradition; he saw his public involvement his life destiny. He argued that a man's unique value is not measured by how many years he lives, but rather by his actions and his service to the public. That idea guided him his entire life. Cruel fate wanted that his life to be short, but that life was accompanied by good deeds and intentions for the benefit of individuals and the community.

Naturally, in a small town a public servant must take care of many public issues, willingly or unwillingly. Our home was open to all and was a destination for every person in need, and to all those in pain, where they found aid and comfort. His heart was always open to assist and encourage.

I am unable to describe all my father's public activities. I will attempt to raise memories from the corners of the past, to demonstrate and shed light on his positive activities.

My father would claim that our existence in the Diaspora is conditioned upon Hebrew education. That is why he energetically fought for the establishment of a Hebrew school, and was fortunate to be among its founders. Each year he was a member of the school board and one of its main activists. He cared for the teachers' salaries and the school's maintenance. Despite financial difficulties, there was no incident where a poor child in town could not attend the school due to inability to pay tuition. My father guarded the school as the apple of his eye, because he knew that in this institution his children must be educated for love of the people and the homeland.

My father was among the initiators and founders of the Hebrew library. Because there was concern that the establishment of that library would damage the Yiddish *VILBIG* library, lovers of the Yiddish language were angered and began bothering him. He was even physically assaulted by them, but that did not deter him – and the Hebrew library became an established fact.

My father was among the administrators of the new *Bet Midrash*. During his time, the synagogue was put in order and the furniture was renewed. For that purpose, a painter was specially brought from Olshan, and he enriched the synagogue with breathtaking oil paintings on topics from the Bible and *Eretz Israel*. To this day the wonderful painting *In the Last Days* on the western synagogue wall remains in my heart.

Considered among the most important roles in town was *Chevra Kadisha*[Ed. Note: Jewish Burial Society] treasurer, because eventually every resident would need a *chesed shel emet*.[Tr. Note: literally the truest act of kindness; refers to the preparation of the deceased for burial] My father successfully served as treasurer for many years, though that role included great responsibility and annoyance. The treasurer had to haggle regarding burial fees with the stingy rich men as their dead lay before them. On the other hand, the company took care of funeral expenses for those in poverty who could not afford it.

The annual *Chevra Kadisha* dinner took place in our home. That Mitzvah was mother's, and grandmother's, pleasure.

My father was very active member on the *Gemach*[Ed. Note: interest-free loan banking] committee. Every Saturday night, with other committee members, he would distribute loans to the needy. Every request was individually considered. That role too was accompanied by annoyance, because every rejection was met with anger, and at times – with swearing and cursing.

My father was also a member of the administration of *The Jewish Bank* – the first and largest financial institution in town. The bank operated as a mutual organization and dispensed loans for business purposes, with interest rates the same as other banks.

In severe instances, when the aforementioned institutions could not provide assistance – such as a coachman's horse failing, which meant a family without a livelihood, or a bankrupt merchant, the problem was solved by a fundraiser. My father, along with his friends, would conduct a rapid fundraiser that was sufficient, say, to buy Chaim Hershovitsh a new horse, or to get that needy merchant back on his feet.

My father was also on the board of trustees overseeing the *Relief* funds from the United States, an organization established by former community residents now in New York, for purposes of aid, education, and culture in Divenishok.

My father's public actions were accompanied by deep awareness of Zionism, likely acquired at the Volozhin *Yeshiva*. His opinions were like those of Herzel and Jabotinski, and he did his best to instill these values in his children. His education bore fruit, and my eldest brother Yaakov reached the rank of commander in the *Betar* chapter of Divenishok.

My father was attached to *Eretz Israel* with every fiber of his being, and did his best to revive the Hebrew language and to encourage and strengthen the Zionist movements, by providing aid to the pioneers making *Aliyah*. I remember, in 1929, when the events began in *Eretz Israel*,[Ed. Note: refers to the Hebron Massacre of 1929 and its aftermath] our home was filled with grief and mourning at the saddening articles in the newspapers and the obituaries in Yiddish newspaper *Der Moment*, of which we were frequent readers.

My father participated regularly in *Chumash* and *Mishnah* courses led by HaRav Yosef Rudnik, sage of blessed memory, and later led by HaRav Aharon Tayts ז"ל, to deepen his knowledge of the values and legacy of Judaism. He also forced his sons to study *Mishnah* and *Talmud* with a special tutor.

He encouraged us to be members of *Betar* and to participate in all the movement's activities. Although he needed our assistance on market days, he did not deter us from going out to *Betar* summer and training camps.

My father was a proud Jew and was diligent in his observance of Jewish tradition and his esteem even towards the Christians. I remember once on

Friday night, while we were making *Kiddush*, the infamous police officer Voytoss appeared in our home and asked for a glass board for window installation. It was Hanukkah and a storm raged outside. "No matter," said the officer, "Kehat the glazier will do this for me, even on *Shabbat*." This is where my father's national pride was ignited, and he approached Voytoss, "listen, my friend, Kehat is a Jew like me and I will not allow him to violate the Sabbath!" The glass was not given, and Voytoss left empty handed.

Rescue of Rabbi Zalman Sorotzkin

Even during the Soviet occupation blessed public activities did not cease in our home. My father was undeterred by the dangers and assisted refugees from the wars and massacres.

In 1939, when Poland was divided between the Soviets and the Germans, Vilne and its surroundings were handed to Lithuania. Our town remained under Soviet control, 15 kilometers from the Lithuanian border. Being a border town, many Jewish refugees from all over Poland who wanted to cross the border to Lithuania, the only window to the free world, arrived in town.

Among the refugees, HaRav Zalman Sorotzkin arrived in our town with his family. He fell prey to border crossing guides in Lida, who had charged him a hefty sum. They took the family to a forest near Divenishok and abandoned them there. Rabbi Sorotzkin and his entourage arrived at the town's synagogue, exhausted and fearful. My grandfather, who was acquainted with the rabbi since the days he served as *Beth Din* chairman in Voronova, invited the whole entourage to our home, with permission from my father, despite the danger of the NKVD.

They stayed in my parents' home for several weeks, until my father got hold of a trustworthy gentile who guided them across the border to Vilne, to a hotel on Chopin Street. From there, Rabbi Zalman Sorotzkin and his entourage succeeded in reaching *Eretz Israel*. Here, he served as chairman of *Moetzes Gedolei HaTorah*[Ed. Note: Rabbinical Council of Haredi Judaism, characterized by the rejection of modern secularism] until the day he died.

In one of his books, *Oznaim LaTorah* (a commentary on the Torah), he wrote a dedication to my father in these words: "to the *kadosh* R' Ben Zion Schneider יה"ד, for the great *Khesed* he performed in hiding me in his home during the Red Army's occupation of Poland, and his assistance in crossing the border to Lithuania."

Even during the terrible days of the Holocaust – under German control, our home was open to refugees. One of them, Trigovov, managed to save himself and make *Aliyah*, and would go on to be on the Israeli Foreign Ministry staff.

My Mother Sarah Hinde, Of Blessed Memory

My mother was a woman with valor and very energetic. She had a natural tendency for quick–witted business management and managed the business with great wisdom. She would travel to Vilne to purchase merchandise, and at home conducted the management of the home and business. She had a unique, charming personality that would attract customers to her, Jews and Gentiles alike.

My mother was gifted with life wisdom. She managed to locate the golden mean between herself and my father, who was mostly devoted to public outreach. My mother had her own personality. Her outlook on life was not the same as my father's. She leaned towards socialist views, not rooted in Humanism, but rather in philosophical and mental perceptions. Still, my father and she did not argue over the subject.

My mother was a noble soul and bound to her family with a strong, loving bond. She was admired by her parents, who moved to our town following her marriage to my father.

My Grandfather Moshe Ber

My grandfather, Moshe Ber,[Ed. Note: Satkolshtsik], was a common man, but was devoted to Jewish values and tradition. He devoted every free minute to prayer and Psalms recitation in the synagogue. On the High Holidays he would be enveloped by holiness, standing all day in the synagogue, communing with his creator. On more than one occasion, I observed him shedding tears for the *Galut*[Ed. Note: exile] of the Nation of Israel and the *Shekhina*.[Ed. Note: divine presence] My grandfather objected to the trend of *Minyanim*[Ed. Note: Jewish prayer quorum] gathering in private homes in place of the synagogue. "We must maintain the holiness of the synagogue," he argued.

His wife, Leah – my grandmother – was a righteous and kind woman, who was sickly and well cared for by the devoted family.

In addition to his only son Yudel, who was an avid Zionist, he had a daughter who married Yaakov Yankelovitsh, and a daughter who was single, Tania. They all perished in the Lida ghetto.

My grandfather's eldest brother emigrated to the Pittsburg area in the United States, the center of steel production. He managed a restaurant and was successful with his business. He brought the family along, who all settled into the restaurant business. Only my grandfather refused to join him, because it came to his knowledge the restaurants served pork dishes.

My grandfather's family was murdered in Lida. Yudel likely found his death in Volozhin, where he had married. My grandfather's two daughters, Nekhama (of blessed memory) and Bilkha, managed to leave town, and established wonderful families in Pittsburgh, USA.

[Page 266]

Ben–Zion Schneider

Avraham Aloni

Translation by Meir Bulman

Ben–Zion Schneider was one of the most exceptional and important activists in town. He excelled not only in his benevolent activity on the Parent Conference, but in all of the town's institutions, such as the bank, the *Gemach*,[Ed. Note: interest-free loan giving bank] the synagogue and the library, as well as providing aid and good advice.

Rabbi Yosef Rudnik, who chaired the town institutions, never made a move before consulting Ben– Zion Schneider, because he knew that he was a straightforward thinking person with sound logic. He always addressed the core of the issues, without favoritism, because in his nature he was honest and guided by wisdom.

His face was always adorned with a smile, though it portrayed seriousness and intelligence. He was well mannered and his speech flowed pleasantly. I never saw him mad or angry, since he was a man of peace, striving to understand, and every person found in him an attentive listener and a shoulder to cry on, as the town did not lack troubled individuals. He always found words of encouragement, hope, and comfort, and his patience and understanding made him beloved to all town residents, and all saw in him a loyal friend.

His three children studied in the school that I managed.

The eldest, Yankele, was a gaunt child, pleasant and gentle–natured, whose father cared for him with great devotion – and when the teachers informed him of his son's progress, he radiated with happiness.

The second one, Shmuel, was a chubby boy, always cheerful and happy, with an analytical and logical mind. He inherited his traits from his father, and already at that time stood out for his straightforward mind and his good qualities, and he excelled in level headed thinking and expressive talent. In the 40's Shmuel made *Aliyah* and was absorbed well into the country, but due to his underground activities he was exiled to Eritrea, where he spent some years. When he returned to Israel, he again joined a productive circle, established a proud home, and today fills important roles in Israel's market.

Nathan Itskovitsh's family (1930)

His sister, Libke, was a beautiful girl, with a noble soul, and a diligent student.

Ben–Tsion had two more girls, Rosa, and Leah. As I heard it, Yankele became hard–working and pleasant, and reached the rank of commander in *Betar* in town. During the Holocaust, he was injured by Polish militia forces on his way to the Partisans, returned injured to Lida, where the Germans executed him.

Ben–Tsion, his wife, and three daughters escaped from the Lida Ghetto, and hid with a gentile in the Divenishok area. He took advantage of them, and extorted all their belongings, and when their funds ran out, informed on them to the Polish militia, who murdered them in their hiding place.

That is how a firmly established Jewish family was extinguished with much cruelty, and only one remnant is in Israel, their son Shmuel, who carries the memory of his beloved family in his bereaved heart.

The Zionist Activist Yudel Satkolshtsik

Avraham Aloni
Translation by Meir Bulman

Yudel came from Voronova to Divenishok with his parents, after his sister Hinde Sarah married Ben Zion Schneider. He quickly became involved in the town's public life, and was among the chief Zionist activists in town. He was a member on the *Keren Kayemet*[Ed. Note: Jewish National Fund] board, secretary of *HaKhalutz*[Ed. Note: Zionist youth movement] and of the main initiators to encourage *Aliyah*. He fearlessly combated the Yiddishists who made efforts to recruit people to their camp.

Yudel was an excellent public speaker, and his speeches were very logically organized, based on ideas of Jewish tradition and the concept of national revival. He attracted the youth to his lectures and had a great amount of influence on them. Yudel was also considered a friend to the school and would take part in all field trips.

The Rav brought him closer to the town's public activities, and he fulfilled all his roles with top quality dedication and understanding. He was affable and had an open, on–the–ball approach to all subjects, and all his friends and acquaintances were in good spirits when near him. Yudel was considered one of the most devoted and vigorous activists in the cultural–Zionist–social scene in town.

For his whole life Yudel planned to fulfill the Zionist vision by making Aliyah, but being occupied with providing for his family, he postponed it from one year to the next. Yudel was an agricultural merchant with Rueven Kartshmer, and was quite successful in his business, until he moved to Volozhin where he married, and continued his Zionist activities. On holidays and festivals when he visited his parents, he did not miss an opportunity to speak to the youth. Listening to Yudel lecture on any topic was a moving and unique experience. His words progressed with ease and reason.

Yudel and his entire family were murdered by the Germans in Volozhin.

(photos of the Schneider and Satkolshtsik families on pages 406-409) [Ed. Note: of this book]

Eulogy for My Father of Blessed Memory

Yosef Meir Itskovitsh

Translation by Meir Bulman

The expression 'a *Yiddishe Mamme*' has been deeply absorbed in the hearts of our people. In happiness and sorrow, when the mother sheds tears, we say: "No wonder! She is a *Yiddishe Momme*". The well-known song '*Mein Yiddishe Mamme*' has been translated to many languages and is sung by many people the world over, black and white alike.

Where is a father's place? It is explicitly written in the scriptures, "As a father has compassion on his children."[1] Why was a song not written for him? Why does he not fulfill his rightful place alongside the mother? I do not understand or accept this injustice.

As my father's youngest child, as an orphan who did not get to attend his father's funeral– a man whose resting place is unknown. I did not get to recite *Kadish* at his tomb. I, the orphaned son, the witness to the loss of the Holocaust, would like to correct that injustice, to repair the distortion, and briefly tell of my father. I wish to recite *Kadish* in writing.

My father was named Natan, Natan Reb Dov.[2] That is what was printed in golden letters on the leather binding of the *Khumash* books, prayer books, *Megilot*, and even the Passover *Hagadot* that were placed in our bookcase at home.

His name suited him.[3] Father gave aid to all those in need. Father had an open hand[4] – was generous– and because his financial state was strong, he had the opportunity to give to the poor. He not only had an open hand, but an open heart as well – a heart empathizing with those in pain.

He had an open mind and was gifted with great intelligence, understanding, and judgment.

My father had the three excellent qualities that not all men are fortunate to have.

He was a handsome man, round faced, with a short nose – and underneath it was a short and thin moustache. He had eyes projecting wisdom and mercy that watched and pierced even the smallest object – without corrective lenses. He had an average stature, a strong, manly, and athletic physique. He dressed carefully, wore a tie even on the weekdays, and wore polished shoes without patches. His walk was pleasant and full of confidence, projecting respect, and illumination.

Father was an observant, God–fearing man, among those who prayed in the early Minyan at the New Synagogue, and a keeper of tradition, in which he saw both meaning and pleasure. [He was] a precise man, carefully observing all customs and laws on holidays and festivals.

He was a public servant, not seeking reward, (א קהלישע קליאמקע)[5] meaning:[6] קהלישע from the Hebrew word קהל[7] – audience, community- and קליאמקע[8] meaning door knob in Yiddish. And what does a knob do? It opens the entrance doors. And indeed, once father took up a certain matter, all doors and entrances were opened to him to fulfill his requests.

The tendency to assist, the inner drive to hastily provide aid, the talent and resources to act would not allow him to rest. Alongside his serene mental nature he was like a volcano when dealing with public issues. We members of the household were not pleased by father's involvement in public matters: we were concerned for his health. A hardworking man, an early riser for the *Shachrit* prayer with the early Minyan, he would not rest all day long. Interfering in every dispute to achieve domestic harmony, on more than one occasion we approached him and requested, "Father, please quit, stop it. What more do you need? You have a home, money, admiration, a wonderful family, you lack nothing. What do you need all this for? Why hear the criticism, the shouting, the weeping, and the swearing, when not directed at you? What for?"

As a merciful father he would answer: "Fine, I will no longer attend meetings." Then after eating the *Cholent on Shabbat*, he would lie down for a nap ("דרימל א כאפן"[9]). When we woke up, dad was no longer home – he went to a meeting.

Father had a unique and captivating speaking talent. At times, on Sabbath days during the Torah–reading break, when town problems were discussed and community binding decisions were reached, a fight, a fiery argument, yelling, swearing and even physical altercations took place. When father decided to go up on stage and say his piece, he would rise from his seat by the מזרח וואנט[10] (eastern wall), he would fix the wrap on his *Talit*, emit a brief, loud cough– to be heard by those nearby– and with slow steps, confidently and calmly, he would begin approaching the stage, calmly climb the steps, approach the table on which the Torah scroll was placed, shoot a piercing look right and left, back and forth, raise his right hand and slam it on the table with great force. The echo reached all corners of the house, to the women's section. He would open by saying, "פנים עזות אן אפילו זיין מעג איך", – "Pardon me, gentelmen, "אומגיט פאר נישט מיר נעמט", – even at the risk of impertinence, I must tell you," – and following an opening like that, all tempers were calmed and all listened attentively.

Father was a figurative father to the town's orphans and widows, and would heed their every call.

In our confection work shop, among others, worked Minkhe Bat Leah – and she had a sister– Rachel. They were orphans, long passed the age of marriage. Father would take the care of fulfilling all the *Mitzvot* and customs in their home. When Passover was approaching he would ensure removal of *Chametz* and preparation of the utensils for Passover *Kashrut*. On Hanukah he would light the candles and recite the blessing.

Father was the representative of the Jewish town residents on the municipal council (gmina), and would represent all needs and problems to the council, and fight for the Jewish residents' rights.

Father was a pursuer of justice, loathed injustice, and was quick to assist his fellow man. He was fearless, and stuck to his goals – until victory.

He was very active in all town institutions: he was a member of the committee for Jewish volunteer firefighters— and later established an all-Jewish wind–instrument band, a member of the board of trustees for the administration of the National Jewish Bank, a member of the Hebrew School parent's committee, in *Gemilut Hasadim*, and an honored representative welcoming special government guests (such as, say, the bishop or the district governor – "וואיעוואדע"). He would contribute to all charity objectives, bridal funds, book repairs, *Bikur Holim*, etc.

Father would greet all the distinguished guests from the Christian community, such as the priest, the mayor, etc., with a sharp mind, an accurate judgment, and a decision–making talent. He acquired a name as mediator in hostilities and squabbles among the Gentiles. When villagers would go to the town priest with claims and complaints regarding neighborly disputes, the priest would often invite father and consult him.

Apart from the priest, the Chief Rabbi in every Beth Din trial would also consult father. And though father was not a Talmudic expert, his vast intelligence and judgment–talent assisted him in solving problems, be they the most severe, complex, and complicated.

I remember instances when disputants would directly approach Father and not the Rabbi. Take for instance Seymme[11] Finklshteyn from Voronova, who produced turpentine from needle–tree roots, and his cousin Moshe Kaplan from our town, who did the same. Every year as the snow melted and the roots were uprooted, problems arose concerning the rightful owner of the roots. The marks on them were unclear and so disputes and squabbles arose until they approached father, who in his wisdom and clear judgment, accepted by both parties, would mediate and decide. Of course, father never accepted pay for his mediation efforts.

He cared for the family endlessly. Once, angered at mother, I left home offended, and father went out to search for me. He patrolled the town streets and not even as he reached the woods was he able to locate me; he did not give up and continued searching. Equipped with Eytta Simme's "בייגעלאך-אייער" (egg bagels) he reached the bathing spot by the קליאטקע (a wooden passage over the river) on Dovozisk Street. When he met me there, he approached me and spoke to me with captivating and pleasant words, hugged me and gave me the bagels, and arm in arm we returned home.

I remember another incident: our parents were invited to attend the wedding of a relative – "שיינע די שאשקע" (beautiful Shoshke) from the town of Ivia – who was about to marry a grain merchant, Reuven Kaganovitsh (brother of the writer Moshe Kaganovitsh, author of *The Jewish Partisan War in the Plains of White Russia*, who lives with us in Israel). The wedding date was set for a Saturday night. The parents left Friday at dawn. Three family members stayed: my brother Eliezer, my sister Bilkhe, and I. One cannot simply be exempted completely, so father commanded us to store the oats from our field in Kekerke's barn, who was a Catholic of Lithuanian origin and friends with father.

We worked our fingers to the bone all day, stacked bundles, tying and storing them at the very top, under the haystack ceiling in the granary. We labored intensively, and when I tired and was drenched in sweat, I approached the spring to quench my thirst. I rested on the grassy meadow and fell asleep. When I awoke my whole body was shivering from cold and my head burned as a furnace. I was brought home and placed on the bed in the guestroom. I was burning up. My sister Bilkhe stood near the bed, gripped with fear, she too shaking and concerned. Gordon the פעלטשער (healer) examined and re-examined me and said what he said, but my sister did not leave my bedside and guarded me from harm. My older brother Eliezer ז"ל also stood by my bed, and tormented me by saying, "I told you not to drink from the cold spring water when you're covered in sweat, I told you so!"

Anyway, I burned up all day Saturday and my body radiated heat waves. My poor sister Bilkhe prayed to God that I hold on at least until our parents returned from the wedding.

After Sabbath was over, by Sunday morning light, father stormed the house asking, "Where is he? Where is Yushke Meir?" No one had notified him of my condition, no one had told him a thing, but he felt something was not all right at home – so he told later – and his inner soul, his intuition, whispered to him, saying, "Hurry home!", and he ran and caught an early chariot, finding me in bed.

Father approached me, put his right hand on my brow, and observed me with merciful eyes; he asked me to open my mouth and stick out my tongue.

He looked inside and exclaimed with complete confidence, "That's it! You have something in your stomach, it will soon pass!" He sat near me on the bed, caressed me, held my head in his hands, and slowly but surely the fever passed. I fell asleep, my head in father's arms.

There are many stories, practically all of which are true, about his great love and devotion to the members of the family. It was enough for his hands to touch the pained area for the pain to disappear, as if it never was.

His care for the family was limitless, and above all he was bound to his daughter – Bilkhe, who was his only daughter, who he loved more than anything, and who resembled his facial features.

I recall that when my sister Bilkhe left home on her way to Eretz Israel, members of the household accompanied her to the forest on Vilne Street. When we returned home, father's expression was like that of a man whose ship has sunken to the depths of the ocean. He could not find a spot to rest and mumbled something to himself.

*

In these paragraphs, written by me – Father's youngest child – I have tried with my meager words to describe his wonderful image, a humanistic and Jewish image. His multi-dimensional, colorful personality, was gifted with all the qualities of a man created in God's image.

I have a deep desire that the life and works of my father ל״ז serve as an example for my family members, my town members, their descendants, and the People of Israel today and generations to come.

Absent the ability to visit my father's gravesite and recite the *Kadish*, may those words serve as an eternal memorial monument.

Editor's and Translator's Footnotes

1. Tr. Note: Psalm 103:13

2. Ed. Note: Literally: 'Nathan Son of Mr. Dov'

3. Tr. Note: Natan is the Hebrew word for "give".

4. Tr. Note: Reference to Psalm 145:16

5. Ed. Note: Transliteration: a kehilishe kliamke

6. Ed. Note: Transliteration: kehilishe

7. Ed. Note: Transliteration: kehil

8. Ed. Note: Transliteration: kliamke

9. Ed. Note: Transliteratin: khapn a driml

10. Ed. Note: Transliteration: mizrah vant

11. Ed. Note: In the original text the name is spelled: samech–tsvey yud–mem–ayen.

[Page 271]

About My Father and My Family

Shulamit Fuchs [Rogol]

Translation by Meir Bulman

My father, Aryeh Leyb Rogol, was a Divenishok native. His mother originated from the Berkovitsh family (she was related to the writer Berkovitsh, Sholom Aleichem's son–in–law)[1]. My paternal grandparents had a restaurant and barely made a living. My grandmother Freda was a woman of valor and assisted my father with the burdens of providing. She baked bread and bagels and sold them at the marketplace. She was a righteous, kindhearted woman who helped her fellow man.

My father was a Torah scholar and in his youth studied at the Lomzhe Yeshiva. At the age of 17 he became a teacher in villages. Among others he worked for a Jewish family at the Navinke[2] Village, near Suvalk.[3] In the evenings he studied secular subjects. A friend once approached him and asked, "What's new?" and Father replied, "As the light outside increases so does the darkness in my heart," meaning: as the days get longer and the nights shorten, he must devote more time to teaching and less to acquiring new knowledge. Father was very saddened by that.

After he matured, father married his first wife, Lyuba Levine from Oshmene, and had two children with her, myself, and my brother Tsvi who perished at the Slonim ghetto.

Father then married a second a time, and had three children: Zelig who lives with us in Israel, Mina, and Eliahu who both perished at the Voronova ghetto. Father owned the only pharmacy in the greater Divenishok area and made a nice living.

Aryeh Leyb Rogol at the time of his illness

My father was very much devoted to Zionist ideals. Zionism was etched deep within his consciousness and being; the fruition of the Zionist vision was his life's focus and he passionately devoted himself to that idea. From the days of his youth he busied himself with Zionism. He and his friend Shmuel Chaim Levine were the only ones in towns who purchsed shekels for the first Zionist Congress. He was active in *Keren Ha'Yesod* and *Keren Kayemet*, and organized and guided Zionist youth movements in our town. Truth and justice were his guiding principles, and he never ceased caring for the needy in town. During WWI, he was active in *Ya'akofu* and distributed food to the poor.

In 1926 a fire erupted in our home. A gasoline container exploded in the pharmacy and father lighted a match to clean the gasoline. The gasoline caught fire and the entire house was engulfed in flames. Fear and grief–stricken, father became ill with Parkinson's and was bed–ridden until the Germans murdered him in the Voronova Ghetto.

Editor's Footnotes

1. Refers to Yitzach Dov Berkovitsh.

2. In the original text this name is spelled: nun–tsvey vovn–yud–nun–kuf–hey

3. This is possibly Suvalki: samech–vov–veyz (or beyz)–aleph–lamed–kuf

[Page 272]

Dov Zandman

Translation by Meir Bulman

Son of Yehoshua and Khaye. Born in Divenishok, near Vilne. He was orphaned from both parents at childhood and was raised and influenced by his older brother. He had a sweet voice, and was an appreciator of song and music. After he matured, he was active in establishing *HeKhlautz*,[Ed. Note: Zionist youth movement] and assisted in establishing a large library. Due to his love of theatre, he was the lively spirit in the town's theater company. In those days he began to show organizational talents and a flare for leadership.

He made *Aliyah* in 1926 and immediately made Jerusalem his destination. Upon his arrival in the holy city he became bound to it with a strong bond of love, and despite the difficult adjustment, which included employment in hard, menial work for which he was not equipped, he refused to leave the city. Those hardships were chastisements of love for him and Jerusalem was holy in his eyes.

Since his arrival he was a member of *HaHaganah*[Ed. Note: Jewish paramilitary organization under the British Mandate of Palestine] and since 1929 he was active in the defense of Jerusalem, and all the danger sites. He was alert and devoted to all who were bound to the spirit of the *Yishuv*,[Ed. Note: Jewish residents in the land of Israel prior to the creation of the State of Israel] and believed whole heartedly in the power nested in the *Yishuv*, fighting for its survival – particularly in the days of the difficult struggle against British Mandate forces post–WWII. He was beloved by his friends, because he radiated love to all who encountered him. He was among the first members in the *HaMekasher* Cooperative, and a member of the administration for several years. Later he was very active in establishing the *HaMekasher* library, because by his nature he was a book lover.

Dov Zandman, one of the first pioneers in Israel from Divenishok.
He went to Israel in 1926 and fell on Mount Scopus in the War of Liberation in 1948

A few months prior to the eruption of Israel's War of Independence he visited the United States to see his beloved family members. But America's wonders did not charm him and a few weeks later, after explaining the concept of *Eretz Israel* to his relatives, he returned there, saying: "all that I have seen – does not belong to us". When the Partition Plan was announced on November 29, 1947, he said wisely, "the implementation will come, we must prepare for a long and difficult struggle." After that his work as a public driver in Jerusalem neighborhoods became a wide-ranging activity, and he served with dedication and *Mesirut Nefesh*.[Ed. Note: self-sacrifice] Even during the bitter days of siege and attack, the smile did not leave his face, even with all the seriousness and responsibility in his heart, and he energetically continued his work. Even in those days he did not cease his care for the *HaMekasher* library and the distribution of good books among friends and children. On April 13th, 1948 he was among the leaders of the *Haddasah* envoy to Mount Scopus, and fell with them while fulfilling that job. He was brought to everlasting rest in a mass grave in the Sanhedria Cemetery in Jerusalem. He was survived by his wife, his son, and his daughter.

(this article was first published in the supplement to the Yizkor Book)

[Page 273]

Dov of Blessed Memory

Rivke Zandman

Translation by Meir Bulman

Since first meeting him, I knew to value Dov's unique personal qualities. He was a lively man, generously providing love and warmth to all he encountered. I knew him in the days when he was still young and fresh, a pioneer in the *Fourth Aliyah* wave, lovingly accepting the labor pains of acclimation, alert and devoted to all things concerning the soul of the *Yishuv*.[Ed. Note: Jewish residents in the land of Israel prior to the creation of the State of Israel]

As days went by, with the years of work and setting roots in the country, he was no longer young, having passed the age of 40. The work and fatigue left their mark on him. Even then he devoted all his senses to the community and to strengthening public alertness. The difficult struggle against the British post–WWII was near to his heart; he knew how to explain calmly and without contentiousness the terrorism problem that was not yet solved. He would often warn of the danger terrorism posed to the *Yishuv*. He was then a driver for public transportation in Jerusalem, the city he was bound to with love from his first days in *Eretz Israel*.

Sitting by the wheel, he was fully devoted to his public role, which he knew how to elevate to a humanistic level with great responsibility, taking a wise approach to his audience. Many friends always surrounded him, and Dov was not one to mince words; at the center of his conversation were issues of the *Yishuv*. People took heed of his words and admired him for being a good and kind man. With the news of the partition plan on November 29, 1947, when the streets were filled with crowds of people drunk with happiness, he knew to control his emotions and remain alert to the pending hardships. "The implementation will come," he said, "We must be prepared for a long and difficult struggle". And indeed, we entered a war, and the first victims on the road to an independent state fell that day. Since then Dov's work as public transportation driver in Jerusalem included a wide range of public activism, and he showed devotion and sacrifice for the sake of public transportation.

Those days were immensely difficult. Death hid at every corner. Dov continued his work, his heart heavy. The bond and responsibility towards the family was great, and even greater was his willingness for sacrifice in the appointed role. Yaakov, his youngest, was detached from home, at *Mishmar HaEmek*, heavily attacked in those days. Despite that, his smile remained as he often joked and laughed, sweetening the bitterness in his heart.

On those difficult days, Dov did not cease caring for the *HaMekasher* library, devoting his precious time to encourage readership among friends and children. The children knew to value their devoted librarian, Dov. He also knew to read and understand well, being a man of the book, and with a great taste and a touch for literature. He quenched his thirst for knowledge by reading wise and renowned authors; he read poems by Tchernichovsky and Bialik, history and biblical books, and Gandhi's *The Story of My Experiments with Truth*.

That was Berrele from Divenishok, his small birth town near Vilne. He fondly remembered his childhood experiences. He knew how to give accounts of those experiences with talent, taste, and special emotion.

His heavy inclination towards the theatre arts was not satisfied. The difficult life transformations and the exhausting work left their marks. Dov was fortunate to be a father and cared for his children with great attention and devotion. "More than anything, the child needs a smile, a word of encouragement, and genuine love from the heart," was among Dov's kind sayings.

Our years together were years of loyal friendship and deep emotional sharing, a path of striving and searching for the truth, for the beauty in daily life, particularly for self-education. In that field, Dov will serve as model and excellent example of a family man of perfection and harmony.

A few months prior to the war, Dov was fortunate to visit dear family members in the United States. Despite his happiness and joy at that opportunity to travel overseas, he could not remain there for more than a few weeks, as the yearning for his family and country overtook him; he returned to the country with renewed energy and dedication to go on. America's wonders had not charmed him. "All that I have seen – does not belong to us," he said. He passionately explained the matter of *Eretz Israel* to his family members.

*

I could not write in his memory without detailing the man who lived a great virtuous life, befitting and eligible to enjoy all that is given in the Creator's world. I would not wish to remember how my dear Dov's life was taken. I will remember him alive, always alive, for he will live on in the hearts of many who knew him.

[Page 274]

Reb Moshe Ben Tsion Khasman

Translation by Meir Bulman

(The first pioneer from Divenishok who made Aliyah on foot in 1911 during the holiday months.)

Moshe Ben Tsion Khasman

I knew R' Moshe the blacksmith from the dawn of my youth – those were the first days of Tel Aviv. At the center of the only neighborhood– *Ahuzat Bayit* – stood the proud Hebrew Gymnasium which looked like the form of the *Mishkan*[Ed. Note: the tabernacle was the portable sanctuary used by the Hebrews during their forty years of wandering following the Exodus] in the dessert. Around it, a few here and a few there, were small houses with red roofs, and beyond these lay an ocean of golden sand. Far beyond, within the sand dunes, a small black dot shined; it was Rabi Moshe's smithy, and from it were emitted and echoed the sounds of the hammer diligently hammering away at the anvil. It was the only smithy in small Tel Aviv, and R' Moshe's hands were always busy. The banisters on the roofs and balconies, as well as the fences and gates for the new homes popping up on the sands, were designed and created by R' Moshe the blacksmith.

He was quick in his work, and full of strength and energy. He was always rushing and he did not even have time to eat his meals calmly. He would swallow an entire loaf of bread in one meal – from end to end. On the scalding hot summer days, as he stood and perspired next to the bellows, he would drink a dozen soda bottles, one after the other, while molding the metal, "like clay in the hands of the potter".[Tr. Note: this is a reference to Jeremiah 18:6, a passage recited in the Yom Kippur prayers]

He was affectionate towards children and as he worked he would converse with us, the children. For us too it was an unforgettable experience to stand and watch the scalding iron sparks flying by Moshe's hands, who worked with it as he pleased.

He too had children of his own, but they were not with him in the country. He had no relatives in the country. He had two daughters abroad, as they were still too young, and he was planning to bring them over when the time came. But meanwhile, WWI broke out, and put to rest the dreams of so many.

As Turkey entered the war, Russian citizens were expelled from the land, and only those accepting Ottoman authority were permitted to remain. R' Moshe like tens of thousands did not leave and he accepted Ottoman citizenship, as few others did, but they were nevertheless exposed to the harms of the war: hunger, disease, wandering, expulsion, and harassments at the hands of a failing and hostile regime.

R' Moshe left his family behind in Russia, and wandered for three years from town to town, from country to country, to reach the Land. He had a holy mission: to hasten the arrival of the Messiah destined to appear soon in the Land of Israel. He whole-heartily maintained total faith, and he yearned to have that destiny. He always carried with him the *Agadot* [Tr. Talmudic legends] and *Midrashim* [Tr. similar legends not included in the Talmud] telling of the King-Messiah.

To his interlocutors he would say "Galut Yishmael"[Ed. Note: the Exile of Ishmael, according to Jewish Theology the final phase of the Exile of Edom which is the fourth and final exile before the arrival of the Messiah] is the final *Galut*,[Ed. Note: exile], and the *Geulah*[Ed. Note: the final redemption] would follow it. To prove his point he used as sources the *Agadot* and the sayings of the sages.

I remember during one of his conversations with us, the children, he said, "Today I was with Mr. Blustheyn who is building two, two-story houses on Lilieinblum Street. He ordered a banister for the stairs. When I told him the price he said, "I agree, but do it well," and he clenched his fist and added, "I want it to stand forever!'"

"And what did you say?" I asked.

"The Messiah will arrive before then."

R' Moshe was a man of short stature, with a thick beard, a powerful physique, and tremendous muscles. He would allow us – the children – to feel his muscles, and we were surprised by their power. We saw him bending cast iron with his bare hands. With great passion we listened to his stories about wrestling various strongmen. That raised both our astonishment and our admiration. In our eyes he was a hero capped by a crown of victory.

When Turkey entered the war, R' Moshe was obligated to be inducted into military service and to serve his majesty, the Sultan. R' Moshe did not want that. "The Turk will not obtain my service in his military," he would say, before escaping and evading. When the Turks allied with the Germans, he saw in that the fruition of the legendary combination of *Edom and Ishmael* – a clear sign of the quickly approaching *Geulah*. At every spot where Jews would gather and gravely ponder the serious situation, R' Moshe appeared with glee, in song and dance to the rhythm of וחותנו שעיר כלה.[Tr. Note: "exterminate the hairy goat and his father-in-law", a reference to Esau and Ishmael and a prayer recited on some days of *Selichot*]

After the *NILI*,[Ed. Note: a ring of Jewish spies working for the British in World War I] events and the death of Sarah Aaronsohn,[Ed. Note: a member of NILI who was captured and committed suicide while being held captive] of blessed memory, the situation took a turn for the worse. The Turkish regime conducted a widespread spy-hunt mission and R' Moshe fell prey. Dozens of other military deserters were also captured and they were marched on foot to Damascus, where he [R' Moshe] was imprisoned and accused of spying for the enemy. I do not know how long the Turkish imprisoned them all, but approximately a year after his capture, when I stood in an olive grove in Zikhron Yaakov,[Ed. Note: place where Sarah Aaronsohn lived and was captured] I heard a voice calling my name. It was R' Moshe. He was broken hearted and his appearance was very pitiable. I did not enquire how he escaped – and why would that matter. His face was drooping and gaunt, like that of an ill person. He told me that more than half of the prisoners on the march to Damascus had passed away, and that he survived miraculously. He made the return journey from Damascus on foot. That happened a few days before the British entered the Land. I tried to cheer him up. "Feel my muscle," he said and presented his arm to me. I felt his upper arm. He looked at me, pondered for a bit and said, "You see, it's like a rag now," and sighed bitterly.

It was not an expression of grief due to his declining health and the loss of his bodily strength. There was much more to it though: a deep disappointment of the faith that had not come into fruition, a disappointment at the Messiah's stalled footsteps.

Who possesses stronger faith: the weak or the strong? It is said that the weak person is more faithful, because he cannot rely on anything but his faith. That is what happened to R' Moshe. After he was released from the prison in Damascus he did not recover his strength. He did reopen his smithy and even bought new tools, but the days of the strong R' Moshe Ben–Tzion Khasman, referred to by all of us as "Rabbi Moshe the blacksmith", did not return.

Despite[Ed. Note: or because of] his suffering and his physical weakness, his faith in the eternity of the nation of Israel, and in the approaching *Geulah* had not decreased, he believed with every fiber of his being that the *Geulah* was indeed near.

Several years later I met him in the alleys of Jerusalem. He was wearing a long *Bekishe*[Ed. Note: a long black coat] and growing long *Payot*.[Ed. Note: side locks of hair] As things turned out he closed his shop and was devoting his time to studying Torah. His religious observance increased immeasurably. "We must repent and bring about the arrival of the Messiah," he would say. He did not like the British but he did not lose his faith in the Messiah's arrival and would wait for him every day.

One of his final actions was buying a plot of land in Bnei Brak, near the Petah Tikvah Road, where he built a small house. He donated the house and the land to the institution that hospitalized him in his final months.

His death marked the departure of one of the most cherished of Jewish figures, one of those who were leaders among pioneers, those who lived for *Mashiach* and *Netzach*.[Tr. Note: victory and/or eternity] The grand enterprise of the State of Israel was established based on their faith, progress, dedication, and self–sacrifice.

[Page 276]

The Daughters Tell About Their Father
In Memory of Moshe Khasman

Sarah Itskovitsh and Grunye Bronshtayn
Translation by Meir Bulman

The first time my father Moshe Khasman traveled to *Eretz Israel* was in 1902. He was attending the Volozhin *Yeshiva*, and along with a group of young men, left the *Yeshiva* and made a pilgrimage to *Eretz Israel*. He stayed there one year and then returned to Divenishok. In Divenishok, he established a family and had two daughters: my sister Grunye, and I. In 1909, my father decided to make *Aliyah* once more, but since he had no money he did it … on foot.

I arrived at the Land in 1923. At the time my father lived in Neve Shalom. His smithy stood where the Lieber Candy Factory now operates. My father was a very righteous man and gave charity to the needy, openly and בסתר מתן.[Tr. Note: 'Matan B'Seter' is "When a person gives without knowing to whom he gives, and the recipient receives without knowing from whom he receives"; in the Talmud it is said this type of charity "delivers a man from an un–natural death."(Baba Bathra 10a–b)]

I remember that occasionally he would close his workshop, go to the Arabs, buy food products, store them in the folds of his *Bekishe*,[Ed. Note: a long coat] and go to one of the impoverished neighbors, saying, "Sirele, take these and prepare a meal for you and your children." And then return with a clear conscience to the smithy.

My father was friendly with the *Chazon Ish*,[Ed. Note: popular name given to Rabbi and author Avrohom Yeshaya Karelitz, (7 November 1878 – 24 October 1953)] and often visited him to study Torah and discuss current events. Occasionally my father would take me along for the visit. His wife would fry *latkes* for me – it was a great honor that only a few received.

During WWI, my father and his friend Y. Rebikov were exiled by the Turks to Egypt,[Tr. Note: Egypt is the country named here but another account in this volume names his imprisonment as having occurred in Damascus] where he suffered greatly. He managed to escape the prison and hid with an Arab until the British entered the Land.

In the days of the British Mandate he brought my sister and I to the Land, and after we had married, father bought himself a yard in Bnei Brak and established the smithy there. He worked there for three years and then traveled to study Torah at HaRav Kook *Yeshiva* in Jerusalem. "I want to be intoxicated by the holy city's atmosphere," he would say. He later returned to Bnei Brak and joined an old-folks home. Instead of an entrance fee he contributed the plot with the shop on it.

My father passed away in Bnei Brak, on 26 Shvat, 5736.[Tr. Note: 28 January 1976] He was dedicated to the Zionist idea and passionately waited every day for the arrival of the Messiah. For that reason he would befriend the *Khalutzim*,[Ed. Note: Zionist pioneers] despite their not being so observant.

He would invite *Khalutzim* to his home and give them food, and if they thanked him he would say: "Do not thank me, thank the *Master of the Universe*, he gave to me and gives to you."

My father told me that Ben Gurion would visit him and sometimes dine with him.

He did his best to befriend and encourage the pioneers to stay in the Land, and his heart ached with every Jew that left. Every day he would pray: "Grant me the honor to see with my own eyes the arrival of the messiah."

*

My father Moshe Ben-Zion Khasman was born in Divenishok in 1890. My father's relatives were men of labor and the blacksmith profession would pass from father to son for generations. My father too was a blacksmith. My mother Feige was from the Trovski family of distinguished lineage. She was the second daughter. The older son Isser made *Aliyah* with his family, and passed away in Jerusalem. Isser Trovski's son was a Rabbi, and passed away in Vishneva, Poland. My mother had another brother named Zechariah. He made *Aliyah* at an old age and passed away here.[Ed. Note: in Israel] He was survived by two sons and a daughter. The sons changed their name to Dorman. One of them was U.S. Consul to Thaliand, and another worked in the American embassy in Russia. My mother's sister, Devorah Blumenthal lives in Arad.

My father was a pupil at the Volozhin *Yeshiva*. He visited Israel as a young man. After he returned, he married my mother, who then died in Ivia, and was survived by two daughters: myself and Sarah. In his grief my father decided to leave town and make *Aliyah*, but because he had no money he decided to walk. The journey lasted two and a half years. The man would walk from town to town, work and earn a living, and go on. At night he would sneak on to a train – until he reached Odessa. There he boarded a ship as a kitchen assistant, but did not succeeded much in that work. The captain expelled him from the ship when they reached the shores of Turkey.

The way from Turkey to the Land was full of adventure and suffering. The roads swarmed with robbers, and once, while walking alone, robbers jumped him and stole all his money. Exhausted, broken down, and penniless, he arrived in the Land.

During his first days, he worked for a blacksmith, then, after he saved some money, he established his own shop and worked independently.

In Israel my father did not marry again, and distributed his profits to the poor and to those learning Torah. In the evenings he would spend his time learning Torah. After he brought his daughters to the Land, he left his work and devoted himself entirely to learning Torah.

My father took care of the daughters he had left in Divenishok and would often send us financial assistance. After my sister Sarah and I grew up he brought us to Israel.

[Page 278]

HaRav Ben–Zion Khasman

Eliahu Netaneli (Itskovitsh)

Translation by Meir Bulman

I was among the first members of the *Third Aliya*, which began in a tidal wave from Poland. In *Eretz Israel* I found an interesting figure from our town who had made *Aliyah* in 1911. His primary motivation to leave his family and make *Aliyah* was a love of the land. He wandered on foot from country to country, until he reached *Eretz Israel* via Iraq.

Even prior to the establishment of *Ahuzat Bayit*,[Ed. Note: name of the settlement that eventually became Tel Aviv] he fearlessly established a smithy in the Jaffa sands. After some time, the area residents grew accustomed to him and provided him their business. He was the first blacksmith in Jaffa, and even the Arabs deeply admired him and brought him their business.

He would close the workshop early to go to the synagogue for prayer and Torah study. He was a deeply devout, religious man, and believed with every fiber in the coming of the Messiah and the *Geulah*.[Ed. Note: period of ultimate redemption] On Friday nights and holiday eves, he would cease work at 12, and *Shabbat* was entirely devoted to Torah study. He abstained from speaking on Shabbat. He would limit himself to a few words if necessary, and even then, he spoke only Hebrew.

The area Jews greatly respected him due to his knowledge of Torah wisdom, and would attend his classes on Talmud. They particularly revered him due to his honesty, righteousness, and his efforts to sustain himself with the fruits of his labor.

He studied Torah his whole life, and in old age he closed his shop and devoted the remainder of his life to Torah and *Mitzvot*. He studied a few years in the old city of Jerusalem, and later in Bnei Brak. He passed at a ripe old age, older than 80.

Sarah Disha Horvits: A Righteous Woman

Henye Harari

Translation by Meir Bulman

Sarah Disha Horvits

Sarah Disha was a valorous woman and labored greatly to provide for her family. After her sons Issac and Chaim Yudel emigrated to America and began sending money, her situation improved. She lived modestly, and a large portion of the money she received from her sons she gave to charity.

She knew of all the town's events, and showed an interest in all of them. She knew all the misfortuned people and would help them whole-heartedly. Be it *Hachnasas Kallah*[Tr. Note: bridal fund] or *Bikur Holim*,[Ed. Note: extending aid to the sick] or just a man in need whose horse had fallen – Sarah Disha's hand was always charitably open.

I remember once, as children, we were sent to fundraise for *Bikur Holim*. We entered Sarah Disha's home. A woman of advanced age wearing a white kerchief on her head, she opened her *knifl* [Tr. Knot] with shy hands and give generously. With a smile always on her face, and bestowing her blessings, she gave encouragement to the public–needs volunteers.

She was a righteous woman and saw it as her duty to prepare for that crucial day. For that purpose, she prepared her own shroud. She would sew and try on her own shroud. I once saw her standing by the window wearing a shroud, and I was afraid and yelled out, "Mom, there's a woman in a shroud for the dead!" The next day we asked her what she was doing and she answered: " לעבן דאס איז אזוי קינדע עס איז אזוי",[Ed. Note: 'azoy iz es, kinder, azoy iz dos lebn'] meaning, "That's how it is, children. That's life."

Despite her old age she was always euphoric and affable. She was alert to everything happening in town. To her last day her mind was clear and to her last day she prayed morning and evening prayers, as was always her habit.

[Page 279]

Hirshl Krizovski

Shlomo Gordon

Translation by Meir Bulman

Tzvi Krizovski was my father's good friend and would often visit our home. In my memory I perceive him as one of the educated Jewish people of that time. This was the prototypical Jewish mind in a small Poland town: with no academic education, even basic – a man independently acquired, as an autodidact, universal knowledge in technical fields, arts, and medicine.

To this day, it is difficult to comprehend how he succeeded in building and repairing radio devices, without training, or a lab, or instruments. In his meetings with my father he strived to acquire knowledge in medicine. He was always thirsting for knowledge, always desiring to learn.

He had a natural talent for directing and he directed almost all of the town's plays. He was active in the library and enjoyed befriending youths – he was young at heart. He had no spiritual counterpart for the physical world, his focus in that regard was humanism and a recognition of nature's wonders.

He studied photography on his own and all the photos that survive from the town are due to his efforts. He produced 200 photos of Divenishok's people and their way of life and sent them to America, where a film about the town was prepared.

His father Kalmen Shepsel, the Torah instructor, was impoverished and cared for so many children that Tzvi was unable to acquire a proper education, which was unfortunate – if he had gotten that education, he would likely have become a great man.

Tsvi and Mikla Krizovski with their sons and daughters (1933)

[Page 280]

Tzvi (Hirshl) Krizovski

Khaye Rivke and Menukha Krizovski
Translation by Meir Bulman

My grandfather's name was Shepsel, and he was a Torah teacher for schoolchildren. My grandmother Roykl helped my grandfather provide for the family by working as a seamstress. They had ten children – only five of whom survived. The eldest daughter, Masha, passed away in America at the age of 90. The second one, Sheyne, was pretty and blonde, and from the age of 10 worked at a shoe factory in Vilne. There, she married university student Avram Moisevitsh.

Some members of Vilbig, with Hershl Krizovski[Ed. Note: Krizovski: top row, far right; Bilke Kherson: middle row, first from left; Yankel Benyakonski: middle row, third from left]

In Vilne, Masha[Ed. Note: the name Masha is used in the original text, but the author is most likely referring to Sheyne] was involved in revolutionary activities, and in 1905 she was imprisoned at the *Lokishki* Prison in Vilne. The custom then was to whip political prisoners, literally – and that was done to her as well. Her health retreated beginning in 1917 when they crossed with the Red Army to Russia;

from then on their whereabouts are unknown. They were likely imprisoned and passed away in a Russian prison.

Aryeh Yaakov was a poet born in 1892, and passed away in New York. The fourth son was Motl, and he too travelled to America and passed away there. He worked as a tailor. The youngest child was Tzvi – our father.

Our Father's Life and Public Works

Because of the poverty and deficiencies at home, at the early age of 12, he had to travel to Vilne to find work. He made a living selling newspapers. He did not have a place to sleep – during the summer he slept on stairs, and in the winter with charitable people. He suffered and lived impoverished like that for several years, and then returned to Divenishok. At the age of 19, he married with my mother Mikleh of the house Gomnits from Ivia – and did not leave the town since.

My father was a very diligent and a man of unusual talents. He had many professions, all of which he learned on his own. At first he was an electrician, but because the town was small and he could not provide with that profession, then he studied photography. He was the only photographer in Divenishok and all surviving photos are the fruit of his labor. With the dawn of the age of radio, he taught himself the profession of radio-technician and was successful at that too.

He very much liked agriculture and devoted much of his time to growing vegetables in the large garden behind our home. In the days of the Poles, he even got an award for beet growing.

In the 30's, with the financial situation of Jewish residents deteriorating, *Yakkofu*[Ed. Note: an aid organization for Polish Jews] recommended to Jews living in towns with land, that they plant quality fruit trees so that in later days they would have a decent income. The *Yakkofu* people brought quality seeds to Divenishok too, and the town Jews planted them. My father was enthusiastic about the idea, planted fruit trees all over the garden, lovingly cared for them, and had unusual success. Three years later they bore excellent fruit that brought us substantial income.

The financial suffering that my father experienced from the dawn of his youth, and his pain over the lack of proper educational and other information-acquiring opportunities, created in his soul a begrudging bitterness for the political and social regime in the state, and he deeply longed for a replacement of the state political regime. His worldview was Socialist. The town folks called him "Hirshl the Bolshevik." They also called him "the Messiah," because once, while making a speech, he expressed, "when the Russians arrive, the messiah for the Jews will arrive."

Truthfully, he was more of a *Yiddishist*[Ed. Note: a political party that sought Jewish national autonomy within the Diaspora] than a communist, a zealot for Yiddish language and literature, who treated Jewish tradition with respect. The fact is that on Passover he would always have a Seder, and would go to the synagogue on the high holidays.

My father would organize all the dramaticals in town. He would choose the play, direct, and provide makeup. At times he also played a lead role. He was the driving force of the *Yiddishists*' cultural activity in town. He was a member of the VILBIG[Ed. Note: ("*Vilner Yidishe Bildung Gezelshaft*"; Vilne Jewish Educational Society] library committee. Not a single important event took place in town without my father's attendance.

My father was interested in medicine as well, and attained most of his knowledge from Gordon the פעלטשער.[Ed. Note: 'feltsher' an uncertified healer]. He successfully administered injections, and 'bonkes' (cupping therapy). He often contributed short articles to פאלקסגעזונט,[Ed. Note: 'Folksgezunt', literally, the people's health] a weekly publication published in Vilne, edited by the famous Dr. Tsemekh Shabad. When one of the neighbors became ill they would first consult with Hirshl.

With the entrance of the Russians, my father was chosen as פרעדסיאטעל–סוביײט של הסיעל (town council chairman),[Ed. Note: 'predsiatel shel khsiel-soveyt'] and did his best to assist the town residents.

Rescue of the Leybman Family

The Leybmans left Divenishok in the late 20's and settled in Smorgon, where they had a steel products store. When the Russians arrived, they feared remaining in Smorgon, and so they moved to Divenishok. They rented half an apartment with the " רצקו פעלטשער "[Ed. Note: Raszko the Feltsher', see above] family on Oshmene Street. In the second half of the apartment lived the *feltsher's* daughter, Yadzha.

Yadzha was a prostitute and contacted a band of thieves to kill the Leybmans and rob all their belongings. The custom at the time was that one person from every home would go for night security patrol at the *Khsiel-Soveyt* building. She scheduled the robbery for the night she had guard duty to create an alibi.

It was a large and organized gang of robbers and they truly intended to carry out their plot.

A farmer from the Krakon village who was a member of that gang, wanted to repent, and so one night he knocked on our door. When Father opened the window and saw a bearded man, poorly dressed, with bloodshot eyes, he was intimidated by him and wanted to shut the window. The man urged him to hear him out: "I came to inform you of an issue with great importance," he said; "I truly am a thief, but I want to repent. I have pity on my wife and children, so I came to inform you of my gang and the plot they plan to carry out tonight at three... I want to repent and ask forgiveness for my bad deeds." (He had once robbed and murdered a priest on the road). My mother was very frightened, but my father convinced her that action must be taken immediately: "I think the farmer is telling the truth," he told my mother. He let the farmer into our home and went out to rescue the Leybmans.

My father gathered a few police officers and NKVD officials, who happened to be in town recruiting soldiers to the military, entered the Leybman home and waited. Precisely at three o'clock the door was opened and the head of the gang entered with a loaded gun in his right hand, and a flashlight in his left. My father shot at him and he shot at my father— the bullet whisked right by Father's ear. When the rest of the robbers saw their leader was injured they ran towards the woods, where an escape carriage awaited them. The next day the injured robber was found in the woods and taken to the hospital, where he later died.

The thief who informed Father had informed on the entire gang, and all of them, about 40, were captured and tried in a large public trial in Baranovich. To be clear, the Soviets were not hesitant to sentence them to many years in prison.

The Leybman family included an old father, his wife, and a daughter and her husband with a five-year-old girl. According to the plan, the old man, his wife, and the little girl were to have been bound in rope and imprisoned, while the daughter and husband were to have been murdered. Among those sentenced to a long imprisonment was Yadzha, who had been the architect of the conspiracy.

Working for the Community

Eliohu Blyakher

Translation by Meir Bulman

For my father Moshe Ben Binyamin, a son to a family of distinguished and respected lineage, who had lived in Divenishok for several generations. I recall that on days of remembrance, my father would show us the gravestones of his father and grandfather at the old cemetery. My mother's name was Khenye, and she originated in in Kovne. She was his second wife.

His first wife died young and childless. My father was a typical Jewish man like many residents of Lithuanian towns. He was a religious Jew, rooted in the

Jewish tradition. Love of Torah and love of humanity were at the core of his life force.

He was a wealthy man, and because he did not have children with his first wife, he devoted part of his fortune to writing two *Sifrei Torah*.[1] He donated one to the Old synagogue, and kept the other in a Torah ark at home. On Shabbat and holidays, *Minyanim*[2] were held in our home. On *Simchat Torah* we went to the synagogue with the *Nevi'im*[3] scrolls, and fulfilled the *Mitzvah* of *Hakafot*.[4] It was a great honor for us, but was envied by neighboring children.

My father was a very observant man. He went to pray at the synagogue three times daily. Between *Mincha*[5] and *Maariv*[6] he routinely participated in learning *Mishnayot*.[7] Prayers were a natural need for him and he prayed with great devotion.

He was a righteous man, quick to fulfill a *Miztvah*.[8] On Fridays he would quickly cease working and go out to the market place to plead, "שבת איז'ס, קינדרלך, געששעפטן די פארמאכט! ("My children, *Shabbat* has begun, close the shops!"). He would urge the late ones, saying: "Nu! Nu! Quickly, quickly, *Chilul Shabbat, Chilul Shabbat!*"[9]

All the town residents would respect my father's request, because they knew his actions arose from a sincere faith in the Torah. When my father would appear at the marketplace all would quickly close down their shops, and if a customer would delay a grocer, then he would tell the customer, "My Jewish friend, can't you see that Moshe the Tinsmith already announced Shabbat? Do you want him to reproach me?"

My father was active in the *Chevrah Kadisha*[10] in town, and was fully devoted to that role. "I am granting those who have passed the *chesed shel emet*."[11] That was the most important *Mitzvah* to him. He would fulfill it with sacred dedication.

He was murdered by the Germans in 1942.

Editor's Footnotes

1. A holographic copy of the Torah, prepared according to strict guidelines, and often commissioned by wealthier members of the congregation

2. A quorum of ten Jewish adults required for certain religious prayers and rituals

3. Refers to the section of the Hebrew Bible comprised of the books of the various prophets

4. Refers to the ritual circle dance around the *bimah* (pulpit) on the holiday of *Simchat Torah*

5. Afternoon prayer service

6. Evening prayer service

7. Lessons from the first section of the Talmud

8. Good deed

9. Literally 'killing the Sabbath', meaning a Sabbath violation is occurring or about to occur

10. Jewish burial society

11. 'the truest act of kindness'

[Page 283]

My Father and Grandfather Loved Working the Land

Yosef Kaplan

Translation by Meir Bulman

My grandfather passed away when I was an infant and so I cannot describe his character, but according to the stories about him he was a strict Jewish man and was not willing to concede one iota.

Our plot of land was the largest in town; it stretched all the way from our house at the market place up until the קודרע¹ (the famous pool on Vilne Street). As was customary in Poland, an unworked strip of land separated ours from and the neighbors' plots. On that strip grew the wood sorrel (*Szczawik zajeczy*, or simply *Szczaw* in Polish) that was among the town residents' favorite food items.

Usually the peasants' wives brought *Szczaw* to sell in town, but at times there were also a *Szczaw* shortages, and then the town's young women would raid the strip of land and pick the sorrel. My grandfather would chase the girls with a stick, but they chose to continue picking the forbidden *Szczaw* to spite him. Then once he tripped and fell mid-chase, became ill, and passed away.

My father loved working the land and in the scalding season the family joined him, be it to harvest grain or uproot the potatoes. We stored the potatoes in the basement and they served as basic nutrition all year.

The family of Mordechai and Khasya (Khasita) Kaplan, in Divenishok in 1928, all killed by the German murderers, except for five year old Yosef, seated at the bottom in the center, who was able to emigrate to Erets-Yisrael with his parents Mordechai and Khasya

In the days of the Russian Czarist regime, my father was secretary of "אופראווא מיעששאנסקאיא"(city administration); my father would assist Jews who needed to change their names or obtain a residence permit. These services were most important to Jews escaping from Russia to Poland.

My father was an observant Jew who was also a public servant. He served as *gabbai*[2] at the synagogue, and for a while as a treasurer and bank administrator after Sholem Yakov Rogol left for America, and Yakov Druck resigned – since the bank was then at the brink of collapse.

I was the youngest of the family and everyone pampered me. We had a tavern at home where we kept beer barrels. I once snuck in and drank directly from the barrel so Father would not notice. My sister brought the entire family and everyone stood in the doorway and watched me drink – and my father stood there and smiled.

Like all town children I too attended the Hebrew school, where the language of instruction was Hebrew. During my time there, a change was enacted and Yiddish became a secondary language of instruction. The *Yidishists*[3] in town likely got the upper hand at that time.

Editor's Footnotes

1. The Kidreh

2. Beadle

3. A political party that sought Jewish national autonomy within the Diaspora

[Page 284]

In Memory of my Father Leyb Dubin May He Rest in Peace

Rachel Zuvitshki (Dubin)

Translation by Meir Bulman

My father Leyb Dubin was born in the village of Dubinke, located on the road from Divenishok to Benakani. My father was in the forestry business. After he married, he moved to Divenishok. My mother Beyleh was from the Kramer family. Moshe Kalmen Kramer, the famous cantor, was my mother's first cousin.

I spent my childhood and young adulthood in Divenishok. Of all my teachers I remember Stutski from Ivia, who was beloved by the town's youth. He organized the *Bund*[1] organization in town, and would give magnificent speeches opposing the Czarist regime. Thanks to him the *Bund* in our town was well organized. Its members were Socialist minded.

Gatherings took place in secret – in the field or the woods— in fear of the government. The *Bund* leader in our town was Bezalel the *Chasid's*[2] son, an educated young man with excellent leadership skills. His family left Divenishok a long time ago.

The family of Leyb Dubin, who lived on Market Street, 1924

In 1909, I married my husband Eliezer Zuvitshki and moved to Vilne. My husband worked at a bank in Bunimovitz.[3] My father too moved to Vilne, but the bond with my birth-town did not cease. We visited the town often and had a special tradition of visiting Divenishok during the summer break. That tradition was kept by our descendants as well. We would always return from Divenishok with many positive experiences and impressions.

My father was a sought-after cantor; he had a sweet, pleasant voice and served in that role his whole life. During our stay in Divenishok, and later in Vilne, he was the cantor at the famous קלויז[4] ס'שאוול synagogue.

Editor's Footnotes

1. Allgemeyner Idisher Arbayterbund in Lita, Poylen un Rusland, a pan-Diaspora labor organization and political movement

2. From the word for 'pious' or 'piety', Chasidism is a mystical Jewish practice founded in the 18th Century in the Western Ukrainian section

of Poland and characterized by an emphasis on prayer, religious zeal, and joy

3. The town of Bunimovitz has not yet been identified. It is presumably a town in the vicinity of Vilne.

4. 'Shavlos Kloyz'; this small synagogue has not yet been identified. There were over 100 synagogues in Vilna at that time.

[Page 285]

Mordechai Blyakher, Of Blessed Memory

Moshe Mintz

Translation by Meir Bulman

Mordechai's father was named Hershl (Tsvi) der (בלעכער the tinsmith), and his mother was named Sarah Ita. They lived near the *Gavya* Stream. After Mordechai's mother Sarah Ita passed away, Tsvi married again, and Mordechai often had to leave the house. He was a leather maker and worked in various locations.

They arrived in Israel in 1925, and being a member of *HaPoel HaMizrachi*,[2] Tsvi found work with a Petah Tikva farmer named Donovitsh, earning enough to fulfill his needs. Once, Donovitsh's young son saw a film in which a horse dragged a man. It left a strong impression on him and he decided to try it on one of his father's workers. One day while unsupervised by his father he commanded the Arab workers to tie Tsvi to a horse, which immediately galloped forward. Tsvi began to scream and the horse was stopped only with difficulty. He was severely injured and taken to the French hospital in Jaffa.

After recovering from his injuries he hired a lawyer and filed a lawsuit against the farmer Donovitsh. Investigators came to the scene, but the investigation yielded no results. The investigators were probably bribed by Donovitsh and did not even deem it necessary to summon Mordechai Blyakher to recount the event. The French hospital was also allegedly bribed and the lawsuit was dismissed.

Donovitsh fired Tsvi, and as if that was not enough– withdrew his recommendation to accept Mordechai Blyakher as a farmer in Netanya; Ben-Ami, the village mayor, expelled him from the co-op.

All those events broke his spirit and he was bedridden for a long while. After recovering he married a woman from Hertzliya and lived there for the rest of his life.

Moshe Mintz, [Ed. Note: sitting on left] *Blyakher and S. Rosenblum,*
[Ed. Note: Sholem Rosenblum, sitting on right] *in Israel (1929)*

Editor's and Translator's Footnotes

1. Tr. Note: 'Of Blessed Memory'; the title of the essay is 'Mordechai Blyakher', but the events described mostly deal with his father Hershl Tsvi.

2. Ed. Note: Literally 'Mizrachi Worker'; HaPoel HaMizrachi, founded in Jerusalem in 1922, was one of the two parties that later in 1955

combined to form the National Religious Party, or Mafdal, in Israel (the other party being HaMizrachi).

[Page 286]

My Family

Kheyne Sutskever

Translation by Meir Bulman

My paternal grandfather, Yosef (Yosl)[1], of a Divenishok family living there for generations, worked as a blacksmith. He married my grandmother Kheyne (I am her namesake). My father, Shimon Leyb, found his beloved, my mother דובה[2], in the nearby town of Ivia.

My eldest brother, Raphael, attended the Stutchin *Yeshiva*, where his uncle was Chief Rabbi of Stutchin, *HaRav* Yehuda Leyb Khasman (also known as R' Leibtshik Stutchiner). The son of the Rav, Raphael Khasman[3], worked for a while for the נייעס[4] newspaper's editorial staff in Kovne, and after that was appointed secretary of the editorial staff at די אידישע שטימע[5]. Raphael made *Aliyah* in 1926 and was appointed secretary of the editorial staff at *HaTzofe*.[6] He passed away in Tel Aviv on 1972.

My brother Raphael married Etl of the house of Abramovitsh. Her brother, Motl Abramovitsh, married in the town of Rudzishok,[7] where he was later murdered. My brother Raphael, his wife Etl, and their three children, perished in Voronova with my father. My brother was a devoted *Torah* scholar, and at the end of each exhausting work day he would study a *Talmud* chapter in the synagogue in front of our home. My sister Shifra arrived in Israel in 1926 and was a guest in the home of our uncle *HaRav* Yehuda Leyb Khasman, then spiritual administrator at the Hebron *Yeshiva*. She was miraculously saved from the massacres in Hebron, where she met her husband *HaRav* Moshe Saritski, who was a student at the Hebron *Yeshiva*. My brother-in-law now serves as Rabbi of Karkur. Shifra passed away in 1967.

I loved public activity and I remember that when I was young I worked at the *Beit Zandman* library. The rehearsals for drama club took place in our home. The biggest attraction was when *HaShomer HaTzair*[8] acquired a radio and rented a space in our home so the youth in town could listen to the radio.

My husband, Lolle Sutskever, was also very active in public service, an active member at the VILBIG[9] library, as well as being a commander at the fire department, devoting the bulk of his time to training these firefighters.

Editor's Footnotes

1. The family being described here starting with Yosef is believed to be of surname Khasman. This is based on the statements in the second and third paragraphs stating that the author's uncle was named Yehuda Leyb Khasman. Yehuda Leyb Khasman is believed to be the blood brother of Yosef, thus justifying the application of the surname Khasman to the whole family.

2. 'Dube' or 'Dobe'

3. Both the article author's brother and her uncle's son were named Raphael

4. 'The News'

5. 'The Yiddish Voice'

6. 'The Oberver'

7. This town has not yet been identified; it is possibly the town also known as Radoshkovitsh

8. 'The Young Guard'; Zionist Youth Movement

9. 'Vilner Yidishe Bildung Gezelshaft'; Vilne Jewish Educational Society

[Page 287]

On Those Who Escaped to Soviet Russia

Rivke Krizovski

Translation by Meir Bulman

Yosef Levine (Son of Yitzach Artzom)

His family was with us when we escaped from Divenishok, but then they returned with my mother. He managed to reach Russia and suffered greatly there. In 1943 he was enlisted into the Lithuanian military and participated in combat. He was wounded eight times and received medals for excellence. He now lives in Kharkov and has two daughters. He often visited me when I was in Vilne. He also helped me a lot in reaching Israel.

Lolle Olkenitski

Lolle snuck across the border in 1933 with Paula, Tsvi Srulovitsh's wife. High quality Jewish youth in Poland were not at all aware of what their fate would be if they crossed the border to Russia illegally. Thousands of our best young men and women risked their lives and faced lengthy prison sentences if the Poles were to capture them while trying to cross. And indeed many were captured and imprisoned, and placed in the Bereza Kartuska Prison Camp. In prison they envied their close friends who had succeeded in crossing the border to Russia and thought they must be the happiest people ever. But they were gravely mistaken! All those who crossed the border from Poland were considered spies in Russia and were exiled to Siberia, which was their final destination in life.

Lolle was lucky; his wife Paula[1] had relatives who lived in Russia and thanks to them they were not sent to Siberia. Paula died four years after they arrived in Russia and Lolle remarried, to a Russian woman. They had a daughter. His in-laws were very anti-Semitic and so they forced their daughter to divorce him. Later he married a third wife and from her too he had a daughter. He passed away a year before I arrived in Israel.

Bilke and her mother Rokhl Leah also succeeded in reaching Russia. Rokhl Leah died there. Bilke married and lives in Romanovka, near Moscow. Her husband is a supervisor at an aviation parts factory. She would often visit me in Vilne. She is no longer the same gorgeous Bilke. Time has left its marks on her.

Translator's Footnote

1. Here Paula is described as Lolle's wife. In the previous paragraph she is described as the wife of Tsvi Srulovitsh.

In Memory of Our Mother
Shoshana (Reyzl) Ben–Dov

Amnon and Yaffa

Translation by Meir Bulman

My heart bleeds as I am about to describe the image of our mother of blessed memory. She was a model of righteousness, humility, honesty, and love for the family.

She inherited her noble soul from her parents, about whom many stories are told. Her father R' Eliahu-Chaim, was a righteous man, and was well-known in town for his fairness and kind heartedness. Her mother Pesye Malka, despite her troubles and woes, never said a bad word about a fellow human. More than that; every Friday, she would cook for the town's poor people, so that they too can feel the holiness of the Sabbath. She also always contributed to *Keren Kayemet*[1] and the town's institutions.

She made *Aliyah* with her husband 50 years ago, residing in Haifa, which according to her was "mountains and stones." There she would care for the bachelors from town who had made *Aliyah* with them and assisted them in those difficult days.

My mother's life goal was devotion to family, aid to her fellow man – particularly those who were connected to her town – and to her final day she mentioned the people of Divenishok and showed interest in their lives.

That is how our dear mother was and it is a shame she passed away so soon.

May her soul be bound in a bond of everlasting life. May she rest in peace.

Editor's Footnote

1. Jewish National Fund

[Page 288]

About A Jewish Family

Dina Lebizuvski[1]

Translation by Meir Bulman

My mother's family tree had many branches and they always lived in Divenishok. My grandfather's name was Matisyahu and my grandmother was Khayne Rishe. Aryeh, Zalman Solodukhe (Zalman Artsiks) Isha (יאש) Nashes (נאש) and Chaim Alferovitz– were grandmother's brothers.

My grandfather Matisyahu was son to a rich family in Minsk. Because there were many men in his family for whom military enlistment was mandatory, he was sent to Divenishok, where he received a passport under a different name— and did not enlist in the military. Instead he remained to live in Divenishok where he married my grandmother. His original last name was Vigudski, but was changed to Levine. He was a great *Torah* scholar who studied *Torah* day and night and passed away with a *Talmud* volume by his heart.

My grandmother had six brothers who lived in Divenishok. My mother had four brothers, among them Chaim Levine, who remined in France. His son Yehezkel Levine is a well-known internal medicine physician in France.

My father, Eliahu[2] originated from a family of scholars in Eshishuk, and he too was a *Yeshiva* student. After he married he had to work a butcher and he found it very difficult to provide for his nine children with his wages. Naturally, the older children emigrated and spread across the globe. One sister traveled to Africa, two sisters and a brother to Boston in the United States, and my sister Yente (Of Blessed Memory) and I made *Aliyah*. Sheynke[3], Lolle Sutskever's wife and her two children, and my brother Aharon, remained in Divenishok, where they perished at the hands of the Germans. One brother lives in Argentina.

I met my husband Yehuda Blezuvski[4] in Divenishok. He was among the heads of *HaKhalutz*[5] in Eshishuk, a group that taught Hebrew to the pioneers, and conducted social activities in the spirit of Zionism. In 1925, we made *Aliyah* as passionate idealists to build the land.

Our first journey was to Afula, where my husband worked paving the road to Zemach. In Afula tragedy struck us: the shack in which we lived burned down with all our belongings and we survived only penniless. After that we moved to Petah Tikva and lived near my in-laws. There, my husband became ill and passed away after being bedridden for over a year. I remained a widow with my infant daughter Deborah. I raised my daughter with great pain and effort until she married and established a home, in which I found some rest – we live together.

Editor's Footnotes

1. This surname is spelled two different ways in this article: Blezuvski and Lebizuvski.

2. The surname of the author's father Eliahu is believed to be Khasman. This is based on the reference to Lolle Sutkever's wife, Shenyke, in this paragraph. Sheynke's maiden name is believed to be Khasman from the article entitled 'My Family' on page 286 of this volume.

3. Also known as Kheine

4. This surname is spelled two different ways in this article: Blezuvski and Lebizuvski.

5. Zionist youth movement

R' Leyb Aharon Engle, Of Blessed Righteous Memory

Eliahu Netaneli (Itskovitsh)

Translation by Meir Bulman

My first *Rebbe* was a short-statured man with a long beard. He was a wonderful man, both God-fearing and a lover of Zion. All day he would teach *Torah* to pupils in his home, which was packed, and he would counsel them with a gentleness as well as serious discipline. On Fridays before Shabbat he would sweetly sing the *Haftara*[1] with his pupils.

His wages were quite low, yet he was never angry. When pupils payed tuition, one Ruble once or twice monthly, he would accept payment with tear-filled eyes and say to the child, "What will become of you? What will you learn? I fear you will leave this room ignorant of Torah. Is that possible? For that I spend all the oil in my house? What outcome will your studies have?"

The students were not pleased by that speech nor by his strict supervision of them. They knew how to behave in his home, respectful and studious, but that did not suffice for him. He wished to establish a generation of scholars.

When my father left to the United States, he fulfilled his role: he was proficient in *Talmud* and the *Poskim*,[2] and he liked to study the *Torah* commentators in depth. The whole audience loved him.

Editor's Footnotes

1. The weekly *Torah* portion
2. Judicial decisions on Jewish Law

[Page 290]

Eliahu Chaim Shkolnik

Eliahu Netaneli (Itskovitsh)

Translation by Meir Bulman

One day, Eliahu Chaim went as he did very day to pray *Shachrit*[1] at the synagogue. When he reached the entrance he did not enter, but instead turned back and quickly walked towards the street. My father, who was in the synagogue at the time, noticed that something unusual seemed to be happening to Eliahu. "Chaim," he called him, and asked, "R' Eliahu Chaim, why are you returning home without praying? Did something happen?"

Eliahu Chaim replied, "On my way to the *shul* I saw a child at the market place who was barefoot, with feet red from the cold, and winter is quickly approaching. On my way I pondered the issue and I got agitated. Until the boy has shoes I will not be able to pray with a clear conscience. In this case, fulfilline the *mitzvah* of clothing the naked takes precedence over the *sacharit*[1] prayer."

My father was very impressed by Eliahu Chaim's actions and he would tell this story every chance he had.

Esther Engle z"l [Tr. Note: may her memory be for a blessing] *on the steps of her house*

Editor's Footnote

1. Daily morning prayer service

One of the Ancient Families

Esther Ala (Blyakher)
Translation by Meir Bulman

Our family is one of most ancient and expansive families in Divenishok. We had many relatives in town, both paternal and maternal.

My paternal grandfather's name was Eli Feyvus. He was a good man from the expansive Kartshmer family. Grandfather worked as a butcher and made a good living. There was a pleasant religious atmosphere in my grandfather's home; he was a traditional God-fearing man. He often led prayers at the old synagogue. He would regularly trill and hum holiday and festival prayers.

My father, Yitzach, son of Binyamin Blyakher, passed away in 1922, leaving behind seven children, and our mother who was pregnant with our sister Khaya Lefte. Our financial situation was quite poor.

Thanks to our sister Zilpa, who made Aliyah with the first *khalutzim*, most of our family succeeded in making *Aliyah* and live here with us. The eldest sister, Radke, stayed in town and perished along with her husband and five children at the Voronova Ghetto.

Our little brother Tevye, the youngest in the family, died a heroic death with our town's last Partisans in the Stoki forest. Tsvi Novoplanski provides a detailed description of that in this book.

Our mother Itte passed away in Israel a few years ago. My brother Shraga, my sister Zilpa, and my sister Khaya Lefte live with me in Peta Tikva. My sister Gitte-Merke lives in Giv'atayim.

We have two sons, the eldest Dani and the second Eliezer, who both established a home. I am happy to have the good fortune to live in Israel, but my heart aches when I remember my sister, brother, and all my relatives who perished in the Holocaust.

[Page 291]

My Husband Yosef Levine: A Multifaceted Man

His wife, Yehudit Levine

Translation by Meir Bulman

I cannot accept the fact that my husband Yosef, or as the members of his town of Divenishok affectionately named him, "Yosele dem muler's", is no longer among the living. He was indeed a man with great energy, active and activating, lively and enlivening.

Yosef had a special touch for literature and his knowledge of Jewish and global literature was astounding. His favorite authors were Mendele Mocher Sforim, Sholem Aleichem, and Karl Marx, whose works he nearly memorized.

Yosef was blessed with a phenomenal memory and memorized all the important historical events in both global and Jewish history. Before final exams, friends of our only daughter Hadassah would gather in our home and study.

Ita Blyakher, Of Blessed Memory   *Yosef Levine*

I met him in Vilne and it was there that our fates intertwined. He worked at an electronics factory, and despite not possessing basic knowledge in electronic science, succeeded very much at his work. He acquired a vast amount of knowledge in that profession and succeeded in improving and devising new operation procedures. That amazed his mangers, who gave him excellence awards and substantial bonuses.

Yosef, my husband, was blessed with excellent musical talent. As a young boy he taught himself how to play mandolin. When he enlisted in the Polish military his talents were recognized and he was accepted as a trumpet player in the military orchestra. That was a rarity in the anti–Semitism ridden Polish military, which routinely blocked Jews from attaining respectable positions. Hadassah, our only daughter, inherited his talent, and she too excelled in the musical field.

He was a man of great traits. His speech always flowed calmly. He was always smiling, cordial, affable, and beloved by people. He never lied once his entire life.

He had a natural flare for public activities and with his strong persistence archived every goal he set. Those talents were expressed boldly in his role as director of culture at the Petah Tikvah retirement home. He wrote and directed plays, organized and conducted the choir at every festive event, lectured on intellectual and literary topics, and instilled in his listeners a love of the arts and culture.

As his town folks told me, Yosef excelled at public activities. He was one of the managers of the public library, was quite familiar with all the books in it, and would amaze all readers with a book recommendation fitting their tailored preferences.

In his town of Divenishok, he was active in the Yiddish youth movement *VILBIG*,[1] and stood out as one of the most important Yiddishist leaders in town. He excelled both with the youth group as well as the cultural activity. He managed to attract youth with his charm and became their spiritual leader.

Following the holocaust in Europe, and after spending many years in the Soviet Union, a substantial shift in his views occurred. He was deeply disappointed by the cruelty of the Soviet regime. "We dreamed of the liberation of the proletariat," he would say, "but in fact the proletariat is now subjected to a repressive authoritarian regime and the Soviet "paradise" is in fact a dark hell."

His soul was especially burdened by the extinguishing of Jewish life in Russia; Yiddish culture ceased to exist, values of preserving Jewish uniqueness seemed to have perished, and Yiddish journalism and literature were unheard of. In sum, the Jewish people in Russia are dwindling, and it will not be long before they completely assimilates and disappear. This hurt and angered him very much.

While still in Vilne, we decided to leave the Soviet Union and make Aliyah. Lively and turbulent arguments took place in our home on that issue with Lolle Olkenitski, who escaped in the thirties to the USSR with Paula and would often visit us in Vilne. In those arguments I was surprised by my husband's deeply rooted Zionist views and I thought about the changes in his political and national views. Indeed, my husband became a conscious Zionist, which was boldly expressed in his essays, one of which appears in this book.

A grave illness put an end to his active life and he left behind a vacant space that will be tough to fill. His good memory will always remain in our hearts.

ה"תנצבב2

Editor's Footnotes

1. ("Vilner Yidishe Bildung Gezelshaft";) Vilne Jewish Educational Society

2. "[...]the soul of my lord shall be bound in the bundle of life[...]"; from 1 Samuel 25:29

[Page 292]

Tsvi Rogol

Shulamit Fuchs (Rogol)

Translation by Meir Bulman

My brother Tsvi was born in 1909. He completed his degree in chemistry and pharmaceuticals in Vilne. He was a tall and strong young man with a gentle soul. Though his father was among the wealthiest men in town, he always favored youth from the lower class and was of the radical intelligentsia camp.

While at university he was a member of leftist student unions- and under surveillance by the Polish secret police.

He was modest and quiet, and his speech flowed calmly and in good taste. Due to this he was beloved and accepted among his peers.

Before WWII, he married in Slonim, and was a manager of a large pharmacy. In addition, he lectured young students in pharmaceutical studies and on other subjects.

*Hershl Rogol, Aryeh Leyb's son,
killed by the German murderers*

In the days of German occupation he escaped with his wife to the Slonim woods, but returned to the ghetto and perished there along with his wife.

[Page 293]

About My Parents and Grandfather

Shlomo Gordon

Translation by Meir Bulman

My Grandfather

My grandfather, Berel Katz (or as the town residents named him "Berel der shooster,[1]"), was a famous figure in Divenishok. My grandmother Feige passed away before I would have the chance to know her. Leybe Idel's, who lived on Girneyner Street, was my grandfather's brother. Hirshl Krizovski's mother was my grandmother Feige's sister.

In his youth my grandfather worked as a shoemaker, hence the "Berel der shooster" nickname. He was naturally skinny and amazingly quick. Once, someone fell into the well at the market place. Nobody wanted to descend into the well to rescue him, but my grandfather risked his life and saved the man.

My grandfather owned a large garden which was admired by the town residents. It was the only garden in town owned by a Jew. My grandfather had a natural gift for gardening since childhood. He knew how to grow two types of fruit on the same tree, care for trees, and heal them when necessary. The garden was very well-kept, and the scent of cherry blossom would spread to the area and fill the people with a feeling of happiness and calmness. He had great success in growing different strains of fruit; the apples and pears were sometimes the size of grapefruit.

In his old age grandfather quit shoemaking and the bulk of his income came from the garden. On market day Thursday he would take out a wagon filled with fruit for sale to the public in front of his house at the market place (which bordered the priest's garden). Even the government clerks would buy high quality apples. In winter he would prepare frozen apples, which was considered by the youth as a delicacy.

The fruits of the garden also enticed the town's children and they were attracted to the juicy apples smiling from the tree; they would sometimes try their luck... but not on Berel's watch! He guarded the garden like the apple of his eye and even built a hut in the garden where he would sleep.

He was a humble man of few words, observant, and a lover of *Torah*. He was a regular member at the *Mishnah* society and prayed daily at the Synagogue. In his old age he would spend many hours praying and reciting Psalms at the Synagogue. My grandfather passed away in 1938.

My Father

My father was born in 1889 in Lida, where he spent his childhood. In 1912 he completed medical school ("fletzeraskia shkola") for which there was a four year study period, and then received the degree of "certified fletser." My father came from a poor family and attained his position on his own merit. He arrived in Divenishok as a "certified fletser" and began practicing medicine. There he also married my mother, Ahuvah. My grandfather gave him the house near the garden as a wedding gift.

The gravestone of Moshe Aaron Katz in the Divenishok cemetery, 1931

With the eruption of WWI my father was enlisted in the military as a medical operative. The military hospital where my father served wandered all across Russia until finally it reached Melitopol, Crimea. My sister was born in Divenishok in 1914, and I was born after we moved to Melitopol, in 1916. There we experienced hardships – we went through the civil war and the Bolshevik revolution, were afflicted by starvation, poverty and suffering. The film *Doctor Zhivago* is a good description the state of our wellbeing while living in Russia.

We resided in the Soviet Union until 1923. My grandmother ל"ז missed her daughter very much and she wrote asking for her return. My father also wanted to leave that prison as soon as possible, but that goal was not easily achievable. At that time in Russia movement between districts was forbidden, let alone traveling abroad.

Syoma Gordon, his sister Rivke, and their grandfather, Berel Katz (z"l), murdered by the Germans

We snuck from district to district like Partisans, and the journey lasted three quarters of a year. We traveled in freight trains, wandering from camp to camp, and then we had to cross the border to Poland illegally.

My mother

My mother contracted tuberculosis due to the travel woes, and reached Divenishok sick and weary. My parents left me at the hospital in Vilne because I was bloated from starvation and exhausted from the long journey. My father had to care for my mother and so could not even travel to Vilne to pick me up, and I, still quite feeble, had to travel on my own from Vilne to Divenishok with a coachman.

My mother passed away in 1923 after much suffering, and my father remained a 34 year–old widower, caring for two toddlers. Two years later my father remarried and the relationship between my grandfather and father intensified— father had to leave Divenishok and move to Smorgon in 1930.

My father was a pleasant and mingled well with people, always calm, and smiling. He had a natural tendency to console his patients and his family. With his devoted, fatherly attitude, he would instill a feeling of serenity and security in the home of the patient. He consciously projected his personality onto his patients and the psychological impact was tremendous. He would explain to the patient the nature of the illness with a smile, lessening its perceived dangers with a good joke or a heartwarming anecdote– and he was successful.

During times of need and on special occasions he would save the sick by conducting home-visits. He did not consider time or money – financial matters were secondary to him. When needed he would sit with the patient for hours to calm the patient and the family. In severe situations he would waive the fee and add medicine at no cost.

I Made *Aliyah*

My father understood the importance of technical fields, even back then, and so he did his best to provide his children with a professional education. I was steered to an *ORT*³ technical college. It was one of ORT's prestigious institutions in Poland; the best teachers and engineers taught there. The language of instruction was Yiddish.

When I completed my studies at the technical college I was unemployed because all gates to government jobs were closed to Jews. Anti-Semitism increased in Poland and the future seemed grim. Instead of sneaking across the border to Russia, like many other youths from town, my father sent me to *Eretz Israel*, even though he was not a Zionist. "The only path for Jewish youth is in Eretz Israel," he would say.

I first met my wife Esther Schwarts in Ivia in 1933, where we had moved for family reasons. She was a seminary student in Vilne. In 1934 I made *Aliyah* as a student at the Technion in Haifa, and in 1937 I returned to visit my family, and then married my wife Esther and made Aliyah. That was how we were saved from the Nazis' claws.

In Israel we started a family and have two children, the oldest Uzi – an architect at the Technion in Haifa, and a daughter, Ahuva, a university graduate.

My father perished in Ivia in 1941 in the extermination of the Intelligentsia. On Tisha B'Av of 1941 many doctors, teachers and the other intellectuals were taken, supposedly to work, but did not ever return. My stepmother perished with my sister Rivke, and her husband Shmuel, and their son, when the Ivia ghetto was disbanded by the Nazis.

Editor's Footnotes

1. Berel "The Shoemaker"

2. 'may her memory be a blessing'

3. Общество Ремесленного Труда, *Obchestvo Remeslenogo Truda*, "Association for the Promotion of Skilled Trades"

Yehuda Satkolshtsik, Of Blessed Memory
Shlomo Aviel
Translation by Meir Bulman

Righteous, honest, humble, lover of Zion and his Nation, with a big warm heart; on men like him it is written in Psalm 15:

> *He who walks blamelessly and does what is right*
> *and speaks truth in his heart;*
> *who does not slander with his tongue*
> *and does no evil to his neighbor,*
> *nor takes up a reproach against his friend.*

It is customary around the globe that when a person passes to the next world, his family, relatives, and friends attend a funeral, feel pain, and eulogize. Then as time passes they grow accustomed to the absence, reconcile, and even forget. But there are others, though they are few and outstanding, who are never forgotten– and one of those people was Yehuda Satkolshtsik ז"ל.

I met Yehuda while I was still young, in my 20's. He was an honest, precious Jew, a devoted lover of Zion, a public servant of high stature, and a member of *HaHistadrut HaTziyonit*[2] in town. Among the founders of the library, the organizers of the theater company, and a loyal and active participant in all Divenishok institutions.

His greatest love was towards the Zionist youth movements, including all factions: *HaShomer HaTzair*[3], *HaKhalutz*[4], etc. He was not only a friend to all, but also a leader, a planner, and operator. He supported and assisted all. He would say, "in my eyes you are all equal, as you are all headed to Zion, and there you will get along."

After some time he married a woman and moved to her home in Volozhin. It was said that he acclimated and immediately became a central figure there in the Zionist movement and its institutions; *Keren Kayemes*[5], *Keren HaYesod*,[6] etc. There, too, he became attached to his life–long devotion to the youth. He contributed much to them. We know he played a central role in the town's social and public scene.

He, as many others, was executed by the cruel Nazi beast, along with his wife and his only daughter. The heart aches that he too did not get to arrive in Zion.

May these few paragraphs serve as a memorial candle in his honor.

Editor's Footnotes

1. 'May His Memory Be A Blessing'

2. World Zionist Organization

3. Zionist self–defense movement

4. Zionist youth movement

5. Jewish National Fund

6. United Israel Appeal

My Father Provided Much Aid to Jews

Yehuda Katz

Translation by Meir Bulman

I was born in 1909. My paternal grandfather, Leybe Katz, was ordained as a rabbi. My maternal grandfather, Leyb Kagan, maintained and managed the ranch owned by the family of Polish Prime Minister Piłsudski. The well–known banker in Vilne, Bonimovitsh, was from my mother's family.

My paternal grandfather[1], Kalmenovitsh, who lived at Niamn Station, was a telegrapher. He was of the Cantonists, or as his nickname stated, "a *Nikolaiist soldier.*" He was kidnapped as a child for service in the Russian military and served for 25 years. During his military service he was a telegraphist in the Czar's castle. It was a respectable position which a Jew could not normally fill, but the Czar was not aware of his Jewish lineage. Then the Czar saw him wearing a *tallit* and *tefillin*. Realizing his career would end, he escaped, but later overcame his fear and presented himself to the Czar, who informed him that his continued service would be impossible. My grandfather's brother requested to settle at Neiman, and that request was granted. He was rich and established a large local sawmill.

About my father David I can say that in 1918, in the days of Bolshevik control, he was chairman of the local MRC (*Voyenno–revolyutsionny komitet* – Military Revolutionary Committee). When the Polish entered he became a wanted man, but he escaped from home. The Poles demanded that Mother turn in my father and hand over the weapon he had supposedly left with her,

The local priest saved my father by testifying that my father always informed him ahead of time when the MRC was preparing to seize some farmer's assets. The priest said, "Do not harm this Jew! He aided us a lot under the Bolsheviks."

My father indeed provided much aid to Jews; on one occasion, he rescued Mordechai Kaplan from prison after he ran into trouble with the authorities. When the Germans entered our town, my father saved the lives of many Russian soldiers the Germans had captured in the woods and had locked in Natan Itskovitsh's basement. My father risked his life by removing the door off its hinges to release the prisoners.

Our family was comprised of four brothers and one sister. The oldest, Yakov, was a carpenter. He perished at the Vornova ghetto along with his wife, and three children, as well as my mother and father. My second brother was an excellent student at a high school in Vilne. In 1923, while in Vilne, he tripped down the stairs, was severely wounded, and passed away at the young age of 14. The third one has been living in the United States. The fourth is Devora–Roykhle, and I, Yehuda Katz am the fifth.

I made *Aliyah* in 1936 and spent the two prior years training with HaKhalutz[2] in Święciany, Poland. There were 66 members who trained there. There was no work and members suffered poverty and starvation. In my occupation as a carpenter, I provided them with many benefits, and I had much work, both at the kibbutz, as well as at external jobs. My wife, Yocheved, was kibbutz manager, and she excelled in diligence and devotion. As a token of appreciation, we were the first of all trainees to receive immigration certificates, and we made *Aliyah* and built a family in Hadera.

In Israel three children were born to us and I was fortunate to have grandchildren too.

Editor's Footnotes

1. The author calls Kalmenovitsh his paternal grandfather. From the context of the article, it is probable that Kalmenovitsh is actually the Grand Uncle of the author (that is, Kalmenovitsh is the brother of the author's paternal grandfather Leyb Katz). Under this theory, Kalmenovitsh would be his surname as a 'Cantonist'.

2. Zionist youth movement

[Page 297]

Our Mother Zipporah (Rashke) of the Levine Family

Shoshana Yudenfreund

Translation by Meir Bulman

Mother, *Of Blessed Memory*, – Zipporah Yudenfreund (of the Levine family), made Aliyah in 1935, listed as her uncle Shlomo Levine's daughter. Shlomo Levine, *Of Blessed Memory*, and his family were among the first pioneers of *Sde Ya'kkov*, the first moshav[1] established by *HaPoel HaMizrahi*.[2] Since her first days in Israel to the day she died she worked in agriculture – raising livestock and working the land. Her work day began early in the day with milking the cows (then done by hand, of course). She spent the rest of the day working the fields, planting corn in the furrows dug beforehand by my uncle.

Bilke Ashman, of the Itskovitsh family, and Kushe Levine, daughter of Pesakh and Khayne (z"l)[Tr. Note: the caption reads "Pesakh Khayne", but as the grammar of the phrase requires more than one person, the "and" is implied]

Even after she married my father, Shlomo, she continued working in agriculture. She worked at the cowshed and chicken coop, and in harvest season in cultivation. Alongside her work there were always refreshments and baked goods, liqueurs, and wines she prepared, and she even found time to pickle olives.

Her devotion to animals is embodied in the following anecdote: every day mother would give milk to the calves. She had to teach the small ones how to drink from the bucket. What did she do? She immersed her hands in the milk bucket and they sucked on her fingers. They bit her, and once, a calf infected with rabies bit her, and she had to be vaccinated— but she was not deterred by all that.

Though she was busy on the farm all day, every needy and poor person found in our home an open heart and generosity in addition to the *tzedakah*[3] boxes in our home. Mother placed much value in *mattan b'seter*[4] and avidly maintained the practice. Her qualities of *hakhnasat orhim*[5] and charity to the poor are demonstrated with the following incident. It was the week before Passover. Preparations for the holiday were at their peak and impoverished Jews were preparing too. I gave them charity generously, but when they asked to eat breakfast, I apologized and said mother was ill and I am still little. But the poor folks claimed, "We have been coming to *Sde Ya'kkov* for 20 years and we always dine with Mother!" The passage in the book of Micah, "He has shown you, O mortal, what is good… [a]nd what does the Lord require of you? To act justly and to love mercy and to walk humbly with your God," was an accurate characterization of Mother, because these were her attitudes towards God and man.

The Gavya River [Ed. Note: Gauja River]

Mother was quiet by nature and never talked much. As is written in *Pirkei Avot*,[6] "Say little and do much, and receive every person with a pleasant countenance." And our sages said, "The righteous say little and do much." And indeed, malcontent people would enter our home to pour their hearts out, and Mother, despite her many activities, would sit in silence, listen, and help as much as she could.

Her passing away was also silent. On Thursday, the 24th of *Iyar* 5734, Mother wanted to get out of bed, in order to bake the dough she had prepared the previous night and then continue preparations for Shabbat, but suddenly she felt ill and in silence closed her eyes, returning her pure soul to God.

Editor's Footnotes

1. A type of cooperative agricultural settlement in Israel

2. Literally 'Mizrahi Worker'; HaPoel HaMizrachi was one of the two parties that later in 1955 combined to form the National Religious Party, or Mafdal, in Israel (the other party being HaMizrahi).

3. 'charity'

4. 'anonymous charitable giving'

5. 'hospitality'

6. 'Chapters of the Fathers'; a compilation of the ethical teachings and maxims from the Talmudic Era (c.190 - c.230 CE)

[Page 299]

In Memory of Itteh Blyakher

Eliahu Netaneli (Itskovitsh) & Bella Ashman (Itskovitsh)

Translation by Meir Bulman

She was the typical image of a 'Yiddshe mamme'[1] from the old generation. She lived her life simply, wisely, and level-headedly. With a righteous heart, and with faith, she reached a ripe old age.

Fate was cruel to her. She was widowed as a young woman and had to bear the heavy burden of raising and educating seven children. Neither did the Holocaust pass over her home: in Divenishok, her son, along with her married daughter with her husband and five children perished at the hands of the Germans.

Despite that, she tolerated her suffering in silence. She battled life's obstacles and pains with immense heroism, never complained about her bitter fate, and always calmly accepted reality in good spirits.

She was aware of every event, loved her relatives very much, loved her townspeople, and was bound to them like a mother. He words were peppered with pleasantries and humor, refreshing to each listener. She would fascinate her listeners with stories from the past.

She was blessed to make *aliyah* before the Holocaust and raised three generations, a blessing which only a few receive. As she was virtuous she reached the very advanced age of 80.

The Blyakher family in Petach-Tikva 1949. In the center: Ita Blyakher z"l

She went to the hospital with a clear mind, ready and able to accept her fate. Her last words were, "This world is like a corridor, and one must prepare to reach everlasting life."

Her loyalty to her people and her family will serve as an example and as a noble image of our glowing past.

Translator's Footnote

1. An endearing term for a typical Jewish mother.

[Page 300]

About My Husband and Our Family

Ida Kaplan

Translation by Meir Bulman

I married at age of 17 as was customary those days. My husband Mordechai (Rest in Peace) was a learned Torah scholar, but particularly excelled in his knowledge of the Russian language, which granted him a special status in town. His handwriting became famous in the region and many people knocked on his door to ask for assistance with appeals and forms in Russian.

My husband worked at the bank and at *Myeshtshanskia Aufrava* (a civic Jewish authority operating with consent from the regime) whose role was to hear all the concerns of Jews in town, and represent them to the Czarist regime. The *Aufrava* was certified to provide Jews with identity cards. The *Aufrava* had three members: my husband Mordechai Kaplan, Kushye Levine (Zalman Kushye's father) and Zvi Bartonovski.

My husband was among the leaders of the community and was familiar with many people. As a typical public activist, he was active in all town institutions. As a man knowledgeable in the laws of the Czarist regime, he always responded to calls for guidance and advice concerning all matters related to the government and the authority.

My husband had a knack for literature and he administered the burial society's notebook where he would record all such events in town. After he arrived in Israel he composed, from memory alone, a detailed list of our town folk who perished in the Holocaust.

My husband's family was wealthy; they owned the land on Dubizishok Street up to Moshe the Blacksmith's home (Moshe der Shmid). The properties were later sold and all that remained for us was the property behind the house. That plot was quite large and spanned several acres.

We had seven children. Three perished in Hitler's time. My daughter Khaya and her husband Mordechai Berman perished in Ivia. The second daughter, Gittel and her husband Chaim Eliashkovitsh along with the third daughter, Tzila, and her husband Aharon Kherson perished at the Vornova ghetto.

One daughter resides in Canada with her husband Mordechai Kupel and their three children. I have two sons in Israel, Natan and Yossef, both high ranking police officers.

In Memory of My Parents, Brothers, Sister, and Family

Bella Ashman

Translation by Meir Bulman

The image of my maternal grandmother comes before me as if in a fog. She was a short–statured woman, but energetic and lively. Her name was Miriam, but was nicknamed Mirle. My grandmother was a righteous woman and every Friday at sunrise she would collect various vegetables in a basket and sneak out of the house. I once followed her and saw her going up to a balcony, placing the basket, and disappearing. She was cautious to not let anyone know about her actions so the mitzvah of anonymous charity would be fulfilled.

My mother Khayne strove for knowledge. As opposed to other town girls, she studied at the Russian public school and later traveled to Vilne to continue her studies. In 1903 she completed the school of art, embroidery, and design and received a licensing diploma. She was the only young woman in town to complete high school level credentials in Russian and art.

My father was a kindhearted public activist. When someone came to request advice or assistance he would take off his work apron and run to lend a helping hand. My father invested his energy and life into public activism. It was simply etched in his blood. It was as natural to him as if he had been born to be a public servant. He was alert to all the issues in town, pleasant, and popular, and was always considered a pillar and leader of the community.

The Gentiles admired my father as well, and he was chosen to be *lawnik in gamina* (council representative). My father did not want to attend meetings on *Shabbat* so he told the chairman, "Hold the meeting without me. I speak broken Polish anyway." The chairman postponed the meeting and told my father, "You and your broken Polish are more important to us than anyone who does speak Polish but has no ability to deliberate."

Though my father was not Orthodox he strictly observed tradition. Every Shabbat he would take his sons to the synagogue for prayers; an unbroken rule he had was to fast on all fast days.

Once, after the Fast of Gedaliah,[1] there was a thunderstorm and my father had not yet returned from the synagogue. I took a sandwich and ran over to the synagogue. I found him at the rabbi's home. The people were surprised and said, "What a good daughter Natan has." I saw it as a natural obligation, because how can one leave a father hungry? It was the result my upbringing and the good spirit in our home. My father was devoted to every child and had a special nickname for each one. My mother used to say, "No effort is too much when your children are concerned— you would bring down a plate from the sky for them."

Eliezer Itskovitsh z"l and Lolik Sutskever
yb"l [may he have long life]

There was once a regional conference of Beitar in Divenishok and a few young men were scheduled to be hosted in our home. At night, I went to see father and did not find him in his bed. In his stead were two young men. I went to the workshop and saw him laying on a table. When I asked him, "Father, why did you leave your bed?" He replied, "I heard the guys standing outside in the freezing cold! I pitied them and brought them to my bed."

In 1908 my father traveled to America, but longed for his family. My mother firmly objected [to his return] and said, "We have no future here in town, I will come to you in America." But my father could not contain himself and returned. My father feared to enter the house and sent a neighbor to prepare her. The man said, "Kheine, what would you say if Natan were to return home?" "He must be crazy! I will travel to him," my mother replied. And at that moment my father entered the house.

*

I was a member of *HaShomer HaTsair*[2] and participated in all tasks given to us. We would make blue–and–white flowers from crepe paper and go in pairs to weddings and other events with *Keren Kayemet*[3] collection boxes to fundraise. Once, the Yiddishists wanted to collaborate with us on a play and give us 30% of proceeds. But my father refused. "I do not want to be involved with the Yiddishists," he would say.

I was a devout Zionist and so wanted to travel for training. "I will not allow my only daughter to travel for training," he said. My brother Eliahu sent a young man to us and we married fictitiously and made *aliyah*. I had a very tough time in Israel. I had been an only daughter pampered by her father and struggled to adjust to the harsh conditions in Israel. I lived with Eliahu and his wife Khayeh, who was like a mother to me, and thanks to them I stayed in Israel.

In Israel I married my husband Shlomo Ashman and we have two sons, the oldest Yossi and the second Avi. I would be happy if only my parents were alive and with me, and my brothers Leyzer and Khaykl who perished in the ghetto at the hands of the Germans.

My Brother Leyzer Itskovitsh

Leyzer was the second, after Eliahu. After Eliahu made *aliyah*, he became the oldest in the home, so naturally he helped father with his business. He was an educated young man, knew Polish well, and would write requests on behalf of residents to the authorities, some paid and some free of charge. He was a nice, well–mannered young man, and was popular. He studied accounting in Vilne and kept my father's books.

There was a time when all the *tandetnikim*[4] established a co–op to sell clothes at a fixed price. The co–op consisted of my father Natan Itskovitsh, Meir Rogol, and Munye Kherson. Meir's son Yitzach[5] kept the books along with my brother Leyzer. Once, they ran into severe difficulties and could not calculate earnings. In the end they had to approach my father who easily made the calculations. My father smiled and told them, "*Nu, kinderlach*,[6] finally you cannot calculate and have to approach the *schneider kopp*?" (a name for a tailor who cannot keep books and can only sew).

The leadership of the HaShomer HaTsair "nest" (1933): Shraga Blyakher (in Israel), Nekhemke Katsev, Esther Rokhel Shkolnik, Uminke Mintz, who were killed in the Holocaust

My parents and brother Leyzer perished in the Lida ghetto. Leyzer was shot in the winter of 1943 when going with Leyzer the miller to prepare a broom for the house.

The Sisters Mineh and Rachel Levine

I see it as a sacred duty to memorialize the sisters Mineh and Rachel Levine. They were orphaned by their father and their mother was ill and bed-ridden. Mineh sewed for us and Rachel for Meir Rogol. I loved them deeply. They were quiet young women with pure souls, kind and gentle. They suffered in silence, were always modest, organized, neatly and cleanly dressed, always smiling, and pleasant to their fellow man. They found their deaths in Voronova with the other Divenishok martyrs.

My Brother Khaykl Itskovitsh

When Khaykl graduated from the Tarbut school in Divenishok, he traveled to Rabbi Elchonen Wasserman's Yeshiva in Baranovich, who was famous as a pedagogue skilled at conveying basic Talmudic knowledge for beginners. Two years later, Khaykl transferred to the Radin Yeshiva where he studied alongside Binyamin Dubinski and Yeshayahu Moshe Katz.

Khakl had a big soul— a kind and dear young man. "Whatever you do on Friday, say it's for *Shabbat*," my brother would tell me. Diligent and studious, he devoted his entire being to the study of Torah. He always stayed in Radin for *Yom Kippur* to absorb the spirit of the High Holidays in the presence of the Chofetz Chaim. My brother Khaykl had the honor of dressing the Chofetz Chaim in his coat. It was a big honor that only a lucky few got.

After the high holidays we would send a coach to bring Khaykl home. Once, my father sent my brother Leyzer to bring him home. When Leyzer reached Radin, Khakl brought him to the Yeshiva and then to the Chofetz Chaim's house. Leyzer was captivated by the holiness imbuing the house which made such an unforgettable impression that he began to go daily to the synagogue even though he was not devout. My father was immensely happy.

My brother Meir Yosef told me that during the German occupation, when Khaykl was starving, he would not touch bread until he could ensure the bread was kosher and not near pork.

Khaykl was the jewel of our family and my father was very proud of him. With much joy and pride would my father go to the synagogue on Shabbat with his son Khaykl, and with much devotion would they pray together and return from the synagogue.

My father deeply wished for his son Khaykl to be a Rabbi in Israel, and had he been so honored there would be no man happier than him. Indeed, Khaykl was very well-versed in Torah and was on the threshold of ordination, but fate was very, very cruel to us and my father did not receive that honor.

Velvel the Butcher's Home

That house on Subotnik Street was one of the few houses in town in which a heartwarming, friendly atmosphere was present for all who visited. The door was always open to all and everyone was greeted kindly. A feeling of tranquility surrounded you in the unique atmosphere present in that house: harmony and good spirits between all family members, always smiling, calm and polite, and always willing to accept any friend or stranger.

There was something special in that house which attracted the town's youth. The house served as a meeting place for the youth of Divenishok. From morning to evening the house was full, be it for card games or checkers or rehearsals for plays.

That house is near and dear to me. It was etched deep in my soul and to this day I dream of it as if I am still in it, spending the beautiful times of my youth. Whenever I felt an empty inside, and sadness surrounded me, I would rush to that house; as soon as I would enter, my mood would change as if by magic wand, and I would become a different person, calmer, all woes far away. I would forget everything and be in a different world. Fate was cruel to that family. Aside from one son, Yitzach, who resides in the United States, not one remained alive. It was a large household of 8 people.

The father, Velvel, was sure to attend daily services at the synagogue and was a regular member of the Psalm Society. Every Shabbat afternoon, after a short nap, he would read the weekly Torah portion, reciting *Shnayim mikra ve-echad targum*.[7]

The burden of providing for the family rested on the shoulders of Yudl and Manke, two strong, kind, and courteous young men. Manke excelled in physical strength, and when the occasional squabble between Jews and Gentiles took place, he always stood guard. The Gentiles treated him with respect, as they recognized his strength

It is said of Manke that when the family was led to their deaths and the Germans began hitting his father, Manke rushed over and began raining blows on the German until a bullet pierced his heart.

Rokhl was a good woman and a kind soul. She would help her mother in caring for the household, and with kindness and conversational talent was the main hostess who made stays pleasant, entertaining guests with a kind word or attractive story.

Nekhamak'e was an active member of *HaShomer HaTsair*. She attended training but was not fortunate enough to make *aliyah*. She studied accounting in Vilne and later worked at a bank.

The youngest and most pampered in the family was Khaykl. He was a talented young man who studied for some time in Radin and then devoted himself completely to the Zionist ideal. He was very active in *HaShomer HaTsair* and became one of its leaders. A very kind young man, he was very popular among the youth in town— kind, courteous, always smiling and calm. The smile on his face did not dissolve until the very last moment.

The group Kfiros[Tr. Note: young lionesses] of the HaShomer HaTsair "nest" with their leader Minke Mintz (z"l) at their farewell to Khaye Blyakher on the occasion of her emigrating to Erets Yisrael (1934)

On Minke Mintz and Her Family

I am obliged to mention my friend Minkeh Mintz. They lived in a warehouse on Geranion Street. Her father, Yosl "the warehouse man", was a merchant who struggled hard to feed his family. His wife Esther was Sarah Leah, Velvel the butcher's, wife [sic].[8] Like her sister, she was a quiet woman, modest, and carried her suffering in silence. The son, Mordechai, was a quiet and kind young man, but weak and sickly from the day he was born. He was a good friend who helped his father with providing for the family.

The daughter Mineh was the most successful in her family. Tall, with dreamy blue eyes, she was beautiful and beloved by all. She attended training, but for various reasons was not fortunate enough to make *aliyah*.

They were honest and tranquil people. They too perished in the Voronova Ghetto.

Editor's Footnotes

1. After Nebuchadnezzar exiled most of the Jews from Israel, he appointed Gedaliah to govern those who remained. Gedaliah advocated submission to Babylon as a means of ensuring continued partial Jewish autonomy, and under his administration, the Jewish colony prospered. When he was assassinated in 423BC by political rivals, the Jews scattered and all remaining vestiges of Jewish autonomy were lost. His assassination is commemorated yearly with the Fast of Gedaliah. ("Gedalia ben Ahikam", in Chabad.org Knowledge Base, http://www.chabad.org/search/keyword_cdo/kid/9673/jewish/Gedaliah-ben-Ahikam.htm, last accessed 18 December 2017.

2. Zionist self-defense movement

3. Jewish National Fund

4. Tailors involved in sewing ready-made clothing, as opposed to made-to-measure clothing, see https://www.jewishgen.org/Yizkor/Capresti/cap030.html, last accessed 18 December 2017.

5. This is likely a misremembered name since Meir Rogol's son Moshe Yakov was a bookkeeper, see p. 328.

6. 'So, children...'

7. A mitzvot, or religious obligation, to twice re-read by recitation the weekly Torah portion along with some commentary to the portion once, outside of the synagogue.

8. An obvious misprint. Esther is Sarah Leah's sister.

[Page 305]

A Daughter and Granddaughter Speaks

Sarah Hinde Movshovitsh [Blyakher]
Translation by Meir Bulman

My grandfather was named Binyamin. I do not know much about him. One action he took was etched deep in my heart. It was on a cold winter day. My mother was sick with pneumonia. Grandfather, then aged 75, left his spot by the fireplace, approached mother, and said, "You are still young and you care for small children. I am an old man. If the heavens wish you any harm I accept your fate and punishment in your stead." He passed a short while following that.

My grandmother Khaveh died aged 93, though she was never ill. On the day she would pass she approached mother and said, "Khenye, are you cooking for the holiday? I would like to taste Passover soup before I travel – I am going home." "What are you talking about?" my mother responded, "We are preparing for the Passover Seder and you will join us." "No," she said, "go call Moshe, I really need him." When my father entered she told him, "Go tell Mikhel the gravedigger to prepare a plot for me, I am going home." Father was startled and refused. My grandmother would not let him evade her, and so he fulfilled her request, teary-eyed. When he returned, Grandmother called him and said, "Moshe, you see, I am sweating. This is cold perspiration, my final perspiration." Father wiped away the sweat and she passed away in his arms in the blink of an eye.

After the final *hessed*[1] was done for her, all sat a brief *shivah*, because *shivah* cannot be fulfilled during the festival.

My father was a manual laborer and worked hard so he could provide for his family, but that did not stop him from dealing in public matters and providing aid to the needy. Father would raise funds for *ma'ot khitim*,[2] and general charity for the poor and the sick – as *matan b'seter*.[3] On Friday nights he would remain in the synagogue and wait for the needy who were not yet invited to the Sabbath meal, and invite them to our home. There were always many poor folks at our Sabbath meals.

After the Germans invaded, father sheltered many refugees in our home—though that required putting his own life on the line. I remember that as he sheltered two Yeshiva students in our home, one of them was practically barefoot. Father removed the boots from his own feet, gave them to the yeshiva student and said, "I am not working, so I can stay at home. You go to work: take the boots."

In the days of Russian control father bought grain and sent my husband to the mill to grind, and then distributed the flower to the poor.

Editor's and Translator's Footnotes

1. Ed. Note: The act of Jewish burial is known as *hessed shel emet* (literally: true kindness).

2. Tr. Note: The Jewish custom of giving charity before Passover to help needy families buy matza and other necessities for the festival (literally: money for wheat) (*from* morfix.co.il)

3. Tr. Note: Anonymous charitable contributions

My Mother Immigrated to Israel in 1922

Sara Kaplan

Translation by Meir Bulman

My mother, Yonah, was the daughter of Eliahu the Butcher (Elyeh der Katzev). She arrived in Israel in 1922.

My grandfather cared for a large family of 11 people. There were many butchers in town and competition was fierce so his financial status was poor. Every child who matured searched for a haven out of the house and most of them dispersed across the world.

My grandfather's origin was in Eyshishok where he had many relatives. Among them was the Schneider family, who decided to make *aliyah*. My [grand]father took advantage of that opportunity and asked the Schneiders to list my mother as a family member, allowing my mother to make *aliyah*. She made *aliyah* with the Schneider family and worked various jobs to sustain herself.

After a while, she met my father, Yehuda Spivak, and married.

After wandering from one *moshav*[1] to the next, they reached Kfar Ma'as where they decided to reside permanently. My mother had three children here: Sima, Eliahu, and myself, Sarah.

Since the Mordechai Kaplan [family] from Divenishok also resided in Ma'as, we were naturally friendly with them, and my future husband Yosef became friendly with me and we married eventually.

While still in Divenishok, my mother owned a small grocery store in Moshe the Tinsmith's house. My future husband Yosef would come to her store to ask for candy. Decades later, when her daughter was grown and Yosef was courting her, he would remind my mother of the candy she gave him in Divenishok and the flavor which remained with him to that day. My mother would smile and say, "I have a realistic view of life: I prepared a husband for my daughter in the Diaspora."

After I married my husband Yosef, we relocated to Ramat Aviv in Tel Aviv. He enlisted in the Israeli Police and reached the rank of officer. We were also fortunate to have three girls: Orit, Liat, and Einat who continue their parents' tradition. Orit received an honor in school for an essay titled *My Father's House* which appears in this Yizkor Book.

Editor's Footnote

1. A farmer's cooperative.

[Page 306]

A Family of Blacksmiths

Zalmen Bronshtayn

Translation by Meir Bulman

The profession of blacksmith was difficult and physically exhausting. Yet it is a historical fact that in Poland, only Jews did this profession. There must have been political and economic reasons for that and I do not wish to examine them here. But it is a fact that must not be denied. I write this to emphasize that the profession of blacksmith was a family tradition spanning many generations. My grandfather, and his grandfather before him, and my father, brother, and I continued that tradition.

My grandfather was a blacksmith and inherited the smithy from his father. My grandmother's name was Sara Feigl.

My grandfather was a Torah scholar and had sons knowledgeable of Torah. He was admired and respected by the area farmers, who came to him to exchange horseshoes, repair wagon wheels and sled blades. He was known as Yehuda the Blacksmith, but one event added to him the description of dentist: a farmer who came to the smithy complained of a severe toothache. In those days, there were no dentists in small towns, and my grandfather wanted to help the poor farmer who was squirming in pain. He searched for a solution and found one; because he knew toothaches are not persistent but rather come and go, he approached the farmer, put his fingers into his mouth, whispered some spell, and promised the farmer that when he will return home the pain will subside. And indeed, that is what happened: the pain diminished. The farmer brought my father a gift and said, "You saved me, Yudtshke." He then told an audience of villagers about the wonders of Yehuda the Blacksmith, who was immediately crowned with the title "dentist."

The family of Moshe Bernshteyn (1930)

My grandmother was known as a kind-hearted and righteous woman. She enjoyed giving to charity and granting others the mitzvah of charity.

My grandfather had six sisters and three brothers.[1] The eldest traveled to the United States after he married. The second, Daniel, also traveled to the United States. The third child was my father Moshe. His sister Rachel-Malka also married in Divenishok and traveled to the States. Tzire Leah (Lyke), a beautiful and intelligent young woman was active in the *Bund* prior to WWI. She was a leader and enthusiastic speaker. Once, while lecturing to a crowd of young men and women, soldiers and police officers appeared and began hitting attendants left and right. Lyke was scared, later developed epilepsy, and after a few months on the brink of death passed away. The remainder of the sisters married, and they too left Divenishok.

My father had eight children: Shakhne-Itshe who passed away in America; Sarah, who married in Warsaw perished at the hands of the Nazis in 1941, along with her husband and three children; Sholom Ber (Dov) who married and moved to Oren, near the border of Lithuania, and became one of the most daring Partisans in the Oren area. Tzirke married Antek from Warsaw, who was the first to offer a taxi service in Divenishok. He drove passengers twice daily from Divenishok to the train station in Benakani and from there they would travel by train to Vilne. My sister Yeintke married Mendel "Kragele [bars]". The sixth child is myself – Zalman Yosef. Dovke and Yehudit had not married and perished in Voronova.

I began my studies at the Hebrew school, which was right across the street from us. My teachers were Ingulski, who taught us according to Manosevits' *Sight for Eyes*, and the teacher Aryeh Leyb who taught us bible and Talmud. My studies were discontinued by my father who took me to work. I objected and escaped to my relatives in Geranion, but my father returned me to work because my assistance at the smithy was very much needed. "The family is large and there are many needs," he would claim, "you must help me work so I can provide for my large family!" In the end I agreed and since then I worked with father at the smithy-- until he passed away. After that I managed the smithy.

In my youth I was a member of *Gordonia*.[2] The activists in that movement were Eliahu Itskovitsh (Netaneli), and Yossef son of Rabbi Movshovitsh. After that, crisis erupted in the land and winds of change began blowing in town.

Luck smiled upon me and I reached Israel by a difficult path, built a home, and now live in Hadera with my wife Rachel and my only child, Moshe.

Editor's Footnotes

1. From the context it is clear that the meaning of this sentence is that the grandfather had 9 children, six girls and three boys.

2. A Zionist youth movement established in 1923 in Galicia. According to the Yivo Encyclopedia of Jews in Eastern Europe: "From the time of its founding, its acknowledged leader and ideologue was Pinchas Lubianniker (Lavon; 1904–1976), who established Gordonia after he left Ha-Shomer Ha-Tsa'ir in disagreement with its ideological developments." Tzur, Eli. 2010. Gordonia. YIVO Encyclopedia of Jews in Eastern Europe.

http://www.yivoencyclopedia.org/article.aspx/Gordonia (accessed August 4, 2017).

[Page 308]

A Typical Jewish Home

Zipporah Yudenfreund (Levine)

Translation by Meir Bulman

Our home was a typical Jewish home like all Jewish homes in town. Father was an ordinary man who made his living by hard work. But behind the ordinary [façade] hid a noble personality and a gentle soul which strove to instill in the hearts of his children a love of Torah and a love of humanity.

Those days from my childhood are etched deep in my heart. There was no kindergarten, nor kindergarten teacher, and my father filled the role of educator. He taught us to memorize the morning blessing. Every morning after the blessing each child had to approach mother and father and say, "Good morning" and kiss their palms, and at night before bed [each child] had to say good night. On Shabbat, we had to sing hymns with father although we barely knew how to pronounce the words.

Father expected great things from his children but regretfully was not so honored. At a certain age children [tend to] go through a crisis and stop studying. This was very painful for father. He attempted to persuade [us] in a charming manner, quoting passages from *Pirkei Avot*.

My father was kind and looked after poor children. When Nahum's class completed its course, the [class] parents wanted to establish a continuing class which the parents would have to fund. Yeshayahu Moshe Katz was in that class; his widowed mother could not afford tuition. There were parents who objected to Yeshayahu Moshe continuing his studies, but my father rose and said, "Be careful about the education of the sons of paupers, as it is from them that the Torah will issue forth.[1] If Yeshayahu Moshe will not study, my son Nahum will also not study." Spirits were calmed and everyone agreed for him to continue.

My father was a man of conversation and liked company. He gladly participated in various cultural activities. I remember my father played the role of Jacob the Forefather, which was the lead role in the *Sale of Yosef* play in town. The play made a good impression on the town and generated substantial revenue for the library.

Translator's Footnote

1. The quotation is from the Talmud: Nedarim 81a.

A Brief Biography of My Friend Avraham Kartshmer

Avraham Aloni

Translation by Meir Bulman

Abraham Kartshmer

Ever since I was a young boy Avraham Kartshmer stood out to me as a talented child. Avarham and his uncle Reuven Kartshmer were similar: talented, sharp, studious, and with a phenomenal memory. As a pupil at the kheyder, Rabbi Aryeh Leyb predicted a great future for him.

After graduating from the local school, Avraham Kartshmer traveled to Vilne where he completed his schooling at the Sophia Gorvits Gymnasium and was hired as a teacher in a town nearby.

Avraham did not see teaching as his life's destiny, but a spring-board to continue his post-secondary schooling.

At school he met his future wife Tamara, who was a Polish-language instructor. He traveled with her to Paris to pursue a higher education. Conditions were harsh; they had no source of income and had to worry about both schooling and work.

Thanks to his willpower and his many talents, Avraham managed to overcome all obstacles and obtained an engineering degree. He specialized in alcohol manufacturing and succeeded in that field beyond expectations. He was appointed manager of the largest beer brewery in Lille, France.

He was considered an expert in that field in France and published many articles on the subject. Avraham visited Israel often and once even came as the leader of a group of expert consultants to the beer industry in Israel.

At the start of the World War, he was enlisted in the French military and was taken prisoner. His wife Tamara suffered much and the burden of raising their daughter fell on her shoulders- a task which she fulfilled with honor until her husband returned. They raised their daughter on the love of humanity and the love of Israel. She completed her university studies with honors and worked as a physics instructor at a university and won an award for her research in the field of physics. Her husband who is from a respected Jewish French family works as a scientist at a university. Avraham was also blessed with a granddaughter who will soon complete medical school.

In his youth, Avraham was somewhat distanced from Zionism, but in recent years became a conscious Zionist and is alert to every Jewish issue in Israel and the world. He retired last year and began taking an interest in cultural and social issues. His wife Tamara is a loyal life-friend to him and has supported him through his struggles.

[Page 309]

Khaneh[1]

Khonen Eyshishki

Translation by Meir Bulman

It was a blessing in disguise. Moshke Rivel's di Blindde informed the NKVD[2] that I had in my possession a gun from the Polish days. The gun was found during a surprise inspection conducted in my house, and after a trial I was sent to two years in prison in Sverdlovsk. In September of 1941 I was released with the Poles from the camps. I could no longer return home and was sent to the Stalingrad District, where I worked 18 months at a kolkhoz[3] named Watero. After that I was transferred to the coal mines near the Mongolian border at Komorowska Oblast and at the order of Vanda Vasilsovka was enlisted in the Armia Ludowa (The Polish People's Army). Thanks to my athletic build, my appearance, and especially my perfect command of the Polish language and style, I gained the trust of my superiors.

After questioning, I was sent to an officer's training course in Razian, and was certified as a Polish officer six months later. I was enlisted in the Polish Brigade headed by General Berling which made its way west with the Russian army. We traveled from Smolensk to Zhitomir and from there to the Barditchev and the Lutskiverts woods in Polish Ukraine. I commanded a platoon of 67 people. We crossed the Bug River and reached Lublin two days after the invasion. Coincidentally, I was transferred from an officer on the front lines to an officer on the rear, and I could patrol freely behind the lines and witness events. In Lublin I visited the death camps. For the first time I saw the horrors the Germans inflicted on Jews. The camp still had human skeletons, piles of eyeglasses, children's shoes, a large hair warehouse, torture cellars, and more. The horrifying sight left an impression on me and I was in shock.

From Lublin we traveled to the Vistula, and while the army was situated in Dumblin Fortress I patrolled the town of Dumblin and saw uprooted tombstones used for sidewalks. The town itself contained no trace of Jews.

Warsaw was under heavy siege by Russian artillery and aerial bombardment. German units were seen roaming through Warsaw by car or on foot, all headed west wearing rags, barefoot, with unkempt beards. On 2/8/1944 we were ready to cross the Vistula, but the Russian offensive was suddenly stopped. Later it turned out that the Armia Ludowa in Warsaw, headed by General Bór-Komorovski, started an uprising against the Germans to take control before the Soviet army and the Polish Brigade fighting alongside it would cross the Vistula. The Russians postponed the offensive and waited until the Germans would [begin to] suppress the uprising. General Berling sent in two para-trooping units that fought alongside the rebels in Zoliborz and Czerniaków, but the uprising failed and on 2 October an envoy of Armia Ludowa signed the surrender. The Russians began an all-out assault on Warsaw and occupied it in a short time. General Berling payed with his life for daring to send para-troopers to the aid of the rebels and command of the Kościuszko Polish Division was taken from him; his whereabouts since are unknown.[4]

I was wounded at the battle on the Vistula and was hospitalized for a few months in a field hospital in Otebsk. After I healed I was once again enlisted in the Polish Brigade and reached Eastern Prussia during the fighting. In one of the battles I took 2 Germans as prisoners. My platoon sustained heavy losses that day and with burning hatred for the Germans I executed the Germans with my own hands.

Khonen Eyshishki, officer in the Polish Army, 1939

In the evening, battalion commander Smitanin contacted me and instructed me to immediately appoint my immediate subordinate and report to the command center at once. When I reached the command center, Smitanin drew his gun from his holster while spouting juicy curses. My blood froze. "You took prisoners?" he asked, and without waiting for my response added, "Where are they?" I answered firmly, "You know I'm Jewish and what the Germans did to my people! You should know that every German I take as a prisoner will not live, and you can do with me as you please." The commander was slightly calmed and then the political first–lieutenant addressed me and said it would have been better if I had at least interrogated them first– since we had sustained heavy losses that day. After that I was sent back to my unit.

I was severely wounded in the town of Miroslawiec and was hospitalized for over four months. I then returned to my unit which was in Biala Podalaska where I was discharged from the army.

Editor's Footnotes

1. The reason for the selection of the name Khaneh for the title of the article is not clear.

2. The leading Soviet secret police organization from 1934 to 1946

3. A collective farm in the Soviet Union

4. In fact Berling was not killed during these events and reached the age of 84; (https://www.hoover.org/news/papers-polish-general-zygmunt-berling-now-available-hoover-institution)

[Page 311]

About the Family of Tsvi Schmidt
(Hershl the Stableman)

Zalmen Dan Kushtulski

Translation by Meir Bulman

After the dismantling of the Vornova Ghetto, Hershl and his family were at Biale Wotzka, near Vilne and not far from Suruk Tatrov. When I went to Vilne to extract an organized group from the ghetto, we also extracted him and his family. On our way back, his wife and his child were killed in a German ambush. Tsvi and his son escaped to Divenishok, where the gentiles murdered them.

Our Mother Khayne
Daughter of Avraham Eliezer and Miriam Levine

Eliahu Netaneli [Itskovitsh]

Translation by Meir Bulman

With these words I memorialize you, mother, and fulfill a sacred obligation. In your memories we include hundreds of mothers in our town.

Although you were not overly ambitious, nor caused any miracles, I want to raise three events that remain in my memory.

At the start of the 20th Century a revolutionary underground countering the Czar expanded and many Jews joined. As in every town, a cell of the Bund organized in Divenishok, which my mother joined at age 15. As a member of the cell, she and three young men were tasked with assassinating the commander of the regional gendarmerie in Oshmene, who was known as a Jew-hating dictator.

In his passage by coach through the Kalvitze Forest on his way to Divenishok, my mother served as a look-out. The men attacked the commander and quickly restrained him, and before he could draw his weapon they tied a rope around his neck and slowly strangled him. They tied up the coachman in the coach and left.

The men were quickly smuggled abroad. My mother returned home half-conscious and was bedridden for a few days. After she recovered she told of what had happened to the gendarmerie commander. My parents quickly moved her to relatives in Vilne, where she began studying handcrafts, and three years later was bestowed the master's degree.

The second event took place during WWI in 1914 when I was seven years old. The Germans expelled us from our house and moved us to a small wooden house plagued by dampness and humidity.

One day, hunger bothered me and I ran to my grandfather's house to ask for a slice of bread. On the way there I passed near the military police station where I saw a full loaf of bread on the window sill. A battle took place within me between the commandment "thou shall not steal" and the sense of hunger. I felt an inner pang and could not contain myself and nicked the loaf of bread from the window.

Before I could move I felt a blow to my face and a German police sergeant appeared before me, raining blows and shouting in German. I fell to the ground, my nose bleeding. The sergeant carried me in his arms and brought me to the commander. He saw me bleeding, took pity on me, and commanded the return of the loaf to me and the supply of a loaf to my family daily.

My mother was not home at that time, as she and the other local women were apple picking at the Albertina Ranch by German decree. She returned shattered and broken because the Germans had assaulted her for not keeping up the pace with the other women. When she saw me, she began to cry, bandaged me with a cold bandage and began consoling me. When she handed me a slice of bread, I refused to eat and yelled, "No! I will not eat stolen bread, God will punish me." My mother consoled me, saying I was young and stole without intent and therefore God will forgive me. The war ended and a few more children were added to our home, and our life returned to its usual course. Our home was spacious. There were laborers in the workshop and merchants came from nearby towns to purchase coats, and my mother conducted the household and ensured the children had all they needed. She made every effort for her children to be raised in the Jewish tradition and to study a profession, so they could make a decent living.

Since I left home many years have passed. Many experiences and memories became blurred, new times have come, everything changed, and only memories remain.

In these words, I dedicate my gratitude to you, mother. You lived a life of financial success, but one of hard work. Raising children and managing a house with many laborers are not trivial matters, and also [you] did everything with love and devotion, never complaining, always silently, calm, and cheerful. As they say, [you were a] "a Yiddishe Mama," until that fateful day arrived.

May her soul be bound in the bond of everlasting life.

They Were So[1]

Binyamin Dubinski

Translation (Introduction) by Meir Bulman

A flame of love blazed in their heart
and by that flame to the loathers of Israel
the sanctity of the Nation they did impart.
Rabbi Yosef Rudnik ZTL[2]

Our town Divenishok was a small town, but a unique aura was draped over it. Its white homes stood atop a tall hill and it was surrounded by pine forests that gave off an enchanting, intoxicating scent.

Life flowed peacefully in that small town, like the crystal–clear river that flowed slowly at the outskirts of town. Day after day went by without change, shakeup, or renewal.

Suddenly, an event took place that shook the town: Rabbi Movshovitsh left town and traveled to the United States, and then many candidates for service in that elevated position arrived in Divenishok. After a tumultuous period of debates, the great Rabbi Yosef Rudnik was chosen as chief town rabbi. To this very day I remember his first appearance: tall, handsome, with a radiant face, his beard magnificently constructed, and his blue eyes projecting warmth and love. It is therefore unsurprising that he won over hearts at first sight. The folks convened an excited greeting ceremony in the suburbs of the town and then accompanied him to his new home with great respect.

A few days went by before the rabbi appeared at the school. There, he examined the students and invited the talented among them to the Talmud classes he would conduct at the synagogue. The rabbi's Talmud lessons were an unforgettable experience; with stories, allegories, and songs he would captivate students on the Talmudic topic at hand. His listeners were elevated to a spiritual world, a world of legend and imagination.

The rabbi labored tirelessly to instill the spirit of the Torah and awareness of the national Zionist ideal among the town youth. With a fatherly, yet closely inspecting, eye he accompanied the footsteps of every youngster in town, and was very happy when he would succeed and manage to send a young man to the famous Radin *Yeshiva* that was not far from our town. Due to his influence, I too spent a few years in Radin. He was especially proud of his two prodigies, Yeshayahu Moshe Katz and Khaykl Itskovitsh, who studied at Radin for many years. Excelling in their talent and their far-reaching knowledge of the *Mishnah* and *Talmud*, they were candidates for rabbinical ordination.

He was not just a man of great words but also a man of great action, and so he sent his son Avraham to Radin as well, where he studied for many years and achieved much knowledge of *Talmud* and *Poskim*.

Yeshayahu Moshe Katz and Khaykl Itskovitsh perished in the Diaspora, but the son of the rabbi, Avraham, is with us in Israel. He participated in the war of independence and now devotes his time to educating the younger generation. Rabbi Yosef Rudnik passed away at the height of his energy and public work, still with many plans in the works. His death caused heavy mourning in town and the surrounding area; all the rabbis from the nearby towns came to eulogize him: Rabbi Rabinovitsh from Lida, Rabbi Rozovski form Eshishuk, Rabbi Perlman from Ivia, Rabbi Shmuelzon from Oshmene, Rabbi Shub from Traby, the two rabbis from Voronova, Rabbi Fein from Bilitza, and Rabbi Eliezer Kaplan – one of the rabbis at the Radin Yeshiva.

Rabbi Yosef Rudnik was busy with various works of public activism. He was active at many religious institutions in the Vilne district and surrounding area and bestowed upon them his good spirit. He was beloved as a rabbi by the town's population. He was not only a spiritual leader, but also a devoted father to his tribe. His door was always open to all those with aching hearts or low sprits. He reserved spiritual assistance for each one of them and in times of need he gave also material aid. Rabbi Yosef Rudnik served as Divenishok's Chief Rabbi from 1925 to 1933.

We mourn for those lost and not forgotten.

Footnotes:

1. Ed. Note: This essay, written by Mr. Binyamin Dubinski is comprised of an informative overview of dozens of Divenishok figures from the rabbis to the common folks.

2. Tr. Note: *Zekher Ttzadik Livrakha*: 'May the Memory of the Righteous Be a Blessing'

[Page 313]

Avraham Abir (Rudnik)

Translation by Atara Mayer

Rabbi Yosef Rudnik's amazing character was most noted for its radiance, not just his love for *Am Yisrael*[1], but also his constant zeal and soulful thirst for the learning of Torah. During one of his small talks he told about the days of his childhood when he studied in the Volozhin Yeshiva, and how once in Vilne he had stood for many hours by the storefront window of a bookstore, reading the titles and authors of the books he saw, yearning to read these books but being unable to acquire them.

The Rabbi passed on this zeal to his young students continuously and steadfastly, stemming from his affection and love for them. In order to serve as a personal example for the youth, the Rabbi included his son, Avraham, in the group of students who studied the Talmud. Avraham was also one of the first students that the Rabbi sent to learn in Ohel Torah Yeshiva in Baranovich, which was headed by Y. Wasserman,[2] who was known as a great pedagogue imparting Talmudic foundations to yeshiva students. Afterward, Avraham continued his studies at the Chofetz Chaim Yeshiva in Radin, and was ordained as a rabbi by Rabbi Pilovski, member of the Rabbinical Council of Vilne.

In order to combine Torah and Science, Avraham matriculated at the high school in Vilne, completing his studies entirely in Polish, and then moved to Israel in 1937, where he was accepted as a full-time student at the Hebrew University in Jerusalem.[3] Simultaneously, he was accepted as a student at the *Mizrahi* School for teachers in Jerusalem, which he successfully completed.

Following his training, he worked as teacher at the *Bilu* State Religious School in Tel Aviv.

During World War II, he enlisted on behalf of the Jewish Agency to the *Nutras*[4], and guarded the territory's beaches while doing his best to assist in the transfer of immigrants to Israel.

When the War of Independence broke out he enlisted with the Israel Defense Forces and participated in many bitter battles against the enemy.

Following the war he founded the *Hemed* Settlement along with other religious war veterans and there he ran the local religious school for the settlements.

The chain of Torah scholars in this family continues. Avraham's son, who was named for his grandfather Yosef, devotes himself to Torah study at a yeshiva in Jerusalem. The son of Rabbi Yosef Rudnik's daughter Breyne, Yosef Aloni, who was also named for his grandfather, is among the significant scientists at the Weizman Institute in Rehovot.

Footnotes

1. Tr. Note: The People of Israel

2. Ed. Note: aka Elchonen Wasserman

3. Ed. Note: in 1937, before the formation of Israel, the area was still called Palestine

4. Tr. Note: Jewish Guards

[Page 314]

Rabbi Aharon Tayts

Translation by Atara Mayer

Rabbi Aharon Tayts, who was appointed as rabbi following the death of his stepfather, Yosef Rudnik, was blessed with several relatively rare basic qualities. Rabbi Aharon Tayts was exalted. His appearance was characterized by nobility and peace of mind. His basic knowledge of *Shas*[1] and scholarly commentary, and his secular education, were vast. His emotional identification with the tradition and the spiritual experience of the Jewish heritage prepared him for the responsibility of being the rabbi of our town.

A love of Torah and Science were embedded in his personality. Once he acquired basic knowledge in the *Mishnah* and the *Talmud*, he made his way to Vilne, the city of Lithuania, aiming to acquire wisdom and knowledge. Following a relatively short period he completed his studies in the "*Mizrachi*"[2] Seminar and the Hebrew *Gymnasium*[3] in Vilne, and continued on to study at the "*Hildesheimer*" Rabbinical Seminary in Berlin.

When the director of the seminary learned that he was a descendent of a rabbinical family, he asked Aharon if he would consent to be tested on a challenging issue in the Talmud. "Certainly," replied Aharon without hesitation. "What if I test you on the *Zevachim* tractate?" challenged the director.[4] "You may also test me on the Zevachim tractate," answered Aharon, even though that is the most difficult of the tractates. And so the director tested Aharon on the Zevachim tractate and marveled at his knowledge and proficiency.

Aharon's stay in Berlin was very short; the German atmosphere of the institution felt at odds with the moral values of Rabbi Yisroyl Salanter.[5] Aharon returned home and departed from there to the Chofetz Chaim Yeshiva in Radin, where he was ordained a rabbi.

His status in the yeshiva was highly respected and was regarded with respect and admiration, though he was humble and not arrogant. He was extremely helpful to all the young persons of Divenishok who studied in Radin. He concerned himself with their welfare, their financial situation, and, most of all, their progress in Talmud and moral doctrines. Among those he cultivated were Khaykl Itskovitsh and Yeshayahu-Moshe Katz, from whom he expected greatness. I am not ashamed to admit that he also shaped my personality and that I saw him as a symbol of morality and Torah wholeness.

After he was appointed as the rabbi of our city he managed to gain the trust of the people of the city and the Polish aristocracy through his noble appearance, his pleasant speech, and his fluent Polish.

In the late 1930's, after Hitler gained power, anti-Semitism in Poland reared its head and the Jews suffered economically and politically. Rabbi Aharon Tayts stood steadfast like a lion and fought every appearance of anti-Semitism, and struggled for the rights of every Jew. His impressive appearance and his glowing visage, his judgement, his fluent conversation, his pleasantness, and his good spirits captured the heart of the *Oshmene Strostev* (local ruler[6]) and, consequently, several severe restrictions were lifted. The heavy taxes imposed on the Jews in Poland were also reduced.

When the Soviets arrived in the town, the Rabbi was forced to leave and he crossed the border into Vilne with his wife and children.

In Vilne, he lived in great distress, like all the refugees who arrived in droves. He searched for a way to go to Israel, but he was not so lucky and he perished along with his family in Ponary, Vilne.[7]

Footnotes

1. Tr. Note: another name for the *Mishnah*

2. Ed. Note: Mizrachi refers to a religious/Zionist organization founded in Vilne in about 1902 by Rabbi Yitzach Yaacov Reines

3. Ed. Note: a gymnasium is a pre-university school

4. Ed. Note: the Zevachim tractate is a section of the Talmud that focuses on various types of animal offerings in the Holy Temple

5. Ed. Note: Rabbi Salanter is one of the founders of Musar Movement, a school of Orthodox Judaism that emphasizes moralistic thinking and ethical conduct

6. Ed. Note: of Oshmene

7. Ed. Note: Ponary was an area on the outskirts of Vilne where many thousands of Jews were massacred and buried in mass graves by German Nazis and their Lithuanian henchmen

[Page 315]

Rabbi Chaim Yudl Horvits

Translation by Atara Mayer

Rabbi Chaim Yudl Horvits was one of the original and most interesting characters in the American landscape. A member of this remote little town, Rabbi Horvits was selected to the respected position of "Secretary of *Kashrut*[1] Inspectors" on behalf of the Jews in New York and the surrounding areas. Rabbi Horvits was appointed to oversee thousands of *kashrut* supervisors and was responsible for tens of thousands of establishments, butcher shops, and food-producing factories. Any establishment under Rabbi Chaim Yudl Horvits' supervision undergoes a *kashrut* inspection, which rewards its founders with the letter U, a widely accepted kosher symbol. Products branded with the letter U were accepted by the Jews and by the Christians, who were also interested in clean, fresh, quality merchandise. The Rabbi is a popular and highly respected character in New York City, and many respected and important people sought his proximity.

Rabbi Horvits was endowed with many virtues: he was intelligent, clever, pleasant, and popular in his community; his knowledge of *Torah* and wisdom about Israel was vast; his words were spiced with writings of *Chazal*[2] which capture the ear and delight the heart. Rabbi Chaim Yudl had a warm, Jewish heart; his whole spirit is tied to his past, particularly to his childhood, which he spent in his hometown. For these reasons, he was a dedicated member of "Relief," which is considered one of the town's main pillars and main facilitators. As long as the town existed, Chaim Yudl's home was the main address for the heads of the town in times of distress and adversity for they found in him generosity and a listening ear.

Our fellow townsman, Rabbi Harry (Chayim) Yehudah Horvits z"l,[Tr. Note: Of Blessed Memory] photographed with President Harry Truman in the US (1945)

Rabbi Chaim Yudl was, naturally, a public figure and a man of action. His extensive public activity he saw as an important task and a mission in life, and he was devoted to it with his entire soul. The Rabbi's contribution to fundraising for the United Appeal was particularly notable. In recognition of his actions and efforts the Jewish National Fund planted a forest in his name.

Translator's Footnotes

1. referring to kosher dietary laws
2. articles by Hebrew Sages

[Page 316]

Avraham Noakh Shlomovitsh, the Town's *Shohet*[1]

Translation by Atara Mayer

Avraham Noakh Shlomovitsh, or as he was known in the town, Avraham Noakh the *Shohet*, was an interestingly unique character. His image was a wonderful blend of scholarship and action. He took care of public affairs and was also active in addressing individual needs.

In our town, it was customary for people to venture to the market on Thursdays to purchase a calf or a lamb for the Sabbath, and then to invite the *Shohet* to slaughter and *kasher*[2] the meat for the duration of the week. Under these circumstances Avraham Noakh tended to visit most of the people in the town and was, therefore, well-aware of their joys and sorrows. He always lent an ear to those who needed someone to listen and to every aching heart, and he tried to help, to condole, and to encourage with his advice and actions to the best of his ability.

It was customary in our town for the *Shohet* to take the spleen of any large animal.[3] It should be noted that the spleen never ended up on the *shohet's* table; there was always a needy Jew who would receive it as a secret gift.

Avraham Noakh was an expert in his field, both in preparation of the knife used for slaughtering and in the slaughtering itself. The butchers were surprised at his efficiency and professional skill. He never once caused a *Terifa*.[4] He was also a very talented *mohel*[5] and was proud that all of the youth in the town were his sons, since it was by his hand that they had entered into the covenant of Avraham our Forefather.

His whole life he blew the *shofar*[6] in the new synagogue. To carry out this sacred task he prepared himself with great care and compassion. On *Rosh Hashanah*[7] when Avraham Noakh ascended the stage dressed in white and as his pleasant voice rang out with the verse "*min hametzar karati yah*",[8] a deathly silence descended upon the synagogue, and the congregation was mute, tense, and full of anticipation for this sacred moment. The sounds of the *shofar* poured and rolled through the synagogue and the congregation stood in awe.

Avraham Noakh participated in all public affairs in the town. He was a member of the school committee where his four children were educated, he was *gabbai*[9] in the new synagogue, a dedicated member of the Jewish National Fund Committee, an active member of *Mizrachi*,[10] and together with Eliahu, he distributed funds for the movement.

In the days of Mrs. Prystor,[11] when Poland banned Kosher slaughter for supposedly humanitarian reasons, Avrahm Noakh traveled to Bialystok, where he studied the process of *nikkur*.[12] He studied the technique even though it was very costly, all to overcome the meat shortage in town.[13]

Reyzl Bartonovski, on the front steps of her house on Vilna Street

Avraham Noakh married Menya Bartonovski, whose father was one of the most respected men in the town. His mother in-law, Reyzl Bartonovski, was a wise and virtual woman, who gave charity both openly and quietly, and warmly welcomed every guest and neighbor. His in-laws' house was a warm, pleasant home, always filled with guests, young and old. Teachers who worked in the school and lived outside the town always stayed with Reyzl Bartonovski.

Avraham Noakh was not lucky in life. His wife, Menya, contracted a malignant disease. She lay on her deathbed for a few years and passed away in her prime. He and his sons died in Voronova, together with all the martyrs of Divenishok.

Avraham Noakh the *Shohet* was originally from the town of Bilitza. Rabbi Yosef Rudnik ZT"L[14] served as the rabbi of this town before he was appointed as the rabbi of Divenishok.

Avraham Noakh's father, Rabbi Shlomo Shlomovitsh, was God-fearing and exalted in Torah, merciful and revered. His mother, Sheyna Reyzl z"l, was a God-fearing woman of virtue, who tried to keep her husband from being interrupted while he learned Torah. Rabbi Shlomo and Sheyna Raisel, his wife, had two sons and two daughters. The eldest son, Rabbi Dov Tzvi, was a *shohet* in Divenishok, and following World War I he emigrated to the United States. His younger brother, Rabbi Avraham Noakh, took over as *shohet* of the town in his stead, until it was annihilated by the Nazis and their accomplices.

May his soul be bound in the bundle of life.

Footnotes

1. Tr. Note: a slaughterer of certain mammals and birds for food according to Jewish dietary laws

2. Tr. Note: to make kosher

3. Ed. Note: the Hebrew word used here is 'gas' and is believed to be short for 'behema gassah' which means 'large mammal'

4. Tr. Note: injuring an animal, which disqualifies the animal from being considered *kosher*

5. Tr. Note: circumciser

6. Tr. Note: a musical instrument made of a ram's horn

7. Tr. Note: the Jewish New Year

8. Tr. Note: "from the depths I called to you"

9. Tr. Note: a person who manages the affairs of the synagogue

10. Ed. Note: Mizrachi refers to a religious/Zionist organization and movement founded in Vilne in about 1902 by Rabbi Yitzach Yaacov Reines

11. Ed. Note: Mrs. Janina Prystor was the wife of the President of the Polish Senate who sponsored the 1936 Kosher slaughter ban and one of its chief proponents

12. Ed. Note: "deveining"; the process of removing forbidden veins and fats from cattle thereby rendering more of the beef kosher than would be under normal koshering processes

13. Ed. Note: The 1936 Polish ban on Kosher slaughter permitted meat to be kosher-slaughtered only in districts composed of 3% or more Jewish population, and only for purposes of consumption by that population. Most of the kosher-slaughtered cattle is forbidden to Jews because it contains too many veins and fats. Normally that would not be an issue where sale of the remaining meat to gentiles was permitted, but without the gentile market to buy the uncertified meat, Kosher slaughtering would be too costly. Avraham Noakh's newly acquired deveining skills would allow for more of the slaughtered animal to be certified as Kosher.

14. Tr. Note: may the memory of the righteous be blessed

[Page 317]

Aryeh Leyb Rogol
the Dedicated, Loyal Zionist

Translation by Atara Mayer

Aryeh Leyb Rogol, a remarkable figure in our town, dedicated his life to realizing the Zionist idea. As a child he absorbed the Zionist atmosphere in his parents' home and decided to dedicate his life to this goal.

Aryeh Leyb was one of the first members of the town who answered Moshe Lilienbloom's call to join the Hibbat Zion movement, and was involved in fundraising on behalf of the first settlements in Israel.

With the declaration of Herzl's political Zionism, he worked to spread the teachings of the state's visionary. Rogol was among the first shareholders of the "Anglo-Palestine Bank". He conducted Zionist activity in the town since the establishment of the Zionist movement. He distributed shekels to all the Zionist congresses and was the first to buy shekels. His house was used as a meeting place for the sages, where Zionist townspeople gathered to read "Hatzfira" and to coordinate Zionist activity.

From the First Zionist Congress he was the Zionist Movement's representative in our town, and with the foundation of the JNF,[Ed. Note: Jewish National Fund] he became the authorized representative in town and worked intensively collecting funds for the Jewish National Fund.

The pharmacy of Aryeh Leyb Rogol

During the First World War, from 1914 to 1919, when hunger spread in the town, Aryeh Leyb organized aid for the needy. He was selected as the delegate from our town to the first regional conference of "Yaakofu"[Ed. Note: an aid organization for Polish Jews] which took place in Vilne on the 8th and 9th of September, 1919, and which discussed the necessary assistance to the towns suffering from starvation.

With the establishment of a Polish government in the town, Aryeh Leyb committed himself even more to Zionist work and to the beloved inhabitants of Divenishok. He particularly devoted himself to the activities of the JNF and served as the head of the National Fund until he fell ill.

Polish authorities regarded the "HaShomer HaTsair" as "communists for export" and demanded a guarantee from the leaders of the Jewish community not to engage in hostile action against the State. Aryeh Leyb Rogol, who owned the only pharmacy in town and was involved with and accepted by the Polish intelligentsia, signed a guarantee for the activities of "HaShomer Hatza'ir" and "HeKhaluts", thereby enabling their regular activities.

I will never forget the scene in the late 1920's when we, 14 and 15 year old youths, sat in the new synagogue's women section and drank in Aryeh Leyb's fiery words about Zionism and the revival of the Jewish State, which was the order of the day. He was already dangerously ill. His hands shook but his voice boomed and his face reddened; he infected us with his Zionist zeal and urged us to take on Zionist activity.

His only wish was to emigrate to Israel with his family and to fulfill this goal, he sent his daughter Shulamit as a pioneer to the Israel, and he was deeply disappointed when his daughter returned from Israel. He hid his pain in public, but continued to plan to emigrate to Israel with his family.

After a fire broke out in his pharmacy and his house went up in flames, he fell ill and did not recover until he was brutally murdered by the Germans in the Voronova Ghetto.

He was one of the rare figures in the landscape of the town, a man who had educated several generations for Zionism and the building of the country, and thanks to him, many young people who survived heard his call and emigrated to Israel.

A malicious hand cut the thread of his life and the murderers of our people will suffer the curse of God.

May his soul be bound in the bundle of life.

[Page 319]

Herman Fuchs Z"l

Translation by Meir Bulman

(Remarks delivered at the unveiling of the monument in the Ben Shemen Forest in memory of Herman Fuchs and his daughter Lilly, who perished in the Lida Ghetto.)

At this moment we are secluded with two pure souls; that of Herman husband of Shulamit and the soul of her daughter Lilly who were executed – their one and only crime: being Jews.

With these two pure souls, rising from the depths are the souls of all our brethren and loved ones from our town Divenishok, with whom we were raised, ate from their bread, and from which we inherited the courage to stand guard and fight for our national and religious uniqueness.

*Herman Fuchs z"l,[Tr. Note: Of Blessed Memory] his wife Shulamit,
and her brother Hersh Rogol z"l, in their pharmacy on Market Street, 1937*

Our heart aches as their bodies were cast in a long line in the trenches of the valley of the slaughter, their eyes reflecting death, and they are forever silenced.

This gentle Shulamit, daughter of R' Aryeh Leyb Rogol, shattered and broken by the big tragedy that befell her, but still of sound mind and spirit, decided to avenge the blood of the innocent that was shed. Shulamit adopted the way of the slingshot with all her might, and with her brother Zelig, she took to the woods of Lipnishok to avenge the blood of the martyrs. She used her pain, unparalleled by any other pain, and cast it into firm metal and steel bullets, and struck the enemy with the vengeance of a pained mother.

After her Aliyah to the homeland, she was resolute in her decision to establish a monument for her loved ones. And indeed, here we are today, participating in the tree planting ceremony in honor of her husband and daughter.

May this monument be a torch for the saints of our town and a living and damning testimony of an apathetic world that stood idly by in the face of the horror.

Memorial stone of Herman and Lilly Fuchs, murdered by the Germans, in the Ben Shemen Woods of Keren Kayemes

[Page 320]

Natan Itskovitsh
(a brief biography and his public works)

Translation by Meir Bulman

Natan was gifted with many qualities that define a public activist. He had a fine presence, a pleasant smile always on his lips, and his big eyes projecting love and care — won over the hearts of his peers. He was a man of conversation; his stories and witty jokes and sayings touched the heart of every person, for they encompassed in them the flavor of life.

Natan Itskovitsh, or "Natan der Schneider" as he was nicknamed in town, was considered one of the most important town leaders, and not a small or large matter went by without his knowledge. He was the only Jewish "Lvnik" in the Gmina (representative in the town council). He was also among the founders of the Hebrew school and one of its main operators, and he did his best to instill in his students a love for the Jewish tradition and the national and Zionist ideals. Natan was among the administrators of the New

Synagogue, ensuring its maintenance and pleasant aesthetic. As was customary in the towns of Poland, important public matters were decided on Shabbat by delaying the recitation of the Torah. At times deep differences of opinion arose in this public and deliberations were lengthy and exhausting. Tensions were high and it seemed matters would never reach a conclusion. Itskovitsh would then ascend to the stage and say, "Gentlemen, we have heard differing opinions, but in my humble opinion (שכל נארישן מיין לויט)[1] this and that solves the matter." And what a sight! Silence overtook the crowd and Natan's opinion was accepted by all.

Natan was full of a passionate Zionist spirit and sponsored the Zionist organizations in town: he nourished, encouraged, and assisted them nonstop with words and funds. He lived up to his principles; his eldest son, Eliahu was among the founders of *HaKhalutz*[2] in town, and among the first to make *Aliyah*. Eliahu Itskovitsh departed from a wealthy and warm home, preferring to work the roads and groves. He suffered from malaria, and hunger more than once, but he swore to build the land so that his wish might come true: the establishment of a Jewish state in *Eretz Israel*. His father's inspiring spirituality is what guided him on that difficult path.

Natan was not satisfied by only his son being in Israel and a few years later sent his daughter Bilkhe to *Eretz Israel*. He himself planned to make *Aliyah*, but fate dictated otherwise.

Natan, who was tolerant in religious matters, had a deep attachment to the Torah and Jewish tradition, and so he also served as a role model for others. He sent his son Khaykl to study at the Baranovich Yeshiva, which was administered by the esteemed rabbi and pedagogue Wasserman, and later to the Chofetz Chaim Yeshiva in Radin. His youngest son, Meir Yosef, was sent to the *Tarbut* seminary in Vilne, where he was licensed as a teacher at the Tarbut schools, known for their high levels in the subjects of Judaism and Hebrew. His son Meir Yosef was among the founders and leaders of the *Betar*[3] movement in town. At that time, frictions erupted between *Betar* and *HaShomer HaTzair*[4] about who would have the privilege to conduct meetings in the school building. Natan, who was gifted with a sharp mind and life-wisdom, effectively mediated between *Betar*, where his son was among its leaders, and *HaShomer HaTzair*, in which his daughter Bilkhe was a member. He would pacify, mediate, and ensure that all went smoothly between the organizations.

Natan Itskovitsh had a sewing workshop (טאנדעט).[5] He was busy with work: measuring, cutting, and preparing the fabrics for the worker-sewers, but he was very attentive to all that happened in town. His home was always filled with people who came to request aid from a place where they knew would never disappoint them. Natan was ready for them, his mouth producing a smile, or encouragement, or a joke to alleviate the pain. When needed he also took off the measuring tape from his neck and the work robe from his body, running to fulfill the *mitzvah* of "If thy brother be waxen poor and fallen in decay with thee then thou shalt relieve him". The drive to assist his fellow man was engraved deep within his blood. He never exhibited signs of being tired by public activity. He was always smiling and lively, always willing to assist.

Natan Itskovitsh was also a member in the administration of bank and the *Gemilut Hasadim*,[6] and always ensured that the merchants (עגלות בעלי)[7] who traveled on Saturday nights to the villages to purchase produce would have at least the minimum funds needed for that purpose.

It is therefore unsurprising that Natan was the most popular and beloved man in town.

Natan was also the Rabbi's confidant. Natan, Ben-Zion Schneider, Shalom Yakov Shkolnik, and Natan Kaplan were those who along with the Rabbi made decisions on all public matters.

It is also worthwhile to mention that Natan possessed a unique mentality, swift assessment capabilities, an ability to adapt to special circumstances, experiential knowledge unattainable by mere studying, and a phenomenal memory which enabled him to remember the sum of the issues confronting him, without needing any type of note-taking. His son Eliahu's words are true: "My father was gifted in rare qualities of leadership, was sharp minded, and sharp witted. If he had studied, he would undoubtedly have become a brilliant lawyer."

Our hearts are filled with grief because one of our town's beloved activists, who devoted a large portion of his life to the public without reward – found his death together with all the Divenishok martyrs in the slaughter conducted by the Nazis in Voronova.

תנצב"ה[8]

Editor's Footnotes

1. Loyt meyn narishn shkhl; literally: according to my foolish understanding

2. A Zionist youth movement

3. A right-wing leaning Zionist youth movement

4. 'The Young Guard'; Zionist youth movement, emphasizing scouting and kibbutz-living

5. 'tandem', use of this word is unclear, could mean jerry-built, second-rate or simply old clothes

6. A charitable fund for the needy

7. 'beli eglut': cart owners

8. Epitaph meaning: *May his soul be bound in the bundle of life*

[Page 321]

Khaykl Itskovitsh: Rabbinical Scholar

Translation by Meir Bulman

One of the wondrous young men in town possessing great qualities was Khaykl Itskovitsh. While the youth of the town were persuing a general education, Natan Itskovitsh's son chose the *Chofetz Chaim* Yeshiva in Radin.

Khaykl spent the majority of his young and flourishing life in Radin, dedicating himself to Torah and *Musar* with his entire passionate being. The study of Torah was at the center of his desires; he wished for the passion to study *Talmud* and *Poskim*.

Because of his qualities and his knowledge of *Talmud* he acquired a great reputation and was on track to be ordained as a rabbi. He did not achieve that due to the political upheaval at that time. The Soviets invaded Radin and put an end to the prestigious Yeshiva. Its administrators were imprisoned and exiled to Siberia.

Khaykl was the crowning glory of his family, and thanks to him a traditional religious spirit was maintained in the household. At home, he strictly observed all the *Mitzvot*,[1] be they large or small, and led the ceremonial religious procedures. To his last day he remained loyal to his path, and even when under German control, when hunger struck home, he did not give up an inch in his observance of *Kashrut*.[2]

Khaykl believed his path was the correct one to take in life and he devoted much effort to garner support for the ideals he championed. He was always cheerful and smiling. That is how young and lively Khaykl was, a flourishing tree in the bud, predicted to have a great future, but severed by the Nazi beast.

Khaykl Itskovitsh

Editor's Footnotes

1. Jewish religious commandments

2. Jewish dietary laws

[Page 323]

Munye the Tailor
(Munye Kherson)
Translation by Atara Mayer

One of the most interesting and prominent characters in the town was Munye Kherson. Munye was attractive and well-mannered and he was endowed with a pleasant voice and an affinity for song and prayer. For many years Munye served as the primary cantor in the new *Beit Midrash*.[1] He was the cantor who led the *Musaf*[2] services on *Rosh Hashanah* and *Yom Kippur*. The sounds of his beautiful voice still echo in the hearts of our townspeople and awaken a longing for this cherished character.

Shmuel 'Munye' Kherson

When Munye began the prayer "*hineni he'ani mima'as*"[3] with a sob in his voice and the cries escaped his heart, the entire congregation trembled with fear of this holy and terrible day, and all hearts were open to this prayer of mercy and gratitude.

The congregation reached an enthusiastic climax when Munye declared "*unetaneh tokef kedushat hayom*".[4] Then, all dams would break and a burst of tears and moans filled the synagogue as the restrained sounds of weeping echoed from the women's section.

Today, only ruins cry out to the heavens, and instead of prayers, deep moans and the sound of deafening sobs emanate from the weeping bricks on the wall that bemoan the divine exile and the holiness that has left, the lives that have been extinguished, and the blood that has been shed.

Munye Kherson had a large family. The eldest son, Yosef, was killed alongside his family in Voronova, together with the other brother, Aharon (Arka), and his family. Today, his daughter, Bilke, married to Yaakov

(Yankele), who was known in the town as a leader of the "Vilbig," live in the United States. His son, Yisrael Kherson, also lives in the United States.

Munye Kherson's home was always full of young persons and the intellectuals among the town's Jews, both due to his status and because of his sons and daughters who were very active in the town's cultural pursuits.

Munye passed away prior to the war and did not suffer through the Holocaust, though part of his family was killed, as stated above, by the Nazi murderers in the mass grave in Voronova.

Translator's Footnotes

1. Jewish study hall

2. an additional prayer service that is recited on the Sabbath and holidays

3. "Here I am, deficient in meritorious deeds" – a prayer chanted by the cantor prior to the *Musaf* service, humbly beseeching G-d to accept his prayers on behalf of the congregation

4. "Let us ascribe holiness to this day" – a poem widely considered to be the pinnacle of the *Rosh Hashanah* prayer services

[Page 324]

Shlomo Kotler
(Shlomo the Coppersmith)

Translation by Meir Bulman

Shlomo Kotler was an impoverished Jewish man caring for his many children. He did not even own his own house; he lived in a rental behind the market. Shlomo was a peddler and every Saturday night he hurried to the nearby villages to buy various agricultural products. Shlomo handled many products: from swine hair, to fox and rabbit fur, to eggs and chicken, to calves and sheep. When his wagon was packed with merchandise he returned home, rested for a day, continued to Vilne and repeated the cycle. Shlomo was busy providing for his large family, but that was not his focus in life. He had a noble soul full of longing for *Torah* and love of Israel.

On the Sabbath, Shlomo prayed at the dais. And although he was not a cantor his great emotional spirit took hold of the crowd.

Our town was not blessed with famous Torah institutions and *Yeshivot*, but was indeed blessed with a twofold thirst for Torah. Every Jew found a unique manner of expressing that thirst according to individual abilities. Among other such activities in our town there was a Psalms-reading club whose members included common folk. They gathered on Shabbat afternoon and read together the "*Borchi Nafshi*"[1] with tremendous devotion and enthusiasm. Shlomo was among the group leaders, and in a sweet voice sang each verse and the crowd replied as a choir. He who has not witnessed these precious Jews enthusiastically reciting the Psalms, their eyes ablaze with God's flame, has never seen holiness in his life.

For the sake of his business he, at times he needed to stay in Vilna over Shabbat. There too he recited "*Borchi Nafshi*" along with the audience.

Etched in my heart is a story I heard as a youth from Zeydke Lubetski about Shlomo Kotler. "Once on a Saturday night," said Zeydke, "I traveled with my brother Simcha to the nearby villages to purchase stock. As we were trekking heavily through the dark woods, the sun began to rise. The whole universe awakened, song birds praised God, an intoxicating spring scent rose through the air, and all was silent. Suddenly we heard a prayer song erupting from deep within the forest. We listened carefully and heard the sweet notes of "*Borchi Nafshi*" ringing through the forest, and the echo of the forest replied as a choir. We stopped our wagon and waited impatiently, wondering. And there came Shlomo, sitting atop his wagon, and singing *Tehilim*[2] with a burning ecstasy, all from memory, and as a great tide."

Those were the common folk in our town, simple peddlers, but full of God's love and an eternal love for the Psalms.

From his entire large family remain Moshe, who resides in Naharia, his son Eliezer, and his daughter Reyzl who resides in Buenos Aires, Argentina.

Editor's Footnotes

1. Literally, 'Praise, My Soul...' (an exhortation directed to the soul of the supplicant). The phrase appears in various Psalms sometimes referred to collectively as the Borchi Nafshi.

2. Psalms

[Page 325]

Leybe the Blacksmith

Translation by Meir Bulman

At the entrance to town on its right side corner, on Vilne Street, stood a smithy, and behind it was the home of Leybe the Blacksmith. He was an average Jew, coarse and tongue–tied, married to Nekhama, who was a dear woman, kind–hearted, and righteous in both public and private. Life was very, very cruel to Nekhama the Blacksmith's wife. On market day, when there was more work than ever, Nekhama would stand with her husband by the anvil and pound the hot steel with a sledgehammer, while Leybe would urge and encourage her, "שטארקער[1] פעסטער,נחמקע קלאפ". And Nekhama would pound faster on the anvil while sparks flew in every direction. She struck the white–hot steel to the astonishment of the villagers who surrounded her, mouths agape and wide eyed. She did not complain about her cruel fate and suffered in silence.

She was one of the strong spirited Jewish mothers in town who bravely carried their pain.

Translator's Footnote

1. 'Pound Nekhamke, faster, stronger'

Zalmen Leyb Lieb

Translation by Meir Bulman

Zalmen Leyb Lieb excelled in his good traits. He was tall, with an impressive outward appearance, bright and captivating at first sight. Since the day he was born he had the energy of a man who was destined to guide and lead. He also possessed a natural, intricate intuition for trade and business. Zalman Leyb stood out since the days of WWI. When the Germans occupied our town, Zalman was appointed *bürgermeister*,[1] and did much to improve the poor financial state of the Jews at that time, and also rescued many Jews sentenced to forced labor camps.

After the war, he relocated to the Free City of Danzig and opened a department store. Fortune smiled on him and his store succeeded and expanded, and became one of the largest department stores in Danzig. After Hitler rose to power, Zalman Leyb had to leave Danzig and return to his hometown of Divenishok.

In 1941, after the Germans invaded the town, Zalman was appointed head of *Judenrat*[2] in town. His basic knowledge of the German language and mentality helped him with that difficult task. On the first days of their governing, the Germans had already arrested a number of town notables, and had led them as hostages to Oshmene. Among those notables were Nahum Lipkunski, Pinche Mintz and others. They were tortured in prison and their fate was sealed. After Zalman Leyb's vigorous lobbying efforts, they were released and returned home.

Zalmen-Leyb Lieb and his wife, killed in the Holocaust

An unruly gang of Poles terrorized the town, headed by the famed robber Truskevitsh from Yurgln Village. Night after night they raided Jewish homes, robbed, looted, and raped. Once, in the dead of the night, Pesye, daughter of Binyamin Mikelson broke out and shouted for help; the gang broke into her home and stole whatever they could lay their hands on. The town residents did not respond, due to their fear of the Germans. Due to Zalman's efforts, the gang members were arrested, and their leader, Truskevitsh was executed at the center of the market place. Germans executing Poles for robbing Jews was an unusual event.

Many Jews from Vilne heard about the relative calmness in our town and began flocking to Divenishok. The German and Polish police banded together to ensure that no outsiders remained in town. Zalman Leyb volunteered to aid those refugees, and using various stratagems succeeded in securing resident status for these refugees from the outside.

The teacher Shmuel Geller from Ivia, who was among the refugees, describes the story of his rescue by Zalman Leyb: "After the situation in Vilne became unbearable, I decided to return to my wife and children in Ivia. I traveled on side roads and narrow paths. After two days I arrived in the town of Divenishok in great poverty, having been robbed on the road. I entered the first house I found and the homeowners there warmly greeted me, inquiring about the state of affairs in Vilne. As I told them the sound of muffled crying filled the house.

I was in town for two weeks before my situation became dire; the police officers were familiar with every Jew in town and I was in grave danger. It was proposed that I join a group of Jews who traveled to work in a sawmill at the ³גיעלז near town, which would increase my chances of being permitted to reside in town. I accepted the offer, but fate did not smile upon me, and the Polish manager greeted me with swears and belittlement, kicking me off the premises. While walking away from the gate, the Poles sicced a large dog on me. I was bitten and bleeding all over with my clothes torn. To the sound of the cheering Poles, I escaped the place running for my life.

I returned to the town both devastated and fearful, at which point two Polish policemen jumped me, and as they struck me with force, demanded to see my papers. They led me, bleeding from my mouth, to the police station for transfer to the Gestapo. Jews who observed the event immediately informed the head of the *Judenrat*, Zalman Leyb Lieb, and he went out and invited me and the two officers to his home. I do not know what Zalman said, but I do know this: Zalman Leyb Lieb saved my life."

A different event was recounted by Sarah Hinde, Moshe the tinsmith's daughter: "One day, the Germans captured two young refugees, brought them to the police, and were about to put them on a truck to an unknown destination. When Zalman Leyb saw what was about to take place, he ran to the station, and with some negotiation managed to free the two young men in exchange for two pairs of boots."

After residents of Divenishok were transferred to Voronova, he was again appointed member of the *Judenrat* and did his best to rescue Jews from the Nazi claws. After the Voronova ghetto was dismantled, he was transferred to the Lida Ghetto, and there too he was among the leaders of the *Judenrat*, making an effort to ease the suffering of Jews and improve their bitter lives. The regime in Lida Ghetto was more lenient than in some other ghettos. Thanks to him there was a freer atmosphere in the ghetto which allowed a large flow of Jews from the ghetto to the woods. Near the time when the Lida

Ghetto was to be dismantled he was permitted to live outside the ghetto's borders, and he easily could have escaped to the partisans. And indeed, the famed Bielski sent him a horse and wagon to bring him there, but Zalman refused, fearing the Germans would conduct a slaughter in the ghetto if he escaped.

After the dismantling of the Lida ghetto he was taken with all Jews to a death train and was executed in one of the death camps along with his wife and his only daughter.

From his large family remains his brother Zvi Ahuvi, יבדל״א[4].

Editor's Footnotes

1. Position comparable to town mayor

2. Jewish Councils mandated by German orders in the occupied communities of Eastern Europe during WWII

3. This word is unknown to the editor and translator in either Hebrew or Yiddish.

4. Long may he live.

[Page 327]

Meir Bolinski

Translation by Meir Bulman

He was a boy from a poor family who emigrated to the United States, where he was quite successful. Though he was not the wealthiest of men, he succeeded in life, and most importantly was content with his lot. While far from his town of origin, he did not forget for a moment the days of his childhood, the strife and the extreme poverty, the humiliation in suffering, and once he reached financial stability he then devoted himself to the poor and the suffering, especially his brethren across the sea, in his hometown of Divenishok.

Indeed, his whole life was dedicated to that goal. For sixty years he was among the chairmen of *The Relief*, and being a furrier he succeeded in raising funds at gatherings of furriers, funds dedicated in full to *The Relief*. Thanks to him, substantial funds were transferred to our town that outpaced even the לנדסמאנשפטים[1] in the large cities.

Meir Bolinski was among the founders of *The Relief* and one of its most dedicated, outstanding leaders. He always excelled in drive and resourcefulness, and was usually the first and most generous donor, serving as an example to the public. A donor and fundraiser, encouraging and motivational– that is how Meir Bolinski was.

Emigrants from Divenishok, in New York, prepare food packages for the Jewish survivors from the town in the refugee camps in Germany and Austria. On the right, Meir Bolinski z"l,[Tr. Note: Of Blessed Memory] in whose factory the packages are prepared. Next to him is Sarah Kartshmer z"l and other women of the Ladies Auxiliary

After the Holocaust, he was contacted by a survivor from our town and assisted him substantially until he reached safe harbor.

He was gentle–spirited and a fair–tempered, a lover of humanity, and a holy soul. Public activity was both the spice of his life and inevitable. He stuck to his life goals to his last day. Even in his will he left a $500 charitable donation to the organization of Divenishok alumni in Israel.

All our town people will carry the memory of their great and devoted friend with longing and pain, he who dedicated his life to his brethren from our town with love, devotion, strength and money. He especially will be remembered by *Sh'erit ha–Pletah*[2] who found in him a loving and caring father figure and devoted friend, overflowing with love, attention, and the will to come to their aid and ease their pain. May his memory be blessed.

Editor's Footnotes

1. Landsmanshaftim: mutual aid and philanthropic organizations composed of immigrants from the same city or region which formed wherever large numbers of Eastern European migrants settled

2. 'Surviving remnant', from Ezra 9:14 and I Chronicles 4:43; refers to Jewish refugees who survived the Shoah

[Page 328]

Meir Rogol
(נאז דער מאיר)[1]

Translation by Meir Bulman

Meir and Fanny Bolinski with their sons and daughters, in New York, 1928

Meir Rogol, a wealthy man, considered one of the town's notables. His home, which was proudly displayed at the center of the marketplace, was a large brick home, a symbol of respect and importance on our town.

He was a tailor by trade and had a sewing workshop for mass production of clothes, where six young women were employed. He never interfered in public matters, being always reserved and a man of few words, calculating and level headed, meticulously dressed, and early to synagogue on the Sabbath. His daughter Mikhle married Yitzach Srulovitsh and lived with him in her father's home. His wife Etl passed away before the war.

Meir Rogol's source of pride was his son Moshe Yakov, an expert bookkeeper who knew Polish and worked at bank in Divenishok. His pride expanded further as his son married Reyzl, daughter of Rabbi Movshovitsh, meaning he was part of the Chief Rabbi's family.

His son Moshe Yakov emigrated with his family to the United States and lives there to this day. He is a very religious Jew, his love for *Eretz Israel* is immense, and he has also visited Israel many times.

Translator's Footnote

1. Meir the Nose

Yosef Aharon Schneider
(who fell in battle in the Yom Kippur War)
(who was the son of Eliezer Nakhum Schneider from יאנישבצינוע)[1]

Translation by Meir Bulman

Yosef Aharon stood out as talented young man since childhood. A war waged on injustice accompanied him all his life. Coupled with t hat, he also excelled in manners and respect for his fellow man. Intelligence, common sense, and sound judgment were his dominant traits.

Yosef was born in Poland and made Aliyah with his parents to Be'er Sheba, where he attended primary school, high school, and being an excellent pupil, was then accepted as a student in the Negev University.

Yosef Aharon excelled in responsibility, punctuality, and dedication to every task he was assigned. He possessed an entrenched Jewish noble spirit and was proud of the Jewish tradition; he was very passionate in his love of the homeland.

During the Yom Kippur War he was enlisted in the Medical Corps and fulfilled difficult missions under enemy hellfire. He risked his life to rescue wounded soldiers from death more than once. He fell during the battle across the Suez, when a helicopter transferring the wounded from the east bank was shot down by a missile: all those in the helicopter were burned alive, including the doctors and medical personnel.

That is how noble youths fall for the sanctity of the homeland, with their youthful spirit and child–like smiles on their lips as they stand at the edge of life. The pure–hearted came from among us: they are the heroes of Israel who devoted their souls and sacrificed their blood and bones at the altar of our freedom and existence.

Editor's Footnote

1. Transliterates to something approximating Yannisev Zintse; meaning remains uncertain

[Page 329]

Yankel the Blacksmith (Yakov Khasman)

Translation by Meir Bulman

The gentiles in town, as in all towns of the Jewish diaspora, complained about Jews working in commercial trades and 'easy' professions, as opposed to those who made a living by doing hard work. So, the gentiles esteemed the Jewish blacksmiths for their ability to stand all day in the scalding heat by the anvil as sparks flew in many directions.

The blacksmith profession was entrenched within the Jewish population for generations. A Jewish blacksmith lived on every street in town. One of the more fascinating figures among the blacksmiths was Yankel the Blacksmith, a small–statured Jew with an athletic body–type, large shoulders, and warty hands. He was a kind man of few words who received with affection the curious children who came to his shop.

Yankel the Blacksmith worked tirelessly. The bulk of his income came from fashioning sickles for the area villagers. The manufacturing was done in a number of stages: first the bending of steel to the shape of a sickle, secondly a sharpening procedure, thirdly fashioning prongs, and finally handle installation.

Yankel's sickles obtained quite a reputation and on market days the smithy was packed with area farmers. The man minced his words and worked quickly and patiently, silently and calmly, with no complaints or criticism. On Shabbat days he would wear a suit and walk slowly from Subotnik Street to the synagogue, then pray serenely and bless the Creator for kindly providing for him.

*The blacksmith Yakov Khasman as a soldier
in the czarist army during the First World War*

At times of need he demonstrated supreme bravery in defending the honor of Israel— to the point of risking his life. One such story was told as follows: Important Polish officials visited the town on occasion and the residents would prepare a gate of honor in front of the synagogue courtyard with a Star of David decorated with flowers adorning its top.

On one of these occasions, the district governor was scheduled for a visit, and as was custom, the Jews erected the honor gate, and the Rabbi and the village notables awaited their guest with bread and salt. This took place in the late 1930's, at the height of anti-Semitism in Poland. The Poles, headed by the anti-Semitic Polish teacher Koitle, tried to remove the star from atop the gate. The Jews expressed their firm opposition and so Koitle summoned armed

Poles from the National Guard (Steshelzi), which he headed, and approached the gate as he waved his sword above his head.

Suddenly, Yankel the Blacksmith burst forth, quickly removed Koitle's sword, and shattered it on his knee, tossing its pieces all around. The awe-stricken Poles retreated from the Jewish gate in shame.

Yankel the Blacksmith symbolized the typical and unique image of the popular Jew in the towns of Lithuania, encompassing a Jewish rootedness in hard work and a love of the People of Israel.

[Page 330]

Rafael the Bricklayer

Translation by Meir Bulman

On Vilne Street lived a dear man named Rafael the Bricklayer. He was a Jew who made his livelihood with hard work; his profession was building fireplaces. He was an artist of the profession, and not every person was fortunate enough for Rafael to build his oven.

R' Rafael was a man who focused on both Torah and work. He was a scholar, with a pleasant voice, and for that reason he led prayers at the old synagogue on high holidays.

He passed away while I was yet a child, but his memory was etched in my heart due to his charming personality; to this day he stands before me as if alive. I find myself morally obligated to memorialize him and his family.

R' Rafael was invited to our house to build a fireplace. I stood near him to watch him work and was amazed by his quick hands. I soon caught his attention and he began testing my knowledge of *Words of our Sages and Midrash*. I was very much impressed by his knowledge. From time to time he would trill holiday hymns in his pleasant voice. He labored and sang, and the sounds of *Kol Nidrei* would mix with the sound of the fireplace being built. R' Rafael passed away a short time after that and our fireplace was his last product. I remember his wife came to us to be paid for the fireplace and it was she who tearfully told us her husband passed away.

R' Rafael was succeeded by two sons and a daughter. His oldest son, Yosef, was a Zionist activist in town who then married out of town. His second son, Michael, was a gentle, disabled man, and spent most of his days praying, and studying Torah. Rafael's daughter Libkhe, worked for Natan Kaplan and passed away at a young age.

After Rafael's death, his family lived a life of poverty. Michael could not afford a shaver and would sit for hours and trim his beard with scissors, which thoroughly depressed me. They were proud people and never complained of their misfortune. On one Friday afternoon I visited their house without notifying them first, and in their oven I saw a small pot of potatoes and nothing more. I told that to Avraham Noakh the ritual slaughterer and he tried to assist them in various ways. Since then, that family was among those who were often given the spleen.

Rafael's son Michael tried to work as a tutor. He taught pupils in the women's section at the synagogue but was not very successful. He excelled at writing beautifully, and many women would request his services in writing letters to America. Among them was Solomon Levine's mother, and he was deeply impressed by Michael's beautiful wording and his impressive handwriting.

That family was unfortunate. The mother, Khaya, and her son, Michael, found their deaths at the Voronova ghetto.

[Page 331]

Shalom Yakov Olkenitski

Translation by Meir Bulman

Shalom Yakov Olkenitski's family was a very enlightened family. They came to us from Subotnik in the 1920s. When they arrived, Shalom Yakov Olkenitski was already a widower and did not want to remarry— so that the children would not have to experience a step mother.

The father was educated, an illustrator and a musician, a devout lover of classical music, who was skilled in playing the violin, and he instilled that talent in his sons. I remember he would come to the home of the ritual slaughterer Avraham Noakh Shlomovitsh, who owned a radio, and sit for hours and hours listening to classical music, without saying a word. At those times he was concentrating and immersed, as if in a different, elevated dimension. He was a man of few words and never shared his musical soul with strangers. With difficulty, he supported his family by etching gravestones and painting.

Fate was unkind to him in regard to his family life. Is oldest son, Lolle, who was a very talented, kind, and charming young man, escaped in the 30's to the Soviet Union with Paula, Leyb Srulovitsh's wife. There he suffered poverty and passed away in 1972, survived by his only daughter in Leningrad.

His second son Aharon was a musician, and played the violin beautifully, and expectations were set high for him, but he suddenly fell ill with pneumonia and passed away at the age of 19.

His father loved him dearly, and though he was estranged from his religion, would run to the synagogue in the dead of night and ask for mercy on his son. He made a special tombstone for his son Aharon. Every letter he etched he would soak in his tears. He framed a picture in glass and an etched violin below. He went to the cemetery weekly where he bitterly wept at his son's grave.

His only daughter Khava was a sympathetic young woman, and was an intensive member of the drama club. She was also a kind and courteous librarian at the public library. Khava married in Vilne and it is there she passed away.

Yekusiel Zhizhemski (Kushke)

Translation by Meir Bulman

My friend from my youth, Yekusiel Zhizhemski, was always smiling, happy, handsome and kind. He was affectionately nicknamed 'Kushke' by his parents and friends. We traveled a long road together. In grade one in elementary school we had already befriended one another, a bond which strengthened as we progressed through the grades. He was a good friend, honest, truthful, and devoted. Kushke was an only child to his parents Yosef and Miriam (Mirele). They loved him and pampered him, but alongside the pampering ensured he was given a traditional Jewish education, and instilled in him the values of friendship and respect for peers— and nurtured within him the love of nation and homeland.

After school a few us friends would do our homework together. His father, a hatter, sat by us, snipping from paper or cloth different designs of hats, supervising us and ensuring we properly completed our homework. He would enjoy his son's proficiency in Torah or mathematics.

When he reached his bar mitzvah he gave up every gift offered by his parents and insisted they buy him an album *Photos of Eretz Israel* published in Tel Aviv. With much love, he browsed through the book, his eyes lighted with happiness and satisfaction. The album was a source of pride and every friend was invited to read and listen to Yekusiel's commentary.

His parents' home was nice and quiet. His mother was a perfect housewife– – order and cleanliness was impeccable. There were always teachers residing in their home. I remember that the teacher Sonnenson (from the town of Lubtsch) taught us in preparation for our studies in Vilne. We did indeed travel to study in Vilne; I at the Hebrew Gymnasium, and Kushke at the *Tsherne* Seminary, which he successfully completed, and was then accepted as a teacher at the Hebrew school in our town.

Kushke was an avid Zionist and from a young age was member of *HaShomer HaTzair*[1], first as student and later as a guide and teacher. He was a brave warrior for the Hebrew language. He and I subscribed to *HaKokhav* [*The Star*] which was published in Lodzh, edited by famed writer and educator Aharon Lubishitski. Due to the dire financial state of Poland in the 30s the paper did not survive long, as there were not even 5000 subscribers among the youth.

When the Soviets entered, Yekusiel was appointed principal of the Jewish school in town and excelled in his devotion, patience, and love for educational work. When the Germans entered, the Jewish school was shut down and Kushke disappeared. He found his death at the Voronova ghetto.

Translator's Footnote

1. Zionist self–defense movement

[Page 332]

Khaykl Katsev
(Khaykl Velvel the Butcher's)

Translation by Meir Bulman

Khaykl was blessed with traits that made him beloved by society. He was humble, pleasant towards all, calm, modest, soft spoken, well–reasoned, always speaking logically and with poise without sentimentality or arrogance.

Khaykl was my close neighbor— our houses were right near each other. We walked to school together and played and spent afternoons together. We were bound to one another,

After graduating from grade school our paths split. I left town to study abroad and he went to work at his father's business.

Khaykl was devoted to Zionist activism, especially to *HaShomer HaTzair*.[1] He educated an entire generation based on principles of practical Zionism, with a socialist vision. His dream was to travel, to train, and then make Aliyah, but he was the youngest in his family and his worried parents did not allow him to leave home. Thus, he stayed in town, his heart filled with yearning and wishing for Aliyah.

Khaykl perished tragically at the Voronova ghetto with his parents, his brothers Yudke and Manke and his sisters Rachel and Nekhama. It was a horrific sight to witness, to see, all of them marching together to death. Eye witnesses stated that that family resisted the murderers angrily and persistently. Manke, who was known in town as a strongman who stood up to gentile–taunting Jews, hit the most intensively. During the banishment he attacked one of the German murderers who harmed his father, punching until falling prey to a bullet.

That is how a whole family was uprooted from its source of life.

A single family member remains, his son Yitzchak, who left town in the 20s.

Translator's Footnote

1. Zionist self–defense movement

[Page 333]

Liba bat Broyne[1] Levine

Translation by Meir Bulman

Liba Levine, daughter of Broyne, murdered by the Germans

Liba was wonderfully beautiful, industrious, kind, gifted with a sensitive soul and an open minded understanding of her peers. She was an exceptional student at the Hebrew school and later in the Polish school, a great athlete who excelled in volleyball, her favorite sport.

As the Germans entered the town, Liba and her mother left Divenishok and relocated to Ivia, where her brother Yudel lived. Liba died with her family in the Ivia ghetto.

After completing her studies at the Polish school, Liba traveled to Vilne, where she completed a yearlong course in bookkeeping, and was then employed in that field. Her temperamental soul found no peace in the small town. She desired with all her heart to reach her sister Khaya, who was among the first pioneers who arrived in Palestine in the course of the *Second Aliyah*. But she was not fortunate; WWII erupted and she remained in town.

The Levine family

Her letters written in neat handwriting, filled with longing, wit, and wisdom, remain to this day with her sister Khaya. From time to time Khaya re-reads Liba's letters and her childhood days are reanimated; images of the family members, especially that of the beautiful Liba, appear in front of her eyes as if they were alive.

(Dictated by her sister Khaya Garvey)

Editor's Footnote

1. Liba Levine, daughter of Broyne

Chaim Leyb Schneider

Translation by Meir Bulman

Chaim Leyb Schneider is the only remnant from a large family. His Grandfather Chaim Leyb (whom he was named for) had three sons; Kalmen – Chaim Leyb's father, Mordechai "the Rod" and Asher Schneider, who owned a large steel store in Leyb Dubin's house.

The entire family perished in the Holocaust. Chaim Leyb was saved by chance. He tried passing the border to Lithuania with a group of young men and was captured in Turgul, a small town beyond the border, and transferred to the Russians, who exiled him to Siberia for five years. After the war, he was released and moved to Poland, and form there to the United States. He established a family and is successful in his business.

[Page 334]

Moshe Blyakher
(Moshe "the Tinsmith")

Translation by Meir Bulman

R' Moshe, or as he was known by the town residents, Moshe "the Tinsmith", was a famous man in town, lively and original, a lover of Torah and respectful of rabbis.

He was a man of small stature, wearing a small yellow beard with white stripes which granted it a special shade. In that small body was nested an endless energy; he was always dynamic and busy either with the woes of providing or with public matters.

R' Moshe was a central figure within the burial society. He viewed the good deed of purifying the dead not just as a true *mitzvah*, but as a sanctified matter which he regarded with holiness and piety. R' Moshe was always the first to summon the other members of the burial society to fulfill the deed. On days of extreme cold and snow he was the first one out in the cemetery to dig the grave with his bare hands. R' Moshe supervised the burial ceremonies so they will be fulfilled carefully in accordance with religion, and respect for the dead was observed by him to a 'T'.

R' Moshe was dynamic and very quick; in my memory he is constantly running, be it to the morning or evening prayers, or to raise funds for the needy, for a guest speaker, or just for a guest who came to town needing assistance. His mind was open to all. He would leave his work and sprint like deer to fulfill the wishes of his creator in prayer or in good deeds.

On Friday nights, he would remain as the last one in the synagogue and ensure that all the poor folks who came to town would be invited to the Sabbath meal. Those were days of poverty and trouble, and the town was flooded with poor folks seeking nourishment. On more than one occasion many poor people stayed in the synagogue without an invitation to the meal. R' Moshe would wait patiently and would invite to his home the ones who did not manage to match with a host.

R' Moshe worked hard to provide for his large family. Despite his difficult work he was always happy with his lot— for that was the Lord's wish.

Between afternoon and evening prayers he would routinely participate in a class on *Orakh Chaim*,[1] and when the subject of the exile of the holy spirit was reached, R' Moshe would weep like an infant: "When will we have the fortune of complete redemption?" he would whisper.

To this day the image of Moshe, wrapped in his *talit*, running from store to store at the marketplace on Friday, urging merchants to close their shops. "My son, it is already Shabbat, the sun is setting." He did that out of honesty and godly devotion, devotion which he would pass to those around him. No man disobeyed Moshe "the Tinsmith", and after a few minutes the holy silence of the Sabbath enveloped the marketplace.

R' Moshe was pure of heart, honest, a man of morals, and a lover of wisdom— always greeting his peers willfully and gleefully. He was smiling and kind-hearted, especially towards children. When we would visit his sons at his home he always greeted us with love and tenderness, his eyes lighted and projecting warmth and love.

That was R' Moshe's character, a rare figure in town, which shed its light on the town's lifestyle and left its mark on each and every one of us. We, the children, learned love for the People of Israel and the Torah from his pure-hearted personality.

R' Moshe Suffered with all the Jews of the Lida ghetto and died in a death camp with his daughter Leah and her husband Shayke, Meir Zalmen's son.

His son Eliahu, who became a glorious partisan in Bielski's militia, was sent by Bielski five times to the Lida ghetto and managed to rescue 253 people from the ghetto, saving them from the Nazi beast. He arrived in Israel before the War of Independence and actively participated in the war. He currently lives in Israel.

Among those rescued from the ghetto were his sister Sarah Hinde and her husband David Movshovitsh. They stayed in Bielski's camp all through the Holocaust and endured the harsh conditions and being chased by Germans. They spent their time sinking in swamps, bloated by starvation and thirst, but their will to live overcame; they came out alive on the other end and now reside with us in Israel.

Editor's Footnote

1. literally 'Way of Life'; refers to the first book of the *Tur* and *Shulchan Aruch* covering the laws of daily living.

[Page 335]

Tuvya Blyakher

Translation by Meir Bulman

Tuvya was my brother Meir's classmate. He would often come over to our house to do homework with my brother, and thus I was able to closely observe his traits and personality.

I knew that his entire family traveled to Israel, but the British consulate refused to allow him to join them, claiming that he was older and needed his own certificate.

Tuvya was a naturally silent type and carried his suffering in silence. His wise, sad eyes reflected his burning pain and immense suffering. With burning dedication he devoted himself to schoolwork, and especially the Hebrew language, in the hope that one day his desire to join his family in Israel would be fulfilled. That was the wish which he constantly dreamed about. He was a studious pupil and would labor by his books for hours. Until his homework was completed he refused even a cup of tea offered by my mother.

He was kind hearted, humble, and ready to assist his fellow man – traits which his family excelled at.

He had a deeply rooted Zionist passion entrenched in Jewish tradition. He was among the few amidst the town's youth who did not once miss daily *tefillin* wrapping or morning and evening prayers.

The partisan Tuvya Blyakher, who fell fighting the German murderers

Exits from the area were sealed Under Soviet occupation and Tuvya's pain and suffering became extremely pitiful. He tried crossing the border to Vilne, but was unfortunately captured. In a search conducted in his few belongings were found a pair of *tefillin*, which he never parted with, and the NKVD[1] officials who assumed they had obtained 'an important spy' put him under maximum security arrest. Only after tireless efforts by heads of the community was he released.

As the Voronova ghetto was being dismantled, Tuvya escaped with my two brothers Meir and Tsvi to the woods in the Divenishok area, where their paths split. My brothers approached the forest ranger at the Poltva village and were executed by Polish militia; Tuvya roamed the woods for over a year and found his death in a dugout, along with the final remnants of our town folks. Polish militia attacked them during the frosty height of a winter storm.

Zvi Novoplanski, the glorious partisan from our town, describes their feelings at the time with admiration and excitement: after they had completed preparing their dugout for the winter and had exhaustedly laid down to rest, fractured words from the slumbering Tuvya reached their ears. In a dream he envisioned meeting his loved ones in Israel as he shouted his emotions gleefully: "Guys, we finally made it to Eretz Israel! Our hopes have been fulfilled! We are all here!" All the other inhabitants of the bunker woke up and gathered around Tuvya, listening to his excited words as their eyes grew teary.

A few months passed until Tuvya fell with his friends in a final battle for freedom and national integrity. His final words echo through the Stoki Forest and we are obligated to fulfill the wills of those who fell for our people. They did not achieve their goal to arrive and live with us, but their souls float among us, demanding vengeance.

By lighting a memorial candle in honor of Tuvya and his friends we fulfill their final wish.

Editor's Footnote

1. the leading Soviet secret police organization from 1934 to 1946

[Page 336]

Khonen Eyshishki

Translation by Meir Bulman

My father was Tsvi, my grandfather was named Khonen and I am named after him. My mother's name was Gittel. She was Kalmen Ilituvitsh's daughter. I do not remember a thing about grandfather's personality. About grandmother father would say she was "a Kozak a froy", meaning a woman of initiative and energy.

My maternal grandmother passed as WWI erupted, and grandfather traveled to Russia, to the town of Rostov–on–Don. There he spent the remainder of his days.

Prior to WWI, my father and uncles leased the Estate in Zemiuslva and Miastova near Kalvitze.[1] The mansion owners were contractually obligated to sell at a fixed rate the milk they produced, and father would prepare yellow cheeses— *Holland Cheeses* as we called them at the time.

After WWI, we moved to the Giluzh village near Divenishok. There we owned a grocery store, and we leased the ranch, and were financially sufficient.

I had two sisters and a brother. My oldest sister, Miriam, married Chaim Kosivitski in Oshmene, who was enlisted in the Red Army during WWII and since then his whereabouts are unknown. My brother, Shimon, hid with a gentile named Zeslav Khruzhy at the Gdini village, later relocated to the Vilne ghetto, and from that point his whereabouts are unknown.

My parents could not stay long in Giluzh, because the gentiles harassed them— a gentile shot and wounded my father— so my parents left Giluzh and moved to Divenishok. They lived there until they were commanded to move with the town residents to Voronova, where they perished. My young sister Fruma also perished there.

I hid in the woods and later in quarantine camps until the war ended. After the War, I left the blood-soaked land and arrived in Israel. I settled in Petah Tikva where I live to this day.

During WWII I served in the Polish military as a lieutenant with the Wanda Wasilevska field army.

Editor's Footnote

1. These places have yet to be identified.

[Page 337]

Shimon Kartshmer

Translation by Meir Bulman

Shimon Kartshmer was born in Warsaw in 1903. He spent his childhood years with his grandfather in the town of Divenishok near Vilne. He loved the small wood houses and the simple, modest lives the Jewish residents led: the Sabbath and holidays, the Jews in their festive clothes, the moon blessing ceremony, the synagogue, market days on which the Jews would go out searching for bargains, the wedding canopy on four poles under the stars, the varied and at time strange figures: the mute water-delivery man, the coach drivers, musicians – all sparked his imagination and influenced him. The Jewish town that is no more remained was etched on Shimon Kartshmer's heart.

Shimon Kartshmer

He drew inspiration from that town's wellspring time and time again and brought us his drawings from every place in which he lived and from every place of arrival.

He studied in Paris at *École des Beaux–Arts* and worked there for twenty years. During Nazi occupation, he was with the partisans in Nice.

After a number of years in Israel, he visited in the United States, after which he returned to Israel to settle in Safed— where he found a new backdrop for his favorite folklore themes. He participated in many exhibitions in the United States, Canada, Paris, Mexico, Tel Aviv and more.

The Horvits Family Tree

Translation by Meir Bulman

Gedalye Chaim and Miriam Yocheved were born in Divenishok in 1849, and there they married. The family lived at the town center in the fine brick building they erected there, nicknamed the *R' Gedalye Building*. They were pleased by dwelling in their town and expected the family to expand in Divenishok. Seven children were born to them: Ida, Shaul (Saul), Yetta, Selye,

Robert, Gertrude, and Esther. Their family life served as a wonderful example for the whole of Divenishok.

Esther (bat Gedalye) Horvits, her husband Reuben Engle, and their child

Gedalye Horvits became a respected man in Divenishok, Vilne, and the surrounding area. He was *gabbai* at the synagogue. Because he was known as an honest man, he was entrusted with maintaining the large forests. His reputation preceded him; he was "Gedalye the building owner".

Ida was the first to leave Divenishok and emigrate to America. At first she resided in New York, and later moved to Scranton, PA, where she married Louis Levine, and thereafter resided in Pittston, PA.

Some years after, Shaul arrived in America. He had been a pharmacist, but after relocating to New York he established a men's clothing factory. He married Florence Cohenson, and they have three children.

Selye and Robert traveled to America together. Selye married Harry Cohen and relocated to Scranton. They have four children. Robert became established in a men's clothes factory, much like his brother Saul, and married Lilian Sheinok. They have two children.

Gertrude married Philip Mintz in Divenishok, where their two children were born. In 1921, Philip and Gertrude Mintz arrived in America so they can be near the family. They brought their two children, and along with them came Gedalye Chaim and Miriam Horvits. Philip and Gertrude Mintz then had a third child.

Esther married Reuven Engle in Divenishok, and they had five children. Esther stayed in Divenishok to guard the building, then nicknamed *The Wall* (*moyer*). Unfortunately, she, Reuven, and their family perished in the Holocaust.

All Horvits descendants – children and grandchildren – followed in the footsteps of their ancestors: religious, honest, loyal, generous, caring for their people, and proud of their Jewish heritage. They were active in many fields, *Yeshivot* and other religious institutions, devoting much of their energy and time in addition to giving financial support. Gedalye and Miriam Horvits' descendants follow indeed the path set by Gedalye and Miriam: Sabbath observers, active in synagogue and Yeshivot, etc. Their activism in the realm of charity is done on a local and national level, and is acknowledged and publicized in many Jewish newspapers. Their professions include experts and businessmen. Many of the great-grandchildren studied in Yeshivot, but most importantly, they continued to observe the Sabbath and are proud of their Jewish heritage. Their devotion to Jewish matters is a source of pride for their parents, and praise and gratitude from their grandparents. The next generation, great-grandchildren to Gertrude Mintz, are yet very young. We are certain that all descendants will be raised in accordance with tradition.

Gedalye and Miriam Horvits' family is the root of a family tree rich with Jewish tradition, a family proud of their Jewish heritage and glorious among the Jewish people.

The president of Divenhok-ites of the greater New York area is Frank Barnett, son of the now deceased Shmuel and Yetta Barnett, grandson to the now deceased Gedalye Chaim and Miriam Horvits. His devotion to the organization is admirable. After many of the founders were unable to continue their activity in the organization, many young folks among Divenishok alumni families took it upon themselves to continue its wonderful activities.

[Page 339]

Aharon Kaganovitsh

Translation by Meir Bulman

Aharon Kaganovitsh

Tall, smiley, and kind-hearted: that was Aharon, or as he was nicknamed in town, Arke Elias. Since childhood he thirsted for Torah and education, but poverty prevented him from attaining a structured education. His biggest dream was to complete the Hebrew Seminary in Vilne and become a teacher, but the heavens did not smile upon him and he did not succeed in his mission. He attempted to teach in his town and was a bible teacher in the nearby town of Olshan.

Aharon was an avid Zionist, among the founders of the local *HaShomer HaTzair* chapter.[1] I remember that in the 30s when I studied at the Heberew Gymansium in Vilne, I met him on *Tu B'Shvat* at a 'fruits of Israel' bazaar that *HaShomer HaTzair* conducted. With much love and devotion, he tasted the fruit and wished me and himself that we would soon make *Aliyah*.

After the Soviets invaded Poland he relocated to Vilne, which had been given to the Lithuanians. We met on occasion. He was saddened by the situation and searched for a way to join his sisters in Israel, but to no avail. Thus, he found his death in Ponar with the Jews of Vilne.

Editor's Footnote

1. Zionist self-defense movement

A Brief Biography of Aharon Bloch (Rest in Peace)

Translation by Meir Bulman

Aaron Bloch, died in 1933 at age 47

Aharon Bloch was born in the nearby town Ivia, and resided in our town after marrying Freide, Itshe Binyamin's daughter.

There were three hatters-furriers in town: Yosef Zhizhemski, Eliezer Schneider- known by his nickname "the governor", and Aharon Bloch. It was a small town so the competition was tough and making a living was very difficult. Of the three, Aharon Bloch stood out as gifted with natural intelligence and a sharp and clear mind. He had a knack for leadership and a personal drive towards public works. He was a bright man, a great speaker who added folk wisdom and the wisdom of the sages, winning over the hearts of his listeners.

Aharon was a fair-tempered man with a great sense of humor and personal charm. At every gathering he stood out as chief speaker, his words flowed patiently and clearly, peppered with allegory and rhymes.

He busied himself with public maters his whole life. He loved and devoted himself to that with every fiber of his being. He tirelessly served the community until a cancerous illness overcame him at a young age.

After WWI and returning from German captivity he was an active member at *Yakkofu*[1] and oversaw cultural and charitable matters in town. He devoted his full attention to assisting the needy and the poor, and provided psychological and financial assistance to the many impoverished town residents.

Aharon Bloch was chairman of the Hebrew school board in the early 1920s. He rented the large bank house on Duvitsisker Street and hired excellent teachers, such as Ingulski, Engle, and the famed instructor Rabbi Aryeh Leyb, who taught the students Hebrew, Yiddish, Judasim, and Polish. Aharon is credited as the first to provide the town with a planned and orderly school with a stable curriculum.

Aharon filled many public positions; he was a member of the bank board, chairman of *Linat HaZedek*,[2] and more. His son Yakov told me that once someone had to be sent urgently to a severely ill patient and Aharon could not find a volunteer. He approached his son Dov and commanded him to fulfill that holy mission, which he refused. And so Aharon preached on the matter and slapped him for refusing the mitzvah mission.

The crown jewel of his public activities was organizing the Professional's Association in town (Hantverker Fareyn). He lovingly and devotedly served as chairman of the organization his whole life. That was an important role carrying much responsibility. He ensured the labor license certifications for the various professionals and ensured a fair distribution of taxes. He was in continuous contact with the officials in Oshmene concerning all matters concerning professionals in town. He served as a mouthpiece and supporter in times of trouble.

Though he was not a deeply religious man he was entrenched in the Jewish tradition. He would regularly visit the synagogue and led prayers on holidays and festivals.

Aharon was a passionate Jew and persuaded folks of the importance of a national awakening among the Diaspora. Later in life he was captivated by the ideas of socialist Zionism and educated his children according to those principles. I hold special nostalgic feelings towards this man due to the reform he enacted in the Hebrew school by adding a special hat with blue stripes on a white background. We wore the hats with pride and self-respect. The Hebrew flag waved atop each student's head. Since that time we never felt inferior compared to the university students who would come to town for vacations wearing colorful formal hats.

Aharon was beloved by town residents including its youth. I remember that once after visiting his home (there were many such visits because his son

Yakov was my classmate) I exited mentally satisfied. I felt I had learned something from that man.

Aharon was not fortunate and did not serve the town's residents for long. He became ill with cancer while in a German prison, suffered for many years, and was overcome in 1933. The town's residents thereafter could no longer enjoy his personality and blessed activism. He died young and was succeeded by his widow Freida and five young children: Dov, Yakkov, Malka, Shaul, and Dube. His oldest son, Dov, reached the Soviet Union after many years of wandering and fell in battle during WWII. He was succeeded by his wife, and daughter. His second son Yakov resides with us in Israel, apparently having inherited his father's traits: he is devoted to social and Zionist activism. The other children perished with their mother at the Voronova ghetto.

We mourn for those lost and not forgotten.

Editor's Footnotes:

1. an aid organization for Polish Jews

2. literally 'justly slumber'; an organization dedicated to visitation of the sick

[Page 341]

Shaye Kaplan

Translation by Meir Bulman

He was a Torah scholar, a personality of the old generation who was deeply rooted in Torah and the love of Israel. He owned a home with a store in the market place and was considered a town notable. The Rabbi encouraged him to participate in public matters. He was among the synagogue's activists.

Shaye was also considered to be among the educated folks in town, because he knew languages like Russian and Polish which few people in town knew. Thus, he was accepted as a teacher of religion at the Polish school (Pubshkhni).

He and Chaim Lubetski took turns teaching Mishna and Bible at the Old Synagogue, lessons that attracted a large audience.

His wife Tsipe-Leah was also an influential public activist, and along with Esther Gedalye's and Pesyeh Krizovski, was on the women's board representing the Ladies Auxilary. Their roles were to distribute funds sent from America to assist families in need.

His nephew Yitzach Segal was a partisan with Zelig Rogol in the Lipnishok woods. Since then his whereabouts are unknown.

His brother resides in the United States and contributed much to the *Relief*, and was among the first contributors in the establishment of the *Gemach*[1] in Israel.

The Barnett Family

Translation by Meir Bulman

The Barnetts are a family with many branches on the family tree, composed of five brothers who are active and devoted to the people of Divenishok and the *Relief* in New York. One of them, Albert, currently serves as chairman of the Relief in New York.

The brothers Barnett originate from Gedalye Horvits. Their mother was Gedalye Horvits' daughter. Esther bat Gedalye was their maternal aunt. Moshe Mintz's brother married Gitte-Reikhel, Gedalye's daughter, and they too reside in the United States.

The Barnett family was very active in public matters, especially in matters relating to our town. They coordinate our memorial services, and because of the sorry state of affairs at the Relief as the elderly are passing away and the younger generation strays further off the path, the tradition-observing Barnetts still fill memorial evenings with content and interest.

Solomon Levine

Translation by Meir Bulman

Solomon Levine was a warm-hearted Jewish man, humble and affable. His father Rafael instilled in him the love for the Torah and the people of Israel at a young age. He devoted his life to the work of the *Relief* to help his brethren at his town of origin. He visited Divenishok with his daughter in the 30s, and was interested in all economic and cultural matters in town.

After he returned to the United States, he passionately devoted himself to providing urgent care to the town residents. He was also a devoted activist for Israel and visited Israel many times with activists of the *Bund* from the United States. He usually timed his visits to coincide with the memorial service for the martyrs of our town, so he could attend the memorial ceremony with the people of our town.

Solomon Levine

His father Rafael was an administrator and cantor at the Old Synagogue. He lived sparingly and sustained himself mostly with funds his son Solomon would send from the United States. His wife Freidel would sell frozen apples to the children during winter, which she called "wine."

Solomon was succeeded by a son and a daughter, both married. The son is a doctor.

Editor's Footnotes:

1. Interest–free loan banking

[Page 342]

Meir Zalman Wiener

Translation by Meir Bulman

Meir Zalman Wiener was a popular figure in town: A tall Jewish man, adorned by a small white beard, full of energy and joie de vivre. He was a great Torah scholar, and had a thorough knowledge of the Talmud. His words were always peppered with wit and the sayings of our sages. He was considered one of the pillars among the attendees at the old synagogue. He also led prayers on high holidays. Those who prayed at the old synagogue regarded him with respect and admiration, and he served as *gabbai* [*administrator*] at that synagogue for many years. I remember that one time, as I attended the morning prayer, he tested my knowledge of Aramaic; he asked that I translate *Yekum Purkan*[1] to Yiddish. At the time, I found it a tough nut to crack, and I translated it partially- but for the most part he translated and explained it to me.

Life was not kind to him. All his life he had to travel to the villages to purchase stock and then travel to Vilne to sell his goods. That was a difficult and exhausting profession which strained all his energy. Despite that, he would make use of any free time he had to run to the synagogue to study a chapter of Talmud.

Meir Zalman was blessed with a large family. He had three boys and three girls. The oldest David, Fyvke second, and the third, Shayke, who married Leah, Moshe the Blacksmith's daughter. The oldest daughter, Rosa, traveled to her mother in America. The second daughter, Hindke, married Shlomo Kotler, and the youngest daughter, Ettke married Zydke. Zalman Meir was assisted by divine providence and passed before the war, but his family perished at the hands of the cursed Nazis.

Editor's Footnote

1. Yekum Purkan is a two-paragraph Aramaic prayer supplicating first for the welfare and well-being of all the Torah leaders of the generation and then for the members of the congregation at large and those actually praying in the synagogue at that time.

Moshe Aaron Katz
(The Tinsmith) [and the road to Benakani]

Translation by Meir Bulman

Moshe Aaron was an interesting and very popular figure in town. Moshe Aaron and Shimon Leyb the tinsmiths had a contract with the Polish government to deliver mail from Benakani to town. Their contract was ongoing and they were favored by the authorities. During the *Endecja*[1] government, an attempt was made to take the contract away from them, but other authorities did not permit it.

Everyone in town knew Moshe Aaron and needed his services. Anyone who wanted to travel to Vilne or Lida had to ride to the Benakani train station on Moshe Leyb's or Shimon Leyb's mail coach. The trip was a noteworthy experience in both summer and winter.

The coach would depart from town in the dead of night and reach Benakani at dawn. You suddenly find yourself between the open fields late at night. All is still and silent. The horse slowly strolls. Here we are in the Duvinke Forest. You are cloaked in darkness, as if you had suddenly slipped into an enchanting, frightening, and curious place. Once in a while a wild animal passes the dirt road in the blink of an eye.

We travel for hours deep into the forest and inhale the intoxicating scent of pine trees. That was a rare opportunity to experience an unforgettable night in a forest full of secrets, then to awaken and witness the waking universe as birds sing.

The family of Moshe Bernshteyn in front of their house in Divenishok (1932)
[Ed. Note: the caption printed here is a correction of the book's original caption that erroneously identifies the photos as the Moshe Aaron Kutz family]

The trip during winter was equally impressive. Moshe Aaron would provide a large sheepskin to everyone. You would cloak yourself in it and your eye would behold a spotless white stretching to the horizon as the moon shone a pale light on the fields. The trees are wrapped in *talitot*[2], as if thanking the creator. Upon reaching the train, countless more experiences and impressions await. Only the whistle of the train would wake you from the enchanted dream.

The trip from Benakani to Divenishok was equally interesting, though it took place during the daytime. Moshe Aaron had many stories. He would entertain you on the road with stories and amusing jokes. He knew the art of storytelling and his passengers' personalities, and would fit the right story for each. Moshe Aaron would encourage his passengers to stretch themselves by running easily down a hill from the coach or sleigh. Your feet would sink in the snow as you would run, huffing and puffing to catch up to the horse.

Moshe Aaron had a unique approach to new people. Carefully and patiently he would begin examining the person's character, be he Jew or Pole. 'What do you do and what brings you to town?' He knew how to gain the trust of guests and strangers. To the Polish clerk he would recommend the best guesthouse, to the teacher he would seek an update on his subject of interest, and as a matter of course he would soon extract the reason for each visit. If the rider was an enforcer, or an alcohol related investigator (Aktzinik), he would immediately notify those concerned to beware and prepare.

The trip to Benakani was truly an unforgettable experience, especially for the youth and for indoor dwellers, for whom the meeting with the mystery-filled woods was unforgettable.

Editor's Footnotes:

1. Alternate name for the Polish political party called National Democracy (*Narodowa Demokracja*, or *ND*). A primary goal of *Endecja* was the defense of Polish sovereignty against invading empires.

2. Plural of *tallit*: prayer shawl.

[Page 344]

Harry Levine

Translation by Meir Bulman

Son of Yitzach Leyb Levine. He left town at a young age, but remained bonded with all his heart to the townspeople and was active in the Relief and *Gemilut Hesed*.[1] He co-founded that charitable organization and gave the initial $1500 for the *Gemilut Hesed*.

The family of Yitzach Levine in their home in Divenishok in 1932

Harry Levine visited Israel on occasion and contributed much to the strengthening of the *Gemilut Hesed*.

Editor's Footnote

1. a charitable fund or service for the needy

Dovid Chaim Lubetski

Translation by Meir Bulman

Dovid Chaim Lubetski was considered a town notable. His store was adjacent to the store owned by his brother–in–law Isser Kovenski. They both owned fabric stores— among the largest in town. The two sisters, Meril and Chana would compete for customers on weekdays. On market days both stores were full of customers and they made a nice living.

Dovid Chaim was a wise and interesting Jewish man. Every conversation with him was accompanied by original philosophical concepts which he expressed often.

Dovid Chaim had a large family. His oldest daughter Khaya married in Navaredok, where she later perished. His son Velvel was an educated, affable young man. Velvl was a devoted Zionist, and served as fire department chief for a long while.

His brother Moshe studied at the school of law in Vilne. He was an avid Zionist, fully devoted to Revisionist Zionism. Moshe co-founded the *Beitar*[1] chapter and was a central figure in that chapter.

Dovid Chaim had another son, Yekutiel, who lived in the United States. He visited his parents before the war and the family was very happy.

Dovid Chaim was a Torah scholar. He taught a bible class between the afternoon and evening prayers. He once gave a lecture on Ecclesiastes and expressed skepticism towards the concept of the afterlife. That very much offended one of the listeners who approached Dovid Chaim and said, "I am a poor old man and a panhandler. I greatly suffered in life— starved at times. My only hope in this life is that I would go on to the next world, and here you are denying me that hope— so what else do I have in life?" His words greatly influenced Dovid Chaim and brought tears to his eyes.

Editor's Footnote

1. Revisionist Zionist youth movement

Moshe Aaron Katz's Father and Family

Translation by Meir Bulman

Moshe Aaron was Kalmen Shepsel the shoemaker's son. Kalmen Shepsel stands before my eyes as if alive: a short, skinny man, with thick eyebrows covering his pupils. Every day I saw him in the New Synagogue sitting in his spot, praying with devotion, and then continuing his study of *Mishnah*. He was elderly and frail, and he did not interact with people being all absorbed by the spiritual dimension. My father's seat faced his seat so I was always able to observe him. His small body shrank from of old age from day to day. He prayed in a whisper filled with sadness and longing, and on the high holidays filled with tearful sorrow.

I do not know why, but Kalmen Shepsel lived and slept at the synagogue. At night he would take out his beddings from the bench-box, organize them on a bench and lay down. What brought him to that and why did he not live with his son Moshe Aaron? I have not figured it out. I remember he passed away at the synagogue and from there he was taken to be buried.

Moshe Aaron had many children, all talented and full of energy and life. The oldest son, Khamke married in Oshmene. His son Zalmen was a smart fellow; he brought the first bus to town with his partners. His third son, Berke, emigrated to the United States and then Canada. His son Meirke married Mariyashke. His daughter Radke married Yankele Shmuels. His daughter Sarah, who was Mordechai Kartshmer's wife, passed away in the United

States. His Daughter Reyzl and her husband Chaim Caleb live in Canada. They have one son, named Yitzchak. Berel also has children, a boy – Chaim, and a girl – Miriam.

[Page 345]

Yankel Schneider (Yankel Leyzer's)

Translation by Meir Bulman

Yankel Leyzer's was a folksy, ordinary Jewish man. He made his living as a peddler, with difficulty, and would patrol the villages so that he can provide for his family. He was not a great Torah scholar, but he possessed a good and noble soul. He was always willing to aid his fellow man without considering the difficulty of the effort.

His son, Eliezer Schneider, who made Aliyah from Argentina at an old age and settled in Naharia, dictated these words prior to passing away:

"It happened on 1917 approximately, while the town was controlled by Germans. Making a living was quite difficult, and starvation stood at the doorstep of many families.

My father once sent my brother Shlomo Yitzchak to Shaul the Cobbler on Dovitshisker Street to repair shoes. Great poverty affected the cobbler's home and his children begged for bread. My brother returned and detailed the state of affairs in the cobbler's home with tears in his eyes. Father quickly dressed in his sheepskin and fur slippers, took a large, woven basket, covered it with a napkin and ran to the neighbors, collected food items and hurried with the full basket to the cobbler's house.

That is how our fathers were," Eliezer concluded, "and so must we behave as well; help one another and live in friendship and harmony."

At an old age, Yankel would tire himself with fundraising using a box of the Yeshivot Council, despite his advanced age. Rain or shine, summer and winter, he would do that work, which he considered a holy mission and a purpose in life.

That is how the ordinary people were in our town; men of effort and labor, lovers of Torah and of the People of Israel.

[Page 346]

Zusye Yankel Shkolnik

Translation by Meir Bulman

Gotlib Shkolnik and Khaykl Yekhezkel Katsev (1937)

Tall, strong, adorned with a small beard and a black moustache, Zusye Yankel walked every morning to pray at the synagogue, cane in hand and *tallit* and *tefillin* under his arm. Rain, whirlwinds, or heavy snow would not deter him. His conscience towards the heavens would not be clean if he would not pray with a community in the synagogue.

After breakfast, Zusye Yankel is often invited to the rabbi's home. A few town notables are invited to discuss public matters. He is wise, energetic, and especially firm; he has a tough approach, and he knows to raise his voice when needed. That grants him the rabbi's esteem, because sometimes it is necessary to be tough and firm to protect the public's rights and funds.

Zusye Yankel is fully devoted with every fiber to the school, which also his children attend, yet he is also alert to all public issues, and plays an active role in loaning money from *Gemilut Hesed*,[1] a loyal and devoted member of the burial society and among its leaders.

Zusye Yankel was considered one of those rooted public figures who were attached to the Torah and a love of Israel. He considered public matters as issues of the utmost importance which require devotion of heart and mind.

Zusye Yankel had a large family. His oldest son, Antshel, married in Vishneva and perished there. His daughter Esther Rokhl married in Vilne and perished there with her family. His son, Tsvi, lives in the United States, was a happy young man, friendly, and popular among the youth in town. He knew how to play the violin beautifully, and was not absent from any cultural or social evet.

His youngest son, Gottleib, managed the *Smolarnia* at Geranion and cared for his father's business. He currently resides in Venezuela.

Editor's Footnote

1. a charitable fund or service for the needy

[Page 347]

Eternal Light for the Souls of My Dearly Beloved

Translation by Meir Bulman

Radin was a small town in the Lida district, cloaked in trees and fauna like all towns in the Vilne area. A special beauty enveloped that town, not due to its scenery or natural beauty which it did not possess, but due to the holiness in which it was immersed: the holiness of the *Chofetz Chaim*, who lived there, penetrated the being of every Jew in town.

My paternal grandfather, Zalmen, was of those people, an innocent man, a lover of *Torah* who did not cease from studying until the day he died. He conducted himself simply and humbly, and instilled within his sons, Yosef, Shmuel, and Israel, a love for the Jewish tradition and People.

My grandmother Gittel was a skinny, short woman, but being a woman of valor she helped my father provide for the family, laboring in her vegetable garden and saving every penny to fund her children's education. She especially showed affection for her youngest child and only daughter, Alte. She was righteous and helped her fellow man in public and private.

My father studied in his youth at the Lomzhe *Yeshiva*, and later trained in forestry, eventually supervising the uprooting of pine trees and their transportation to the Benakani train station; from there they were sent to Germany and England to serve as telephone poles. In the course of his work he traveled to Geranion, near Divenishok. At the recommendation of friends he met my mother Blume and their fates were intertwined ever since. My father relocated to Divenishok with my mother's parents and established a family there.

My Mother's Family

Translation by Meir Bulman

The image of my maternal grandfather, Hershl (Tsvi), stands before me as a pleasant experience from those days. As a young man I would lead my old and blind grandfather to pray in the synagogue every Sabbath. He was a small-statured man, adorned by a small brown beard with white stripes woven through it, giving it a unique appearance. My grandfather was the only child of his father, Meir Berel, who spared no effort to provide his son with a religious education. Indeed, my grandfather studied at the Slabodke *Yeshiva* for many years and became a great Torah scholar and was ordained as a rabbi.

Luck did not smile down upon him and he had to struggle for existence, yet he was content with his lot and prayed daily, and studied *Mishna*. Because of his deep knowledge of the *Talmud* and *Poskim*, he was among those who stood out in the *Talmud* study group and on many occasions conducted fierce debates with the chief rabbi about different topics in the *Talmud*. He was quite generous and was happy to explain a *Talmud* chapter to all who asked.

My grandmother, Khaya-Basya was a gentle and kind hearted woman, who was alert to the needs of those in pain or poverty, and approached those in need with open arms. She helped provide for the family with much talent. She was pure-hearted and provided bedding on credit to town residents who would travel to America, thinking they would send the money when they arrived there. As for the most part those people forgot the town, so too they forgot their debt and my grandmother.

During WWII under German occupation, when famine struck, my grandmother walked to a nearby village to bring a bottle of warm, fresh milk for her eldest grandson. By chance, on her way back, the Germans caught her and violently assaulted her. As a result, she lost her ability to speak and passed away after being two weeks on the brink of death.

My mother was the youngest child in her family. She had two brothers—Gottleib, and Avraham-Yitzchak, and two sisters – Toyveh and Esther. Her brother married in Russia, as did her sister Toyveh, and after the Soviet regime was established contact with them ended. Her sister Esther married Tsvi Liberson from Divinsk and travelled to America, where he served as rabbi and ritual-slaughterer in the town of Portsmouth to the day he died. He was succeeded by his only daughter, Frances (Freidel).

My father was a modest and pleasant man with a sensitive and gentle soul. He experienced illness and poverty and fiercely battled the stormy waves of his life. Despite that, he was strong-minded and always expressed kindness and wisdom. As a student at the Lomzhe *Yeshiva* he was always content with his life. He discarded material matters and considered a man's spiritual entity a primary force. He educated his children that spirit and projected onto them from his wise and kind personality.

Alongside his difficult struggle for being, he longed to see his children becoming Torah scholars. He was willing to limit his food to achieve that goal. Despite the financial difficulties, he sent me to study at the Hebrew Gymanaiusm in Vilne and then to the Chofetz Chaim *Yeshiva* in Radin. My father was not fortunate to see his children blossom, as he was cruelly murdered by the Germans at Lipufke, a suburb of Vilne. He was on his way to attempt the rescue of my brother Michael, who was jailed in the notorious *Lokishki* Prison in Vilne for the crime of Zionism.

My mother Blume was a beautiful woman, honest and modest, known to all as a woman of valor. Even at a young age she would assist my grandfather in preparing slaughtered cattle, dividing, and distributing to customers.

My mother helped a lot in providing for the family. Each year, she would rent a garden overflowing with apple and pear trees. I was always impressed by her wisdom, and courage to walk alone in remote properties, to patrol the garden and correctly estimate the expected yield. An error in predicting the yield could result in heavy financial loss after many months of hard back-breaking labor.

Tsvi Ahuvi told me about my mother's courage and intelligence, who once heard the following at Rabbi Movshovitsh's home:

My mother once leased a garden from Count Milvski in Geranion. Once, while in a good mood, he asked my mother, "Say, is it true that the Jews use Christian blood on Passover?" Mother replied instinctively, "If that were true there would be Jewish informants who would notify the authorities." Her honest response made such a deep impression on him, that it was etched deep in his mind, and at the first meeting with the rabbi he decided to share the story with him and to compliment Mother's wisdom.

Strong in mind and spirit, she did not surrender to her fate, and energetically, without tiring, industriously and persistently, she participated in the harsh struggle to sustain the family.

Having a gentle soul and a kind heart, she was always prepared to understand her fellow man and to listen to his heart. She happily and kindly greeted every guest who came to the Sabbath meal, projecting her kind-heartedness, and wishing well all the people— that is how my mother was.

Yosef Dubinski z"l

She humbly and pure-heartedly educated her children, she was absorbed in Jewish values, and she spared no effort to educate her children in that manner. But her fate was very bitter; as stated, her husband was murdered by the Germans on the second day of their occupation and became the town's first victim. Her son Michael was murdered by an angry mob at the *Lokishki* prison in Vilne. Her two sons Meir and Tsvi escaped from the Voronova ghetto and found their deaths at the hands of Poles who used to be our best friends. She herself had to suffer greatly, alone and abandoned, and her life was ended in the valley of death, along with all the martyrs from Divenishok, Voronova, and the surrounding area.

From the large family there remain only a few. From my family I alone remain, from my uncle Shmuel's family remained only his young son Michael, and from my uncle Israel's family remained two children who currently reside in the Soviet Union.

I raise my eyes to the heavens, with praise and thanks that against the odds I was fortunate to reach Israel and establish a family here. God has blessed me with a beautiful wife, Mina, and three children: the eldest Yosef, the second Tsvi, and the third, Asher, who proudly carry the memory of their family. With a heavy heart and much sadness we mourn for their loved ones who did not reach the promised land— which was their desire all the days of their lives.

May their memory be blessed and their souls be bound in the bond of everlasting life!

–Binyamin Dubinski

[Ed. Note: Here ends the 'They Were So' section.]

[Page 349]

My Grandfather
R' Yitzchak (Itshe) Binyamin Rudnik,
(Of Blessed Memory)

Yakov Bloch

Translation by Meir Bulman

My grandfather Itshe Binyamin originated in the town of Navaredok to the Kovneski family, men of labor and trade. In his youth, because of his status with the Russian military, he had to change his last name from Kovneski to Rudnik in order to be released from his duties, and he stayed with that name, even though all his brothers and the family were named Kovneski.

He chose blacksmithing as a profession, manufacturing agricultural tools, as well as copper and steel work–instruments. He remained in that profession and made a nice living for the remainder of his life.

I remember him as a tall man, projecting strength, and self–confidence, overflowing with wisdom and life lessons, with a sense of humor. He was familiar with Jews as well as peasants, and also with landowners for whom he conducted administrative business concerning livestock, fruits and vegetables, and grain.

He built a number of buildings on Oshmene Street; a large residential building, and a smithy, where he employed his sons and other workers. He established a large family, comprised of two sons and seven daughters. He was widowed at a young age (my grandmother Sarah Malkeh passed away at the birth of her son Elimelech) and left him with five children. He married a second time, and with his wife Rivkah of house Kartshmer had four daughters (one of whom is Henye Harari, residing in Israel.)

Yitzach Binyamin Rudnik

It should be noted, that my step-grandmother, Rivkah Zmel had a gentle soul. She cared for and nurtured the young orphan as a mother, with much love and devotion.

My grandfather's home was open to many, and his reputation preceded him as a wonderful host. In times of trouble, such as WWI, he shared with his neighbors as though they were his children. His family knew no poverty during his lifetime. He also excelled at *matan b'seter*[1].

Being a brave and a strong man, he stood up to the loathers of Israel more than once.

He was among the administrators and a member at the Old Synagogue. In the twilight of his days he was devoted to *Shulkhan Arukh*[2] and the study of *Torah*.

He passed away in 1928 after a brief illness. I still remember the large funeral the community organized for him.

May this essay serve as a memorial to my grandfather— 'Of Blessed Memory'.

Translator's Footnotes

1. Anonymous charity

2. Literally, 'Set Table'; a highly influential book of everyday Jewish law

[Page 350]

The 'Tel-Hainik': M[eir] Y[osef] Itskovitsh

Chaim Lazar

Translation by Meir Bulman

After the bloody events which have just occurred before our very eyes, which we have felt in our bones, and after losing all that was dear: family, friends, the Jewish masses executed by thousands of methods, it is very difficult to return to the image of God overnight, to adorn the dear crown of freedom and to shout to the world, and yourself, that you are liberated. The toughest thing is to forget! Memory is perhaps the most valued asset secured by this freedom. It is a gift from fate to those remaining and their only consolation for the suffering of the era of horror. Memory is the dynamic motivating force which calls and obligates action, the Memory which accompanied us across borders and winding roads throughout the blood-soaked European Continent. From the cold and grey north to the sunny south, from the distant Ural Mountains to the Alps with snow covered peaks, through deserts, forests, rivers, checkpoints, soldiers, and guards from dozens of nations and languages, through permanent fenced camps and temporary halfway camps, with all their merciful caregivers which the "enlightened and progressive" world has generously given us.

* * *

In those days during the winter of 1945, Lublin was the central city in Poland. Those remaining flocked to it, survivors from the camps, from the hiding places. Partisans emerged from the forests, Jewish fighters who raised the flag of resistance and went to fight the German enemy for the nation's honor and avenge the bloodshed of our nation.

Lublin had three public houses to accommodate the refugees which were supposedly maintained by the Jewish Council. One was named "*Bet Peretz*", the second on Lovratovska Street, and the third on Nerutovitshe Street. While in one house the conditions were somewhat acceptable, as there were youths living there and it was maintained by *HaBrikha,* conditions in the other two were unbearable. The rooms were crowded at full capacity and beyond.

The people were laid across the cold floors, under them some hay which smelled like mold. It was very crowded. In every available spot, the corners, the hallways, and the corridors there were living corpses which had recently left the death camps, starving, disease-ridden, and wearing rags. The small portion of soup they were being given was not enough to nourish them. The cold howling wind which flowed in through bare windows and doors penetrated the bones. All yearned for their wounds to heal-- to no avail.

Is that the liberation and freedom which we had dreamed and prayed for? Is there a difference between the crowded wooden huts in the concentration camps and the persistent stench standing in the air from all the horrifying dirt filling the house, rising from puss-filled wounds and from the living corpses decaying in this cursed and wretched place?

Lublin, previously was a Jewish town- a town rich with tradition, the town where *Maharshal*[1], *Maharam*[2], *ha-Chozeh*[3], and other great rabbis had once lived, the town which honorably hosted the sessions of the Council of Four Lands.[4]

At the end of 1944 the Germans still controlled and oppressed Warsaw. The liberated region was already under the control of the new Polish government. Most of the survivors who reached Lublin crowded the narrow alleys and walked between its ancient walls. It was as if they had come to resurrect the Lublin Jews who perished, and the souls of the town's rabbinic geniuses, whose influence was far-reaching among the Jewish Diaspora. These Jews were not concerned with ideology at that time; they wanted to travel to Israel. They wanted to vote with their feet, to get up and leave, leave the blood-soaked land, the mass graves in which their relatives and Jewish masses were buried, to leave those who were destroyed in that cursed land.

At that time, in a situation few of those remaining traveled through Europe, I met in Lublin the Partisan, the "Tel-Hainik," Meir Yosef Itskovitsh and his Partisan wife Esther.

At that time, being a man of *Beitar*[5] in Poland was a risk to freedom and life. The *Beitar* people were like "conversos."[6] Only a few knew who was a *Beitar* person, their past and group affiliation. Under the Communist national regime in Poland, it was only permitted to be a Zionist of the Left, ideologically compatible with the regime, which began to show its influence in all facets of life. Being a member of *Beitar* was not mentioned, as it could lead to jailing, interrogation, torture, and exile. Despite the many dangers, this man of *Beitar* suddenly appears – a "Tel-Hainik" in public, without signs of fear or anguish. And indeed, why now, after Liberation, being a free man should he fear publicly expressing his opinions, if while being in the woods with the Partisan battalions, where the Communists ruled, he had not hesitated and was not deterred from walking among the Jewish and Gentile Partisans, and their Russian commanders, with the greeting of 'Tel-Hai' on his lips-- a customary greeting between friends in his youth?

Shortly thereafter, I became aware of the biographic details of this "strange" *Beitar*-Partisan, who had crossed my path in those days of renewal and revival for the survivors of the terrible Holocaust.

Meir Yosef's origin is in Divenishok, Oshmene District, Vilne metropolitan area. He was a son of a respectable lineage, fifth in his family. Meir's father, Nathan, was a respected, God-fearing Torah-observing man who faithfully served the public and who was widely respected and admired by them. He was an active in the Jewish and charitable organizations in his town and known as a warm-hearted, generous Jew who supported every needy person – be it in secretive charity or in his contributions to public matters. Meir's father was a member of the parents' council at the Hebrew school, the administration of the local bank, the *Gemilut Hesed*[7] societies, the bridal assistance society, the Passover food bank, and the rest of the institutions, which were ample in the Jewish town. During most of the years between the World Wars, he was a member of the Polish city council representing the Jewish residents, by which he earned also the respect of Gentiles for his contributions to benefit of the whole population.

Meir was raised in a traditional Jewish home and his young soul absorbed all that is good, beautiful, and honest, as it was entrenched in his home. That national-spiritual heritage is what guided him in his life's journey with all its trials and tribulations – the sign of our time. That heritage is what guarded him from veering off the path of Judaism so he would not fall, so he could stand tall in the face of every wind and storm which washed away everything in its path.

R' Nathan ensured that his children receive a national-traditional education, based on both enlightenment and Torah. After completing their studies at the Hebrew school, he sent his children to the Hebrew Gymnasium in Vilne, except for one of his sons, Yehezkel, who since childhood was attached to Torah and mitzvot and was sent to learn at the Yeshiva in Baranovich and later to the Yeshiva *Chaffetz Chaim* in Radin.

When Meir was a student in middle school, word reached their town of the establishment of the "Language Guardians Brigade" as a result of the "culture war" then in style. He decided to establish a branch of the Brigade in town with his friends. They published a copy of a Hebrew newspaper and vowed to conduct their friendship by communicating exclusively in Hebrew. Meir's love of the Hebrew language also guided him through his life.

When he completed primary school he was sent to Vilne to study at The Epshteyn Hebrew Gymnasium. In Vilne, a large Torah town, a town of wise men and writers and Torah, the Jerusalem of Lithuania, Meir absorbed the beauty and depth of pure Judaism. His character was composed there. There he matured and became a proud Jewish young man, uncompromising, aware of his nation's eternal values: the renewal of the ancient spirit of bravery of the conquerors of Canaan.

It was no wonder, then, that when news came of the riots in the Land, he left *HaShomer HaTzair*[8], of which he was a member according to the present fashion, and joined the ranks of *Beitar*, the Hebrew youth movement, which had begun spreading and taking hold of the youth across Poland.

When he returned home for summer vacation he would gather his friends around, and with Ze'ev Lubetski, a local resident and law student, established the local *Beitar* chapter. Meir was chosen as the chapter's first commander, and his blessed activism made its mark in a short while.

Meir's leadership abilities were well developed. He felt he had found his calling. He left the Gymnasium and began learning at the Tsherne Teaching Seminary in Vilne, and in 1936 he received a teaching certification. Over the next year, Meir served as a teacher in Amdur, near Grodne. The chairman of the school board was a pharmacist who was one of Ze'ev Jabotinski's enthusiastic followers. He insisted the teacher hired would have Zionist views. Who else but Meir Yosef would fit that role?

A year later he taught Torah to Jewish children in Horodok, near Molodetchno by the Russian border. As 1939 approached, Meir, born in 1917, would soon have to report for duty with the Polish military. His father and relatives encouraged him to obtain proper documentation to release him from duty for health reasons, but Meir declared that he is in good health and wished to serve in the military. He must have hidden his true intention for enlisting. As a man of *Beitar*, he would heed the call and prepare for the battle to free the homeland and establish a Jewish state. Therefore this would be a good opportunity to obtain military know-how.

That decision was destined to be useful and produced many future benefits, perhaps even saving his life. WWII erupted. The 85th Sniper Brigade of Vilne, stationed at New Vileyka near Vilne, was sent to the front. They managed to reach Piotrokov near Lodzh, but all the same the Polish military was defeated and sustained heavy losses. The Polish military began disintegrating and many escaped to the rear. Meir arrived in Varshe. In Zhetl, new brigades were composed of the remnants of the defeated military. His brigade was stationed to guard the capital Warsaw. The siege on the city tightened. The guardians manage to hold on for a few days, but could not withstand the bombardment and immense pressure from Hitler's army. The city surrendered and Meir was captured by the Germans. He was held with the rest of the prisoners at a school building near the train station. Typhus broke out in the camp, taking many lives. They were transferred from place to place and eventually moved towards Brisk-Litovsk, where a prisoner exchange took place between the Russians and Germans. The Soviets promised that they would soon be released and could return home, but in the meantime would be performing various jobs while being housed in freight cars. A Polish man told Meir that this transport is destined to be sent to the depths of Russia. An escape plan formed in Meir's mind and within a short while he succeeded. He eventually found out that his group had been transported to Katyn, where, as is well known, the Russians murdered all the POWs, many Jews among them.[9]

Meir reached his hometown, now under Soviet control. He consulted with *Beitar* friends from his town and towns nearby, Oshmene and Voronova, and they decided to cross the border to Vilne illegally. A border patrol agent captured Meir, but he was already experienced, and once more he evaded his captor, escaped custody, and reached Vilne. Meir found himself a refugee among many other refugees who had reached that town from all over Poland.

Vilne was then under Lithuanian control and a free regime was still in place. Meir was among the few, perhaps the only one, who received a work permit from the Lithuanian Education Ministry and served as a teacher at the Hebrew school in Olkenik, Professor Klozner's town of origin. Prof. Klozner's wooden shack still stood there. There was also Napoleon's gift to the old synagogue, an ancient ornamental curtain etched in gold, complimenting the beautiful decorative carvings on the wooden ark. A lively small Jewish community was still in place, maintaining a standard routine.

Meir did not confine himself to studying Torah. He communicated with the men of *Beitar* in Vilne. He visited Vilne frequently and was involved with events taking place within the refugee community.

The calm period of Lithuanian control also reached its end. The Soviets occupied Lithuania. *Beitar* went underground. At the home of Meir's friend Leybeh Katz they secretly listened to radio broadcasts from abroad. One day they heard the bitter news of the death of *Beitar* leader Ze'ev Jabotinski. Their world darkened. Who would they look to now?

With his friend Ehrlikh, a *Beitar* member and refugee from Lodzh, he rode a bike towards Vilne. Meir brought the bitter news to the attention of Ysroel Epshteyn. Ysroel took out from his pocket a picture of the *Beitar* leader and said, "No, it is not true. Ze'ev Jabotinski did not die, he will live forever."

Within a few weeks, even that time would seem ideal compared to what was about to take place. In the summer of 1941 Hitler's forces invaded the Soviet Union. Within a few days German troops occupied Lithuania and White Russia. Meir left Olkenik and made his way towards his hometown, passing through the evergreen forest of Rudniki. Local villagers followed him, robbed him of his few belongings including the clothes he was wearing, and wanted to murder him. Nearly naked, he managed to evade them and reached his home – just as the German occupation began and the German military and local Gentiles began their rioting. They did everything in their power to prove to the Jews that they could anything to them: torment them, dishonor them, break into their homes, steal, and murder, and especially when a Jew dared to protect his family, his honor, and his belongings. Jews were kidnapped for work. They were assaulted and humiliated, tortured, and starved – their lives became worthless.

Some alumni of the youth movements, among them Meir as one of the primary speakers, consulted one another, held discussions, and searched for ways to ease the situation, to protect their honor, to stand up to those wishing to end their lives. Deliberation, and ties to the underground, yielded results: in 1942, Meir and his friends traveled into the woods and connected with Partisan groups which later became the acclaimed "Bielski Brigade."

Then began a time of guts and glory, with many battles-- a relentless war of vengeance waged upon the German enemy. Meir Yosef, with his military expertise, became one of the stand-out fighters.

For a long time, they operated around the towns of Navaredok and Lida, trying to liberate Jews from the ghettos and to gather Jews who had escaped the slaughter. They maintained contact with the towns and prepared a place of refuge for survivors.

Meir Yosef and his friend Yakov Strudvorski breached the Lida ghetto and rescued a group of 30 Jews.

Later he was designated to serve as a messenger between the Bielski Brigade and the neighboring Baltiets Brigade and later was permanently placed within that group, based on active combat.

As the days went by everyone became acquainted with the Tel Hai-nik Meir Yosef Itskovitsh. When he appears before a commander, even a general, Meir greets him with "tel hai," the *Beitar* greeting, and parts ways with "tel hai," all in the territory of the Red partisans.

Meir Yosef in his role as messenger met many Jewish youths, whom he would gather together in the evenings and on the sabbath to tell them of the Promised Land. He gave classes on Jewish History and geography and instilled them with Zionism. He recounted the recent past and fostered dreams of the future in front of them.

And that was how Meir Yosef upheld the oath of *Beitar*, "Whether in light or in darkness/ Always remember the crown …For silence is filth/ Worthless is blood and soul /For the sake of the hidden glory." He revolted "Through all obstacles and enemies."[10] He influenced hundreds of youths in the camp with his faith and ideas and served as a role model.

* * *

As the snow melted at the end of the winter of 1945, when the spring sun began to illuminate the world-- for spring had reached even those remaining after the horrific destruction-- I met Yosef Meir Itskovitsh, the loyal *Beitar* member, the proud Jew, the fearless fighter flowing with ideas, energy, and a deep willingness to continue rescue operations and to take a place in the genesis of the nation's renewal. I felt that with young men like him miracles could be achieved and we have not parted ways since. We went on to pave the road for escape, the road leading to Zion.

There he was with the survivors of the sword, of the fire, those singed by the gas chambers, hungry and thirsty, wearing rags, who wandered on crooked paths, climbed snow covered mountains, survived the frost, descended hot and dry valleys, snuck across borders, and reached Italy so they could ascend to the mountaintop, to their one and only destination, their homeland of Israel. And who guided them, who offered them warm words of encouragement? The Jewish Partisans whose appearance was like a breath of fresh air. The Partisans were the only facet of the survivors inner spirit that was not destroyed, the Partisans were the energizing force supporting the ideology, because of their need to continue their past activities [into the present]- be it vengeance plots against the Germans or organizing the lives of the survivors of the camps. The Partisans were fortunate to be stationed as the first guard, scouts watching out for the People of Israel on their meandering path. The Jewish Partisans understood the importance of their new destiny. They educated the public, strengthened the people, mended them as if in a furnace, instilled passion within them. They knew that this was the road leading to Zion, and so they worked night and day and devoted themselves completely to sustaining the existence of those remaining, maintaining their physical and spiritual needs, and training them for the coming war to establish the State of Israel.

When we reached Treviso, Italy, a large camp administered by the Hebrew Brigade Divisions was located beneath the Alps. That spot, breathtakingly beautiful, quickly became a reception center for hundreds and thousand of refugees who were brought there by soldiers of the Brigade, or reached it via the usual escape routes. The arrivals were greeted with an abundance of brotherly love so rare they had not encountered anything like it since they were uprooted from their families. Sometimes the unjustified impression was made that the Brigade soldiers were trying to redeem themselves of their heavy burden of guilt from not having come to their brothers' aid in their time of need since they had not been with them as they suffered, and that they had not shared the suffering. Sometimes it seemed that the Brigade soldiers were unable to look one in the eye without pangs of conscience that fate had placed them on the other side of the bottomless blood pit.

We watched, in astonishment, the soft and gentle treatment of the survivors by the soldiers. With much caution they unloaded them from the cars as if they were gentle and expensive glassware. Such happiness was reflected in the soldier's eyes when a Holocaust survivor smiled at him. We thought, "If such love and devotion exist, it was worth it to pass through hell to then have the good fortune to reaching such elevation." And indeed those were moments of great rising and genesis, a period of renewal rising from the ruins, a period which passed with the clearing of the ruins and the rebuilding. A special excitement was reserved by the Brigade soldiers for when they met the Jewish Partisans, their brothers in arms. The reputation of the Partisans, the Jewish avengers, had reached them long ago. They long knew that there had been young men and women in the Diaspora towns who had risked their lives to save the nation's honor, who had climbed the barricades in the burning ghettos to rebel, to resist, to fight and avenge, that there were young men and women who had breached the tall and well-guarded ghetto walls, found their way to the woods, and fought against the German destroyer who murdered swiftly, against his regime, his military, his police, and laws. There were Jews from many places who had escaped the slaughter of their communities and they too reached the forests and joined the ranks of the fighters. Stories had reached the Brigade men of the wondrous, immense bravery of the Jewish Partisans, who struck their nation's enemies and instilled fear, but they had yet to meet those Partisans and heard from them about their actions. And there they stood before them, wearing crowns of glory, their minds made up to continue their fight and to overcome obstacles, to achieve the dream – the raising of the people from its ruins and the establishment of a state which would gather all the survivors and the Jewish masses from their countries of exile.

As opposed to the short restful time in Treviso, the harsh reality existed in the refugee camps that were established across Italy in Bologna, Mestre, Padua, Cinecittà, and Modena near Rome, and in the Bari area of southern Italy. In most of the camps conditions were poor with scarce nutrition, an unvaried diet with no fat or sugar. Especially poor were conditions for the weak and the ill. Especially harsh conditions were found in Modena, which is where Meir Itskovitsh arrived. It was a halfway camp for refugees of various nations making their way to their homes and homelands, and therefore all arrangements were temporary. What was fitting for other nationals was tough on the Holocaust survivors. In the camp designed for 2500 people, there were 5000, among them approximately 4000 Jews. Conditions were harsh, [including] a lack of mattresses with most folks on the cold stone floors. Nutrition was starvation portions for malnourished people. The camp was at the center of town in a large building which formerly served as a military academy. The building had been partially destroyed by shelling during the war, the windows were broken, and despite that, there was no air to breath at night because of the overcrowding. Hundreds slept in the yard without mattresses and blankets. Representatives of the Jewish Council pressured representatives of the British Red Cross, who administered the camp, and requested improvement. But camp officials rejected their pleas with various excuses. Firstly, they did not recognize the Council as representing the refugees as it was not based on the Jews' countries of origin. Secondly, they did not recognize the Jews as a nation but rather a religious class, and thirdly, "What did the refugees want from them? There are Jews in the camp who have two pairs of pants or an extra shirt, they should share amongst themselves." The only agreement by officials of the Red Cross was an addition of a cup of milk for children below the age of 14. Food portions were very small: for breakfast some white liquid made from milk powder without bread or any other food item, for lunch soup and a roll, repeated for dinner. The distribution of this pitiful food was also conducted in unfathomable conditions. At first there was only one distribution spot and people stood in line for hours on end to get their portion. The dining hall had a capacity of only 300 and people had to eat hastily so the others could take their places. Most of the refugees were still wearing the clothes they had worn in the death camps or the ghettos or the woods. There were no laundry services. Medical assistance was almost nonexistent. Sometimes ill people slept on the floor and there was only one doctor and one nurse.

That's how the "honey moon" for the survivors transpired. Despite all that, the Partisans and *Beitar* members did not despair. Meir Yosef was among the first camp leaders to turn the horde of abandoned survivors into an organized Zionist national force. With much passion and energy he began organizing life at the camp to ease the stay, and was among the first to gather the few [remaining] members of *Beitar* to reestablish an organized *Beitar* movement. That is how Itskovitsh became a *Beitar* leader in Italy for the next two years. He was among the organizers of *Beitar* gatherings in Florence and Milan, and later among the organizers of the first *Beitar* conference, which was also the first *Beitar* conference in Europe post-WWII and took place in Castel Gandolfo, the Pope's summer residence near Rome, in January 1946. In that conference, Itskovitsh was appointed culture and education commander, an especially difficult role in the absence of explanatory literature or guidebooks. Itskovitsh was also among the founders of the *HaMa'apil* and *LaNitzahon* newspapers which *Beitar* published in Florence, the first papers published by the survivors in Italy, made possible thanks to the immense devotion of the activists, among them Meir Yosef. Leaders of other Zionist movements who had more financial and technical resources did not mange to do what the small group of *Beitar* in Italy managed to do at that time. The literature prepared by Meir Yosef reached all *Beitar* units in Italy and beyond. *Beitar* in Italy had 2000 members. Meir Yosef was also active in maintaining close contact with members, Italian Jews for many generations, among them *Beitar* commissioner Leona Carpi,[11] Esq. in Milan, Mr. Tedeschi in Florence, Mr. Bassani in Rome, and many others. Close cooperation and contact developed amidst the survivors from the movement and Italian Jewry.

The story of Meir Yosef Itskovitsh is the story of an extremely eventful period, full of tribulations, in the history of our nation, and one which left a deep impression on our future. It was a time of holocaust and rebuilding, the loss of a third of our nation, and then the achievement of the dream of establishing the State. Itskovitsh's part [in this history] is immense. He and his friends, those Jewish youngsters with a deep Jewish consciousness, men of vision and bravery ready to sacrifice, fight, and struggle, that helped us through the most terrible of times, and paved the road to Israel's independence with their blood. Since those days and to this day he symbolizes the persistence and the deepening of the idea of revival, its dissemination and achievement. As a teacher, guide, and fighter, he serves as an example to his generation and the generations to come.

Editor's Footnotes

1. Solomon Luria ("MaHaRSHaL"; d. 1573), author of "Hiddushe Maharshal" (Cracow, 1581), from "Hiddushim (or Novellae)" by Solomon Schechter, Max Schloessinger, in *Jewish Encyclopedia*, New York: Funk & Wagnalls Co., 1906;

2. Meïr Lublin ("MaHaRaM"; d. 1616), author of " Ḥiddushe Maharam Lublin" (Sulzbach, 1686), from "Hiddushim (or Novellae)" by Solomon Schechter, Max Schloessinger, in *Jewish Encyclopedia*, New York: Funk & Wagnalls Co., 1906;
http://www.jewishencyclopedia.com/articles/7682-hiddushim, last accessed 5 Dec 2017.

3. Jacob Isaac Horowitz, known as "The Seer of Lublin", *ha-Chozeh MiLublin*; (c. 1745 - August 15, 1815) was a Hasidic rabbi from Poland, from "Yaakov Yitzchak of Lublin", (2017, March 12), In *Wikipedia, The Free Encyclopedia*;
https://en.wikipedia.org/w/index.php?title=Yaakov_Yitzchak_of_Lublin&oldid=769966121, last accessed 5 Dec 2017.

4. The central body of Jewish autonomy in Poland for nearly two centuries—from the middle of the sixteenth to that of the eighteenth… The four lands that sent their representatives to the council were Great Poland (with its capital, Posen), Little Poland (Cracow), Polish or Red Russia (Podolia, and Galicia with its capital, Lemberg), and Volhynia (capital, Ostrog or Kremenetz). Lithuania seemed to have its regular or extraordinary representative in the Polish-Jewish Council until 1623, but in that year it established its own central organization which acted independently, from "Council of Four Lands" by Herman Rosenthal, S. M. Dubnow, in *Jewish Encyclopedia*, New York: Funk & Wagnalls Co., 1906; http://www.jewishencyclopedia.com/articles/4705-council-of-four-lands, last accessed 5 Dec 2017.

5. A revisionist Zionist youth movement

6. Conversos were Jews forced to convert to Christianity in the Spanish Empire. The members of Beitar in Poland at that time had to hide their true identities in much the same way.

7. A charitable fund or service for the needy

8. Zionist self-defense movement

9. Note: Reference is to the Katyn Massacres, a series of mass executions of Polish nationals carried out by the Soviet secret police, see Katyn massacre. (2017, December 2). In *Wikipedia, The Free Encyclopedia*. Retrieved 22:00, December 6, 2017, from
https://en.wikipedia.org/w/index.php?title=Katyn_massacre&oldid=813216771

10. The lyrics here are from *Shir Betar*, the *Beitar* Song.

11. The surname in the original name is spelled: kuf-reysh-peh-yud.

[Page 358]

Ben-Zion Schneider hi"d   Hinda Sara Schneider hi"d

*From the right: Yehuda Satkolshtsik, Ben-Zion
Schneider, and Avraham Krivitski hi"d*

[Page 359]

Satkolshtsik family Seated: Moshe Ber and his wife Leah z"l and their children.[Tr. Note: all the children are standing] *Standing, from the right: Tonia, Yehuda (Yudl), Rokhka hi"d, and Bilha tb"l*[Tr. Note: May She Have Long Life]

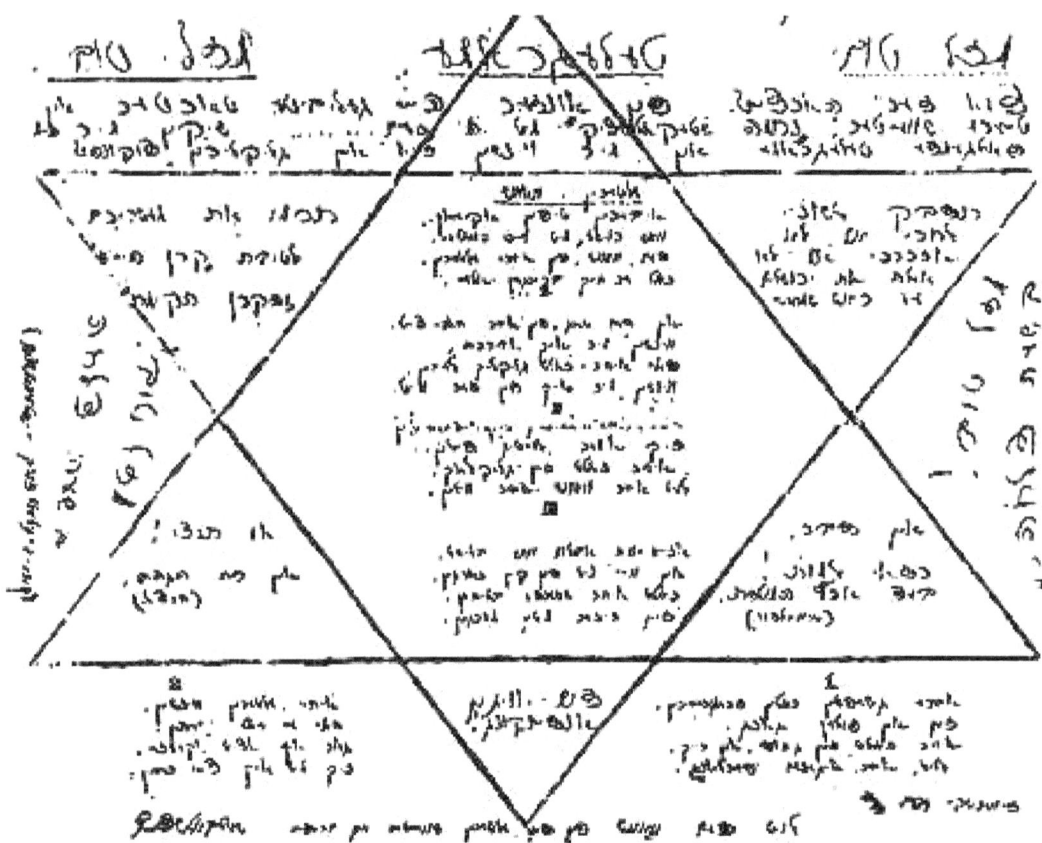

Congratulatory telegram which Yudl Satkolshtsik sent from Divenishok for the wedding of his sister Nekhama in the United States in 1924

[Page 360]

MEMORIAL CANDLE

For a beloved family murdered during the Holocaust by the enemies of Israel 5704–5:

The martyr Rabbi **Ben–Tsion** ben R' **Shabtai** z"l **Schneider**

his honorable wife Mrs. **Sarah Hinde** bat R' Moshe Ber z"l née **Satkolshtsik**

Their eldest son the martyr **Yakov** (who fell while battling the murderers in the woods near Lida)

Their daughters **Liba** (Ahuva), **Rozhe**, and **Leah**

From the town of Divenishok near Vilne

May we witness God avenge their blood and may their souls be bound up in the bond of life with the souls of all of Israel's martyrs

Dedicated by their grieving son

R' **Shmuel** ben R' Ben–Tsion **Sharon** (Schneider) and his family, Ramat Gan

---

~~~~~~~~~~~~~~~~~~~~~~~~~~~~~~~~~~~

God bless the martyr R' Ben-Tsion Schneider, God avenge his blood, among the leaders of the Divenishok community, lover of the Torah and Torah scholars, for the charity and kindness he showed me during the Holocaust when he hid me in his house along with other rabbis, as I escaped the persecutors of faith and religion when Poland was occupied by the Red Army. I found shelter in his home and much aid in crossing the border to Lithuania, from which, by the grace of God, I was able to make *Aliyah* and dwell in the house of *Hashem* in Jerusalem, May it be rebuilt and re-established speedily in our own days, Amen.

<div align="right">The Author</div>

(From the dedication to the book of Genesis with *Oznaim Latorah* commentray by the great and righteous rabbi Zalmen ben Rabbi Ben-Tsion zt"l Sorotzkin, formerly ABD in Lutsk, Zhetl, and Voronova. Second Edition with addiditons. Jerusalem, 5721)

[Page 361]

Yiddish Section

1. The Town and its Development

[Page 363]

The end of Vilne Street

Divenishok-The History of a Town

Binyamin Dubinski

Ed. Note: This article appears in both Hebrew and Yiddish in the original Yizkor Book; only the Hebrew version has been translated and published in this book. The title of the Hebrew version is "Divenishok- From the Founding" and may be found at page 10 of this book. Photos appearing within the Yiddish version of the original book are included here without their accompanying text.

[Page 364]

The market place at twilight. In the background - the Eastern Orthodox church

[Page 366]

The old synagogue on Vilne Street

[Page 368]

The Catholic church

[Page 370]

Mikla Krizovski, Esther Engle, and Leah Kaplan, the authorized representatives of the Divenishok Ladies Auxiliary in New York for the distribution in Divenishok of the aid sent from America

[Page 373]

The pump at the market place, constructed by the Germans during the First World War

[Page 376]

Divenishok town hall

[Page 377]

The house where the post office was located and a cooperative was set up by Polish anti-semites to fight Jewish commerce

[Page 378]

The Shtetele Divenishok

Meir Yoshke Itskovitsh (Son of Nosn)

Translation by Tina Lunson

With the help of this pen and my memory, I will bring to paper – partly in verse and partly in prose – my recollections of Divenishok: her streets and lanes, homes and people. This is my last stroll through the town where I was born, grew up, studied in *kheyder* and *shul*, played, dreamed and struggled – until the German murderers wiped everything away. Therefore I want to revive on paper various figures and events from Divenishok.

1

There was a shtetl by the name of Divenishok, near the Gavya River, where Jews lived, various kinds, poor and rich, all were equal: Aba the shoemaker, Leybl the smith, Bentshe the wealthy. One person lived in want, hoped for a better future, and strove towards that. Meanwhile the fish that were plentiful in the Gavya River sufficed and a second person was pleased that he lacked for nothing and ate to his fill.

But on *shabes*[Tr. Note: Jewish sabbath] in the *besmedresh*[Tr. Note: study house] little Frume from the poor house and Khiene, wife of Nosn, prayed from the same book and benefited from the prayers. And not only on *shabes* – when all the Jews ate *khale*,[Tr. Note: braided white-bread loaf] even Yankl "the aeroplane"[Ed. Note: a nickname] sought out a bit of chicken and forgot that he was the ultimate pauper.

As I said, there was a *shtetl* Divenishok – and we will not see it again. My little shtetl, similar in some ways to others, to me you are unique. I will not forget you in joy and in good times, or in sorrow, in German captivity without food, when I sat full of memories about food, dreaming, hoping and never forgetting. In the long, sleepless nights of cold to break my bones, my heart terribly bitter, I always had this prayer: God, I beg you, could I just see my *shtetl* again?

The black berries in the big clay jugs, the moss-covered straw roofs, and on them stalks of rye and white goats. Red berries, sour but juicy, sweet raspberries full of worms but tender. And red strawberries with little cheeks of white literally pleading 'take me and eat'! And where are the bilberries at Mikhal the blind's that grew on shrubs in the mud, but had an unexpected taste . And the fish, pike and tench – *Got mains*,[Ed. Note: My God!] how could I ever get that taste back?

And the yellow *lisetskes*[Ed. Note: possibly a type of mushroom] and other mushrooms (I have already forgotten their names!). The spring water from the pump, sparkling in the copper wash basin. The awful soot and Hukshe the chimney sweep with his broom and flue.

Our wagon drivers, butchers with their fat arms, the inept tailors with their needles and waistcoats, and the water carrier Elka the mute.

The watercarrier Elka (Eliohu) the Mute

2

Now the eve of Passover is coming and people are preparing for the *seyder*,[Tr. Note: ritual before the festive Passover meal] but not before they try to get rid of the bedbugs that danced freely around in the beds. Each person did it according to his "patent": one found them with a candle and burned them; a second used kerosene smeared here and there with a ladle. Then later in the night someone got the idea to play a prank on a friend and carried a mattress over to another's house.

Thursday was market day, and Jews, rich, poor or stingy, made partnerships for buying fruit. And who, do you think, were the partners? Shaye Kaplan (nicknamed the cat) and Koheles the *shames*[Tr. Note: beadle] (who never had a *groshen* to his name) made a partnership. One of them paid and the other carried-- and they did not buy only fruit.

As winter approached with its biting cold, Jews turned the world on its ear in search of a partner for a sheep or a calf. The rich one paid and the poor one got half.

Now let's jump from the market to the women's section of the shul, which on *shabes un yontiv*[Ed. Note: Sabbaths and holidays] was always full with women and girls, clad in dresses from American packages (because not everyone could afford to buy new clothes). The clothes were sent by whomever had an uncle, an aunt, or a cousin who was concerned about them. The praying and the prayers were not familiar to everyone, but their faces were always turned toward towards the eastern wall. When Munye the tailor began the prayer it was as quiet as on *yonkiper* [Tr. Note: Yom Kippur] for *neile*. [Tr. Note: the evening's final pleading prayer] It was no wonder that everyone loved his singing, since his voice was sweet and tender.

Divenishok figures: [Ed. Note: back row, left to right] Eliezer Mintz, his daughter Itka z"l, and Moshe Mintz (in Israel); [Ed. Note: front row left to right] their sisters Golda, Gitl Rivke; Pesah Mintz (died in America)

3

If a Jew from the *shtetl* had to travel overseas it was an unusual event. As soon as he would start packing his baggage someone would start baking sweets for him to take along-- but finding a suitcase? Who in town had such a thing? Or a handbag? I remember that Rive Leye's daughter Minke had such a thing. But packing was a specialty of Peysakh the shoemaker, he could put the proper squeeze to it. He got everything in, closed and bound, nice and fine.

Do you remember Leyble the Smith and his wife Manke, who always had that heavy hammer in her hand, standing in the forge and fanning the fire, even pounding on the anvil, and not letting in her husband: because Leyble, the moment he earned one zloty from a peasant, got the desire for a shot of brandy, and one-two he was through the garden, harnessed up, and off to Tsalke Hinde's restaurant, downing a whole liter of hooch until his head spun and trembled like a bell.

Where are you, my Jews, the simple and the wise, where is Yankl the *artshom*[Tr. Note: meaning unknown] and the manufacturer Yatke from Seltz? Where is Leyzer the Guide, where are the wooden houses, Lolke Sutskever, the pendulum, and the *shabes* candlesticks of polished nickel? I remember Dobke Rivele's and Minke, their walls decorated with pictures. Eli the worm and Shaye the cat, Slove the little and Slove the big, their cries, tears and laughter and play – who can make a reckoning of all that, dear God!

4

In summer we boys slept on the porch at Elke Meyshe's and when Vikte the gentile went at dawn to the river with laundry and our fathers went to pray with the first minyan, we, quite to the contrary, took an interest in Zoshke the *plataver's*[Ed. Note: unknown word] daughter; and along the way bought bagels made with eggs from Itke-Sime. It did not matter who paid, Altlik, Arke, or Meir. After that we went jumping around in the water, not far from the flax warehouse, in the enclosure. There, our little group watched the gentile Zoshke, and especially Meir-Yoshke.

She was blonde and beautiful, and did not differentiate between Jews and Christians. She was not disturbed by my long nose or profile. She knew what I meant, and decided for herself the intent. Zoshke's father was not a friend of Jews, or a chum, but Jews from the *shtetl* brought their cows to him (excuse me, not to him but to his bull).

If we are going to talk about bathing, it is no wonder in a *shtetl* such as ours that women and men bathed separately. Reyshke the Rov's, as lovely as the world, bathed in the hot and in the cold weather. We boys, hidden, marveled at her body from a distance.

*Farewell for Moshe Yakov[Ed. Note: Rogol] and Reyzl Rogol
on the occasion of their emigration to America (1933)*

I will indulge in mentioning Alter Yashe Nashe's, who had "recipes" for every illness and fever. If a Jew encountered misfortune, or if someone delivered him a hard blow (may we not know about such things), if in the middle of the night an only daughter disappeared and the whole house went crazy – people turned to Mr. Alter and he went to the patient, quietly and calmly, without a question and answer, and with something cooked up from pap that he smeared on here and there, after a few days only a memory remained of the irritation. But instead of incantations and spells Mr. Alter swung a black hen around over his head and soon the problem disappeared.

Itshe Levine was a dear man, but cursed, poor thing, with a humpback. Zeydke Lubetski said of him: and it was evening and it was morning...on the front a hunch and on the back a hump.

Meyshe the tinsmith, even in the midst of his work hammering holes out of a grater, would push his glasses up higher, to his cap, and take an opportunity to recite a few psalms by heart. But when someone had a toothache he knew what to do: he dipped a wad of cotton into vitriol and placed it in the tooth hole like a patch. It burned in your mouth but the ache was calmed. Meyshe the tinsmith was a saint of a Jew, upholding the holy

Torah, doing only good deeds, and shielding himself against wrong-doing. When Jews hurried from *shul* on Friday evening to go home for supper, Meyshe never forgot to invite a guest home for *shabes*.

Hirshel Krizovski, a relative of our family, the genius of the town and an accomplished romantic, was a photographer by trade and by retouching he could transform a Jewish pauper into a Polish nobleman. Hirshel was also a revolutionary, but an honest one, with idealism. Even more, he played in the theater, also directing and carrying out his activity of conspiracy. He was a quiet Jew, modest and proper, so that even on the eve of *shabes* as the *Rov* hurried through town calling out *"Yidn, bentsh likht!"*,[Tr. Note: Jews, (light and) bless the candles!] Hirshel turned and went straight to the *besmedresh*.

I recall how Hirshel used to search each face for the "photogenic profile", turning the head to all sides as it was warm or cool, and then said "Look into the camera". And everyone obeyed him. My heart is heavy, very heavy, as I think about Hershel: the young man with the curly forelock, clever eyes and serious mien, who died trying to better the world – until that world was exterminated and destroyed.

Market day in the town

5

Ah, I can certainly not forget how we used to fight a fire in our town. The fire fighters' brigade consisted of only Jews, so it is no wonder that more than one house burned down. As soon as a fire, a conflagration, broke out, or some other kind of plague, either the wagon shaft for the horse was missing, or she was out grazing in a field, and you could talk to a lamp or to the wall because the fire was burning, as everyone knew. The only one who appreciated and understood, as is said, a fat groshen, was the insurance agent, Anisim's son from Malinovke. I recall that many years ago the chief Velvke Lubetski attended a course, dressed up in a red uniform with shiny buttons, and the Jews in the shtetl danced with joy. He came back from the course full of enthusiasm and related what he had learned there, including some praise for himself: "They set a ladder up against a five-story building and asked who was prepared to climb up. No one answered, everyone remained silent. The only one who would take up and answer the challenge with a loud "Good" was I, Velvke. I started up the ladder, while everyone else was in a cold sweat. But they looked at me with respect – and no wonder, because heroes always arouse childhood fantasies."

Some time went by after that story when the alarm siren suddenly sounded. Women wrung their hands, "Woe is me, where is the fire? Who is burning?" No one saw any fire – and indeed there was no fire (as they say there: no bears and no woods... [nothing of the kind]). It was just an attempt to see how a Jewish fireman would manage. The regional chief inspector, visiting from another town, had arranged for a false alarm. [Velvke] looked in the book that the course had provided. Seeing that his firefighters were not as fast as he had thought, his blood began to boil, he started to shout and spit, curse and swear, move worlds with the Polish *psiakrew* and *cholera*[Ed. Note: both are Polish expressions of strong annoyance, anger, and irritation, akin to 'damn' or 'heck' in English] and asked himself, what is the wonder that the barrel and the horse are so far apart? The hose is torn, water put into it does not come out the other end. The tools are not prepared, nothing is where it should be. As the leader, so goes the soldier. He couldn't climb the ladder to the first floor...

6

In Divenishok where there was a house, there was some kind of hole under the cooking oven. Hens were kept in there, to lay eggs and for some meat. Now that so many years have gone by, the secret can be told:

A strange rooster once came to visit at my father Nosn and mother Khiene's house. There was tumult and screaming, the hens did not lay one egg. "Cockadoodle-doo, craw, craw. Who is this stranger here?" One clever hen, no fool, went to the rooster and gave him a peck. It landed a rip by his upper lip, and she went away satisfied, in peace. Another, a speckled hen, thought that she was a peacock, began turning her tail around to him. But the rooster gave a look, a sniff, and quickly got away from her. Another hen, ready for anything, but holding herself large, with a torn nose – the rooster circled her a little, then gave a flap with his wings – and to this day that hen eats grass. This really is the case with hens – but there is a moral in it for people too!

Some Jews, youths, children in front of Meir Zalman Sloboda's (z"l) house on the market place

7

In every town, one day of the week is a market day. Divenishok was no exception. On the appointed day tens (and sometimes hundreds) of peasants came into town with the produce of their fields, gardens, orchards and livestock. From the pre-dawn hours caravans of wagons drew in, harnessed to one or two horses. There was no lack of those coming by foot, with packs on their shoulders or baskets in their hands.

At the entrance to the town, officers of the council collected a special fee, according to the quantity of merchandise each was bringing to sell. The Tatars came up from Subotnik Street, where they lived not far from Ivia. Their specialty was pelts and leather goods, although they also brought vegetables to sell. After harnessing their horses, they had all covered the horses with *adzerushkes*[Tr. Note: meaning unknown] to keep the flies from biting them; and afterwards they raised the wagon shaft where they hung a pelt or a piece of a sole so that people could see from a distance what they had to sell.

Wagons drove in from Oszmiana and Dubizishok Streets with cattle tied to them, and calves or horses to sell. The wagons also held baskets of eggs and bound chickens. Opposite from Vilne Street the action was weaker, because the payment in that section was smaller.

There could be no doubt that almost all the merchants, shopkeepers, artisans, peddlers, *zardarmnikes*[Tr. Note: meaning unknown] and even the thieves had been waiting for market day for their "guest appearances" from Vilne, in order to take advantage of the small-town innocents and peasants. Jews pleaded to God that it would not rain, because the market would be bad, but rather on a fine day the profits would be very different. There were several Jews who had their signs for rain:

If on Wednesday, the day before market day, the cows came in from the pasture and Meir Nozi's black cow was leading, it was certain that it would rain in the morning. But if a heifer was in the lead – it was certain to be a nice day. In our house there was a flower pot that foretold rain a day earlier by showing on its leaves drops of water like tears. It is likely that there were still other signs.

As the anti-Semites in Poland raised their heads and were encouraged by the government, a Christian cooperative food store opened in Divenishok, the so-called *"Spul-Dzhelnie"* on Subotnik Street, besides a Polish satellite business on Vilne Street, and even a Polish restaurant, in order to weaken Jewish business, to compete with Jewish merchants and market dealers. The anti-Semites also demanded to move the market outside the town, with the argument that the gathering of the masses and the filth would be the cause of disease among the residents, let alone the disrupted quiet. In truth, however, they sought to distance the Market from the center of the town, where the majority of Jewish shops were located. Thanks, however, to the energetic intervention of Jewish representatives with the sheriff,[Ed. Note: Starosta, the chief administrator of the county] and then the mayor,[Ed. Note: Voyvode, an official entitled to sit in the Polish Senate] the market remained in its old place. However, the partitioning of the market was altered:

Near the houses and shops, only carts with chickens, eggs, fruits, vegetables, and the like were allowed to stand. In the middle of the market a large place for cattle, calves, and sheep was designated-- and another place for pigs. In the middle of the square, they set aside a special house with a large scale for the weighing of those four-footed creatures. The horse market was moved to behind the church, in a large area that stretched from Oszmiana Street, near the pig place, up to Dubizishok Street. All the horse dealers went around here, known as *koniukhes*, some of whom were Christians with their horses, but most importantly came the Gypsies, who were well-known specialists in horse trading.

8

The sale of a horse took place like this: First you looked him in the eyes, to see whether he was blind; then in the teeth, in order to ascertain the age; and finally you drove him to see how he ran and be sure that he did not limp. Interestingly, the Gypsies' horses literally galloped during the trial run. Even a *konine* (what we called a horse of just skin and bone) galloped. Experts explained that with the help of pepper or alcohol in an unmentionable place, the Gypsies could spur any horse to run.

Commercial zone between Market and Subotnik Streets

A Divenishok Jew named Itshe Gitlits (nicknamed Zshagin) was an even greater specialist in selling horses than the Gypsies. Although he was walleyed – people said that one eye looked at Oszmiana Street and the other looked at Dubizishok Street – he could run very fast with his little horse in a straight line, never veering from the path. One *simkhes toyre* when a gang of drunken pranksters promised Itshe a bottle of brandy if he could translate *"eyn k'eloheynu"*[Tr. Note: "There is no God like ours", a part of the Jewish liturgy] into the Gypsy language. He agreed and did get the brandy – because who knew enough to check if the translation was correct?

The old men were also among the accomplished horse dealers. Such were Pesakh the elder and his son Broyna, who wore boots the whole year round, even in summer, and was never without a whip in his hand – except for *shabes*, of course. A very different type of horse dealer was Leybl from Warsaw, a tall, broad-shouldered Jew who possessed extraordinary strength. The Christians in town were afraid of him and not one of them dared to start up with Leybl. Yet his area of greatest knowledge was equine diseases and the healing of them. This "Leybl Varshavski" as the Poles respectfully called him, had once taken a bet with some ten Christians to see who was the strongest. They made a big hoop out of old reins and put ten Christians inside on their knees with their heads sticking up through the reins. Leybl did the same thing on the other side. From the huge crowd that gathered around, the Poles encouraged their brethren while the Jews prayed for a miracle that Leybl would not fail. We heard the order "Pull!" – and our Leybl dragged on the reins and all ten Christians fell into the sand.

Leybl also broke iron chains. I recall how once, with a wagon shaft in his hand, he drove away a market-square full of peasants. For us children it seemed as though he stuck a pointed knife into the drawn muscles of his hand and then the knife was withdrawn as if by a spring.

For the horse dealer Hirshel the tall, the Poles also had a great deal of respect too...and fear. He was blonde and tall, nothing like a Jew, with red, full-blooded cheeks. He spoke Polish like a born Pole and in town it was said that he once put a piece of "that other thing"[Tr. Note: pork] in his mouth. Hirshel's boots were always polished and he always had a whip in his hand.

No Jews were seen in the part of the market that was designated for hog dealing. Instead, the hog dealers and the other peasants, and the traveling Christian buyers and sellers, filled the Jewish shops and stalls, purchasing clothing, fur coats, shoes, boots, hats, manufactured goods, tin and metal products, household tools and foodstuffs.

9

The biggest earners on a market day were the restaurants. Tsalke Hinde's ran sweating and harried from one table to the next, serving brandy with snacks and not being shy about asking someone to pay upfront because he knew that after all was said and done there was no one left to talk to. He was also not afraid to tell a drunken *goy*, "enough", and not serve him another glass.

More proper Christians ate and drank at Itshe Levine's. People also drank and stuffed themselves there, but there were no scenes or fistfights.

At Yankele Olkenitski's public house, people drank beer from the Papirmaysters and Pupkos breweries in Lida.

As night fell the police began to shoo the remaining peasants towards home. While the peasants were laying in their village homes, snoring, the Jews in Divenishok counted their takings and wished that the next market day would be a better one.

10

People in the shtetl said about Hershel Krizovski that he had a brilliant mind. He certainly did have rare abilities, read many books, and also studied from them. Thanks to them he was able to assemble a radio apparatus, the first in town. The box was set up in the *"Vilbig"* [acronym for the Vilne Education Organization] meeting place. Two wires came out of the box and led to two poles on the roof. They brought a big battery with another storage battery and the box acquired a 'tongue': it spoke and played music, and people came running to look and hear as if at some evil wonder. Whoever was speaking, even if the radio was just saying what the weather would be tomorrow, it was a sensation. The Jews were smarter than the radio though and always predicted when the meteorological station announced rain, it would surely be a lovely day.

11

The Oszmiana Forest got its name from the road that went through it to the provincial capitol [Oszmiana], where the most important state offices were located, offices where Jews always had to take care of dozens of district matters.

The youth, worry free, used the dense pine forest to stroll around, amuse themselves, and spend time together. Especially on *shabes* after the *tsholent*[Tr. Note: a stew left to cook overnight in the cooling oven, as no fires may be lit or extinguished on the sabbath] when our parents were indoors taking a nap, we boys and girls went off to the forest, in groups, in pairs, or individually. The groups were called "companies" and they were mostly girls: Ferke Alte Noyekh's company, Bilke Peysi the beggar's company, and others.

The forest was an ideal place to play hiding games, or to chase each other among the trees, or the lie back on the grass and read a book or simply rest. Those who were tired from running around and from the games picked and ate berries that grew on bushes in the part of the forest where it was damp and dark, because the sun did not reach there due to the thickness of the trees. One could never be satiated with the delicious berries, because part of the pleasure of them was that they did not cost any money. The pleasure was not completely without care, because picking and eating the berries left black stains on our hands that would not go away for a long time. The berries also left telltale signs on our lips. Since these pleasures of the forest were only on *shabes*, some were afraid that on going home they would be punished by observant parents for violating *shabes* by picking berries. So we first went to the Gavya River, took wet sand from the water and scrubbed our stained hands with it. More than one person rubbed off skin and made a wound.

A group of youths from town

In time though, progress began to permeate even to Divenishok. Yankel Namiot, the supplier's son from Rogols' pharmacy – who studied in a *gimnazie* – brought a new invention to town: a special washing medium of sour salt whose application made the stains from the berries disappear. But where could one get sour salt? Most of our mothers could not afford to buy lemons, and so for cooking sorrel soup or beets they would buy sour salts at Rueben Kartshmer's pharmacy store. We children sniffed out where our mothers kept that "merchandise" and when we went off to the forest and the berries, we took along a few pieces of sour salt in our pockets. We did not always succeed in getting the sour salt to the forest because our pockets were full of holes from the pants being washed so much.

I remember that once when my mother was cooking sorrel soup and needed to add a little sour salt, she could not find any. There was an uproar in the house. My father said angrily several times that he did not know what kind of housekeeper forgets where she has put things away.

My mother did not know what to answer, although she was very annoyed because she did remember where she had put the sour salt. I did not have the courage to confess to the theft. After that around the shtetl it was said that sour salt was very helpful in washing stains from the hands, but that more than once it had disrupted the peace of a home.

[Page 394]

A Jewish Life that is No More...

Motke (Moshe Leyzer's)[1] Kartshmer

Translation by Yael Chaver

Introduction

I must thank my *landslayt*[2] in Israel who convinced me to recount my memories of the *shtetl*, its people, my home and my family, for the Divenishok *Yizkor-Bukh*. I confess, this is no easy task for me, because I left Divenishok 45 years ago, as an 18-year-old young man, and not many events remain in my memory. What I want to recount, although it consists of individual experiences, constitutes a significant reflection on the social and community Jewish life there, to the degree that I belonged to several communal organizations. I also believe that my biography is, after all, very similar to and characteristic of most young people in the pre-Holocaust period.

Now I live in Florida, in America. Thanks to a visit to Israel, I was able to meet with many comrades and friends from my old homeland in Divenishok. I learned from them about the preparations to publish a memorial book to preserve for all time the murdered *shtetl* and its Jews. As I sit in a Tel-Aviv hotel and carry on a pleasant conversation with the editor of the Divenishok book, I make efforts to present as many details as possible about a Jewish life that existed - and is no more.

Home and Family

I would like to start with my home and family. I was born in 1912 in Divenishok to my parents Moshe-Leyzer and Itta, both also natives of Divenishok. My father died when I was 6 years old. I don't remember my father, but people from the town would always say that Moshe-Leyzer Kartshmer had a good heart; as Jews say, he was a "good soul." When he drove his wagon to the train station he would give a free ride to people along the way.

My mother was a quiet, gentle woman as well as very religious. She prayed three times a day, and observed all the commandments. After her husband died, the burden of making a living fell upon her.

We were three sisters and three brothers. The oldest brother, Meirke, left for America the year I was born. My brother Shmuel died of tuberculosis during the First World War. He got this sickness after he spent several weeks digging trenches for the Germans, who were occupying the town. The dampness and forced labor made him sick and he left this world at a young age. My sisters Kilke, Braynke and Khayke were murdered, along with their husbands and children, by the Germans and their helpers during the Second World War. I managed to get a postcard from them as late as 1941, letting me know that our mother had died in the month of Kislev.[3] She simply died of hardship, as well as because there were no remedies in the ghetto to heal her.

The football team "Gloria"

My sisters were seamstresses by profession and helped our mother to make a living until they got married. My brother in America would often send a few dollars. We lived on Oshmene Street.

I began studying in *kheyder* with Kalmen Shepsel, when I was five years old. My second teacher was Leyb Bareh, and later I studied with Isaac Horvits and Rogulski, from Vilne.

In the Organization and Trade Union

In 1926 I joined *HeKhaluts*.[4] I was only 14 years old, but I was attracted to the company of comrades, the bright space, the singing [of Zionist songs], and the *Eretz-Yisro'el* atmosphere[5] that dominated all our meetings and gatherings. I forget now why I suddenly exchanged *HeKhaluts* for *HaShomer HaTsair* and became active in the latter youth organization, with which I was not familiar.[6] They were located on Vilne Street. About 30-40 children and young people would gather there. *HaShomer HaTsair* was headed by Shraga Blyakher, who now lives in Israel. Our goal was to go to *Eretz-Yisro'el* and help build the country. The lectures and group meetings educated us about Jewish history and Zionism, as well as scouting.[7]

The HeKhaluts organization in Divnenishok (1925)

I was a member of *HeKhaluts* for one year, and a *HaShomer HaTsair* member for two years. That was long enough to foster a Zionist awareness in me, as well as a love for *Eretz-Yisro'el*, and the desire to become a settler there.[8] Unfortunately, the number of "certificates"[9] that the British government issued to Jews was so small that thousands of people could not realize their dream. Yet we all lived with the hope of settling in *Eretz-Yisro'el*.

As I was drawn to performing in the theater, I joined the drama club and appeared onstage in several roles. I remember that there was an ongoing argument and fight between the A.G. Yiddishists, who were influenced by the Left, and the Hebraists, the supporters and members of the various Zionist groups.[10]

I also want to emphasize that daily relations with the Christian population were tolerable, with no particular conflicts or clashes. After the Holocaust, I soon found out that these non-Jewish neighbors had expressed their hatred of Jews while the town was under German rule by actively assisting them murder the Jewish population of Divenishok.

However, it is no secret that the young Jews in Divenishok felt the ground burning under their feet even before the Second World broke out. Those who didn't get the desired "certificate" sought to emigrate overseas by any means, or leave for the big city. This was also my case.

The last year I was in the *shtetl* I joined the volunteer firefighters of Divenishok. I was too young to put out fires, but I was accepted because I was very tall. I remember how, one Friday night, a fire broke out in the neighboring town of Olshan. The Divenishok firefighters were also called in. We labored there for several hours and didn't return home until Saturday at daybreak, when our Jews were going to the synagogue. My mother was awake all night and waited in the street for the firefighters to come back safely. You can imagine her joy when she saw me return unharmed and very happy too, as I was very proud of myself. This was no small matter: a 15-year old boy and already a firefighter!

The moment a sports club was organized in the town, I too wanted to kick the ball. I was a member of the children's group and was very glad that we, too, did sports. My mother, though, understood that putting out fires or playing football was not a good future for her son. She sent me to Gronem Melamed, where I was supposed to learn a trade: tailoring. As was then customary, I was mainly busy with babysitting the tailor's child, cleaning the house, bringing water, and doing other chores - on top of which my mother had to pay the tailor for teaching me how to use a needle.

After that my mother had the notion that it would be only fair to send me to a *yeshiva*, but I declared firmly and clearly that I was not prepared to eat at other people's tables, so nothing came of this plan.[11] I decided to emigrate, even more so because my time to be drafted into the Polish army was nearing.

Divenishok youths who served in the Polish Army at Vilna

I Leave Divenishok

In 1930 I managed to emigrate to Cuba, thanks to my cousin Finke Munis. My first occupation in Havana was working for 5 dollars a week. When I managed to save my first 70 dollars, I bought a wagon for ... peddling. After two years of peddling, I opened a small "department store," improved my finances a bit, and sent [emigration] papers to Sarah Katz in Divenishok. We got married in Havana in 1935.

In 1941, my brother sent us the documents we needed in order to move to the United States. I did not know this brother, because he had left Divenishok when I was ... six months old. You can imagine our meeting in Trenton, New Jersey. We later left for New York, where I opened a children's clothing store.

In 1943-45 I served in the U.S. army, in General Patton's Third Army, and took part in the battles against the Hitlerian enemy in Europe. When I was at the front in Germany, my feet got frostbitten, and I was hospitalized in

England and America for four months. Now I am a member of the Jewish War Veterans of America.

In 1956 my only brother Meirke died, and a year later - my wife. Among Divenishokans she was known as "the mother," because after the terrible Holocaust she cared for the town survivors and sent them packages, help, and letters.

A class of students from the Talbut School in Divenishok (1930) with their teachers Betsalel Petukhovski and Sonnenson, during the visit of the 'landsleit' [Ed. Note: fellow townsfolk] *from America: Meir Bolinski and G. Levey*

For about 30 years (1942-1973) I was active in the Divenishok Society of New York and served as President. Throughout this long period I helped the town's Jews, before the destruction and later - helped the few survivors to get back on their feet in the Displaced Persons camps of Germany and Poland, and in Israel.

Now I live in Miami Beach, and am still busy with community work, as I used to be in the Divenishok that was…

Translator's Footnotes

1. The name in parenthesis is that of his father Moshe-Leyzer, along with a possessive suffix. People were often familiarly known by their mother's or father's names.

2. A loose translation would be - "my fellow Divenishokans."

3. This Jewish month roughly corresponds to December.

4. "The Pioneer," a center-Left Zionist youth organization that was geared towards training young people to settle in Palestine.

5. Kartshmer uses *Eretz-Yisro'el* (Land of Israel) to describe the atmosphere of the Zionist settlements, rather than in the traditional Jewish sense of a God-given land.

6. *HaShomer HaTsair* ("The Young Guard") was a more left-leaning youth movement with the same Zionist goals as *HeKhaluts*.

7. These and other Zionist youth movements were modeled on the British Scout movement at the turn of the 20th century.

8. He uses the term *oleh*, literally "one who ascends," following the Jewish traditional view that settling in the Land of Israel means reaching a higher plane of existence.

9. Refers to immigration permits. At this time, the British Mandate authorities severely limited the number of permits allowing Jews to settle in Palestine.

10. I have not been able to find the meaning of "A.G." "Yiddishists" most likely refers to members of the non-Zionist, Socialist Jewish Labor Bund, which considered Yiddish the major language of the Jewish people. Zionism espoused the adoption of Hebrew as a linchpin of its ideology.

11. This custom, often termed "eating days" (Yiddish "*esen teg*") was a community system whereby students from out of town ate their meals in a different home each day.

Social and Political Life

Shraga Blyakher
Translation by Leybl Botwinik

Divenishok was a small, quiet *shtetl*.[Tr. Note: village] I left it in 1934 and made *aliya*[1] to the Land of Israel. I loved the *shtetl* and its streets, houses and institutions. Like all its inhabitants, I knew almost every Jew there.

A

The Jews in the *shtetl* drew their livelihood from commerce and various professions: there were cobblers, tailors, carpenters, tinsmiths, and blacksmiths. Some lived from the monetary support and packages they received from relatives in America. There were also those that did not want to teach their children a profession because they believed it was beneath their dignity to have a craftsman in the family. Some of the youth continued their studies in Vilne, or in the Yeshivas of Radin and Volozhin, or just wandered around shiftlessly.

There were several philanthropic institutions in the *shtetl*: The *Gmiles-Khsodim*,[Tr. Note: charity fund] *Bikur-Khoylim*,[Tr. Note: for visiting and assisting the ill] and *Linos Hatsedek*.[2] I remember *Rebitsin*[Tr. Note: Rabbi's wife] Rudnik and the lady Sore-Dasya sending out pairs of youngsters to collect money for the poor. This mutual help was on occasion very significant. For example, if a coachman's horse expired, they would buy him a new one the next day.

Every Thursday, Market day, the merchants, retailers, and craftsmen were busy buying and selling. That single day would provide the *shtetl's* livelihood for an entire week. On the other days, one could see the bearded *shtetl* Jews sitting near the doorways of Zalmen Ortshik, Zalmen Kushes, or Nasan the Tailor, carrying on conversations about various issues. Gossip was not lacking.

The old and new *Beys-Medresh*[Tr. Note: a synagogue that was both a house of worship and of learning] were to be found at the *Shulhoyf*,[Tr. Note: synagogue courtyard] as was the Rabbi's hovel. When my father, z"l[Tr. Note: of blessed memory] prayed in the old *Beys-Medresh*, he did so in his usual spot in front of the *Orn Koydesh*.[Tr. Note: place where the Torah scrolls are kept] In the new *Beys-Medresh* he would stand to the right of the *Orn Koydesh* near the Rabbi, *reb*[3] Yosef Rudnik, ZTs"L.[Tr. Note: of saintly and blessed memory] The most esteemed residents of the *shtetl* sat in the first row and among them the *Gabay*,[Tr. Note: manager of synagogue affairs] Munye the tailor. *Mishnayes, Sha"S*, and *Kitser Shulkn Orekh*[Tr. Note: various holy books] were studied on tables near the stove in the old *Beys-Medresh*. Every early evening, between *Minchah*[Tr. Note: afternoon prayer] and *Maariv*[Tr. Note: evening prayer] the merchants left their stores and the craftsmen their workshops, gathering in the *Beys-Medresh* to study a *Blat Gemore*,[Tr. Note: passages from the Gemarah or Talmud] or *Mishnayes*.[Tr. Note: passages from the Mishnah]

Hannuka performance by the children in the first grade at the Tarbut School (1930)

It would also be appropriate to recall the bath that was located at the *Shulhoyf*. We used to visit every Friday and derive great pleasure from the hot, refreshing vapor that steamed out of the stove, as well as the beatings on the back with the little sauna brooms. Jews, naked as the day they were born, would lie on the benches and breathe in the steam of the red-hot stones on the stove. During the summer, we abandoned the bath and went for a swim in the river off Ozsmiana Street. There were separate areas for women and men (without bathing suits). If an inquisitive eye happened to take a peek, the girls would hide among the bushes.

B

The *Shulhoyf* also contained the *Tarbus* Hebrew school, where the entire curriculum was taught in Hebrew. The *HaShomer*[Tr. Note: Zionist self-defense movement] and *HeKhaluts*[Tr. Note: Zionist youth movement] carried out their activities in the school too. After a meeting, my brother Tevye z"l and I would go to the synagogue to recite a chapter of *T'hilim*.[Tr. Note: Psalms] The *shtetl* also contained the *Bund* organization[Tr. Note: a Social-Democratic movement] that opposed Zionism, but its influence on the youth was minimal. The majority of the youth were Zionist oriented.

The Zionist organizations joined forces to set up the *HeKhaluts* to prepare the youth for *aliya* to the Land of Israel. The *HaShomer HaTsair*[Tr. Note: youth division of HaShomer] and *HeKhalutdz* did much for the *Keren Kayemes*[Tr. Note: Jewish National Fund] and the *Keren Hayesod*.[Tr. Note: United Israel Appeal] I recall that we once invited Shimon Vishnitski of the *HaShomer HaTsair* to our *shtetl*. His talk at the school stirred listeners.

A group of young HeKhaluts students and teachers (1925)

We should also mention the teachers Avraham Aloni and Dubkin that did much to help the two above mentioned youth organizations carry out a large number of activities. We should also highlight the name of reb Aryeh Leyb

Rogol, the chairman of the Zionist organization in Divenishok, who was the person responsible for facing the authorities with respect to all Zionist activity in the *shtetl*. During our meetings with him we spoke only in Hebrew. He had always wanted to make *aliya*. May his memory be honored!

The HeKhaluts organization in 1925, at the farewell for the emigrants to Erets-Yisrael: Nathan Kaplan, Sholem Rosenblum, A. Itskovitsh, Moshe Mintz, Dov Zandman z"l, Khaya Garvey, David Leyb Berkovitsh, and others. The activity of HaShomer HaTsair and HeKhaluts continues in the town. Zelig Rogol also came to Israel and we hoped that after him others would come. Unfortunately they did not live to do so

We should also remember, in particular, the *Rav Hagoyen*[Tr. Note: Rabbinical scholar] reb Yosef Rudnik ZTs"L, that did much to further the Zionist activities. This was a gentle figure, loved by everyone in the *shtetl* because he was known as an honest *Dayen*[Tr. Note: rabbinical judge] who cared for the suffering. He was devoted to the settlement of the Land of Israel, and both religious and secular Jews valued him greatly. He excelled as a speaker and stirred hearts with his words. The night he passed away, I sat with my brother Tevye reciting *T'hilim* all night. His memory will always accompany us!

I must also mention the amateur drama group that played dramas such as: *Mekhires Yosef*,[Tr. Note: The Sale of Joseph] *Di Makhasheyfe*,[Tr. Note: The Witch] *Di*

Puste Kretshme,[Tr. Note: The Empty Inn] *Der Vilder Mentsh*,[Tr. Note: The Wild Man] *Der Batlen*,[Tr. Note: The Idler] and others. The role of the old woman was played by Bilke, Nosn's daughter, and Ester Rokhke z"l.

C

Thanks to the blessed work of *HaShomer HaTsair* and *HeKhaluts* many made *aliya* to the Land of Israel and were thereby saved from death during the years of the Second World War. It is worthwhile to mention the case where Yakov Bloch, Shloymke, and I - committee members of *HeKhaluts* - plucked a few young people from the Communist youth organization and sent them through *Hakhshara*.[Tr. Note: preparation for *aliya*] Today, they are with us here in Israel.

I remember what happened to Shloymke, the son of Itshe and Pesakh from Geranion.[Ed. Note: this is possibly a reference to Geranion Street in Divenishok] When we sent him for *Hakhshara*, his parents sat *shive*.[Tr. Note: seven day mourning period for the newly dead] They then approached me and Yakov Bloch, and wailed and pleaded that we shouldn't send their child to *shmad*...[Tr. Note: to convert away from Judaism] Shloymke rebelled, completed his *Hakhshara*, and finds himself today with us in Israel.

The anti-Semitism in Poland grew in strength from day to day, and also reached our *shtetl*. We became convinced that our place was not in that country and began to immerse ourselves in *aliya* issues. Yakov Bloch, Ester Rokhke, Nokhmke, Minke, and I left for the *Hakhshara* camps in Lomzhe and in Grodne, and then made *aliya* to the Land of Israel. Here, news reached us that the activities of the *HaShomer HaTsair* and *HeKhaluts* were continuing. Zelig Rogol also came to the Land of Israel and we were hoping that after him others would arrive. Unfortunately, they did not make it...

D

As a youngster, I was a devoted Zionist and, with the creation of *HaShomer HaTsair*, gave my all to the movement. The following were outstanding members of *HaShomer HaTsair*: Yakov Bloch, Shloyme Levine, Aharon Kaganovitsh, Liovke Namiot. They carried out the cultural and organizational activity of the movement together with us.

After a certain period of time there was a split in *HaShomer HaTsair*. Friend Pundak (now a brigadier in the Israeli army) came to Divenishok and took a group of *HaShomer HaTsair* members with him to his *HeKhaluts HaTsair*.[Tr. Note: Zionist Youth young pioneers] The difference between the two movements wasn't great, but there were certain ideological dissimilarities.

The *HaShomer HaTsair* emphasized educational and ideological activities, while the *HeKhaluts HaTsair* leaned towards more practical work.

We had not yet recuperated from this fragmentation when there appeared on the scene Moshe Lubetski (the son of Khayim-Dovid) - a student at the Faculty of Law at the Vilne University - and he founded a branch of *Betar*.[Tr. Note: Revisionist Zionist youth movement] Shmuel Sharon, Meir Yosef Itskovitsh, the Solodukhe brothers, and the sons of Pinkhas and of Betsalel Mintz joined him.

E

With the coming of *Betar*, interactions among the youth in the *shtetl* became aggravated. The *Betar'ists* would sometimes charge into the school and a fistfight would break out between the parents who had children in *HaShomer HaTsair* and those who had children in *Betar*.

Once, there was a meeting of *HaShomer HaTsair* with the participation of Shimon Vishnitski from the central leadership in Vilne. It's possible that the *Betar'ists* denounced us - suddenly policemen appeared and ordered everyone to disperse. One policeman arrested me, Orke Kaganovitsh, Liovke Namiot and Yakov Bloch. Later, Aryeh Leyb Rogol came to the police, calmed everyone down, and on his responsibility, those arrested were freed.

All organizations and institutions required official certification from the authorities in order to carry out their activities. This was particularly true concerning Jewish organizations. The *HaShomer HaTsair* had a lot of trouble getting its authorization because the Poles did not like the word 'socialism' and were in no hurry to hand over the certification. As long as the gatherings took place inside the school building, they were still kosher. However, if there needed to be a gathering in an open space outside, that became suspect as far as the police were concerned.

When Yakov Bloch and I went away for *Hakhshara*, the following were elected to run the *HaShomer HaTsair*: Khaykl Katsev, Moshe Levine, Tevye Blyakher, Sorke Levine, and Sore Teybke Hershovitsh. The cultural work was led by the teachers: Avraham Aloni, Sh. Dobkin, Betsalel Petukhovski, and others.

We would very often carry out a "Blossom Day" on the streets of the *shtetl*. The money that was gathered was marked for the *Keren Kayemes*. Such a "Blossom Day" began with a folks-gathering where the Zionist leadership of Divenishok would speak.

I made *aliya* in 1934 with the assistance of the *Hakhshara* group, but my contact with friends in Divenishok did not stop. I continued to follow what was happening in the *shtetl* with great interest, particularly concerning *HaShomer HaTsair*.

F

Oh, my tiny *shtetl*, cradle of my life, and home. The few that remain of you are like forlorn leaves of a beautiful tree. I recall the large marketplace and the surrounding houses with their beauty and charm. In the center, the tall white post with its boot-tree that shone like a golden crown. From all sides, the streets and passageways stretched, where old Jews, youth and children buzzed like in a beehive and blossomed like flowers.

During *Shabes*,[Tr. Note: the Sabbath] the daily burdens and noise disappeared, and in their place drifted in the *Ruakh Hakoydesh*.[Tr. Note: the Holy Spirit] The youth that left the *Beys-Medresh* (after services) took advantage of the day to go for a walk, meet in groups, romance, and wanted in one breath to understand all the problems of the world. This was a youth that strove to know and dreamt a dream of a better tomorrow.

Two Jewish women in Divenishok: Libe-Itteh (on the right) and Sheyne-Itteh, with a grandchild

If the *Shulhoyf* was a place for the children to frolic and wile away the time, for the youth it was a spiritual corner where discussions were held, and news of the *shtetl*, the Land of Israel, and other countries were talked about. Inside, in the *Beys-Medresh*, Hassidic youth argued over a *Blat Gemore*.

I remember the cold Autumn days in the still dark early mornings when over the shtetl there carried the call of the Shames[Tr. Note: like the *Gabay*, the Shame dealt with synagogue affairs] accompanied by a banging on the shutters: "Wake up, *Yidelekh*,[Tr. Note: Jews] to *Slikhes!*"[Tr. Note: a series of atonement supplications recited during each early morning of the period just before and during the Jewish High Holidays]

G

But all has vanished in great suffering, pain, oppression and shootings. No remains are left of the victims of the German massacres, other than the stones and silent walls that could not tell their tales. The trees in the woods, not far from the *shtetl* heard the final screams of agony of the unfortunate ones, but could not come to their aid. The leftover mass grave is the sole monument to the *Kdoyshim*.[Tr. Note: holy martyrs]

The helpless cries and wailing, as well as the pleading to God for mercy - were answered with contemptuous laughter and devilish sadism by the murderers.

We, the *Sharis Hapleyte*[Tr. Note: survivors] will forever remember the martyrs of Divenishok. They will never disappear from our memory. The recollection of all of you will be carried by us deep down in our hearts and will always accompany us.

Translator's Footnotes

1. "*Aliya*" - Literally, "to go up". In this context, to go up (i.e. immigrate) to the Land of Israel. Also means to go up to and bless the Torah and be blessed in return (during the reading of the Torah).

2. "*Linos Hatsedek* - Charitable aid was handled differently in each community, ranging from financial assistance, to physical care, to providing sleeping accommodation for the family of a patient or even for strangers in town.

3. "reb" - Used as a sign of respect, similar to "Mr./Dr.", but used only for the first name. For example, "Dr. Moyshe Vays", might be referred to as: "reb Moyshe Vays", "reb Moyshe", or "Dr. Vays" - but never as "reb Vays".

Zionist and Cultural Activity

Avraham Aloni

Translation by Yael Chaver

As principal of the Hebrew school of Divenishok, I had the chance to look at the town *pinkes*,[Tr. Note: Town record book] then kept by Mordkhe Kaplan. He came up to me one day and said, "Look at my *puchork*.[Tr. Note: probably 'manuscript', possibly a variant of *puchok* from Russian, which translates as 'bundle, packet'] Kaplan used to note, in his ornate script, all the events that took place in the town. On the same occasion he gave me the name of the person who managed the *pinkes* before him, but I don't remember that name.

Unfortunately, the *pinkes* was lost, and Mordechai Kaplan, too, passed away. In addition, a previous *pinkes* was lost, which contained notes on all the events in the town since its establishment. Thus, many things have been forgotten and there is no one to fish them out of the abyss of forgetfulness.

More than forty years have passed since then, but I will nevertheless try to write down some memories.

Avraham Aloni,[Ed. Note: first from right]*, Bruria z"l,*[Ed. Note: first from left] *and other teachers*

Testimony from the *Pinkes*

The *pinkes* contained information such as the following:

"The unmarried woman Feyge L. fell from the attic and lost her virginity. We, the leaders of the community, examined the matter and we testify that she lost her virginity. Signed...."

Another item written in the same style followed a great fire that broke out in the town in 1912: "A great fire broke out this year and consumed the entire town. All the residents were left naked and with no possessions. There were no fatalities, but there was great loss of property."

Another incident was noted in the *pinkes*: "A family with many children collected mushrooms in the forest, cooked and ate them. The entire family suffered severe stomach pains, and they all died after terrible suffering."

After I emigrated to Palestine, a representative of YIVO[1]

came to our town to write down the town's history. He was given access to the town's *pinkesim*[Tr. Note: Plural of *pinkes*] and other important historical material, but his work seems to have stopped part way through, because no monograph about Divenishok was ever published.

I deeply regret that these authentic sources about the town's history were lost, as they contained much material that would have illuminated important events of the town's founding and development—material that is now lost forever.

The Hebrew School

The Hebrew school was the center of the town's cultural life: all the Zionist offices, the library (which included Hebrew and Yiddish books), the free loan society, the art-lovers' club, etc. Theater rehearsals also took place in the school.

The school was comprised of seven grades, and almost all the town's children attended. A few studied at the *Pawszechna*,[Tr. Note: Polish public school] especially those who opposed Hebrew, such as Krizovski's daughters.

The Hebrew school had a high educational and pedagogical level, even higher than in the Polish school. I specialized in natural sciences, and learned how to catch snakes, lizards, and butterflies. I organized a wonderful natural-science room. One day I caught a snake on the school grounds; all the students and myself were extremely anxious until I caught it...

The Hebrew public school (Tarbut) in Divenishok (1934)

Planting

As the town was bare of all greenery or trees, I initiated a letter to the *gmina*[Tr. Note: Municipality] and asked for tree saplings. After my request was answered, I went out with the children to plant the trees in the town's streets, especially on the Vilne Street, where the school was located. We planted a decorative garden around the school and at the rabbi's house. The garden was amazing— really beautiful— and this school garden encouraged people to plant similar gardens near their homes. Malkaleh, Yakov Bloch's sister, wrote me later, when I was in Palestine, "We kiss the fence you built around the schoolyard."

Another initiative I began was medical examinations. I contacted Dr. Weisenfeld, the town doctor, who would come to the school every week to examine the children. Those who needed medications would get a discount at the only pharmacy, that of Aryeh Leyb Rogol. The childrens' standard of health thus improved.

As we were all relatively poor, we set up a kitchen, funded by our theatrical performances, help from America, from the bank, and from donations. The poor children received breakfast and lunch every day. The kitchen committee consisted of Sholem Yakov Rogol, Ben-Zion Schneider, S. Y. Shkolnik, and others.

Plays and Trips

We used to organize plays for every holiday and special day, and the teachers invested much effort in preparations. As I could play the violin, I set up music and singing, along with Yosele Levine (the builder's son) and his brother Leybkeh. The plays were performed in the school auditorium. Khaneleh Lipkunski, Tsvi Novoplanski and his sister, and Khane Engle's son were particularly good actors.

The harness maker Avraham Gliat z"l in his workshop in Divenishok (1931)

After Passover we went on trips to the towns in the area.[Tr. Note: Trips earlier in the year were not feasible because of the harsh winters] We visited Oszmiana, Traby, Voronova, Olshan, and even the village of Kalvitze, where Tsvi Ahuvi had a tar factory. We visited all the historical and public places, which the children were very curious about.

So that all the townspeople would appreciate the school— there were some Yiddish-lovers in the town who fought us— we held public examinations. We prepared questions about the curriculum, and an examination was held in each class, with parents present. The parents were allowed to ask questions and test the children. We were extremely successful; it was a cultural activity that parents and children looked forward to impatiently.

The star graduates went to Vilne to study, or to the yeshivas of Baranovich or Radin. Those who couldn't continue academic studies learned a trade.

I was the principal of the Hebrew school in Divenishok. Those were glorious days that provided great spiritual satisfaction. I enjoyed the polite, pleasant attitude of the townspeople toward the teachers, and the warm atmosphere and the longing for culture and science that permeated the town, as well as the children's love for the teachers and the school. These experiences have stayed with me all my life.

Cultural Activity

We mounted cultural activities, such as public "trials"[2] about Zionist and literary topics. The "trials" were held before an audience, and all the townspeople were invited by means of advertisements in the synagogue and on the street. The standard of these "trials" was high, and they attracted many people, who asked questions and received answers.

Teachers would give talks to young people about current events. One of the speakers was Rueben Kartshmer, leader of the town's Yiddishists[3]. Kartshmer was very intelligent and knowledgeable, extremely talented, and had an amazing memory. Though he spoke slowly, his talks were serious and very interesting.

HaShomer HaTsair would organize plays and cultural events.

I directed the plays, together with other teachers. Before each performance, the son of Attorney Dilinski would come from Olshan and "polish" the play. The performances were successful and attracted the young people of the town to the Zionist camp—and the influence of the Yiddishists declined. They started to hamper our activities.

Krizovski was a good person, but strongly opposed to Zionism. He was in charge of the Fire Brigade building. We often quarreled with him before performances because he wouldn't give us the keys. We had to talk to other people so that we would get the key.

Krizovzski once threatened to expel me from town. In order to make an impression, the Yiddishists brought members of the Vilna Yiddish Association for Yiddish Culture ("Vilbig") to town, in order to show us that they had their own youth group. It was useless. Zionist awareness was deeply embedded in the young people of Divenishok.

HaShomer HaTsair would hold meetings every Friday. Every meeting included a cultural or political talk by a teacher. The work of our teachers Dubkin and Eliohu Mazeh was especially outstanding.

The talk would be followed by a question-and-answer session, and the meeting ended with Zionist songs and an enthusiastic *hora* dance. Afterwards we would spend time in the forest.

Letter to Shmuel Dubkin from HaShomer HaTsair

20 September 1932[4]

HaShomer HaTsair Organization
In Poland, Dzirnishki[5] branch
From the leadership of the local branch

A. Y. Shmuel, "hazak!"[6]

Please forgive us for not having answered your last card. We shall not make excuses ...[7] There were reasons for not answering you: There is no news at the branch, everything is fine. Details about the home.[8] You may know about the death of Nathan Goldberg ...[9] the leadership of the Vilne region. When we heard of his death we gathered next to the home to hold a memorial meeting inside. We found the home is closed and an announcement is pasted to the wall prohibiting all organizations from entering. We looked at everything, opened the home, and started our branch meeting. As we were singing the "Tehezakna" anthem,[10] suddenly three wealthy people[11] — [...[12]], Ben-Zion[13], Nathan – came in, headed by Ben-Zion, who called out "Halt!" And it was precisely then that we vented our emotions in a burst of song. They saw that we weren't stopping, and [they] extinguished the fire and the candles. They also tore up some of our banners, and we were left in the dark. They started to throw us out of the home, and of course one of our "halutzim"[14] gave them 'money for the road' (a beating). The ending was that they handed over five of our brothers to the police: Aaron, Shrage, Yakov, Moyshe, Yisroel Shatsitnitski,[15] [...[16]], who had given the beating. We were summoned to the police to frighten us off from going to the home again. We wanted to get it into the newspapers but everything calmed down. Yet people were excited about it in the town.

The *Shulhoyf*

The *shulhoyf*[Tr. Note: synagogue courtyard] was the nerve center of the town. It was the location of both houses of study[17] (the old and the new), the school, the Rabbi's home, and the *Hekdesh*[Tr. Note: Community guest house] where poor out-of-towners would stay. The community guest house was run by Avreml the Shoemaker. At its back was an ice-house, which supplied ice to the sick.

The *shulhoyf* was always humming with Jews hurrying to pray and children going to school. There were also people who were on their way to the Rabbi to take care of their affairs, and that was where the youth organizations held their night-time meetings.

Translator's and Editor's Footnotes

1. Institute for Jewish Research, founded in Vilnius in 1925 and relocated to New York in 1940.

2. Such public debates concerning controversial historical figures and events were popular among Zionist youth groups at the time. They were couched in the form of a "trial," presenting pros and cons, culminating in a vote by the audience.

3. Yiddishism was a major European Jewish cultural and linguistic movement in the late 19th century, which considered that the status of Yiddish reflected the status of the Jewish people. Its proponents believed that only Yiddish could save Europe's Jews as a people from the onslaught of assimilation, and did not consider Zionism a viable option.

4. Tr. Note: year digits are ambiguous in the original text

5. Tr. Note: unclear as to whether this place name is a variant of Devenishok

6. Tr. Note: "*Hazak*" ("be strong") is an abbreviation of the full greeting and farewell phrase *hazak ve–ematz* ("be strong and courageous"), adopted by "HaShomer HaTsair" from Moses's parting words to Joshua (Deut. 31,7).

7. Tr. Note: two illegible words follow the word 'excuses'

8. Ed. Note: the word 'home' in this letter appears to refer to a meeting place or clubhouse

9. Tr. Note: one illegible word follows 'Goldberg'

10. Ed. Note: The opening word of a popular poem of 1894 by the major Hebrew poet Haim Nahman Bialik (1894). The poem, which praises the efforts of 19th–century proto–Zionist settlers, was set to music and adopted as the anthem of the Zionist labor movement.

11. Tr. Note: The Hebrew term here, "*ba'ale batim*" (pl. of *ba'al bayit*) literally means "owners of the house; but in this Eastern European Jewish context also meant, in a more general sense, "property owners" or just "wealthy people" who were anathema to left–wing ideologists. The absence of a definite article seems to indicate the latter meaning.

12. Tr. Note: first name in the list illegible

13. Ed. Note: probably Ben–Zion Schneider

14. Tr. Note: plural of Hebrew *HeKhaluts* (scout), adopted by Zionist youth movements to denote people intending to immigrate to Palestine.

15. Ed. Note: using evidence derived from the image on p425 these names are further identified as follows: Yakov Bloch and Moshe Mintz; Shraga is likely Shraga Blyakher, Aaron is still uncertain but could be Aaron Bloch or Aaron Krizovski.

16. Tr. Note: an illegible word in quotes, possibly nickname

17. "House of Study" is the English translation of "Bes-Medresh," where young men would spend hours studying, mainly the Talmud.

How I Remember You, Divenishok...

Khanan Lefkovitsh

Translation by Tina Lunson

It is possible that because I am not from Divenishok myself, I am more suited to write about this particular *shtetl*. It is not important whether I stem from Oshmene or Ivye. It is sufficient to mention that I visited Divenishok and spent a long time there, simply intoxicated by its beauty and the striking landscape.

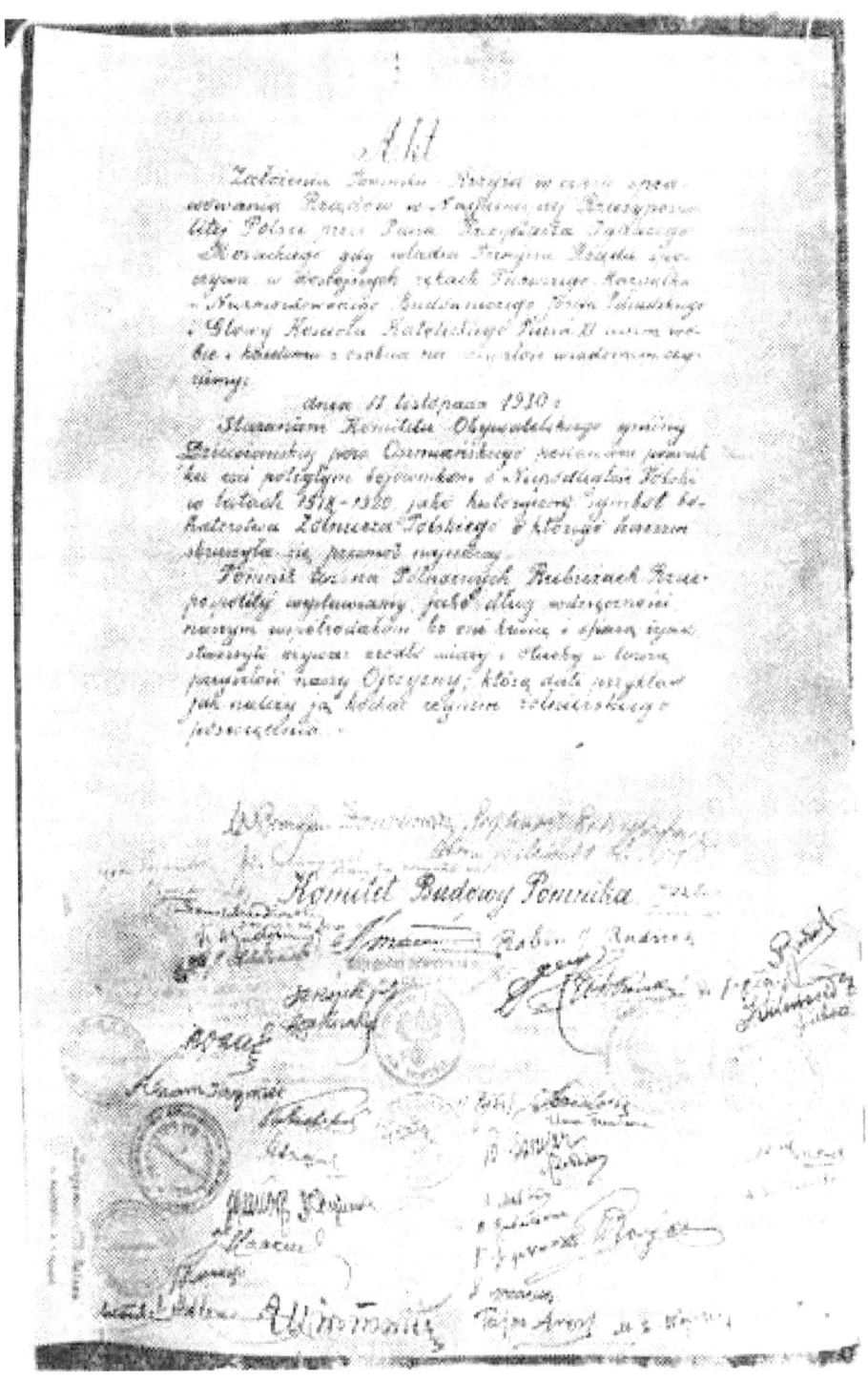

Document of the committee to build a monument for combatants who fell for the sake of an independent Poland, signed by Jewish and Polish council members.

I was also enchanted by the lovely Jewish young people with their various organizations, the Jewish school with the ebullient children. The beauty of the landscape was apparent: the pond, the meadows, the fields and beautiful forest where we used to meet to enjoy time together, singing, dancing and being happy.

One must not forget any of this, but speak of it, describe, and immortalize Jewish Divenishok.

*

How fine it would be if Zipe's grandchild could sometime read how her grandmother described the village, or how she went into the forest to gather black and red berries there, and then cook them on the wood-fired oven in a pot – and how from that, there came the best preserves which today one could not produce from the best electric stove. Especially delicious were the strawberry preserves, which served not only as a tasty dish but were the best medicine for the flu, serving to sweat out the illness and make you well.

How I remember you, Divenishok . . .

[Page 419 – Yiddish] [Page 28 – Hebrew]

Those Days Are Well Remembered

Yakov Bloch

Translation by Leybl Botwinik

The 25th of January 1975, marks the 40th year since I left my home and my mother z"l,[Tr. Note: Of blessed memory] brother and sisters, the family, friends who shared the school bench, the movement ("*HaShomer HaTsair*") and my birth *shtetl*[Tr. Note: Jewish town or village] Divenishok in the Vilne circle – and made Aliya to *erets yisroyl*.[Tr. Note: The Land of Israel] To this day, I remember those wonderful days of spending time with my parents, with the family, in a warm and snug home, mixed with worries. Even now, there is nostalgia of that tiny *shtetl* where not one Jew is left, just like in hundreds of *shtetlekh*[Tr. Note: Plural of *shtetl*] in Poland and Lithuania, which have been emptied of their Jewish inhabitants, after the majority had been slain by the Nazi murderers and their helpers during the years of the Second World War. Only a small handful of these Jews managed to escape from the murderers, and the majority of those survivors are to be found in Israel.

The Family

My mother Frieda, two sisters, Malka and Duba, and my younger brother Saul perished with the martyrs of the *shtetl*. My oldest brother Dov, who managed to run away to the Soviet Union, fell in battle against the Germans in the Moscow hinterlands.

My mother, Frieda *bas*[Tr. Note: Hebrew for 'daughter of'] Yitzhak Binyumen and Sarah Malke nee Bernshteyn, was born in Divenishok. My father Aaron z"l was born in Ivia. I was born during the years of the First World War, the second son in the family. My older brother, Dov, was born two years earlier. When the war broke out, my father was mobilized into the Russian army where he served without interruption for five years. My mother remained with her two sons.

The yoke of making a living and educating the children fell on her. Our fate was the same as for all the *shtetl* inhabitants. My mother ran a workshop for hat making and was also supported by our grandfather the smith, Yitzhak Binyumen, who worked mostly for the peasants and received potatoes, wheat, vegetables, and fruits for his work, which was enough to feed the family and help out the needy.

My Father – in German Custody

In the wretched days of the First World War, the economic situation of the Jews in the small *shtetlekh* turned for the worse. Many Jewish settlements in Eastern Europe were transformed into battlefields where the armies of Tsar Nikolas the Second and those of Kaiser Wilhelm and Franz Josef fought. The population was miserable, particularly in the small villages. Commerce and crafts ceased and it was not possible to get raw materials or even combustibles.

Refugees of the war wandered over the roads of Poland and Lithuania seeking safety and food. The Russian soldiers, in particular the Cossacks, broke into homes, robbed what was there, and if anyone tried to oppose them, they were heavily beaten.

The fronts moved eastward. At Tannenberg, in Eastern Prussia, the Tsarist army suffered a resounding defeat and Poland and Lithuania were occupied by the Austrian and German armies. The German occupation army was less severe in oppressing the Jewish population that understood German. As the battles moved further away, the restrictions on private trade remained. Communication was renewed and high quality German and Austrian construction appeared. The rapport with the powers-that-be was normalized.

Aaron and Freida Bloch z"l with their family. On the right:
Yakov Bloch as a boy scout (1930)

In the beginning, we had no news from our father. Then a rumor spread that he was alive and had been incarcerated by the Germans. This rumor was confirmed when we received a post-card through the Red Cross. He had been captured at Tannenberg where the army of General Samsonov met a brutal defeat. Afterward, a correspondence began between my mother in Divenishok and my father in the prisoner camp. On the letters to my father, my mother would draw my and my brother's hand outlines in order to show my father how much we had grown. We also sent him photos that were taken by the German military commander of Divenishok who expressed a particular affinity toward the children of a prisoner of war.

German "Decency"

Even though the Germans had a more-or-less good rapport with the *shtetl* Jews, they still mobilized the youth to dig trenches, inter-connecting channels, and bridges. Those who had cows were required to provide milk quotas.

During the period of the German occupation, almost no social or cultural activity was carried out because there were few youths in the *shtetl* and it was also cut off from the cultural center at Vilne. The Germans used to organize performances of their wind orchestra in the market place, or show films.

The situation in the *shtetl* became particularly difficult in 1917, after the Germans stopped their distribution of wheat to the inhabitants and hunger let itself be felt in every house. Various illnesses also wreaked havoc in the *shtetl*, predominantly stomach typhus.

After the October revolution in Russia in 1917, and the upheaval in Germany in 1918, skirmishes began again between the Red Army and the Germans, who retreated in great panic, and the *shtetl* passed back and forth between them. Later, there were battles between the Red Army and the Polish military. In the end, Divenishok was taken over by the Polish Military that was led by General Haller.

His first task was – to bully the Jews. A great Fear again befell the *shtetl*, and no one knew what the morrow would bring. At that time a youth watch was organized whose task was to maintain order and prevent robbery and pogroms. Little by little, things began to quiet down.

At the end of 1919, my father returned home from the war and prison. I was about 4 years old then, and my brother, 6 years old, when he appeared at the entrance of our house, accompanied by 3 other soldiers, who, together with him had lived through the war and imprisonment. Mother almost didn't recognize Father after all that he had gone through. We, the children, behaved coldly and with reservation towards him. He showered us with a lot of love and presents and we soon began to accustom ourselves to him. A few days later, after a rest, his friends left our home to return to their own families.

During the period of 1923-1929, our sister Malka, our brother Saul, and our sister Duba were born. They all perished together with our mother, at the hands of the German murderers. My older brother, Dov, as mentioned earlier, fell in battle in the Moscow hinterlands.

Restoring our Family Life

Father then began rebuilding the family, as well as the workshop. He also became involved in the social and cultural life of the *shtetl* and helped found the cooperative bank, the school, and the first kindergarten. Together with Tzvi Krisovski and some others, he organized a drama circle and a library with Yiddish, Hebrew, Polish, and Russian books.

In those days it was not easy to convince the Jews of Divenishok to alter their old lifestyle of sending the children to learn in *kheyder*,[Tr. Note: Religious school for children beginning at a very early age], where the *melamdim*[Tr. Note: Religious, male, teachers] ruled. Only after a great deal of initiative and clarification did the parents' committee succeed in renting a house that would serve as a school.

The teacher Ingulski was selected as administrator. He was stern and pedantic and threw fear into the children and demanded that they show him respect.

The bridge over the Gavya River

In my memory is deeply etched the *melamed* Leib-Aryeh, who taught for many years, even before the First World War, and later ran a *kheyder mesukn*[Tr. Note: Traditional children's school, but with a slant towards more enlightened learning] where *khumesh, gemore* and *psukim*[Tr. Note: Standard Jewish religious texts] were taught. On more than one occasion he would strike the slower learning children with his stick. However, we learned a lot from him. I remember that both Leib-Aryeh and Ingulski also wore "Jewish hats".[Tr. Note: Probably the simple "Kashket" style worn daily by Khasidim of Eastern Europe] Ingulski was always dressed elegantly, as opposed to Leib-Aryeh who wore a long *kapote*[Tr. Note: Black robe of the Khasidim] with *arbe kanfes*[Tr. Note: A white undershirt (sometimes worn over a shirt) whose four corners were tied with sashes called *tsitses*], a white beard, and lived in solitude with his wife. He was a *boki*[Tr. Note: Religious authority] on *tanakh*[Tr. Note: The Bible] and knew exactly where each *posek*[Tr. Note: Quoted text from the Bible] could be found. During the school year 1922-1923 there were between 100-120 students in 6 classes.

Political-Social Awakening

From that past, reminiscences pop up of the experiences of the various youth organizations in the *shtetl* – and I ask myself: How did it start?

Nowadays when we talk of a political movement we know its ideological platforms as well as the names of its leaders. In a *shtetl* like ours it was difficult to arrive at clear definitions. Such figures as Herzl, Jabotinski, Yitzhak Gruenbaum, Ben Gurion, Berl Katzenelson and others, lived inside the awareness of the youth. The opponents were not always capable of formulating a position against whom or what they were fighting – was it against a political notion or against a specific personality?

However, one institution was clear for everyone: The *keren kayemes leyisroyl (kkl)*,[Tr. Note: Jewish National Fund (JNF)] whose goal everyone knew: to gather *groshns*[Tr. Note: Very small coins, e.g. pennies] for festivities, get-togethers, and various events; emptying the *kkl* alms boxes that were to be found in the majority of the Jewish homes in the *shtetl*. And all this – in order to liberate the terrain of the Homeland.

Young people who learned in the "*tarbut-shul*",[Tr. Note: Hebrew language Zionist oriented school] in the Polish ("Povshechni") school, and elsewhere, all belonged to one or another youth-organization.

The "*HaShomer HaTsair*"

The *ken*[Tr. Note: Hebrew for "nest" – similar to a Boy Scout "den"] of the youth organization "*HaShomer HaTsair*" was established in 1929 thanks to the teacher Betsalel Petukhovski from Vilne, who administered the "*tarbut-shul*" in Divenishok. I was in the 7th grade at the time. He called together all the pupils in class, as well as graduates – some of whom were already learning a trade in the *shtetl* or in Vilne. The movement was already carrying out its activities in the entire Vilne circle. Instructors were invited from the regional management and after they became acquainted with our *ken*, the appropriate advisory literature was sent. This movement had at its disposal every method and possibility to attract the youth: uniforms, flags, scouting, and the duty to self-development via *kibbutz*,[Tr. Note: The *kibbutz* was a model for collective social living and working] the *hakhshore* (preparation).

Of the initial founders of the *ken*, we must with warm recognition recall: my brother Dov Bloch, Liovke Namiot, Ester Rokhl Shkolnik, Minke Mintz, Nekhemke Katsev, Yekusiyel Zhizhemski (these are no longer among the living) – and may they live long: Shraga Blyakher (in Israel), Nahum Levine and Sh. Levine (United States), and the writer of these words. All were devoted to the goals of formation and of instructional effort. We were united by the passion for the movement and each one contributed with whatever they were able to.

Some youths from HaShomer HaTsair in Divenishok (1932) Standing, from the right: Nahum Levine (now in the United States), Moshe Mintz (Petah-Tiqva), and the teacher S. Dubkin (Israel). Seated: Yakov Bloch (Tel-Aviv), A. Aloni z"l (Tel-Aviv), and Aryeh-Lyubka (died in the Holocaust)

The *ken* was composed of 150 young men and women, and was the center of social activity for the youth. Their goal was to realize the Zionist-Socialist ideal, and life in the *shtetl* was considered a "corridor" to the future life in the Land of Israel. If not for this yearning on the part of the youth for the land of their fore-fathers, to escape the reality of the *golus*[Tr. Note: 2000 years of wandering in the Diaspora without a homeland] with its dark companion-events, our joie-de-vivre would have been shattered. The energetic youth infected everyone in the *shtetl*: the parents, the teachers, and even the Rabbi, Reb Yoysef Rudnik, *zts"l*.[Tr. Note: of Blessed and saintly memory]

Regional convention of the HaShomer HaTsair organizations of Divenishok, Olshan, Vishneva, Traby, and Smorgon, summer of 1933

The *Lag Ba'Omer* trip,[Tr. Note: Lag Ba'Omer: Holiday falling on the 33rd day after Passover eve] the street manifestations on the 3rd of May (a Polish national holiday), and the uniforms and flags of the *ken*, were transformed into an impressive experience, and everyone, adherents as well as opponents, felt fatherly warmth and respect for the group.

The ken effervesced with social and cultural activity. The majority of the members and their *madrikhim*[Tr. Note: Guides or mentors] expanded their education, bought and read books with great enthusiasm and understanding. The younger members also became infected by this atmosphere, and they also yearned for knowledge and scholarship.

The movement implanted in everyone's hearts a feeling of responsibility and attachment to a collective, gave a purpose and scope in life, and produced moments of joy and elation. We, the few who managed to make Aliya, remember the spiritual and physical compensation that the *ken* – our second home –provided us with.

A group of Jewish female students from the Polish State School (Pawszechna) playing volleyball (1929)

The *ken* in Divenishok remained in close contact with parallel organizations in the surrounding *shtetlekh*. We went on trips, went boating on the waters, and participated in Scout activities. Our members participated in all the regional get-togethers in the Vilne circle, and carried out the activities that were organized by the main leadership in Warsaw.

During the Summer of 1933, some of the members of the *ken*, together with the leadership, left for *hakhshore*, and in the years 1934 and 1935 succeeded in making Aliya to the Land of Israel. Those that stayed behind in the *shtetl* continued the work, and in this way, a second muster took over the leadership, although with less enthusiasm than their forerunners.

Their names need to be recalled: Yekusiel Zhizhemski z"l, graduate of the "Tarbut" seminar in Vilne, that led the *ken* in 1936; Minka Rogol, Yehudis and Sime-Etke Levine, two sisters, also graduates from the same seminar; Tevye Blyakher, z"l, who perished as a Partisan, and Malka Bloch, z"l.

The "*Betar*" Ken

The first founders of "*Betar*"[Tr. Note: A right-wing leaning Zionist youth movement] in the *shtetl* actually came from the "*HaShomer HaTsair*", such as Meir Itskovitsh and others. As far as I can remember, one of the initiators was Yisroyl Berkovitsh from the nearby *shtetl* Voronova. He was the Commander of "*Betar*" in that *shtetl*. While visiting Divenishok in 1933, he swayed some of the youth to the ideals believed in by Ze'ev Jabotinski – of a Land of Israel on both sides of the Jordan River.

Jewish coachmen from Divenishok with coaches loaded with merchandise on route to Vilna (1932)

The *ken* in our *shtetl* was composed of several tens of members and sympathizers. The *ken* was internally consolidated around the Revisionist ideology. They used to organize get-togethers and circles where concerns in the movement were discussed, as well as Jewish history and current issues concerning Zionism. Amongst the activists, the most prominent were: M. Itskovitsh, Schneider (Sharon), Solodukhe Aaron and Y. Kotler (both now in the United States), Lubetski-Lutski, and others.

[Page 429]

On Communal Life

Lolik Sutskever
Translation by Tina Lunson

Divenishok belonged to the category of very small towns. The Jewish population was very poor; there were no rich people in Divenishok. Anyone with property was considered a person of great wealth.

Occupations

The Jews made their livelihoods from the following sources:

The shops were all in the market square and served the shtetl population and the surrounding villages. Once a week, on Thursday, there was a market day when all the peasants from the surrounding villages gathered, and that provided the livelihood for the whole week.

Among the Divenishok Jews there were many tailors, shoemakers, tinsmiths and blacksmiths in poor workshops of which 90% consisted of the artisans alone, without any helpers. These artisans also drew their livings from the market day, because they prepared ready-made tools to sell. The village peddlers worked very hard. They were on the road the whole week, not acknowledging the difference between day and night, but always going from one village to another trying to earn a little bread. But on Shabes they came home to rest their bones. They were very poor. If his horse failed a peddler, he did not have any means to buy another. They had to collect money to buy a horse.

The whole area consisted of poor peasants engaged in a backwards agriculture, in sandy soil. Thus making a living was very hard for the town Jews. Nevertheless the town carried on a very intensive social life.

Der Shulhoyf [Tr. Note: The shul courtyard]

The shul and the study houses were located in the shul courtyard.

In Divenishok there was a Hebrew school in which 100% of the Jewish children studied even though there was a Polish school where one could study for free. One had to pay tuition to go to the Hebrew school, but all the Jews did so in order to send their children to the Hebrew school, which was located in the new building constructed with great difficulty on the place of the old shul and with special permission of the rabbis. American *landslayt*[Tr. Note: natives of the town] had a special part in building the school.

In the two shuls - a new one and an old one - prayers took place three times a day. People also studied there, a chapter of the *Mishne*, the book *Ein Yaakov* [ethical and inspirational teachings of the Talmud by Rov Yaacov ibn Chaviv, 15th century], and others like it. The *rov*'s house was in the shul courtyard, alog with the *rov*'s court chamber, a bathhouse and a *mikve*.

Communal Life

The following organizations, institutions and societies were active in the town:

The burial society, the Jewish *folksbank*, a poorhouse, societies for visiting the sick and to provide for poor brides, a library, private donation fund, fire fighters, a *Keren Kayemes* group, a department of the Vilne VILBIG,[Tr. Note: Vilner Yidishe Bildung Gezelshaft/Vilna Jewish Educational Society organized in Vilna in 1924] a fund to provision the poor for Passover, a free loan society, and *Beta"r* and *HaShomer HaTsair* groups.

The burial society was well organized. The distinguished Jews in town participated in it, because they considered it the biggest *mitsve*. Older Jews presented themselves voluntarily to dig a grave, even in the rain, snow, frost or blizzard. The burial society kept its own budget. When a rich person died the family was charged a high price for burial so that a poor person could be provided with burial shrouds for free.

Every year the 29th of Kislev was the day for the burial society. None of the members worked on that day, they fasted and recited psalms. At night there was a feast fit for a king, fried goose and duck and whisky and wine flowed like water.

*

The *folksbank* was a cooperative society, founded just before the First World War. The bank gave out loans, took deposits, administered promissory note collections, dealt with foreign currency and securities. It was the only institution that had a paid administrator.

*

When someone in the town was sick for a long time and the family members became weary of caring for the patient, a man or woman was sent to sit by the patient's bed all night in order to relieve the household family. As far as I recall, no one ever refused a call to come and sit with a patient overnight.

The members of the "hospital" for the poor did everything voluntarily. The group was headed by Gad Levine (son of Gute Itshe).

No sick fund existed in the town. A private doctor used to charge 5 zlotys for a visit, for rich or for poor. The poor had no possibility of paying for a visit. The society for visiting the sick had an agreement with the doctor that he should treat the poor people and they paid him for the necessary things. The society also lent out a rubber bottle to apply ice to the head, and cupping glasses, and thermometers. In very severe cases the society contributed to send the patient to Vilne.

The visiting society was headed by Chaim Eliashkovitsh, along with several volunteer youths, like Binyamin Dubinski, Khaykl Katsev, Gad Shkolnik and others. The visiting society needed a lot of money. Part of the expenses were covered by relief from America, part by donations, and also from the so-called "Friday Actions". Each Friday two youths went around from house to house with a charity box and collected money. The visiting society was the only institution in town that not only took, but also gave. Almost every Jew in town had to call on the society at some time.

The provision for poor brides was one of the quietest and most modest organizations, providing the means for poor girls to celebrate a wedding, or to buy a dress for the bride. It is hard to determine who was involved with this.

*

The Yiddish public library was located in a rented space (in later years, at Avrom Meir Lubetski's in Subotnik Street). The library possessed more than 6,000 books in Yiddish and Hebrew--- the greatest classics. A special purchasing commission had assembled the lists and acquired new books on the recommendations of experts. One of the experts was the manager of Shimon Funk's bookstore in Vilne. That is also where we bought the majority of the books.

The library brought light into the grey life of the shtetl. Generations of youths were drawn to the library, youth who had no education but achieved a good deal of learning thanks to the library and the reading room. From time to time presentations were given there on various topics in culture, literature, medicine, politics and science. Periodical publications were also received there.

Every year we had to send a list of the books to the central authorities. In 1935 a letter arrived from the ministry of education, in which it was stated that they could not understand that such a serious and rich library contained no Polish books. So they sent us, at no charge, a beginning set of 200 of the best Polish classics -believing that we would then buy more Polish books. And that is what happened: we bought Polish books each year too and thanks to that we had a few dozen readers from among the Christian *intelligentsia*.

Up to the year 1930, the library was for everyone. But that year the Zionists demanded more Hebrew books. The dispute lasted until 1933. Every member of the library had voting rights. The Yiddishists had the majority in the general meeting that year, and the library went over to their hands. Fayvke Blyakher broke out in a hysterical wail in his great vexation.

*

Library administration and board (1933)

In Divenishok there was a benevolent organization that quietly carried loans for impoverished householders who were ashamed to hold out their hands. There were such householders in town who had fallen on hard times and who would rather die from hunger than ask for support. The private donation society helped those people in secret.

*

The firefighter command consisted of volunteer Jews, although the chairman was the local priest. Members of the administration were Nathan Itskovitsh, Ben-Zion Schneider, Dovid-Khaim Lubetski, and others. The firefighter command was sustained by the "chimney tax". Other than that their budget was overseen by the community board, in order to keep the management of the firefighter's out of Jewish hands.

The head of the firefighter command was Zev Lubetski ('Velvke', son of Dovid Khaim). I was also among the leaders of the firefighters, did exercises with the firefighters and went through the firefighting courses in order to raise the level of the command.

The firefighters also created a wind orchestra which was the pride of the youth. The Poles were not pleased that a Jewish band played for all the Polish national holidays and parades. They could not rest until they had wrested the firefighter command from Jewish hands.

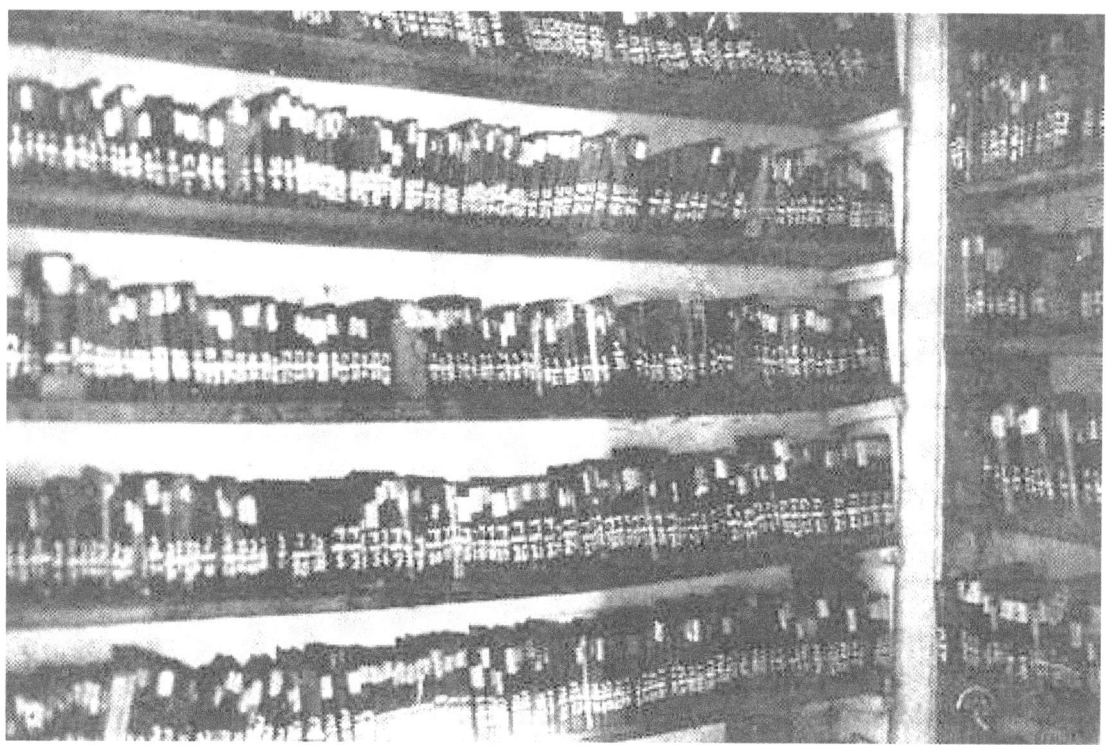

Part of the library bookshelves (1933)

VILBIG

At the beginning of the 1930s when the crisis in *Erets Yisroel* was coming to a head, and many of the youths who had gone there came back to Divenishok, the influence of communism became stronger in the town. The VILBIG was created then, and it also took over the library. VILBIG carried out two tiers of cultural activities. The Polish government "kept an eye on" them. And one morning we received an announcement from the sheriff rescinding our legitimization. Still the VILBIG remained active until the outbreak of the war in September 1939.

Temporary Help

Every year, 'Divenishok Relief in America' sent money for all the institutions in the town. A certain amount of that was specified for the Passover Fund. But the main fund for that purpose was gathered right there in the town itself. Every Jew was taxed for the Passover Fund so that poor Jews would be able to observe the Passover holiday properly.

The free loan society was established with both American monies and membership dues. The loan society was very important for poor Jews. I cannot imagine how they could have existed without that institution. Any Jew could get a loan of 500 zlotys, which at that time was a lot of money. As soon as a Jew had repaid one loan, he could receive another.

One of the managing members of the free loan society fund, Avraham Krivitski, used to borrow money from his friends and every Friday afternoon distribute a free loan to the poor peddlers, as an addition to the loans that they received. Krivitski was also a regular Torah reader at the new study house, and a distinguished householder in the town.

Beta"r summer camp, led by M.Y. Itskovitsh (1935)

Moshe Lubetski ('Moshele', son of Dovid Khaim), a student in Vilne, created the *Beta"r* in Divenishok. Respected householders helped them. Their meetings were held in the school.

HaShomer HaTsair and *Beta"r*

The *HaShomer HaTsair* in town was very strong; the majority of the Zionist youth belonged to it - idealists who did not only talk but took action. Many of them went to Zionist preparatory camps and emigrated to *Erets Yisroel*.

It must be mentioned that the town rabbi, *Reb* Yosef Rudnik, gave the *HaShomer HaTsair* his full support, which strengthened the position of the organization.

Keren-Kayemet Activity

Although not all Zionist organizations co-existed in peace, at least the *Keren-Kayemes l'Yisroel* were all united. In almost every Jewish home hung a blue and white charity box for the *KKL*. Each week youths from the Zionist organizations emptied the boxes. The head of the *KKL* was Aryeh Leyb Rogol.

*

With this short, general overview of the social life in town, I want also to immortalize the social workers, the idealists, and activists who encouraged the cultural and political activity among the Jewish population.

[Page 437]

The "Bees" and "Vilbig" Organizations

Khaye-Rivke Krizovski

Translation by Tina Lunson

The "Bees" in Divenishok was founded in 1930. Officially it was considered a scout organization, but in fact is was a leftist youth group that educated its members in a communistic spirit. To the Polish authorities it was described as a non-political scout organization since otherwise the "Bees" would have been shut down.

While the "Bees" was for younger children, the older youth belonged to the VILBIG,[Tr. Note: *Vilner bildung gezelshaft* (Vilna education society)] which had the same political positions as the "Bees". Both the Vilbig and the Bees were founded by the Yiddishists, or as they were called in Vilne, the *folkists*. Among the leaders of the *folkists* was Dr. Tsemekh Shabad and his son-in-law Max Weinreich, president of the YIVO[Tr. Note: *yiddisher visenshaftlekher institut* (Yiddish scientific institute)] in Vilne.

The heads of the Vilbig were Hirshel Krizovski, Moshe Stul (today in Minsk) and others. And the head of the "Bees" was Yisroel Kherson. He also directed the cultural activities of the "Bees".

Vilbig, the "Bees", and the folks-library were located in the home of Avrom Meir Lubetski, on Subotnik Street. The Vilbig meetings were held there, as well as the activities of the "Bees". That was the cultural center of the Yiddishist circle in our town.

The "Bees" were conducted like all scout groups, organizing summer and winter camps. I was an active member in the group and participated intensively in all the activities.

Once we arranged a winter camp in the village of Renkatsinski.[1] The poet Avrom Sutskever and his wife visited us there. His wife had an accident there and broke her leg.

It is worth mentioning that at the camp we enjoyed the moral and intellectual support of a group of writers known as the *Yung Vilne* [young Vilne].

I was 16 years old at the time. We spent two weeks at the camp. We slept on the ground, cooked and roasted potatoes, went on outings and sledding.

In the summer of 1932 there was a summer camp of "Bees" groups from Vilne, Oshmene and Divenishok.

In 1933, in Oshmene, there was a "swarming" together of "Bees" organizations from the Vilne region (there are photographs of both the Divenishok camp and the Oshmene "swarm" in the book *Yerushlayim d'Lite*[Tr. Note: Jerusalem of Lithuania] by Leyzer Ran.

Despite the fact that the Polish authorities looked askance at the activities of the Vilbig and the "Bees", we involved at large number of young people and carried out multi-branched activity in the town. We fought for Yiddish and for Yiddish-Jewish education.

After the Soviets occupied our town in 1939, the Vilbig and the "Bees" were liquidated and several of our leading members were taken in by the Communist Party, among them my father, who was nominated as chairman of the town council.

The "Bees" members were taken in by the KomSoMol.[Tr. Note: *Kommunisticheskii Soyuz Molodyozhi*, Communist youth group] The activities of all remaining youth groups was forbidden, among them of course the activities of YIVO and of our Yiddish cultural institutions.

Editor's Footnote

1. The specific location of this village has not yet been determined as of the date of this translation in 2013.

[Page 439]

The Torah Reading Was Stopped

Eliahu Itskovitsh

Translation by Leybl Botwinik

Summer, a *shabes*[Tr. Note: Sabbath, the Jewish day of rest] morning in the month of May. The dew still lays on the fields that smell of fresh mown hay. It's quiet in the *shtetl*. The cattle have gone into the fields.

The populace has gone *davenen*.[Tr. Note: To pray] The first *minyan*[1] has finished, and the second is about to start. Everyone, even those from the first *minyan*, however, remains. No one goes home. There is a feeling that something is about to happen. In the meantime the people begin to pray. They now reach *kriyes toyre*.[Tr. Note: reading from the Torah scroll] Suddenly everything is quiet. Mikhl the *shamesh*[Tr. Note: Manager of synagogue affairs] bangs on the pulpit and says "*nu, nu*"[2]! No one moves from his place.

The *rov*[Tr. Note: Rabbi] looks towards the *bale-batim*,[3] those at the eastern wall. What is going on here? The mood is stressful. The reading has stopped. Munyc Kherson, the regular *bal-tfile*[Tr. Note: Person who leads the prayer service] stands leisurely, but wipes the perspiration from his brow, and waits for a command.

Suddenly, from the other side of the heating oven there is a murmur, mumbled words:

– We will not allow them to carry away... cut off a livelihood ... gradually, one another ... *kupkes* ... *kupkes*...[Ed. Note: The meaning of kupkes has not yet been discovered]

Then louder shouting, voices crying out:

– *Raboysay, raboysay*...[Tr. Note: Gentlemen, gentlemen]

Moshe Kalmen, breathless, sweaty, with foam on his lips, his hands trembling, cries out:

– *Raboysay*, this must be the work of a *sheygets*...[Tr. Note: A male gentile (female is *shikse*);. used here in a derogatory manner meaning a "troublemaker"] people should know what is happening here, no ... it will not be ... transporting meat from the *shtetl*, the *katsovim*[Tr. Note: Butchers] are gathering money, they should be uprooted!

Moshe Kalmen doesn't finish and the noise grows louder. The doors open wider and the "*alte gvardye*"[Tr. Note: "Old guard" or veterans] of the old *beys hamedresh*[Tr. Note: Synagogue or house of learning] come in.

The battle grows stronger. Hands are raised and slaps are thrown. When the *rov* sees that things have gone bad, he gets really angry: *raboysay*, a *khilel-koydesh*,[Tr. Note: Blasphemy] the *toyre* has been lying on the table an hour long. How can one suspend the *kriye*,[Tr. Note: Reading] let us call an *aseyfe!*[Tr. Note: Meeting] – He calls out in his weak voice.

Others look at the large wall clock. Young men do not dare speak a word. The gathered become rambunctious, crying out. Things become suspenseful.

Suddenly a voice is heard, getting louder and louder: "*veyehi binsoya hooroyn*"...[Tr. Note: Prayer said while the Torah ark is being opened] and tens of voices continue "*veyefutsu oyvekho*"[Tr. Note: From the same Torah ark opening prayer, "and your enemies shall be driven away..."] and they begin to read.

However, who it was that stopped the reading is still unknown.

One thing is well known, however – and it was talked about all week – more than one *cholnt*[Tr. Note: Traditional *shabes* meat-potato-and-bean fare left on a burner overnight to avoid cooking on the Sabbath] was burnt because of what went on that *shabes*.

Translator's Fotonotes

1. Minyen – A gathering of 10 Jewish males (who are at least 13 years old) for purposes of praying and other rituals. Here: A specific gathering for the morning prayer services. Normally, if there is more than one minyen in the morning, the first one is very early, possibly even starting at daybreak.

2. Nu – There are many uses and translations for this word. Often the meaning is dependent on the expressed mood and intonation of the speaker. In this case, it may be a query: "Come on already, what are you waiting for?", or "What's up?", or "What gives?", or even an admonition: "Be still/quiet".

3. Bale-batim [s. bale-bos] – Usually refers to owners or 'bosses'. In this case, the well-to-do (or leading figures) of the community. They normally sit up front in the first rows, with a select few sitting towards

the congregation. Praying is normally done facing eastwards (towards Jerusalem). When required by the service they turn around and face eastward.

[Page 440]

Jewish Livelihoods in Divenishok

Translation by Tina Lunson

From the book *On the Ruins of Wars and Unrest,* Vilne, April 1931.

Report of the Labor Committee "YEKOPO"[Tr. Note: Acronym for an organization dedicated to assisting the victims of World War I, active in Eastern Europe.] For Vilne and the Provinces, in the years 1919 – 1931, under the editorship of Moyshe Shalit, published in 1931.

Divenishok (Oshmene region):

520 families, 140 of them Jewish. Chief occupation – shop-keeping, village merchandising, craftsmen in workshops and second-hand goods. In the town – 60 Jewish shops; two Polish cooperatives for groceries, haberdashery, leather, footwear. These had the support of the community. Goods from the Polish cooperative were often brought to the train station in Benakani (21 kilometers away).[Ed. Note: The purpose of bringing goods to the Benakani train station is unclear; this may have been an efficient way to distribute goods more widely throughout the region.]

The Jewish shop-keepers brought goods by wagon from Vilne (63 kilometers away). Shop-keeping was in a poor stead because of limited transport and also because of the surplus of shops. There was a market [open air] once a week.

Twenty to twenty-five families lived from village merchandising. In town, five Jewish workshops operated, producing inexpensive men's clothing and coats and fur coats for men and women. They employed 40 workers, men and women. They earned between 20 and 30 zlotys a week. The goods were sent to the surrounding villages of Vishneva, Trok, Olshan, Volozhin, Oshmene and so on.

In the town itself there were two Christian shoe specialists. Except for one carpenter there were no Jewish construction workers in the town.

Five Jewish families in town owned their own land, each two acres. They worked their lands for their own accounts, using for the most part hired labor. Besides the land work, the landowners also had other employment.

Daniel Schneider "packs up" hens and eggs to sell them in Vilne

Among the Jews there were also some *"luft-mentshn"*.[Tr. Note: people without livelihood] They lived from the fairs.[1] There were also Jews who dealt in boar bristles, earned a living as matchmakers, or who got money for pasturing animals, raising calves, and as farmers.

On *Tish B'av* people played *berelakh*.[2] A fascination for soccer developed. There was a children's teacher, and also a teacher for even younger children, and the *kheyder*[Tr. Note: elementary school] lasted from early in the morning until late in the evening.

Activities of the "Yekopo" in 1917 – 1918

In 1918 those who had fled into Russia returned. Vilne was occupied by the Polish military.

Divenishok is mentioned among the towns that undertook to help the suffering war victims. Divenishok sent a delegate, among 83 delegates from 74 villages, to a conference in the Vilne region.

The help was expressed in the creation of cooperatives, orphanages, schools, hospitals, aid committees on the community councils, help from

ORT,³ and from OZE.⁴ The representative from the "Joint"⁴ was Isadore Hirshfeld.

The delegate from Divenishok to the first regional conference of "Yekopo" in Vilne in 1919 was Ira-Leyb Rogal. The second regional conference was in Vilne, the 5th, 6th and 7th of December 1921. The delegate from Divenishok was the Rov Yisroel Movshovitsh. The Rov was also the delegate to the third regional conference, the 9th and 10th of March, 1924.

Translator's Fotonotes

1. Fairs in Eastern Europe were large regional markets where goods were bought and sold wholesale. At the fairs (the big ones were usually held at fixed locations) there were lots of temporary jobs to be had. People with no real jobs could be employed peddling small wares, helping with customer services, working as porters, and so on.

2. This word literally means little bears, but is also the diminutive for the name Berl. To my knowledge it is a game that included the phrase "Berele, Berele, kum aroys!"

3. The name ORT is an acronym for the Russian words Obshestvo Remeslenofo zemledelcheskofo Truda, meaning the Society for Trades and Agricultural Labour, founded in 1880 in Tsarist Russia.

4. An organization devoted to the promotion of health, hygiene, and childcare among Jews. Founded on August 7, 1912 in Saint Petersburg as the Society for the Protection of the Health of the Jewish Population, (Obshchcstvo okhraneniia Zdorov'ia Evreiskogo naseleniia; and later, Obschestvo Zdravookhraneniia Evreev).

5. This refers to the American Jewish Joint Distribution Committee, Inc. (JDC), a non-political humanitarian aid organization headquartered in New York that is an overseas arm of the North American Jewish community. Committed to the rescue of Jews in danger, relief of those in distress, renewal of Jewish community life, and support of Israel.

[Page 443]

2. Destruction and Bravery

[Page 445]

*Memorial plaque for the martyrs of Divenishok,
in the Vilne immigrant house in Tel-Aviv*

[Page 446]

Left: *Pinkhes Lipkunski, partisan in the Bielski brigade*
Right: *The partisan Sarah Hinde Movshovitsh*

Left: *The partisan Sholem Ber Bernshteyn, now in Israel*
Right: *The partisan Khonen Lefkovitsh, born in Traby*

Khaim Danoyker, from a village near Divenishok

[Page 447]

All That Remains is a Name

Solomon Levine

Translation by Leybl Botwinik

Somewhere far on the Lithuanian plane, surrounded by green woods, fields, and crystal–clear streams, a little town existed not too long ago – a Jewish *shtetele* [Tr. Note: shtetl is a village and *shtetele* is a smaller village. The diminutive is used here to emphasize endearment] teeming with life.

For generation upon generation, our fathers and mothers, brothers and sisters, and our dear families lived out their lives in that *shtetele*.

For all of us, that birthplace and place of our roots was precious.

However, with the destruction of one third of our people at the bloody hands of the Amalekite–Hitler folk[Tr. Note: The Amalekites were the biblical arch–enemy of the Jewish Nation] our *shtetele* was annihilated and uprooted.

What remains is only a name, "D–I–V–E–N–I–SH–O–K", carved into this gravestone[Ed. Note: This book] as a memorial for future generations.

How I Remember You, Divenishok...

As related by Shoel ben Natl Kaplan

Translation by Tina Lunson

> From the book *Khurbn Vilne* [The Destruction of Vilne], Edited by Szmerke Kaczerginski, New York, 1947 Published by the United Vilne Relief Committee in New York TSYKO Book Printing

Voronova

According to an order from Hanveg, the Area Commissariat in Lida, Jews were driven into Voronova from the surrounding towns of Divenishok, Benakani, Great Soletchnik, Yashny, Kalelishok[1]. Altogether there were 3,000 Jews in the town.

On the 9th of May 1942, the town was encircled by a three-part chain of SS, police, and local residents. We were encircled for three days. Jews were not even forbidden from going outdoors, because there was constant shooting.[Ed. Note: No official curfew was declared].

For the Jews it was already clear what was meant. Some had tried to run away, but many were shot along the way. There were cases where the guards took money from Jews to let them through, but then as soon as the guards took the money they would shoot the payers anyway.

On the 10th of May, in the evening, some Jews organized themselves to run away. But that evening Staff Officer Vintsus, from the Lida Area Commissariat, came specifically to announce to the *Judenrat* that in the morning there would be a document check for all Jews, who would have to go orderly out to the market square, because in Radin there had been misunderstandings this same day with the Jews there who had not behaved.[Ed. Note (Kaczerginski): they had made a rebellion]

In the morning, at five o'clock, before dawn, a troop of drunken Lithuanian SS arrived in Voronova and they drove all the Jews into the market square. In the square, the Jews had to lie down with their heads on the ground.

Survivors from Divenishok at the memorial in Voronova for the victims of the Nazi murders

At the crossroads that led to Lida, by the railroad tracks and Herman Lane, Hanveg was stationed along with Vintsus and other high officers from the area commissariat as well as a representative of the SD (security detail). An order was given to the Jews to lie down according to family. After that they made individual groups stand up to be taken to a sorting place at the crossroads. Each family was led to Vintsus, who decided their fate. Vintsus simply asked the man of the family about his vocational ability and accordingly made the selection. He did not generally ask about larger families. He sorted people into three groups: "straight, left and right."

"Straight" meant to the mass grave by the right highway to Lida, a kilometer and a half from town, near Balerovski's forest. There, were the prepared pits, four meters deep and fifty meters long, which some peasants had dug-up during the time the Jews had been encircled. Those who went there had to pass through two columns of peasants who beat them horribly with rakes and iron bars.

"Left" meant that if Jews who had been sentenced "straight" began to run away or mount a rebellion, Jews on the "left" would be shot, like hostages.

"Right" - the smallest number were sorted here. Small families and such specialists for whom the Germans might have had a strong need.

I said that I was a miller and was sent with my wife and child to the left, quickly separating me from my parents and my sister Sore.

After the sorting we heard a lot of shooting and, so that the voices of the unfortunate could not be heard in the town, the Germans started up the motor of a truck, the noise drowning out the cries.

The shooting happened like this: the victims were told to undress completely, to nakedness. Only the elderly could stay in their underwear (the Germans were disgusted to look at them). The naked had to go into the grave in groups, lie face down head-to-foot and foot-to-head and as so they were shot. On top of that group, another group was ordered to lie, and so on. This is how they shot 1,800 Jews - men, women and children.

Those who refused to go were rushed with pitch forks by town-dwellers who stabbed the victims through the body and slid them into the pit. They also stabbed children with the pitch forks and pitched them into the pit.

Those left on the right and left were counted. There were 840 Jews. We were taken to the market square, and set down on our knees. Town officials wrote the names of each of us on a list.

Eventually many wagons came from the mass grave with the clothing of those who had been murdered. Some of us even saw the clothing of our own relatives. I recognized my father's jacket.

Hanveg and Vintsus, with his retinue, arrived. Vintsus delivered a speech to us: "You Jews are guilty for all the wars and so you must be exterminated. The Jewish people are like a snake that will poisoned by its own poison. The rest of you will live for a while and will be sent to work in Lida."

[Page 450]

In a few days those remaining were sent to the Lida ghetto, where they were killed during the liquidation of the ghetto in October 1943.

Related by Shoel ben Natl Kaplan (Voronova), Vilne, August 31, 1944

Translator's Footnote

1. As of this writing (09/14/2011), this town is unknown to the JewishGen Communities Database. The town name has been transliterated to English from the original text and thus may be an inaccurate translation of the original name.

The Amputee of Divenishok
Meir Yosef Itskovitsh

Ed. Note: This article appears in both Hebrew and Yiddish in the original Yizkor Book; only the Yiddish version has been translated and published in this book and may be found at page 203 of this book.

[Page 454]

A Dream
Meir-Yosef Itskovitsh
Translation by Tina Lunson

I dreamed a dream
that peace finally came!
No more fear, no trembling,
Messiah's time – *ve-gar ze'ev im keves*[1]
as written in the holy Torah.
When human no longer treats human like animal.
Life full of joy and goodness, literally a *mekhaye*.[2]

I had the desire, as can happen to anyone,
to see my hometown Divenishok again:
Fathers, mothers, sister and brother –
to meet with them again.
I traveled through forests,
I raced over fields,
dragging on day and night by train,
and only saw faces of Stefan and Ivan.[3]

Arriving in Vilne, the Litvak Jerusalem,
leaping through streets, one, a second, a third,
seeking a Freydl, a Sheyndl, a Frume, an Itteh,
a Khiene-Reyzl, a Khaye-Shite,
stuck in my state of longing and pleading –
For finding a Jew maybe is possible –
just once in a blue moon.

For nothing I looked in the Benakani station
for the gossipers Meyshe-Aron and Berele-Zalmen
but I could only find
… the mug of Mr. Pole.

On to Divenishok, my town,
where my crib and my little bed stood.
I visited the lock, full of water, not dry,
the frogs observing me with oversized eyes.
They sat in the muddy water,
croaked wearily and slow,
croak, croak, croak –
what are you doing here, Mr. Jew?!
An old frog gave a rumble
and everything grew quite still.
She said to her youngsters:
"Don't talk so much, hold your tongue!
Give this Jew respect and honor,
because his parents raised my parents,
here, in this lock..."

From the lock I walked to Vilne Street,
the houses old and new.
I looked askance to the right and trembled
my glance should not meet an exchange
while my heart was full with pain, and bitter.
Looking left, to the *shul* courtyard –
from the ruins I felt a dead shiver...

I began to go further – and at the *sheykhet's*[4] wooden house
I stood still.
Recalling memories of childhood years,
summer in the fields, after the rye had been cut,
we stole into his orchard, on the trees
grew little pears, small and fine,
juicy, delicious and sweet,
so eating them was never a shame.
After the *sheykhet* – Eltshik the tinsmith,
and Eli the maid, somewhat higher.
Across from the Polish food store,
where I am reminded – breaking my heart.
Who could manage to think of it all?
The terrible tumult of our dear brothers?
The misfortune in town, the great breach,
when a wire pierced the eye of Eltshik the tinsmith?

And I go on further, I run.
Here is Sore-Hinde's and Ben-Zion's yard.
In the front a shop with iron goods and linens,
then the big construction over the wall

which served the non-Jews as a restaurant.
Ach, overlooked, forgot to take a look,
as I went by Feygele and Yankl Druck's apartment.

On Subotniki Street I stand still
because I can go no further.
Unwillingly I am drawn there,
perhaps to find a token of *"Vilbig"* or the *"Bees"*.[5]
I search at Leybke Olkenitski's restaurant,
the locale of *"Betar"*.
I search and search – and stand still
like an idiot, a fool – totally alone.
No memories remain, no memory,
only an ache, a sickness, in my heart.

In the market square I stand mute
taking it in, round and round.
I search for the house of Meyshe the tinsmith,
I seek his *shabes* sanctifying silver goblet.
I want to see his sabbath table,
set with delicious gefilte fish,
lots of out-of-towners and local guests.
But they no more drink, no longer eat.
There's no more blessing…
just the singular surprise
that on Meyshe's chair
sits an Ivan full of joy.

I search further in the market
the short, narrow sidewalk,
and seek there my heart's desire,
my friends Sheynke the rabbi's, Bilke the beggar's.
I turn here and there,
craving just a glance of them.
I talk, I call out, but don't hear an answer.

* * *

As I said, I dreamed a dream,
I saw a vision – that is how peace came.
I stood a long time there in one place,
awaiting a response – but never heard a word.

Footnotes

1. "And the wolf shall dwell with the lamb" (Isaiah: 11:6) [Ed.]

2. A real joy, a pleasure, something to be greatly enjoyed. [Ed.]

3. 'Stefan' and 'Ivan' are used here as generic names for Lithuanians and Russians. [Ed.]

4. Jewish ritual slaughterer of comestible animals. [Tr.]

5. Vilbig and Bees were both Yiddishist, socialist-leaning educational and scout groups for young people. The Bees was for the younger children, the older youth belonged to the Vilbig [*Vilner bildung gezelshaft* (Vilna education society)]. Both the Vilbig and the Bees were founded by the Yiddishists, or as they were called in Vilne, the *folkists*, and both espoused the same political positions. [Ed.]

The many branched Olkenitski family, destroyed by the Nazi murderers. A survivor, Leyb Olkenitski of Ramat-Gan (third from the right, seated), provided the photograph, which was taken in 1935

[Page 457]

3. Figures

[Page 459]

The Rabbi and Great Scholar Yosef Rudnik,
May His Memory Be For a Blessing

*(Dos Vort, Orthodox Weekly,
Vilne, May 25, 1933 - 1 Sivan 5293)*

Translation by Yael Chaver

Last Friday, after a long and serious illness, the Divenishok rabbi, our Rabbi, Great Scholar, and Teacher, died at the age of 58.[1]

The deceased was one of the most prominent rabbis in the Vilne area and active in community affairs. He took an energetic, active role in all the rabbinic and other Orthodox conferences in Vilne during the recent postwar years. He was also a delegate to many different central Orthodox institutions in our region.

As Rabbi, he was very beloved by the entire population, regardless of conviction and political tendency. To his congregation, he was truly like a dear father, interested in each individual, and concerned with the needs and requirements of each person, without exception. He was greatly loved in all the surrounding communities, which also benefited from his activities and kindness.

His funeral was attended by, in addition to the whole town [Divenishok], large numbers of people from surrounding towns: all the important people from Bilitza (Bielica), where he previously served as rabbi, came led by their current rabbi, Rabbi Shabtai Fein (long may he live). A large group of prominent residents also came from Benakani, where the deceased had founded a *mikveh*.[Tr. Note: Ritual bathhouse]. Other participants included rabbis from the vicinity, such as Rabbi Rabinovitsh from Lida, Rabbi Rozovski from Eshishuk, Rabbi Perlman from Ivia, Rabbi Shmuelzon from Oshmene, both rabbis from Voronova, Rabbi Sakharov from Traby, Rabbi Khadash from Olshan, the supervisor of the Radin yeshiva, Rabbi Eliezer Kaplan, the *Maggid*[Tr. Note: Preacher] of Oshmene Rabbi Yehuda Leyb Farfel, and others.

Rabbi Yosef Shub, long may he live, participated in the funeral as a representative of the Council of Yeshivas, in which the deceased was a devoted activist.

The deceased was eulogized by all the above-mentioned rabbis, as well as by his son, Rabbi Avrom Rudnik. In moving terms, they described the enormity of the loss, the Rabbi's moral stature, qualities, and good deeds.

By decision of the entire town, his stepson Rabbi Aaron Tayts, long may he live, was appointed as his substitute.

With the death of the Divenishok rabbi, our region lost one of its best and noblest rabbinical personalities. His absence will be sorely missed by all those who came into contact with him.

Chaval al de'avdin.[2] May his soul be bound up in eternal life.

Translator's Footnotes

1. These titles, presented in acronym form in the original text, are commonly used when referring to a rabbi.

2. A traditional Aramaic phrase that concludes the eulogy of a great person or leader.

Aaron-Leyb Baron

Translation by Yael Chaver

Born in 1886 in Kalelishok (a village near Divenishok). His first poems were published by A. Reyzen in *Dos Yidishe Vort*, 1904, and later in *Veker - a Folk-newspaper*. In 1906 he emigrated to America, where, in addition to lyrical poetry published in *Forverts* and *Tsukunft*, he also wrote humorous poems under the pseudonym *Der Litvisher Baron*.[Tr. Note: The Lithuanian Baron] A selection of his poems titled *Libe un Benkshaft* (Love and Longing), published by H. Sheifer, 32 pages) appeared in New York in 1910. He later abandoned literature altogether.

> Sources: Sh. Niger, *Fraynd*, 1910; Y. S., "Magical Experiments," *Literatur* collection, I; *Dos Naye Lebn*, 1910, V; *Der Shtral* 1910, 13; Basin, *Antologye*, 11.

[Page 460]

Reb Moshe Ben-Zion Khasman,
May His Memory Be For a Blessing

(The first *chalutz* from Divenishok, who walked for three years to reach *Eretz-Yisro'el*.)[1]

Translation by Yael Chaver

Moshe Ben Zion Khasman

I knew Reb Moshe Koval since my earliest childhood. Those were the first days of Tel-Aviv. In its center stood the white structure of the *Gymnasia*, like the biblical Tabernacle in the desert.[2] There were only a few small houses around the building, with a sea of sand stretching behind them. A small black dot was visible on the sand, far from the houses. This was Reb Moshe's smithy, from which loud clangs of the hammer on the anvil were heard.

This was the only forge in the small town of Tel-Aviv, and Reb Moshe was therefore overwhelmed with work. Balustrades and supports for terraces, balconies, and stairs, as well as fences and gates, were all made of iron, and Reb Moshe was their maker.

He worked quickly and energetically. Those who saw him outside the smithy recounted that he was always in a hurry and had no time even to eat his meals in peace. He would eat an entire loaf of bread, from end to end, at each meal. On hot days, when he stood at the fire and hammered the glowing iron, he would drink up a dozen bottles of *gazoz*.[3]

In the middle of his work he would stop to talk to us children. He loved children very much. He too, had children, but they were not with him in *Eretz Yisro'el*. He had come by himself and lived a lonely life. He did not even establish a home. He told us that in the old country he had left behind two small daughters and was going to bring them over when the time was right. Meanwhile, the First World War broke out, which put an end to all his dreams and hopes.

When the Turks entered the war, all Russian citizens had to leave the country, if they had not taken Turkish citizenship. Reb Moshe, like tens of thousands of other Jews, did not leave the country. He, along with a small number of Jews, became a Turkish citizen and stayed in the country, exposed to all the horrors of war, such as hunger, disease, homelessness, expulsions, and enslavement to a decaying regime.

***

Reb Moshe had immigrated to *Eretz-Yisro'el* to greet the Messiah. He firmly believed that the Messiah would come soon, and would first arrive in *Eretz Yisro'el*. The topic of conversation with anyone he met was the imminent arrival of the Messiah. He carried around legends that spoke of the Messiah. He claimed that the Turkish exile ("Exile of Ishmael"[4]) would be the last, and would be followed by Redemption.

I remember a conversation that he had with us children while working. He recounted:

"Today I visited Mr. Blushteyn, who is building two two-story houses on Lilienblum St. He needs an iron fence around the stairs. I told him how much it would cost. 'But make it well,' he tells me. He clenched his fist and waved it in the air: 'It has to be strong, for eternity!'

'And what did you say?' I asked.

'It will outlive the coming of Messiah,' I answered."

Reb Moshe was short, with a thick black beard. He was solidly built, with strong muscles. He would let us kids feel his muscles, and we were astonished by them. We watched him bend thick iron bars with his hands and eagerly listened to his stories about his fights and wrestling matches with other men. In our minds he was a real hero and we had true admiration and respect for him.

When the Turks joined the war on the side of the Germans, Reb Moshe was drafted into the Turkish army to serve the Sultan. He did not want that. "He won't live so long, the Turk, as to have me serve in his army," he would say. He actually hid and evaded the draft in every possible way.

He considered the alliance of Germany and Turkey to be like the partnership of Edom and Ishmael.[5] According to the *midrash* on the Redemption, this was a clear sign that redemption through the Messiah was near.[6] Wherever Jews would gather and anxiously discuss the evolving situation, he would be very joyful and would even dance and sing the merry song: *kaleh se'ir ve-chotno*.[7]

But things kept getting worse. After the NILI[8] affair and the death of Sarah Aaronsohn, the Turkish authorities in *Eretz-Yisro'el* started chasing after spies - and Reb Moshe was caught. They placed him together with dozens of army deserters and marched them to Damascus where they were imprisoned under the charge of spying for the enemy.

I don't know exactly how long they spent in prison, but about a year after he had been caught, I was standing in an olive orchard in Zichron Ya'akov, when I heard someone calling my name. It was Reb Moshe-broken, tired, in sad condition.

I didn't ask him whether he had escaped from prison - and what did it matter? I saw before me a sick man with a swollen face. He told me that more than half the people who had been marched to Damascus had died. He had stayed alive by a miracle. He had also walked the whole way back from Damascus.

This happened a few days before the British marched into *Eretz-Yisro'el*. I tried to cheer him up. "Feel my muscle," he said, and stretched out his arm. When I had done as he asked, he said, "You see, now it's a rag," and heaved a sigh. He wasn't mourning his lost health, only his ruined strength.

***

Who has greater faith, the strong man or the weak man? I believe it is the weaker, because as he has no more strength, faith is his only support. That is what happened to Reb Moshe. After he returned from the Damascus prison, he never regained his former strength. True, he took up his post in the smithy again and bought new tools, but the might of Reb Moshe Ben-Zion Khasman -- known as Moshe the Blacksmith - never returned. Those days were gone.

Years later, I met him in the alleys of Jerusalem, dressed in a long *kapote* and with long *peyes*.[9] He no longer worked, but his religious conviction had greatly strengthened. "We must repent and bring the Messiah," he told me.

He did not like the British, but never lost faith in the Messiah. He was sure that Messiah would come any day, and waited for him...

His last deed was buying land on high ground in Bene-Berak, not far from the main road to Petach Tikva.[10] He built a small house there. Later, he gave the house and land to an institution that supported him in his last days.

With the death of Reb Moshe, one of those dear pioneering Jews who set out ahead of the community passed into eternity; these were Jews who had a Messiah and had an eternity. Their faith, devotion, and readiness for sacrifice gave rise to the great accomplishment that bears the proud name of the State of Israel.

May the memory of Reb Moshe be honored!

Translator's Footnotes

1. The biblical *chalutz* is the term for a Zionist pioneer. *Eretz-Yisro'el* (the Land of Israel) is used here in the traditional Jewish sense of the land given by God to the Israelites.

2. Refers to the "Herzliya Hebrew High School" (founded 1905), the first modern secondary school of the Zionist community in then-Palestine.

3. A fruit-flavored fizzy soft drink.

4. In the Zohar, the fifth and final exile.

5. In the Bible, peoples who were the two archetypal enemies of Israel, hearkening back to the stories of the Patriarchs.

6. *Midrash Ge'ulah*, in the 7th-century apocalyptic *Book of Zerubavel*

7. This is a phrase from a religious song (*piyyut*) that is part of the *selichot* (penitential prayers). The phrase expresses a wish that God should annihilate Sei'r -a biblical term for Edom - and his father-in-law Ishmael, traditional enemies of Israel The phrase is corrupted here, possibly due to various errors and/or dialectal variations.

8. NILI is an acronym for a secret group of Palestinian Jews who spied for the British during the First World War, and were caught by the Turkish authorities in September 1917. One of its principal members, Sarah Aaronsohn, committed suicide while undergoing torture.

9. *Kapote* (a long coat) and peyes (sidelocks) are hallmarks of a religiously observant Jewish man.

10. Bene-Berak is an ultra-orthodox town; Petach Tikva is one of the first proto-Zionist settlements in the country. Both are suburbs of Tel Aviv today.

[Page 463]

Krizovski, Aaron Yakov— of blessed memory

Translation by Yael Chaver

Born in Divenishok, May 20, 1891. Taught himself Yiddish. Started writing poems at age 12. Started publishing his poems and stories in Vilne and Varshe. Emigrated to America in 1913, where he published work in various newspapers and journals. Published a book comprised of a collection of poems, entitled "My Sincere Songs," and other collections of poetry. (According to Avrom Reyzen's *Lexicon of Yiddish Literature*)[1]

Below, we present two poems by the deceased poet, poems that express his close relationship with Divenishok.

Translator's Footnote

1. The "Lexicon" was compiled by Zalmen Reyzen, not Avrom.

Two Poems by Aaron Yakov Krizovski
Translation by Yael Chaver

At the Divenishok Bridge

Reflected in the pond: the sky, the forest, and the world around,
The washerwoman stands, upside–down, with laundry–beater and red knees.
The water burns – and burns – but water cannot douse the flame!
Nor does it look to see whether the sun cares not or disapproves.

Soft, like a cat, the sky snuggles up under the bridge,
And sails onward with gold and amber ships, blending into green,
And rushes to find absurdity, asking the mind,
"What does this beater beat in the forest? What does the forest beat back?"

And swallows preen, take wing, on and off the water,
And snack on quickly snacking water spiders, fly–haters,
That snack on beauty marks kissed by the wind on the waters –
The sun sets in red, the sky blanches paler.

Etrog[1] aroma ascends, heating the blood –
From the land of the sun, nearby, the tamarind blooms —

Back Home

From the world's river willows – songs of hanging harps,
With Mendele's mare – a cartful of poems – with Fishke the Lame,
From grandpa's mill, along the "Devenishski" river willows
Splendid shtetl, river, from under a rock–hung mountain spring.

To the wounded mountains of Judea, twenty centuries of weeping,
Mother's bosom embracing you, motherland:
"If I forget thee–may my tongue cleave to my palate,
Scattered over an alien world – St. Vitus dance " –
Imprisoned, separated.

With Holy Land soil – rolling through the ground,
From Christ's pretend–"forgiveness" cheek – through blood libels,
From "killing God" to "pound–of–flesh
heart" – through crypts – mysterious…

Through the prophet's call, to the dance of Miriam's hopeful tambourine,
On stingy mountains – through branded crosses and the cross's scorn,
From "fleshpot," "melting pot", through flame –
Homeward…

(From *Sonnets*, published in New York, 1953)

Translator's Footnote

1. The *etrog* (Yiddish pronunciation esreg) is the fragrant citron, one of the "four species" used in the Succot festival ritual.

[Page 464]

The Poet Aaron Krizovski

Menukha Peykhova (Krizovski)

Translation by Yael Chaver

My uncle, the poet Aaron Krizovski, was the third child in the family of my grandfather Kalman Shepsel[1] the *melamed*.[Tr. Note: teacher] My father Hirshl was the fifth child.

As a young child, Aaron distinguished himself as a good student, and exhibited a talent for poetry. However, the home was very poor and his father did not pay attention to his poetic ability. In addition, the small-town atmosphere of Divenishok did not help him develop his talent. When he would recite his poems to girls, they mocked him: "Look at this guy, he speaks only of the sun and the moon, and only in rhymes." The young folk didn't understand him, his father was oblivious to his talents and inclinations, and instead sent him to learn tailoring in Vilne.

Aaron eventually became acquainted with a girl from Soletchnik and fell in love with her. When he left for America, he promised that he would bring her over. He was true to his word, and brought her to America. But when she got to New York, she left him and married someone else.

In America, my uncle Aaron was a tailor, and in his free time wrote poems. He published several books. In his first book, *My Sincere Songs*, he dedicates many poems to his birthplace, Divenishok. He portrays the young people of the shtetl in "Felix's Barn," the poem's title referring to the location of the town's makeshift playhouse. The volume is dedicated to his former girlfriend from Soletchnik.

In America, he lived alone for many years. In 1937 he formed a relationship with a younger woman. She robbed him of everything and left. This shattered him. He became ill, underwent several operations, and died in New York.

Contact with him was scant. For long periods of time, he did not write to my father, but when "the muse came alive" a 20-page letter would arrive.

All his life he was a leftist, but during his final years his nationalist feelings strengthened and he prepared to go to Israel.

My uncle was born luckless. He worked hard for every crumb of bread. In literature, as well, he was unlucky. His work made no strong impression and did not achieve its rightful position in Yiddish poetry.

He published all his books at his own expense and distributed them himself in America and other countries.

Editor's Footnotes

1. The difference in names here may reflect the official naming policy that was adopted by government decree in the 19th century, with Krizovski being the officially adopted name and Shepsel belonging to the pre-decree period.

[Page 465]

Our Poet A. Y. Krizovski

Binyamin Dubinski

Translation by Yael Chaver

Four of A. Y. Krizovski's poetry collections were published during his lifetime: *My Sincere Songs* (1919), *Blood and Tears*[Tr. Note: or *Blood and Wine*] (1933), *Daily Bread* (1946), and *Sonnets* (1953).

In addition, as the poet writes in his "Foreword" to *Sonnets*, two more volumes of sonnets were ready for publication, as well as five volumes of ballads, essays, and poems. His unpublished works probably included even more material awaiting publication.

Before all else, I wish to root out the mistake in Reyzen's *Lexicon* stating that Krizovski was born in Voronova. He was born in Divenishok, brought up and educated there. That is where his parents and ancestors had lived for generations.

All his writing is rich in biographical details about his family, Jews and non-Jews, the river, "Felix's Barn," the forest, the great fire, the shtetl. These supply us with a clear picture of the strong bonds linking the poet with his home town. Voronova is never mentioned in his books.

Already as a child he would carry around notes on which his poems were written and recite them to his friends. The young folks laughed at the "rhymester," but he paid no attention to those who mocked him and continued his own way.

In his teens he left his poverty-stricken home in the shtetl and went to seek good fortune[2] in Vilne, where he started to learn tailoring. He went to America before the First World War and lived there for the rest of his life. In America, too, he made a living by tailoring, writing poetry in his free time.

He published his first collection of poems in 1919. It includes several biographical motifs, such as the memory of his grandfather blessing the Hanukah candles, and a description of his mother lighting the Sabbath candles with a tear trembling on her pale face.

In 1908 a conflagration broke out in Divenishok which consumed the entire shtetl and devastated the residents, both materially and spiritually. The poet depicts the great fire in powerful strokes: the entire shtetl is in ruins, confused people wander around among the chimney stumps mourning their misfortune. Reb Leyb Balbirishker went insane with grief and his wife hanged herself. The synagogue was consumed along with its ten Torah scrolls, as was "Felix's Barn."

His second collection, *Blood and Tears*,[Tr. Note: See note 3] of 1933, contains no biographical motifs. America was then overwhelmed by a great crisis. Social slogans appeared among the Jewish working masses. The Civil War in Spain and the general conditions had a powerful effect on our left-leaning poet, and so the book is characterized by social concerns.

The Second World War and the great tragedy that the Hitlerian murderers brought upon our people caused turmoil in the poet's style of thinking. It aroused within him longings for his lost family and the murdered shtetl.

His third book, *Daily Bread* (published in 1946), includes many poems dedicated to his family and the shtetl, as well as descriptions of the beautiful natural surroundings of Divenishok.

In his poem "My Lineage Merits the Crown" he describes his poverty-stricken childhood. His father, Kalmen Shepsel the *melamed*, had to provide for thirteen children. At age 4, the poet himself had to watch over children in order to earn a piece of bread. He also had to go out to the fields and forests to collect bones and sell them to Leyb the grocer, who would pay "a fortune" for them: a small herring and a bit of brine. The brine was no less important than the small herring, which by itself could not suffice for thirteen hungry mouths. In the brine, though, many could dip their potatoes and gulp them down with pleasure...

Loneliness and the poverty at home influenced the political leanings of the children. All were affiliated with the political left wing and played an active role in revolutionary organizations that fought the Czar. His oldest brother was exiled to a prison camp. His sister was arrested for participating in a prohibited First of May demonstration. According to the rules of Czarist Russia at the time she was sentenced to receive thirty lashings in the prison courtyard.

His father was a *melamed* of very young children, but not extremely observant. He would read *Hatzfira*, and get through the *Shemoneh-Esreh* prayer early.[3] In the study-house he would arm himself with letters and verses in order to prove to the rabbi that "the Messiah is just about to come." Kalmen Shepsel was a scholar, as his son wrote, who was "steeped in learning."

Motifs of the Holocaust and mass murder appear in the first chapter of the book *Daily Bread*, where they comprise 25 pages. The first poem is titled "Comfort Ye My People."[4] The poet's imagination is set in Europe, where God's fiery curses coil around, snake-like, and the chain treads of tanks roll over towns and *shtetls*. Varshe is burning - and the ghetto walls collapse.

The poet pours forth his wrath over the world, which has abandoned us and flung us into the claws of the Nazi beast. The world looks on and is silent, our blood gushes like water, while the world's conscience naps...

Although the poet lives in New York, his soul and being are with his brothers in his home town, and he walks in spirit with them on their last road towards death: "I go with you, with your wives and children / uphill to the shtetl, with shovels to dig the graves..."

The terrible tragedy awakened the nationalist spark in him, and he wrote the poem "Forward With Torah Scrolls": "Forward with our famous light-heavy weapons / fear not, with *tallis* in hand / and a tear in our eye."

Just as the poet begins to address the Holocaust and mass murder motifs in "Comfort Ye My Nation," he ends his treatment of these motifs with two poetic elegies: "My People" and "I Come To You, My People" - a blending of heartfelt nationalistic motifs. "With a small-great people, with your Sinai-Torah light, you will light up the world, and I turn towards you with my whole being, in full prophet-light."...

The poet's views changed drastically after the mass murder of Europe's Jews. He prepared to go to Israel. In the following letter to his nieces Menukha and Khaye Rifke in Russia,[5] dated in Brooklyn, Saturday, April 19, 1958, he writes, among other things, "As I have already informed you, my assets are in a fund created by my literary admirers, for them to publish my literary legacy. But if I settle in Israel, send all the assets to me there."

A. Y. Krizovski was a multifaceted poet. He left, as I have mentioned, a significant legacy, which has not appeared in print. His poems and articles are also scattered in various periodic publications.

Translator's Footnotes

1. The Yiddish orthography in the original text is unvoweled; the second word of the title could therefore be either 'wine' or 'tears'.

2. The Yiddish word "glik" can mean both "luck" and "happiness."

3. *Hatzfira* was the first Hebrew newspaper in Poland, founded 1862, which became sympathetic towards Zionism in the 1890s. *Shemoneh-Esreh* is a key portion of the daily morning prayers.

4. The title is a quote from Isaiah: 40, 1.

5. By this time, Russia had become the USSR.

[Page 468]

Shtetelekh[1]

Shloyme Kazjimirovski

Translation by Leybl Botwinik

My father was from Bobroisk
Always lived in commotion.
My mother from a *shtetl* Grodne
He took to the city.
There was a *shtetl* "Shok"[2]
I had family there
Three aunts, kosher and frum[3]
A dove of an uncle, like a flower.

A Rivke in Kalelishok
Also Libe in Subotnishok,
A Leye in Lipnishok
And Hirshel in Divenishok.

As a child I didn't have it easy
Just trouble from my wet-nurse, a fear!
A wish for happiness and laughter

I can remember to this day.
A difficult childhood I had
Wanting to meet up with a 'nash-brat,'[4]
Meeting up with family, going to friends
I would find sun and shine.

Into the small shtetl Kalelishok
A drop into Lipnishok
A hop into Subotnishok,
And didn't sidestep Divenishok.

(From the book "Shadow and Light",
Songs and Poems, Published by
"Nay Lebn", Tel Aviv, 1973)

Translator's Footnotes

1. *Shtot* is city, *shtetl* is town, *shtetele* is small town (*shtetelekh* - plural)

2. There is no known *shtetl* by the name of "Shok". There are, however, numerous towns and villages that have '-shok' as the suffix in the town name. This seems to be a play on that: He had family in the 'one' town of Shok, when in fact he lists 4 different town names, implying that all of Lite was one big *shtetl*. "Shok", in Yiddish also means 60 – which also implies 'many', while at the same time being a single unit – like 'Dozen', or 'Score' There were therefore shoks of 'Shoks' in the region at that time.

3. Religiously observant

4. Buddy

One Cannot Forget Them

Sore-Teybke and Nahum Levine

Translation by Leybl Botwinik

It has been 35 years already since I left the *shtetl*, family, and friends. It's difficult to remember it all. Our Divenishok is remembered like in a dream.

One cannot forget fathers and mothers, brothers and sisters, and the friends of my youth. It's difficult to objectively place a value on the personally close ones, with whom we were connected by threads of love and devotion.

I would like to write-up some episodes of my husband Nahum's family.

His father Pesakh Levine, his mother Reyne, and the sisters Sore-Rivke and Libe-Merke, and the boy Meirke – were murdered all too early by Hitler's henchmen.

My mother-in-law, Reyne, was a very quiet, introverted and religious woman. She never raised her voice. My father-in-law was an intelligent person with liberal leanings. They lived together like two doves, and regardless of their harsh conditions, and barely making a living – they were involved in the doings of the *shtetl*. If someone needed a favor, or was in need of advice – they came to Pesakh. If a poor person needed to sign a promissory note, Pesakh would sign for him, and quietly pay off the loan.

They had an open house, where not only the adults, but also the youth of the *shtetl* could find advice and assistance and lively discussions. Their daughter Tsipoyre with her husband Shloyme, two daughters and a son and grandchild live in Israel.

My husband (their son Nahum) and I, with our daughter and two grandchildren, live in California. Also their son, Moshe and his wife Pearl with a son and two daughters live in America.

We hold very dear the reminiscences of all those martyrs who perished in our *shtetl*, particularly all our dear and close ones who with their respectable and honest way of life have left memories in us – and these will be passed on from their children to the future generations.

May their memory be honored!

[Page 469]

My Shtetl, Home, and Family

Moshe and Perke Levine-Kartshmer

Translation by Leybl Botwinik

At the end of 1939, on a cold early morning, I left my home *shtetl*, as well as my dear father and mother and my three sisters. My oldest sister Leye was already living in America and my brother Avraham – in France.

With a deep feeling of longing and love, I write these lines about my father Noyekh Kartshmer and my mother, may she rest in peace. They lived near the marketplace, not far from the church, together with their daughters and only son.

My father was a modest person: Calm and intelligent, and a keen student of the *Shulkhan Orekh*.[Tr. Note: Jewish code of laws] My mother – a very intelligent woman who worked very hard, would read a book or a newspaper in her free time.

Noakh and Alte[Ed. Note: Rokhl Solts] *Kartshmer, Of Blessed Memory*

Unfortunately my parents are among those who perished. Together with them, the following were murdered by Hitler's thugs: My sister Dvoyre with her husband Yoysef Gitlits and their two children – a little girl, Khayele, and a boy Shmulikl, my sister Bashke, my sister Broyna with her husband and their little daughter.

My sister Leye (her husband has since passed away) lives in America with her two married daughters and four grandchildren; My brother Avraham, with his charming wife Tamara, live in France. They have a daughter and a son-in-law. Their granddaughter is studying medicine. My brother Avraham is a unique person – it's the dream of each father and mother to have such a son. Avraham contributed much to the social and cultural life in Divenishok. Whenever he was on vacation in the *shtetl*, he would organize performances and present lectures.

I, Perele, am the youngest – the *Mezinke*.[Tr. Note: youngest daughter] I'm married to Pesakh and Reyne Levine's son, and we live in America, in Fresno, California. We have two daughters, a son-in-law and a son.

It is difficult to express in words everything that my heart feels – the childhood years, the home, our small *shtetl* Divenishok with its beauty. The small shtetl was surrounded by green fields, meadows, and a lovely pine forest. People used to come to us to spend their summer (*Datshe*[Tr. Note: summer country house]), because one could rest very well there, and refresh oneself in the river, during the hot days.

I carry in my heart a great love and longing for my home *shtetl* Divenishok.

I also want to mention the following people: My Grandmother Khaye-- she was a very pious woman, always ready to give charity; she passed away when I was still a small girl...my aunt Rodl and her husband Gershn and their daughter Zlatke...my aunt Dvorke with her husband Osher and their two little children...my uncle Rueben and his wife. He was a person of great intelligence and sharp mind. When he would lecture on some topic, he would mention dates from memory, like a "walking encyclopedia".

May these few words about my friends and loved ones be an eternal memorial to them all.

[Page 470]

In Memory of My Father, My Mother, and My Family

Sore-Toyve Hershovitsh-Levi
Translation by Leybl Botwinik

My father Chaim Hershovitsh was born in Lipnishok, a *shtetl* that was about 30 kilometers from Divenishok. Of the six children – 3 boys and 3 girls – five remained. They, along with their entire families, perished during the Hitler period. I do not know under what circumstances.

In his very early youth, my father studied at the *Yeshive*[Tr. Note: A theological seminary] in Mir, together with one of his uncles. My father did not like to stay in one place. He strove for freedom and had an inclination towards business. When he married my mother he settled in Divenishok and occupied himself with business. He would travel to fairs and to markets, and come home only for *Shabes*[Tr. Note: Saturday, the day of rest]. He was a year-round-Jew,[1] a good husband, and a loving father.

My mother, Rokhl-Leye Glazer (or Shklar), was the daughter of Alter the glazier. She had five brothers: Ayzik and Tevye in America, Moshe and Leybe in Argentina, and Eltsik the tinsmith – in Divenishok. In her youth, my mother was a tailor.

My parents had seven children. I was the oldest. Three died very young. A sister of mine, Khaye, died when she was 10 or 11 years old. My two brothers, the older one Alterke, and Zalmenke the younger one, were not even of *Bar-Mitsve* age[2] when the war broke out.

My mother, Rokhl-Leye, was a very intelligent woman, a good soul, an *Eyshes Khayil*.[Tr. Note: A woman who could handle anything] She never complained, was always willing to help others, never boasted, and never gossiped about others. "Look, my children, downwards – and you will always be happy in life. If you look upwards, you will always be unhappy". This was my mother's motto that indeed guided me in life. When my mother took ill, our small world shattered. We remained like a ship without a rudder.

My older brother Altke was a good-natured fellow, took nothing to heart, and accepted life as it went. He was always with his younger brother, like a twin, never a minute apart.

Zalmenke, my younger brother (by two years), was very sensitive, and took everything to heart. Already during his earliest years he knew about responsibility in life, and took everything very seriously. The sadness of life and the difficult living conditions were mirrored in his mournful eyes.

I remember my childhood with love, my earliest youth, the devotion and togetherness of our family.

Nahum and I were wedded in 1938. Two weeks later, he left for America and settled in Fresno, California. When the Russian army marched into Divenishok, I managed – via all sorts of back ways – to make my way to Vilne, which was already under Russian-Lithuanian control. After nine months of wandering, I miraculously managed to make it to America – via Moscow, Vladivostok, and Japan. I reached the shores of San Francisco in November 1940. We have a daughter Rosalyn Levi-Blum, and two grandchildren that continue to follow the Jewish tradition.

The Levine family at the farewell for Nahum, Sarah, Moshe, and Pearl, on the occasion of their emigration to the United States (1938)

Translator's Footnotes

1. Devout and consistently religiously observant on a daily basis, as opposed to some Jews that were not observant all year.

2. The age of 13, when a boy takes on the religious responsibilities of a grown-up male Jew.

[Page 471]

In Memory of My Father

Sore Shklar

Translation by Leybl Botwinik

I, Sore Shklar of Buenos Aires, daughter of Moshe ben Alter and Sore, would like to recall in goodness the memory of my blessed father who dedicated every waking minute of his entire life to society – to the needy. He was a good hearted person, a dear Jew who was concerned only for others and could be a role model for other Jews in Divenishok, and later – in Argentina.

He supported his family honorably, and his honesty and sensitivity to Justice were renowned among all his friends and family who knew him from near.

Our mother Paulina, the daughters Sore and Royze-Leye, the sons-in-law Julio and Mario, as well as the grandchildren Graciela, Dina, Jerarda and Viviana, will always remember the gentle figure of this man, father, father-in-law and grandfather Moshe Shklar.

May his memory be honored.

[Page 472]

Horav[1] Khaim Yehudah Horvits, Of Blessed Memory

N. Gordon

Translation by Leybl Botwinik

Leader of the *Mashgikhim*[2] Union

Sometimes, great things happen as a result of some event that people describe by the title 'chance'.

This chance occurrence may in itself be a small, negligible event that no one pays any attention to. However, this triviality can sometimes grow into a very, very significant development, that manages to attract everyone's attention.

For *yidn mayminim*– [Tr. Note: Observant Jews] for whom there is no such thing as 'coincidence' – it is particularly worthwhile to seek out the unnoticed and hidden reason that is in essence the first round of all subsequent events.

In the case of the *Agudes*[Tr. Note: Union of] *Hamashgikhim* that is currently a vital factor vis-a-vis the issue of Kashres[3], and in the lives of hundreds of Jewish kosher inspectors – there are enough logical motives why *kashres* needs *hashgokhe*[Tr. Note: supervision] and *mashgikhim* need to be organized.

If you were to calmly confer with the living 'nerve' of the *Agudes Hamashgikhim*, and its director Horav reb' Khaim Yehudah Horvits, you would also be faced with – in addition to all the other open and logical motives – a minuscule trifle that happened to him by chance just over twenty years earlier. This was a passing happenstance that turned out to be of extreme significance in the history of *kashres* in America and in the life of Horav Horvits whose twenty year jubilee as founder and leader of the *mashgikhim* union was marked by the publication "*Amerikaner*".[Tr. Note: The American]

The young Horav Horvits, while a groom to be married, went out to find a hall for the wedding celebration. He didn't, however, get to visit many wedding-halls, since the very first one he entered convinced him of what he could expect there.

A Jew with a white beard and rabbinic wrinkles on his forehead stepped out of the kitchen, with an apron around his waist. The owner of the hall wanted to show him that his place was kosher, and for proof – here was the *mashgiakh*.

"You see him? The rabbi?..." the owner asked him, with the triumphant smile of a circus performer when the monkey dances to the rhythm of his baton.

"Go rabbi. Go back to your kitchen and don't forget what you need to do: peel enough potatoes for the entire kettle ... Don't forget, rabbi..."

And with that, the owner sent the *mashgiakh* back to the kitchen, and began preparing himself to sign the contract for the party.

The old *mashgiakh* with the white beard returned to the potatoes in the kitchen like a loyal slave. He managed, however, to throw a glance at the young groom, a look that expressed so much the pain of an old and broken *talmid-khokhem*– [Tr. Note: Learned scholar] and this particular gaze accompanied Horav Horvits the entire two decades that he led the *mashgikhim* union.

His fighting spirit imbibed as a youngster in Shutchin by Navaredok under the auspices of reb' Leybtshe Telzer, the Navaredok stubbornness of not being surprised by the greatest impossibility – all this came awake that evening, looking upon the *mashgiakh* with the apron. He had decided to bang on the table and let out a cry: "Gevald yidn,[Tr. Note: "Be aware Jews!"] the *mashgiakh* is also a human being!"

A tiny trifle touched the heartstring in a highly sensitive Jewish heart that broke out in a revolt against the shaming of a *talmid-khokhem* and he decided that such as this could not continue.

Kashres is in particular the *mitsve*[Tr. Note: Commandment or deed] of "*beyn odem lemokoym*".[Tr. Note: Between Man and God] It is a commandment that has to do with the *kibiyoykhl*[Tr. Note: The omnipotent one (God)] himself. But with what right – asked Horav Horvits – may Jews deal with *mitsves* at the expense of a *mashgiakh* that must scrub floors and then goes home with more shame than money?...

Reb Yisroyl Salanter did not want to use even one drop of unnecessary water for *vashn*[4] before eating, out of pity for the poor servant girl that had to fetch the water...

Where is the heart of Jews that observe *kashres* – Horav Horvits demanded of himself – when they allow Jewish *talmidey khokhomim* to undergo such shame, and suffer from hunger as well??...

Horav Horvits plunged into his work. The work consisted not only of convincing the owners that they would benefit from having a free, independent, and loyal Union member as the *mashgiakh*. The work consisted also in persuading the *mashgikhim* to dare to become free persons who perform *malokhes hakoydesh*[Tr. Note: Holy work] with dignity and honor.

Even though in character he was of kind heart, a person with no malice to others, Horav Horvits was nevertheless a very stubborn person when it came to *kashres*. Here, *tokhnunim*[Tr. Note: Pleas or petitions] did not help. Everything must be according to the rules of religious law.

Horav Horvits cooks up a prodigious plan, a "Committee for the Spreading of *Kashres*", with the assistance of rabbis and owners who would step up to the task with a true desire to free *kashres* from its imprisonment and instead place it at the center of Jewish public life.

When one takes a look back at what this quicksilver Jew has managed to do until today, it would be more than correct to believe that all the dreams that he still carries around with him will also very soon be realized.

The most prominent person for him is the *mashgiakh*.

*

Our *bal-yoyvl*[Tr. Note: Person being celebrated] was born in a small *shtetl*, named Divenishok, Vilne region. His father was a bricklayer. However, besides this business, he also arranged for his son – who was studying at the *yeshive*[Tr. Note: Jewish theological seminary] to tutor a little and send home the few rubles.

From Shutchin by Navaredok he traveled to Slabodke to continue his studies, where he took with him the "*Altn's*"[5] *muser-nign*.[Tr. Note: melody of edification] Quite often, while seated in his office, he would draw out the "*Altn's*" mournful melody. This, at a moment when bricks were falling on the *mashgikhims* heads... the bricks coming from a source that should have instead provided encouragement to the *mashgikhim*, assisting them to organize *kashres* on a more independent basis...[6]

He is a person with an unlimited dynamism.

This is the way he was in his youth overseas when he organized a "*sama-abrane*", a Jewish self-defense against Denikin's and Petliura's brigands[7]. The dignity of a Jew was always deemed holy by him, and he was ready to go out and join in battle for it.

The deceased Zionist leader, Khaim Greenberg o"h[8] recounted on more than one occasion, how Chaim Yehudah Horvits came to the prison where he was being held, and rescued him from who knows how many years in Siberia, or even worse...

During those *Beyn-Hashmoses*[Tr. Note: Twilight] years when Jewish settlements would go over from the control of one authority to another, the young Chaim Yehudah Horvits was a *malakh hamoyshiyo*[Tr. Note: Delivering angel] for many a family, who he, together with other youths, rescued from bandit attacks.

Prior to his coming to America, in the year 1922, he managed to study a few years in Lida, under Horav Raynes, z"l[9], such that his *yeshive* background consisted of an amalgam from Navaredok, Slabodke, and Lida.

He learned a great deal from each one of his *rabeyim*[10], and not just in *toyre* [Tr note: Bible and Talmud], but in all aspects of supervising the world and people. To do a favor for a fellow Jew is a good trait and this was inscribed in his heart, because the '*beyn odem lekhaveyro*'[Tr. Note: (deeds) between man and friend] and his care for the *mashgiekh* were *geknipt un gebundn*.[Tr. Note: went hand-in-hand]

He brought *sharis-hapleyte*[Tr. Note: Holocaust survivors] into his union, many who were *rabonim*, that had important rabbinic positions before the *khurbn*.[Tr. Note: Yiddish for "The Holocaust" (in Hebrew it means "destruction")] He gave these *talmidey khokhomim* a source of honorable livelihood, while at the same time these *talmidey khokhomim* helped to raise the prestige of *kashres* and the dignity of the *mashgiekh*.

Horav Chaim Yehudah Horvits looks back at the past 20 years of his life as if they were part of a greater framework: that which is named the *agudes-hamashgikhim*. Indeed, the future of the *agudes-hamashgikhim* has become a part of his own personality

He lives 24 hours in a *mes-les*[Tr. Note: One full day cycle] with the problems, successes and failures of the *agudes-hamashgikhim*.

And he is full of faith that the following 20 years will bring even more awareness that *kashres* requires inspection and inspection requires a *mashgiakh* that is looked upon as an *oysek malokhes hakoydesh*[Tr. Note: Partaker of consecrated labor], and is subjected to the authority of the *shulkhan orekh*[Tr. Note: Authoritative coded book of Jewish daily rituals and laws] not the caprices of an owner.

And all this – adds Horav Horvits – in the conditions that we live under today, cannot take place except through the existence of a very strongly organized union of *mashgikhim*, a union whose objective is organized *kashres* by, through, and for the general populace.

Nisn Gordon
("Der Amerikaner", NY, 1-Aug-1960)

Translator's Footnotes

1. Rabbi

2. Inspector of food products to ensure that they are kosher - i.e. conform to the Jewish dietary laws - and are prepared according to those laws (pl. mashgikhim).

3. Kashres – The domain of kosher food

4. Washing of the hands in a special pre-meal ritual before partaking of bread

5. "Alter" (Literally, "old (one)") – Rabbi Nosson Zvi (Nota Hirsh) Finkel known as the Alter of Slabodke

6. The writer seems to be hinting that someone who should be helping the *mashgikhim* is in fact working against them. The "falling bricks" and the "Altn's" sad melody further enforce this thought – that Horav

Horvits was depressed at the thought of 'authority' figures acting counter-productively.

7. Ed. Note: Symon Petliura was a Ukrainian national leader who was unable to prevent anti-Jewish pogroms at the hands of his own forces. Anton Denikin was a Czarist general and leader of the anti-Bolshevik White Army whose troops were also responsible for large scale pogroms.

8. Olev hasholem (o"h) – Literally: "may he ascend (to heaven) in peace". Said about someone who has passed away. See also z"l and zts"l

9. Z"l and zts"l – z"l (*zikhroyno livrokho*), "of blessed memory" is the equivalent of o"h (above). Zts"l (*zikhroyno tsadik livrokho*), "of blessed and saintly memory" is used for rabbis, scholars and other great learned persons.

10. The plural for rabbi (also: rabonim)

[Page 476a]

APPENDIX

Divenishok Jews, Community Workers and Fighters, who Live in Israel and America

Left: *Eliahu Nathaneli (Itskovitsh), founder of HeKhaluts in the town, arrived in Israel with the third "aliya"* ***Center:*** *Dr. Menachem Weisenfeld, the town physician* ***Right:*** *Michael Dubinski, son of Samuel, partisan*

Left: *The survivor, the engineer Mintz, Toronto, Canada* **Right:** *Nathan Kaplan, police officer during the British Mandate and in the State of Israel*

[Page 476b]

Left: *Eliohu Blyakher, partisan in the Bielski unit*
Right: *Seyba Griner, partisan*

Gedalye Horvits, Of Blessed Memoryl, Philip Mintz, and his family

Tsvi Ahuvi (standing at the left) at a meeting in New York of workers in the Divenishok emigrants organization

[Page 476c]

Philip Mintz, his wife, and Ida Levine, United States

Menukha Krizovski, officer in the Red Red Army

Gedalye Horvits z"l (center) and Sam and Vita Barnett in the U.S.

[Page 476d]

Standing, from the left: Shmuel Sharon, Meir Yosef Itskovitsh, Yakov Bloch, Binyamin Dubinski **Seated:** David Shtokfish (editor) and Shraga Blyakher

People from Divenishok in Israel at the wedding of
Rokhl and Shmuel Sharon (Tel Aviv, 1949)

[Page 477]

4. Landsmanshaftn

[Page 479]

Memorial evening for the martyrs of Divenishok, in Vilne House in Tel-Aviv, 1975

Our Landsmanshaft[1] in Israel

Khaya Garvey

Translation by Leybl Botwinik

I want to tell you about our *landslayt*[2] in *erets–yisroyl*,[Tr. Note: The Land of Israel] the first pioneers who left our *shtetele*.[Tr. Note: Diminutive of *shtetl* (town), a very small town]. In 1925, a small group came to *erets–yisroyl* – Eliahu (Eylke) Itskovitsh, Nosn Kaplan (Leybe), Zilpa Blyakher, Moshe Mintz (from the store), David–Leyb Berkovitsh, Khaye Shifre Blyakher, Mirke Mazeh, Dov Zandman *z"l*.[Tr. Note: *zikhroyno livrokho* – "of blessed memory"]

Dov was one of the finest people, the first pioneer of communication in Jerusalem, and a person of high education. He organized the library in the bus co-operative *"Hamekasher"* that exists to this day.[Tr. Note: Created in 1931, absorbed by a larger cooperative – "Egged" – in 1967] He died *oyf kidesh hashem*[Tr. Note: A martyr to God and Judaism] enroute to the university on Mount Scopus and the Hadassah Hospital, before the creations of the State of Israel. He perished with tens of other educated individuals – professors and doctors, nurses, and others. There were five buses traveling – and all the passengers perished. To this day all of Jerusalem remembers "our Dov" (as they called him).

Several of the first pioneers returned home because those were difficult times in *erets-yisroyl*, as it says in the *Toyre*:[Tr. Note: Bible] *"ve hoorets oykheles es yoyshveho"* ["and the land devours its inhabitants"]. It was difficult, very difficult, and not everyone could surmount these hardships. However, our land was built upon these adversities until we attained our own country.

Our small group of *landslayt* was concentrated in one area and we always sought each other out to help one another with whatever each of us could. When Hitler conquered Europe and all our dearest loved ones in the old home perished horribly, calls for assistance reached us from the few surviving *landslayt* – broken both physically and spiritually, having endured the horrors of the second world war. Our *landslayt* in America helped them out with packages, with money, and with comforting words. These were the fine and noble deeds that originated in our old home, when those from Divenishok in New York always supported our *shtetl*, where poverty reigned – with an article of clothing, shoes, with help buying a horse for someone whose old nag had fallen, assistance for the *shil*,[Tr. Note: Also called *shul* – The house of prayer and learning] for the *gmiles khesed*[Tr. Note: Charity fund] and for all of the cultural institutions.

Our tiny group in *erets-yisroyl* lived in friendship and harmony. We were, after all, left with no one else, and therefore supported one another both materially and morally.

After the war, *landslayt*, survivors of the *shoah*,[Tr. Note: Hebrew for Holocaust] began arriving as *olim khadashim*,[Tr. Note: Hebrew for new immigrants to the Holy Land] and they needed assistance. Therefore, the idea of creating a *gmiles khesed* fund was born, since the newcomers would need an apartment – and that required a large sum of money. Thus, we created a fund and each contributed what he could, and when a *khaver*[Tr. Note: Friend] would arrive, we would provide him with rent money for three months in advance and the bare essentials for the apartment, until the newcomer could start working and stand on his own two legs. Our fund has been in existence for quite a few years.

Since 1944 we have gathered yearly for the annual remembrance ceremony to honor the martyred.

Translator's Footnotes

1. *Landsmanshaft* – Fraternal organization of people who were born or lived in the same town or geographic area. Often, the second and even third generation are included in the membership. See *landslayt*.

2. *Landslayt* – People who were born or lived in the same town or geographic area.

[Page 481]

Memorial evening in Tel-Aviv (May 1963) in memory of the martyrs of Divenishok

American Relief[1] Creates the *Gmiles Khesed*[2] Fund

Tsvi Ahuvi (Lieb)

Translation by Leybl Botwinik

After the proclamation of the State of Israel, Divenishok *landslayt*[Tr. Note: People who were born or lived in the same town or geographic area] living in America began to visit Israel. The first was Harry Levine, who received his last regards from his father Yitshak–Leib through me. He had died of great anguish three days after the Soviets arrested me.

Harry Levine interested himself with the situation of the *Divenishokers* in Israel and asked what they required. I explained to him that the most urgent issue was a roof over one's head, and that a fund needed to be set up so that any needy *Divenishoker* could take a loan from it to pay for an apartment.

Praesidium of the memorial evening in Tel-Aviv (1975) **From the viewer's right:** *Meir Yosef Itskovitsh, Binyamin Dubinski, Nathan Kaplan, Tsvi Ahuvi, Shmuel Sharon, Shraga Blyakher, Yakov Bloch*

Very soon after, his son Leo Levine came from America and brought 1,500 dollars from Relief to create the *gmiles khesed* fund. After him, Meir Bolinski came to visit (twice), Solomon Levine (Raphael's son), Shmuel Kamenitski, Khayim–Yidl Horvits, and others that brought money for our loan fund.

Still later, Milton Kartshmer and Jack Kaplan came.

It is worthwhile to point out the Barnett family – four brothers that actively participate in Divenishok aide–giving. They are my close friends, and so I brought up the question of the *gmiles khesed* fund, and they helped us.

Thanks to the fund, many of our *landslayt* acquired their own apartment. In addition to that we also assisted needy *Divenishokers*.

As the head of the *gmiles khesed* fund, I am in a position to appropriately evaluate the importance of this institution that our brothers in America set up here in Israel.

Translator's Footnotes

1. Relief – Refers to the relief fund that the Divenishokers in America set up to assist their brethren in need, both in Israel and elsewhere.

2. Gmiles Khesed (kase) – Charity and self–help loan fund

[Page 483]

(DOCUMENT)

An Appeal From Former Divenishok Residents in the Land of Israel to their Townspeople in America

Translation by Leybl Botwinik

Brothers, Sisters, Jews!

The Divenishok *landslayt* in *erets–yisroyl*, appeal to you:

The war is over. The European continent that was cut off during the war years is again open, but with the consequences of five years of the Hitler– regime in the occupied countries: Destruction and death, cities and hundreds of towns wiped out – along with densely populated Jewish settlements. Among them, our small *shtetele*[Tr. Note: Diminutive of shtetl, which is a small town] Divenishok, that had stood for hundreds of years cloaked in peace and tranquility, where Jews led a life of high quality from the social aspect as well as the cultural, with schools, libraries, savings–and–loans funds, and organizations. There, a body of youth grew up instilled with national and cultural values. Everything, however, was wiped out, crushed.

Our *shtetl* was annihilated in the Jewish month of Iyar of the year *tof–shin– beys*,[Tr. Note: 5702 according to the Jewish calendar] the 11th of May, 1942. Our parents, brothers and sisters were murdered in a most brutal manner: Burnt and shot, and the small children suffocated. A black layer of ash covers the earth. The wheat flourishes and sprouts on the fields enriched by our brothers' flesh and blood.

From this gruesome catastrophe, just over forty persons managed to save themselves – some of them partisans – they are now dispersed over all of the military occupation zones in Germany, Austria, and Italy.

They stretch out their hands for help – their only goal is *erets–yisroyl*, the place where they will find a home, after their painful suffering. We have lived to see the moment when we can take in the first of these "swallows" from our *shtetl*: a former partisan who has reached us after a long journey of wandering from the White Russian forests, through Italy, to finally reach us.

All the *landslayt* immediately helped him to settle in and helped him to get back on his feet. We await other survivors that we expect to reach us with the passage of time. We are in need of assistance for them.

Annual Memorial (1955) in 'Melutzot' Hall in Tel-Aviv, with the participation of Solomon Levine and Wife from New York.

Today, the 11th of May, 1946, the fourth *yortsayt*[Tr. Note: Annual memorial day in memory of the passing of an individual or group] for our *kdoyshim*,[Tr. Note: Jewish martyrs] we – the *landslayt* of Divenishok – stand deeply broken at a solemn gathering with tears in our eyes and with words that are too meagre to describe the great calamity.

We have decided, in the holy memory of our *kdoyshim*, to assist the remaining survivors of our town, still wandering across Europe on their way to reaching us, with all our potential.

We have also decided to erect a monument to commemorate our *shtetl*. There are few of us here in Israel and we are therefore limited in the possibilities to carry all this out.

You, *landslayt* from Divenishok in America, who have with your efforts and compassion built a synagogue, a library, and all the cultural institutions in the last 20 years through your financial support – we appeal to you: Help us. Call together a mass meeting, carry out an act, to enable the *sharis-hapleyte*[Tr. Note: Survivors of a calamity – in this case, the Holocaust] to come to us.

Correspondence and money transfers can be sent according to the following address:[Tr. Note: The actual address was presented in Hebrew, except for the word "PALESTINE"] Eliahu Itskovitsh and Khaya Levine, Borokhov neighborhood, haMefane street, PALESTINE.

These two persons are authorized by all participants in the gathering to administer all opportunities and to maintain correspondence with you, brothers in America,

Every year, Yud Iyar[Tr. Note: The 10th of the Jewish month of Iyar] we will congregate in the place where the monument will be erected. We here in *erets–yisroyl*, and you in America will be consoled by the *sharis–hapleyte* that have survived.

Assist us in rehabilitating our unfortunate brethren.

In the name of the Divenishok *landslayt* in *erets–yisroyl*
–Eliahu Itskovitsh

[Page 485]

Landsman[1] in Israel
Tells About the Landsmanshaft [2] in America

Yakov Bloch / Tel Aviv

Translation by Leybl Botwinik

On the 31st of July, 1950, I arrived in New York from Tel Aviv, where I have lived since 1935 (that is, approximately 15 years). I lived through all of the events in that land, until the creation of the State of Israel.

A few years ago, I lost my right hand in an accident at work. In order to undergo an operation to attach an artificial hand, I came here, thanks to the noble assistance of my *landslayt*[3] and the so called "Ladies Auxiliary". They have made, and are continuing to make, every effort for my sake, to assist me in the particular circumstances at the hospital where I now find myself.

Being aware of the activities that have been carried out by the "Divenishok Ladies Auxiliary" for various purposes in their 20 year existence; being aware of the aid that through them was provided the rescued Hitler–victims and *pleytim*[Tr. Note: Refugees] in the camps in Germany and Italy, and later – the new arrivals to America and Israel, and their ongoing aid to this day; being aware of their warm response to the "United Jewish Appeal" and other achievements – I cannot ignore my duty to present an assessment and express my high estimation for these "unknown soldiers" that have loyally served, for many years, our needy brother–*landslayt* and their people.

Who are these auxiliary ladies? Where do they come from? What has moved them to organize themselves and to carry out their bountiful activity?

Committee of the Divenishok emigrants organization in the United States, at the time of the visit of Yakov Bloch[Ed. Note: not in picture] from Israel in 1950

The *shtetl*[Tr. Note: Small town] Divenishok is located far far off the beaten track, on the border between White Russia and Lithuania, a distance of 60 *vyorst*[Tr. Note: Old Russian measurement (*verst*) – Approximately 60 km, or 39.8 miles] from Vilna, that was once the *yerushalayim d'lite*.[Tr. Note: "Jerusalem" of Lithuania] According to certain historical research, Jews have lived there since the 17th century, creating a Jewish community that has been subject to various governments and regimes— Lithuanian, Russian, German, Soviet, and during the period of 1921 until August 1939, Polish sovereignty.

During these several hundred years the Jewish community suffered greatly at the hands of their Christian neighbors. More than once the Jewish community suffered pogroms, incineration, and destruction. However, after each such calamity Jewish inhabitants returned to their foundations and made a united effort to rebuild the *shtetl*, reconstruct their Jewish life, build *shiln, besey midroshim, khadorim*–[Tr. Note: Houses of prayer, places of learning, children's schools] and in this manner, carried on from generation to generation.

A gathering of Divenishok emigrants in New York (1949)

In their tiny enclave, they lived out their Jewish lifestyle far from the wide world. The *haskalah*[Tr. Note: The phrase refers to the enlightenment of the Jewish "renaissance period"], however, reached even the smallest of communities, including this *shtetl*. The Jewish youth thirsted for a resurgence, for renewal, for enlightenment, and they opened their vistas to the world–at–large.

At the same time, there emerged a desire for emigration, and young Jewish men and women from Divenishok were swept into the stream going towards America during the latter part of the previous century (the 1880s). They became pioneers and dreamers for a new and free life, ideas instilled in them by socialistic–democratic philosophies prevalent at the time.

In America many of them joined the labor movement and fought for worker's rights. Few in numbers but adamant in their will to stay connected to the old home, they did everything to stay in touch with the backward and impoverished birth–*shtetl* they had recently abandoned. They remembered the great privation of their brothers, sisters, parents, and friends across the sea.

In 1903, they founded the "Divenishok Society" in America, whose goals were: Mutual assistance for *landslayt* immigrants, and aid for needy individuals and institutions back in the *shtetl*. The old country was like a wailing wall for them, a source of comfort. They yearned for their days of youth and for the experiences of *shtetl* life.

They began by sending money to the needy. They brought in many relatives to America. Thanks to their assistance, libraries were established in the *shtetl*, as well as the construction of a modern school. At this school the youth received instruction, including a Jewish education and exhortations to settle in *erets–yisroyl*[Tr. Note: The Land of Israel] in order to revitalize our nation and its land. A large number of these youths did indeed realize their aspirations and immigrated to *erets–yisroyl*, and struggled in the building of our land.

I remember that in 1929 several of the officers of the Devinishok Relief fund came to visit us in our *shtetl*: Mr. Meir Bolinski, his wife Fene, and family, Mr. Joseph Levey and his wife, *z"l*.[Tr. Note: *zikhroyna livrokho* – "of blessed memory"]. They were all very warmly received in the *shtetl*. The guests expressed their truly paternal love and enormous devotion.

There was not a single institution in our *shtetl* that was not been assisted by them. They all visited, and as a result, rejuvenated our activities. We have a very great deal of gratitude to express to them, because thanks to them progress was introduced to Jewish Divenishok in those years.

After returning to America, Meir Bolinski and his wife, with the assistance of dear Nellie Brown, Penny Sbeyski and her husband, Mr. Davey, Lina Cohen, Rose Becker, and others – established the "Divenishok Ladies Auxiliary" with the goal of assisting the poorer class of Divenishok inhabitants in all matters: with food and heating, with medicines and various materials, getting the war victims back on their feet, etc.

In this manner they continued their holy work – until the outbreak of the Second World War that brought an end to Jewish life there. Among the various Jewish settlements in the vicinity of Vilne destroyed by the Hitlerian beasts and their henchmen, our old and dear home, our birth–*shtetl* Divenishok was also destroyed.

Our dearest ones, our dear parents, our brothers, our sisters, perished tragically at the hands of the bloody murderers, on the 11th of May, 1942, together with 2000 other Jews from the nearby *shtetl* of Voronova.

The despair is immense. Every contact with the *shtetl* has been cut off. The war continues and the messages received are very sad. We hear about the death and destruction and we are helpless.

However, the "Ladies Auxiliary" does not give up its work regardless of the apathy that has fallen over certain members. On the contrary! At this time, the young activists – Milton and Sara Kartshmer who had just arrived (re-immigrated) from Cuba – stand up to the task. They throw themselves into their work raising money and searching and inquiring everywhere: Maybe someone has survived the holocaust?

They succeed in uncovering traces of surviving *landslayt* from the *shtetl* and the surrounding area. Parcels of food are shipped to them, as well as clothing and money. Letters of comfort are sent as a balm on the wounded hearts of those who survived. More than 30 survivors have been tracked down, and the "Ladies Auxiliary" via Mr. Bolinski, Mr. Kartshmer, and Miss Sara K., carry on a correspondence with each and every one of them.

I had the opportunity to look at tens of letters from survivors that were sent to the "Ladies Auxiliary". These letters are pages from the history of the holocaust tragedy, the suffering, the dismay, the victims— and the miraculous rescue and comfort of the *pleytim* who were practically reborn, having to regain their trust in humanity and friendship. The activities of assistance for the *pleytim* continue for those who come to America, Canada, and *erets-yisroyl*.

The "Divenishok Ladies Auxiliary" is now entering its 21st year of existence. She carries on her shoulders the weight of many years of activity and positive deeds that greatly aided the *sharis-hapleyte*. In the name of the *landslayt* in the State of Israel, and in the name of the surviving *pleytim* that have found a home with us in *erets-yisroyl*, I laud you, dear friends, and wish upon you the strength to continue your holy efforts for many more years with renewed strength, a more steadfast belief, laying brick upon brick, and achieving through fruitful work the rebuilding, renewal and rebirth of our People in the State of Israel.

**

I present here the letter I published in the New York "Forverts", the 18th of September 1950. I wrote the letter while in the Hasbrouck Heights Hospital and it was a great satisfaction for me that the aforementioned daily Yiddish newspaper in the US published these warm words concerning our *landsmanshaft*, who truly earned it.

This picture of the blessed work of the Divenishokers would not be complete without a recounting of their activities – particularly since there exists a rich source of documentation in the form of Anniversary booklets. I will therefore expand the letter in the "Forverts" with a more meticulous account of the Divenishok activities in the United States of America – as detailed in the archive material – and there is indeed much to recount !

**

Here is one of their invitations to the farewell evening in honor of my return to Israel:

"Worthy sisters, brothers and *landslayt*!

Convention of Divenishok emigrants in New York

It is with great joy that we invite you to participate in a special gathering that will take place Sunday night, the 4th of February [1951], at our locale in the Central Plaza annex, 40 East 7th street, New York.

The get–together is given in honor of Yakov Bloch, on the occasion of his returning to the State of Israel.

The "Divenishok Ladies Auxiliary" expresses its pride and joy with an achievement that surpasses all its prior achievements.

At the same time, we send out our heartiest words of admiration and thanks to our praiseworthy sister and brother, Fene and Meir Bolinski, for the faithful accommodation and determination that have made Yakov feel at home and close. Therefore let us join together to make this farewell evening a joyous and unforgettable one. Fine refreshments will be served."

And now – what the publications and documents recount.

[Page 492]

10th Anniversary of the Divenishok *Landslayt* in New York [Tr. Note: 1903–1913]

1.1 Message from the President Martha Zalkin

Today, the 7th of December, 1913, we are celebrating the 10th Anniversary of our Divenishok Ladies Auxiliary.[Ed. Note: The year given here is the year for the 10th anniversary of the Divenishok Society; the 10th anniversary of the Ladies Auxiliary is believed to have occurred in late 1939 or 1940]

Ten years have passed swiftly because we were immersed in good and important work. Is there anything more vital than assisting the needy and striving to still their hunger and warm their frozen limbs? The Auxiliary has not waited for those suffering to ask for assistance. The Auxiliary has continuously taken care to oversee that the disadvantaged should receive aid in time.

It is now my pleasure to inform you that the Auxiliary today honors the brother and sister, Meir and Fene Bolinski – with a testimonial dinner. If not for Meir Bolinski's great contribution to the Auxiliary, we would not have had this 10th Anniversary. These two wonderful people have not spared anything: Time, money, and hard work. We therefore celebrate our 10th Anniversary with a dinner for our beloved good friends Meir and Fene. They deserve it. We wish them health and prosperity for many, many years to come.

It is of the utmost importance to note that since the Auxiliary cannot physically reach Divenishok, we have united with the following Jewish institutions: HIAS, Jewish Congress, and the Joint. The HIAS has contacts with the entire Jewish community in Europe. If our *landslayt* require aid they are surely receiving care. The Auxiliary has contributed a nice sum to these institutions, and will continue to do so as long as will be necessary. We also help the Deborah Tuberculosis Sanitorium[Ed. Note: Today this institution is known as the Deborah Heart and Lung Center] and the Jewish Guild for the Blind. As you can see my friends, the Auxiliary does not sit with folded arms. It goes out and helps wherever it is needed.

Let us all together, both members and those gathered here – live to see the 25th Anniversary.

1.2 Greetings from the Organizing Committee of the 10th Anniversary of the Divenishok Ladies Auxiliary

The Organizing Committee has taken upon itself a great responsibility. We are celebrating our 10th Anniversary of our auxiliary with a banquet and testimonial dinner. We see the figure of our beloved president, sister Martha Zalkin. We do not have enough words to praise the excellent and hard work you have carried out under your nine years of administration. Thanks to your energy and logic, the Auxiliary has continued to soar. Therefore, beloved and dear sister Martha, we express our deepest and most heartfelt wishes that you should always be with us. Be well and strong, and live to a ripe old age, together with you wonderful husband.

With sisterly regards: Mrs. Fene Sverski, chairman of the Organizing Committee; Mrs. Rose Land, Editor.

1.3 Heartfelt Regards for the 10th Anniversary

I want to express my festive feelings for today's celebration. My heart spills over with joy that the Auxiliary has endured to celebrate its 10th year. These years have not flowed by easily. The Auxiliary has gone through difficult moments. I recall how we needed to appeal to everyone's heart to convince them of the good work carried out by the Auxiliary. The work was indeed fruitful – and my heart is therefore filled with joy.

A special good word for the president Martha Zalkin. You have truly earned the credit for the success of the Auxiliary.

Your friend, Meir Land.

1.4 Three Active Women across the Sea (In the Old Home)

With much joy and the greatest of honor do we present three photographs in our journal of the women's committee in Divenishok–across–the–sea. They make sure that everyone receives the necessary aid. These are: Mikla Krizovski, Esther Engle, and Tsipe Leah Kaplan. The three sisters are an embodiment of our Auxiliary. They are three branches of the same tree. We share with them our great celebration. We drink a toast to your health – that you should continue your good work for our unfortunate ones.

It is a divine act for us to seize this opportunity of expressing a thousand thanks to our dear friend Hirsh Krizovski, who has enabled us to show the pictures of Divenishok. Today at the banquet we will show all the pictures, and we believe that everyone will be roused.

With heartfelt wishes from all the Auxiliary officers and members,

Mrs. Rose Land, Editor.

1.5 Extra announcement

Dear friends and *landslayt*,

We have managed to acquire photographs of our old home, our fathers, mothers, brothers, sisters, friends and good friends. All of the pictures have been very well photographed and you can get these pictures at the gathering and also at the Divenishok Ladies Auxiliary meetings.

Come to the gathering and get a picture of your loved ones. Contact Jacob Zalkin.

Following are the photographs:

Patzlof, the Mill, Sore Ditse, Bere Hirsh, the *hekdesh*,[Tr. Note: hospital for the poor] the harness-maker, Itsik Leib, Zalmen Kushes, the pharmacy, the church, Surles palace, Geranion Street, Peysekh the Shames,[Tr. Note: Sexton managing and maintaining the synagogue] Daniel Shloymes, the Rabbi's house, Meir Zalmen Vayner, the Polish school, Sore Ditse's house, holiday dress, Leyb Dubin's house, the bathhouse and the well, the roof chimney, the library building, Meyshe the tinsmith, the market well, Abba the shoemaker, Meir the tailor, Meir Zalmen's house, Itsik Leib's house, Zalmen Kushe's house, Elke the Mute, Sore Feygl Mikels, Moishe Mamke's houses, the *shtetl* from a distance, the new *beys hamedresh*,[Tr. Note: Synagogue or holy place of learning] Itteh Avreml's house, Yankl Artshom's house,

The gate of the cemetery, the '*kudre*'[Tr. Note: Literally a curved object; could refer to a curved portion of the street or some other unknown landmark] on Vilne street, Zelda daughter of Peysekh the beggar, Khana Leye is embroidering a sack, the old *beys hamedresh*. *Shabes*, going to *shul*[Tr. Note: Synagogue] on *shabes*, Elke Magaziner's house, Khana Leye Kaplan's house, Gedalia the wall builder's house, Vintse the water carrier, Velvl Khaykl's at the butcher's,

The forest and Oshmene Road, Shmuel the kettle maker's house, the tailor and his wife, Nosn the tailor and his wife, Shmuel Yankl the beggar's house, Libe Itteh – left, Sheyne Itteh, the coachmen are traveling to Vilne, Dubizishok street with the cemetery, Elke the warehouse keeper at her house, Peyshe the beggar with Berl Kalmen, Zalmen Aharon with some Jews.

The post and Motele Roshkes' wall,[Tr. Note: The word "*moyer*" here may also be a 'brick house'] the Hebrew school with the teachers, Hirsh the 'red haired' at work, Old Shloyme with a calf at the market, Shloyme the Butcher's house with his family, Bartonovski's house, Leybe the Coachman, Are Yankl Krizovski as he's planting tomatoes, Reyzl the daughter of Leybe Bartonovski on her porch, Leybl the Smith with Nokhemke at work. Eli the Tinsmith lets the cow out for the first time, Yankl the *Aeroplane*,[Tr. Note: A nickname meaning 'flighty'] Elinke the

Tinsmith's and son–in–law, Kahas and his mother, and Dovid the Shoemaker and his wife.

1.6 A Greeting for the 10th Anniversary

A few words to our beloved brother and devoted friend Jack Zalkin.

We are all sure that this festive day is one of the deepest and most impressive celebrations for our brother, Zalkin. All of us who have worked with him over the years express our most heartfelt appreciation for the continued loyal and unswerving work that he carries out at every opportunity.

Much of that credit goes to our 'mother' – as we are wont to call her – Martha.

We are sure, however, that she would have been unable to accomplish much of what was so wonderfully and precisely carried out if it were not for our brother and devoted folks–person, Jack Zalkin. His entire being is immersed in his work. He does everything with heart and soul, and spares no effort or time. For him there is nothing too difficult nor any hour too late. There are nights he has not slept and days he has not eaten, running from one end of New York City to the other – and all for the benefit of the Ladies Auxiliary, to ensure assistance for the needy. He never asked for any honor. And so, we therefore wish brother Zalkin many long years of health.

With Sisterly Regards, On Behalf of the Divenishok Ladies Auxiliary, Ada Silverblank.

[Page 496]

30th Anniversary of the Divenishok Society of Greater New York [Tr. Note: 1903–1933]

2.1 Greetings by Yoysef L. Levey, first, and now current president

As the first president of the Divenishok Society, I greet you my brothers at this 30th anniversary and wish you a heartfelt welcome.

I feel that I will continue the difficult but satisfying work that I had taken upon myself with love and devotion – of course also with your assistance – for the progress and enhancement of our society.

The 30 years of existence of our Divenishok Society reminds me of the hard work, toil, and sacrifice that I, both as founder and as a member, have invested in realizing our aspirations to reach our goals. We see that our work has not been in vain— to the contrary. We have managed to erect a building that makes the Divenishok *landslayt proud*.

We come to this 30th anniversary at a time when the Divenishok Society is flourising, with a membership of 150 persons, with a guaranteed financial success, with a good reputation, and full of enthusiasm and hope for the future.

2.2 Ben Shloyshim Lekoyekh – Meir Zusman Ex–President

I step up with great reverence to the task of describing briefly the history of this wonderful moment that we now witness proudly – the Divenishok Society of New York. Fully 30 years of work have gone into reaching this glorious monument.

When one looks at a firm in existence for 30 years no one asks questions about its achievements. Instead, the general public relies on the firm's activities with complete trust, justified by its 30 years of existence.

Certain of our brothers who were for some time passive as to the activities of the society – and I would even dare say they were unreceptive to the society and its activists – will now have to respect it, whether they want to or not, if they themselves expect to be respected. This is because we are now a *ben shloyshim lekoyekh*, and when faced with such prominence one must, as a rule, show respect.

2.3 In Memorium

The special publication in honor of the 30th Anniversary of the Divenishok Society of Greater New York contained a list in memory of the members who had passed away: Morris Goldfein, Khaim Alter Horvits, Sam Trackel, Reuven Rabinovitsh, Yeshayahu Kartshmer, Ike Levine, Meir Pruzan, Benjamin Tublitski, Joseph Ross, Moyshe Yakov Daytsh, Nathan Smith, Morris Anshelovitsh, Isaac Levine, Morris Goldberg, Philip Levine, Abbie Talal, Jacob Gershonovitsh, Louis Rothman, Binyamin Alter Dubin, Sarah Rudnik, Yete Levine, Ida Dubin, Libe Levine, Yete Bayevitsh, Roze Cohen, Bessie Forman, Rosie Parson, Line Blumgarden, Freyde Kartshmer, Ida Levine, Ene Kraus, Bela Levine, Fene Horvits, Yete Salit Horvits, Khaye Dvoyre Smith, Feyge Toybe Horvits, Rebecca Rabinovitsh, Mrs. Tushitski.

The 35th Anniversary of the Divenishok Society
[Tr. Note: 1903–1938]

3.1 Greetings by Yoysef L. Levey, first and current president

It has again fallen upon me as president of the Divenishok Society to greet all friends and members to our 35th anniversary celebration. I am honored by the yoke[Ed. Note: the role of president] placed upon me by the Divenishok Society. The task has been pleasant. The harder the work has become, the more the need for it – and it must be done. Helping the needy has been both a joy and a pleasure.

During these 35 years, the Divenishok Society has undergone various periods. During these past 5 years there has been a difficult period of unemployment. In these same 5 years we have spent about 5,000 dollars for death benefit endowments and health benefits. We also contributed to general charities such as the Federation for Jewish Philanthropic Societies, American Jewish Congress, the Joint, and various other institutions.

I am very happy that we will be opening our "Old Age Fund". Beginning with the year 1939 an elderly member in need will no longer have to approach anyone about not being able to pay his dues.

The Divenishok Society has also paid cemeteries to the tune of about 10 thousand dollars and remains in a healthy financial state. We have about 160 members. When we add their family members we can say that the membership is over 300.

I am pleased that there is now peace in our organizations. May there never again be flare-ups and may we all work in harmony. When peace reigns amongst us then we will continue to progress.

3.2 Greetings from Meir Land

It is an outstanding moment for me to write this greeting, my dear brothers. We gather again to celebrate out 35th anniversary – with magnificence and elegance.

For us members it is a historic moment because during these 35 years worlds have turned upside down. Powerful leaders have been eliminated. Many nations have lost their civilization and were set back a full generation. Many societies have perished, but the Divenishok Society continues to move forward.

From year to year our society has grown.

It sounds fantastic: from Divenishok, a small *shtetele*, immigrants came to New York and found the society in 1903 with a handful of people. Who could foresee then, that from that small sprout a giant tree would grow with 160 new branches. Yes, the society is the pride of Divenishok. The society has made it possible that all Divenishokers would be able to gather together.

At age 13 [TR Note: 1916], the society gave birth to a child – that was the 'Relief'. For the several and twenty years since its creation, the Relief has sent thousands of dollars over to Divenishok, rescuing hundreds of people from poverty. Without the Relief, tens of children would have been left without an education. To this very day the Relief assists our destitute. This is the fruit borne by our society.

Another great creation has emerged from our society, in the 27th year [TR Note: 1930] since its founding, the Divenishok Ladies Auxiliary was born. The Auxiliary is like having a grandchild for the society and the Auxiliary also has many deed of which to be proud. It sends hundreds of dollars a year for bread and wood. In a word, all the branches do noble work.

It is important to point out, that the society also has a great–grandchild – the "Junior League". These institutions are our children. They have united and committed themselves to the destitute in Divenishok.

3.3 Society Activity (In relation to the 35th anniversary)

By Rabbi Israel Movshovitsh, for over 20 years rabbi in Divenishok, and to this day, a rabbi in Bronx New York.

During a period of political twilight there arose an idea to create a Divenishok Society in order to unite all the brothers and sisters who saw their first light in a small *shtetl* in what was once Russia, and to join together all those whose cradles stood in those tiny, meager, and dark dwellings in Divenishok. The idea of the founders was that at brotherly gatherings members would recount their joys and their tribulations. Unfortunately, the causes of suffering were more than those of joy, particularly for the hard working immigrants.

It is not easy to present an overview – especially a short one – of everything that the Society has achieved. However, one thing does remain fresh in my memory: during the period when the population of Divenishok lived through the worst trials of the war,[Tr. Note: First World War] the evacuation under the Russians, the hunger under the Germans, the terrible forced labor, pogroms and oppressions. During this lengthy period of isolation from the greater world around (and even from the closer surrounding area) there suddenly appeared a ray of light: The leaders of the society decided to establish a 'Relief', whose purpose would be to aid fallen home–owners, to provide a Jewish education for poor children, and to ease the situation of needy widows and orphans.

With this concise overview, I have perhaps managed to bring up certain memories, but these far from encompass the diverse activity of the society during its 35 years of existence.

Mordechai Milton-Kartshmer, his wife Sarah z"l, and Rosa Becker-Wiener in New York

[Page 500]

Greeting to the 45th Anniversary of the Divenishok Society of Greater New York
[Tr. Note: 1903–1948]

Celebrated the 18th of December 1948, at the Paramount Mansion, 183rd Street and St. Nicholas Avenue, New York.

From President Yosef Levey:

Dear brothers and sisters,

I greet you all with pride and love, brothers and sisters, to the celebration of our beloved Divenishok Society. 45 years have passed since our society was founded – great, stormy years in the history of our people.

It was at the beginning of the 20th century. Our parents and brothers in the old home were oppressed, and in great streams they made their way as

immigrants to the new, unfamiliar world – America. They wandered around, lonely, over the streets of New York, and sought the hand of friendship so as appease, together, the spiritual longing for the old home, for parents, for wife and child.

And then the Divenishok Society of New York was created. Our beginning was humble. Seven *landslayt* came together on the 7th of October, 1903, at the house of Simon Levine at 137 Market Street on the East side of New York, and laid the foundation of our Divenishok *landsmanshaft*.

The purpose of the society was to help with health benefits and burial plots and funerals. However, for the members, it meant more than just the material help. It meant brotherly, spiritual support, mutual aid, fellowship at times of joy, and God forbid, in times of sorrow. It meant help for the sick and the poor as well as money, counseling, and practical assistance.

Very quickly our society became loved and grew in membership. The society drew in *landslayt* and friends with their wives and children. As numbers increased so also did the charitable activities of the society for noble causes.

Tens of years have passed. The First World War came and the Divenishok Society threw itself into the Relief's work; it helped rebuild what was destroyed in the old homeland, and brought it back to life, set the suffering brothers back on their feet, aiding them with money, food and clothing.

Our women and sisters stepped up and established the Ladies Auxiliary, and together with the Relief, threw themselves with devotion into the task of performing good deeds. They helped bring over immigrants and took them in, and sought to support them and help them find work.

Again, a number of years passed, and the great tragedy of our European brothers came to pass – The Second World War. Our old home had been burnt and became desolate. Our ill–fated brethren were treacherously slain at the hands of the enemy. Again, it became urgent to offer aid and succor. Again, our Relief together with the assistance of the Ladies Auxiliary, displayed a commitment to offer help to the misfortunates.

The actions of our 'Relief' shall be engraved in golden letters in the annals of the Devinishok society. We may be proud for our children and future generations, and serve as an example of benevolence and heartfelt goodwill.

Yenta Spivak z"l (born Kaganovitsh), her husband, brother, and his wife, from the U.S, at the time of their visit to Israel

I express my wish that our currently large group consisting of 150 members will continue to increase. Our dear and beloved family should grow in scope and significance. May all of our brothers and sisters and their families live happily to see *nakhes*[Tr. Note: Pride and joy] from their children and grandchildren for the *zkhus*[Tr. Note: Privilege] of doing *maasim toyvim*.[Tr. Note: Good deeds]

Greetings unto you my dear brothers and sisters of the Divenishok Society on this day of our great celebration – the 45th anniversary of our Divenishok Society of New York.

***

[Tr. Note: The following note is by Y. Bloch (or possibly the editor of the Yizkor book)]:

Even though the older generation of activists of the Devinishok *landslayt* in New York is now in the *oylem hoemes*,[Tr. Note: Place of truth – Heaven] their children continue the beautiful tradition and continue the blessed work, albeit not in the same scope or with the same enthusiasm as their fathers and grandfathers...

Translator's Footnotes

1. *landsman* – Person who was born or lived in the same town or geographic area as others (plural is: *landslayt*).
See *landslayt, landsmanshaft*.

2. *landsmanshaft* – Fraternal organization of people who were born or lived in the same town or geographic area. Often, the second and even third generation are included in the membership.
See *landsman, landslayt*.

3. *landslayt* – Plural of landsman. See also *landsmanshaft*.

[Page 503]

The 70th Anniversary of the Divenishok Relief in America

Binyamin Dubinski

Translation by Emma Karabelnik

It is hard to determine when the first Divenishok immigrants come to America. The fact that the 'Relief' was established in 1903 clearly proves that emigration from Divenishok started long before. It began back in the 19th century. In the beginning of the current century[1] there was already a quite large amount of Divenishker in America— enough to establish a 'Relief'.

This fact proves that our compatriots back then were blessed with initiative, intelligence, temperament – and talent, and also with a strong commitment to social and philanthropic activity.

There were three factors that caused emigration flow to America. First, there was the severe poverty of the Jews living in the "Pale of Settlement" in Tsarist Russia. The poverty was hard, especially among laborers. It's not surprising that young laborers looked for a way to reach the free world.

The second factor was the revolutionary wind spreading like a storm in Tzarist Russia, reaching even to our little shtetl. A branch of the "Bund"[2] was established in Divenishok, and all the fine young boys and girls, and also the intelligentsia, devoted themselves passionately to revolutionary activity. Jewish youth demanded equality, freedom and justice –they didn't have any of these in Divenishok.

Convention of Divenishok emigrants in New York

The third factor increasing the flow of immigrants to America was the repressive policy implemented by the Tsarist regimes towards the whole Jewish population. It was strictly forbidden to employ Jews in government or municipal positions; a Jew couldn't live in Moscow or [St.] Petersburg. The discrimination caused a lot of hatred towards the Tsarist regime; and Jews did everything to avoid military service. Whoever had the opportunity got out illegally, abroad, across the "green border".

As a result of all the factors mentioned above there gathered a significant amount of Divenishker in America. Most of the immigrants were unprofessional workers and they experienced great difficulties. The conditions were bad, the system of "sweat–shops" was common everywhere, people worked long hours for low wages – and they felt bitter and desperate.

Some of Divenishok young fellows who had an interest in social activity took the initiative of establishing a Divenishok relief in America. It is hard for me to determine who were the first founders because the relief records are not in my possession – they are in America – but there is no doubt that initial credit belongs to Joseph Levi and Meir Bolinski. Their productive activities lasted for almost their entire lives. The special edition in honor of the 50th anniversary of Divenishok relief in America (1903–1953) was largely dedicated to the activity of the first president of our relief, Joseph Levi, where he wrote about the goals and achievements that he succeeded to accomplish:

To give new immigrants financial aid; To help them find work; And most important – a social basis [a foundation] to help the surviving brothers from the Old Country to build a new life.

Mordechai Milton Kartshmer, president of the organization of Divenishok emigrants in the U.S., with his wife Sarah z"l, in the New York office of the appeal for Israel

The Relief performed the duties that it took upon itself with great dedication, and did intense extensive work in different areas in order to organize and stabilize the lives of new immigrants. For this purpose they organized campaigns for the unfortunate ones: medical aid was given to those in need, and also visitation of the sick at homes or in hospitals [was arranged]. The relief also organized discussion nights, along with various activities, celebrations and cultural events.

This fruitful work by the relief brought good results. Till this day, all the ex-"rookies" are grateful for the vital aid that they received as soon as they stepped on American soil, and they are tightly connected to their Relief.

*

1914. The shot in Sarajevo fires the start of a bloody world war that lasts 5 long years. The regime in the shtetl constantly changes. The Russians retreat and the Germans come in their place. Famine in the shtetl is great. The Germans grab youngsters and send them to "labor–battalions" – forced labor. After 2 years the Germans retreat and their places are taken by Poles. The "*halertchikes*"3 cut the beards of Jews and imposed terror on Jewish populations. Suddenly the Poles desert our town, and the Bolsheviks come—again famine and diseases. There is an epidemic of typhus in the shtetl, with a lot of victims.

The Bolsheviks run away and the Lithuanian cavalry comes to town. It doesn't take long before the Poles occupy the town again – and finally the regime gets stabilized.

The American Relief instantly reacted to the call for help from their Divenishok brothers and generously sent money to individuals and organizations. In New York the "Ladies Auxiliary" was established as part of the Relief, and with common effort, hundreds of dollars flew to Divenishok year after year. All of Divenishok's institutions, such as the *Talmud Tora*, the bank, the library, [several] *Beth Midrash'es*, the "Tarbut" school which was almost entirely funded by the Relief, contributions for poor, *bikur cholim* [aid to sick people], *hachnasat-kala* [Jewish weddings], *hachnasat-orhim* [hospitality] and others, remained operational thanks to these monetary contributions.

When the American aid didn't come on time, Rabbi Joseph Rudnik and other important shtetl leaders would go around worried and disturbed: What will be? Where will we take money to pay the teachers? Pesakh is coming – where will donations for the poor come from?

*

In 1930 two Relief board members, Joseph Levi, of blessed memory, and Meir Bolinski, of blessed memory, came to visit the old town; they were shocked by the extent of poverty and misery in town.

Upon their return to America they enlarged the aid for their brothers in the old country even more enthusiastically. As a result of their visit there was established a "*gmilut-hasadim*" fund with the help of American money, which provided great help to Divenishok Jews. Every merchant, peddler, or wagon-owner who lost a horse, or any Jew who was in trouble, hurried to take a loan from the "*gmilut-hasadim*" fund.

In this manner the aid continued year after year. The American brothers with great [devotion] established funds for their hometown.

*

The year is 1939. On September 1, Hitler's Germany attacks Poland. The European Jews are persecuted and exterminated. Their desperate heartbreaking call "help us, save us" – didn't reach the free world.

[Page 508]

*Mordechai Milton-Kartshmer as an American soldier
in the Second World War, with his wile Sarah z"l*

It so happened that one of the most active members of the relief board, Milton Kartshmer, was mobilized in the American Army and took active part in the fighting in France, and came with the liberation army to the gates of Berlin. He saw with his own eyes the big tragedy that had befallen the European Jews. His Jewish heart trembled from the pain and suffering, and he decided to do everything to help Divenshok Jews who had survived [the Holocaust].

On his return to America he became the Head of our Relief and devoted himself to philanthropic work to help the last survivors of our shtetl, scattered on the roads and camps across Europe. As soon as a [new] living Divenishker was discovered, he would be contacted, and necessary aid would be sent to him. Every Divenishker found a warm heart, an open hand, and a brotherly aid.

Later, when most of the survivors had been concentrated in Israel, the relief established a *"gmilut–hasadim"* fund. Thanks to this, many of our compatriots were able to buy a flat, which was the greatest problem for the new *Olim* in Israel.

*

Seventy years is a long period of time not only in the life of an individual, but even in the life of an organization – that's why our American brothers can be proud of their Relief, which has stood out with its social and philanthropic work, with lots of energy, enthusiasm, love and fellowship.

We would like to hope, that the young generation of Americans will honor their parents and continue the important work of fellowship towards their Israeli brothers. Our prayer is that the young generation will not fall from their parents' [deeds].

Editor's Footnotes

1. This article was written in the 1970s so the writer refers to the 20th Century.

2. A Social–Democratic movement of the time

3. In the original text, the word 'halertchikes' is spelled: hey–aleph–lamed–ayen–reysh–tes–shin–yud–kuf–ayen–samekh. The exact meaning of the word is not yet known.

Report from the Divenishok Ladies Auxiliary

Nellie Brown

Translation by Leybl Botwinik

Divenishok, where I was born, is in the vicinity of Vilne. My father's name was Alter Solodukhe. He taught both small children and adults. My mother's name was Itteh, one of Berl Zelik's daughters. Our family was, as the saying goes *"tsu got un tsu layt"*.[Tr. Note: Honest, decent, and god–fearing]

I have been in America for many years and lived through many periods, but I have always been drawn to my *landslayt*.[Tr. Note: People who were born or lived in the same town or geographic area]

In 1930, our *landslayt* joined forces to create a women's organization – the Ladies Auxiliary. Our work consisted in sending money to Divenishok for heating, bread, maintaining the houses, and *gmiles khsodim*.[Tr. Note: Charity and charitable efforts] Our first chairperson was Lina Schwarts who excelled in her activism – to this day. The second was Libe Bolinski, always friendly and devoted, together with the wonderful Rose Aaronsohn (sister of Meir Bolinski), who played an important role in building up the Auxiliary. There was also Martha Zalkin and her finance secretary, my sister Molly Krits and myself as recording secretary. We held these positions for 10 years.

During the 10 years that Martha Zalkin was president, our undertakings grew from day to day. Of course, this was with the participation of all the members, and in particular the Bolinskis who were always the greatest communal volunteers in the organization.

Martha Zalkin greatly excelled in her work. When she was no longer president we honored her and gave her the title of honorary president of the Divenishok Ladies Auxiliary. She absolutely earned it for her capable work. Also her husband Yakov Zalkin added immensely to the community activity.

In 1943, Sarah and Motl Kartshmer arrived from Cuba. It did not take long and they threw themselves with all their fervor into the activities of the Divenishok Ladies Auxiliary because they became convinced that the Auxiliary carried out earnest and wonderful work.

In 1943, I was elected as chairperson of the Ladies Auxiliary together with the outstanding Penny Sbeyski as finance secretary, and the devoted Rose Becker as protocol secretary. This was during World War II. Our sons were mobilized in the army, as well as our brother Motl Kartshmer. Everyone walked about despondent and without energy. Of course this hampered the work and we had the impression that the Auxiliary would go under. It should be underscored here that the Bolinskis did not allow this to happen, because for Mrs. Bolinski, helping the needy was a part of her very existence. She, together with her husband, was adamant that the Divenishok Ladies Auxiliary should and must exist, even more than before.

As chairperson, I did everything I could to motivate and explain to the membership that we must now be united, come to the meetings, actively participate in the work, and live with the hope that the day of peace would arrive. It was successful. With new strength we again started to work and send packages. We would receive responses full of gratitude that positively affected our members.

Later we sent good packages of food and clothing to each *landsman*,[Tr. Note: Singular form of *landslayt*] wherever he was to be found. These parcels, according to what we heard from the camps, kept our *Divenishokers* alive. We did this until our last *landsman* left the camps in Germany.

Correspondence with those who were in the camps was handled by Sarah Kartshmer and Meir Bolinski. They would send letters of consolation and hope. When the *pleytim*[Tr. Note: Survivors] succeeded in emmigrating to America we gave them presents, money, and other necessary things in order to help them set themselves up.

When we found out that our *landsman* in Israel, Yakov Bloch, lost a hand at work, our Ladies Auxiliary decided to bring him over to America to help him with anything we could in order to obtain a new prosthetic 'hand'. Each and every member took to the task. The main roles were "performed" by Mrs. and Mr. Bolinski, as well as by Mrs. and Mr. Kartshmer. The Bolinskis watched over him as if he was their own child. After 8 months, Yakov received his new prosthetic 'hand', and we wish him – from a distance – that he should be able to manipulate it as best as possible.

Yakov has left us. Annie Levine, his aunt, still believes that she will meet up with him under better circumstances. The Divenishok Ladies Auxiliary – all the members – accompanied him to the ship, wishing joy and friendship to his land and family.

I complete my report with a heartfelt greeting to all the members for their diligent work during the 21 year existence of our "Divenishok Ladies Auxiliary".

[Page 512]

Organization of Former Divenishok Residents in Israel

Tsvi Ahuvi (Lieb)

Translation by Leybl Botwinik

Until just after the *shoah*[Tr. Note: Hebrew term for "Holocaust"] there were few people from our town in Israel. They would get together from time to time and a strong rapport existed between them, but they were not organized as an association.

When I arrived in Israel with the Polish "General Anders army", a strong flow of people from our town began to stream to Israel, and there was then a need to create an organization of the people from our town.

The first memorial days in commemoration of the martyrs of our town were held at the house of Shloyme Levine (Leshchinski) on Bar-Kokhba Street in Tel Aviv. Candles were lit on the table, all the townspeople sat around on the beds, and that is how the memorial ceremony was carried out. This made a very disheartening impression on me, and when more survivors of our town began to arrive[Tr. Note: in Israel] the place was too constricted to accommodate us all.

First memorial for our martyrs, victims of the Nazi murders. The memorial took place in May 1946 in Tel-Aviv, in the home of the family Leshchinski - S. Levine

[Page 514]

We initiated a working committee and decided to carry out the memorial day in "*Bet HaKhalutsot*".[Tr. Note: The NY Women's League set up "Women's Pioneer Houses" across Israel to support women immigrants]

On the 23rd of the Jewish month of Iyar in 1946 (May 24), we carried out the memorial ceremony in the Tel Aviv *Bet HaKhalutsot*. All our townspeople were present: Man and wife, elderly and toddler. It was a moving occasion since there were present people who had not seen one another for twenty–five years. The enthusiasm and emotion of unity was greater than expected. Since then the bond among the people of our town strengthened, remembering the good days of our town.

Since then, the memorial days of our town takes place each year on the 23rd of the Jewish month of Iyar, [Tr. Note: The date that is marked is according to the Jewish calendar. In 1942, it was the 11th of May] that is the day the Nazis, *yemakh shemam*,[Tr. Note: May their name be wiped out] annihilated our community. We would unite with the memory of the martyrs of our town and exchange reminiscences from the past.

Divenishok emigrants in Israel at the memorial evening for our martyrs, in Tel-Aviv, May 1949

Presidium of the Tel-Aviv memorial service, with the participation of guests from America, Solomon Levine and his wife z"l

Later, our friends from abroad – Meir Bolinski, Khaim Yudl Horvits, Milton Kartshmer, Kamenitski, and others – visited us in Israel and contributed a lot of money to set up the *g'makh*.[Tr. Note: abbreviation for *gmilat khesed* – a charitable fund or service for the needy] The *g'makh* distributed loans to many of our town's people, and this further strengthened the fraternal bonds among our townspeople.

[Page 515]

MEMORY CANDLE

[Page 517]

In memory of the martyrs and
warriors lost from Divenishok.

[Page 518]

We mourn together for all the martyrs of Israel who fell for the sanctification of HaShem at the hands of the murdering Germans, may their names be erased, and their assistants.

The list includes only the names of the family elders.

The list was compiled from memory after more than 30 years. There are very possible omissions of names-- so we have left blank spaces to add the missing names.[Ed. Note: Blank lines ommitted from this translation]

[Ed. Note: On this page, the same message is printed in Hebrew then Yiddish.]

[Page 519]

List of Martyrs

Transliterated by Ellen Sadove Renck
Edited by Sara Mages
Standardized by Adam Cherson

Surname	First name	Family or note	Partisan
Abramovitsh	Tzvi	and family	
Aloni	Bruriah (daughter of Rabbi Rudnik)	died in Israel	
Aloni	Abraham (a school teacher and principal)	died in Israel	
Baksht	Binyamin		
Bolinski	Meir, chairman of Relief	died in the US	
Bolinski	Fenny (wife Meir Bolinski, chairman of the Leeds Auxiliary)	died in the US	
Bolinski	Yehudit (sister of Meir Bolinski)	died in the US	
Baran	Moshe		
Barnett	Sam, one of the important activist of the relief in the US	died in the US	
Bartonovski	Chaya Reizel		
Becker	David	and Chana	
Bender	Naftali	and family	
Ben-Dov	Shoshanna, daughter of Eliahu Chaim	died in Israel	
Berman	Mordechai	and family	
Bernshteyn	Yehudah	photo p. 558	
Bernshteyn	Bluma	and family	
Bernshteyn	Chaya Ita		
Bernshteyn	Chaya	and family	
Bernshteyn	and her children (sister of Zalman Yosef)		
Bernshteyn	Miriam		
Bernshteyn	Daniel	photo p. 558	
Blyakher	Gershon		
Blyakher	Sonia		
Blyakher	Meir	and family	
Blyakher	Mikal	and family	
Blyakher	Moshe	and family	
Blyakher	Rafael	and family	

Blyakher	Shimon Leib		
Blyakher	Yita	died in Israel	
Blyakher	Mordechai (son of Hirshel the blacksmith from Pazlup?)	died in Israel	
Blyakher	Mina (daughter of Shimon Leib)	died in Israel	
Blyakher	Sima (wife of Shraga Blyakher)	died in Israel	
Blyakher	Tuvia http://www.partisans.org.il/Site/site.card.aspx?lang=en&id=9581	killed in the Stuki forest	partisan
Blyakher	Gershon	fell in the defence of Warsaw	partisan
Bloch	Fridl	and family	
Bloch	Dov	fell in the defence of Moscow	partisan
Bloch	Frida and her children: Malka, Doba, and Shaul	photo p. 558	
Bzura	and Breina (from the family of Chaim Noah Kretzmer)	and family	
Chasman (Khasman)	Moshe Ben-Zion (immigrated to Israel by foot 60 years ago)	died in Israel	
Deiches	Chaim	and family	
Delatishki	Naftali	and family	
Deich(es)	Leib	and family	
Druck	Yakov	died in Canada	
Dubin	Shmuel	died in South Africa	
Dubinski	Yosef, Bluma and their sons Meir, Michael and Tzvi		
Dubinski	Shmuel (from Byenyakoni)	and family	
Dubinski	Meir	killed in the village of Letuviza?	partisan
Dubinski	Michael http://www.partisans.org.il/Site/site.card.aspx?lang=en&id=9736	killed in Vilna	partisan
Dubinski	Tzvi	killed in the village of Letuviza ?	partisan
Dubinski	Nachman	killed in Klyetsk	partisan
Engle	Reuben	and family	
Etzkovitz (Itskovitsh)	Natan	and Heina-Motla and family	
Gershovitsh (Hershovitsh)	Chaim	and family	
Gershovitsh (Hershovitsh)	Chaim and his sons	killed in the vicinity of Devenishki	partisans

Gerson (Kherson)	see Herson		
Ginzburg	Avigdor	and family	
Ginzburg	Alter	and family	
Gitlits	Debora	and children	
Gitlits	Yitzchak	and family	
Gloit	Efraim	and family	
Gol	Masha	and daughter	
Gordon	Rivka	and family	
Graber	Khat	and family	
Grabia	Shalom	and family	
Gridzovtza	see Shults		
Herson (Kherson)	Aharon	and family	
Herson (Kherson)	Yosef	and family	
Herson (Kherson)	Michel	and family	
Herson (Kherson)	Ikel	and family	
Horvits	Chaim Yodel	died in New-York	
Horvits	Yulius	photo p. 558	
Horvits	Shmuel	photo p. 558	
Horvits	Ajzik	photo p. 558	
Inklbitz	Eliahu	and family	
Inklbitz	Yakov	and family	
Jankelewicz	Eliahu	and family	
Jankelewicz	Yakov	and family	
Jutan (Yutan)	Etel	and children	
Jutan (Yutan)	Yisrael	and family	
Kaganovitsh	Aharon son of Eliahu		
Kaganovitsh	Eliahu (the butcher)	photo p. 558	
Kaganovitsh	Sima, wife of Eliah	photo p. 558	
Kamenitski	Shmuel, one of the important activist of Relief	died in the US	
Kaplan	Yeshayahu	and family	
Kaplan	Moshe	and family	
Kaplan	Natan son of Yosef	and family	
Kaplan	Natan	and family (Alter Yashe Nashes)	
Kaplan	Chaya-Sheta	died in Israel	
Kaplan	Mordechai	died in Israel	
Kartshmer	Abraham-Gutl	survivor	
Kartshmer	Sam	survivor	
Kartshmer or Kretzmer	Ita		

Kartshmer or Kretzmer	Berl		
Kartshmer or Kretzmer	Hinda (wife of Kalman)	and children	
Kartshmer or Kretzmer	Noah	and family	
Kartshmer or Kretzmer	Reuben	and wife	
Kartshmer or Kretzmer	Feivel	and family	
Katz	Yeta/Eta		
Katz	David	and family	
Katz	Zalman	and family	
Katz	Yakov son of R' David	and family	
Katz	Yeshayahu Moshe (fell in the defence of Warsaw)		Partisan
Katz	Leiba son of Idel	and family	
Katz	Meir	and family	
Katz	Yeshayahu Moshe (fell fighting the Germans)		
Katz	Berl	died in Canada	
Katsev	Zev	and family	
Kozlovski	Abe (Abe the cobbler)		
Kramer	Moshe Kalman	and family	
Kretzmer	Avraham-Gutel	survivor	
Kretzmer			
Kretzmer	see Bzura		
Krichevski	Shtirke, husband Meir	and family	
Krisovski	Hirshl	and family	
Krivitski	Abraham	and family	
Kubanski	Shoshana	photo p. 558	
Kubanski	Iser	and family	
Kuniak	Gedeliah	and family	
Kupshits	Mendel (from the village of Gridzvza?)	and family	
Kusbitzki	Miriam daughter of Tzvi Oshinski	and husband and children	
Kutler (Kotler)	Alter	and family	
Kutler (Kotler)	Yakov	and family	
Kutler (Kotler)	Leib	and family	
Kutler (Kotler)	Shlomo	and family	
Kutler (Kotler)	Shlomo	killed in the Stuki forest	partisan

Lapida	Israel	and family	
Leybman	Leib	and family	
Levine	Aizik	and family	
Levine	Alter (from the village of Daniuka?)	and family	
Levine	Alter (from the village of Giranyoni?)	and family	
Levine	Alter	and family (Dziar)	
Levine	Eliahu	and family	
Levine	Batya, daughter of R'Yekutiel		
Levine	Breina from Subotnik		
Levine	Gad (Gutka) son of R' Yitzchak	and family	
Levine	Hirshl son of Pesach	and family	
Levine	Hirshel (the cobbler)	and family	
Levine	Zvi (the cobbler from Traby)	and family	
Levine	Velvel from Subotnik	and family	
Levine	Zalman son of Aharon	and family	
Levine	Chaim the miller from Pazlup		
Levine	Moshe the miller from Pazlup		
Levine	Chaim Heshel	and family	
Levine	Broina	wife Feiga and daughter Liba	
Levine	Yehudah son of R' Broina	and family	
Levine	Yakov	and family	
Levine	Yitzchak son of R' Bezalel		
Levine	Yitzchak from Giranion?	and family	
Levine	Leibe son of Moshe	and family	
Levine	Lea	and family	
Levine	Meir	and family	
Levine	Mina and Rachel	(sisters)	
Levine	Moshe (son-in-law of Sara Dishe)		
Levine	Moshe	and family	
Levine	Natan		
Levine	Feivel		
Levine	Pesach	and family	
Levine	Feivel		
Levine	Peshka from Subotnik		
Levine	Rivka	and daughter	
Levine	Rachel Lea		
Levine	Simcha son of Zalman	and family	

Levine	Shimon Leib	and family	
Levine	David	and wife Feiga and daughter Liva	
Levine	Dvora	and children	
Levine	Zalman Leib	and family	
Levine	Tsila her husband and children from Subotnik		
Levine	Yitzchak from Dnuke?	killed in the Stuki forest	partisan
Levine	Chaim from Dnuke?	killed in the Stuki forest	partisan
Levine	Gad (Gutke)	killed in the vicinity of Giranion?	partisan
Levine	Yosef (Yosele), son of R' Moshe Levine	died in Israel	
Levine	Harry, one of the important activists of Relief and the Bonds	died in the US	
Levine	Levi, from the founders of Relief. Was the first chairman and served in the course of years.	died in the US	
Levine	Solomon son of Rafael, from the founders of Relief and one of its important activists	died in the US	
Levine	Heshe (Heni) daughter of Yitzhak Benyamin	died in the US	
Levine	Ida	photo p. 558	
Levine	see Yudenfreund	survivor?	
Lipkovski	Yekutiel/Jekutiel	and family	
Lipkunski	Nachum	and family	
Lipkunski	son of Yekutiel/Jekutiel	killed in a forest near Devenishki	partisan
Lubetski	David Chaim	and family	
Lubetski	Zev son of R' David Chaim	and family	
Lubetski	Zeidl	and family	
Lubetski	Sara Leah	and daughters	
Lzelman	see Saladuka	survivor	
Maroch	Leib	and family	
Mazeh	Eliahu	and wife Feiga and daughter Liba	
Mazeh	Michael	and family	
Melamed	Eliahu	and family	
Melamed	Eliahu	and family	

Melamed	Gabriel	and wife	
Melamed	Grunem	and family	
Mikelson	Benyamin		
Mievski	Yehoshua	and family	
Mintz	Itka		
Mintz	Elka		
Mintz	Bezalel	and family	
Mintz	Hinda		
Mintz	Hirshel (the tailor)		
Mintz	Yehudah (brother of Mintz, Hirshel)		
Mintz	Yosef (from Agazin?)	and family	
Mintz	Pinchas	and family	
Mintz	Pesach son of Eliezer	died in the US	
Movshovitsh	Rabbi Yisrael of Divenishuk	died in the US	
Movshovitsh	Rachel Leah (Rebbitzen), wife of Rabbi Israel Movshovitsh	died in the US	
Movshovitsh	Nachum, son of Rabbi Yisrael Movshovitsh	died in the US	
Namiot	the pharmacist	and family	
no surname	Leibel the Varshever (Leibel from Warsaw)	killed in a forest near Devenishki	partisan
Noviazki	Rachel, daughter of Leib Dubin	died in Israel	
Novoplanski	Aba-Leib	and family	
Olkenitski	Chaim	and family	
Olkenitski	Yosef	and family	
Oschinski	Tzvi	and family	
Portnoi	Eliahu (Eltzik the mute)		
Rosenblum	Menucha (from Pazlup?)		
Rudnik	Alter son of Gedalia	and family	
Rudnik	Rivka	and family	
Rudnik	Rivka (wife of Itshe Benyamin)	and family	
Rudnik	the Rabbinet Sheina, daughter of Rabbi Yosef Rudnik		
Rogol	Aryeh Leib	and family	
Saladucha (Solodukhe)	Michael great-grandson of Zalman Levine Aharon	died in the US	
Segal	Yitzhak	killed in the Liptshan forest	partisan
Shklar	Eliahu	and family	
Shklar	Moshe (uncle of Sara Teibka)	died in the US	

Shkolnik	Eliahu Chaim	and family	
Shkolnik	Teiba	and family	
Shkolnik	Chaim, son of Zusia Yakob	died in Cuba	
Shkolnik	Zvi (Hirshke) son of Zusia Yakob	survivor	
Shlubski	Gershon		
Schmidt	Hirsh	and family	
Schneider or Sznajder	Ben-Zion and Sara Hinda	and family	
Schneider or Sznajder	Asher	and family	
Schneider or Sznajder	Daniel	and family	
Schneider or Sznajder	Yakov		
Schneider or Sznajder	Meir	and family (Zekela)	
Schneider or Sznajder	Mordechai	and family	
Schneider or Sznajder	Kalman	and family	
Schneider or Sznajder	Yakov son of Ben-Zion http://www.partisans.org.il/Site/site.card.aspx?lang=en&id=678	shot in the Naliboki forest	partisan
Schneider or Sznajder	Aharon son of Eliezer Nachum (from the village of Yanushevshchizna) Fell in the Yom Kippur war	died in Israel	
Schneider or Sznajder	Eliezer son of Bezalel (?)	died in Israel	
Schneider or Sznajder	Eliezer (son of Yakel Liezers)	died in Nahariya Israel	
Shlomovitsh	Abraham Noah (ritual slaughterer)	and family	
Shrira	Mina	and family	
Shtzitnitzki	Eliahu	and family	
Shubski	Gershon	and family	
Shults	Moshe	(from the village of Gridzvza?)	
Shults	brothers from Gidzwze?	killed in a forest near Devenishki	partisans
Sidoriski	Fruma		
Sidoriski	Leizer	and family	
Skkolnik (Shkolnik)	Alter son of Eliah Chaim	and family	
Smulkin	Yosef		

Solodukhe	Michael, great-grandson of Zalman Aharon Levine	died in the US	
Solodukhe	Z'nia	and family	
Solts	Hirsh	and family	
Solts	Leiba		
Spivak	Yona, daughter of Eliahu the butcher	died in Israel	
Srulovitsh	Yitzchak	and family	
Stekolshchik (Satkolshtsik)	Feigin Nachama, Pittsburgh, PA	died in the US	
Stekolshchik (Satkolshtsik)	Yehudah		
Stekolshchik (Satkolshtsik)	Tania		
Stzitnitzki	Zalman	killed in the village of Surkatzi?	partisan
Stzitnitzki	Feivel	killed in the village of Surkatzi?	partisan
Sutzkever	Sheina and her children		
Swartz (Schwarts)	Zev	and family	
Swintelsky	Aba		
Szkaliar (Skhlar)	Eliezer	killed in the Stuki forest	Partisan
Tayts	Aharon (the city's Rabbi)	and family	
Umpelin	ha khushubim	survivor	
Wiener	Meir Zalman	and family	
Wiener	Yeshayahu	and family	
Wolfovitz (Vulfovitsh)	Rivka	and family from Kolyshki	
Yehudah	and Mere and their son Yosef (son-in-law of Sara Dishe)		
Yudenfreund	Zipora daughter of Pesach Levine	died in Israel	
Yushinski	see Kusbitzki		
Zaika	Ben-Zion	and family	
Zandman	Dov (Fell in the War of Independence with the convoy to Mount Scopus)	died in Israel	
Zhizhemski	Yosef	and family	
Zlibinski	Zev	and family	
Zusman	Ber son of Leib	and family	
Zusman	Chaim son of Leib	and family	
Zusman	Moshe	and family	
Zusman	Leiba	and family	

[Page 529 (misprinted as 527)]

IN MEMORIAM

Yehudah Bernshteyn

Eliohu Kaganovitsh (the butcher)

Shmuel Horvits

Simha Kaganovitsh, wife of Eliohu

Julius Horvits

Daniel Bernshteyn

Ida Levine

Isaac Horvits

Shoshana Kubanski

*Yosef Aaron Schneider
fell in the Yom Kippur War*

*Shmuel Dubinski
(cousin of Binyamin Dubinski)
murdered by the Poles*

*Avraham Aloni
principal of the Tarbus School
in Divenishok*

Frieda Bloch and her children, Malka, Duba, Saul

Moshe Shklar z"l, from Argentina (see p. 472) [original pagination]

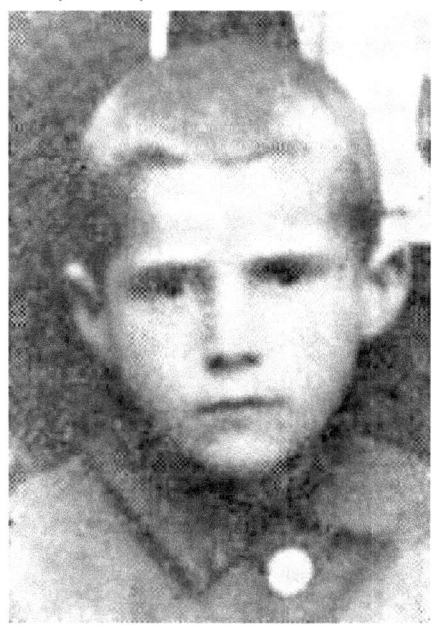

Tsvi Dubinski, partisan fell in the woods near Divenishok

Khaye Rivka Dubinski (Rogov) murdered by the Poles

Tsvi Hirshl Krizovski, who fell near Minsk in the war against the Nazis

Gedalye Horvits z"l and his son yb"l in the U.S.

Tsvi Krizovski's brother Aaron Krizovski, a poet, died in the U.S.

*Hannah Lipkunski
and Libka Schneider hi"d*

*Sonia Bernshteyn z"l
(daughter of Sarah)
from New York*

*Slova, Nakhum and Binyumin Lipkunski, hi"d,
Pinkhas and Akhim Levine, yb"ll*

פוקס הרמן ז"ל
(בעלה של שולמית תב"ל)

Herman Fuchs, z"l
(spouse of Shulamit, tb"l)

פוקס לילי
(בתם של הרמן ז"ל ושולמית יב"ל)

Lilly Fuchs (daughter of Herman and Shulamit z"l)

In Memoriam: Ladies Auxiliary in the U.S., at work on behalf of emigrants from Divenishok. Six have since passed away

[Page 536]

Memorial for the martyrs of Divenishok in New York

Annotated Name Index

Prepared by Adam Cherson

Note: Page numbers are for the first pages of the original Yizkor Book articles in which the references may be found, **not** the page numbers from this translation; please use the original page numbers shown in marginal brackets in this translation to locate the references (e.g., *[Page 509]*)

Surname	Given Name	Comments	Other names	Other towns	Page no.
AARONSOHN	Rose				509
AARONSOHN	Sarah				460
ABIR	Avraham	Rov			62, 251, 258 photo, 312, 385, 459
ABRAMOVITSH	Eytl				286
ABRAMOVITSH	Mordechai Motl				92, 286
AHUVI	Tsvi				219, 325, 347, 410, 477 photo, 481, 482 photo, 512
ALA	Dani				290
ALA	Eliezer				290
ALA	Esther	nee Blyakher	BLYAKHER		290
ALEICHEM	Sholom				271, 291
ALONI	Avraham		ZHOLONDZH		62, 71 photo, 85, 108, 258

				photo, 259, 266, 308, 401, 410, 410 photo, 425 photo, 533 photo
ALONI	Breyneh	nee Rudnik	ZHOLONDZH / RUDNIK	40 photo, 71 photo, 385, 410 photo
ALONI	Yosef		ZHOLONDZH	62, 85, 251, 385
ALPEROVITSH	Chaim			259, 288
ALPEROVITSH	Minkeh Mineh			130 photo, 169, 271, 419
ANDERS	Vladislav			219, 512
ANIEL	Basyeh Bashke	nee Kartshmer/ Kretchmer / Carczmer	KARTSHMER/ KRETCHMER / CARCZMER	469
ANSHELOVTISH	Yitzach Moshe			485
ARKIN	Hershl			219
ARKIN	Tsileh	nee Lieb	LIEB	219
ARTSHOM	Gutka			186
ARTSHOM	Yakov			186, 378, 485
ASCH	Sholom			5

ASHMAN	Avraham			300
ASHMAN	Beilah Bilkhe	nee Itskovitsh	ITSKOVITSH	72, 92, 108, 297 photo, 299, 320, 401
ASHMAN	Shlomo			30, 299
ASHMAN	Yosef			300
ASHPON	Avraham			165
ASHPON	Khayeh	nee Preski	PRESKI	165
AVIEL	Shlomo			296
BALBARISHKER	Leyb			465
BALEROVSKI	[NONE]	Landowner		447
BARAN	Aharon Leyb			459
BARDICHEVSKI	Aharon			90, 92
BAREH	Leyb			394
BARNETT	Chaim Shmuel			337, 476 photo
BARNETT	Eyta Vita	nee Horvits	HORVITS	337, 476 photo
BARNETT	Frank			5, 337
BARTONOVSKI	Leyb			485
BARTONOVSKI	Menya			316
BARTONOVSKI	Reyzl			316, 317 photo, 485
BARTONOVSKI	Tsvi			300
BASTOMSKI				259
BECKER				162
BECKER	Reyza Rose	nee Wiener	WIENER	342,

				502 photo, 509
BEN–AMI				285
BEN–DOV	Amnon			287
BEN–DOV	Shoshana	nee Shkolnik	SHKOLNIK	287
BEN–DOV	Yaffa			287
BEN–GURION	David			276, 419
BEN–TSVI	Yitzach			101
BENYAKONSKI	Chaim			106 photo
BENYAKONSKI	Yacov			106 photo, 110 photo, 280 photo, 323
BERKOVITSH	Barukh Leyb			115
BERKOVITSH	Blumeh Blanche	nee Movshovitsh	MOVSHOVITSH	259
BERKOVITSH	Dovid Leyb			62, 97, 115, 406 photo, 479
BERKOVITSH	Freda			271
BERKOVITSH	Yitzach Dov			271
BERKOVITSH	Ysroel			419
BERLING	Zygmunt			309
BERMAN	Khayeh	nee Kaplan	KAPLAN	52, 284 photo, 300
BERMAN	Mordechai			300
BERNSHTEYN	Daniel			527 photo

BERNSHTEYN	Duba			66 photo
BERNSHTEYN	Grunye	nee Khasman	KHASMAN	276
BERNSHTEYN	Miryam	nee Lipkunski	LIPKUNSKI	190
BERNSHTEYN	Moshe			307 photo
BERNSHTEYN	Sarah			535 photo
BERNSHTEYN	Sheyneh Yokhl	nee Rudnik	RUDNIK	123
BERNSHTEYN	Shlomo Sholem			190
BERNSHTEYN	Sholom Ber			446 photo
BERNSHTEYN	Sonia			535 photo
BERNSHTEYN	Tsireh Leah Lyke			111, 306
BERNSHTEYN	Tsirl Zirkeh			190
BERNSHTEYN	Tsvi			190
BERNSHTEYN	Yehuda			190, 527 photo
BERNSHTEYN	Yenteh	spouse Mendl "Kragele"	KRAGELE	306
BERNSHTEYN	Zalmen			111
BERNSHTEYN	Zalmen Yosef			190, 306
BIALIK	C. N.			251, 273
BIAVITSH	Eyta Leah		BAYEVITSH	485
BIELSKI	Asael			175
BIELSKI	Tuvyeh			136, 175, 186, 325, 334
BIELSKI	Zusyeh			175

BIZHESKI		Doctor			72
BLAUSHTEYN					460
BLEZUVSKI	Dina	nee Khasman	KHASMAN / LEBIZUVSKI		288
BLEZUVSKI	Dvorah				289
BLEZUVSKI	Yehuda				288
BLOCH	Aharon			Iwye	72, 339, 339 photo, 419, 420 photo
BLOCH	Dov				339, 419
BLOCH	Duba				339, 419, 527 photo
BLOCH	Freda	nee Rudnik	RUDNIK		123, 339, 419, 420 photo, 527 photo
BLOCH	Leyb				72
BLOCH	Malkeh				339, 410, 419, 527 photo
BLOCH	Shaul				339, 419, 527 photo
BLOCH	Shmuel				339, 419, 527 photo
BLOCH	Yakov				5, 50, 72, 130

				photo, 136, 339, 349, 401, 410, 419, 420 photo, 425 photo, 476 photo, 482, 485, 486 photo, 509
BLUM	Rosalyn	nee Levine	LEVINE	470
BLUMENTHAL	Dvorah	nee Trovski	TROVSKI	276
BLUMGARDEN	Linah			485
BLUSHTEYN				274
BLYAKHER				299 photo
BLYAKHER				286 photo
BLYAKHER	Bella	nee Olkenitski	OLKENITSKI	186
BLYAKHER	Binyamin			282, 290, 305
BLYAKHER	Eliohu			169, 175, 186, 186, 228, 282, 477 photo
BLYAKHER	Eltsik			136
BLYAKHER	Esther			290
BLYAKHER	Gitteh Merkeh			118, 290
BLYAKHER	Hershl Tsvi			285

BLYAKHER	Itke		66 photo
BLYAKHER	Itteh	KARTSHMER / KRETCHMER / CARCZMER	290, 291 photo, 299, 299 photo
BLYAKHER	Khayeh Shifreh Lifsheh		66 photo, 115, 290, 304 photo, 479
BLYAKHER	Khenyeh		108, 282, 307
BLYAKHER	Mordechai		285
BLYAKHER	Moshe		282, 307, 334, 378, 454, 485
BLYAKHER	Roda		290
BLYAKHER	Sarah Eyta		285
BLYAKHER	Shraga Feivel		5, 72, 108, 118, 269, 290, 303 photo, 394, 401, 410, 419, 429, 476 photo, 482 photo
BLYAKHER	Tuvyeh		66 photo, 72, 136,

				259, 290, 335, 335 photo, 401, 419
BLYAKHER	Yitzach			290
BLYAKHER	Zilpeh			118, 290, 479
BOGOSHOVITSH				219
BOGOSLAV				200
BOLESLAV				162
BOLINSKI				485, 509
BOLINSKI	Fenne			245 photo, 328 photo, 485
BOLINSKI	Libe			509
BOLINSKI	Meir			245 photo, 252 photo, 326 photo, 327, 328 photo, 481, 485, 503, 509, 512
BONIMOVITSH				296
BOR-KOMOROVSKI				309
BOTVINIK	Aryeh Leyb			72
BOYARSKI	Yekutiel			175
BROWN	Nellie	nee Solodukhe	SOLODUKHE	485, 509

BROYDE	Nisn		BRAUDE	251
BURAKAS		Lithuanian Commander		136
CALEB	Yitzach			344
CHERNO		Doctor		62, 72
COHEN	Leah Malkeh Lina			485
COHEN	Reyzl Rose			485
COHEN	Selye Celia	nee Horvits	HORVITS	337
COHEN	Yacov			62, 251
COHENSON	Florence			337
DAKH		brothers		219
DANISHEVSKI	Sarah Malkeh	nee Rudnik	RUDNIK	349
DANOYKER	Chaim			446 photo
DAVEY				485
DAVEY	Penny	nee Sbeyski	SBEYSKI	485, 509
DAVIDOV				169, 190, 194
DAYTSH	Moshe Yakov		DEICHES / TAYTS	485
DELATISHKI	Naftali			119, 175
DENIKIN	Anton			472
DIAMONT		Count		219
DILINSKI		Attorney		410
DONOVITSH				285
DONSHEVSKI	Moshe	Rov		251
DORMAN			TROVSKI	276
DRUCK	Feigeh			240, 454

DRUCK	Moshe				240
DRUCK	Yakov				240, 283, 454
DRUCK	Feigeh	nee Kaplan	KAPLAN		72, 228
DUBIN	Alte				347
DUBIN	Beilah	nee Kramer	KRAMER		284
DUBIN	Binyamin Alter				485
DUBIN	Ida				485
DUBIN	Leyb				285 photo, 485
DUBINSKI	Asher				347
DUBINSKI	Binyamin				5, 165, 186, 300, 312, 335, 347, 385, 429, 465, 476 photo, 482 photo, 533 photo
DUBINSKI	Esther			Tel Aviv	200
DUBINSKI	Khayeh Rivke	nee Rgov	ROGOV		200, 553 photo
DUBINSKI	Meir				121, 162, 169, 335, 347
DUBINSKI	Michael				200, 347, 476 photo

DUBINSKI	Mineh				347
DUBINSKI	Rivkeh			Tel Aviv	200
DUBINSKI	Shmuel				165, 533 photo
DUBINSKI	Tsvi				162, 169, 347, 533 photo
DUBINSKI	Yosef				200, 347, 348 photo
DUBINSKI	Ysroel				347
DUBINSKI	Zalmen				347
DUBKIN	Shmuel				71 photo, 85, 108, 259, 401, 410, 416 photo, 425 photo
DZIENCIELSKI					186
EDELSHTEYN					228
EFORYKIN					259
EHRENBURG	Ilya	Writer			200
EHRLIKH					350
EISENSHTAT					228
ELIASHKOVITSH	Breyneh	nee Levine	LEVINE		333, 333 photo, 378
ELIASHKOVITSH	Chaim				300, 429
ELIASHKOVITSH	Gittel	nee Kaplan	KAPLAN		300

ELIASHKOVITSH	Yakov				62
ENGLE	Aryeh Leyb		INGEL		50, 190. 219, 306, 308, 339
ENGLE	Esther	nee Horvits	HORVITS		290 photo, 337, 338 photo, 341, 370 photo, 485
ENGLE	Leyb Aharon		INGEL		50, 90, 92, 288, 339
ENGLE	Reuven		INGEL		337, 338 photo
EPSHTEYN	Ysroel				350
EYSHISHKI	Frumeh				336
EYSHISHKI	Gittel	nee Ilituvitsh	ILITUVITSH		336
EYSHISHKI	Khonen				309, 310 photo, 336
EYSHISHKI	Miryam				336
EYSHISHKI	Shimon				336
EYSHISHKI	Tsvi				336
FARFEL	Yehuda Leyb	Rov			459
FEIN	Shabtai	Rov	FAYN		312, 459
FINKLSHTEYN	Shimon Sheyme	cousin to Moshe Kaplan		Voranava	267
FLUDERMAKHER			PLUDERMAKHER		162
FORMAN	Basyeh	nee Saritski	SARITSKI		485

	Ettie			
FRANKFURTER	Felix			162
FRISHMAN	David			72
FUCHS	Herman			169, 194, 319, 319 photo, 320 photo, 535
FUCHS	Lilly			169, 194, 319, 320 photo, 535 photo
FUCHS	Shulamit	nee Rogol	ROGOL	169, 194, 271, 292, 317, 319, 319 photo, 535 photo
FUCHS	Zelik			194, 319
FUNK	Shimon			429
GARVEY	Khayeh	nee Levine	LEVINE	50, 115, 219, 333, 406 photo, 483, 479
GARVEY	Sholom		GARBER / GARVIYE	72, 228
GARVEY	Yehuda		GARBER / GARVIYE	115
GASZTOLD				162
GEDGAUDAS		Priest		47

GEDMINAS				162
GELLER	Shmuel			136, 325
GERSHONOVITSH	Yakov			485
GITLITS	Dvorah	nee Kartshmer/ Kretchmer / Carczmer	KARTSHMER/ KRETCHMER / CARCZMER	469
GITLITS	Khayele			469
GITLITS	Shmulikl			469
GITLITS	Yitzach Itshe			378
GITLITS	Yosef			469
GLAZER	Alter			470
GLIAT	Avraham			414 photo
GLOMB		Writer		259
GOGODZINSKI	Liza			190
GOGODZINSKI	Yitzach			190
GOLDBERG	Moshe Dovid Morris			485
GOLDBERG	Nathan			410
GOLDENSKI	Avraham			215
GOLDFEIN	Moshe Morris			485
GORDON		Doctor	Iwye	136
GORDON	Avraham			186, 194, 279, 280, 295
GORDON	Esther	nee Schwarts	SCHWARTS	107, 295
GORDON	Nisn			472
GORDON	Rivkeh			294 photo

GORDON	Shlomo Syoma				107, 279, 294 photo, 295
GORDON	Uzi				295
GORDSVATSER	Maishke		GOLDWATER		162
GORVITS	Grushe		HORVITS		136
GOTTFRIED	Hershl				52
GOTTFRIED	Nasan Notl				52
GOTTFRIED	Yitzach Leyb				52
GREENBERG	Chaim				472
GREENBERG	Uri Tsvi				72
GREVETSKI	Borukh			Voranava	136
GRINBOIM					419
GRINER	Taubeh Toyve				131, 477 photo
GROSSMAN	Meir				72
HACOHEN	David		COHEN / KAHAN / KAGAN		136
HACOHEN	Shlomo	Rov	COHEN / KAHAN / KAGAN		251
HALLER		General	HELLER		419
HARARI	Binyamin				119
HARARI	Eliezer				119
HARARI	Khanita				119
HARARI	Khenye	nee Rudnik	RUDNIK		119, 278, 349
HARARI	Rina				119
HERMAN	Dov				118
HERMAN	Miryam Gitteh Merkeh	nee Blyakher	BLYAKHER		118

HERSHMAN					101
HERSHOVITSH			GERSHOVITSH		190
HERSHOVITSH	Alter		GERSHOVITSH		470
HERSHOVITSH	Chaim		GERSHOVITSH		36, 97, 162, 175, 217, 262, 470
HERSHOVITSH	Elisha		GERSHOVITSH	Voranava	200
HERSHOVITSH	Khayeh		GERSHOVITSH		470
HERSHOVITSH	Reyzeh Leah	nee Glazer / Shklar	GLAZER / SHKLAR		470, 471
HERSHOVITSH	Zalmen		GERSHOVITSH		470
HERZL					72, 262, 317, 419
HINDS		German Officer		Voranava	175
HIRSCH	Berel				485
HIRSCH	Maurice de	Baron			259
HOCHMAN				Salcininkai / Soletchnik	240
HORVITS	Chaim Alter				485
HORVITS	Chaim Yehuda Yudl	Rov			62, 278, 315 photo, 315, 472, 512
HORVITS	Feigeh Taubeh Toyve	nee Schneider	SCHNEIDER		485
HORVITS	Fenne	nee Reinberg	REINBERG		485
HORVITS	Gedalye Chaim George				338 photo, 476 photo, 477

				photo, 535 photo
HORVITS	Julius			527 photo
HORVITS	Lillian	nee Sheinok	SHEINOK	337
HORVITS	Miryam Merah Yokheved			337
HORVITS	Reuven Robert			337, 481, 535 photo
HORVITS	Sarah Disya			105, 278, 278 photo, 401, 485
HORVITS	Saul			337
HORVITS	Shmuel			527 photo
HORVITS	Yitzach			105, 259, 278, 394, 527 photo
ILITUVITSH	Kalmen			336
INGULSKI		School Principal		306, 339, 419
ITSKOVITSH	Dov			92
ITSKOVITSH	Eliahu Netaneli		NETANELI	90, 92, 278, 289, 299, 300, 306, 311, 320, 454, 476 photo,

				483
ITSKOVITSH	Eliezer			228, 300, 302 photo, 406 photo
ITSKOVITSH	Khayeh			92
ITSKOVITSH	Kheyne	nee Levine	LEVINE	92, 378
ITSKOVITSH	Meir Yosef Yoshke			5, 45, 72, 72, 136, 217, 228, 239 photo, 240, 259, 267, 300, 320, 350, 378, 401, 419, 436 photo, 454, 476 photo, 482 photo
ITSKOVITSH	Nathan			62 photo, 72, 85, 92, 118, 246, 267, 268 photo, 296, 300, 320, 378, 429
ITSKOVITSH	Nellie Nili			246

ITSKOVITSH	Sarah	nee Khasman	KHASMAN		276
ITSKOVITSH	Yekhezkel Khaykl				50, 228, 300, 312, 314, 320, 321, 322 photo
JABOTINSKI	Zev				72, 262, 350, 419
JADKA		Polish Marshall			17
KACHERGINSKI	Shmerl		Kaczerginski		447
KADAP	Leyb				175
KAGAN	Yakov Leyb		COHEN / KAHAN		121, 296
KAGANOVITSH	Aharon				50, 339, 339 photo, 401
KAGANOVITSH	Eliahu				305, 527 photo
KAGANOVITSH	Moshe			Iwye	175, 267
KAGANOVITSH	Reuven			Iwye	267
KAGANOVITSH	Simkha				527 photo
KAKRAKA		Councilman			
KALMEN	Berl				228, 485
KALMEN	Moshe				439
KALMENOVITSH					296
KALMENOVITSH	Aharon				72
KAMENITSKI	Shmuel				481, 512

KANTROVITSH		know as "the orangegrower"			97
KAPLAN	Einat				305
KAPLAN	Eliezer	Rov			251, 312, 459
KAPLAN	Frumeh	nee Gottfried	GOTTFRIED		52
KAPLAN	Jack				481
KAPLAN	Khaneh Leah				485
KAPLAN	Khasyeh Eyta	nee Lieb	LIEB		101, 284 photo, 296, 300
KAPLAN	Leyb				228
KAPLAN	Liat				305
KAPLAN	Mintz				85
KAPLAN	Mordechai Mordkhe				284 photo, 296, 410
KAPLAN	Moshe				267
KAPLAN	Nathan				36, 52, 55, 101, 219, 300, 320, 330, 406 photo, 476 photo, 479, 482 photo
KAPLAN	Orit				41, 305
KAPLAN	Sarah	nee Spivak	SPIVAK		305
KAPLAN	Shoel ben Notl			Voranava	447

KAPLAN	Tsipe Leah	nee Alperovitsh	ALPEROVITSH	341, 370 photo, 485
KAPLAN	Yeshayahu			62, 228, 341, 378
KAPLAN	Yosef			101, 136, 283, 284 photo, 300, 305
KARTSHMER	Avraham		KRETCHMER / CARCZMER	55, 92, 108, 308, 309 photo, 469
KARTSHMER	Breyneh		KRETCHMER / CARCZMER	394, 469
KARTSHMER	Freda	nee Kherson / Cherson / Herson / Cohen	KHERSON / CHERSON / HERSON / COHEN / KRETCHMER	485
KARTSHMER	Itteh		KRETCHMER / CARCZMER	394
KARTSHMER	Kalmen		KRETCHMER / CARCZMER	136
KARTSHMER	Khaneh	nee Engle / Ingle / Levinson	INGEL / LEVINSON	410
KARTSHMER	Khaneh Khayke		KRETCHMER / CARCZMER	394
KARTSHMER	Kilkeh		KRETCHMER / CARCZMER	394
KARTSHMER	Leah Leye		KRETCHMER / CARCZMER	469
KARTSHMER	Meir		KRETCHMER / CARCZMER	394
KARTSHMER	Mordechai Motl Motke		KRETCHMER / CARCZMER	5, 115, 344,

	Milton			394, 481, 485, 502 photo, 503, 506 photo, 508 photo, 509, 509, 512
KARTSHMER	Moshe Eliezer Leyzer		KRETCHMER / CARCZMER	115, 119, 394, 469
KARTSHMER	Naftali		KRETCHMER / CARCZMER	72
KARTSHMER	Noakh		KRETCHMER / CARCZMER	47, 394, 469
KARTSHMER	Pinyeh		KRETCHMER / CARCZMER	240
KARTSHMER	Reuven		KRETCHMER / CARCZMER	62, 266, 308, 378, 410, 470
KARTSHMER	Roda Rodl		KRETCHMER / CARCZMER	469
KARTSHMER	Sarah	nee Katz	KATZ / KRETCHMER / CARCZMER	58 photo, 326 photo, 344, 394, 485, 502 photo, 506 photo, 508 photo, 509
KARTSHMER	Shimon		KRETCHMER / CARCZMER	337, 337

				photo
KARTSHMER	Shmuel		KRETCHMER / CARCZMER	394
KARTSHMER	Tamara		KRETCHMER / CARCZMER	469
KARTSHMER	Yeshayahu		KRETCHMER / CARCZMER	485
KASATSHENKOVA			KRETCHMER / CARCZMER	131
KATSEV	Man Manke			300, 332
KATSEV	Nekhama			108, 300, 303 photo, 332, 419
KATSEV	Rokhl			300, 332
KATSEV	Vulf Velvl			300
KATSEV	Yehuda Y			300, 332
KATSEV	Yekhezkel Khaykl			169, 300, 332, 346 photo, 401, 429
KATZ	Avraham			121
KATZ	Basyeh Pesyeh	nee Rudnik	RUDNIK	119
KATZ	Berko			344
KATZ	Berl	known as der shooster (shoemaker)		293, 294 photo
KATZ	Chaim			344
KATZ	Dovid	known as "the shoemaker"		296, 485
KATZ	Dvorah			121,

KRIZOVSKI	Masha			280
KRIZOVSKI	Mikleh	nee Gomnits	GOMNITS	279, 280, 370 photo, 410, 485
KRIZOVSKI	Mordechai Motl			280
KRIZOVSKI	Rokhl			280
KRIZOVSKI	Tsvi Hersh			62, 72, 87, 105, 110 photo, 136, 169, 217, 280, 293, 378, 378, 410, 419, 437, 464
KROSHKIN				36
KUBANSKI	Shoshana			527 photo
KUHN				162
KUSHTILSKI	Zalmen			311, 401, 485
KUTILAH				62
LAND	Meir			485
LAND	Reyzl Rose			485
LESHCHINSKI				512 photo
LESHCHINSKI	Taubeh Toyve			50
LEVI	Joseph			485, 503

LEVINE					333 photo, 471 photo
LEVINE	Akhim				534 photo
LEVINE	Alexander Sender				136
LEVINE	Alter				115
LEVINE	Avraham				200
LEVINE	Avraham Eliezer				92, 311
LEVINE	Beileh Bella	nee Kartshmer/ Kretchmer / Carczmer	KARTSHMER		485
LEVINE	Betzalel				50
LEVINE	Borukh			Salcininkai / Soletchnik	136
LEVINE	Chaim	known as der Milners			72, 136, 288
LEVINE	Gad				50, 62, 429
LEVINE	Gad				50, 62, 429
LEVINE	Hadassah				291
LEVINE	Harry				481
LEVINE	Ida				337
LEVINE	Ike				485
LEVINE	Khayeh				50, 469
LEVINE	Khayeh Feigeh Ida	nee Cherkiss	CHERKISS		476 photo, 485, 527 photo
LEVINE	Khayeh Sarah				162
LEVINE	Khayke				130

LEVINE	Kheyne Rayse	nee Alperovitsh	ALPEROVITSH / VIGUDSKI	288 photo
LEVINE	Kheyne Reyneh			297 photo, 468, 469
LEVINE	Leo			481
LEVINE	Leyb			410
LEVINE	Liba			333, 333 photo, 468
LEVINE	Libe Merkeh			485
LEVINE	Louis			337
LEVINE	Matisyahu		VIGUDSKI	288
LEVINE	Meir			92, 136, 468
LEVINE	Miryam			92
LEVINE	Moshe			50, 401, 468, 469, 471 photo
LEVINE	Moshe	Rov		251
LEVINE	Nachum			305, 419, 425 photo, 468, 470, 471 photo
LEVINE	Payeh			50
LEVINE	Perele	nee Kartshmer/ Kretchmer / Carczmer	KARTSHMER/ KRETCHMER / CARCZMER	468, 469, 471 photo
LEVINE	Pesakh			297

				photo, 305, 378, 401, 468, 469
LEVINE	Phillip			485
LEVINE	Pinkhes			534 photo
LEVINE	Rafael			341, 481
LEVINE	Sarah Rivke			468
LEVINE	Sarah Sorke			401
LEVINE	Sarah Tuabeh Toyve	nee Hershovitsh / Gershovitsh	HERSHOVITSH / GERSHOVITSH	401, 468, 470, 471 photo
LEVINE	Shimon			485
LEVINE	Shlomo Shloymke			50, 62, 72, 108, 297, 300, 332 photo, 341, 401, 419, 447, 481, 512 photo, 512, 514 photo
LEVINE	Shmuel			136
LEVINE	Shmuel Chaim			271
LEVINE	Shmuel Yakov			115
LEVINE	Shoshana Reyzl	nee Yutan	YUTAN	66 photo

LEVINE	Sima Itka		378, 419
LEVINE	Tsvi		271
LEVINE	Ukushe		297 photo
LEVINE	Yehuda Yudel		333
LEVINE	Yehudit		107, 130 photo, 292, 419
LEVINE	Yekhezkel		50, 288
LEVINE	Yekhutiel Kushe		300
LEVINE	Yetteh		485
LEVINE	Yitzach		92, 136
LEVINE	Yitzach Artsom	ARTSHOM	287
LEVINE	Yitzach Itshe	known as Gutte Itshe	378, 401, 429
LEVINE	Yitzach Leyb		217, 344, 345 photo, 481, 485
LEVINE	Yitzach Meir		175
LEVINE	Yosef		72, 136, 169, 287
LEVINE	Yosele	known as dem Muler's or Bricklayer's son	61 photo, 72, 108, 291 photo, 291, 410

LEFKOVITSH	Khonen			446 photo
LIEB	Dovid			219
LIEB	Moshe Aryeh			219
LIEB	Tanyeh	nee Katz	KATZ	219
LIEB	Tsvi Ahuvi		AHUVI	136, 219, 325, 347, 410, 477 photo, 481, 482 photo, 512
LIEB	Yitzach			485
LIEB	Zalmen Leyb			136, 186, 219, 325 photo
LILLIENBLOOM	Moshe			317
LIPKUNSKI	Binyamin			136, 240, 534 photo
LIPKUNSKI	Khaneh			240, 410, 534 photo
LIPKUNSKI	Nachum			45, 240, 325, 534 photo
LIPKUNSKI	Pinkhes			169, 175, 240, 446 photo
LIPKUNSKI	Slova	nee Schneider	SCHNEIDER	240, 534

				photo
LIVAY (LEVEY)	G.			252 photo
LIVAY (LEVEY)	Yosef L.			485
LOTOVITSH	Carolina			131
LUBETSKI			LUTSKI	62, 419
LUBETSKI	Avrham Meir			429, 437
LUBETSKI	Dovid Chaim			72, 341, 344, 401, 429
LUBETSKI	Khayeh			344
LUBETSKI	Moshe			55, 72, 259, 344, 401, 429
LUBETSKI	Sarah Leah	nee Schneider / Sharon	SCHNEIDER / SHARON	262
LUBETSKI	Simkha			324
LUBETSKI	Yekhutiel			123, 344
LUBETSKI	Zev Velvke			344, 350, 378, 429
LUBETSKI	Zeydke			175, 262, 324, 378
LUBISHITSKI	Aharon			331
LYTNENT	Mishka			136
LYUBKA	Aryeh			425 photo
MAGAZINER	Elkeh			485
MAMKE	Moishe			485

MANESS					228
MANOAKH	Yehoshua				90, 92
MASHKEVITSH	Shaul				240, 291
MATNOI	Ahuva	nee Gordon	GORDON		293, 295
MAZEH	Eliahu				115, 410
MAZEH	Michael				115
MAZEH	Miryam Mirke				479
MEIR	Golda				136
MEIR	Leyzer			Belitze	194
MEIRSON	Shlomo	Rov			251
MELAMED	Eliahu				90
MELAMED	Grunem				87, 90
MELAMED	Khava	nee Popisko	POPISKO		90
MELINOVSKI		Doctor		Kallelishok / Konvalishki	200
MELKHOVSKI	Vladek				136
MENSKI	Yitzach			Lida	165
MERLINSKI	Zalmen				219
MIASNIK				Lida	194
MICKIEWICZ	Adam				41
MIKELSON	Basyeh Pesyeh				325
MIKELSON	Binyamin				175, 325
MIKELSON	Sarah Leah				175
MILVSKI		Polish Count			347
MILVSKI		Polish Countess			219
MINDITS	Gauleiter				228
MINTZ	Betzalel				401

MINTZ	Eliezer			382 photo
MINTZ	Gittel Rivke Gertrude	nee Horvits	HORVITS	337, 476 photo, 477 photo
MINTZ	Golda			382 photo
MINTZ	Itkeh			66 photo, 382 photo
MINTZ	Moshe			285, 286 photo, 341, 382 photo, 406 photo, 425 photo, 479
MINTZ	Peysakh			382 photo, 476 photo, 477 photo
MINTZ	Pinkhes			325, 401
MINTZ	Uminke Minkeh			300, 303 photo, 304 photo, 378, 419
MOISEVITSH	Avraham			280
MOISEVITSH	Sheina	nee Krizovski	KRIZOVSKI	280
MOTSKOVITZ		Polish Town Councillor		47
MOVSHOVITSH	Dovid			175, 187, 334

MOVSHOVITSH	Khedveh			186
MOVSHOVITSH	Khenyeh			186
MOVSHOVITSH	Nachum			55, 92, 259
MOVSHOVITSH	Rokhl Leah	Rebbitsn, nee Rabinovitsh	RABINOVITSH	115, 261 photo
MOVSHOVITSH	Sarah Hindeh	nee Blyakher	BLYAKHER	66 photo, 175, 186, 305, 325, 334, 446 photo
MOVSHOVITSH	Yosef	Rov		162, 259, 306
MOVSHOVITSH	Ysroel	Rov		115, 162, 219, 259, 260 photo, 312, 347, 485
MUNIS	Finkeh			394
NAMIOT	Liovke			401, 419
NAMIOT	Yakov			378
NAZARESKI				162
NIMTSEVITSH	Yitzach			47
NOVOPLANSKI	Sheineh	nee Yutan	YUTAN	136
NOVOPLANSKI	Tsvi			410
NYUNKE		brothers		200
OLKENITSKI	Aharon			47, 331
OLKENITSKI	Aryeh			72, 105

OLKENITSKI	Khava				331
OLKENITSKI	Leyb				105, 454, 470 photo
OLKENITSKI	Lolle				287, 292, 331
OLKENITSKI	Meir				175
OLKENITSKI	Shmuel				108
OLKENITSKI	Sholem Yakov				47, 200, 262, 331
OLKENITSKI	Tsipeh	nee Sharashevski	SHARASHEVSKI		105
OLKENITSKI	Yakov				378
OMIASTOVSKY	Graf				219
ORTSHIK	Zalmen				401
PANTZENK			PACHENKO		169, 194
PARSON	Rosie				485
PARVAR	Kalmen				251
PAULEITISS		Lithuanian teacher		Voranava	194
PERETZ	I.L.				90
PERLMAN					312, 459
PETHOVSKI					115
PETLIURA	Symon				472
PETUKHOVSKI	Betzalel				32 photo, 115, 401, 419
PEYKHOVA	Menukha	nee Krizovski	KRIZOVSKI		61 photo, 108, 279, 279

					photo, 280, 410, 464, 465, 476 photo
PEZKOVSKI	Alexander Oless				45
PEZKOVSKI	Helenka				45
PILOVSKI					385
PILSUDSKI					47, 162, 296
PINKOVSKI					215
POPISKO	Dov				90
POPISKO	Reyzl Shoshana				90
PORTER	Shoshana	nee Yudenfreund	YUDENFREUND		297
PORTNOI	Eliohu Elkeh	known as "the mute"			378, 379 photo, 485
PRESKI	Mendel				165
PRESKI	Shmuel				165
PROTZHENOV		Captain			136
PRUZAN	Meir				485
PULITRUK					200
PUNDAK	Frend				401
PUPKO	Leah			Voranava	200
RABINOVITSH	Asher Shabtai	Rov			259, 312
RABINOVITSH	Boris	Sculptor		Smarhon	125
RABINOVITSH	Dinah				200
RABINOVITSH	Reuven				485
RABINOVITSH	Tsvi Hersh	Rov			251

RABINOVITSH	Yosef Yehuda	Rov		259, 459
RAKOVER		Doctor		194
RASZKO		Feltsher		47, 280
REBIKOV				276
REIDER	Eyta			131
REIZEN	Zalmen Avraham			459, 463
REZNIK				215
RODZIVITS				165
ROGOL	Aryeh Leyb			92, 162, 228, 251, 259, 271 photo, 317, 318 photo, 319, 378, 401, 410, 419, 429
ROGOL	Eliohu			136, 169, 271
ROGOL	Etta Etl			328
ROGOL	Hersh Tsvi			194, 292, 293 photo, 319 photo
ROGOL	Khasyeh Esther Reyzl	nee Movshovitsh	MOVSHOVITSH	259, 328, 378, 385 photo
ROGOL	Lyuba Liba	nee Levine	LEVINE	271

ROGOL	Meir	haLevi		92, 136, 175, 300, 328
ROGOL	Mineh Minkeh			130 photo, 169, 271, 419
ROGOL	Moshe Yakov	haLevi		62 photo, 300, 328, 385 photo
ROGOL	Sholem Yakov			283, 410
ROGOL	Zelik			169, 271, 319, 341, 401, 406 photo
ROGOL				
ROGOVSKI	Binyamin			190
ROGULSKI				394
ROSENBLUM	Menukha			87
ROSENBLUM	Shlomo			286 photo, 406 photo
ROSENBLUM	Tsvi			87
ROSOVSKI		Rov		312, 459
ROSS	Joseph			485
ROTHMAN	Louis			485
RUBIN	Lucia	nee Preski	PRESKI	165
RUBINOVSKI	Sheinah Reyzl	nee Shlomovitsh	SHLOMOVITSH	316

RUDNIK	Avraham Abir	Rov		62, 251, 258 photo, 312, 385, 459
RUDNIK	Beileh			119
RUDNIK	Breyneh			40 photo, 71 photo, 410 photo
RUDNIK	Dvorah	Rebbitsn, nee Davidovitsh	DAVIDOVITSH	251, 258 photo, 401
RUDNIK	Elimelekh			123, 349
RUDNIK	Khasyeh			123
RUDNIK	Rivkeh Zmal	nee Kartshmer/ Kretchmer / Carczmer	KARTSHMER	349
RUDNIK	Sarah			251, 485
RUDNIK	Sarah Malkeh	nee Bernshteyn	BERNSHTEYN	419
RUDNIK	Shcynch Jofa			40 photo, 258 photo, 454
RUDNIK	Yehoshua			123
RUDNIK	Yitzach Binyamin	Rov	KOVNENSKI	97, 175, 186, 339, 349, 349 photo, 419
RUDNIK	Yosef	Rov		50, 62, 62 photo,

				85, 85, 125, 251, 252 photo, 262, 266, 269, 312, 314, 316, 385, 401, 401, 419, 459
RUDNIK	Yosef			313, 353
RUSCINSKY		Major		240
SAKHAROV		Rov		459
SALANTER	Ysroel			314, 472
SAMSONOV		General		419
SARITSKI	Moshe			286
SARITSKI	Shifreh	nee Khasman / Blyakher	KHASMAN / BLYAKHER	286
SATKOLSHTSIK				80 photo
SATKOLSHTSIK	Beileh			262, 359 photo
SATKOLSHTSIK	Leah			262, 359 photo
SATKOLSHTSIK	Moshe Ber			262, 359 photo
SATKOLSHTSIK	Nekhama			262, 359 photo
SATKOLSHTSIK	Tanyeh			262, 359 photo

SATKOLSHTSIK	Yehuda Yudl			92, 262, 262, 266, 296, 358 photo, 359 photo
SATSITNISKI	Leah			162
SATSITNISKI	Tsvi			136
SATSITNISKI	Ysroel			410
SCHMIDT	Khayeh Dvorah	nee Horvits	HORVITS	485
SCHMIDT	Moshe	known as "the blacksmith"		300
SCHMIDT	Nakhum	haLevi		485
SCHMIDT	Tsvi	known as "the stableman"		311
SCHNEIDER	Asher			333
SCHNEIDER	Ben–Tsion		SHARON	62, 62 photo, 72, 85, 219, 262, 266, 320, 358 photo, 376, 410, 416, 429, 454
SCHNEIDER	Binyamin			240
SCHNEIDER	Chaim Zalmen Leyb			169, 333
SCHNEIDER	Daniel			442 photo
SCHNEIDER	Dovid			136
SCHNEIDER	Eliezer			36, 339,

				345
SCHNEIDER	Eliezer Nakhum			328
SCHNEIDER	Hinde Sarah	nee Satkolshtsik	SATKOLSHTSIK	72, 262, 266, 358 photo, 376, 454
SCHNEIDER	Kalmen	known as "the cripple"		169, 333
SCHNEIDER	Khayeh Sarah		SHARON	262
SCHNEIDER	Leah			266, 376
SCHNEIDER	Libke Ahuva			262, 266, 376, 534 photo
SCHNEIDER	Malkeh	nee Rudnik	RUDNIK	119
SCHNEIDER	Mordechai			333
SCHNEIDER	Rokhl		SHARON	476 photo
SCHNEIDER	Roshke Shoshana			262, 266, 376
SCHNEIDER	Shabtai Shepsel		SHARON	262, 376
SCHNEIDER	Shlomo Yitzach			345
SCHNEIDER	Shmuel			136
SCHNEIDER	Shmuel		SHARON	5, 72, 80 photo, 186, 225, 262, 266, 401, 419, 476

					photo, 485 photo
SCHNEIDER	Yakov				72, 225, 227 photo, 259, 262, 266, 345, 376
SCHNEIDER	Yitzach				36
SCHNEIDER	Yitzach Zekl				136
SCHNEIDER	Yosef Aharon				328, 533 photo
SCHUCHMAN					36
SCHWARTS	Lina				509
SCHWARTS	Rivkeh	nee Lieb	LIEB		219
SCHWARTS	Velvl				219
SEGAL	Yitzach				194, 341
SENDER	Shapiro	Rov			259
SENDER	Zalmen	Rov			259
SFORIM	Mendel Mocher				291
SHABAD		Doctor		Vilnius	251
SHABAD	Tsemakh				280
SHAPIRO	Masha	nee Shamir	SHAMIR	Voranava	130 photo
SHAPIRO	Rafael	Rov			259
SHARET	Moshe				136
SHARON	Gitteh Leah				262
SHATSIGLOSKI					219
SHEIFER					136
SHEFTEL		Rov			251

SHEFTEL	Yerakhmiel			251
SHEIFER	H.			459
SHEKNEH		Platoon leader		169
SHIMANSKI	Pyotr			186
SHKLAR	Alter		GLAZER	470
SHKLAR	Dovid	known as der Zekel		175
SHKLAR	Eliahu Eltsik		GLAZER	454, 470, 485
SHKLAR	Leyb		GLAZER	470
SHKLAR	Leyzer			136
SHKLAR	Moshe		GLAZER	470, 533 photo, 471
SHKLAR	Paulina			78
SHKLAR	Sarah		GLAZER	471
SHKLAR	Tuvyeh		GLAZER	470
SHKLAR	Yitzach			470
SHKOLNIK	Antshel			346
SHKOLNIK	Eliahu Chaim			290
SHKOLNIK	Esther Rokhl			108, 303 photo, 401, 419
SHKOLNIK	Gad			429
SHKOLNIK	Gottlieb			72, 346 photo
SHKOLNIK	Sholem Yakov			320, 410
SHKOLNIK	Shoshana	nee Ben-Dov	BEN-DOV	287
SHKOLNIK	Tsvi			346
SHKOLNIK	Zusyeh			62

	Yakov Zisha			photo, 346
SHLOMOVITSH	Avraham Noakh			72, 85, 85, 228, 259, 316, 330
SHLOMOVITSH	Dov Tsvi			316
SHLOMOVITSH	Shlomo	Rov		259, 316
SHLUBSKI	Gershon			228
SHLOYMES	Daniel			485
SHMERKOVITSH	Meir Meytshik			175
SHMUELZON		Rov		312, 459
SHRIRA	Zalmen			136, 228
SHTEYNBERG				72
SHTOKFISH	David			476 photo
SHTUL				228
SHTUL	Moshe			55, 108, 437
SHUB	Yosef	Rov		459
SHURIN	Ruth	nee Davidovitsh	DAVIDOVITSH	251
SHVINTOLSKI	Zeytse			136
SILVERBLANK	Ada			485
SIPKA	Khenyeh			131
SKYVISS	Kasiuk			136, 162, 175
SLOBODA	Meir Zalmen			388 photo
SLONIMSKI		Attorney		47

SMITANIN				309
SMOLOVITSKI	Yakov			240
SOBOTSH	Yosef			162
SOKOLOSKI	Eliahu			251
SOKOLSKI	Leyb Lipa			190
SOLODUKHE		brothers		401
SOLODUKHE	Aharon			72, 419
SOLODUKHE	Alter			509
SOLODUKHE	Itteh			509
SOLODUKHE	Michael			72
SOLTS	Myshke		SZULC / SHULTS	72
SOLTS	Rivkeh		SZULC / SHULTS	130 photo
SONNENSON	Sholom			108, 331
SOROTZKIN	Elkhanan			219
SOROTZKIN	Zalmen Ben-Tsion	Rov		219, 225, 262, 376
SOVLOVITSH	Rivkeh	nee Rabinovitsh	RABINOVITSH	485
SPIVAK	Eliahu			305
SPIVAK	Sima			305
SPIVAK	Yenteh	nee Kaganovitsh	KAGANOVITSH	305. 502 photo
SRULOVITSH	Leyb Tsvi			287, 331
SRULOVITSH	Mikleh			328
SRULOVITSH	Paula			287
SRULOVITSH	Yitzach			328
STANKVITSH				190
STASKES	Barsolka			186

STAVITSKI	Max			Warsaw	194
STESHELZI					329
STOLITSKI					175
STOTSKI	Casimir				219
STRUDVORSKI	Yakov				228, 350
STUTSKI	Khava				136
STUTSKI	Moshe				111, 284
STUTSKI	Rokhl				136
SUTSKEVER	Avraham				437
SUTSKEVER	Eliezer				169
SUTSKEVER	Kheyneh Sheyneh	nee Khasman / Blyakher	KHASMAN / BLYAKHER		286, 288
SUTSKEVER	Lolle Lolik				286, 288, 302 photo, 378
SUTSKEVER	Ra"aya				169, 194
SVERSKI	Fenneh				485
TALAL	Abbie				485
TAYTS	Aharon	Rov	RUDNIK / DEICHES / DACH / DAYTSH / DAKH		62, 125, 169, 219, 262, 314, 459
TCHERNIKOVSKI					219, 273
TELERENT	Yitzach				200
TELZER	Leyb				472
TENENBAUM		Doctor			228
TENER	Alteh				121, 165, 186

TENER	Yonah				121, 165, 186
TIKTNISKI					90
TOVAH	Gitteh	nee Gottfried	GOTTFRIED		52
TRAUB	Chaim				215
TRESHKAVITS					136
TRIGOVOV					262
TRIVITSKI	Berl				175
TROSKEL	Shimon Yosef				485
TROVSKI	Ysroel Isser				276
TROVSKI	Zechariah				276
TRUMPELDOR	Yosef				72, 92
TRUSKEVITSH					186, 325
TUBLITSKI	Binyamin				485
TUSHITSKI		Mrs.			485
USISHKIN	Khanneh		EYSHISHKI		169
USISHKIN	Tsvi		EYSHISHKI		169
VARSHEVER	Leyb				162
VASILSKY					219
VASSERMAN	Elchonen				50, 219, 251, 300, 320, 385
VAZYOCK					186
VELVELSKI	Sarah	nee Lieb	LIEB		194, 325, 325 photo
VIGOSH	Kalmen				136
VINDISCH		German Officer		Vorananva	136

VINTSUS		Staff Officer		447
VISHNITSKI	Shimon			401
VORONOVSKI	Feigeh			219
VORONOVSKI	Khayeh	nee Lieb	LIEB	219
VOYTOSS		Police Officer		262
VULFOVITSH	Basyeh			215
VULFOVITSH	Khanneh			215
VULFOVITSH	Khenyeh			215
VULFOVITSH	Reuven			215
VULFOVITSH	Rivkeh			215
VULFOVITSH	Yeshayahu			215
VULFOVITSH	Ysroel			215
VYTAUTAS	Witold			17
WARNER		German Officer	Vorananva	175
WASILEVSKA	Wanda Halszka	Writer		200, 309, 336
WASILNIKO		Partisan Commander		200
WIENER	Dovid			123, 342
WIENER	Eliahu			36
WIENER	Etta Etl Itka			66 photo, 342
WIENER	Feivel Feyvke			342
WIENER	Leah	nee Blyakher / Khasman	BLYAKHER / KHASMAN	66 photo, 175, 186, 334, 342
WIENER	Leyb			36
WIENER	Meir Zalmen			342, 485

WIENER	Tsireh Leah Sarah			36
WIENER	Yeshayahu Shaykeh			66 photo, 175, 342
WIENER	Yoel			36
WEINREICH	Max			437
WEINTRAUB	R.			85
WEISENFELD	Menachem Mendl			47, 62 photo, 410, 476 photo
WEISENFELD	Rosa	nee Ostrinski	OSTRINSKI	47
WILCZYNSKAS	Jonas			190
YANKELOVITSH	Rokhl	nee Satkolshtsik	SATKOLSHTSIK	359 photo
YANKELOVITSH	Yakov			262
YOFFE	Tsvi			136
YUDENFREUND	Shlomo			297
YUDENFREUND	Tsiporah Zipporeh	nee Levine	LEVINE	297, 308, 468
ZALKIN	Martha			485, 509
ZALKIN	Yakov			485, 509
ZANDMAN	Dov Ber			92, 115, 273, 273, 479
ZANDMAN	Rivkeh			273
ZANDMAN	Yakov			273
ZANDMAN	Yehoshua			219, 272
ZELIK	Berl			509

ZELIK	Itteh			509
ZHIZHEMSKI	Yekhutiel			169, 186, 331, 419
ZHIZHEMSKI	Yosef			62, 331, 339
ZHOLONDZH	Avraham Aloni			62, 71 photo, 85, 108, 258 photo, 259, 266, 308, 401, 410, 410 photo, 425 photo, 533 photo
ZHOLONDZH	Yosef Aloni			385
ZUCKERMAN	Shmuel Avinoam			251
ZUKOVSKI	Moshe			215
ZUSMAN	Meir			485
ZUSMAN	Moshe			169
ZUVITSHKI	Eliezer			284
ZUVITSHKI	Rokhl	nee Dubin	DUBIN	111, 284
	Baoshke	known as "the drunk"		175
	Peysakh	known as "the beggar"		378, 485
	Betzalel	known as "the Hassid's son"		111, 284
	Gedalye	known as "the blacksmith"		186
	Meirke	known as "the		136

	blacksmith"		
Yankl	known as "the blacksmith"		87, 108
Yekhel	known as "the blacksmith"		62
Mikhal	known as "the blind"		378
Rafael	known as "the bricklayer"		330
Leybke	known as "the builder's son"		410
Shlomo Shloyme	known as "the butcher"		485
Hukshe	known as "the chimney sweep"		378
Leybl	known as "the coachman"		485
Hershl	known as "the cobbler"		215
Peysakh Peyshe	known as "the cobbler"		108, 375
Shaul	known as "the dyer" or "the varnish"		97, 105, 219
Elkeh	known as "the warehousekeeper"		485
Gedalye	known as "the wall builder (mason)"		485
Leyzer	known as "the guide"		378
Hershl	known as "the red-haired"		485
Hershl	known as "the tall"		378
Leyb	known as "the grocer"		465
Leyb	known as "the ironsmith"		325, 342
Leyzer	known as "the miller"		118
Yatke	known as "the manufacturer from Seltz"	Seltz	378
Koheles	known as "the shammes"		378

Peysakh	known as "the shammes"	485
Shmuel	known as "the kettle maker"	485
Shmuel Yankl	known as "the beggar"	485
Abba	known as "the shooster (shoemaker)"	50, 97, 378, 485
Avreml	known as "the shooster (shoemaker)"	410
Slove	known as "the big"	378
Slove	known as "the little"	378
Meir	known as "the tailor"	485
Nasan	known as "the tailor"	84, 401, 485
Vintse	known as "the water carrier"	485
Bentshe	known as "the wealthy"	378

NAME AND PLACE INDEX

refers to the pagination of **this** translation

(**bold**=places)

A

Aaronsohn, 267, 490, 492, 544, 567
Abali, 228
Abir, 46, 228, 237, 238, 332, 567, 609
Abramovitsh, 75, 286, 549, 567
Acre, 95
Africa, 290, 550
Afula, 290
Ahuvi, 118, 196, 355, 391, 446, 513, 518, 519, 545, 567, 600
Ahuzat Bayit, 265, 271
Ala, 567
Albertina Ranch, 329
Aleichem, 259, 294, 567
Alita, 168
Almpina Swamps, 182
Aloni, 48, 55, 65, 66, 89, 231, 237, 240, 251, 253, 324, 333, 437, 440, 443, 459, 549, 560, 567, 568, 621
Alperovitsh, 568, 588, 597
Amdur, 398
Anders, 568
Andreas, 201
Aniel, 568
Anshelovtish, 568
Aran, 168, 170, 171
Argentina, 290, 351, 387, 503, 505, 561
Arkin, 132, 202, 568
Artshom, 568, 599
Asch, 568

Ashdod, 221
Ashman, 305, 307, 310, 312, 569
Ashpon, 569
Atlit, 137
Aviel, 302, 569
Avinoam, 228, 621

B

Baksht, 61, 122, 549
Balbarishker, 569
Balbirishker, 496
Balerovski, 569
Baltic Village, 139
Baltobitze, 139
Bankover, 74
Bar Kochba Street, 39
Baran, 549, 569
Baranovich, 17, 26, 38, 142, 222, 278, 314, 332, 345, 398, 447
Bardichevski, 71, 76, 569
Bareh, 430, 569
Barnett, 8, 375, 380, 514, 519, 549, 569
Baron, 20, 242, 487, 583
Bartonovski, 309, 338, 530, 549, 569
Bastomski, 245, 569
Bastuni, 139, 143, 149, 156, 212
Bayevitsh, 532, 571
Becker, 16, 525, 535, 544, 549, 569
Beit Ha'haluzot, 39
Belaruski Woods, 119

Ben Shemen Woods, 344
Ben Yehuda Street, 95
Benakani, 10, 17, 20, 36, 62, 118, 142,
　143, 155, 177, 184, 194, 211, 236, 282,
　322, 382, 383, 384, 390, 473, 479, 482,
　486
Ben–Ami, 570
Bender, 549
Ben–Dov, 288, 549, 570, 614
Ben–Gurion, 570
Ben–Tsvi, 570
Benyakonski, 2, 86, 89, 275, 570
Bereza Kartuska Prison Camp, 288
Berezina River, 102, 179, 222, 223
Berkovitsh, 51, 79, 94, 95, 259, 261, 438,
　462, 516, 570
Berling, 326, 328, 570
Berman, 309, 549, 570
Bernshteyn, 4, 47, 92, 102, 321, 383, 454,
　477, 549, 558, 559, 564, 570, 571, 609
Biala Podalaska, 327
Biale Wotzka, 328
Bialik, 571
Bialystok, 36, 99, 198, 338
Biavitsh, 571
Bielski, 122, 123, 125, 156, 157, 158, 159,
　160, 161, 165, 166, 223, 355, 369, 400,
　401, 477, 511, 571
Bilitza, 149, 173, 230, 233, 234, 235, 331,
　339, 486
Bizheski, 572
Blaushteyn, 572
Blezuvski, 290, 572
Bloch, 8, 21, 38, 56, 57, 62, 102, 106, 107,
　116, 377, 378, 393, 439, 440, 445, 451,
　453, 455, 458, 459, 462, 515, 519, 522,
　523, 527, 537, 545, 550, 561, 572

Blum, 573
Blumenthal, 573
Blumgarden, 532, 573
Blushteyn, 573
Blyakher, 8, 42, 47, 56, 57, 90, 94, 121,
　122, 126, 127, 131, 148, 152, 209, 214,
　240, 278, 284, 285, 293, 294, 307, 308,
　313, 316, 318, 367, 369, 370, 430, 435,
　440, 451, 458, 462, 466, 511, 515, 516,
　519, 549, 550, 567, 573, 574, 575, 582,
　592, 604, 610, 617, 619
Bobroisk, 115, 498
Bogoshovitsh, 575
Bogoslav, 182, 183, 184, 575
Boleslav, 575
Bolinski, 224, 229, 355, 356, 357, 433,
　519, 525, 526, 527, 528, 539, 541, 544,
　545, 547, 549, 575
Bonimovitsh, 303, 575
Borokhov, 522
Boston, 290
Botvinik, 575
Boyarski, 161, 575
Braude, 576
Brisk, 12, 399
Bronshtayn, 168, 269, 320
Brown, 525, 543, 575
Broyde, 576
Buenos Aires, 351, 505
Bug River, 326
Burakas, 132, 576
Bzura, 550, 552

C

Cahn, 6
Caleb, 576

Chasman, 550

Cherkiss, 596

Cherno, 48, 61, 576

Chopin Street, 249

Cohen, 50, 231, 239, 375, 525, 532, 576, 582, 586, 588, 592, 593

Cohenson, 576

Constanta, 68

Cressy, 242

Cuba, 432, 526, 544, 556

Cyprus, 221

D

Dakh, 199, 576, 617

Damascus, 267, 268, 269, 490

Danishevski, 576

Danoyke, 59, 62, 126, 127, 129, 130, 131

Danoyker, 576

Danzig, 54, 118, 352

Davey, 525, 576

Davidov, 150, 170, 171, 174, 576

Davidovitsh, 609, 615

Daytsh, 576, 617

Deiches, 532, 550, 576, 617

Delatishki, 98, 153, 550, 576

Denikin, 508, 510, 576

Dganya, 71, 76

Diamont, 576

Dilinski, 447, 576

Dobkin, 440

Dogalishok, 219

Donovitsh, 576

Donshevski, 228, 576

Dorman, 270, 576

Dovinski Forest, 59

Dovitshisker Street, 387

Dovizishok Street, 117

Dovozisk Street, 257

Dowichitzki Street, 74, 163

Dowicz Forest, 169, 170

Dowitshok, 169

Drosknik, 169

Druck, 222, 225, 281, 482, 550, 576, 577

Dsalel-Abad, 201

Dubin, 282, 283, 367, 530, 532, 550, 555, 577, 621

Dubinski, 8, 10, 88, 100, 139, 142, 143, 144, 147, 148, 165, 177, 178, 314, 330, 331, 392, 393, 410, 465, 495, 510, 515, 519, 538, 550, 560, 561, 562, 577, 578

Dubizishok Street, 164, 309, 423, 424

Dubkin, 55, 65, 89, 240, 437, 448, 449, 459, 578

Dubtshinski, 32

Durniak, 169

Duvinke Forest, 383

Dziencielski, 578

E

Edelshteyn, 211, 213, 578

Eforykin, 578

Ehrenburg, 190, 578

Ehrlikh, 578

Eisenshtat, 216, 578

Eliashkovitsh, 578, 579

Engle, 38, 72, 74, 197, 291, 292, 374, 375, 378, 412, 446, 529, 550, 579, 588

Epshteyn, 579

Eshishuk, 61, 70, 71, 147, 290, 331, 486

Eyshishki, 325, 327, 371, 579, 618

F

Farfel, 486, 579
Fayn, 579
Fein, 579
Finkel, 509
Finklshteyn, 579
Florida, 428
Fludermakher, 579
Forman, 532, 579
Frankfurter, 580
Frishman, 580
Fuchs, 147, 171, 259, 296, 342, 343, 344, 565, 580
Funk, 404, 405, 465, 580

G

Galicia, 33, 73, 216, 322, 405
Garvey, 62, 93, 95, 201, 216, 217, 219, 367, 438, 516, 580
Gasztold, 580
Gauja River, 83, 92, 306
Gavya River, 10, 55, 92, 306, 415, 427, 457
Gaza, 201
Gedara, 201
Gedgaudas, 580
Gedminas, 581
Geller, 123, 354, 581
Geranion, 29, 34, 37, 38, 39, 77, 85, 86, 90, 95, 105, 118, 162, 209, 242, 246, 317, 322, 389, 390, 391, 439, 530
Geranion Street, 29, 34, 39, 77, 90, 95, 105, 209, 242, 246, 317, 439, 530
Gershonovitsh, 532, 581
Gershovitsh, 24, 550, 598
Gerson, 551
Giluzh, 141, 147, 372
Ginzburg, 15, 20, 551
Girneyner Street, 298
Gitlits, 424, 502, 551, 581
Glazer, 581, 583, 614
Gliat, 581
Gloit, 551
Glomb, 245, 581
Glubok, 80
Gobernik, 84
Gogodzinski, 170, 581
Gol, 551
Goldberg, 449, 451, 532, 581
Goldenski, 581
Goldfein, 581
Goldwater, 582
Gomnits, 595
Gordon, 4, 87, 123, 165, 172, 204, 257, 273, 277, 297, 300, 505, 509, 551, 581, 582, 602
Gordsvatser, 139, 582
Gorvits, 582
Gottfried, 582, 587, 618
Graber, 551
Grabia, 551
Green Forest, 222
Greenberg, 59, 508, 582
Grevetski, 132, 582
Gridzovtza, 551
Grinboim, 582
Griner, 108, 511, 582
Grodne, 13, 17, 24, 38, 132, 150, 151, 168, 171, 175, 177, 194, 398, 439, 498
Grossman, 62, 582
Gruenbaum, 458
Gvidon, 117, 136

H

HaCohen, 137, 228, 582, 592, 593
Hadera, 169, 304, 322
Haifa, 66, 72, 97, 137, 171, 221, 289, 301
Haller, 582
Hamutsi Village, 140
Hanveg, 479, 480, 481
Harari, 98, 272, 394, 582
Havana, 432
Hekdesh, 210, 450
Heller, 582
Hemed, 333
Herman, 96, 147, 148, 172, 342, 343, 344, 405, 480, 565, 580, 582
Herman Lane, 480
Hershman, 82, 583
Hershovitsh, 78, 139, 161, 189, 195, 248, 440, 503, 550, 583, 598
Herson, 551, 588, 592, 593
Hertzliya, 284
Herzl, 60, 239, 340, 458, 583
Hinds, 583
Hirsch, 583
Hirshfeld, 475
Hochman, 583
Homl, 223
Horodne, 12
Horodok, 116, 228, 230, 398
Horowitz, 405
Horvits, 53, 243, 272, 335, 336, 373, 374, 375, 380, 430, 505, 506, 507, 508, 509, 510, 512, 514, 519, 532, 547, 551, 558, 559, 562, 569, 576, 579, 582, 583, 584, 603, 611

I

Ilia, 202
Ilituvitsh, 371, 579, 584
Ingulski, 322, 378, 457, 584
Inklbitz, 551
Itskovitsh, 8, 32, 38, 46, 56, 59, 66, 70, 71, 72, 80, 90, 97, 117, 195, 203, 206, 218, 223, 225, 226, 240, 252, 254, 269, 271, 291, 304, 305, 307, 311, 312, 314, 322, 328, 331, 334, 344, 345, 346, 347, 348, 395, 397, 401, 403, 404, 414, 438, 440, 462, 466, 468, 471, 482, 510, 515, 516, 519, 522, 550, 569, 584, 585, 586
Ivanitz, 25, 26
Ivia, 38, 54, 55, 60, 82, 92, 122, 123, 125, 149, 164, 167, 195, 225, 257, 270, 276, 282, 286, 301, 309, 331, 354, 366, 377, 422, 454, 486

J

Jabotinski, 60, 61, 62, 63, 248, 398, 400, 458, 462
Jacobs, 10, 33, 77, 88
Jadka, 586
Jaffa, 82, 84, 271, 284
Jankelewicz, 551
Japan, 504
Jerusalem, 38, 50, 76, 79, 95, 111, 168, 175, 206, 261, 262, 263, 268, 269, 270, 272, 285, 332, 333, 398, 409, 470, 473, 482, 491, 516, 523
Jezreel Valley, 38
Juraciski, 87
Jutan, 551

K

Kacherginski, 586

Kaczerginski, 479, 586

Kadap, 586

Kagan, 101, 303, 582, 586

Kaganovitsh, 38, 56, 162, 257, 376, 439, 440, 537, 551, 558, 586, 616

Kahan, 582, 586

Kakraka, 586

Kalelishok, 126, 127, 128, 129, 130, 131, 155, 172, 177, 178, 180, 182, 236, 487, 498

Kalmen, 586

Kalmenovitsh, 59, 63, 303, 304, 586

Kalvitze, 329, 371, 446

Kalvitze Forest, 329

Kalwariski Street, 194

Kamenitski, 519, 547, 551, 586

Kantrovitsh, 587

Kaplan, 24, 28, 40, 41, 47, 54, 59, 61, 66, 75, 81, 123, 128, 134, 148, 201, 211, 214, 231, 256, 280, 281, 304, 309, 319, 331, 346, 361, 379, 412, 416, 438, 443, 479, 481, 486, 511, 516, 519, 529, 530, 551, 570, 577, 578, 579, 587, 588, 593

Karelitz, 269

Karkur, 286

Kartshmer, 8, 35, 44, 50, 54, 63, 75, 89, 93, 95, 98, 126, 129, 130, 131, 132, 138, 220, 253, 293, 324, 356, 372, 373, 386, 394, 427, 428, 434, 447, 500, 501, 519, 526, 532, 535, 540, 542, 544, 545, 547, 551, 552, 568, 574, 581, 588, 589, 590, 596, 597, 609

Kasatshenkova, 111, 112, 113, 590

Kasheti, 168

Katsev, 90, 313, 364, 388, 440, 458, 465, 552, 590

Katyn, 399, 405

Katz, 24, 38, 50, 79, 101, 152, 153, 297, 299, 300, 303, 304, 314, 323, 331, 334, 382, 383, 386, 400, 432, 552, 589, 590, 591, 600

Katzenelson, 15, 20, 458

Katznelson, 591

Kazjimirovski, 498, 591

Kfar Ma'as, 31, 319

Kfar Saba, 82

Khadash, 486, 592

Kharkov, 287

Khasman, 4, 67, 265, 268, 269, 270, 271, 286, 287, 290, 359, 360, 488, 491, 550, 571, 572, 586, 592, 610, 617, 619

Kherson, 47, 56, 88, 89, 117, 207, 229, 236, 275, 309, 312, 348, 349, 350, 471, 470, 549, 551, 567, 588

Khmelnytsky, 12, 593

Khruzhy, 593

Kibbutz HaCovesh, 68

Kidreh, 282

Kiejstutowicz, 593

Kishniev, 242

Kivelevitsh, 593

Klodna Street, 165

Klooga, 42

Klozner, 399, 593

Kobilnik, 18, 109, 113

Koitle, 360, 361, 593

Kollishok, 193, 194

Kolonie Lvovo, 68

Komorowska Oblast, 326

Konigsberg, 190

Konvalishki, 62, 602

Kopel, 593

Kościuszko, 326

Kosivitski, 372, 593

Kostya, 593

Kotler, 54, 85, 117, 122, 126, 129, 130, 131, 350, 351, 382, 462, 552, 593

Koval, 488

Kovenski, 385, 593

Kovne, 85, 151, 223, 228, 242, 278, 286

Koydenovah Camp, 25

Kozlovski, 552

Kragele, 571

Kramer, 66, 85, 282, 552, 577, 594

Kramina, 201

Krasnaya Gorka, 166

Krasnei, 195

Kraus, 532, 594

Kretchmer, 568, 574, 581, 588, 589, 590, 597

Kretzmer, 550, 551, 552

Krisovski, 456, 552

Krits, 594

Krivitski, 46, 66, 70, 406, 468, 552, 594

Krizovski, 1, 45, 51, 56, 67, 85, 89, 93, 114, 147, 195, 196, 199, 202, 273, 274, 275, 287, 298, 379, 412, 420, 426, 444, 447, 451, 469, 470, 492, 493, 494, 495, 498, 514, 529, 530, 562, 563, 594, 595, 603, 605

Kroshkin, 595

Kubanski, 552, 560, 595

Kuhn, 595

Kuniak, 552

Kupshits, 552

Kusbitzki, 552, 557

Kushtilski, 595

Kushtulski, 328

Kutilah, 595

Kutler, 552

L

Lahoisk, 115

Land, 8, 56, 60, 63, 65, 69, 71, 87, 88, 97, 104, 266, 267, 269, 270, 271, 280, 398, 401, 434, 435, 437, 438, 439, 442, 453, 460, 461, 462, 491, 493, 516, 517, 520, 525, 529, 533, 595

Lapida, 553

Lazar, 395

Lebizuvski, 290, 572

Lefkovitsh, 451, 477

Leizer, 95, 556

Lekoyekh, 532

Leningrad, 147, 362

Leshchinski, 38, 545, 546, 595

Levi, 503, 504, 539, 541, 554, 595

Levi-Blum, 504

Levine, 16, 37, 38, 39, 45, 51, 56, 58, 62, 72, 85, 90, 93, 107, 112, 114, 121, 122, 126, 127, 129, 130, 131, 132, 139, 146, 162, 186, 187, 188, 189, 195, 232, 259, 260, 287, 289, 290, 294, 305, 309, 313, 323, 328, 362, 365, 366, 367, 374, 380, 381, 384, 385, 419, 425, 439, 440, 446, 458, 459, 462, 465, 478, 499, 500, 502, 504, 514, 518, 519, 521, 522, 532, 536, 545, 546, 547, 553, 554, 555, 557, 559, 564, 573, 578, 580, 585, 594, 596, 597, 598, 599, 607, 620

Levinson, 588

Leybman, 277, 278, 553, 592

Liberson, 391

Lida, 10, 16, 18, 20, 24, 27, 38, 54, 55, 70, 82, 86, 87, 98, 118, 119, 120, 121, 122, 123, 124, 126, 135, 142, 143, 145, 148, 149, 155, 156, 157, 158, 160, 165, 166, 167, 168, 172, 173, 175, 182, 185, 194, 195, 203, 205, 211, 213, 215, 217, 220, 221, 222, 223, 225, 249, 250, 251, 252, 298, 313, 331, 342, 354, 355, 369, 382, 389, 400, 401, 409, 426, 479, 480, 481, 486, 508, 602

Lida Street, 119, 155

Lieb, 118, 164, 172, 196, 352, 353, 354, 518, 545, 568, 587, 600, 613, 618, 619

Lillienbloom, 600

Lipkovski, 554

Lipkunski, 4, 32, 117, 151, 161, 197, 219, 353, 446, 477, 554, 564, 571, 600

Lipnishok, 16, 54, 57, 63, 121, 144, 175, 343, 380, 498, 503

Lipuvke, 180

Livay, 601

Livorno, 16

Lodzh, 136, 177, 364, 399, 400

Lomzhe, 259, 390, 391, 439

Lovratovska Street, 396

Lubetski, 52, 54, 58, 103, 157, 240, 246, 351, 379, 385, 398, 419, 421, 440, 462, 465, 466, 467, 468, 470, 554, 601

Lubishitski, 364, 601

Lublin, 326, 396, 397, 405

Lubtsch, 363

Lutsk, 206, 409

Lutski, 601

Lytnent, 128, 131, 601

Lyubka, 601

Lzelman, 554

M

Mackevic, 221, 222

Magazin, 15

Magaziner, 530, 601

Mages, 163, 168, 193, 195, 219, 225, 549

Malinovke, 73, 421

Mamke, 601

Maness, 602

Manoakh, 71, 76, 602

Market Street, 30, 283, 343, 536

Maroch, 554

Marzikanza Station, 169

Mashkevitsh, 602

Masukutnik, 85

Matnoi, 602

Mazeh, 93, 94, 96, 448, 516, 554, 602

Meirson, 230, 233, 602

Melamed, 70, 431, 554, 555, 602

Melinovski, 189, 602

Melitopol, 299

Melkhovski, 124, 125, 602

Menski, 145, 602

Merlinski, 197, 602

Miasnik, 175, 176, 602

Miastova, 371

Mickiewicz, 602

Mievski, 555

Mikelson, 153, 353, 555, 602

Milvski, 602

Mindits, 213, 602

Minsk, 17, 20, 114, 115, 135, 178, 179, 180, 200, 203, 289, 470, 562

Mintz, 47, 66, 77, 284, 285, 313, 316, 317, 353, 375, 380, 417, 438, 440, 451, 458, 459, 511, 512, 514, 516, 555, 587, 602, 603

Mir, 26, 50, 503
Mnashye, 84
Mogilev, 196
Moisevitsh, 93, 275, 603
Molodetchno, 18, 398
Moscow, 145, 147, 160, 170, 171, 174, 176, 223, 288, 454, 456, 504, 539, 550
Movshovitsh, 16, 19, 47, 54, 75, 76, 95, 157, 163, 197, 241, 244, 318, 322, 330, 358, 369, 391, 475, 477, 534, 555, 570, 603, 604, 607
Munis, 604
Myopglen, 164

N

Naharia, 351, 387
Naliboki Forest, 163
Namiot, 427, 439, 440, 458, 555, 604
Navaredok, 102, 121, 160, 161, 172, 385, 393, 400, 506, 508
Nazareski, 604
Neman, 10, 11, 149, 151, 173, 174
Neman River, 10, 173
Nerutovitshe Street, 396
Netanya, 232, 284
Neve Shalom, 269
New York, 21, 51, 54, 102, 104, 146, 243, 245, 248, 276, 335, 356, 357, 374, 375, 380, 404, 405, 412, 432, 433, 450, 475, 479, 487, 493, 494, 497, 513, 517, 521, 522, 524, 526, 527, 528, 531, 532, 534, 535, 536, 537, 538, 539, 540, 541, 564, 566
Niamn Station, 303
Nibosha Village, 148
Nimtsevitsh, 604

Noviazki, 555
Novoplanski, 37, 114, 214, 293, 371, 446, 555, 604
Nyunke, 604

O

Olkenik, 147, 170, 399, 400, 593
Olkenitski, 36, 60, 85, 90, 157, 185, 246, 288, 296, 362, 426, 482, 485, 555, 573, 604, 605
Olshan, 54, 82, 102, 202, 247, 376, 431, 446, 447, 460, 473, 486
Olszanica, 20
Omiastovsky, 198, 605
Oren, 322
Ortshik, 605
Oschinski, 555
Oshmeme, 10, 16, 17, 20, 34, 92, 102, 203, 423, 424, 426, 446
Oshmene, 34, 35, 54, 55, 59, 67, 82, 102, 104, 115, 116, 122, 147, 184, 195, 199, 200, 220, 241, 259, 277, 329, 331, 334, 335, 353, 372, 378, 386, 394, 397, 399, 429, 451, 470, 473, 486, 530
Oshmene Forest, 426
Oshmene Street, 92, 102, 116, 277, 394, 423, 424, 429
Oshmene Street Bridge, 92, 102, 423, 424
Ostrinski, 35, 620
Ostrovits, 104
Otebsk, 326

P

Pachenko, 605
Pantzenk, 605
Paris, 325, 373

Parson, 532, 605

Parvar, 232, 605

Patzlof, 67, 530

Pauleitiss, 605

Pawszechna, 444, 461

Penza, 196

Peretz, 605

Perlman, 331, 486, 605

Pethovski, 605

Petliura, 508, 510, 605

Petukhovski, 22, 433, 440, 458, 605

Peykhova, 605

Pezkovski, 32, 606

Pharmacy, 4

Pilovski, 606

Pilsudski, 606

Pinkovski, 606

Pinsk, 12

Piotrokov, 399

Pitma, 200, 201

Plashevitsi, 124, 125

Pludermakher, 579

Podolia, 13, 405

Poltva, 370

Ponary, 232, 334, 335

Popisko, 602, 606

Porter, 606

Portnoi, 211, 555, 606

Preski, 142, 569, 606, 608

Protzhenov, 132, 606

Pruzan, 532, 606

Prystor, 338, 339

Pulitruk, 606

Pundak, 606

Pupko, 189, 606

R

Rabinovitsh, 104, 178, 179, 228, 241, 331, 486, 532, 604, 606, 607, 616

Radin, 25, 38, 50, 119, 147, 177, 219, 231, 232, 314, 315, 331, 332, 334, 345, 347, 389, 391, 398, 435, 447, 479, 486

Radoshkovichi, 114

Rakover, 175, 607

Rakovi, 195

Ramat Rachel Kibbutz, 38

Ramot Remez, 221

Raszko, 36, 277, 607

Raynes, 508

Razian, 326

Rebikov, 269, 607

Rehovot, 333

Reider, 607

Reinberg, 583

Reizen, 607

Renkatsinski, 470

Reyzen, 487, 492, 495

Reznik, 607

Rodzivits, 145, 607

Rogol, 19, 34, 46, 73, 76, 107, 117, 146, 158, 210, 236, 242, 259, 260, 281, 296, 297, 312, 313, 317, 340, 341, 343, 357, 358, 380, 419, 438, 439, 440, 445, 446, 462, 469, 555, 580, 607, 608

Rogov, 177, 562, 577

Rogovski, 608

Rogulski, 430, 608

Romanovka, 288

Rosenblum, 67, 285, 438, 555, 608

Rosovski, 608

Ross, 532, 608

Rothman, 532, 608

Rozovski, 331, 486

Rubin, 67, 142, 203, 608

Rubinovski, 608

Rudnik, 28, 38, 46, 55, 65, 66, 102, 106, 153, 228, 229, 237, 238, 240, 248, 251, 330, 331, 332, 333, 339, 393, 394, 435, 438, 460, 469, 486, 487, 532, 541, 549, 555, 568, 571, 572, 576, 582, 590, 609, 610, 612, 617

Rudniki Woods, 132, 141

Ruscinsky, 610

Russia, 13, 14, 16, 25, 26, 27, 50, 56, 84, 91, 95, 102, 114, 145, 152, 172, 177, 178, 190, 195, 198, 200, 201, 228, 232, 238, 242, 257, 266, 270, 275, 281, 287, 288, 295, 299, 301, 371, 391, 399, 400, 405, 456, 474, 475, 497, 498, 523, 534, 538

S

Safed, 373

Sagla, 122, 123, 125

Sakharov, 486, 610

Saladucha, 555

Salanter, 334, 335, 507, 610

Salki, 132

Samsonov, 610

San Francisco, 504

Saritski, 579, 610

Satkolshtsik, 64, 75, 250, 253, 302, 406, 407, 408, 409, 557, 610, 611, 612, 620

Satsitniski, 611

Sbeyski, 525, 544, 576

Schmidt, 328, 556, 611

Schneider, 24, 46, 47, 48, 51, 59, 63, 66, 121, 122, 126, 128, 131, 199, 203, 205, 206, 219, 240, 246, 249, 251, 253, 319, 344, 346, 358, 367, 377, 387, 406, 409, 446, 451, 462, 466, 474, 556, 560, 564, 583, 600, 601, 611, 612, 613

Schuchman, 613

Schwarts, 202, 301, 544, 557, 581, 613

Sde Ya'kkov, 305, 306

Segal, 148, 149, 150, 173, 174, 380, 555, 613

Seltz, 418, 622

Sender, 121, 242, 596, 613

Sforim, 613

Shabad, 238, 277, 469, 613

Shalit, 20, 473

Shamir, 613

Shapiro, 613

Sharashevski, 85, 605

Sharet, 137, 613

Sharon, 9, 62, 64, 165, 245, 409, 440, 462, 515, 519, 601, 611, 612, 613

Shatsigloski, 199, 613

Shatsitnitski, 131, 139, 140, 449

Sheftel, 230, 613, 614

Sheifer, 487, 613, 614

Sheinok, 584

Shekneh, 614

Shfayim, 83

Shimanski, 163

Shklar, 121, 126, 129, 131, 153, 503, 505, 555, 561, 583, 614

Shkolnik, 46, 58, 90, 93, 291, 313, 346, 388, 446, 458, 465, 556, 570, 614

Shlomovitsh, 60, 219, 243, 337, 339, 362, 556, 608, 615

Shloymes, 615

Shlubski, 556

Shmerkovitsh, 615

Shmuelzon, 331, 486, 615
Shrira, 120, 213, 556, 615
Shteynberg, 615
Shtokfish, 615
Shtul, 615
Shtutchin, 24, 27
Shtzitnitzki, 556
Shub, 331, 486, 615
Shults, 551, 556
Shurin, 230, 615
Shvintolski, 117, 615
Sidoriski, 556
Silverblank, 615
Sipka, 615
Skkolnik, 556
Skyviss, 117, 140, 153, 615
Slabodke, 228, 242, 390, 508, 509
Sleski, 126
Sloboda, 615
Slonim, 36, 145, 259, 296, 297
Slonimski, 615
Slutsk, 12
Smitanin, 616
Smith, 418, 530, 532
Smolensk, 148, 326
Smolovitski, 616
Smorgon, 22, 23, 104, 277, 301, 460
Smulkin, 556
Sobotsh, 140, 616
Sokolski, 171, 616
Sol, 200
Solodukhe, 58, 62, 289, 440, 462, 543, 555, 557, 575, 594, 616
Solts, 58, 107, 501, 557, 616
Soltsin Village, 139
Sonnenson, 89, 363, 433, 616
Sorktzi Village, 140

Sorotzkin, 199, 206, 249, 409, 616
Sovlovitsh, 616
Spivak, 319, 537, 557, 587, 616
Spravstsishuk, 139
Srulovitsh, 288, 358, 362, 557, 616
Stankvitsh, 170, 616
Stashiles, 100, 142, 145, 155, 165, 193
Staskes, 167, 616
Stavitski, 173, 617
Stekolshchik, 557
Stephen Street, 194
Steshelzi, 617
Stoki Forest, 127, 131, 371
Stolitski, 617
Stone, 177
Strudvorski, 214, 401, 617
Stul, 54, 89, 211, 470
Stutchiner, 286
Stutski, 92, 282, 617
Stutthof, 42, 190
Stzitnitzki, 557
Subotnik, 10, 16, 45, 60, 64, 70, 77, 85, 90, 93, 163, 167, 196, 202, 242, 314, 359, 362, 422, 423, 424, 465, 470, 482, 498, 553, 554
Subotnik Street, 45, 60, 64, 70, 77, 90, 93, 167, 196, 314, 359, 422, 423, 424, 465, 470, 482
Suruk Tatrov, 328
Sutskever, 147, 148, 172, 286, 290, 311, 418, 463, 470, 617
Sutzkever, 557
Sventzion, 67
Sverdlovsk, 325
Sverski, 529, 617
Svir, 110
Swartz, 557

Swintelsky, 557
Synagogue, 4, 50, 66, 76, 80, 82, 207, 243, 244, 255, 298, 345, 379, 381, 386, 395, 472, 530
Szkaliar, 557
Sznajder, 556

T

Tambov, 196
Tannenberg, 454, 455
Tayts, 52, 106, 146, 198, 248, 333, 334, 487, 557, 576, 617
Tchernikov, 200
Tchernikovski, 617
Tel Yosef Kibbutz, 38
Telerent, 617
Telzer, 506, 617
Tenenbaum, 215, 617
Tener, 617, 618
Tiktniski, 72, 618
Toronto, 511
Tovah, 618
Traby, 54, 67, 94, 165, 197, 331, 446, 460, 477, 486, 553
Trackel, 532
Traub, 193, 618
Treshkavits, 117, 618
Trieste, 97, 136
Trigovov, 618
Trivitski, 618
Troskel, 618
Trovski, 573, 576, 592, 618
Truman, 336
Trumpeldor, 56, 58, 59, 60, 75, 618
Truskevitsh, 618
Tublitski, 532, 618

Turgel, 131
Tushitski, 532, 618
Tzvik, 232

U

Ukraine, 13, 75, 326
Umpelin, 557
Ural, 200, 395
Usishkin, 618

V

Varshavski, 425
Varshe, 399, 492, 497
Varshever, 139, 555, 618
Varzhan, 228
Vasilishok, 164, 204
Vasilsky, 199, 618
Vasserman, 618
Vayner, 530
Vazyock, 618
Velvelski, 618
Vienna, 36, 238
Vigosh, 618
Vigudski, 74, 289, 597
Vileyka, 111, 113, 399
Vilija River, 11
Villach, 136
Vilne, 10, 12, 13, 15, 17, 18, 19, 20, 24, 27, 28, 35, 40, 41, 42, 48, 49, 51, 54, 55, 56, 57, 58, 61, 65, 71, 72, 73, 74, 76, 81, 82, 93, 100, 111, 112, 113, 115, 116, 118, 128, 132, 133, 134, 135, 136, 142, 145, 146, 147, 152, 153, 168, 170, 172, 181, 184, 189, 190, 194, 197, 200, 207, 208, 214, 221, 225, 228, 232, 237, 238, 242, 243, 245, 249, 250, 258, 261, 264,

275, 276, 277, 280, 283, 284, 287, 288, 294, 296, 300, 301, 303, 304, 310, 312, 315, 322, 324, 328, 329, 331, 332, 333, 334, 335, 339, 341, 345, 350, 352, 353, 354, 361, 363, 366, 370, 372, 374, 376, 382, 386, 389, 391, 392, 397, 398, 399, 400, 409, 410, 411, 423, 426, 430, 435, 440, 445, 447, 449, 453, 456, 458, 461, 462, 464, 465, 468, 469, 470, 473, 474, 475, 476, 479, 481, 482, 485, 486, 492, 494, 496, 504, 508, 516, 525, 530, 543

Vilne House, 516

Vilne Street, 42, 51, 163, 193, 207, 208, 242, 258, 280, 352, 361, 410, 411, 423, 430, 445, 482

Vindisch, 618

Vintsus, 479, 480, 481, 619

Vishneva, 20, 47, 54, 78, 94, 102, 270, 389, 460, 473

Vishnitski, 437, 440, 619

Vladivostok, 220, 504

Volozhin, 178, 228, 241, 248, 251, 253, 269, 270, 302, 332, 435, 473

Vonzdova, 199

Voronova, 38, 54, 57, 59, 70, 72, 82, 87, 98, 102, 118, 119, 120, 125, 128, 131, 132, 134, 138, 139, 142, 143, 147, 148, 153, 154, 155, 156, 160, 161, 162, 165, 170, 172, 179, 180, 181, 182, 184, 185, 189, 192, 193, 194, 201, 204, 211, 213, 217, 245, 249, 253, 256, 259, 260, 286, 293, 314, 317, 322, 331, 338, 342, 346, 349, 350, 354, 362, 364, 365, 370, 372, 379, 392, 399, 409, 446, 462, 479, 480, 481, 486, 495, 525

Voronovski, 619

Voytoss, 619

Vulfovitsh, 193, 557, 619

Vytautas, 619

W

Warner, 619

Warsaw, 20, 59, 60, 67, 68, 73, 75, 97, 146, 149, 152, 173, 322, 326, 372, 396, 399, 425, 461, 550, 552, 555, 617

Wasilevska, 191, 619

Wasilniko, 189, 619

Wasserman, 38, 201, 231, 314, 332, 333, 345

Wazyock, 164

Weinreich, 36, 469, 620

Weintraub, 620

Weisenfeld, 33, 46, 445, 510, 620

Wiener, 24, 47, 158, 381, 535, 557, 569, 593

Wilczynskas, 620

Windisch, 120, 155

Wolfovitz, 557

Y

Yagur, 71

Yankelovitsh, 250, 620

Yanushevits, 118, 125

Yardova, 201

Yashuny, 155, 172

Yehuda HaLevi Street, 84

Yoffe, 118, 620

Yorzishok, 161

Yudelevitsh, 63

Yudenfreund, 305, 323, 554, 557, 606, 620

Yugoslavia, 136

Yurglan Village, 126

Yushinski, 557

Yutan, 47, 551, 598, 604

Z

Zaika, 557
Zakrevtsizne, 86
Zalkin, 528, 529, 530, 531, 544, 620
Zandman, 75, 94, 197, 261, 262, 263, 286, 438, 516, 557, 620
Zelik, 620, 621
Zemach, 290
Zemiuslva, 371
Zheludok, 27
Zhetl, 175, 399, 409

Zhitomir, 326
Zhizhemski, 49, 69, 163, 363, 377, 458, 462, 557, 621
Zhizhimi, 57
Zholondzh, 567, 568, 621
Zichron Ya'akov, 490
Zlibinski, 557
Zoliborz, 326
Zuckerman, 228, 621
Zukovski, 194. 621
Zuravna, 33
Zusman, 147, 532, 557, 621
Zuvitshki, 91, 282, 283, 621
Zvedsky, 199

www.ingramcontent.com/pod-product-compliance
Lightning Source LLC
Chambersburg PA
CBHW082009150426
42814CB00005BA/265